The supply of banking services by clearing banks to small and medium-sized enterprises

A report on the supply of banking services by clearing banks
to small and medium-sized enterprises within the UK

Volume 2: Background Chapters 3–7

COMPETITION COMMISSION

The supply of banking services by clearing banks to small and medium-sized enterprises

A report on the supply of banking services by clearing banks to small and medium-sized enterprises within the UK

Volume 2: Background Chapters 3–7

Presented to Parliament by the Secretary of State for Trade and Industry and the Chancellor of the Exchequer by Command of Her Majesty
March 2002

Cm 5319   £134·55
(four volumes not sold separately)

Web site: **www.Competition-Commission.org.uk**

Volume 2 contents

Note by the Department of Trade and Industry

In accordance with section 83(3) and (3A) of the Fair Trading Act 1973, the Secretary of State and the Chancellor have excluded from the copies of the report, as laid before Parliament and as published, certain matters, publication of which appears to the Secretary of State and the Chancellor to be against the public interest, or which they consider would not be in the public interest to disclose and which, in their opinion, would seriously and prejudicially affect certain interests.

The omissions are indicated by a note in the text or, where space does not permit, by the symbol ✂.

Part II

Background and evidence

3 The markets

Introduction

3.1. This chapter begins by looking at various definitions of SMEs and summarizes the clearing system. It then examines the product and the geographical markets and barriers to entry. Next the chapter estimates the shares of the main providers in 1999 and 2000, looks at shares over time and assesses new entry. Finally, the extent of shopping around and switching by SMEs is considered.

3.2. The information in this chapter and in Chapter 4 is based on responses to our economic questionnaires, our survey of SMEs[1] and comments of the main clearing groups and other parties. We asked the four largest clearing groups, namely Barclays, HSBC, Lloyds TSB and RBSG (for NatWest), to provide us with economic information for the period 1989 to 2000. We asked Abbey National, Alliance & Leicester, BoI, BoS, the Co-operative Bank, First Trust, NAB (for Clydesdale and Northern) and RBSG (for RBS and Ulster Bank) to provide economic information for the period 1997 to 2000. We asked a number of smaller banks, building societies and other financial institutions to provide information for their latest year. We asked for information for different time periods as, from discussions with some of the clearing banks, it became apparent that some of them would be unable to provide data for longer time periods.

3.3. During the early part of our inquiry, 1999 was the latest year for which most of the banks that provided us with data had full-year information to discuss with us. We have, however, updated our findings for results in 2000 and 2001 as such information became available.

3.4. In this chapter and in Chapter 4 we summarize some of the comments of the main clearing groups and other parties. The views of BoS and Halifax were made prior to their planned merger. Fuller versions of the views of various parties are contained in the relevant views chapters—Chapter 8 contains views of third parties, Chapter 9 contains views of smaller clearing banks, and the views of Barclays, HSBC, Lloyds TSB and RBSG are contained in Chapters 10 to 13 respectively.

SMEs and banking services

3.5. There is no widely accepted definition of SMEs. Table 3.1 shows the definitions used by the Department of Trade and Industry (DTI), the European Commission and the Companies Act 1985.

TABLE 3.1 **Definitions of SMEs**

		Classification of SME		
Organization	Criteria used	Micro	Small	Medium
DTI	Number of employees	0–9	0–49	50–249
European Commission*	Number of employees	Max 10	Max 50	Max 250
	Turnover	N/A	Max €7m	Max €40m
	Balance sheet	N/A	Max €5m	Max €27m
	Independence criteria†	N/A	25%	25%
Companies Act‡	Number of employees		Max 50	Max 250
	Turnover		Max £2.8m	Max £11.2m
	Balance sheet		Max £1.4m	Max £5.6m

Source: DTI and European Commission.

*Both the employee and the independence criteria must be satisfied and either the turnover or the balance sheet total criteria. Using the average £:€ exchange rate in 1999 and 2000, the turnover ceilings for small and medium firms are £4.4 million and £25.3 million respectively and the balance sheet ceilings are £3.2 million (small) and £17.1 million (medium).
†Refers to the maximum percentage that may be owned by one, or jointly owned by several enterprises not satisfying the same criteria.
‡Has to meet two of the three criteria in any year.
Note: N/A = Not applicable.

[1]We commissioned BMRB to carry out a survey of SMEs. The survey was carried out by telephone in September 2000. 1,211 SMEs took part in the survey.

3.6. The DTI's definition shown is used in its statistical publications.[1] In practice, government schemes that are nominally targeted at small firms adopt a variety of working definitions depending on their particular objectives. For example, the Small Firms Loan Guarantee Scheme defines SMEs as having not more than 200 full-time equivalent (FTE) employees and turnover of not more than £3 million and £1.5 million in the previous 12 months in manufacturing and in other industries respectively. For the European Commission's definition, both the employee and the independence criteria must be satisfied and either the turnover or the balance sheet total criteria. Using the average £:€ exchange rate in 1999 and 2000, the turnover ceilings for the European Commission's definition of small and medium firms are just over £4 million and just over £25 million respectively and the balance sheet ceilings are just over £3 million (small) and just over £17 million (medium). Businesses have to meet two of the three criteria (number of employees, turnover and balance sheet) in any year to be SMEs under the Companies Act. The BBA collects and publishes data on SMEs' use of banking services where it defines SMEs as having annual turnover of up to £1 million through (each of) its accounts. The BBA, like the banking industry, uses debit turnover that relates to payments from the business's current account. It is therefore a measure of a business's expenditure and can be thought of as a measure of activity through a business's current account. It does not, however, include all payments. For example, RBSG told us that NatWest's data excluded transfers, for example repayments to its loan accounts. Debit and sales turnover may differ. For example, the total sales turnover of an SME using more than one bank will be greater than the individual debit turnover at one of its banks. We have used debit turnover as our measure of turnover. This was a pragmatic approach and for the reasons set out in Chapter 2 (see paragraph 2.10) we do not believe that the difference between debit and sales turnover, or any inconsistency between the banks, has any material effect on our analysis.

3.7. RBSG stated that NatWest divided its business customers into three distinct groups based on annual turnover bands. These are small businesses, middle market companies and larger corporates. A small business is defined as any non-personal account with an annual debit turnover through its bank account of less than £1 million. Firms with between £1 million and £100 million annual turnover are classified as middle market companies and those with over £100 million annual turnover are larger corporates. RBSG said that businesses with an annual turnover below £1 million were primarily serviced within NatWest's Retail Banking division and those with an annual turnover in excess of £1 million within Corporate Banking division. RBSG told us that RBS was split along similar lines to NatWest.

3.8. Other banks also categorize their business customers on the basis of annual turnover. Barclays manages all its SME customers within its Business Banking business unit, up to an annual turnover of £100 million. It and NatWest have different tariff packages for SMEs with annual turnovers up to and beyond £100,000. Lloyds TSB defines its Business Banking customers as broadly those with an annual turnover up to £2 million and its Commercial Banking customers as those with an annual turnover of between £2 million and £100 million. HSBC has a tariff package for SMEs with an annual turnover of up to £100,000. It has no published tariffs for its larger SMEs. BoS told us that it defined SMEs as any business enterprise (sole trader/partnership/limited company) that had an annual sales turnover of up to £10 million. Alliance & Leicester classifies business customers with annual turnover of up to £1 million as small businesses and large corporates as businesses with an annual turnover of over £1 million.

3.9. RBSG told us that NatWest used turnover as a proven primary indicator of the range and complexity of services that an SME customer was likely to require. It said that although turnover did not always reflect the complexities of a business, it had the advantage of being applicable across the marketplace (except in some sectors such as financial services and property) and was therefore a useful starting point.

3.10. For the reasons set out in Chapter 2 (see paragraph 2.13), throughout this report we use the term SMEs to mean those enterprises with an annual turnover of up to £25 million and with a business bank account.

3.11. We use the term 'banking services' to mean any of (a) acceptance of deposits, whether on current accounts or on deposit accounts of various types; (b) lending (including overdrafts, mortgage lending, factoring, financing of commercial transactions, asset finance, and letters of credit); (c) financial leasing; (d) money transmission services (including buying and selling foreign currency); (e) issuing and administering means of payment, such as cheques, credit cards, travellers' cheques, bankers' drafts, and merchant acquiring; (f) giving guarantees; or (g) related administration services. Such banking services are not necessarily supplied only by clearing banks or other banks.

---

[1]DTI Statistical Bulletin, *SME Statistics for the UK*, a regular annual series published each summer.

3.12. We use the term 'bank' to mean an institution that conducts current accounts and pays, and collects payment of, cheques for customers. We use the term 'other banks' to mean banks that are not clearing banks.

3.13. There is no accepted definition of a clearing bank. CCCC is one of three companies operated under the umbrella of APACS, the other two being BACS and CHAPS. CCCC operates the high-volume paper (cheques and credits) clearings in England, Wales and Scotland. A separate clearing system operates in Northern Ireland. BACS carries out electronic clearing of direct debits, standing orders and direct credits such as salary payments. CHAPS provides electronic same-day transfer of high-value payments[1] through-out the UK in sterling and globally in euros. It began in February 1984 and was originally restricted to payments of £10,000 to £100,000; however, the upper limit was progressively raised and was removed in May 1984. The minimum value of payments was reduced in stages and was removed altogether in January 1993. Settlement for all three companies takes place across accounts held at the BoE. All members of CCCC are also members of BACS; only three members of BACS do not belong to CCCC—Coutts, Halifax and Northern Rock plc, whose activities in providing services to SMEs are limited. CHAPS' only members at the time of our inquiry were generally overseas companies also with only limited activities in providing services to UK SMEs. For the reasons set out in Chapter 2 (see paragraphs 2.7 and 2.8), we use the term 'clearing bank' as a bank which is a full member of CCCC (excluding the BoE for the purpose of this inquiry) or a member of the Northern Ireland clearing arrangements. Appendix 3.1 provides a list of the members of CCCC, BACS and CHAPS.

3.14. It is useful at this stage to briefly describe certain aspects of the clearing system. In simple terms, the clearing process *(a)* identifies whether customers using, say, cheques have enough money in their account so that payments can be made or that the bank is willing to advance money on overdraft, and *(b)* transfers funds from the payer's account to the payee's account. Using cheques as an example, there are two clearing dates—cleared for value (the day from which interest is payable) and cleared for fate (the day that the money can be withdrawn). Where the transfer of money takes place between accounts held in the same country, the clearing banks normally clear funds for value on day three and for fate on day four. The clearing cycle is normally extended by one day for cheques drawn in one country of the UK and paid in at a branch in another country of the UK. This is due to the extra time taken to transport and present the cheque at the branch on which it is drawn. Anglia Business Associates Ltd told us that in Scotland, Scottish clearing was two days and English clearing in Scotland was three days. It said that mixed clearing (ie a combination of English and Scottish cheques) was three days, thereby giving the Scottish banks one day's value on Scottish cheques. BoS told us that it did not operate a mixed clearing system. RBSG said that RBS gained one day's value on the intra-country (for example, Scotland–Scotland) elements of mixed clearing credits. Lloyds TSB told us that mixed clearings did not generate a float (see paragraph 3.16), either in its favour or the customer's favour. It said that it had recently implemented a new counter system which accepted credits with mixed origin cheques and automatically applied the correct clearance period on a cheque-by-cheque basis.

3.15. The length of the clearing cycle is related to the work undertaken by the banks to ensure that payment can be made. The following sets out a summary of the work undertaken by the clearing banks during a normal clearing cycle for cheques drawn and paid in the same country of the UK:

(a) On day 1, the collecting bank takes delivery of cheques from customers. It physically transports all the cheques collected during the day to its clearing centre and starts processing them and physically sorts them by paying bank. Processing entails preparing an electronic file of data derived from the cheques.

(b) On day 2, the electronic files and the cheques are exchanged among banks. Each cheque is physically delivered to the branch or other processing area of the paying bank on which it is drawn over-night on day 2/3.

(c) On day 3, paying banks decide whether to honour cheques. The paying bank gives notice by post to the collecting bank of any cheques which it will not honour. Paying banks submit claims to collecting banks for reimbursement of dishonoured cheques. All banks settle their accounts through the BoE. Settlement is effected on the assumption that all cheques submitted for clearing are to be honoured. The paying bank debits the drawer's account with the amount of the cheque that has been paid. Normally, the collecting bank treats the funds received through settlement with the BoE as cleared for value for the benefit of its payee customers.

---

[1]APACS told us that its latest CHAPS traffic survey showed that 47 per cent of CHAPS payments were for less than £10,000.

(d) On day 4, the collecting bank processes cheques dishonoured and returned by the paying bank. This entails cancelling the credit to the payee's account and notifying the payee of the dishonour. Otherwise, the cheque is cleared for fate. Generally, the collecting bank considers the cheque to be finally cleared at this stage but there remains a risk that the paying bank may seek to reclaim the monies (for example, as monies paid under mistake of fact) or that the unpaid cheque has been delayed in the post.

(e) On day 5, the collecting bank's customer may generally withdraw the proceeds of the cheque from ATMs. This reflects the fact that balances on the account are generally updated and input to the ATM system late at night on day 4 and, until then, the ATM system will be unaware of the fact that the cheque has been cleared for fate.

3.16. The main clearing groups told us that on the whole when they received money during the clearing cycle they immediately passed it or interest on it on to their customers, ie they did not hold on to the money and derive income from it, known as 'float income'. APACS told us (see paragraph 8.144) that some banks, but probably not the four largest clearing banks, could currently derive float income, however briefly, from interest earned on money passing between customers' accounts in the following circumstances:

(a) as a result of a competitive decision taken by the collecting bank in relation to its customer proposition as regards any delay in clearance for value (this could be either by direct clearing or clearing by an agent);

(b) standing orders (which were debited from customers' accounts at the outset) going via BACS from one account to another (and were credited two or more days later);

(c) some bank giro credits between accounts;

(d) bankers' drafts; and

(e) one-off payments initiated by telephone, e-banking etc.

3.17. HSBC said that there were only two ways it achieved float income. The first was for customers paying in collection credits (payment of utility bills) at their own branch—in this case, because of a system deficiency at present, the customer's account was debited on day 1 although the funds were not received by the utility until day 2. However, it stated that where an HSBC customer paid its bill at an HSBC branch other than its own, the customer's account was debited on day three but the utility was credited on day 2, thus creating a float loss for HSBC. Secondly, standing orders (via BACS) were also debited on day 1 but in this case not credited until day 3 (except where an HSBC customer was crediting another HSBC customer, where same-day value was provided). It stated that these two exceptions were of little or no significance to SMEs, the float income from the exceptions was negligible and it was in the process of correcting both.

3.18. Lloyds TSB said that, following changes to its internal systems in March 2001, it did not generate float income on its internal standing orders (transfer of funds between two accounts maintained with Lloyds TSB) but it did generate float income for external interbank standing orders. Lloyds TSB told us that float income arose because the paying banks had to manage the credit risk of the paying customer—the paying bank took funds out of the paying customer's account to meet the standing order so as to avoid the paying bank finding that, by the time the standing order had been paid to the payee, there were no funds in the paying customer's account to meet the standing order. It stated that bank giro credits did not generally create float income. However, it said that such income would arise when a bank giro credit was paid in, accompanied by a cheque, by the paying customer at his or her own bank branch. In that event, the paying bank would take the funds out of the customer's account on day 1 and hold them on float, pending transfer to the recipient bank on day 3. Similarly, if a bank giro credit was paid in, accompanied by cash, then the bank held the benefit of the cash from day 1, until transfer to the recipient bank on day 3. For bankers' drafts, Lloyds TSB told us that the paying bank would take monies from the paying customer's account on day 1, when the bankers' draft was drawn, but would pay out only when the draft was presented for payment by the payee's bank via the normal cheque-clearing cycle. The paying bank would hold monies on float in the interim. Lloyds TSB said that one-off payments operated in the same way as standing orders. It told us that it recognized there was no good reason for it to enjoy the benefit of float income and it was working to resolve the issue as soon as practicable. To that end, it was cooperating in an APACS project with a view to eliminating float income generated by certain existing payment systems. Lloyds TSB stated that it earned relatively little float income and had no desire to retain the existing arrangements any longer than strictly necessary.

3.19. Barclays told us that there was an anomaly, which it planned to eliminate, relating to interbank standing orders where its customers were debited on day 1 with the beneficiary account not being credited until day 3. It said that this did not apply to standing orders between two Barclays accounts. Barclays stated that there was no float income with ordinary bank giro credits. However, it offers a service called Automated Bulk Credits, aimed at high-volume recipients of credits, such as mail-order companies and utilities. Barclays told us that ordinarily there was no float income but it could occur where cash was paid in on an Automated Bulk Credit. In these cases, the beneficiary received the value on day 3. Barclays said that with bankers' drafts, the paying bank took monies from the paying customer's account on day 1, when the bankers' draft was drawn, but paid out when the draft was presented for payment by the payee's bank via the normal cheque-clearing cycle—the paying bank holding monies on float in the interim. It stated that one-off payments via telephone or Internet (not its BusinessMaster software package) operated in the same way as standing orders but it was seeking to remove this anomaly.

3.20. RBSG told us that for standing orders, bank giro credits, bankers' drafts and one-off payments its banks adopted the normal industry practice of debiting the drawer on day 1 and crediting the beneficiary on day 3. RBSG estimated that the value of this float income from personal and larger corporate customers as well as SMEs accounted for less than 0.1 per cent of its reported combined income.[1]

3.21. BoS said that in Scotland it did not gain value until the banknotes issued by the other Scottish banks had been exchanged. It stated that the customers, however, received full value from the date of lodgement for banknotes issued by the other Scottish banks.

Market definition

3.22. We begin this section by setting out the framework for an analysis of market definition. We then look at the importance of banking costs to SMEs. Finally we provide the information (including views of various parties) that we took into account in order to reach our conclusion on the relevant product and geographical markets.

The framework for the analysis

3.23. In deciding the appropriate market for competition analysis we have to determine the products that compete in the market and the geographical extent of the market. In order to do this we consider in particular what would be the extent of substitution away from products sold in various locations from the standpoint of consumers (demand-side substitution) and suppliers (supply-side substitution), in response to a small but significant non-transitory price increase above the competitive level. Such a test is normally referred to as the hypothetical monopolist test, and is widely used by a number of competition bodies throughout the world. When applying the test, consideration has to be given to whether current prices are above competitive levels—even a monopolist would find it unprofitable to raise prices further at some level. Applying the test to prices above their competitive levels would be inappropriate and is known as the cellophane fallacy after a US case involving cellophane products.[2]

3.24. In order to gain an understanding of the possibilities for demand- and supply-side substitution the degree of responsiveness of demand or supply to price changes should be examined where observable. This analysis should be supplemented by an examination of the following:

(a) the products' characteristics;

(b) the products' price levels;

---

[1] Reported combined income of Retail Banking, CBFM, Retail Direct and Ulster Bank.
[2] *US v El Du Pont de Nemours & Co* (1956), 351 US 377.

9

(c) the products' relative price changes; and

(d) changes in the pattern of demand of the products.

Evidence on each of these areas is rarely complete and care has to be taken in ensuring that like-with-like comparisons are carried out. Like-with-like comparisons are particularly difficult in lending where the rate of interest is adjusted for a number of factors, for example risk, size of loan, period of repayment, and the extent to which the loan is backed by security. Therefore, the eventual decision on market definition typically involves an element of judgement.

3.25. A concept relevant to market definition in this inquiry is that of a continuous chain of substitution in demand. This can be applied in the banking industry context both in relation to banking services (ie the product) and to the geographical market. As regards banking services, the concept can be illustrated by using the argument put forward by Barclays. Barclays argued that business current accounts provided the starting point in a chain of linked credit and debit products. On the credit side Barclays stated that the chain started from the business current account through business deposit accounts to personal deposit accounts and the equivalent deposit accounts provided by non-bank suppliers. On the debit side its view was that business current accounts were linked to overdrafts which in turn were linked to other forms of debt finance such as loans, leasing and factoring. On this basis, on the credit side an SME's non-interest-bearing current account is a substitute for an instant access account paying a small rate of interest and the instant access account is a substitute for a deposit account with more restricted access but with a higher rate of interest. In this example, the non-interest-bearing current account, the instant access account and the deposit account are links in a chain of substitution. This raises the question as to whether the non-interest-bearing current account and the deposit account should be in the same market even if the non-interest-bearing current account is not itself a substitute for the deposit account. Barclays told us that at the centre of this chain of substitution was the customers' need for liquidity management services. It said that because their cash flow was highly volatile, SMEs needed access to a range of products to manage their liquidity, which included money transmission, short-term deposit and short-term borrowing facilities. The concept of the chain of substitution also applies to the geographical market. If some SMEs see two towns A and B as substitutes and some other SMEs see two towns B and C as substitutes, are towns A and C in the same market? It is only legitimate to treat chains of products as part of the same market if each link in the chain of substitutability is sufficiently strong to ensure that all products in the chain are affected by a common price constraint.

3.26. In assessing the strength of chains of substitution the standard question should be asked: would a hypothetical monopoly supplier of one element of the chain find it profitable to raise its price out of line with those charged by suppliers of supposedly linked products?

3.27. Even if the demand-side links are not strong, a wider market definition might still be justified for supply-side reasons, for example the ability of a supplier of banking services to personal customers to switch to supplying banking services to SMEs if the price of the latter rose relative to the former.

3.28. Before analysing the definition of the market we look at the importance of banking costs to SMEs as this will tend to influence their price sensitivity.

Importance of banking costs to SMEs

3.29. One factor in determining whether SMEs are price sensitive with regard to changes in the prices they pay for banking services will be the amount of money they spend on banking services and the proportion of their total costs (or turnover) accounted for by these charges. A small amount or proportion should imply a low incentive for SMEs to be concerned with these charges given the opportunity costs of their time in seeking to obtain better terms. Some of the main clearing groups did not accept this statement. For example, Lloyds TSB told us that the fact that banking costs were low as a proportion of overall costs did not mean that SMEs would not be price sensitive. It said that if SMEs valued service quality (or non-price factors generally) and providers differentiated their service, then searching would be worth the effort even if it was relatively time consuming. Barclays stated that the importance of banking to SMEs was not just a matter of the costs of the services, because their whole business viability rested on their being able to make all payments they needed to whenever they needed to.

3.30. We asked the four largest clearing groups for estimates of the average amount of money spent by SMEs on banking services and for these amounts as a proportion of the total costs and/or turnover of SMEs. Most of the banks provided estimates of the average annual amount spent on money transmission services. These estimates, all for 1999, ranged from just over £200 to about £550. They accounted for on average less than 1 per cent of turnover of SMEs. Barclays and HSBC estimated that the cost of interest to an SME accounted for, on average, less than 1 per cent of its turnover of SMEs.

3.31. HSBC told us that the average annual (per account) money transmission charge was £232 for SMEs with accounts at its bank. RBSG gave a figure of £546 for SMEs banking with NatWest with an annual turnover of between £100,000 and £1 million, and of about £105 for its SMEs with an annual turnover of up to £100,000, giving a weighted average of just under £300. Barclays' estimate was £282. Lloyds TSB estimated that the average annual money transmission charges for existing SMEs was about £213.

3.32. Lloyds TSB told us that, as part of a recent review, it had examined the costs of money transmission services as against the account debit turnover (which, in its view, approximated to a business's own costs) for a sample of over 4,000 of its Business Banking customers using one of its accounts. It provided us with summary data from this survey. From this data we have calculated that, on average, the cost of money transmission services accounts for less than 1 per cent of Lloyds TSB Business Banking SMEs' debit turnover.

3.33. Barclays estimated that the average annual money transmission cost and account management charges to SMEs accounted for about 0.1 per cent of an SME's own costs. HSBC estimated that money transmission costs accounted for about 0.3 per cent of turnover of smaller SMEs, falling to 0.2 per cent for larger SMEs. Barclays estimated that the average cost of interest to an SME, with an overdraft, was £1,694 a year, on average 0.3 per cent of an SME's own costs. HSBC said that on average borrowing charges might be as high as 1 per cent of turnover but that the use of averages could be highly misleading.

3.34. We begin our analysis of market definition by looking at the product market. We then look at the geographical market.

The product market

The views of the main clearing groups and others on market definition

3.35. Lloyds TSB told us that there were essentially three product markets. These were: deposit accounts and similar savings products; credit products (other than that part of overdraft facilities which formed an integral part of the SME's day-to-day cash-flow management which, in its view, formed an integral part of a current account service), including loans and other debt products such as factoring, invoice discounting, leasing and hire purchase; and current account services (with and without overdrafts).

3.36. Lloyds TSB said that there was a single market for the provision of a package of elements together making up the current account service. It stated that the package included the provision of facilities for the customer to pay in cash and cheques for credit to his account, the receipt of direct transfers of funds to his account, the making of payments to third parties (by withdrawal of cash, the drawing of cheques, the effecting of electronic transfers), and the storage of funds pending such disbursement. It said that, in theory, a customer could buy some of these elements separately but, in practice, the convenience to both the customer and the provider of having all the elements supplied together were such as to mean that it would be difficult for a supplier of just one or two of these elements to compete effectively with suppliers providing the whole package as a unified current account product.

3.37. Lloyds TSB told us that there were numerous personal and SME customers who were confident that they would be able to manage their personal and business affairs in such a way that they would not need an overdraft facility. It said that suppliers could compete effectively to supply such customers without offering an overdraft facility. However, it stated that there were many SMEs which recognized that, however prudently they managed their business affairs, there would be times when they required immediate access to short-term funding to smooth over the irregularities in their cash flow. This, said Lloyds TSB, was simply a fact of business life. Lloyds TSB told us it was arguable that, for the customers that might require an overdraft, there were few, if any, substitutes for the provision of a limited overdraft facility by the provider of the remainder of their current account requirements. It said that the current account provider was, in many cases, uniquely well placed to offer competitively-priced credit to meet urgent, short-term funding needs. This was because, according to Lloyds TSB, the current account provider could: monitor the SME's cash flow; use its day-to-day knowledge of the SME's business to price the overdraft more accurately; and make funds available to the SME by simply advancing funds on the current account to meet cheques and standing orders and so on as they were presented to it for processing, thereby incurring no administrative cost to the SME in having funds transferred by a third party into the current account.

3.38. HSBC defined the markets in a broadly similar way to Lloyds TSB. However, it said that the money transmission market included current accounts but excluded overdrafts and that the market for debt included overdrafts as well as all other forms of debt finance. HSBC took the view that debt finance was in a separate market from current accounts/money transmission, in that the ability to compete in the market for debt was independent from the ability to offer money transmission services. A large proportion of SME customers did not require debt finance but would nevertheless require a current account to make and receive payments: their choice of current account providers would not be affected by the type of debt finance products offered by those providers (if any).

3.39. HSBC told us that products designed for the personal sector should be included within each of these relevant markets (see paragraphs 3.49 and 3.50). It also said that the market could not be constrained to include only SMEs with an annual turnover of below £25 million, because the banks did not distinguish between such SMEs and other larger businesses when pricing their services, and there was a chain of substitution running from personal through small businesses to large businesses.

3.40. RBSG believed that the relevant markets for SME customers should be defined in terms of four separate product categories: money transmission, debt, deposits and merchant acquisition. It said that the market for money transmission included suppliers to personal customers as these suppliers could equally well supply these services to SMEs. It stated that at least overdrafts, bank term loans, asset finance and factoring should be considered part of the market for SME borrowing. It told us that at a minimum the deposit market should include instant access savings accounts to term deposits of up to a period of a year and that it was possible that investment options of a year or more were also part of the relevant market.

3.41. Barclays told us that there was one product market—the SME banking market. It said that at the heart of the SME banking market was the SME customers' need for liquidity management services, which were necessary for them to manage their highly volatile cash flows. Barclays stated that these included money transmission services, short-term deposits and access to short-term borrowing. It said that the three broad product categories—money transmission, deposit products and debt products—should all be included in any analysis. Barclays stated that money transmission consisted of three elements: true money transmission services (for example, paying bills by various means of payment such as cheques and cash), deposit balances and overdraft credit, and that each of these services faced substitution from alternative products. It used the chain of substitution concept to argue that the business current account provided the starting point in a chain of linked credit and debit products. It said that a chain started from the business current accounts through the business deposit accounts to personal deposit accounts and the equivalent deposit accounts provided by non-bank suppliers. Similarly it stated that business current accounts were linked to overdrafts which in turn were linked to other forms of debt finance such as loans, leasing and factoring. Barclays told us that the SME market was constrained by products offered to personal customers.

3.42. BoS stated that there were three product markets—current account services (money transmission market), deposits and bank debt. It told us that it discounted the money transmission market as this was not influential in determining which provider the SME selected. It said that the provision of debt facilities was more significant and would frequently determine the selection of a bank to manage the entire banking relationship.

3.43. SMEs saw overdrafts, asset finance and business loans as alternative ways of borrowing to fund the operations of a business according to BoS. It did not see factoring and invoice discounting facilities as competing against overdraft facilities. It regarded factoring and invoice discounting as complementary to traditional bank finance and for certain SMEs as being the best type of facility for debt/working capital finance.

3.44. The Co-operative Bank said that there were three major product markets: money transmission, debt and deposits. It stated that on the basis of characteristics and uses, each of these major product markets could be split into smaller markets where there was doubt about the degree of substitutability. It told us that the money transmission market could be split into two markets: standard tariff transmission accounts and negotiated tariff transmission accounts. It stated that the debt market could be divided into three markets: short open-term lending products (cards and overdrafts), medium fixed-term lending products (unsecured business loans) and long-term lending products (larger secured loans). The Co-operative Bank told us that the deposit market could be two markets: instant access deposit accounts and notice/bond deposit accounts.

3.45. Abbey National told us that there was one SME banking market that included current accounts, lending and deposits. Alliance & Leicester stated that asset financing/invoice discounting and traditional bank lending were traditionally run as separate businesses from mainstream banking because they were specialized. It said that with asset finance it was necessary to understand taxation regulations and the value of the underlying asset. However, it defined the relevant market as the provision of all banking services for businesses. In its view, a specific market did not exist for SMEs, it being part of a wider offering to business customers. NAB emphasized that the mix of functions in products meant that the traditional distinctions between products (such as overdrafts, current accounts and term loans) were increasingly blurred from the viewpoint of the SME and readily substitutable. It said that, for example, NAB variable rate loans allowed SMEs to redraw monies from the loan, change repayment options and make early repayment at no charge, and that business credit cards provided a payments service displacing cheques and cash as well as a substitute line of credit for SMEs.

3.46. With regard to overdrafts, First Trust acknowledged that overdrafts were a different type of debt product, being a flexible arrangement to cover working capital and short-term requirements. It said that factoring and invoice discounting also had different characteristics from other forms of debt. As regards other asset finance, First Trust regarded this as differing from general purpose business loans only up to a point. Within debt, BoI thought it a fair assessment that factoring and invoice discounting had distinct features from other debt products. Similarly as regards deposits, BoI broadly accepted that whereas SMEs would look around to find the best deposit rates on sizeable and stable sums, for small volatile funds they were more likely to put them on deposit with their main bank.

3.47. We noted that the Cruickshank report concluded that there were two relevant economic markets for SMEs: local markets for money transmission services and local markets for bank debt where bank debt included overdrafts and term loans but excluded other debt products such as factoring, invoice discounting, leasing and hire purchase.[1] The Cruickshank report also stated that in practice in the UK the supply of overdrafts and bank loans was tied to the supply of money transmission services; and for the purpose of analysis, the supply of current accounts could be taken with the supply of overdrafts and term loans.[2] As regards savings, the Cruickshank report stated that in principle SMEs faced the same conditions as retail customers in the savings markets, with a free choice from a large number of suppliers, and as a result it did not analyse the savings market for SMEs alone.[3] It concluded that the savings market (along with the three product markets for personal customers[4]) were national and would remain so for the foreseeable future.

3.48. We consider whether SME customers with personal accounts are part of the same market as SME customers with business accounts in two ways. First we look at the customers themselves, and secondly we look at the relevant products.

SMEs with and without business accounts

The views of the main clearing groups

3.49. HSBC and Barclays believed that, for the purpose of this inquiry, the relevant market should include personal accounts used by SMEs for business purposes. They said that some SMEs, especially start-ups and others within the lower turnover bands that had relatively simple banking requirements very similar to those of personal customers, in terms of transaction volumes, were able to satisfy their requirements by using banking products designed for personal customers. They believed that about one-quarter of SMEs used personal products.

---

[1]*Competition in UK Banking*, A Report to the Chancellor of the Exchequer, March 2000, paragraph 5.24.
[2]Ibid, paragraph 5.25.
[3]Ibid, paragraph 5.22.
[4]Money transmission, unsecured lending and secured lending (ibid, paragraph 4.3).

3.50. HSBC said that there had been and would be many instances where an SME customer, for various reasons, decided not to declare his or her business status and either opened a personal account, or used an existing personal account, for business purposes. It told us that it offered different products to businesses and to personal customers because their banking services requirements and their utilization of the bank's resources were different. However, it said that, although all SME customers were likely to utilize money transmission services more than personal customers, the needs of some SMEs (for example, sole traders with low turnover and a limited cash-handling requirement) were often much closer to those of personal customers than they were to the needs of larger SMEs.

3.51. Lloyds TSB stated that for some SMEs (generally sole traders running certain types of small businesses), banking products designed for personal customers were suitable substitutes for SME-specific products. (In Lloyds TSB's case the income from such SMEs was not separately identifiable.) It told us that the availability of personal banking products acted as a competitive constraint on firms supplying banking services to such SMEs. It stated that for other SMEs, however, access to a relationship manager, be it for advice or at times when cash flow was tight, was a definite advantage, which would not be available to them via a personal account. Hence, in its view, only SMEs with the simplest banking requirements, the characteristics of which were not very different from those of personal customers, in practice chose to run their business through a personal account. Lloyds TSB therefore accepted that business accounts were the proper focus of our inquiry.

3.52. RBSG said that personal banking was a fundamentally different type of activity to business banking; it involved fewer and less complex transactions of a less risky nature.

3.53. First Trust believed that only a very small proportion of its SMEs operated personal accounts for business purposes and so were not relevant for our inquiry. BoI believed it was a fair assumption that businesses operating through personal accounts were not particularly relevant to the market we were looking at, given their different characteristics.

Policy on personal accounts being used for business purposes

3.54. HSBC told us that it did not have a formal policy that SME customers must not use a personal account for business activities. It stated that it would not open a personal account in the name of a limited company. For sole traders and partnerships, personal accounts would only be opened if the individuals concerned used their own name(s) rather than a trading name. HSBC said that certain restrictions arose as a result of legal considerations, for example in the use of cheque cards (under APACS rules, limited companies could not be issued with cheque guarantee cards). It told us that where the pattern of the transaction made it obvious that a personal account was being used for business purposes HSBC might occasionally close a loss-making personal account which had 'average business' levels of money transmission usage if the customer refused, on request from the bank, to open a business account. But HSBC said that it would first suggest that it would be more appropriate for that customer to use a business account and its general approach in this area would always be to try and encourage SME use of business accounts.

3.55. RBSG told us that NatWest's personal current account products were designed specifically for personal customers and were not intended for use by SMEs. It said that NatWest generally relied on its staff for detecting SMEs masquerading as personal customers—by seeing a large number of transactions going through a (supposedly) personal account. In such a case, RBSG stated that the issue would be discussed with the customer who would move on to an SME account or would change his or her behaviour (ie use the personal account as just a personal one).

3.56. Barclays told us that it was not its policy to prevent SMEs from using a personal account in preference to products specifically designed for businesses. However, it said that it actively encouraged customers it knew to be SMEs to use business products as they offered SMEs a substantial advantage over personal products.

3.57. Lloyds TSB told us that at the highest level within its organization it drew a distinction between personal and non-personal customers for the purpose of both its internal organization and in categorizing products and/or services provided. It said that where it identified an SME using a personal account it would encourage the customer to open a business account based on the benefits of holding such an account. It stated that this reflected the fact that products and services were tailored, and priced, to suit the particular usage of different customer groups. Lloyds TSB said that there were differences in the way in which personal and business customers made use of their bank. On the one hand, the vast majority of genuinely personal users generated very few money transmission services (they paid in few cheques, and rarely used the branch counter to pay in large amounts of cash). On the other hand, SMEs were generally larger users of money transmission services. It told us that policy and procedures did not allow a personal current account to be opened in the name of an incorporated entity. It stated that a customer operating a business through a personal account would not be able to access products in its business range. Lloyds TSB told us that it would not advise an SME to take out a personal loan for a business purpose. However, it said that it would allow an SME to take out such a loan for such a purpose if the SME insisted. Lloyds TSB told us that as part of the consolidation of the former TSB and Lloyds IT systems, it was reviewing accounts.

3.58. BoS told us that its personal banking products were not available to SMEs. It said that individuals who owned or managed SMEs might use these products and services, but only in their personal capacity, and that business use of personal products was negligible. It stated that a different price structure was in operation for Personal and Business Banking products.

3.59. The Co-operative Bank said that it had no policy restrictions that would prevent an SME from obtaining services designed for personal customers unless the SME was a limited company. It stated that on occasion it would become aware that customers were directing business turnover through a personal account and would encourage them to open designated business accounts.

Advantages and disadvantages to SMEs of their using a business and not a personal account

3.60. The main advantages to the SMEs as told to us by the four largest clearing groups were the following: -

(a) SMEs have access to the expertise of the relevant staff of the bank who are trained to serve such customers.

(b) SMEs have access to a wider and more flexible range of products and services.

(c) SMEs have lower unauthorized borrowing charges.

(d) Interest received by limited company SMEs would be paid without deduction of tax.

(e) Business and personal transactions go through separate accounts making bookkeeping easier.

3.61. The four largest clearing groups told us of the following main disadvantages to SMEs of using a business account compared with using a personal account:

(a) SMEs would incur money transmission and other charges. However, the banks pointed out that new SMEs (start-ups) and those switching banks might not have to pay money transmission charges for an introductory period.

(b) SMEs would not receive interest on their current accounts.

Advantages and disadvantages to banks of SMEs using a business and not a personal account

3.62. The main advantages to banks as told to us by the four largest clearing groups were the following:

(a) The banks received revenue from the charges to SMEs using business accounts.

(b) Some of the banks would have lower costs as they did not pay interest on current accounts.

(c) The banks had a better understanding of the risks involved when dealing with SMEs and therefore had better credit control.

(d) The banks could develop products and services that were more suited to SMEs.

3.63. The four largest clearing groups told us of the following main disadvantages to banks of SMEs using a business account compared with using a personal account:

(a) The banks incurred costs of providing the various services to SMEs.

(b) The banks lost income, for example from lower unauthorized borrowing fees.

Estimates of number of personal account holders that use personal accounts for business purposes

3.64. Lloyds TSB told us that it did not hold data on the number of SMEs holding personal current and/or deposit accounts for business use. However, it stated that in practice there were likely to be some incorporated SME customers who, because they did not generate large volumes of money transmission services transactions, generated a similar pattern of usage to a personal customer, and hence, used a personal account without their banks noticing or objecting. It also gave the example of certain kinds of sole traders, for example self-employed consultants. It said that in contrast to these types of sole traders, other sole traders, for example those running retail shops, would be likely to generate a very different pattern of account usage unlike a personal customer, with frequent deliveries of cash to the local branch and regular payments from accounts to suppliers.

3.65. Barclays estimated that in 1999 it had a maximum of 230,000 personal customers that could have been operating a business without a business account with Barclays. It estimated this figure by multiplying the DTI's estimate of the number of small and medium-sized businesses by Barclays' share of business current accounts and deducting the actual number of business customers held by Barclays. Barclays recognized that some of the 230,000 customers could hold business accounts with other banks. Barclays' estimate compares with its total number of SME customers which stood at about 560,000 at the end of 1999. SMEs with personal accounts therefore represent, according to Barclays, a maximum of 29 per cent of all small and medium-sized businesses with current accounts at Barclays. Barclays also estimated that in 1992 it would have had a maximum of 165,000 personal customers that could have been operating a business without a Barclays business account according to the same methodology. In 1992 Barclays had 677,000 SME customers with business accounts. Therefore at that time, small and medium-sized businesses with personal accounts would have represented a maximum of 20 per cent of all such businesses with current accounts at Barclays. It told us that, in an annual survey of small business drawn from various sources, about 20 per cent of firms with an annual turnover under £0.5 million did not have a business bank account. It said that, in a survey of start-ups, in the year to September 2000 about 16 per cent of start-ups did not have a separate business account. Barclays also estimated that the revenue from its customers using its personal accounts for business purposes accounted for about 7 per cent of its revenue (less provisions for bad debts) from SMEs.

3.66. RBSG estimated that in 2000 some 30,000 of NatWest's retail customers used a personal account for business activities. It told us that it had no reason to believe that this number had significantly changed since 1989. It stated that, given the total number of its accounts, it viewed the number of NatWest's retail customers using their account for business purposes as insignificant (about 3 per cent of the number of SME current accounts).

3.67. HSBC estimated that about 25 per cent of SMEs and about 40 per cent of SMEs with an annual turnover of up to £100,000 used their personal accounts for business activities. Its 25 per cent estimate was based on a market research report of July 2000 and DTI statistical publications (see paragraph 3.6). HSBC told us that the high usage of personal accounts for business transactions was supported by survey evidence. It said that a survey conducted for HSBC in 1996[1] indicated that 17 per cent of SMEs made some use of

---

[1]*Public Attitude Survey*, 1996.

personal accounts for business purposes and one in 1999[1] found that 36 per cent of sole traders/partnerships sometimes paid business revenue directly into a personal account. HSBC stated that the regular annual surveys of start-up businesses conducted by a market research company showed that, for three of the four largest clearing banks, the proportion of their business start-up customers using personal accounts for business purposes had been 9 or 10 per cent for each of the last three years. However, HSBC said that these figures, high as they were, were probably underestimates; a higher proportion of SMEs as a whole probably used their personal accounts for business purposes because start-ups benefited from a period of free banking on their business current account.

3.68. In contrast, a number of other banks, for example BoS, the Co-operative Bank, First Trust and BoI, told us that the number of their personal account holders that used their personal accounts for business purposes was insignificant.

3.69. Some of these estimates are based on DTI statistics, in particular the DTI's estimates for the number of businesses with no employees (sole traders). The DTI estimated that in 1999 these sole traders accounted for 63 per cent of the total number of businesses. In its annual statistical publications the DTI points out that its estimate of sole traders 'is the greatest potential source of error which is due to the assumptions necessary in estimating businesses that do not appear on the official register and to sampling error with the self-employment data on which these estimates are based'. The publications also state that 'only data for businesses with at least one employee are suitable for detailed analysis. Data for businesses with no employees (and hence the total number of businesses) may be regarded as a broad indicator of the level of business activity'. Businesses with at least one employee account for 37 per cent of the DTI's estimate of the total number of businesses.

3.70. We have estimated the number of small and medium-sized businesses without a business current account by using the DTI's estimate of the number of these businesses and our estimate of the number of SMEs (ie those with business current accounts). We have adjusted the DTI's estimate to remove those businesses with an annual turnover of more than £25 million—this makes very little difference to the total. We have taken into account that, on the basis of data provided to us by the main clearing groups, small and medium-sized businesses have, on average, about 1.2 business current accounts. Using this data, we estimate that 19 per cent of small and medium-sized businesses do not have a business current account.[2]

3.71. A market research report on SMEs (see paragraphs 4.259 to 4.263) estimated the proportions of the value of lending and credit balances accounted for by small and medium-sized business with no business current accounts. It used data from the BBA (on the value of credit balances and lending by SMEs with an annual turnover of less than £1 million) and from the DTI (estimates of the number and turnover of small and medium-sized businesses). In producing its estimates, the report used the ratio between deposits and turnover and between lending and turnover, and it estimated that 38 per cent of sole traders did not have a business current account. It estimated the value of credit balances and borrowing by medium-sized businesses (data not collected by the BBA) by increasing the ratios between deposits and turnover and between lending and turnover. Our approach differed from that of the market research report in that, because we had data on medium-sized businesses and on all SMEs broken down by turnover (provided by the banks), we used ratios for the smaller businesses to estimate the value of credit balances and lending of businesses with no business current accounts and the data for SMEs provided by the companies. Our results are based on our estimate that 29 per cent of sole traders do not have a business current account.[3] Table 3.2 shows our results and those of the market research report.

---

[1] HSBC's *Liability Research*, 1999.

[2] DTI statistics show that there were 3.67 million small and medium-sized businesses (less than 250 employees) in the UK in 1999. HSBC provided us with its analysis where it used less than 200 employees from DTI data. This makes very little difference to the total number of small and medium-sized businesses. We estimated that there were 3.54 million SME business current accounts in the UK in 1999. Using the ratio of the number of current accounts per SME (based on data provided by the main clearing banks), we estimated that there were 2.99 million SMEs with business current accounts in the UK in 1999. Therefore, we calculated that there were 0.68 million SMEs with no business current accounts (3.67 million − 2.99 million) which accounts for 19 per cent of the number of small and medium-sized businesses (0.68 million / 3.67 million).

[3] DTI statistics show that there were 2.32 million sole traders in the UK in 1999. Using our estimate of the number of SMEs with no business current accounts (0.68 million), we calculated that sole traders with no business account accounts for 29 per cent of the number of sole traders (0.68 million / 2.32 million).

TABLE 3.2 **Proportion of credit balances and lending accounted for by sole traders with no business account, 1999**

per cent

Type of account	CC	Estimates by: Market research report
Current account	1.2	⎫
Deposit account	1.8	⎬ 2.1
Overdrafts	1.0	1.2
Term lending	2.7	2.0

Source: CC calculations on data provided by the main clearing groups.

3.72. Our estimates and those of the market research report are very similar—small and medium-sized businesses with no business current accounts account for very small proportions of the value of credit balances and borrowing by small and medium-sized businesses.

3.73. We asked the four largest clearing groups how many SMEs had switched from operating a business account to operating their business through a personal account. All the banks that responded told us that there were very few instances of this type of switching. Barclays provided us with evidence that actual switching from business accounts to personal accounts does take place, although this amounted to a relatively small proportion of accounts—less than 0.5 per cent of the number of its SME business current accounts. It also investigated those SMEs that closed their business account but increased the number of their transactions through their personal account. Adding these SMEs to the number of SMEs that did switch increased the proportion of switchers to about 1 per cent. Barclays said that switching from personal accounts to business accounts was a much more common and established pattern than switching from business to personal accounts, as the former reflected the fact that the banking needs grew as businesses matured.

3.74. HSBC told us that sometimes, an SME on its Small Business tariff that had money transmission usage patterns indistinguishable from those of the average HSBC personal account customer would ask to switch its activity over to a personal account, and this would be agreed if HSBC found that the level of cost recovery would still be acceptable. It said that although it was harder to demonstrate switching from business to personal accounts than vice versa, this did not invalidate its view that personal and business products were part of a single market, since two products could be considered substitutable even if customers did not show an equal propensity to switch between them in both directions. It stated that the fact that SMEs actively compared business and personal current accounts for their money transmission needs was reflected in its offer of up to 24 months' free banking to start-ups. HSBC told us that this was designed to make the business current account more attractive to these customers relative to the personal current account and so provided direct evidence of its prices for business accounts being constrained by the potential for SMEs to use personal accounts for business transactions.

3.75. We now look at the prospects for demand- and supply-side substitution. The evidence is presented under each of the four aspects listed in paragraph 3.24.

Characteristics of SMEs

3.76. The DTI estimated that there were 3.7 million small and medium-sized businesses in the UK in 1999.[1] The DTI's estimates include all private sector businesses, even if they sell their products exclusively to the Government, and exclude central and local government, charities and other non-profit-making organizations. Table 3.3 shows how this number is broken down by number of employees, by number of businesses and by annual turnover. We have excluded from DTI estimates those businesses employing 250 or more staff.

[1]*Small and Medium Enterprise (SME) Statistics for the UK, 1999*, September 2000.

TABLE 3.3 **Small and medium-sized businesses broken down by number of businesses, number of employees and annual turnover, 1999**

	Total	Number of employees		
		None	1–49	50–249
		per cent		
Businesses (m)	3.7	63.3	36.0	0.7
Employment (m)	12.0	22.5	56.8	20.7
Turnover (£bn ex VAT)*	967.9	9.3	63.8	26.8

Source: CC calculations based on DTI national statistics, September 2000.

*Percentage totals do not sum to 100 because of rounding.

3.77. Sole traders account for the majority of the businesses in the UK (63 per cent) but a smaller proportion of the number of employees (23 per cent) and an even smaller proportion of turnover (9 per cent). As a proportion of all businesses in the UK, SMEs account for some 55 per cent of employment and 45 per cent of turnover.

3.78. Barclays produced estimates of the number of start-ups and business closures in England and Wales. These estimates, together with its estimates of the number of mainstream firms in England and Wales, which are defined as full-time businesses with the sole objective of making a profit, are shown in Figure 3.1. Barclays includes all sizes of firms, although it states that the vast majority of firms have annual turnover of less than £1 million.

FIGURE 3.1

Start-ups, closures and the stock of mainstream businesses in England and Wales, 1988 to 1999

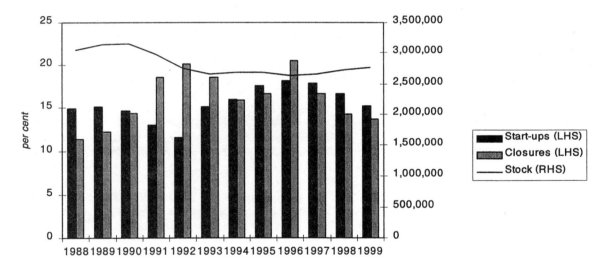

Source: Barclays and CC calculations based on data provided by Barclays.

3.79. Figure 3.1 shows that the trend in the stock of mainstream businesses in England and Wales increased between 1988 and 1990, fell between 1991 and 1993 and has been fairly flat between 1994 and 2000. The rates of start-ups and closures of businesses were broadly in line with each other, except for the period between 1991 and 1993. During this period, the rate of closures was greater than the rate of start-ups, resulting in a fall in the stock of businesses. Over the period from 1988 to 1999, the percentage of start-up businesses to the stock of businesses averaged 15.5 per cent and closures averaged just over 16 per cent of the stock of businesses.

3.80. Barclays also produced estimates of the average lifespan of businesses over the period 1988 to 2000 and this data is shown in Table 3.4.

TABLE 3.4 **Business lifespan***

	Months since formation					
	6	*12*	*24*	*36*	*48*	*60*
Percentage of businesses surviving	91	79	58	45	36	30

Source: Barclays.

---

*Businesses in England and Wales, excluding second occupation and non-trading businesses. Looking at the lifespan of each current account where the business closed, not the complete business relationship or just ceasing to trade.

3.81. Table 3.4 shows that 91 per cent of start-ups have survived at least six months, with nearly 80 per cent trading for one year and 58 per cent still in operation after two years. 70 per cent of businesses have closed after five years. HSBC told us that the average lifespan of a business was about eight years.

3.82. We applied the proportion of start-ups (15.5 per cent) and the proportion of switchers (5 per cent—see paragraph 3.357) to our estimate of the number of SME current accounts in the UK (3.5 million[1]) to estimate the number of new SME current accounts (725,000) (see Table 3.5).

TABLE 3.5 **Breakdown of new SME current accounts**

	%	*Number**
Start-ups	75.6	548,000
Switchers	24.4	177,000
Total (excluding CACs)	100.0	725,000

Source: Data provided by the banks and CC calculations based on data provided by the banks.

---

*Rounded to the nearest 1,000.

3.83. Table 3.5 shows that about three-quarters of new SME current accounts are start-ups.

Characteristics of banking services

Current accounts

3.84. Many SME customers can use their business current accounts to make and receive payments in a number of different ways (over the counter, by post, by telephone and by PC) and through a number of different means of payment (for example, cash, cheques, and automatic methods such as direct debit and standing orders).

3.85. SMEs with a business current account generally have access to a relationship manager. A relationship manager is the SMEs' main contact at the bank for discussing the financial requirements of their business including deciding on overdraft facilities and other lending requirements and associated rates of interest, all within set guidelines. Lloyds TSB told us that relationship management duties included monitoring the day-to-day operations of the customers' current accounts to ensure that they were within agreed guidelines and taking decisions on whether to honour or return 'over-limit' payments.

3.86. Relationship managers are responsible for a number of SMEs, the number depending upon the size of the SME and the complexity of their needs. Lloyds TSB stated that each of the (1,820) relationship managers in its Business Banking division (serving SMEs with an annual turnover of less than £2 million) was responsible for, on average, just over 300 SMEs. However, it told us that the average number of business customers for the (220) relationship managers in its Commercial Banking division (serving business with an annual turnover of between £2 million and £100 million) was 75. These average numbers of SMEs per relationship manager are also broadly found in Scotland and Northern Ireland. In Scotland, each of RBS's relationship managers in its Retail division (handling SMEs with an annual turnover of up to £1 million) is, on average, responsible for 273 SMEs. In its Commercial and Mid-Corporate division

---

[1]Excluding charities, associations and clubs (CACs). Including CACs does not alter the proportions.

(business with an annual turnover of between £1 million and £100 million) each relationship manager is, on average, responsible for 158 businesses. Regarding Northern Ireland, Northern told us that each of its relationship managers for smaller SMEs was responsible for about 200 customers whereas each of its relationship managers for larger SMEs dealt with about 100 customers.

3.87. Except for their credit assessment duties, for which the costs are generally recovered via loan arrangement fees, the costs of relationship managers are mainly covered by revenue derived from operating current accounts—money transmission charges, for example pence per cheque and revenue from credit balances—and not by specific charges related to the use of relationship managers. Barclays told us that some costs were also recovered by interest on credit facilities and interest on deposits. There are exceptions to this charging policy. Lloyds TSB said that since January 2000 it had provided its Commercial Banking customers with three different types of relationship management, each addressing a different customer need. The first option, 'Banking Solutions', was close to the general service described in paragraph 3.85 and was focused only on meeting the financial needs of the SME customer. Costs were recovered from the revenue derived from operating the current account. Lloyds TSB told us that the two other offers provided additional services, designed to offer support to the customer in the general development of the customer's business, rather than being limited to dealing with the financing of the enterprise. These services, 'Industry Focus' and 'Business Strategy', carried additional charges of £4,200 a year and £10,000 a year respectively and were provided by the customer's relationship manager who also provided the required core banking service.

3.88. Lloyds TSB said that a similarly segmented relationship management service was to be offered to its Business Banking SMEs and completion of the roll-out of the new strategy was anticipated to occur in October 2001, with Scottish SMEs and SMEs on one existing TSB account receiving the new offerings thereafter. SMEs would be offered the choice of four relationship manager options (presently being offered on a pilot basis), depending on the level of involvement which they wanted with the bank and the way in which they wanted to deal with the bank. Lloyds TSB told us that these four options would offer an increased range of services and a greater intensity of relationship for an appropriately higher charge. The first option, 'Business Express', offers a telephone banking relationship with access to a team of relationship managers (and access to all products and services as well as access to branches and ATMs). There is no monthly fee for this service. The second option, 'Business Response', provides a named relationship manager available by telephone. Lloyds TSB told us that where the SME or the bank required face-to-face contact, for instance when an SME was borrowing larger amounts of money or had a more complex financial requirement, a separate team of business finance managers was available to see the SME. SMEs pay an account maintenance fee for this relationship of £2.50 a month. 'Business Focus' is the third option and this provides a face-to-face relationship with a specific relationship manager. A monthly relationship fee of £10 is charged for this service. The fourth option is known as 'Business Partner' and this provides a fuller relationship than Business Focus. A monthly relationship fee of £50 is charged for this service. [

Details omitted. See note on page iv.

]

3.89. RBSG stated that its banks did not charge separately for relationship managers but for SMEs that did not want face-to-face relationship management RBS and NatWest offered an alternative, cheaper direct banking service via the telephone and the Internet. For NatWest this involved a telephone-based relationship manager with no account maintenance fee but with the same money transmission charges as its branch-based service. RBS's business banking direct offering, which was used by about [✂] per cent of SMEs banking with RBS Retail Banking at May 2001, has no relationship manager, free money transmission until 1 January 2002 and, at the end of this period, will on the whole have lower money transmission charges than its branch-based accounts. From 2002, for existing customers, its direct service will charge a flat rate of 20p for each type of standard transaction. This will offer savings on all standard-type transactions (apart from paying in cheques in Scotland which has a price of 19p per cheque) ranging from 20 to 69 per cent (see Table 3.6). RBS's direct service has the same charges as its branch-based accounts for non-standard types of transactions such as stopping a cheque and banker's drafts. [
Details omitted. See note on page iv.   ]

TABLE 3.6 **Money transmission charges for RBS's direct and branch-based services**

pence per transaction

	Direct debit	Standing order	Auto credit	Cheque in	Cheque out	Credit in
England and Wales						
Branch-based	40	43	25	25	55	64
Direct	20	20	20	20	20	20
Difference (p)	20	23	5	5	35	44
Difference (%)	50.0	53.5	20.0	20.0	63.6	68.8
Scotland						
Branch-based	31	45	27	19	46	46
Direct	20	20	20	20	20	20
Difference (p)	11	25	7	−1	26	26
Difference (%)	35.5	55.6	25.9	−5.3	56.5	56.5

Source: CC calculations on data provided by RBS.

3.90. Barclays said that it did not seek to impose any separate charges for relationship managers. It said that in the past it did charge for relationship managers' time but these charges were phased out in March 1995 in response to customer pressure. Barclays told us that research it had carried out had identified a segment of SMEs that would prefer not to have a relationship manager in return for lower charges. It said that it was responding to this finding by introducing a business direct service that would offer SMEs a banking service without access to relationship managers in a branch (although they would be available over the telephone) at prices about 20 per cent lower than those to branch-based customers.

3.91. HSBC said that staff costs, including the costs of relationship managers, were reflected in its product pricing. It stated that separate charges for relationship managers would not only be complex and costly for HSBC to administer but would reduce this transparency to the customer. It told us that it was also important to note that an important part of the role of a relationship manager was the general 'behind the scenes' work, for example considering whether to telephone the customer when a payment was required which exceeded the authorized overdraft limit, or, if the customer was not available, deciding whether to make the payment. HSBC said that it charged customers separately for the services of relationship managers, or any other staff costs or expenses, only in very limited circumstances. It stated that this would be for completion of a special task which was over and above the level of service that the bank could reasonably be expected to provide without recouping some of the additional cost to the bank, such as supplying copy bank statements for an extensive period (and this particular circumstance, and others, were explained in HSBC's Business Banking Charter). Such charges would always be agreed with the customer in advance.

3.92. Another characteristic of most current accounts is access to an overdraft facility. An overdraft facility comprises an agreement between the bank and the customer that the bank will advance funds to the customer on demand, up to an agreed overdraft limit, on terms that the customer will pay interest on the amounts from time to time outstanding. In most cases the principal and interest will be repayable forthwith on demand by the bank. However, in October 2000 NatWest announced the introduction of committed overdrafts for one year that it introduced in March 2001. BoS introduced them in January 2001. Within the overall overdraft limit, the borrower will be free to draw, repay and redraw funds at its discretion, to meet its day-to-day funding requirements. Where a bank agrees to make an overdraft facility available, it generally agrees that the facility should remain available for 12 months or some shorter specified period (albeit normally subject to repayment on demand at any time). However, in practice a facility agreement will often be renewed from one year to the next, and overdrafts may therefore remain outstanding for a number of years. In other cases, the SME will repay the overdraft very quickly, using it only as a short-term stopgap to cover a temporary cash-flow shortfall. Lloyds TSB told us that it actively encouraged SMEs not to depend on overdraft facilities for their medium- to long-term funding requirements, as it was frequently in the customer's interest to arrange finance for these needs through a facility with structured repayments. In its press release announcing its committed overdrafts, BoS noted that SMEs used overdrafts as working capital, ie to fund day-to-day activity of their business, paying supplies and wages, and not to fund permanent items such as premises and machinery. The FPB survey asked SMEs with overdraft facilities to allocate the main use of these funds to working capital, fixed assets or both. The same question was asked to those with fixed-term loans. The FPB survey found that most SMEs with overdraft facilities (84 per cent) used these funds as working capital whereas most SMEs with fixed-term loans (59 per cent) used these funds to acquire fixed assets (see Table 3.7). A number of SMEs (15 per cent of those with overdrafts and 18 per cent of those with term loans) used these products for both working capital and for acquiring fixed assets.

TABLE 3.7 **Purpose of overdrafts and term loan**

per cent

Categories of spend	Overdraft	Term loan
Working capital	83.7	22.4
Fixed assets	1.5	59.3
Working capital and fixed assets	14.8	18.2
Total*	100.0	100.0

Source: FPB survey, *Private Business and their banks*, 2000.

*May not sum because of rounding.

3.93. Table 3.8 shows the proportions of SME current accounts with each of the main clearing groups (Northern did not provide data) that had overdraft facilities at the end of 1999 (left-hand side of the table), the proportions of SME current accounts that were overdrawn for the whole of 1999 and those that were overdrawn for part of the year (right-hand side of the table).

TABLE 3.8 **Proportion of SME current accounts with overdraft facilities and overdrafts, 1999**

per cent

	Proportion of SMEs with overdraft facilities*	Proportion of SMEs with overdrafts		
		All year	Part of year	Total†
Barclays	28.3	5.1	46.7	51.8
NatWest	27.5	8.1	42.7	50.8
HSBC	31.8	10.5	33.9	44.4
Lloyds TSB‡	34.2	10.6	49.2	59.8
RBS	21.9	7.2	41.6	48.9
BoS	22.1	10.1	27.8	37.8
Clydesdale	18.5	8.2	N/A	N/A
Ulster Bank	50.0	11.1	59.0	70.1
BoI	36.6	16.6	28.8	45.4
First Trust	25.0	0.4	43.6	44.0

Source: CC calculations based on data provided by the main clearing groups.

*As at December 1999.
†Totals may not sum because of rounding.
‡Business Banking only.

3.94. Table 3.8 shows that, on average, about 30 per cent of SMEs have an overdraft facility, ranging from 19 per cent for Clydesdale to 50 per cent for Ulster Bank. Lloyds TSB told us that 62 per cent of its Commercial Banking customers had overdraft facilities. These proportions underestimate the extent to which SMEs have overdrafts because they are calculated at a point in time, ie they do not take account of the swings in the value of accounts during the year. The proportions of SMEs that were overdrawn for the whole of 1999 ranged from 0.4 per cent (First Trust) to 17 per cent (BoI). The proportion of SMEs overdrawn for part of 1999 was about 40 per cent, ranging from 28 per cent (BoS) to 59 per cent (Ulster Bank). In total (combining those overdrawn all the year with those overdrawn for some of the year) about 50 per cent of SMEs were overdrawn for at least part of 1999. However, these proportions also underestimate the extent to which SMEs have overdrafts at some point in their lifespan because they only relate to one year. During the life of SMEs it is likely that most of them will require an overdraft facility. Indeed, Lloyds TSB told us that relatively few SMEs would have no need for an overdraft facility. It said that although a significant number of its Business Banking SMEs might remain in credit for a full year, the identity of those customers changed from one year to the next. Barclays said that it had evidence suggesting that only 13 per cent of new SME customers would reach the age of three years and would have remained in credit for the whole period and of firms that would survive five years, only about 25 per cent would have remained in credit for the whole period. HSBC's interpretation of its data in Table 3.8 was that very few SMEs have 'permanent' overdrafts and that only a minority even go overdrawn at any point during the year.

3.95. The proportions of SMEs that are in credit and debit for part of the year provides an indication of the volatility of an SME's cash flow. Other indications were provided by Barclays. It told us that based on a sample of its business customers with an annual turnover of less than £1 million, [✂] per cent of SMEs who were in debt at some point in the year (irrespective of whether the overdraft was arranged or not) exceeded their limit in at least one month during a 12-month period. Also, based on the same sample, Barclays stated that whilst the majority of SMEs (with an annual turnover of less than £1 million) had debit:credit ratios (ie value of payments to value of receipts) in their accounts of between [✂] and [✂] per cent over the year, the month-by-month ratios varied considerably. It said that more than [✂] had experienced a minimum debit:credit ratio of less than 50 per cent in at least one month whilst [✂] per cent had experienced maximum ratio of more than [✂] per cent in at least one month. It illustrated this volatility by dividing the maximum ratio by the minimum. This showed that about half of SMEs had a maximum ratio that was at least five times their minimum ratio and, for more than 15 per cent of them, the maximum ratio was more than 20 times higher than the minimum. RBSG provided us with data that showed that the vast majority of accounts which go overdrawn fluctuate between credit and debit balances during the course of a full year. On the basis of this data, RBSG told us that most overdrafts could not be substituted by term loans. It said that it regarded them both as forms of debt finance: overdrafts to finance short-term financing needs and term loans for medium/long-term financing. HSBC said that some overdrafts could be substituted with term loans and some could not, as some overdrafts were used for medium/long-term financing. It stated that it was irrelevant for the purposes of market definition whether or not most overdrafts could not be substituted for term loans: as long as there was sufficient substitutability by SMEs between overdrafts and other forms of debt such as term loans (which there was), it was inappropriate to include overdrafts (even those overdrafts that were used for working capital) within the same relevant market as money transmission/current accounts.

3.96. Unauthorized overdrafts occur when the SME pays a third party by cheque or by automated debit which, if honoured, will cause the account to go over its overdraft limit or to go overdrawn when no limit is in place. In such cases, the bank will have to decide, when presented with the request for funds in the course of clearing, whether to dishonour the request (on the basis that the bank has not agreed to advance funds to honour the request) or to pay it, and thereby to grant or extend an overdraft to the SME customer. In such cases, the bank will aim to regularize the position after the event, by agreeing or increasing a formal overdraft limit with the customer, or by requiring the customer to bring his account back within its existing limit. An overdraft may be offered either on an unsecured basis, or subject to the giving of security. The proprietors of an SME may be asked to give security over business or personal assets. Proprietors, directors or other family members may be asked to give guarantees[1] of the SME's liability in respect of the overdraft (both principal and interest) and, in some cases, to give security in support of the guarantee such as personal property.

3.97. SMEs with overdrafts pay a rate of interest (see Tables 4.21 and 4.22 for the margins on these rates of interest) and various fees (see Table 4.23).

Term loans

3.98. Term loans differ from overdrafts in that, instead of being repayable on demand, and capable of being drawn down, repaid and redrawn at the borrower's discretion within the overall overdraft limit, they are granted for a fixed term (subject to accelerated repayment in the event of default by the borrower). Generally, the borrower is required to draw down the amount of the principal in accordance with an agreed timetable (for example, drawdown of the total amount on a specified date, or drawdown of an agreed number of tranches at agreed intervals). The borrower will also agree a schedule for repayment, and will pay agreed interest on the amounts outstanding. Such loans may be secured or unsecured, and may be supported by guarantees from third parties.

---

[1]Technically, a guarantee is not security, but it serves to enhance the bank's prospect of recovery in the event of the SME's payment default.

3.99. The borrower may agree to pay interest at a fixed rate, or at a variable rate. For fixed-rate loans, the bank will expect to fund the loan by itself raising the amount of the principal from time to time outstanding for a similar period (for example, if the loan is priced at a fixed rate for a 12-month period, then the bank will work on the basis that it must also borrow at a fixed rate for the same period). In consequence, the bank will expect the borrower to agree that, if it wishes to prepay the loan, then it should also pay an additional amount to compensate the bank for the costs that it has incurred in funding the advance for the scheduled period of the loan.

3.100. In some cases loans are linked to current accounts. NatWest's policy is that SMEs taking out loans with NatWest also have to open a current account with NatWest. RBSG told us that NatWest's policy was a technical requirement, driven by systems constraints which would cease to be an issue when NatWest's accounts were migrated on to RBS systems. Lloyds TSB stated that its policy was that SMEs taking out loans with Lloyds TSB also had to open a current account with Lloyds TSB to facilitate the servicing and repayment of the loan. Barclays told us that in some circumstances a Barclays current account was required to service a loan. It stated that this arose from the fact that it was easier to make payments from an external account into a current account than into a loan account and it arose in the case of a debenture securing the loan. Table 3.9 shows the proportions of SMEs with loan accounts that also had a business current account with the same bank. It shows that, even for banks that do not require SMEs with loan accounts to hold a business current account, most SMEs with a loan account also hold a business current account with the same bank.

TABLE 3.9 **Proportion of SMEs with a loan that also have a business current account at the same bank, 1999**

	%
Barclays	93
HSBC	87
NatWest	100
Lloyds TSB	100
RBS	90
BoS	98
Clydesdale	N/A*
Northern	100
First Trust	N/A†
BoI	85
Ulster Bank	100

Source: CC calculations based on data provided by the main clearing groups.

*NAB told us that the vast majority of SMEs that had a loan account with Clydesdale also had a business current account with it.
†First Trust said that its systems did not record this data but its best estimate was over 90 per cent.
Note: N/A = Not available.

Deposits

3.101. Banks provide a range of deposit products to their SME customers, differing in terms of minimum and maximum amounts of the deposit, length of term, and limits on amount and mode of withdrawals. Interest may be quoted as either gross or net of tax and paid at different intervals, which can make comparisons between quoted rates difficult. RBSG told us that annual equivalent rates (AERs)[1] must appear more prominent than the gross interest rate quoted, thus allowing customers to compare like with like.

3.102. Business deposit accounts are generally not designed to handle day-to-day transactions, but rather are designed to operate as savings vehicles. For example, deposit accounts may be free of service charges, provided the account is not used for trading turnover.

[1]A notional rate that shows the gross interest rate (excluding any reward payable) as if paid and compounded on an annual basis.

3.103. The deposit accounts offered by some of the four largest clearing groups have a condition attached to them that the account can only be used in conjunction with a current account. Barclays said that its Business Premium Account, one of its business deposit accounts, was designed to be linked to a business current account. Barclays told us that SMEs had the choice of its other business deposit accounts—such as its High Interest Business Account—if they did not have or want a Barclays business current account. However, Barclays Business Premium account is used by more SMEs than any of Barclays' business deposit accounts—it accounts for [✂] per cent by number ([✂] per cent by value) of Barclays' deposit products. Barclays' Treasury deposits, a money market product, have the largest proportion by value— [✂] per cent ([✂] per cent by number).

3.104. An SME with either HSBC's Business No-Notice deposit account or its Business 14-day Notice account must have a business current account. HSBC told us that this condition existed for operational reasons because these deposit accounts did not currently carry a cheque book. Therefore, if a customer did not have a current account, outgoing payments would need to be effected electronically. These two accounts represent about three-quarters of business deposit accounts held by HSBC's SMEs by number and about two-thirds by value.

3.105. Lloyds TSB stated that it did not require SMEs to hold its business current accounts alongside any of its business deposit accounts. However, Lloyds TSB told us that the majority of its SMEs with business deposit accounts did nonetheless have a business current account with Lloyds TSB.

3.106. RBSG told us that RBS did not require SMEs using its business deposit accounts to have a current account with RBS. It stated that NatWest no longer required its SME customers to maintain a current account with NatWest in order to operate any of its deposit products. It said that before it acquired NatWest, a number of NatWest's business deposit accounts required SMEs to hold a business current with NatWest.

3.107. Table 3.10 shows the proportion of SMEs with business deposit accounts that did not have a business current account at the same bank.

TABLE 3.10 **Proportion of SME business deposit accounts that had no business current account at the same bank**

	%
Barclays	6.8
Lloyds TSB*	1.4
HSBC	6.8
NatWest	2.9
RBS	10.9
BoS	10.0
Clydesdale	<1†
BoI	29.9
Northern	22.0
Ulster Bank	0
First Trust	N/A

Source: CC calculations based on data provided by the main clearing groups.

*Commercial Banking customers.
†Based on a sample of its SMEs.
Note: N/A = Not available.

3.108. Very few SMEs that have business deposit accounts with the six largest clearing banks and Clydesdale do not have a business current account at the same bank. The proportions are much higher for BoI and Northern but not for Ulster Bank.

3.109. An advantage of having a business current and deposit account at the same bank is that funds can be transferred quicker between the two accounts for a smaller or no charge than they can between a current and a deposit account held at different banks. The transfer of funds between these two types of accounts would occur on the same day if they were both held at the same bank but would take the normal three-day cycle if the accounts were held at different banks. If the accounts were held at different banks, transfer could still take place on the same day if made by CHAPS (transfer of high-value payments which would cost the SME about £20) or if cash was physically withdrawn from one account and paid into the other; the latter might be inconvenient for the SME.

3.110. Apart from deposit accounts, banks offer money market products where SMEs, mainly larger SMEs, invest their surplus monies direct on the money market, normally doing this via a bank. Whereas most of the deposit accounts offered by the main clearing groups to SMEs have standard rates of interest, rates on money market products offered by them tend not to be published. A number of these accounts require a minimum credit balance ranging from £5,000 (HSBC for deposits over six months) to £250,000 (NatWest for Call (no notice) or overnight money). There are, however, a number of no-notice money market accounts with lower thresholds, for example £10,000 for Barclays and £25,000 for BoS.

Factoring and invoice discounting

3.111. SMEs are provided with finance from a factoring company (factor) which agrees to purchase the sales invoices of the SME as they arise in the normal course of trading. The factor also administers and controls the SME's sales ledger and collects the debts from the SME's customers. Factoring may be with recourse, where the factor does not provide bad debt protection, and therefore has recourse to the SME to recover monies advanced when the SME's customers do not pay. Alternatively, the factor may provide non-recourse finance, whereby the factor absorbs such bad debt losses.

3.112. Invoice discounting is used by SMEs requiring finance but not requiring sales ledger administration or credit protection. The SME does not need to notify its customers of the sales finance arrangement—hence it is known as confidential invoice discounting—and the debts are normally subject to full recourse. This is a primarily financial service where the SME maintains the sales ledger and collects from debtors on behalf of the factor to whom the debts have been assigned.

3.113. Factoring and invoice discounting, which we refer to collectively as sales finance, are based on credit sales. Lloyds TSB told us that sales finance was restricted to businesses operating in sectors which generate trade debtors, such as manufacturing, wholesale, distribution and the business-to-business service sector. A recently published report[1] stated that certain types of businesses were not suitable for factoring. It gave the following examples: businesses that invoice in stages, such as those in the construction industry; businesses that sell to the general public or otherwise for immediate settlement; businesses that sell on a sale-or-return basis; and businesses whose goods or services are of a complex nature where there may be a high level of rejection or after-sales service required. It stated that factors also liked to see a good spread of debtors, with no single customer representing a high proportion of the sales ledger. RBSG told us that NatWest required invoice discounting clients sold to a minimum of five other businesses on short-term (up to 120 days) credit.

3.114. The report gave a number of advantages and disadvantages of sales finance. It gave four advantages. First, sales finance provides finance for working capital thereby eliminating or reducing cash-flow problems. Secondly, attractive balance sheets or substantial net worth are not required. The report states that in contrast to other forms of lending, factors tend not to be as concerned about balance sheet strength. The factor's main source of security lies in the trade debts of the business. Thirdly, finance is provided in proportion to sales, reducing the risk of overtrading. The report notes that the amount of finance available grows with the business that permits the SME to plan its future working capital requirements without the burden of having to allow for facility renegotiation. It notes that factors will set limits to a facility but states that these should take into account expected short-term growth. Fourthly, factoring relieves SMEs of the burden of credit control and sales ledger maintenance. The report notes that this service allows the SME to concentrate on its core business activities leaving the chasing of debts and other sales ledger functions to the factor. The report lists three disadvantages. First, the cost of the service: the reports notes that the service is thought to be expensive. It refers to surveys in 1977 and 1981. Secondly, loss of control: the report states

[1]*Factoring in the UK, 2000, Report and guide to the factoring industry*, BCR Publishing, 2000.

that many companies are concerned over the loss of control of the sales ledger and in particular the prospects that a third party will have access to their customers in respect of the often sensitive issue of debt. Thirdly, image: the report notes that since its inception in the UK, factoring has been associated with last resort financing. Potential clients have been concerned that factoring may be seen as a sign of financial weakness by suppliers and customers. However, the report states that in recent years this concern has lessened considerably.

3.115. Factoring normally involves two types of charges: an administration fee and a finance charge. The administration fee is expressed as a percentage of the business turnover. It is designed to cover the costs of debt collection, sales ledger administration and bad debt protection (where the arrangement is non-recourse) by the factor. The fee will vary depending on the factor, the service offered, expected sales volume, average invoice value, and number and status of debtors. Factors may make an additional administration charge in respect of any invoice that remains unpaid for a specified period after the due date, usually 90 days. There will be an administrative charge for invoice discounting to cover the cost of monitoring the account and other non-credit-control administrative functions. The finance charge is levied on the value of the initial payment from the factor to the client. The range of margins on sales finance is discussed in paragraphs 4.143 and 4.144.

Asset finance

3.116. Asset finance provides a medium- to longer-term form of funding for SMEs to finance various forms of capital equipment specific to their businesses. The asset is more important in securing the finance in this funding option than it is in other options such as overdrafts and term lending. The main types of asset finance products are finance leases, operating leases and hire purchase.

3.117. With a finance lease, the full cost of the asset plus finance costs is amortized by way of lease rentals paid by the SME to the lessor. Legal ownership of the asset rests with the lessor but the economic risks and rewards of ownership reside predominantly with the lessee. With an operating lease, the lessor also retains ownership of the asset and leases it to the client, but only a proportion of the asset's capital cost is amortized over the lease period, which is typically less than the physical life of the asset. At the end of the lease, the asset is returned to the lessor, who takes the residual risk of disposing or rehiring the asset. Hire purchase is an agreement to hire an asset that includes the option to purchase, often for a nominal sum, at the end of the contract period.

Use of these products by SME and personal customers

3.118. Some of the characteristics of use associated with money transmission services, debt and deposits for SMEs using business accounts and using personal accounts are similar and some are not. There are two main differences in the characteristics associated with money transmission services for SME and personal customers: first, the extent to which these two groups of customers use the services; and second, there are additional products and services, and related costs associated with business accounts. We deal with these in turn.

3.119. HSBC said that the nature and extent of the use of services by personal and business customers was generally different—SMEs varied considerably but many SMEs used substantially more money transmission facilities than personal customers. HSBC said that, on average, its SME customers with up to £100,000 annual turnover paid in twice as many cheques as personal customers, and made 20 times as much use of HSBC's cash-handling facilities. It stated that deposit accounts also showed a differential—activity levels on business deposit accounts exceeded those on personal accounts by a factor of up to 10. A similar point about the difference in usage was put to us by Lloyds TSB and RBSG. However, HSBC estimated that some 35 per cent of customers on its Small Business tariff had usage patterns that were indistinguishable from the average personal customer. It also said that it was reasonable to assume that many of the estimated 20 to 25 per cent of all SMEs operating through personal accounts also had usage patterns indistinguishable from personal users.

3.120. Barclays also provided some estimates on usage of transaction services by personal and SME customers (see Table 3.11).

TABLE 3.11 Average number of annual transactions by Barclays personal and SME customers

		Average number of annual transactions: categories of customer	
Type of transaction	Personal	SME with annual turnover of less than £1m	SMEs with annual turnover of between £10m and £25m
Cheque and cash deposit			
Cheque debit	*	Figures omitted. See note on page iv.	
ATM withdrawal			
Direct debit/standing order			

Source: Barclays.

*Includes both in-bank debits and connect debits.

3.121. Table 3.11 shows that larger SMEs (an annual turnover of between £10 million and £25 million) make greater use of cheque and cash deposits and cheque withdrawals than smaller SMEs (an annual turnover of less than £1 million) who in turn make greater use of these banking services than personal customers. The reverse is true for ATM withdrawals. Larger SMEs make greater use of direct debits and standing orders than smaller SMEs and personal customers who make broadly the same use of these banking services. Data from RBSG (for NatWest and RBS)[1] and Lloyds TSB[2] showed broadly the same results as those for Barclays, and BoI told us that the data in Table 3.11 was representative estimates of relative usage.

3.122. Regarding additional products for SMEs, businesses operating through a personal account will not have access to a relationship manager. Barclays told us that any business that operated via a personal account would not be permitted to process high volumes of cash and cheques through that account, nor would they receive fact sheets or be able to attend its seminars that provided advice and information on a wide range of topics. RBSG said that none of its business products and services would be available to businesses operating through a personal account. Lloyds TSB stated that businesses without a business account would not be able to use any of its business loan products.

Price levels

3.123. This section on price levels and the next one on changes in prices discuss the comparison of prices between but not within possible markets. Chapter 4 contains a fuller discussion of prices—how they vary between banks and other providers of banking services to SMEs and how they have changed over time.

Money transmission services

3.124. On the whole there are differences in money transmission prices for SMEs operating through a business account and for those operating through a personal account. Lloyds TSB told us that such price differences reflected the fact that personal customers used their accounts less than SMEs and did not have to contribute to the costs of relationship managers through such charges.

3.125. Providers of banking services normally make charges for the main money transmission services used by SMEs but some smaller providers (for example, Fleming and Abbey National) do not charge SMEs

---

[1]RBSG provided data for personal customers, SMEs with an annual turnover of less than £1 million, SMEs with an annual turnover of between £1 million and £10 million and SMEs with an annual turnover of between £10 million and £100 million for cheque and cash deposits, cheque withdrawals, ATM withdrawals (for NatWest only) and direct debits and standing orders (for NatWest only).

[2]Lloyds TSB provided data for personal customers, SMEs with an annual turnover of less than £1 million and SMEs with an annual turnover of between £2 million and £25 million for cheque withdrawals, ATM withdrawals and direct debits and standing orders.

if they operate within specified criteria (see paragraphs 4.27 to 4.29). Under various free banking packages, new SMEs are generally not charged for their main money transmission services. This applies to a lesser extent to some recent switchers—only two (Barclays and HSBC) of the four largest clearing groups have a standard policy of not charging for main money transmission services for switchers (see paragraph 4.8). There are no such charges for SMEs operating through a personal account. As a result SMEs banking with one of the larger providers of banking services will typically pay some hundreds of pounds more each year if they operate through a business account than if they operate through a personal account (paragraphs 4.43 to 4.52 discuss charges to SMEs). SMEs operating through a business account with Fleming or Abbey National will not pay more than SMEs operating through a personal account if they stay within the criteria for free banking of these two providers. HSBC told us that for an SME with an 'average' level of business money transmission activity, the products of the smaller providers were probably not available as they were aimed at levels of money transmission activity similar to that of the typical personal customer. It stated that for SMEs with a lower level of money transmission activity, the difference in money transmission charges would not be hundreds of pounds: it was true that SMEs with these smaller providers were likely to pay less than SMEs with HSBC (assuming they were not receiving HSBC's free banking package) but they would receive a much more basic service. It said that SME customers using a personal account also received a more basic level of service than SMEs using a business account.

3.126. Generally SMEs operating through a business current account will not be paid interest on this account (see Chapter 4). However, this is not always the case; for example, Fleming and Abbey National offer business current accounts that pay interest. Fleming's Investment account pays net per year rates of 0.4 to just over 3 per cent. Its Corporate account pays slightly lower annual rates of interest. Abbey National pays net annual rates of interest of between 1 and 5 per cent with its Business Reserve Account and between 0.5 and 3.5 per cent with its Business Bank Account. Personal account holders also receive interest on their current accounts, although generally the rates are small: 0.1 per cent is paid, for example, by Barclays in England and Wales and by BoS in Scotland. Personal account holders in Northern Ireland do not receive interest on their current accounts but banks offer current accounts under different names that do pay small amounts of interest, for example Ulster Bank pays 0.25 per cent on its Current Plus account.

Debt products

3.127. Like-with-like comparisons are difficult when comparing rates of interest/margins and fees for different types of debt products where the rate of interest is adjusted for a number of factors, for example risk, size of debt, period of repayment, the extent to which the debt is backed by security. HSBC told us that in the debt market each individual lending proposition would have different characteristics of credit risk. It stated that most of its debt pricing was therefore negotiated so as to take account of the different credit risks and individual customers' preferences as to repayments. Barclays said that it would not be easy for us to assess average relative prices in aggregate from published tariffs for different products, because the services varied between products and interest margins were set in relation to individual business propositions. However, it told us that, for the customer, the credit interest margin element of the charge was usually specified separately, allowing them to compare the costs of credit across different products for their individual business propositions. It stated that leasing finance was secured against a very specific asset, often with a well-defined value (such as vehicles), and sales finance involved a high degree of debtor management service as well as finance. Table 3.12 shows the average margins and the main fees on debt products in 1999. A fuller discussion of the prices of debt products can be found in Chapter 4.

3.128. Rates and margins vary for authorized and unauthorized overdrafts. Average margins for agreed overdrafts range from 2.1 to 3.8 per cent in England and Wales. Average margins in Scotland and Northern Ireland are within this range but they tend to be at the lower end of the range. Arrangement and administration fees can be a cash amount or a percentage of the value of the overdraft facility. For example, in 2000 Lloyds TSB charged a tiered arrangement, administration fees ranging from a cash amount of £50 for facilities up to £1,500, to £225 for facilities up to £15,000 and a percentage amount (1.5 per cent) for facilities over £15,000 up to £25,000. The fees for facilities over £25,000 were negotiable. These fees are paid at the outset of the facility and when the facility is renewed. These fees tend to be between 0.6 and 1.3 per cent in England and Wales. As with average margins, fees in Scotland and Northern Ireland tend to be at the lower end of the range in England and Wales. SMEs may have to pay other fees to those shown in Table 3.12, for example an acceptance fee, a commitment fee, an early termination fee, a non-utilization fee, a prepayment fee and/or an account control fee.

TABLE 3.12 **Average margins and fees on debt products, 1999**

per cent unless otherwise shown

	England and Wales			Scotland			Northern Ireland		
		Fees			Fees			Fees	
	Margin	Initial	Ongoing	Margin	Initial	Ongoing	Margin	Initial	Ongoing
Unauthorized overdrafts	15–24	£10–£12	£2–£3.50 per day, £27–£30 per unpaid cheque	21–24		£30–£32 per cheque* £90 per day	12–15	£0–£9	£10–£35 per cheque*
Overdraft†	2.1–3.8	0.6–1.3	0.8–1.3	1.6–2.3	0.5–1	0.4–1	2.1–2.6	1	0.25
Loans	2.1–2.3	0.8–1.6	N/A	1.8–2.2	0.4–1	N/A	1.4–2.4	0.5–1	N/A
Asset finance‡	1–3	£40–£80	N/A	1.9–2.9	£50–£100	N/A	1–3	£50–£100	N/A
Sales finance§	1.6–2.6	N/A	0.1–1.2	1.4–4	N/A	0.2–1.1	2–2.8	N/A	0.1–1

Source: The main clearing groups, *Business Money£acts* and CC calculations based on data provided by the main clearing groups.

*Dishonoured cheques.
†There may also be other fees, eg an acceptance fee, a commitment fee, an early termination fee, a non-utilization fee, a prepayment fee and an account control fee.
‡There may also be a commitment fee, option to purchase fee (HP), agency purchase facility and progress payment facility.
§There may be an arrangement fee.

3.129. The margins for unauthorized overdrafts range from 15 to 24 per cent in England and Wales. They are towards the top end of this range in Scotland and towards the bottom of the range in Northern Ireland. These margins are much higher than those for authorized overdrafts. BoS told us that its facility letter would specify the margin for unauthorized borrowing. It said that these margins were negotiable and in practice were set at a figure substantially below the published rate for unauthorized borrowing. In addition to the rates of interest, SMEs may have to pay fees, for example £2 for every day of the unauthorized overdraft, £30 for each unpaid cheque.

3.130. Average margins for loans in England and Wales—2.1 to 2.3 per cent—tend to be lower than those for authorized overdrafts. The same is true for Northern Ireland, though the margins tend to be at the lower end of this range. In Scotland, average margins for loans (1.8 to 2.2 per cent) seem to be broadly the same as those for authorized overdrafts (1.6 to 2.3 per cent). A major price difference between financing debt by overdraft or by loan is that there tend to be fewer annual charges for loans.

3.131. Unlike unauthorized overdrafts which incur a much higher interest rate than authorized overdrafts, there is little or no difference between the agreed rates of interest on term lending and the default rate (ie the interest rate payable if the borrower breaches the terms of the loan). Lloyds TSB told us that its default rate on loans to its Commercial Banking customers was generally 3 per cent above its agreed rate. It said that there was no difference between its agreed and default rate for its Business Banking customers. HSBC stated that it did not apply default rates to loans. It told us that in some cases, an increased rate of interest might be negotiated with the SME as a result of increased risk but that the main focus would be on resolving the underlying problem causing the default. RBSG stated that for most SMEs the same loan rate applied irrespective of whether the account was in default, but for larger SMEs the facilities letter might specify a higher rate for overdue interest and repayments.

3.132. The structure of charges for asset finance—margin and a set-up fee—is similar to that for loans. The range of average margins for asset finance is 1 to 3 per cent. This is a little wider than the range for loans. SMEs may incur additional charges for asset finance, for example a commitment fee, an agency purchase facility and an option to purchase fee in the HP agreements.

3.133. The range of average margins for sales finance is 1.4 to 4 per cent. In addition, SMEs will pay between 0.1 and 1.2 per cent of turnover, the former charge being for invoice discounting which involves a lesser administration service than factoring.

Deposit products

3.134. Table 3.13 compares the published interest rates paid by the main clearing groups by length of notice period—no notice, 14 days and 30 days.

TABLE 3.13 **Rates of interest on business deposit products of various length, 2000**

per cent

Amount invested

	£1	£500	£1,000	£2,500	£5,000	£10,000	£25,000	£50,000	£100,000	£250,000
England & Wales										
No notice										
HSBC	2.25	2.25	2.25	2.25	2.50	2.50	2.75	2.75	3.00	3.25
NatWest	1.10	1.96	1.96	2.22	2.22	2.22	2.57	2.57	3.03	3.17
Barclays	2.12	2.12	2.12	2.32	2.32	2.32	2.73	2.73	2.88	3.14
Lloyds TSB	1.97	1.97	2.22	2.22	2.22	2.53	2.53	2.89	2.89	3.09
14 days										
HSBC*	2.25	2.25	2.25	2.25	3.65	3.65	4.65	4.65	4.75	4.85
Barclays†	-	-	-	3.55	3.55	3.55	4.06	4.06	4.42	4.68
NatWest†	-	-	-	3.39	3.39	3.39	4.06	4.06	4.42	4.68
Lloyds TSB	2.53	2.53	2.53	2.53	2.53	3.76	4.18	4.18	4.44	4.65
30 days										
NatWest‡	-	-	-	-	-	3.97	4.49	4.49	4.75	5.01
Lloyds TSB	1.00	1.00	1.00	1.00	1.00	3.92	4.44	4.44	4.75	4.80
Scotland										
No notice										
BoS	2.63	2.63	2.63	2.63	2.63	2.63	3.51	3.51	4.65	4.65
Clydesdale	2.02	2.02	2.02	2.02	2.02	2.27	3.03	3.03	4.06	4.58
RBS†	0.25	0.25	0.25	2.26	2.26	2.40	2.65	2.65	2.95	3.17
30 days										
BoS§	-	-	-	-	-	-	-	5.64	5.90	6.04
Northern Ireland										
No notice										
Northern	1.51	1.51	1.51	2.52	2.52	3.03	3.55	4.01	4.01	4.78
BoI¶	-	2.15	2.15	2.45	2.70	2.70	3.60	4.00	4.70	4.70
First Trust	0.85	1.10	1.10	2.75	2.75	3.25	4.25	4.25	4.25	4.25
Ulster Bank	-	-	0.5	1.5	3.0	3.0	4.0	4.5	4.5	4.5
30 days										
BoI#	-	1.7	1.7	3.05	4.3	4.65	5.25	5.35	5.5	5.5
Ulster Bank‡	0.25	0.25	0.25	0.25	0.25	5.00	5.00	5.50	5.50	5.50

Source: Business Money£acts and data provided by the main clearing groups.

*Minimum opening balance of £5,000.
†Minimum balance of £2,000.
‡Minimum balance of £10,000.
§Direct account requiring a minimum balance of £50,000. [
Details omitted. See note on page iv.   ]
¶Minimum balance of £500.
¤Minimum balance of £1,000.
#90 days. SMEs can withdraw funds without notice and without interest penalty where a balance of £5,000 remains in the account after the withdrawal.

3.135. Table 3.13 shows that higher rates of interest tend to be paid on larger amounts of money deposited and, subject to requirements for a minimum balance, for longer terms of notice.

3.136. Rates offered by the banks on money market products are usually set at a discount to the prevailing wholesale market rates. Margins on money market products tend to be less than 1 per cent, much lower than the margins on deposit products (see Chapter 4 for more details).

3.137. We found a mixed picture in relation to the difference in rates between personal and business deposit accounts (see Chapter 4 for more details).

Changes in prices

3.138. Prices for money transmission services for SMEs operating through a business account have been broadly constant in nominal terms over the last few years, falling in real terms—the Bannock

Consulting indices show real falls in bank charges, the 'Big Four' index falling by about 30 per cent in real terms between June 1992 and August 1999 and the 'non-Big Four' index falling by about 20 per cent over the same period (see paragraph 4.54). HSBC told us that the average annual (per account) money transmission charge for its SMEs had fallen in nominal terms from about £298 in 1995 to about £230 in 1999, an annual average fall of 6 per cent in nominal terms and 8.5 per cent in real terms.

3.139. Different debt products have each experienced broadly similar trends to each other (see Chapter 4 for more details).

3.140. The same is true for the different deposit products—their trends being broadly similar (see Chapter 4 for more details).

Changes in demand

3.141. BMRB asked SMEs whether they would switch to another particular type of funding if all banks and financial institutions increased the price of the type of funding they used (for example, if all banks only increased the rates of interest on loans, would SMEs switch to overdrafts or another particular type of funding). 45 per cent said that they would switch to another particular type of funding in response to a 5 per cent price rise and a further 15 per cent said they would do so in response to a 10 per cent price increase.[1] BMRB asked which particular types of funding SMEs would switch to in response to a 5 per cent price rise. 21 per cent said loans, 10 per cent said overdrafts and 6 per cent said leasing.

3.142. BMRB's finding on how SMEs would behave can be compared with its findings on how SMEs have behaved. Lloyds TSB disagreed—it said that as BMRB's question as to how SMEs would react to price changes was purely hypothetical, the results could not readily be compared with evidence as to actual behaviour, since, in the case of the actual price change, the customer would be responding with fuller knowledge of the facts (for example, the basis/cause/nature of the price changes), whereas in the hypothetical case, customers would be responding to a different assumed set of facts. 37 per cent of SMEs told BMRB that their charges, fees and interest rate had changed over the last year. Of these SMEs, 73 per cent said that their businesses did not respond to these changes. HSBC said that this proportion should not be taken as evidence of unresponsiveness to price changes. It gave three reasons for its view. First, for a number of SMEs these changes in relative prices might have been favourable. Second, if these changes were due to changes in the base rate, they were likely to affect pricing of most debt finance products offered by most financial institutions in the same way. Third, if these changes were due to renegotiations of prices to be more in line with costs, the relevant charges were unlikely to be different at any other financial institution.

3.143. The BMRB survey breaks down how SMEs responded to changes in charges, fees and rates of interest alone by whether such changes resulted in the SMEs paying more or less or about the same to their bank. These results, however, have to be viewed with some caution as, for example, SMEs that experienced little overall change in their charges, fees and rates of interest could have experienced increases in some prices and reductions in others which might influence how they responded. 59 per cent of SMEs that said their charges, fees and rates of interest had changed over the last year told BMRB that these changes alone had resulted in their businesses paying more to their bank. 28 per cent said that the changes had resulted in them paying less and 11 per cent said that the changes resulted in them paying about the same, ie no nominal change (which amounts to a real price fall, albeit by a small fraction on an annual basis). Table 3.14 shows how these different groups of SMEs responded to whether changes in their charges, fees and rates of interest alone resulted in their businesses paying more to their bank.

---

[1] A 5 per cent price rise would be represented, for example, by an interest rate increase from 10 to 10.5 per cent.

TABLE 3.14 **Proportion of SMEs that responded to changes in their charges, fees and rates of interest over the last year**

How responded	Changes in charges, fees and rates of interest alone resulted in SME paying:		
	More	Less	About the same
Made no difference	69	76	88
Used bank/service less	10	1	6
Used bank/service more	2	15	2
Actively looking for a new bank	6	-	-
Switched bank/service	4	1	2
Not applicable	-	1	
Don't know	2	3	2
Other	8	3	-
Total*	100	100	100
Sample size	261	126	49

Source: BMRB survey.

---

*Totals may not sum because of rounding.

3.144. 88 per cent of SMEs that told BMRB that their overall charges, fees and rates of interest had not changed did not respond but 10 per cent did. The equivalent proportions for SMEs that experienced overall reductions in charges, fees and rates of interest were 76 and 17 per cent respectively and for those that experienced overall increases the proportions were 69 and 22 per cent respectively.

3.145. BMRB asked SMEs how often they reviewed their charges, fees and interest rates. 38 per cent said that they did so at least once a year and about an additional 10 per cent each said at least once a month, at least once a quarter or at least once every six months. Thus about 70 per cent in total reviewed their charges, fees and interest rates at least once a year. 12 per cent of SMEs said that they never reviewed their charges, fees and interest rates. Of those that reviewed prices (80 per cent of the sample), 51 per cent said that they did so by comparing past bank statements and 27 per cent said that they did so by comparing prices at other banks.

3.146. Just under 80 per cent of SMEs were aware that other banks or building societies might provide banking services more cheaply than their main bank, just under 16 per cent were unaware and just under 5 per cent did not know if this was the case. Of those unaware and those who did not know, 48 per cent said that this information would not make them more likely to consider switching banks and 39 per cent said it would.

3.147. We have not seen any comprehensive data on substantial changes in the number of businesses operating through business accounts and those operating through personal accounts over time. We would have expected, all other things being equal, the narrowing difference in money transmission charges—falling in real terms over time to SMEs—to have led to a fall and not an increase in the number of businesses operating through a personal account. Barclays, however, estimated that the number of its personal customers that could have been operating a business without a business account had risen from 165,000 in 1992 (20 per cent of its businesses with and without business accounts) to 230,000 in 1999 (29 per cent). Barclays told us that the apparent increase in the number of SMEs using personal accounts was the result of increases in SME liquidity, such that they had less need to borrow in recent years. Lloyds TSB said that any reduction in the number of existing businesses operating through personal accounts due to the falling incremental cost of using a business account was likely, in practice, to be masked by the increasing number of individuals working as SMEs in sole trader/consultant-type roles, for whom a personal account was perfectly adequate.

3.148. Figure 3.2 shows the trend in the aggregate value outstanding of different debt products for SMEs with an annual turnover of less than £1 million in nominal terms between 1995 and 2000.

FIGURE 3.2

Value of outstanding debt finance to SMEs with an annual turnover of up to £1 million, 1995 to 2000

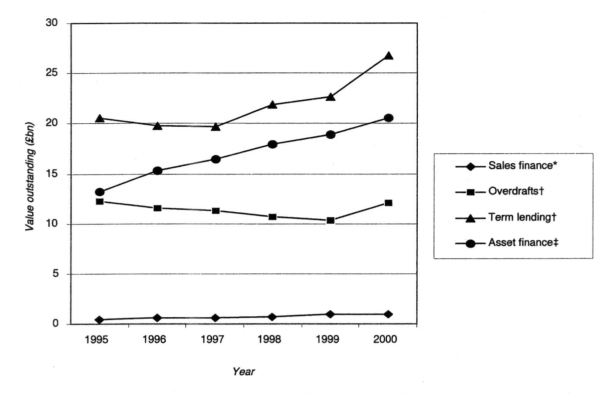

Year

Source: CC calculations based on data provided by the BBA, the Factors & Discounters Association and the Finance & Leasing Association.

*Actual data for 1998 to 2000. 1995 to 1997 are estimates based on the average proportion of total value accounted for by SMEs with an annual turnover of up to £1 million between 1998 to 2000.

†Estimates which are based on the proportion of new lending accounted for by SMEs with an annual turnover of up to £1 million in 1999.

‡Includes the six largest clearing banks for 1995 to 1997, Clydesdale added in 1998 and the Co-operative Bank, Girobank and Yorkshire added in 2000.

3.149. The value outstanding for sales finance has doubled between 1995 and 2000, although it fell slightly between 1999 and 2000. However, it still accounts for the smallest proportion of debt finance. The value outstanding for asset finance experienced the second largest increase between 1995 and 2000—55 per cent. In 1995 there was little difference between its value outstanding (just over £13 billion) and that for overdrafts (just over £12 billion) but by 2000 this difference had grown to about £8.5 billion, the value outstanding for overdrafts having fallen between 1995 and 1999 before recovering in 2000. The value outstanding for term loans increased by 30 per cent between 1995 and 2000. It started and ended the period as the largest value outstanding.

3.150. Table 3.15 shows the type of external funding held by SMEs in the last two years and which was the largest source.

TABLE 3.15 **Proportion of SMEs with types of external funding**

per cent

	Types of funding	Largest type of funding
Loan	38	28
HP	22	10
Leasing	22	9
Overdraft	23	8
Overdraft facility	24	6
Commercial mortgage	7	5
Invoice discounting	5	3
Factoring	3	1
SFLGS*	2	1
Cards	7	1
Other	10	8
Don't know	16	18
Total†		100
Sample size	427	427

Source: BMRB survey.

---

*Small Firms Loan Guarantee Scheme.
†Totals may not sum because of rounding.

3.151. The main types of external funding were loans (held by 38 per cent of SMEs), leasing, HP and overdrafts (each held by about one-fifth of SMEs). Loans were by far the largest type of external funding (held by 28 per cent of SMEs). Leasing, HP and overdrafts were each the largest source of external funding for about one-tenth of SMEs. Invoice discounting and factoring were the largest source for very few SMEs (3 and 1 per cent respectively).

3.152. 46 per cent of SMEs said that their largest type of external funding was with their main bank, the same proportion saying it was with another source. These proportions differed for different types of external funding (see Table 3.16).

TABLE 3.16 **Source of funding by type of funding**

per cent

		Types of funding*			
Source of finance	All	Loans	Overdraft	Leasing	HP
Main bank	46	69	92	8	9
Other	46	31	8	93	91
Don't know	8	-	-	-	-
Total†	100	100	100	100	100
Sample size	427	121	36	40	44

Source: BMRB survey.

---

*Sample sizes for the other types of funding were too small to analyse reliably.
†Totals may not sum because of rounding.

3.153. Table 3.16 shows a marked difference in the use of the main bank by type of funding. For loans and overdrafts the majority of SMEs use their main banks (69 and 92 per cent respectively). The opposite is true for leasing and HP—over 90 per cent do not use their main bank.

3.154. The Centre for Business Research (CBR) at the University of Cambridge also carries out a regular survey of small and medium-sized businesses which looks at external finance (see Table 3.17).

TABLE 3.17 **Proportion of small businesses approaching financial institutions for external funding, 1997 to 1999**

	Approached %
Banks	84.2
Venture capital	6.8
HP/leasing	46.3
Factoring	10.6
Trade customers/suppliers	4.6
Partners/working shareholders	10.0
Other private individuals	7.4
Other sources	8.0

Source: British Enterprise in Transition, CBR, 2000.

3.155. Table 3.17 shows that five out of six small businesses approach banks for external finance (84 per cent). The only other source approached by significantly more than 10 per cent of small businesses is HP/leasing.

3.156. The CBR work also shows the proportion of small businesses that receive external finance from a bank and from other sources, and the proportion of finance from these sources (see Table 3.18). The CBR told us that the proportions attributable to banks might be underestimated because in some cases certain categories of finance in the table (for example, HP/leasing) were in fact obtained from subsidiaries of banks.

TABLE 3.18 **Source and proportion of external finance, 1997 to 1999**

	Proportion of:	
	Small businesses	Finance
Banks	75.9	61.2
Venture capital	4.8	1.3
HP/leasing	44.9	22.7
Factoring	8.6	2.6
Trade customers/suppliers	4	0.8
Partners/working shareholders	8.4	4.4
Other private individuals	6.4	2.1
Other sources	6.8	4.9
Total		100.0

Source: British Enterprise in Transition, CBR, 2000.

3.157. Table 3.18 shows that most small businesses use banks as a source of external finance (76 per cent) and that this finance accounts for 61 per cent of all external finance used by small businesses. This latter proportion has risen back to that recorded in the CBR's 1987–1989 survey (61 per cent), having been 47 per cent in its 1995–1997 survey.

3.158. BMRB asked SMEs what other types of funding they considered when taking out the type of funding actually used (see Table 3.19).

TABLE 3.19 Proportion of SMEs considering different types of external funding when taking out their external funding

per cent

| Types of other external funding considered | All | Types of external funding taken out | | | |
		Loan	Overdraft	Leasing	HP
Loan	11	11	14	12	11
Overdraft	5	7	6	3	3
Leasing	4	4	4	7	12
HP	3	2	5	9	3
Overdraft facility	3	3	3	2	3
Factoring	2	1	2	2	2
Commercial mortgage	2	2	4	1	-
SFLGS	1	1	1	2	-
Cards	1	2	1	1	-
Business Angels	1	2	3	-	-
Invoice discounting	-	-	-	1	-
None	55	58	48	52	61
Other	5	4	4	3	3
Don't know	16	11	14	17	10
Sample size	427	161	100	95	92

Source: BMRB survey.

3.159. Table 3.19 shows that when taking out external finance, about half the number of SMEs did not consider alternative types of finance, ranging from 48 per cent for SMEs taking out overdrafts to 61 per cent for those taking out HP. Although about half of SMEs in total did consider alternative types of finance, very few considered particular types of other external finance. In the case of overdrafts, only 14 per cent of SMEs considered a term loan and no other type of external finance was considered by more than 6 per cent of SMEs. On the whole, smaller proportions of SMEs with loans considered other types of external funding—the highest being 7 per cent which considered overdrafts.

3.160. BMRB asked SMEs why they had chosen the supplier of their external funding (see Table 3.20).

TABLE 3.20 Reasons why SMEs chose the supplier of their main external funding

Reasons	%
Best deal/package	22
Always use main bank	17
Best price	13
Easier to use main bank	13
Existing relationship	8
Availability/only one available	5
Don't know	19
Other	11
Sample size	427

Source: BMRB survey.

3.161. 13 per cent of SMEs said that they chose their supplier because it offered the best price. Price could have been part of the reason for the 22 per cent of SMEs that said they chose their supplier because it offered the best deal/package. 17 per cent said that they always used their main bank and 13 per cent said it was easier to use their main bank.

3.162. SMEs with external finance were asked by BMRB if there were any types of finance they would not use. 50 per cent said factoring, 45 per cent said invoice discounting, 31 per cent said commercial mortgages, about one-quarter said HP with the same proportion saying leasing, 10 per cent said overdrafts and 9 per cent said loans.

3.163. We now look at the geographical market.

The geographical market

The views of the main clearing groups and others

3.164. We have to establish whether the market is local, regional, national (UK) or international. A concept relevant to geographical market definition in this inquiry is that of the chain of substitution (see paragraph 3.25).

3.165. Lloyds TSB told us that there were elements of both national and local influences in pricing but that the choice of geographic market definition should not be a pivotal issue in our investigation. This was because, in its view, the vast majority of customers had the choice of a range of competing financial providers even if markets were defined locally.

3.166. Lloyds TSB acknowledged that, although a decision-making framework was imposed on a national basis, local managers had some discretion in the setting of terms and conditions. Lloyds TSB said that this discretion applied particularly to its Commercial Banking customers where prices for money transmission services and lending were negotiated on a case by case basis. For its Business Banking customers, Lloyds TSB told us that money transmission charges were set by tariff and interest charges were set at standard rates according to the risk category applicable to a particular borrower/borrowing. It said that this approach was driven by customers: Lloyds TSB had a decision-making structure that allowed it to respond as flexibly as possible to each client's individual needs. In its view, this local discretion did not mean that there was a problem because the vast majority of customers had the choice of a range of providers. It said that there were few captive customers in this market who did not have the credible threat of using an alternative provider.

3.167. HSBC told us that the precise geographical market delineation was unclear. It said that competition clearly took place at both a national and local level. It stated that, on the one hand, for many SME customers the choice of bank might to some extent be affected by branch location, and local HSBC branches had significant flexibility with respect to many price elements. On the other hand, all pricing decisions were carried out within nationally-agreed guidelines, and in some cases would need to be centrally authorized. It said that other key dimensions of competition such as branding and reputation were also carried out nationally, and certain products were largely sold by direct sales units rather than at the branch level. At the same time, it noted, the growth of telephone banking and electronic banking—and in particular Internet banking—was greatly reducing, and had already reduced, the importance to customers of branch location.

3.168. RBSG told us that each of the four product markets—money transmission, debt, deposits and merchant acquisition—were national. The principal reasons for its view were, first, that the products themselves were national. Secondly, RBS and NatWest both had national pricing policies (although RBS pricing might be different from NatWest pricing). One exception, for historic reasons, was that RBS had different money transmission tariffs across Scotland and across England and Wales. Ulster Bank had its own pricing across Northern Ireland. Thirdly, distribution arrangements were national. Finally, the BMRB survey showed that SMEs were relatively mobile, with most being willing to travel up to 30 minutes to visit a branch if necessary and a very significant number being willing to travel further if necessary to achieve a cost reduction.

3.169. Barclays told us that the SME banking market was a national market. It said that in some product areas such as bank finance, merchant acquiring and charge cards the market was international. Market conditions were, in Barclays' view, relatively homogeneous across the country and should therefore be analysed at the national level. Barclays told us that on the whole it had operated a national pricing policy for at least ten years. In respect of money transmission prices, the published tariff rates had historically provided for some price premium in London and the South-East on the grounds of higher service delivery costs (see paragraph 3.175). It said that most SME banking products were sold on a national basis by all providers.

3.170. BoS said that the geographical market was local. It stated that the location of these markets was partly governed by the ongoing requirement for SMEs to use the services of the local branch for money transmission purposes. NAB told us that that competition clearly took place at both a UK-wide and local level. It said that new entrants were also competing without a branch network and the associated costs, which meant that access to products and services to SMEs were increasingly available from a wide range of providers anywhere and at any time throughout the UK.

3.171. We noted that the Cruickshank report concluded that the two relevant product markets for SMEs—money transmission services and bank debt—were local markets. The Cruickshank report based its view on:

(a) the essential access to a local facility for those SMEs with high volumes of cash and cheque transactions;

(b) its finding that half of SMEs used their closest provider and over 80 per cent were less than 30 minutes' travel time from their main provider of finance;

(c) its finding that two-thirds of SMEs believed that their branch had local discretion over prices and terms, although the Cruickshank report did not find a systematic variation in prices by locality; and

(d) the perceived importance of local knowledge for lending decisions.

Variation in prices by region

3.172. The structure of prices—money transmission charges, rates of interest on debt and rates of interest on deposits—is discussed in Chapter 4. In this section we examine whether prices differ by geographical region. This is more straightforward to ascertain when prices are published, as they are for certain banking services, for example money transmission services. It is more difficult to ascertain where prices are determined by negotiation or where they are related to individual circumstances. Both of these situations arise in banking. The six largest clearing banks told us that on the whole they set UK-wide prices. The Cruickshank report did not find that prices differed systematically between geographical regions. The existence of national prices does not necessarily mean that there are no local markets. If demand is of a similar nature and the different localities share major elements of cost and have similar cost structures, each locality is likely to generate similar prices. If such a situation existed, the absence of major price difference would not necessarily constitute evidence that there is a single market: it might reflect similar local markets behaving in similar ways.

3.173. Table 3.21 shows prices for money transmission services to SMEs for different groups with subsidiary banks operating in more than one country in the UK (see Table 4.6 for a fuller comparison of prices for money transmission services).

TABLE 3.21 **Money transmission charges of groups with banks operating in the different countries of the UK, 2000**

	Pence per transaction						Pence per £100	
	Direct debit	Standing order	Auto credit	Non-auto credit	Cheque in	Cheque out	Cash in	Cash out
RBSG								
NatWest*	40	40	40	67	0	67	0	0
NatWest†	40	40	22	95	28	67	49	57
RBS (England and Wales)	40	43	25	64	25	55	49	53
RBS (Scotland)	31	45	27	46	19	46	61	59
Ulster Bank	38	49	38	49	33	49	60	60
NAB								
Yorkshire*	37	37	37	53	53	15	25	25
Yorkshire‡	35	35	20	75	75	28	50	50
Clydesdale	21	47	24	47	20	47	61	61
Northern	38	49	38	49	33	49	58	58
AIB								
AIB (GB)	55	55	35	65	22	65	55	55
First Trust	37	50	37	50	33	50	63	63
BoI								
BoI—Northern Ireland§	38	49	32	47	33	49	60	60
BoI—GB§	55	55	16	39	39	71	64	58

Source: The banks and *Business Money£acts*.

*Annual turnover up to £100,000.
†Annual turnover over £100,000 to £1 million.
‡Turnover over £100,000.
§Taken from *Business Money£acts*.

3.174. Table 3.21 shows a large variation in money transmission prices between countries. None of the prices shown are the same in the different countries.

3.175. There are also some differences in prices between geographical regions within countries. Barclays told us that its standard money transmission tariff for businesses with an annual turnover of over £100,000 was between [✂] and [✂] per cent higher in London and the South-East of England. Barclays stated that its price premium started in the mid-1980s and became more formalized in the early 1990s. It told us that the premium was not highlighted in its published material nor raised proactively in discussions between SMEs and relationship managers but that it did discuss tariffs face to face with its customers. During the course of our inquiry, Barclays said that, as a result of competitive pressures in the market, it had decided that it was no longer sustainable to seek to apply this premium and had therefore made a decision that the price premium would be withdrawn. It estimated that the achieved price premium in this region was 6 per cent.

3.176. First Trust told us that interest margins available in Northern Ireland for similar types of business with the same type of risk were a lot finer than in England, Wales and Scotland. BoI believed charges in broad terms and margins to be lower in Northern Ireland than in Great Britain. These views are supported by Table 4.25 that shows that average margins for loans are lower in Northern Ireland than in Great Britain. The same is true for overdrafts in Scotland compared with England and Wales (see Table 4.21).

Variation in coverage of banks by region

3.177. The main clearing groups, though not necessarily the groups that own them, tend to have a greater presence in certain parts of the UK. The four largest clearing banks have a greater presence in England and Wales with little presence in Scotland and Northern Ireland. In Scotland there are three main suppliers: RBS, BoS and Clydesdale. These three suppliers are not widely represented throughout England and Wales nor in Northern Ireland. There are four main suppliers in Northern Ireland: BoI, First Trust, Northern and Ulster Bank. These four banks are not widely represented in England and Wales nor in Scotland. There are also some banks that are have a greater presence in certain regions of England, for example Yorkshire in northern England and the Co-operative Bank in the North-West of England. Following acquisitions, a number of groups are well represented in different countries of the UK. RBSG is well represented in England and Wales (by NatWest), in Scotland (by RBS) and in Northern Ireland (by Ulster Bank). NAB is well represented in Scotland (by Clydesdale) and in Northern Ireland (by Northern) and is represented in England and Wales (by Yorkshire). As well as being well represented in England and Wales, Lloyds TSB is represented in Scotland mainly as a result of the merger between Lloyds and TSB. In 1998, the last year for which Lloyds TSB had separate data on the number of its SME customers in Scotland held by Lloyds and TSB, TSB accounted for 92 per cent of Lloyds TSB's SME customers in Scotland.

3.178. Barclays told us that Scottish customers tended to have a particular attachment to Scottish providers, but that it was clear from the success of RBS and BoS in England and Wales that this was not an issue for English and Welsh SME customers. It said that it had not invested more in developing its business in Scotland because its priorities had been elsewhere. Barclays has four branches in Scotland, plus 19 Woolwich Plc (Woolwich) branches following its recent acquisition. In Northern Ireland Barclays does not operate any counter-based branch services but has a small representative office with business banking relationship managers, based in Belfast. Woolwich has nine branches in Northern Ireland providing services to personal customers. Barclays told us that its approach to the SME market in Scotland had focused mainly on larger companies within the SME market, either large Scottish companies or the subsidiaries of English and Welsh companies operating in Scotland. It said that its strategy in Scotland was to [

Details omitted. See note on page iv.

].

3.179. HSBC has three branches in Scotland serving some 700 commercial customers. It is represented in Northern Ireland through the five branches of its subsidiary HSBC Equipment Finance Ltd. HSBC has about 5,000 business customers with total lending balances of about £[✂] million in Northern Ireland.

3.180. RBS is the only one of the six largest clearing banks that has a broadly even distribution of its branches between England and Wales, and Scotland. Of its 647 branches, 339 are in Scotland and 308 are in England and Wales. Twenty-six out of BoS's 350 branches are in England and Wales. The same is true for nine of Clydesdale's 269 branches.

Time taken to visit branches

3.181. BMRB asked SMEs a number of questions about the time it took them to travel to their banks and the maximum amount of time they would be prepared to travel to them (see Table 3.22).

TABLE 3.22 **Travelling time**

per cent

		How long to travel to:		Maximum time willing to travel to:		
	Own branch	Branch where make cash/ cheque deposits/ withdrawals	Person at bank dealing with financial aspects	Nearest branch	Person who deals with financial aspects	Furthest bank visited when opening account
Up to 10 minutes	56	79	46	42	17	44
11 to 20 minutes	18	12	16	33	25	23
21 to 30 minutes	10	6	12	17	25	14
31 to 45 minutes	4	1	4	2	5	5
46 minutes to 1 hour	3	1	4	1	13	5
More than 1 hour	7	1	7	1	8	6
Don't know	1	-	11	4	6	4
Never visit branch	1	-	N/A	N/A	2*	-
Total†	100	100	100	100	100	100
Sample size	726	688	318	721	318	80

Source: BMRB survey.

---

*Not willing to travel.
†Totals may not sum because of rounding.

3.182. In terms of actual travelling time, most SMEs travel up to 10 minutes: 56 per cent of SMEs when visiting their own branch, 79 per cent when making cash or cheque deposits or withdrawals and 46 per cent when visiting the person at the bank they use to discuss the financial aspects of their business. Between about one-fifth and about one-quarter of SMEs travel between 11 and 30 minutes. 76 per cent of those visiting their own branch said that it was important that they could reach their branch within the time they specified.

3.183. In terms of maximum travelling time, most SMEs are not willing to travel more than 30 minutes: 92 per cent of SMEs visiting their nearest branch, 67 per cent when visiting the person at the bank they use to discuss the financial aspects of their business and 81 per cent when opening an account.

3.184. BMRB asked SMEs in business for more than two years that visited their bank how much further they would be willing to travel to their nearest branch to obtain a 5 and 10 per cent reduction in their banking costs (see Table 3.23).

TABLE 3.23 **Proportion of SMEs* that would travel further in response to a 5 and 10 per cent reduction in their banking costs**

	Reduction in banking costs	
	5%	10%
No further than at present	48	36
Up to 5 minutes further	10	10
More than 5 minutes up to 10 minutes further	12	14
More than 10 minutes up to 20 minutes further	10	14
More than 20 minutes up to 30 minutes further	7	9
More than 30 minutes up to 1 hour further	3	6
Over 1 hour further	2	3
Don't know	8	8
Total	100	100
Sample size	726	726

Source: BMRB survey.

---

*Aged two years or more that visited their bank.

3.185. For a 5 and 10 per cent reduction in banking costs, the most frequent answer given by SMEs was that they would not travel any further: 48 and 36 per cent respectively.

3.186. Use of branches could indicate a local or national market; the latter would involve the concept of the chain of substitution (see paragraph 3.25). Use of telephone, post and/or electronic means for banking could indicate a national market. The use of branches and other delivery channels is covered under barriers to entry in paragraphs 3.195 to 3.215.

Barriers to entry

The importance of branches

3.187. The four largest clearing groups told us that not having a branch network was not a barrier to entry. For example, HSBC told us that branches need not be used at all in the supply of debt and deposit products, although, for certain money transmission services, in particular cash handling, they were at present the most convenient distribution channel to some types of SME. It said that new entrants either already possessed branch facilities which could be used to retail such services (for example, if they were (ex-) building societies), or could acquire them without placing themselves at a cost disadvantage compared with incumbent suppliers or could use branches/retail outlets of another bank/retailer. As regards the requirement of certain customer groups for cash handling, HSBC stated that certain categories of SME made very infrequent use of branch facilities for cheque and cash handling: for example, about half of its SME customers paid in cash, on average, no more than once a fortnight. HSBC said that an alternative to a branch cashier service (particularly for paying in coins) was third party collection by a provider of secure transport and rather than handing cheques in at a branch, these could be sent directly to the relevant regional or central processing centre. Lloyds TSB acknowledged the somewhat greater difficulty of new entrants in the supply of current accounts with overdrafts where, it said, new entrants would need access to a branch network (either its own, or one which it used under contract). HSBC stated that the importance of technological change, and the growing proliferation of new distribution models over recent years, should not be under-estimated—the new entrant could adopt a completely branchless distribution strategy based on direct, but remote, customer access (for example, over the Internet). While recognizing this development, HSBC said that it was committed to maintaining its current spread of branches.

3.188. However, HSBC also told us that in order to operate its cash service for SMEs, not only was a network of branches required, but it was also necessary to have regional cash centres for sorting, counting, packaging, securely storing and distributing both notes and coins. It said that larger retail chains used security carriers to transport cash to and from the regional cash centres, but such an approach was not favoured by SMEs as they found it too expensive and restrictive for their needs, preferring to use the local branch.

3.189. HSBC also referred to the non-counter or 'back-room' cash-handling activity carried out by the major clearing banks, for example storing and redistributing banknotes and distributing new notes and coins. HSBC said that the provision of these cash services by the major clearing banks was one of the reasons why the new entrants into the banking market (for example, former building societies, Internet banks, major foreign banks) had not been keen on providing full service banking to SMEs.

3.190. BoS stated that start-ups were attracted to it in Scotland because of the existence of an extensive branch network with locally-based empowered staff. It told us that one obstacle to its growth in England was the high cost of developing a branch network. It said that it would be much less easy to lend through loans or overdrafts to SMEs without some sort of local presence. BoS told us that for many SMEs, growth of direct and Internet banking would be complementary to, rather than a replacement for, their traditional relationship with a locally-based manager. It said that, certainly for the next two to three years, demand from SMEs for a bricks and mortar network and a designated relationship manager who understood the needs of their business would remain high.

3.191. Alliance & Leicester stated that SMEs had a key requirement for the physical depositing of cash and to a lesser extent cheques. It said that cheques could be sent to the bank by post but many SMEs were reluctant to do this. First Trust said that a branch network was an absolute necessity in the way that the market was structured, in order to provide relationship banking with a local bank representative, important to businesses. BoI stated that convenient access to a bank branch was essential for SMEs to service their cash depositing and withdrawal needs. We discuss the importance of cash and cheques in paragraphs 3.199 to 3.202.

3.192. Abbey National told us that the structure of its branches historically was around the personal customer and that changes would be necessary in order to serve the business customer effectively. This point was also made by Halifax. HSBC told us that it was not aware from its own experience that there was any difference in the requirements of branch layout for the provision of personal and business current account services. It was also unaware that any (ex-) building societies which had chosen to offer personal or business current accounts had had to make changes to their branches' layouts in order to do so. Halifax did not believe its existing branch network put it in a position readily to enter the SME market. It said that as branch networks were used primarily for personal savers and depositors rather than current account activity and, with increasing use of the telephone, Internet and ATMs, the branch networks of all banks, particularly banks with the largest networks, might get smaller. Halifax told us that only the smallest businesses, in its view, would deliver cash to branches, larger businesses using carriers. Halifax concluded that branch networks were not therefore necessary for business banking, except possibly for very small businesses requiring nearby cash and cheque deposit facilities, but that some local support for businesses was clearly needed. Abbey National told us that with less time/capacity at branches being used by personal customers and given that some 80 per cent of its Business Banking customers were introduced through its branch network, greater use of branches for SME banking would be required to meet its target of achieving a market share of 5 per cent.

3.193. The CCBS told us that post offices were generally unsuitable to act as multiple banking agent for business customers as many were small, unsecure and independently owned. A recent report[1] stated that 'many post offices are already criticized for congestion and lack of privacy—hardly surprising given that all but 600 or so of the 18,000 post offices are franchises and most of these are in small privately-owned shops'. In contrast, RBSG told us that there were about 8,000 post offices that could effectively provide a full banking service. The Post Office held a similar view—it said that most of the 18,000 post offices could effectively provide a full banking service and of these some 8,000 were best suited in terms of size and capacity. The views of the main clearing groups and other parties are set out more fully in the relevant views chapters.

3.194. We look in turn at branches, direct alternatives to using branches and the use of the Post Office.

Branches

3.195. Table 3.24 shows how the number of branches for the main clearing groups have changed over the last ten years.

TABLE 3.24 **Number of branches, 1990 to 1999**

	1990	1991	1992	1993	1994	1995	1996	1997	1998	1999	Change %
Lloyds TSB*	3,600	3,328	3,253	3,181	3,034	2,854	2,793	2,638	2,510	2,308	−36
Barclays	2,563	2,465	2,274	2,112	2,067	2,033	1,997	1,975	1,950	1,895	−26
NatWest	2,805	2,683	2,541	2,545	2,410	2,215	1,920	1,754	1,727	1,712	−39
HSBC	-	1,827	1,734	1,732	1,731	1,722	1,698	1,675	1,671	1,676	−8
RBS	841	805	786	752	732	687	665	673	652	647	−23
BoS	515	502	490	455	430	411	385	349	359	350	−32
Clydesdale	350	346	330	314	322	322	312	297	276	269	−23
Ulster Bank	89	89	90	90	90	90	108	106	105	99	+11
Northern	105	107	107	107	107	107	106	101	98	96	−9
First Trust	N/A	96	96	94	89	80	73	71	71	72	−25
BoI	43	43	43	45	48	48	48	48	47	47	+9

Source: CC calculations on data provided by the main clearing groups and the BBA.

*Excludes Cheltenham & Gloucester Building Society (Cheltenham & Gloucester).

3.196. Table 3.24 shows that the six largest clearing banks and Clydesdale have reduced the number of their branches, HSBC having the smallest reduction. This pattern of reductions is seen to a lesser extent in Northern Ireland, First Trust and Northern having reduced the number of branches during this period but BoI and Ulster Bank having increased the number of their branches.

[1]*The Case for Community Banking*, D French, New Economics Foundation, ISBN 1 899407 30 8.

3.197. Table 3.25 shows the number of branches held by the main clearing groups that provide banking services to SMEs and the number held by other banks or building societies that the four largest clearing groups see as having the potential to grow their SME business.

TABLE 3.25 **UK branch networks, end December 1999**

England and Wales		Proportion of the average number of branches (%) (b/a)
Lloyds TSB	2,122	
RBSG*	2,013	
NatWest	1,705	
RBS	308	
Barclays	1,891	
HSBC Bank	1,673	
Average (including RBS)	1,925(a)	
Halifax	820(b)	43
Abbey National	765(b)	40
Nationwide	682(b)	35
Alliance & Leicester	319(b)	17
Scotland		
RBS*	339	
BoS	324	
Clydesdale	260	
Lloyds TSB Scotland	186	
Northern Ireland		
Ulster Bank	99	
Northern	96	
First Trust	72	
BoI	47	
Groups		
Lloyds TSB Group†	2,529	
RBSG*‡	2,458	
NAB§	615	

Source: The companies and *Banking Business, An Abstract of Banking Statistics*, BBA.

---

*April 2001.
†Includes Cheltenham & Gloucester.
‡Includes NatWest's branches in Scotland.
§Includes Yorkshire and Clydesdale's branches in England and Wales.

3.198. Alliance & Leicester, Abbey National, Halifax and Nationwide, which are the providers that the four largest clearing groups see as having considerable potential to increase their SME business, all have smaller branch networks than the four largest clearing groups. Halifax has under half the number of branches of the average number held in England and Wales by the four largest clearing groups. The equivalent proportions for Abbey National, Nationwide and Alliance & Leicester are 40, 35 and 17 per cent respectively. HSBC said that suppliers could compete successfully with networks smaller or less dense than those of the largest banks. It stated that Halifax and Abbey National, for example, had a large enough branch network to provide wide-ranging coverage across the UK and there were other smaller networks, for example Yorkshire—which had a 3.4 per cent market share with only 246 branches—with sufficiently dense coverage to compensate for the smaller size of their network. HSBC told us that BoS had achieved a material level of penetration among SMEs, particularly in the North-West of England with only 29 branches. Barclays said that there was no longer a need to have an extensive branch network to compete effectively due to the advent of new distribution channels.

3.199. The importance of cheques and cash to SMEs was shown by the BMRB survey which asked SMEs which means of payments they used to make deposits and withdrawals and which means they used most for deposits and withdrawals (see Table 3.26).

per cent

	Deposits and withdrawals	Main method of making:	
		Deposits	Withdrawals
Cheque	89	67	74
Cash	46	16	10
Direct debit/standing order	34	4	6
Debit card	18	2	2
ATM/cashpoint machine	9	2	2
BACS payments	4	2	2
Transfers	2	1	2
Credit cards	2	1	-
Not applicable	-	-	-
Other	4	3	2
Don't know	1	2	2
Total*	N/A†	100	100
Sample size	1,211	1,211	1,211

Source: BMRB survey.

*Total may not sum because of rounding.
†Respondents could give more than one answer.

3.200. Table 3.26 shows that 89 per cent of SMEs told BMRB that they made some deposits and withdrawals using cheques and 46 per cent using cash. Cheque was the main method of withdrawal and deposit for 74 and 67 per cent of SMEs respectively. The equivalent proportions for cash were 10 and 16 per cent. 22 per cent of SMEs that used cash as their main way of making deposits were retailers.

3.201. 85 per cent of SMEs aged 2 years or more visited branches of their main bank. BMRB asked SMEs aged 2 years or more that visited branches to make cash or cheque withdrawals or deposits how often they used their main bank's branches to make withdrawals or deposits by cash or cheque over the counter (see Table 3.27). Such SMEs accounted for 39 per cent (cash) and 76 per cent (cheque) of all SMEs aged 2 years or more in BMRB's sample.

TABLE 3.27 **Proportion of SMEs aged 2 years or more visiting branches to make cash or cheque deposits or withdrawals**

	Cash	Cheque
More than once a day	4	5
Once a day	21	24
Two to three times a week	40	40
Once a week	17	17
Less than once a week	16	12
Don't know	3	2
Total	100	100
Sample size*	334	653

Source: CC calculations based on BMRB survey.

*Totals may not sum because of rounding.

3.202. Table 3.27 shows that 40 per cent of these SMEs said that they visited the branches of their main bank two to three times a week to make cash or cheque deposits or withdrawals. Over 20 and 17 per cent did so once a day and once a week respectively. In all, over 80 per cent of these SMEs visited their main bank's branches at least once a week to make cash or cheque deposits or withdrawals.

3.203. Figure 3.3 shows the trend in the number of personal and business cheques between 1985 and 1999 and a forecast by APACS of the trend between 1999 and 2009.

FIGURE 3.3

Use of cheques, 1985 to 2009

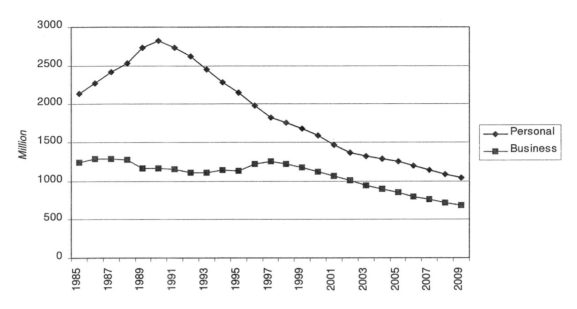

Source: APACS.

3.204. Unlike the number of personal cheques which has fallen every year since 1990 and is forecast to continue doing so, the number of business cheques fell from 1986 to 1992, then rose to 1997 and fell to 1999 when it was 5.6 per cent lower than the number in 1985. APACS is forecasting an annual average fall of just over 5 per cent in the number of business cheques between 1999 and 2009, slightly higher than its forecast for the decline in the number of personal cheques (4.7 per cent).

Electronic and other forms of direct banking

3.205. Table 3.28 shows the proportion of SMEs banking with the main clearing groups that use electronic banking (Internet and PC banking) for any part of their banking services at these banks.

TABLE 3.28 **Proportion of SMEs with electronic* access to their accounts**

Banks	%
Barclays	29
NatWest	15
Lloyds TSB	4
HSBC	8
RBS	13
BoS	8
NAB†	2
Ulster Bank	3
BoI	4
First Trust	1

Source: CC calculations on data provided by the main clearing groups.

---

*Internet and PC banking.
†Includes Clydesdale, Northern and Yorkshire.

3.206. Barclays has the highest proportion of SMEs (29 per cent) who use electronic banking for any part of their banking services. It has no SMEs that only have direct access (electronic and/or telephone) to their accounts. Proportions for HSBC, Lloyds TSB and NatWest range from 4 to 15 per cent. BoS and RBS have similar proportions to HSBC and NatWest (8 and 13 to 15 per cent respectively). NAB (which includes Clydesdale, Northern and Yorkshire), Ulster Bank, BoI and First Trust have much lower proportions (1 to 4 per cent). NAB told us that its low penetration for PC banking might be explained by the fact that in the UK it did not yet have Internet banking, albeit this would become available for Clydesdale and Yorkshire in September 2001.

3.207. HSBC said that rates of Internet use for banking purposes among respondents to the FPB survey almost doubled between 1998 (14.4 per cent) and 2000 (27.3 per cent). It stated that a market research survey published in October 2000 had found that Internet penetration among smaller SMEs had grown by 22 per cent in the previous six months ('equivalent to around 70,000 new Internet connections among businesses with fewer than 10 employees'), and that 42 per cent of those not yet online were certain or likely to be so in the next year. HSBC told us that these results were also broadly consistent with those of a recent OFTEL survey on SME use of the Internet. In contrast, RBSG said that the number of customers using the Internet for business banking was still so small that it was not possible to draw conclusions about the viability of the Internet as a principal distribution channel for new entrants to business banking.

3.208. BMRB asked SMEs about their use of branches and other delivery channels. 92 per cent of SMEs told BMRB that their main business account was branch-based. 4 per cent said that it was a PC account and 2 per cent said that it was a postal account with the same proportion saying it was a telephone account. BMRB asked all respondents the extent to which they used the telephone, post and PC for their banking services (see Table 3.29). These proportions highlight the importance of multi-channel banking.

TABLE 3.29 **The proportion of SMEs that use post, telephone and PC for their banking services**

	Post	Telephone	PC
None of banking	69	55	68
Up to a quarter of banking	18	31	16
Up to half of banking	3	7	7
Up to three-quarters of banking	4	3	3
All or nearly all of banking	5	3	4
Don't know	1	1	1
Total*	100	100	100
Sample size	1,211	1,211	1,211

Source: BMRB survey.

*Totals may not sum because of rounding.

3.209. The majority of SMEs told BMRB that they did not use post, telephone or PC for any of their banking services with their main bank—55 per cent did not use the telephone, 68 per cent did not use PCs and 69 per cent did not use post. Responses varied by size of SMEs. For example, 63 per cent of SMEs with an annual turnover of up to £100,000 stated that they did not use the telephone for any of their banking services with their main bank compared with 39 per cent for SMEs with an annual turnover of between £5 million and £25 million. The respective proportions for post were 78 and 44 per cent and for PC 81 and 36 per cent.

3.210. However, a sizeable minority of SMEs made some use of these different delivery channels. The survey revealed that 44 per cent of SMEs did some of their banking by telephone and 30 per cent did some by PC. It also showed that 31 per cent of SMEs used the telephone for up to one-quarter of their banking with their main bank and 16 per cent used PCs.

3.211. Respondents were asked whether their future use of these different delivery channels would make them more or less likely to visit branches of their bank in the next two or three years. 45 per cent said that their future use would make them less likely to visit branches, 40 per cent said it would make no difference and 13 per cent said it would make them more likely to visit branches.

Post Office

3.212. The Post Office provides for cash and cheque deposits, cash withdrawals and change-giving services for Girobank customers throughout the UK.[1] It provides deposit and change-giving facilities for

[1]The Universal Banking Service Agreement between the Post Office, the Government and banks will provide personal services for banks' basic bank account customers and Post Office card account customers. The Post Office also provides personal banking services for all customers of six banks under separate contracts.

Lloyds TSB SME customers at 11 branches in Reading, a trial that has been running for one year. On a limited trial basis, it also provides deposit and withdrawal facilities for Abbey National SME customers. It has been providing services for the Co-operative Bank for over ten years, both deposit and withdrawal facilities across the UK.

3.213. The Post Office told us that the corporate banking contract with Girobank contained an exclusivity clause that restricted POCL from unilaterally offering cash-processing services to business customers of any bank or building society other than through Girobank. It said that the trials with Lloyds TSB and Abbey National had produced only low volumes and the current process used was not seen as helpful from either a customer or a banking prospective, for example the need to opt for the Post Office service and use Girobank stationery. The Post Office stated that it was discussing with Girobank how to resolve these issues and expand the services offered to business customers, but its room for manoeuvre was severely constrained by the contract with Alliance & Leicester.

3.214. [

Details omitted. See note on page iv.

]

3.215. [

Details omitted. See note on page iv.

]

The need to provide a range of banking services

3.216. Halifax told us that most SMEs expected a single bank to provide a package of services, for example current accounts with overdraft facilities, lending and deposit products. Providers such as Abbey National and Fleming that have no money transmission charges when less than a certain number of transactions are carried out and that pay interest on business current accounts have a relatively small number of SME business current accounts in England and Wales (about 1 per cent for Fleming and less than 1 per cent for Abbey National). One of the reasons why they do not have more SME customers could be that these two providers do not offer authorized overdrafts or term loans although during the course of this inquiry Abbey National decided in March 2001 to establish a programme of overdraft facilities. HSBC said that few SMEs obtained all their banking services from one supplier. It said that market research data showed that, on average, HSBC's business current account customers held 4.6 banking products in addition to their main account from all providers including HSBC of which only 1.7 (excluding the current account) were held with HSBC.[1] Insurance and pension products accounted for over 85 per cent of the products held by these customers at providers other than HSBC.

3.217. We also investigated as a possible barrier to entry whether there was any relationship between the need for finance and the belief that better terms, prices or service can be obtained from an established relationship with a bank. In particular, whether SMEs may be more reluctant to switch banks or banking services if they believed that they would receive better access to funding at more favourable rates of interest the longer they had had their account with their bank or the better the relationship they had with the staff at their bank. Lloyds TSB told us that it was simply a fact of business life that many SMEs, however prudently they managed their business affairs, would, at times, require immediate access to short-term funding to smooth over irregularities in their cash flow. BMRB asked SMEs about their banking relationship and how this affected the availability of funding and the rates they paid.

3.218. BMRB asked SMEs aged 2 years or more whether they agreed or disagreed that they would receive more favourable interest rates, fees and charges, and would receive easier access to funding in the following three situations: a long-term relationship with their bank; a good relationship with a person at their bank; and having a business account. Table 3.30 shows the results.

---

[1]Market research syndicated telephone survey of small businesses (defined as business with an annual turnover of up to £1 million and up to 50 employees), April 2000.

TABLE 3.30 Proportion of SMEs agreeing and disagreeing with the following statements

(a) A long-term relationship with the bank means:
(b) A good relationship with an individual at the bank means:
(c) Having a business account means:

per cent

	(a)	(b)	(c)	(a)	(b)	(c)
	More favourable rates, fees and charges			Easier access to funding		
Agree strongly	16	14	11	32	31	23
Tend to agree	32	26	32	42	41	46
Tend to disagree	29	36	29	14	15	15
Disagree strongly	17	17	17	8	6	7
Don't know	6	6	12	5	6	9
Total	100	100	100	100	100	100
Sample size	856	856	856	856	856	856

Source: BMRB survey.

*Totals may not sum because of rounding.

3.219. Between 40 and 50 per cent of SMEs agreed that any of the three situations would result in more favourable rates, fees and charges. The equivalent proportion with regard to easier access to funding was about 70 per cent. Lloyds TSB told us that as the SMEs' answers to BMRB's questions were purely speculative, without experience and knowledge of these situations, they were of little if any evidential value.

The need to offer lending and the ability to assess risks

3.220. The four largest clearing groups said that there were plenty of off-the-shelf models that would enable new entrants to assess the risks of lending. Many of the main clearing groups provided us with the manuals and guidelines they use for assessing requests for debt finance. However, some of them pointed out that assessing these requests was not just a mechanical process but that it required staff to use their discretion which in turn required staff to have experience and expertise and to take sufficient steps to ensure that they knew their customers. In contrast, HSBC stated that skilled decisions were relevant to judgemental decisions on larger facilities but the majority of its lending to SMEs was assessed using credit scoring. It said that the characteristics used on all scorecards tended to be fairly similar, whether they were developed in-house or by a third party supplier. HSBC told us that an in-house system would not necessarily be any more effective, or cheaper, than software which a new entrant could acquire off the shelf from third parties.

3.221. However, RBSG told us that, although developments in application credit scoring and behavioural credit scoring for personal customers meant that the personal credit process could be largely centralized and automated, the same was not true of SME customers. It said that their businesses and risk profiles were not homogeneous and it was necessary to evaluate individual situations and to apply judgement as well as routine credit analysis. It stated that a new entrant would not be able to rely only on automated credit scoring, but would need to have people with appropriate credit skills, judgement and experience. It said that these people could be recruited from existing banks.

3.222. Halifax told us that the greatest barrier to entry was on lending where particular skills were necessary, and would have to be acquired from within the established banking community. It said that lending to SMEs would require a shift in focus from looking at asset value to factors such as ability to repay, including credit scoring, a different skill base for evaluating risk, particularly for unsecured lending or lending against equity, and with a further requirement to monitor accounts.

3.223. The need for expertise was also cited by Alliance & Leicester which told us that what SMEs probably needed the most was to feel they had access to somebody who understood their business, who was traditionally in their community and to whom they could go if they needed to borrow money. It stated that to meet the requirements of SMEs it would have to create a new sales force specifically aimed at SMEs which it would have to recruit from the existing banks.

3.224. The Co-operative Bank said that to fully understand all the risks that might affect a business, close involvement with the SME was a necessity. It stated that less information about, or contact with, the SME would mean that propositions concerning the SME would generally carry more risk thereby increasing the cost of funding to the SME. It said that it was vital to understand the local economic environment in which the SMEs were operating. The Co-operative Bank told us that lending to SMEs was more complex than providing finance to the consumer market and that traditional lenders had developed both the experience and resources to deal efficiently with applications for loans and overdrafts. It said that credit and behavioural scoring techniques were being considered by many financial institutions, although this required investment in new technology and would probably only be used successfully to assess funding applications up to a relatively modest level.

3.225. We asked Barclays whether its policy which prevents its staff that deal with SMEs from joining a rival organization for a period of 12 months could hinder the ability of a new entrant to hire experienced staff. Barclays said that it had found no instance of ever enforcing such a covenant. During the course of our inquiry, Barclays told us that it was in the process of removing any restrictions in its contracts of employment for all relevant staff grades on working for, or being involved with, a competitor bank. BoS told us that one of the obstacles to it growing in England was the shortage of suitably qualified staff to support its English business.

3.226. Barclays, Lloyds TSB and HSBC provided us with estimates of the number of their FTE staff that dealt with SMEs. We have estimated the increase that could be needed in staff numbers at one or more entrants if, in total, they were to account for, say, 20 per cent of the number of business current accounts and they operated in the same way as the four largest clearing banks currently operate (see Table 3.31).

TABLE 3.31 **Numbers of staff* dealing with SMEs, 1999**

	SMEs
Barclays	9,733
Lloyds TSB	5,746
HSBC	12,000
NatWest	9,184e
Total	36,700
Average	9,200
Employment required by potential entrant or entrants achieving a market share of:†	
20 per cent	8,600‡
5 per cent	2,200§

Source: CC calculations on data provided by the Barclays, HSBC and Lloyds TSB.

---

*FTE staff.

†Calculated on the unrounded data and rounded to the nearest 100.

‡Total SME employment (36,700) divided by their share of supply (85%) multiplied by an assumed share for the potential entrant or entrants (20%).

§Total SME employment (36,700) divided by their share of supply (85%) multiplied by an assumed share for the potential entrant or entrants (5%).

Note: e = estimated by CC.

3.227. Table 3.31 shows that one or more entrants would require over 8,000 additional staff if they were to achieve a 20 per cent share of the number of business current accounts on the basis of the current practices of the four largest clearing banks. A share of 5 per cent would require over 2,000 additional staff.

3.228. HSBC said that this analysis was not relevant to barriers to entry as it did not consider whether or not staff were available and/or difficult to obtain and at an asymmetric cost. It stated that the exact number of staff required would depend on the service proposition of the entrant and, in particular, what delivery channels were to be used. It told us that there was no reason why an entrant should have to pay correspondingly more than HSBC nor would it be required to train these staff overnight. HSBC said that staff were available (particularly given the number of recent branch closures) and/or could be trained, and, if the clearing banks lost customers, some of their staff would become surplus to requirements. Barclays stated that it disagreed with this analysis. It said that as a business grew, its staff levels would increase naturally.

Information asymmetries between existing providers and new entrants

3.229. We considered whether knowledge of an existing SME's business by its current bank might enable it to price a loan more accurately than other banks. Such information might be gained from having a relationship with the SME, the information not being fully reflected in bank statements and financial accounts.

3.230. RBSG told us that there were two main situations where it gathered data from SMEs: opening an account and requests for borrowing. It said that it also used data on SMEs collected by market research companies. All SMEs were subject to credit reference searches (in the case of limited companies, it said that searches were also made on the names of principal directors) when they applied to open an account. With regard to requests for borrowing, it required recent and projected trading information on the SME (for example, audited accounts (where appropriate), management accounts and projections of cash flow, operating budgets and profit and loss etc) and details of the specific proposition for which funding was required. It also required information on non-financial aspects of the SME's performance. The amount of information sought from the SME varied according to, for example, whether the bank already had information on the SME's history because it was an established customer.

3.231. BoS stated that general information about SMEs, their markets and how they (and their competitors) conducted themselves within that marketplace would be received in the ordinary course of business. It told us that it was extremely important to have a sound relationship with, and as much knowledge as possible about, the SMEs. It said that if it did not have access to information provided by the SME then the assessment and decision-making process would be longer and more difficult. It told us that, although the lack of information might not prevent it reaching a decision, the basis for the decision might be flawed. BoS said that in the case of existing SMEs, it might have immediate access to information on which to base a decision, resulting in an ability to make a faster decision. It told us that the challenge and possible common barrier was the ability to develop and maintain an effective Customer Management System through which long-term relationships with SMEs were created to mutual benefit.

3.232. Abbey National told us that a pool of information on credit for business customers across the UK would much assist entry or expansion of SME activities. It acknowledged that there were companies such as credit-rating agencies which provided fairly detailed information, but they only covered part of the SME sector: it was not aware of any comprehensive credit database which extended, for example, to sole proprietors and small partnerships. It stated that limited companies with a turnover of less than £1 million were also no longer required to register audited accounts. Therefore, although it was able to get information on defaulting customers, this was extremely limited and there was no comprehensive database available that could be used positively as a basis upon which to make lending decisions to certain SME customers. In contrast, it believed that existing bankers of SMEs had the benefit of knowing the history of their performance and payment record which other potential providers of banking services did not. This in turn made it more difficult for SMEs to switch since potential competitors might conclude that they did not have enough information upon which to base credit decisions.

3.233. HSBC did not believe that lack of information on SMEs in general, or on the performance of individual SMEs, constituted a barrier to entry. It focused its comments on the importance of information in the debt market since it had not seen any suggestion that information on SMEs was necessary for a new entrant to offer deposit products or money transmission facilities. HSBC stated that all the information on individual SMEs which was relevant to a lending decision could be obtained either from the SMEs themselves (whether directly or indirectly, for example through their existing bank) or from third party sources, such as credit reference agencies, Dun & Bradstreet Ltd, or Companies House. There was no information which an SME's existing bank possessed that could not be obtained from one or other of these two sources. This view was shared by Barclays which stated that it regularly used information available in the public domain to compete for and win customers from competitors. It said that a credit reference agency search could be made against the personal address of a sole trader, individual partners or the directors of a limited company, in the same way as they were conducted for personal customers. HSBC stated that there was no reason why it should cost a new entrant more to obtain any of the relevant information than it would cost an incumbent (with the possible exception of the SME's existing bank)—there were, for example, very few economies of scale associated with individual information gathering.

The process of switching

3.234. This section looks at the process of switching. The extent of switching is considered in paragraphs 3.352 to 3.368.

3.235. The four largest clearing groups believed that switching banks, or one or more of their services, was not difficult. HSBC said that one of its small SME customers setting up a business current account and not transferring any secured lending would normally be able to complete the switching process in seven to ten days. It stated that this was reflected in the seven-day timescale contained in the terms of its Account Opening Guarantee, under which HSBC promised to pay a new business current account customer £10 for each error if HSBC had not done the following within seven days: provided a cheque book, paying-in book, business self-service card and PIN; correctly set up all standing orders and direct debits; and assigned a named business banker. HSBC also told us that on average it took SMEs 55 days to switch their accounts. However, HSBC said that this figure was taken from a particular piece of analysis, based on a study carried out in 1995, in which the mean was biased (perhaps due to the inclusion of some large businesses) and that it reflected, in part, customer preferences to transfer their banking arrangements gradually. It said that the analysis showed a median time to switch of 28 days.

3.236. Lloyds TSB told us that, although the cost of switching was small, it would take longer for businesses with borrowings to switch, given the need to transfer security and compensation on early redemption of fixed-period loans where, as a result, the bank would face a mismatch between its borrowing and its lending. It provided us with data that suggested that 37 per cent of switchers took more than one month to switch and that of these, less than half (16 per cent of the total switchers) took more than three months. Lloyds TSB said that, even if an SME could not close down its account with its old bank immediately, it could open the new account with the new bank immediately. The SME could then use the new account to undertake money transmission activity, even before it had closed its old account. Lloyds TSB told us that market research on small business banking for 2000 suggested that some 4 per cent of small businesses diverted their banking to some other arrangement (perhaps a secondary account) during the previous two years.[1]

3.237. Barclays told us that there was no evidence of any overt limitation on switching. It said that the new bank did the bulk of the work and it believed that all banks made this easy for SMEs. Barclays stated that it went to considerable lengths to make switching to itself trouble free and had instituted a customer account switching service in order to make it as simple as possible. Barclays pointed out that BACS required members to provide lists of standing orders and direct debits within ten days and that BACS members were committed to deploying automated switching arrangements for all customers by the end of 2001.

3.238. RBSG did not believe that switching was particularly difficult in any of the product markets. In money transmission, RBSG responded to customers' instructions, and had service standards for doing so. It said that there were no costs, with one exception, where Ulster Bank charged for cancelling regular payments. Switching debt could be done quickly and with no costs—except for a charge if fixed-rate debt was repaid early. Variable-rate debt customers could repay early, at no cost. In practice, the transfer of security lengthened the time taken to switch debt but, in RBSG's view, this was not a reason for switching not to be undertaken.

3.239. Alliance & Leicester told us that, depending on the size of the SME, the difficulty with switching was in changing paying-in arrangements, for example organizing new paying-in books, creating contacts, not only with salesmen, but with the Post Office or the branches being used, and creating relationships with back-office people in the new bank. It stated that, as a small business gained in complexity, moving became more arduous. An overdraft or security resulted in other complications. It said that probably the biggest difficulty about moving was if houses or life policies were mortgaged to the bank as security for lending.

3.240. BoS said that there were a number of problems that could occur when SMEs switched banks. First, there could be delays in closing an account which could be due to Letters of Credit/Documentary

---

[1]The market research showed that during the previous two years 10 per cent of small business (excluding homeworkers) had stopped using their main bank account and 6 per cent had started using a new bank account.

Collections still being outstanding. Secondly, there could be disputes/errors with standing orders and direct debits. Thirdly, BACS credits might be returned to the originator, not forwarded to the new bank. Fourthly, excessive closing charges could be imposed by the transferor bank.

3.241. BoS told us that the average time to transfer or receive an account was ten working days, assuming there was no security involved and allowing time for the customer to receive cheque books and paying-in books. It said that this could increase to about six to eight weeks if security was required. If there was no borrowing, BoS stated that a transfer from it should take no longer than five days. BoS said that where sales finance facilities were involved transfers to/from BoS were usually subject to a three-month standard termination period, although this could be longer on occasion.

3.242. The Co-operative Bank stated that SMEs believed there were difficulties in changing banks.

3.243. The FPB told us that the significant constraints on actual switching were bundling, the cost penalties of switching, a lack of knowledge of the new supplier and fear of reprisal from the existing bank. It said that a business needed immediate and seamless transfer of services such as direct debit payment/receipt and standing order processing; where delays were evident, whether deliberate or unintentional, the creditability of a business could be irretrievably damaged. The fear of this risk might often mitigate against a decision to change banks. The FPB provides its members with a range of guidance and information on running a small business and on relationships with banks. One such piece of information advises SMEs to 'think again very hard' about changing banks. It states that 'changing banks requires careful thought and is not a decision to be taken lightly' implying, in its view, that the business owner must be sure of the full nature of the existing arrangement and the future arrangement before changing banks. The FPB said that constructive negotiation with the existing bank might result in better terms. However, it believed that the removal of many of the switching constraints would lead to better relationships in the first place.

Use of security

3.244. Many SMEs taking out loans and overdrafts have to provide security to their lenders. This security can be in the form of granting the lender first access to the assets of the business or of the owner's own assets or both. In some cases if the SME wants to take out another loan from a different lender it will have to obtain permission from the first lender.

3.245. We asked the main clearing groups to provide us with the number and value of their loans to SMEs that were backed by security. Only Barclays and NatWest were able to provide the data although some of the other banks provided us with estimates of the proportion of their lending that was backed by security. Table 3.32 shows the proportions of lending to SMEs by Barclays and NatWest that were backed by security.

TABLE 3.32 **The proportions of lending to SMEs by Barclays and NatWest backed by security**

per cent

| | Barclays* | | NatWest† | |
		All‡	Retail	Corporate
Total value of loans outstanding				
Type of security:				
Full				
Partial				
Full and partial				
Value (£bn)				
Total number of loans outstanding		*Figures omitted.*		
Type of security:		*See note on page iv.*		
Full				
Partial				
Full and partial*				
Number ('000)				

Source: CC calculations on data provided by Barclays and NatWest.

*Data for 2000. Excludes all the loans priced by means of the Small Firms Pricing Policy (either with annual sales of less than £250,000 or with borrowing of £25,000 or less). In addition, the number of secured/partially secured loans maybe understated because not all loans have amendments applied to them.

†Data for 1999. Includes businesses with an annual turnover of up to £100 million. Unable to provide data for partially secured.

‡Totals may not sum because of rounding.

3.246. Barclays told us that with the exception of unsupported guarantees, security would not be taken for borrowings of £5,000 or less, except possibly as a condition of further support when dealing with an account in difficulty. Table 3.32 shows that [✂] per cent of the total value of loans outstanding from Barclays to SMEs had full security. [✂] per cent was partially secured giving Barclays some security for [✂] per cent of the total value of its loans outstanding to SMEs. Barclays had less security in terms of number of loans outstanding—[✂] per cent in total comprising [✂] and [✂] per cent of fully- and partially-secured loans.

3.247. In terms of value, NatWest had full security for [✂] per cent of its loans outstanding to SMEs but there was a marked difference between its Retail (annual turnover of up to £1 million) and Corporate (annual turnover of between £1 million and £100 million) customers—for the former, NatWest had full security for [✂] per cent of its loans, but for the latter, the equivalent proportion was [✂] per cent. NatWest had full security for about [✂] per cent of the number of its loans outstanding to SMEs. [

]

Details omitted. See note on page iv.

3.248. HSBC estimated that the value of security from its SMEs was [✂] per cent of the value of their debt. HSBC was not able to provide a figure for the value of debt secured but noted that it was common for it to take partial security.

3.249. Lloyds TSB stated that, in most cases, it did not take security from its Business Banking customers to secure their borrowings. It said that this reflected the fact that most of these customers borrowed less than £10,000 and it did not generally take security for loans or facilities below this figure. It told us that Commercial Banking took security in some [✂] per cent of the number of its loans.

3.250. RBSG said that, based on high-level management estimates, approximately [✂] per cent of the number of loans and overdrafts awarded by NatWest to SMEs in its Retail Banking business were fully or partially backed by security. It stated that the proportion was about [✂] per cent for NatWest's smaller SMEs. The equivalent proportions by value were about [✂] and [✂] per cent respectively. NAB told us that [✂] per cent of its lending book was fully secured.

3.251. The proportions of loans backed by security underestimate the cover that the banks have as the figures do not take account of personal guarantees. Barclays stated that most very small businesses were sole traders or partnerships where the principals were liable for the debts of the business. It told us that for many very small limited companies, their financial position was not separate in practice from that of the owner(s) and director(s). It was therefore appropriate to take a guarantee for borrowings by such companies. Barclays told us that for limited companies that had banked with it for less than 12 months a personal guarantee was required from the director(s). The guarantee would be limited in amount to the agreed facility (all money and liabilities of the named customer present and future including contingent liabilities, interest and cost, subject to any specified limit). For limited companies that had banked with it for 12 months or longer a personal guarantee was required from the director(s) where a facility was requested for £2,000 or more.

3.252. HSBC told us that in the case of many SMEs, the only security available would be the personal assets of the owner of the business. It said that for limited company borrowers, its policy was to take a debenture (including a fixed and floating charge) and, wherever possible, the personal guarantee of the principal directors. As regards sole traders and partnerships, it would commonly take some form of security over personal assets, such as by way of a mortgage on a house.

3.253. Lloyds TSB said that loans of less than £10,000 were generally offered without the need for personal guarantees. It stated that subject to this, it was its normal (if not universal) practice to take personal guarantees from the directors of corporate borrowers: in practice, this was a necessary step to secure the directors' continuing commitment to the success of the business. It told us that many small businesses had limited assets to provide as security, and frequently all that was available was either business premises (if owned) or the proprietor's own home.

3.254. RBSG stated that personal guarantees did not provide the banks with tangible collateral for debt, unless they were themselves backed by tangible collateral. It said that mortgage debentures and directors' guarantees were always considered when lending to limited companies. It told us that directors' guarantees would be more typically seen where the strength of balance sheet alone was not proportional to the weight of external borrowing or the company had been in existence for less than three years. However, it said that no hard and fast rules existed.

3.255. Provision of security was covered by the BMRB survey. BMRB asked SMEs whose largest type of external finance was a loan (28 per cent of SMEs with external finance and 10 per cent of the whole sample) whether the bank required security and if so whether this security was personal, business or a mixture of personal and business. Table 3.33 shows the results.

TABLE 3.33 **Proportion of SMEs with security**

Type of security	%	
Business	27	
Personal	16	
Personal and business	15	
Total*		59
None		26
Don't know/not stated		16
Total*		100
Sample size	121	

Source: BMRB survey.

*Totals may not sum because of rounding.

3.256. Of those SMEs for which loans were the largest type of their external finance, 59 per cent were required to provide security—27 providing business security, 16 per cent providing personal security, and 15 per cent providing both types of security.

Access to the wholesale network and wholesale charges

3.257. The wholesale network is the agency arrangements whereby members of APACS provide clearing services to financial institutions that are not direct members of APACS (agency banks). The charge for such services is the wholesale charge. The four largest clearing groups told us that neither access to the wholesale network nor the size of wholesale charges were barriers to entry.

3.258. Barclays told us that banks that were members of APACS were not protected from competition from non-members. It said that there was no barrier to non-members becoming members but a substantial cost. It stated that agency arrangements were offered to non-members so that they could avoid the costs of direct membership. Barclays told us that since 1995 14 institutions had joined APACS and six had left. It told us that it did not know of any recorded instances of any financial institution being barred from APACS.

3.259. Barclays said that where non-members chose not to seek membership there were alternative routes for them to access the payment systems. It said that they could have an agency arrangement that would enable them to offer clearing services to their own customers. Barclays stated that an SME should not see any difference in service or performance whether its bank was a direct or indirect member of APACS.

3.260. Barclays provided us with data on the number of agency agreements it had tendered for between 1990 and 2000. In all, Barclays had made [✂] tenders, seven being successful and [✂] being unsuccessful. Of the [✂] unsuccessful tenders, one was partially successful in that services were split between clearing banks including Barclays. In [✂] cases Barclays had bid lower than the winning bid but had not won the tender. However, this had only occurred once in the last [✂] unsuccessful bids between 1998 and 2000. Since 1996 it had lost four clearing agency customers to other banks and gained seven new agency customers, a mixture of those new to the industry and those gained from other banks.

3.261. APACS provided us with data on the number and value of items cleared and the shares held by the six largest clearing banks (see Table 3.34).

TABLE 3.34 **Number and value of cheques and automated items cleared and shares held by the largest clearing banks, 2000**

	Interbank*	Inter-branch†
Cheque clearing in London		
Number		
Four largest clearing banks (%)	75	93
Total number (m)	1,704	367
Value		
Four largest clearing banks (%)	78	N/A
Total value (£bn)	1,214	N/A
Cheque clearing in Scotland		
Number		
Two largest clearing banks‡ (%)	65	82
Total number (m)	116	25
Value		
Two largest clearing banks‡ (%)	74	N/A
Total value (£bn)	115	N/A

	Direct debits	Standing orders	Direct credits
Automated clearing in UK			
Four largest clearing banks (%)	78	69	78
Six largest clearing banks (%)	90	78	88
Total number (m)	2,010	247	1,060

Source: APACS.

*Items cleared drawn on the reporting bank for payment through the branches of another bank.
†Items cleared drawn on the reporting bank for payment through the branches of the reporting bank itself.
‡RBS and BoS.

3.262. Table 3.34 shows that the six largest clearing banks account for the majority of the items cleared.

3.263. The Federation of Small Businesses (FSB) told us that it had had discussions with Wells Fargo some years ago on the understanding that the bank was to enter the market, but because of the four largest clearing banks' domination of the money transmission system Wells Fargo decided that the venture would not be worthwhile.

3.264. Table 3.35 shows the main agency (wholesale) money transmission charges for the four largest clearing banks in 2000.

TABLE 3.35 **Wholesale money transmission charges,* 2000**

	Minimum	Quartile 1	Median	Quartile 3	Maximum	Total number of banks/ building societies	Number of banks/ building societies used in this analysis†
NatWest							
BACS transactions							
Direct debit/standing order input							
Direct credit input							
Direct credit/standing order received							
Automated credit entries							
Cheque transactions							
Cheques paid into customer account							
Cheques drawn on customer account							
HSBC‡							
BACS transactions							
Direct debit/standing order input							
Direct credit input					§		
Direct credit/standing order received					§		
Automated credit entries							
Cheque transactions							
Cheques paid into customer account							
Cheques drawn on customer account							
Barclays‡							
BACS transactions							
Direct debit/standing order input							
Direct credit input							
Direct credit/standing order received							
Automated credit entries							
Cheque transactions							
Cheques paid into customer account							
Cheques drawn on customer account							
Lloyds TSB							
BACS transactions							
Direct debit/standing order input							
Direct credit input							
Direct credit/standing order received							
Automated credit entries							
Cheque transactions							
Cheques paid in to customer account							
Cheques drawn on customer account							

Figures omitted.
See note on page iv.

Source: CC calculation based on data provided by the four largest clearing groups.

*Pence per transaction.
†Banks/building societies which had most of the above services.
‡Larger agency customers. Barclays told us that such customers accounted for [✂] per cent of all agency transactions produced by Barclays.
§Standard tariff of 9p per transaction.

3.265. Table 3.35 shows a wide range of wholesale prices (see Appendix 3.2 for more detail on the charges of these banks). NatWest has a far greater range of wholesale prices than the other three banks shown in Table 3.35 but it has provided data on many more banks which could widen the distribution of its wholesale prices. For example, Barclays provided us with pricing data for only nine out of its 69 agency arrangements. It said that these nine arrangements accounted for 98 per cent of all agency transactions produced by Barclays. Possibly due to the larger number of banks for which it has provided data, NatWest's median wholesale prices are much higher than the other three banks. RBSG told us that in the main NatWest dealt with low-volume agencies that would, together with the larger sample of data it provided, account for its higher charges relative to other banks. It said that it would expect NatWest's prices to be in line with the market when compared on a like-with-like basis. Some of NatWest's fellow group companies—Lombard Bank Ltd and Lombard North Central plc—pay the lowest wholesale prices for direct debit/standing order and direct credit input. RBSG told us that low rates for these companies were not surprising given their high volumes of transactions.

3.266. For most money transmission services the wholesale charges of these four banks are much lower than their retail charges. This is always the case for Barclays' tariffs for retail money transmission prices. For HSBC, it is always the case with regard to its standard tariff retail charges to small business. HSBC told us that both the variable costs of the particular service provided by HSBC and the price of that service to the customer varied according to the extent to which the customer carried out certain processing functions for itself. For example, if cheques were paid in at HSBC branches, the costs and price were greater than if the customer delivered its cheques to HSBC's processing centre. Similarly, the costs and the prices to the customer were lower if the customer encoded the cheques itself. [

Details omitted. See note on page iv.

]

NatWest's wholesale charges for standing orders and auto credit for a number of its agency customers (and for one customer for cheque withdrawals) are higher than its retail charges but again these customers either offer no or very limited banking services to SMEs.

3.267. BoS said that membership of APACS was its lowest-cost option for offering money transmission services and allowed it to compete on a level playing field with all clearing banks.

3.268. Triodos Bank NV (Triodos—see paragraph 8.104) stated that it was difficult to change the bank that provided its clearing system, since it would necessitate it changing its sort code.[1] It said that this would be highly complex, because all of its customers who had standing orders and automated payment instructions such as direct debits set up had a coding which went through its provider's sort code: if it went to another bank all its customers would have to have the sort code of the new wholesale bank. It stated that new cheque books and paying-in books would have to be issued to all its customers. Triodos said that this whole process would be hugely time consuming and expensive to do and almost impossible.

3.269. HSBC said that if a bank were to switch to a different supplier of agency clearing services, it would not only have to supply all its customers with new cheque books containing the sort code of its new supplier; it would probably also have to renumber its customers' accounts. It stated that so long as institutions use agency clearing arrangements, no change to the sort-code system alone could remove this obstacle to agency customers switching suppliers: the only way of solving this problem would be to introduce a system of universal account portability. HSBC also told us that the present account-numbering system did not present a barrier to switching by agency clearing customers, and such switching did occur. It said that even where agency clearing customers did not actually switch supplier, the threat of switching remained sufficiently credible to ensure that in a tender situation they were able to play their supplier off against a rival tenderer and secure a price reduction.

3.270. BoI told us that the process of having to withdraw all its cheque books from SMEs and issuing them with new cheque books with a different sort code on them would preclude it from even considering changing the agency arrangement in Great Britain.

The policy of bundling

3.271. BMRB asked SMEs a number of questions about bundling, exclusive arrangements and conditions limiting SMEs' ability to obtain funding from another bank. These questions and the responses of SMEs are shown in Table 3.36.

---

[1]Every account identification code has two parts: the six-digit sort code and the eight-digit account number. The sort code identifies the bank where the account is held, and the branch of that bank at which it is held; the account number identifies the customer's account. Virtually all banks which acquire clearing services under agency arrangements do not have sort codes of their own (Halifax is one of the exceptions). Thus the sort codes which appear on cheques issued by such a bank will be sort codes of the bank through which it clears its cheques.

TABLE 3.36 **Proportion of SMEs with and without certain conditions agreed with their main bank**

	No %	Yes %	Sample
SME required to take out a service as a condition of taking another service	90	8	963
SME obtained services at reduced price when taking out another service	87	7	963
Bank insisted on exclusive arrangement	90	6	1,019
Bank indicated exclusive arrangement would be advantageous	87	6	955
SME agreed to this arrangement	76	19	59
Funding included conditions limiting SMEs' ability to obtain funding from other banks	89	4	1,136
SMEs prevented from obtaining funding from another bank in last 3 years	80	12	41
Bank tried to dissuade SMEs from obtaining funding from another bank in last 3 years	93	4	1,131

Source: BMRB survey.

3.272. Table 3.36 shows that most SMEs said that they did not experience bundling—being required to take out one service as a condition of taking out another service or obtaining services at a reduced price when taking out another service. Most SMEs said that their banks had not insisted on exclusive arrangements nor had they indicated that such arrangements would be advantageous to the SMEs. Most SMEs said that their banks did not prevent nor dissuade them from obtaining funding from another bank or financial institution. Lloyds TSB told us that where SMEs reported bundling, they might well mean no more than that the bank might offer them a better deal if they took out two or more products which might simply reflect genuine economies of scope. HSBC said that generally, the BMRB survey gave strong evidence of a lack of coercive selling by the banks and of a lack of bundling. It stated that the BMRB survey indicated that only 4 per cent of respondents said that their bank limited the business's ability to obtain funding from another source and only 4 per cent said that their banks tried to dissuade the business from obtaining funding elsewhere in the last three years.

3.273. BMRB gave all respondents a list of aspects of banking and asked them to decide which, if any, they felt would have an adverse impact on business: 46 per cent of respondents said arrangement fees, 43 per cent said bundling of services, 43 and 39 per cent respectively said the need for personal security/security for loans and 32 per cent said the influence by the bank in business decisions.

Source of new SMEs

3.274. Banks recruit new SME customers from four main sources: from their own personal accounts, recommendations or contacts of relationship managers, from intermediaries such as accountants and solicitors and by word of mouth. Many SMEs open a business current account at the bank where they have a personal account. HSBC told us that it was likely that the bank at which the customer held its personal account would be its 'first port of call' when it was considering starting a business and if it was offered satisfactory terms by that bank (including an initial period of free banking) and had a good relationship with the bank there was a strong likelihood that the bank would gain the current account business, although the customer would be likely to use other suppliers for some or all of its banking needs. HSBC provided us with survey data that shows the proportion of start-up customers that opened a business current account at the bank where they had a personal account (see Table 3.37).

TABLE 3.37 **Proportion of new SMEs that open a business account at the bank where they have a personal current account, 1999**

	%
Barclays	71
HSBC	69
Lloyds TSB*	67
NatWest	66

Source: HSBC from a Start-up Business Research Survey.

*Business Banking.

3.275. Table 3.37 shows that about two-thirds of start-up customers with the four largest clearing banks opened a business current account where they held their personal account. These proportions are consistent with data provided to us by other banks. Abbey National told us that 60 per cent of its new Business Banking customers were personal customers of Abbey National and approximately 80 per cent of new business was referred from its branch network. Lloyds TSB told us that the fact that start-ups might open their business accounts with their personal bank did not necessarily imply that they had not been influenced by the other three sources—recommendations or contacts of relationship managers, from intermediaries such as accountants and solicitors and by word of mouth.

3.276. The size of these proportions suggests that banks with a larger share of personal current accounts are in a stronger position to recruit new SMEs than banks with a smaller share of personal current accounts. Table 3.38 shows the share of personal current accounts in Great Britain held by the four largest clearing groups and by the banks that these groups see as having potential to grow their SME business.

TABLE 3.38 **Shares of personal current accounts in Great Britain, 2000**

	%	Proportion of the average share of the four largest clearing groups (%) (a/b)§
Lloyds TSB	22	
Barclays*	18	
RBSG†	18	
RBS	4	
NatWest	14	
HSBC‡	14	
Average (including RBSG)	18(b)	
Abbey National¶	5(a)	28
Halifax	5(a)	27
NAB	4	
Alliance & Leicester¤	3(a)	19
Nationwide	3(a)	16
BoS	2	
Other	6	
Total	100	

Source: Market research data and CC calculations based on market research data.

*Includes Woolwich.
†Includes Virgin Direct.
‡Includes First Direct.
§Calculated on unrounded data.
¶Includes Safeway.
¤Includes Girobank.

3.277. Abbey National, Halifax, Alliance & Leicester and Nationwide all have far smaller shares of personal current accounts than the four largest clearing groups. Abbey National and Halifax each have less than one-third of the average share held by the four largest clearing groups. The equivalent proportions for Alliance & Leicester and Nationwide are 19 and 16 per cent respectively. HSBC provided us with market research data showing shares of personal current accounts at April 2001. Using these data, we re-estimated the proportions of the average share of the four largest groups accounted for by Halifax (46 per cent), Abbey National (34 per cent), Alliance & Leicester (27 per cent) and Nationwide (23 per cent). HSBC told us that Table 3.38 showed considerable scope for banks such as Halifax with substantial personal customer bases to build substantial SME customer bases. Barclays stated that personal current accounts did not provide the only source of access to personal customers who started a business. There were other relevant personal accounts—mortgage accounts and savings accounts. Barclays told us that while Abbey National had 5 per cent of personal current accounts, it had 13 per cent of personal savings accounts and 13 per cent of personal mortgages. It said that Halifax had 17 per cent of savings accounts and 19 per cent of mortgages, and Nationwide had 11 per cent of savings accounts and 8 per cent of mortgages. Barclays stated that in virtually all cases, these shares were higher than those of the four largest clearing banks.

3.278. With regard to the other three sources for recruiting SMEs—contact with relationship manager, recommendation by intermediaries and word of mouth—Lloyds TSB told us that, in 2000, at least the following percentages of its Commercial Banking's new customers were introduced to Lloyds TSB from the following sources: recommendation of existing customers (34 per cent), intermediaries (24 per cent) and work by relationship managers (15 per cent). Lloyds TSB said that as most of its Commercial Banking customers were likely to be established businesses (since they had an annual turnover of more than £2 million), they were likely to be switchers, rather than start-ups, and accordingly were unlikely to be introduced from the personal customer base.

Regulatory requirements

3.279. Since 1997 the EC has introduced a number of directives intended to coordinate the laws, regulation and administrative provisions relating to the financial services industry.

3.280. Some of the more important of these directives, such as the First and Second Banking Directives, the Own Funds Directive, the Solvency Ratio Directive and the Large Exposures Directive, have been consolidated into Directive 2000/12/EC known as the 'Credit Institutions Directive'. Other important directives are the Capital Adequacy Directive and the Investment Services Directive.

3.281. For a new entrant to be able to accept deposits from an SME, it must be authorized under the Banking Act 1987, as amended by the relevant EC Directive. From a regulatory stance, entry as a deposit taker is possible through three main routes as are set out in paragraphs 3.282 to 3.287 below.

3.282. First, entry is possible by application to the FSA to become a UK-authorized institution under the Banking Act 1987. The authorization criteria are interpreted by the FSA according to its 'Statement of Principles'. The Guide to Banking Supervisory Policy complements the Statement of Principles and details the FSA's prudential policy for its supervision of institutions authorized under the Banking Act 1987. These requirements and standards reflect the requirements of both the Banking Act 1987 and the relevant EC Directives.

3.283. The Banking Act 1987 requires that the FSA reach a decision within six months of receipt of a duly completed licence application, although the FSA may extend this period for a further six months where it requires additional information or documents to be furnished by the new entrant. A fee of £25,000 has to be submitted with the licence application.

3.284. Secondly, under the Credit Institutions Directive mutual recognition of bank authorizations granted by different national authorities known as the 'single licence' or 'passport' means that any EC bank can carry on activities set out in Annex 1 to the Credit Institutions Directive in the UK.

3.285. FSA authorization would therefore not be required for a new entrant which is a bank incorporated and authorized in another member state or within the European Economic Area. Such banks can carry on a wide range of banking and other financial services businesses in the UK either through the establishment of branches or by the provision of services on a cross-border basis. In order to avail itself of the 'passport', such a bank would be required to go through a fairly simple notification process. No fee is currently payable for this. However, when the Financial Services and Markets Act 2000 comes into force on 1 December 2001 European Economic Area banks that go through this notification process will automatically become authorized persons for the purposes of the Financial Services and Markets Act 2000 and a fee equivalent to half the fee charged to a UK authorized bank will be payable.

3.286. The FSA (and other UK regulators) retains the responsibility for supervising the day-to-day operation of the various financial markets for which they are responsible. However, the responsibility for supervising the financial soundness of such banks lies with the supervisory authority of the member state in which the bank is authorized.

3.287. Finally, entry is possible by application for change of control under the Banking Act 1987 through a takeover of an existing UK-authorized institution.

3.288. Providers (both banks and non-banks) wishing to make loans of £25,000 or less to individuals or unincorporated bodies are required to be licensed under the Consumer Credit Act 1974. An application for a licence would have to be made to the DGFT under the Consumer Credit Act 1974. The licence is issued if the DGFT is satisfied that an applicant is fit to hold one. The cost of the licence fee is negligible— currently £175 for a limited company or partnership. No authorization is required to lend money where the amount of each individual debt exceeds £25,000.

3.289. Triodos told us that the process it had to go through in order to be able to supply banking services in the UK took it about two years because of the protocol between the BoE and the Dutch Central Bank, and probably cost about £150,000 (see paragraph 8.107). HSBC said that evidence suggested that the UK had a relatively open and low-cost regulatory regime. It told us that the general position was that the key authorization required in the UK was for deposit-taking and an EC financial institution which had authorization in its home state was not required to have such authorization as the EC 'passport' regime enabled it to provide such services in the UK without authorization. It stated that such institutions merely needed to register with the FSA.

Conclusions on market definition

3.290. Our conclusions on market definition, and reasons for our conclusions, are given in paragraphs 2.16 to 2.61.

Shares of the main providers in 1999 and 2000

3.291. We now look at the sizes of, and the shares of the main suppliers in, each of the markets we have defined. There are four such markets: a liquidity management services market (including current accounts, overdraft facilities, and short-term deposits[1] that are provided by suppliers of business current accounts); general purpose business loans market (term loans excluding asset and sales finance and commercial mortgages[2]); an other lending market (segmented into asset finance, sales finance and commercial mortgages); and an other deposits market (including money market products). We look at the position in 1999 and 2000. We have based our estimates on data given to us by financial institutions that provide business accounts to SMEs. In the case of asset and sales finance we have made use of data collected by the Finance & Leasing Association (FLA) and the Factors & Discounters Association (FDA) respectively. We have calculated the shares including and excluding CACs. However, we only show shares excluding CACs unless there is a sizeable difference between those with and without CACs. We have been unable to estimate shares over time for the markets we have defined as we did not receive data from all the banks. We examine the trends in some of these services in paragraphs 3.315 to 3.323.

Liquidity management services market

3.292. For the reasons set out in Chapter 2 (see paragraphs 2.32 to 2.47), the liquidity management services market consists of current accounts, overdraft facilities and short-term deposits that are provided by suppliers of business current accounts. There are separate markets in England and Wales, in Scotland and in Northern Ireland.

Liquidity management services market in England and Wales

3.293. Table 3.39 shows our estimates of the size of this market (by number of accounts and value[3]), the shares held by the main suppliers and the HHI. The HHI is a widely-used measure of market concentration. An HHI of 10,000 indicates that there is only one supplier in the market, and the lower the number the lower the concentration. The CC has used the HHI in past inquiries as a way of providing a single index of the degree of concentration in a market but has not regarded it as the only indicator of the extent of competitive pressure. In merger inquiries, the US Department of Justice distinguishes different levels of concentration by the size of the HHI. Markets with an HHI of less than 1,000 are regarded as having a low level of concentration. A market with an HHI of between 1,000 and 1,800 is viewed as having a moderate degree of concentration and over 1,800 signifies a high level of concentration.

---

[1]Less than 30 days' term or notice.

[2]Data on commercial mortgages are included with data on general purpose loans because a number of the banks were unable to provide separate data for these two categories.

[3]Amount of money in current account credit balances plus amounts of overdraft facilities plus the amount of money held in short-term deposit accounts.

TABLE 3.39 **The liquidity management services market in England and Wales, 1999 and 2000**

per cent

	1999 Value	1999 Number	2000 Value	2000 Number
RBSG*	35	29	34	29
NatWest†	25	24	24	24
RBS†	9	5	10	5
Barclays	28	24	28	24
Lloyds TSB†	17	21	17	21
HSBC	11	17	11	17
Yorkshire‡	2	3	2	2
BoS	2	1	2	1
Alliance & Leicester	≤0.5	1	1	2
Co-operative Bank	1	1	1	1
Abbey National	1	≤0.5	1	1
Nationwide	1	1	<0.5	1
Other	2	2	2	2
Total§	100	100	100	100
Value (£bn)/number (m)	75.7	5.4	80.3	5.5
HHI¶	2,410	2,190	2,370	2,180
Four largest clearers‡¤	91	92	90	91

Source: CC calculations on data provided by the companies.

*Also includes Coutts.
†Includes businesses with annual turnover up to £100 million.
‡Excludes SMEs with an annual turnover of less than £100,000.
§Totals may not sum because of rounding.
¶Rounded to the nearest 10.
¤Includes all of RBSG.

3.294. Table 3.39 shows that there are over 5 million SME accounts in this liquidity management services market with a value of over £75 billion. Barclays and RBSG are the two largest suppliers, each with 24 per cent or more. HSBC and Lloyds TSB are the other two large suppliers. In all, these four suppliers account for about 90 per cent of the market. The HHI is over 2,000, which using US Department of Justice's criteria signifies a market with a high level of concentration.

Liquidity management services market in Scotland

3.295. Table 3.40 shows our estimates of the size of this market, the shares held by the main suppliers and the HHI.

TABLE 3.40 **The liquidity management services market in Scotland, 1999 and 2000**

per cent

	1999 Value	1999 Number	2000 Value	2000 Number
RBSG*	38	40	37	41
RBS†	37	39	37	40
BoS	32	31	32	30
Clydesdale‡	22	18	21	18
Lloyds TSB†	2	4	2	4
Other	7	7	7	7
Total§	100	100	100	100
Value (£bn)/number (m)	10.6	0.5	11.3	0.5
HHI¶	2,910	2,900	2,890	2,910
Three main clearers‡	91	89	91	89

Source: CC calculations on data provided by the companies.

*Also includes NatWest.
†Includes businesses with annual turnover up to £100 million.
‡Excludes SMEs with an annual turnover of less than £100,000. NAB estimated that Clydesdale's share in 2001 was 14 per cent by value and 23 per cent by number.
§Totals may not sum because of rounding.
¶Rounded to the nearest 10.
¤Includes BoS, Clydesdale and all of RBSG.

3.296. There are 0.5 million SME accounts in the liquidity management services market in Scotland with a value of over £10 billion. RBSG and BoS are the largest two providers, each with over 30 per cent of the market. Clydesdale is the other large supplier, its share being over 18 per cent. In all, these three suppliers account for about 90 per cent of the market. The HHI is just under 3,000, a market with a high level of concentration according to the US Department of Justice's criteria. Lloyds TSB's share, which is mainly a result of TSB's presence in Scotland, is less than 5 per cent.

Liquidity management services market in Northern Ireland

3.297. Table 3.41 shows our estimates of the size of this market, the shares held by the main suppliers and the HHI.

TABLE 3.41   **The liquidity management services market in Northern Ireland, 1999 and 2000**

per cent

	1999		2000	
	Value	Number	Value	Number
Northern*	36	22	36	21
Ulster Bank	30	38	28	37
First Trust	18	22	20	22
BoI	12	15	12	15
Other	4	4	4	4
Total†	100	100	100	100
Value (£bn)/number (m)	2.7	0.2	3.0	0.2
HHI‡	2,680	2,610	2,650	2,580
Northern Irish banks†	96	96	96	96

Source: CC calculations on data provided by the companies.

*NAB estimated that Northern's share in 2001 was 30 per cent by number of accounts.
†Totals may not sum because of rounding.
‡Rounded to the nearest 10.

3.298. There are 0.2 million SME accounts in the liquidity management services market in Northern Ireland with a value of over £2.5 billion. Northern and Ulster Bank are the two largest suppliers. First Trust and BoI are the other large suppliers, First Trust being the larger of the two. Together these four suppliers account for approximately 96 per cent of the market. The HHI is over 2,500, a market with a high level of concentration according to the US Department of Justice's criteria.

General purpose business loans market

3.299. For the reasons set out in Chapter 2 (see paragraphs 2.32 to 2.47), the general purpose business loans market comprises loans that are not contractually related to specific assets, ie they exclude asset and sales finance and commercial mortgages. Data on commercial mortgages is included with data on general purpose business loans because a number of the banks were unable to provide separate data for these two categories. There are separate general purpose business loans markets in England and Wales, in Scotland and in Northern Ireland.

General purpose business loans market in England and Wales

3.300. Table 3.42 shows our estimates of the size of this market, the shares held by the main suppliers and the HHI.

per cent

	1999		2000	
	Value	Number	Value	Number
RBSG*	39	31	39	31
NatWest†	28	25	27	24
RBS†	11	6	12	6
Barclays	23	23	22	22
Lloyds TSB†	10	25	11	27
HSBC	12	12	12	11
Yorkshire‡	4	4	4	4
BoS	1	1	1	1
Co-operative Bank	1	1	1	1
Alliance & Leicester	<0.5	<0.5	<0.5	<0.5
Nationwide	<0.5	<0.5	<0.5	<0.5
Other	9	2	9	2
Total§	100	100	100	100
Value (£bn)/number (m)	44.3	0.7	47.7	0.7
HHI¶	2,330	2,280	2,320	2,300
Four largest clearers‡	84	90	84	91

Source: CC calculations on data provided by the companies.

---

*Also includes Coutts.
†Includes businesses with annual turnover up to £100 million.
‡Excludes SMEs with an annual turnover of less than £100,000.
§Totals may not sum because of rounding.
¶Rounded to the nearest 10.
¤Includes all of RBSG.

3.301. Table 3.42 shows that there are 0.7 million general purpose business loan accounts with a value outstanding of over £44 billion. In terms of number of accounts, RBSG, Barclays and Lloyds TSB each have much larger shares (ranging from 22 to 31 per cent) than HSBC (about 11 per cent). However, Lloyds TSB has broadly the same share of the value of accounts as HSBC (10 to 12 per cent), both being much lower than the shares held by RBSG (39 per cent) and Barclays (about 22 per cent). The shares of the four largest clearing groups are much larger than any other suppliers. In all they account for about 90 per cent of the number accounts and 84 per cent of their value. The HHI is over 2,200, and using the US Department of Justice's criteria this signifies a market with a high level of concentration.

General purpose business loans market in Scotland

3.302. Table 3.43 shows our estimates of the size of this market, the shares held by the main suppliers and the HHI.

TABLE 3.43 **General purpose business loans market (including commercial mortgages) in Scotland, 1999 and 2000**

per cent

	1999		2000	
	Value	Number	Value	Number
RBSG*	39	33	39	34
RBS†	37	33	37	33
BoS	23	25	22	24
Clydesdale‡	31	31	31	31
Lloyds TSB†	3	4	3	5
Other	4	6	5	6
Total§	100	100	100	100
Value (£bn)/number (m)	5.1	0.07	5.5	0.08
HHI¶	2,970	2,730	2,990	2,740
Three main clearers§¤	92	89	92	89

Source: CC calculations on data provided by the companies.

*Also includes NatWest.
†Includes businesses with annual turnover up to £100 million.
‡Businesses with an annual turnover of more than £100,000. NAB estimated that Clydesdale's share would be 19 per cent (by value and number) excluding its businesses with an annual turnover of more than £25 million.
§Totals may not sum because of rounding.
¶Rounded to the nearest 10.
¤Includes BoS, Clydesdale and all of RBSG.

3.303. There are over 0.07 million general purpose business loan accounts in Scotland with a value of over £5 billion. RBSG is the largest supplier (33 per cent or over of the market). Clydesdale (31 per cent) has a larger share than BoS (between 22 and 25 per cent). Together these three suppliers account for about 90 per cent of the market. The HHI is over 2,700, a market with a high level of concentration according to the US Department of Justice's criteria.

General purpose business loans market in Northern Ireland

3.304. Table 3.44 shows our estimates of the size of this market, the shares held by the main suppliers and the HHI.

TABLE 3.44 **General purpose business loans market (including commercial mortgages) in Northern Ireland, 1999 and 2000**

per cent

	1999		2000	
	Value	Number	Value	Number
Northern	26	28	25	27
Ulster Bank	28	28	28	28
First Trust	19	23	18	23
BoI	20	14	23	15
Other	7	7	7	7
Total*	100	100	100	100
Value (£bn)/number (m)	2.5	0.03	3.2	0.03
HHI†	2,240	2,330	2,240	2,290
Northern Irish banks*	93	93	93	93

Source: CC calculations on data provided by the companies.

*Totals may not sum because of rounding.
†Rounded to the nearest 10.

3.305. There are about 0.03 million general purpose business loan accounts in Northern Ireland with a value of over £2 billion. The largest four suppliers account for over 90 per cent of the market. The HHI is over 2,200, a market with a high level of concentration according to the US Department of Justice's criteria.

Other lending market

3.306. For the reasons set out in Chapter 2 (see paragraphs 2.32 to 2.47), other lending consists of loans that are related to specific assets, ie they include asset and sales finance and commercial mortgages. Data on commercial mortgages are included with data on general purpose business loans because a number of the banks were unable to provide separate data for these two categories. There is a UK-wide other SME lending market.

3.307. Table 3.45 shows our estimates of the size of this market and the two segments (by value outstanding only), the shares held by the main suppliers and the HHI. Our estimates are based on data provided by the companies and by the FLA and FDA, two trade bodies representing asset finance and sales finance companies respectively. We adjusted the data from the trade bodies because they do not include all companies and the data is not restricted to financing SMEs.

TABLE 3.45 **Other lending in the UK, 1999 and 2000**

	Value					per cent
	1999 Type of finance			2000 Type of finance		
	Asset	Sales	Total	Asset	Sales	Total
RBSG	16	20	16	14	20	15
Lloyds TSB*	16	12	16	16	14	15
BoS	10	4	10	10	5	10
Barclays	8	7	8	8	10	8
HSBC	4	12	5	4	11	5
Other	46	45	46	48	40	48
Total†	100	100	100	100	100	100
Value (£bn)†	49.6	4.4	54.0	49.8	5.2	54.9
HHI‡			790			750
Four largest clearers†	44	51	44	42	55	43

Source: CC calculations on data provided by the companies, the FLA and the FDA.

*In the final week of our inquiry Lloyds TSB provided us with revised data for asset finance which reduced its share of asset finance to about 5 per cent and its total share to 6 per cent.
†Totals may not sum because of rounding.
‡Rounded to the nearest 10.

3.308. Table 3.45 shows that the value outstanding of other lending was about £54 billion, the majority being accounted for by asset finance (over 90 per cent). The share of the four largest clearing groups (about 43 per cent) is much smaller than in the liquidity management services market and the general purpose business loans market. The HHI is below 800, and using the US Department of Justice's criteria this signifies a market with a low level of concentration.

Other deposits market

3.309. For the reasons set out in Chapter 2 (see paragraphs 2.32 to 2.47), other deposits consist of SME deposits from suppliers that do not offer an SME current account, long-term SME deposits,[1] and money market products held by SMEs. There is a UK market.

3.310. Table 3.46 shows our estimates of the size of this market, the shares held by the main suppliers and the HHI.

---

[1]30 days or more term or notice.

TABLE 3.46 **Other deposits in the UK, 1999 and 2000**

per cent

	1999		2000	
	Value	Number	Value	Number
RBSG*	30	15	28	15
RBS†	6	6	5	6
NatWest†	19	8	18	8
Barclays	23	9	24	10
Lloyds TSB†	20	12	21	13
HSBC‡	15	10	15	10
BoS	2	1	3	1
NAB§	3	1	2	1
First Trust	1	5	1	5
BoI	1	<0.5	1	<0.5
Other	6	47	5	46
Total¶	100	100	100	100
Value (£bn)/number (m)	32.7	0.2	38.1	0.2
HHI	2,090	690	2,060	710
Four largest clearers¶#	88	46	88	47

Source: CC calculations on data provided by the companies.

*Also includes Ulster Bank and Coutts.
†Includes businesses with annual turnover of up to £100 million.
‡Includes money market products held by businesses with an annual turnover of up to £100 million.
§Excludes SMEs with an annual turnover of less than £100,000 for Clydesdale.
¶Totals may not sum because of rounding.
¤Rounded to the nearest 10.
#Includes all of RBSG.

3.311. Table 3.46 shows that there are 0.2 million other SME deposits accounts with a value of over £32 billion. There is a marked difference in the shares of the four largest clearing groups when the size of the market is measured by the number of accounts as opposed to the value of these accounts. This is because money market products, which are primarily offered to SMEs by the four largest clearing groups, account for about 90 per cent of the value of the market but only about 40 per cent of the number of accounts. Building societies and ex-building societies account for about 80 per cent of the number of other deposits held by SMEs excluding money market products. The four largest clearing groups account for over 45 and 88 per cent of the number and value of these accounts respectively. The HHI is about 2,000 when measured by value and using the US Department of Justice's criteria this signifies a market with a high level of concentration and about 700 when measured by number which signifies a market with a low level of concentration.

SME banking services

3.312. Barclays told us that the market consisted of all banking services to SMEs—current accounts, overdrafts and other types of lending, and all SME deposits—and that some personal accounts should also be included in the market (see paragraph 3.41). Barclays believed there was a UK market.

3.313. Table 3.47 shows our estimates of the value of SME banking services, the shares held by the main suppliers in the UK and the HHI.

TABLE 3.47 **The value of SME banking services in the UK, 1999 and 2000**

| | per cent | |
	1999	2000
RBSG*	31	30
NatWest†	17	16
RBS†	12	12
Barclays	19	19
Lloyds TSB†	14	15
HSBC‡	9	9
BoS	6	6
NAB§	4	4
First Trust	1	1
BoI	<0.5	1
Other	16	16
Total¶	100	100
Value (£bn)	228	244
HHI¤	1,640	1,620
Four largest clearers#	73	73

Source: CC calculations on data provided by the companies.

*Also includes Ulster Bank and Coutts.
†Includes businesses with annual turnover up to £100 million. In the final week of our inquiry Lloyds TSB provided us with revised data for asset finance which reduced its share of banking services to about 12 per cent.
‡Includes money market products held by businesses with an annual turnover of up to £100 million.
§Excludes SMEs with an annual turnover of less than £100,000 for Clydesdale and Yorkshire.
¶Totals may not sum because of rounding.
¤Rounded to the nearest 10.
#Includes RBSG.

3.314. Table 3.47 shows that SME banking services had a value of over £225 billion. RBSG is the largest supplier (about 30 per cent), followed by Barclays (19 per cent), Lloyds TSB (14 per cent) and HSBC (9 per cent). BoS had a 6 per cent share. The four largest clearing groups accounted for just under three-quarters of the value of SME banking services. The HHI was about 1,600, and using the US Department of Justice's criteria this signifies a market towards the higher end of a moderate level of concentration.

Shares over time

3.315. We have been unable to estimate shares over time for the markets we have defined as we did not receive data from all the banks. However, a number of the main clearing groups provided us with their estimates of the trends in shares of the number of main business accounts held by banks. These estimates were based on market research data, which the banks provided to us, that also showed the trend in shares held by banks. Figure 3.4 shows the trends in shares between 1990 and 2000 of the number of main business accounts in England and Wales for businesses with an annual turnover of up to £1 million held by the four largest clearing banks and by the other suppliers in aggregate.

3.316. NatWest's share fell by over four percentage points between 1990 and 2000, most of its fall occurring in the late 1990s and in 2000. HSBC increased its share by over two percentage points between 1990 and 2000. Its share fell in the early 1990s, was broadly stable in the mid-1990s and increased in the late 1990s and in 2000. Barclays' share fluctuated over the period, falling by just under two percentage points between 1990 and 2000. Including TSB's share with that for Lloyds for the whole period shows that the share of Lloyds TSB fluctuated over the period but its share in 1990 was broadly the same as that in 2000 (20 per cent). The overall share of these four banks fell by over three percentage points between 1990 and 2000. Their overall share fell in the early 1990s, was broadly constant in the mid-1990s, fell in 1995 and has been broadly constant since then. Taking into account the acquisition of NatWest by RBSG, the share of the four largest groups in 2000 was slightly higher than their share in 1990.

FIGURE 3.4

Shares of the main business banking account for businesses with an annual turnover of less than £1 million in England and Wales, 1990 to 2000

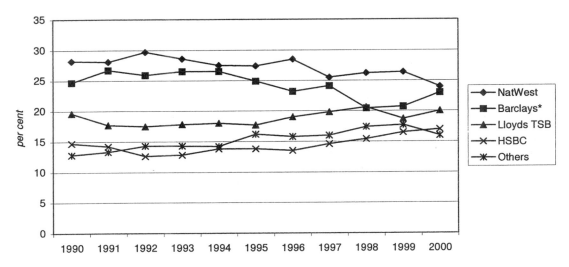

Sources: Market research data and CC estimates.
*Using one market research company's data, Barclays' share would be broadly constant (about 23 per cent) between 1997 and 2000.

3.317. Figure 3.5 shows the trends in shares for businesses with an annual turnover of between £1 million and £100 million. NatWest's share has been broadly constant between 1990 and 2000. Barclays' share fell by over three percentage points. It was broadly constant between 1990 and 1992, fell to 1996 and has been broadly constant since then. Lloyds TSB's share (including TSB's share for the whole period) has fallen by over two percentage points. Its share fell to 1992, was broadly constant to 1996, rose to 1998 and fell to 2000. The share of HSBC rose by nearly two percentage points, most of this rise occurring in 1999. The aggregate share of these four banks has fallen by three percentage points between 1990 and 2000. Their share fell in the early 1990s, was constant in the mid-1990s, rose in 1998 and fell to 2000. Taking into account the acquisition of NatWest by RBSG, the share of the four largest clearing groups in 2000 was two percentage points higher than their share in 1990.

FIGURE 3.5

Shares of the main business banking account for businesses with an annual turnover of between £1 million and £100 million in England and Wales, 1990 to 2000

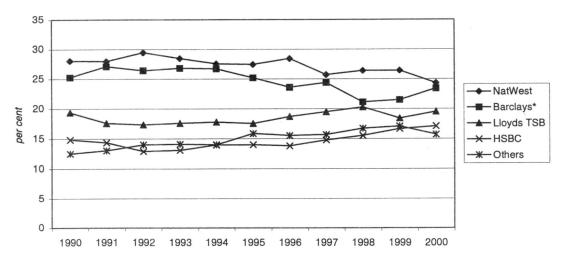

Source: Market research data and CC estimates.

3.318. Using data provided to us by the four largest clearing groups for 1999 and 2000, we have combined the data on the trend in shares for businesses with an annual turnover of less than £1 million and for businesses with an annual turnover of between £1 million and £100 million. We have applied a weighting factor of 0.9 for the smaller businesses. Figure 3.6 shows the trend in shares for the combined businesses.

FIGURE 3.6

Shares of the main business banking account for businesses with an annual turnover of up to £100 million in England and Wales, 1990 to 2000

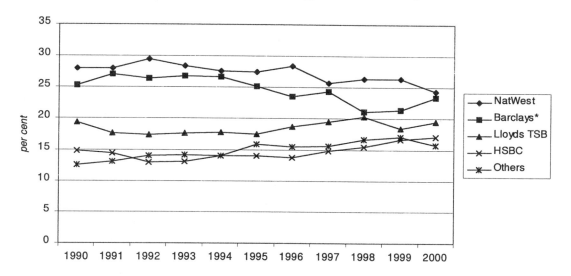

Source: CC calculations based on market research data provided by the banks.
*Using one market research company's data, Barclays' share would be broadly constant (23 to 24 per cent) between 1997 and 2000.

3.319. As we have applied by far the largest weighting to the smaller businesses, Figure 3.6 is very similar to Figure 3.4—NatWest and Barclays have experienced a reduction in share, HSBC has increased its share and the share of Lloyds TSB has been constant. The aggregate share of these four banks fell by just over three percentage points between 1990 and 2000 but rose by one percentage point after taking account of RBSG's acquisition of NatWest.

3.320. RBSG provided its own estimates of the trend in shares between 1990 and 2000 but its estimates were for businesses with an annual turnover of up to £25 million in Great Britain (see Figure 3.7). The main differences between RBSG's estimates and those of the market research company and our estimates based on those of the market research company is that RBSG's estimates show a constant share for NatWest and a slightly declining share for HSBC. The shares of BoS, Clydesdale and RBS in Scotland are constant over this period. These constant shares in Scotland are consistent with the views of BoS. It told us that the shares of these large three suppliers had remained broadly constant over the last ten years but that there had been some growth by Lloyds TSB.

FIGURE 3.7

Shares of the main business banking account for businesses with an annual turnover of up to £25 million in Great Britain, 1990 to 2000

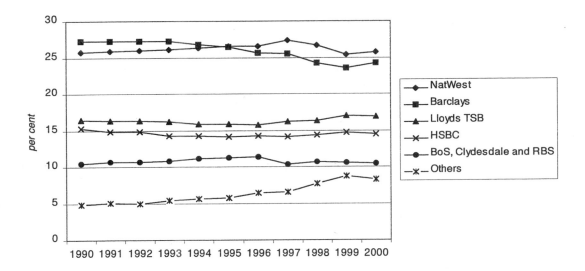

Source: RBSG.

3.321. Table 3.48 summarizes the change in the shares held by the four largest clearing groups between 1990 and 2000. It takes into account the changes in ownership by including Barclays, NatWest, HSBC and Lloyds in 1990 and by including Barclays, RBSG, HSBC and Lloyds TSB in 2000.

TABLE 3.48 **Shares of the number of main business current account held by the four largest groups in 1990 and 2000**

per cent

	England and Wales						Great Britain	
	Less than £1m		£1m–£100m		Up to £100m		Up to £25m	
	1990	2000	1990	2000	1990	2000	1990	2000
Barclays	24.7	23.0	30.2	27.0	25.3	23.4	27.2	24.2
NatWest/RBSG*	28.2	28.1	26.5	32.0	28.0	28.5	25.8	31.5
Lloyds/Lloyds TSB†	16.6	20.0	16.6	15.0	16.6	19.5	13.6	16.9
HSBC	14.7	17.0	16.1	18.0	14.8	17.1	15.3	14.5
Four largest	84.2	88.1	89.4	92.0	84.7	88.5	81.9	87.1
Other	15.8	11.9	10.6	8.0	15.3	11.5	18.2	12.9
Total‡	100	100	100	100	100	100	100	100
Percentage point change in shares held by the four largest groups‡		3.9		2.6		3.8		5.3

Source: CC calculation based on market research data provided by the companies.

---

*NatWest in 1990 and RBSG in 2000.
†Lloyds in 1990 and Lloyds TSB in 2000.
‡Totals may not sum because of rounding.

3.322. Table 3.48 shows that between 1990 and 2000 the share of the four largest clearing groups, taking into account mergers during the period, has risen by between 2.5 and 5.5 percentage points.

3.323. BoI told us that, except for changes in ownership of the TSB Bank Northern Ireland plc, there had not been any significant changes in aggregate share held by the Northern Irish banks over the last ten years.

New entry

3.324. There are no examples of large-scale entry, other than by acquisition, into the liquidity management services markets and the general purpose business loan markets in recent times. This is demonstrated by the broadly constant trend in the size of the shares of the number of business current accounts held by companies other than the six largest clearing banks and Clydesdale. There are examples of entry but these companies are either no longer independent or they do not currently offer a full range of banking services to SMEs or they account for a small market share, particularly in the liquidity management services market and the general purpose business loans market.

3.325. HSBC stated that there had been successful, albeit mainly recent, entry in each of the relevant markets. Both new entrants and existing smaller players had succeeded in significantly increasing their market share. It said that a number of new providers of business current accounts had emerged, and had succeeded in attracting substantial numbers of customers in a relatively short time. These included the Co-operative Bank, Alliance & Leicester and Abbey National. In addition, (ex-) building societies (such as Nationwide and Halifax) had begun to offer personal current accounts and other money transmission facilities, and had attracted large numbers of customers for these services—some of whom were likely to be using their accounts for business as well as personal purposes. It told us that some financial institutions had recently begun to target SMEs, including Birmingham Midshires Building Society (Halifax-owned, targeting commercial mortgages to SMEs, and also accepting loan applications through its web site) and Euro Sales Finance. HSBC said that new entrants providing deposit products included Standard Life Bank (a telephone-based service) and, as with money transmission and debt products, it was also necessary to take account of new suppliers of personal products, such as Egg.

3.326. Lloyds TSB provided us with a brief history of TSB that it said proved that successful market entry was genuinely possible. It told us that in 1979/80, the trustee savings banks gradually started providing banking services to SMEs. Lloyds TSB said that although the TSB brand was well known and had a good reputation, it was a mixed blessing—it was strongly associated with personal savings. The lending decisions taken by inexperienced branch managers in the early 1980s proved to be poor in some instances and TSB sustained losses when some of these debts turned bad. TSB instigated a more rigorous credit policy in about 1983/84. It recognized that it required personal and technical skills to generate and control its commercial business and that those skills were substantially different to those possessed by its existing staff who dealt predominantly with non-credit products. By 1987 many of TSB's staff had undergone training but TSB recognized that the training was not sufficient—it still did not have enough expertise to undertake commercial lending on a day-to-day basis. In the mid- to late 1980s TSB reviewed its strategy regarding the SME market and commissioned reports from management consultants. The consultants endorsed TSB's strategy of establishing corporate business centres, separate from TSB's personal branches, as this was considered to be the optimal means of achieving and exceeding target growth in the medium and long term. TSB would also focus on building up deposits and developing niche markets and safe lending. By the late 1980s TSB was offering a full range of banking services to retail customers, SMEs and corporate customers. In 1988 TSB's business banking was reorganized into two divisions: retail and personal banking, and corporate banking. By the time of the merger between Lloyds and TSB in 1995, Lloyds TSB said that TSB had adopted a segmented approach to business banking, had successfully recruited staff from other banks and was recording profits on its small business banking credit business. Lloyds TSB told us that TSB attracted business customers—predominantly sole traders, small to middle market businesses and professionals—through the success that TSB had in niche segments through the exploitation of its online real time system which enabled the bank to successfully recruit among, for example, solicitors. Success with these customers provided access, indirectly, to other customers. According to market research data, between 1989 and 1995 TSB accounted for about 3 per cent of the number of business current accounts held by businesses with an annual turnover of less than £1 million and less than 1 per cent of such accounts held by businesses with an annual turnover of between £1 million and £100 million.

3.327. Halifax told us that it had become involved in one aspect of SME business in the mid-1980s—lending to housing associations and builders—such loans being secured. Halifax said that the subsequent downturn after 1989 reflected that it lacked a branch infrastructure containing people who were experts in the risk diagnosis of business. It stated that, after its earlier experience, development of an approach to small businesses, given it did not have the core competency, was not a priority. Halifax told us that it currently had very little involvement with the SME sector. However, it said it envisaged that its new Internet banking operation Intelligent Finance would seek to provide banking services to the small business sector, and it was also considering how it might more widely enter the SME market but as yet it had no firm plans. As noted in paragraph 3.4, this comment was made prior to the planned merger of BoS and Halifax. Halifax told us that the new group—HBOS plc—would be in a position to use the skills and experience of BoS to increase its presence in the SME market throughout the whole of the UK.

3.328. Citibank told us that it first began to offer banking services to SMEs some ten years ago but was unsuccessful because it had very few branches, and so had to withdraw from the market. It said that it had subsequently re-entered the market during the late 1990s, but was again unsuccessful because of its lack of a branch network, and so had exited once more. It told us that it had no current plans to re-enter the market.

3.329. Nationwide told us that its primary mission was the provision of financial services for private customers. Its account 'BusinessInvestor' offered SMEs an instant access account with a business cheque book and interest paid on credit balances. Nationwide offers secured loans for small businesses but not overdrafts, which it said was due to its lack of expertise. Nationwide told us that it was soon to make a decision on whether or not to expand its services to SMEs. It told us that it would be likely to focus on smaller businesses—sole traders, for instance, and small partnerships. It stated that its biggest challenge would be providing lending facilities on current accounts, because it did not have that expertise, but could maybe do so through use of a score card as it did for personal borrowers; alternatively it would initially only offer a current account without borrowing facilities.

3.330. Many of the four largest clearing groups told us that they were expecting new providers to enter the markets in the next few years and that some of the smaller providers would grow. Many referred to Alliance & Leicester, Abbey National, Halifax and Nationwide. We have summarized the views of Halifax (see paragraph 3.327) and Nationwide (see paragraph 3.329) with regard to their current and possible future offerings to SMEs (see Chapters 8 and 9 for a fuller discussion of their views) and we now examine the current and future offerings of Alliance & Leicester and Abbey National.

Abbey National

3.331. Abbey National, which towards the end of our inquiry was subject to a contested takeover bid from Lloyds TSB, began providing banking services to business customers in 1997. One year later it established a business asset finance division within First National Bank, one of its subsidiaries. At the time of writing this report Abbey National offered current accounts for two-person partnerships and sole traders, deposit accounts for a wider range of SMEs including limited companies and larger partnerships, asset finance and leasing, factoring and invoice discounting, and commercial mortgages. It does not offer term loans to SMEs. At the start of the inquiry Abbey National told us that its current account was only available to two-person partnerships and sole traders because, inter alia, the technology on which the account was modelled was taken from its personal banking offer which was only configured to deal with up to two individuals as signatories. Abbey National said that it would be upgrading its software shortly so that limited companies and larger partnerships would be able to hold its current accounts by the end of 2001. Historically, SMEs with current accounts with Abbey National have had to maintain a credit balance, ie Abbey National did not offer overdrafts with its business current accounts. Abbey National stated that it had been a commercial decision not to offer overdraft facilities as part of its business banking package based on research showing that 65 per cent of all businesses operated permanently in credit and the difficulty in obtaining adequate credit histories of companies in order to assess the risks involved in making such facilities available to them. However, Abbey National said that as its product offering to business customers developed it intended, in due course, to offer overdraft facilities. As part of its stated ambition to capture 5 per cent of the SME market within five years, board approval for engaging in small-scale short-term overdrafts on current accounts was granted in March 2001 with the intention of rolling out the programme shortly.

3.332. Abbey National's Business Bank account was free of charges until 1999. In 1999 Abbey National began to offer indefinite free banking to SMEs subject to transaction limits—up to 25 cheques for credit, up to 25 cheques for debit per month and up to £500 cash deposits per week via ATMs. There are no limits on automated credit and debits. It also pays interest on its current accounts, ranging from 0.75 per cent gross AER for balances of less than £2,000 up to 4.25 per cent for balances of more than £0.5 million.[1] Abbey National's present charges apply to existing SMEs and start-ups. Abbey National told us that it did not negotiate money transmission charges with SMEs.

---

[1]The following gross AERs also apply: 1 per cent for over £2,000 to £25,000; 2.4 per cent for over £25,000 to £50,000; 2.6 per cent for over £50,000 to £100,000; and 3.4 per cent for over £100,000 to £500,000.

3.333. Abbey National's bank account offering to business customers is currently primarily remote, ie not branch-based but operated through the post, over the telephone and over the Internet. In Business Banking it has about 40 to 50 relationship managers covering the whole of the UK.

3.334. Abbey National's product offering to business customers does not currently allow for cash deposits as the accounts are not branch-based. However, there is a pilot process for its SMEs which allow them to make deposits over post office counters. Abbey National told us that there were about 20 users in the pilot scheme which was not being extended at present. It said that as a general rule it would actively discourage SMEs with large cash-handling requirements from using its current accounts as these, being postal, telephone or Internet, were not designed to deal with large amounts of cash. It told us that this position could change as it broadened its business banking offer.

3.335. Abbey National recently announced its intention to endeavour to capture some 5 per cent of business banking customers[1] by 2005. It expects the number of its Business Banking accounts to increase from [✄] in 2000 to [✄] in 2001, [✄] in 2002, [✄] in 2003, [✄] in 2004 and [✄] in 2005. Abbey National told us that its plans, which include growing its existing asset finance business, required an additional one-off investment (predominantly IT) of £[✄] million to £[✄] million (on top of the £[✄] million already approved) and an ongoing incremental cumulative investment (which is heavily marketing dominated) of £[✄] million in total to 2005. It said that any further growth within this timescale would have to be through acquisition.

3.336. Abbey National's growth plans are based, in part, on its free Internet and telephone-based proposition—it told us that there would be no charges for standard services within defined transaction limits and that interest would be paid on current and deposit accounts. It said that customers would be charged for heavier transaction volumes and for additional services.

Alliance & Leicester

3.337. Alliance & Leicester told us that it classified business customers as small businesses (with an annual turnover of up to £1 million) and large corporates (with an annual turnover of over £1 million). Its Small Business current account is operated on a direct basis—telephone, fax, post and Internet. Cash and cheques are banked at the Post Office, the cheques being passed over the counter in a sealed envelope which is then remitted to the bank via Royal Mail to the bank's processing centre. Post office counters act purely as a collection point. Cheques can also be sent to the bank by post but Alliance & Leicester told us that many customers were reluctant to do this. It said that it would be increasing its branch staff's knowledge and awareness of its small business offering as the Alliance Business Banking product developed. Alliance & Leicester's business customers with annual turnover of over £0.5 million have relationship managers. Those businesses with an annual turnover of £0.5 million to £1 million contact their relationship managers by telephone whereas relationship managers visit those businesses with an annual turnover of over £1 million. Alliance & Leicester has about 70 relationship managers throughout the country.

3.338. Alliance & Leicester launched a new current account for businesses with an annual turnover of less than £0.5 million called Businessplus in August 2000. The account was targeted at businesses that dealt in lower cash volumes. Prior to the launch of Businessplus Alliance & Leicester operated one account (Girobank Direct) for small businesses with a turnover up to £0.5 million. The Girobank Direct tariff was specifically designed for businesses dealing in large volumes of cash. Businesses with an annual turnover of up to £0.5 million have a fixed tariff with day-to-day customer contact via a dedicated call centre. There are no negotiations on these tariffs. Alliance & Leicester told us that the main components of these tariffs had not changed during the last five years; there was an increase in miscellaneous charges in 1999. Alliance & Leicester had 34,535 fixed tariff accounts at December 1999 out of a total of 68,633 current accounts (50 per cent). Businesses with an annual turnover between £0.5 million and £1 million have negotiated tariffs. These tariffs are negotiated annually through a call centre team. Businesses with an annual turnover over £1 million are assigned to a sales manager who looks after the account and deals with the annual negotiations. Day-to-day customer contact is via a call centre.

3.339. Alliance & Leicester offers interest for those customers using its Internet banking service. However, it told us that in January 2001 it launched a package to attract businesses that had been with their

---

[1]Defined as all business customers.

existing bank for over three years. It said that its main reasons for initially targeting this group of business customers were that they were potentially receiving poorer service and pricing than start-ups and that established businesses were a lower credit risk for Alliance & Leicester for offering full banking services. Part of this package includes offering interest on business current accounts.[1]

3.340. Alliance & Leicester rebranded its business offerings from Girobank to Alliance Business Banking in quarter 4, 2000. In October 2000 Alliance & Leicester began to offer overdraft and loan facilities to its existing Small Business customers. These facilities were offered to its new SMEs in early 2001 although Alliance & Leicester said that a highly conservative lending stance was adopted towards a number of lending categories, including start-ups. Alliance & Leicester told us that within Alliance Business Banking the maximum unsecured exposure was limited to £25,000 and the maximum secured exposure was restricted to £200,000.

3.341. Alliance & Leicester said that it aimed to acquire a 10 per cent share of new small businesses (an annual turnover of £1 million) by 2005. It stated that due to the higher risk of lending to start-ups, the initial focus of its marketing activity would be on established businesses wishing to change their banks. It told us that over the coming years start-ups rather than switchers were expected to represent an increasing number of its new account acquisitions. It said that it had historically not targeted start-ups but had only targeted existing SME customers with other banks (switchers).

3.342. Alliance & Leicester told us that its projections were based on it offering rates of interest on current account balances, simple fixed tariff banking and transparent pricing, 24-hour telephone banking and the provision of unsecured loans and overdraft facilities to sole traders, partnerships and limited companies, up to a value of £25,000, although larger facilities, for example secured lending, would be introduced in the near term. It said that it also offered a service to make it easy for SMEs to switch banks. The projections would require an increase in its cost base from about £25 million to just over £100 million.

Future plans of some of the six largest clearing banks

3.343. Some of the six largest clearing banks provided us with their plans for the next few years and some told us how they saw their business developing. We summarize the information given to us by Lloyds TSB, Barclays, HSBC and BoS.

Lloyds TSB

3.344. Lloyds TSB's 2000 Group Strategic Plan showed its estimate of its share of the number of Business Banking (annual turnover up to £2 million) and Commercial Banking (annual turnover between £2 million and £100 million) accounts over the period 2000 to 2002 (see Table 3.49).

TABLE 3.49 **Lloyds TSB's estimate of its shares of Business and Commercial banking, 2000 to 2002**

per cent

	Actual	Forecast		
	1999	2000	2001	2002
Business Banking* Commercial Banking†	[Figures omitted. See note on page iv.			]

Source: Lloyds TSB.

---

*Annual turnover up to £2 million.
†Annual turnover of between £2 million and £100 million.

3.345. [*Details omitted. See note on page iv.*

         ]

---

[1]Its current rates were 0.5 per cent for credit balances up to £3,999; 2.75 per cent for credit balances of £4,000 to £99,999 and 4.75 per cent for credit balances of £100,000 and over.

Barclays

3.346. Barclays' 2000 Strategic Plan for its Business Banking business (annual turnover up to £100 million) does not include data showing its projections for its share of this business but in support of its aim to increase its economic profit of its Business Banking business from over £[✂] million in 1999 to over £[✂] million in 2003, the Plan states that Barclays will [

Details omitted. See note on page iv.

].

HSBC

3.347. In its 2000 Plan for its Commercial Banking business (annual turnover up to £100 million) HSBC is projecting that it will increase the number of its accounts by over [✂] per cent a year between 2000 and 2003.

BoS

3.348. BoS told us that it would feel it had done well if over the next three years it managed to triple its market share in England and Wales to about 3 per cent. It said that this would take a lot of effort, a lot of marketing and a lot of sales effort. It believed it could achieve this increase a lot faster if it had more branches in England and Wales. As noted in paragraph 3.4, this comment was made prior to the planned merger of BoS and Halifax.

Shopping around

3.349. Barclays said that on average, start-ups contacted 1.8 banks in person and 2.3 banks by telephone when choosing a new business bank. BMRB asked SMEs that had been operating for two years or less and which had not switched banks (26 per cent of the whole sample) whether they had obtained information from other banks or building societies before making their decision to hold their main account with their bank. 53 per cent said that they had not obtained information and 43 per cent said that they had. The SMEs that had obtained information from other banks and building societies were asked by BMRB to name these banks and building societies. The results are shown in Table 3.50.

TABLE 3.50 **Banks and building societies used by SMEs when shopping around**

Banks*	Percentage of SMEs
Lloyds TSB	41
NatWest	36
Barclays	32
HSBC	28
RBS	13
BoS	9
Halifax	6
Abbey National	4
Sample size	136

Source: BMRB survey.

*No other bank or building society was contacted by more than 3 per cent of SMEs.

3.350. Of those that obtained information, most did so from the four largest clearing groups (41 per cent used Lloyds TSB, 36 per cent used NatWest, 32 per cent used Barclays, 28 per cent used HSBC and 13 per cent used RBS). 9 per cent of SMEs obtained information from BoS. However, this proportion is reduced to 6 per cent by excluding SMEs in Scotland. Very few SMEs obtained information from banks or building societies that the four largest clearing groups saw as having potential to grow their SME business. Only 6 per cent of SMEs obtained information from Halifax, 4 per cent from Abbey National, just under 3 per cent from Alliance & Leicester (including Girobank) and just under 1.5 per cent from Nationwide.

Lloyds TSB told us that it was to be expected that these banks/building societies would not yet attract as many SMEs as the main clearing groups as they did not presently offer as full a range of services as the main clearing groups.

3.351. BMRB asked SMEs that were less than two years old and had not switched banks what source of advice, other than banks or building societies, they had used when taking out their main business account. The most frequent answer was accountants, given by 36 per cent of SMEs.

The extent of switching

3.352. Barclays, HSBC, Lloyds TSB and NatWest provided us with data on the number of SME business accounts they had won and lost (see Table 3.51).

TABLE 3.51 **Gains and losses in number of SME current accounts, 1999**

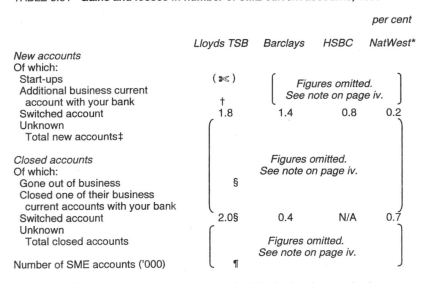

				per cent
	Lloyds TSB	Barclays	HSBC	NatWest*
New accounts				
Of which:				
Start-ups	(✂)			
Additional business current account with your bank	†	Figures omitted. See note on page iv.		
Switched account	1.8	1.4	0.8	0.2
Unknown				
Total new accounts‡				
Closed accounts				
Of which:		Figures omitted. See note on page iv.		
Gone out of business	§			
Closed one of their business current accounts with your bank				
Switched account	2.0§	0.4	N/A	0.7
Unknown				
Total closed accounts		Figures omitted. See note on page iv.		
Number of SME accounts ('000)	¶			

Source: CC calculations based on data provided by the four largest clearing groups.

*Excludes transfers between branches.
†Less than 0.1 per cent.
‡Totals may not sum because of rounding.
§Proportions for Business Banking are for 1998.
¶Number of SME customers.

3.353. There are problems in analysing the data in Table 3.51 as the banks have allocated the data in different ways. However, the data on the number of switchers seems to be broadly comparable. This data shows that, in 1999, switchers accounted for 2 per cent or less of SME business current accounts. Barclays used its internal data that record reasons for changes in the number of its SMEs. On this basis, switchers accounted for less than 2 per cent of Barclays' SME business accounts in 1999. Barclays told us that its figures for switchers were inaccurate and should not be used as they relied on SMEs telling Barclays that they were switching banks and many failed or were reluctant to do so. It stated that out of its [✂] closed accounts ([✂] per cent), [✂] were recorded as switchers (less than 0.5 per cent), [✂] were recorded as having closed their business or one of their accounts ([✂] per cent) and that there was no reason recorded for the remainder ([✂]—[✂] per cent). Barclays believed that [✂] of these SMEs were probable switchers (3 per cent) and [✂] were possible switchers (9 per cent), giving a possible total of switchers of 12 per cent. HSBC initially estimated that just over [✂] SMEs switched to its bank in 1999. On reviewing the source of this data, it told us that the figure of just over [✂] was a significant underestimate. It told us that it did record internally the number of switchers to it but, for various reasons, considered that its internal data under-represented the true number of switchers, partly because of the way in which switchers were recorded and partly because some SMEs maintained accounts for a period at more than one bank, for example. It therefore provided a revised estimate of the number of switchers. It did this by taking the difference between the total number of its new accounts (which it estimated at just under [✂] per cent of the number of its SME business accounts) and the total number of its new start-up accounts in 1999 (which it estimated at just over [✂] per cent of the number of its SME business accounts): it considered this to be a reasonable estimate. This method showed that just over [✂] SMEs had switched to HSBC in 1999, accounting for just over 6 per cent of its SME business accounts. Using HSBC's method (switchers being a residual) on Barclays' and NatWest's data shows that switchers accounted for about 5.5 and 6.7 per cent respectively of their SME business accounts in 1999. Using either method for Lloyds TSB shows that in 1999 switchers accounted for about 2 per cent of its SME business current accounts. RBSG told us that it did not regard its data as accurate as it relied on SMEs telling the bank the reasons for their actions. Lloyds TSB said that the 2 per cent figure was an underestimate as it excluded CACs and SMEs did not always inform Lloyds TSB of the reasons for closing an account. It told us that most surveys suggested a switching rate closer to 5 per cent and that this figure was rising.

3.354. RBSG told us that data on SMEs switching their accounts understated the reality of the number of switchers as NatWest monitored only closed accounts and did not take into account dormant accounts which in its view equated to accounts which had been replaced with active (switched) accounts elsewhere. RBSG estimated that between January 1999 and June 2000 approximately 21 per cent of NatWest's small business accounts were dormant. It said that a significant proportion of these accounts would equate to SMEs that had switched banks. HSBC told us that survey results had suggested that 45 per cent of businesses began a secondary relationship while retaining their existing bank relationship. 84 per cent of SMEs told BMRB that they did not have another business account with any other bank or building society.

3.355. Another way to look at the degree of switching is to look at the duration of relationships between SMEs and their banks. Barclays, HSBC and Lloyds TSB provided us with data on the duration of relationships and NatWest provided us with data on the duration of SME business current accounts. For Barclays and HSBC the average duration of banking relationships was about nine years for SMEs with annual turnover of more than £1 million. For SMEs with an annual turnover of less than £1 million the duration of banking relationships was about seven years. The average duration for Lloyds' Business Banking customers was about seven years.[1] Lloyds TSB told us that the median length of time a relationship was held by its Commercial Banking customers was over ten years.[2] It stated that many of its Commercial Banking customers had been with Lloyds for over 25 years. The average duration of NatWest's SME business current accounts was about seven and a half years. These averages, which on the whole are between seven and nine years, can be compared with the average life of an SME, about eight years. Barclays told us that the average lifespan of a business relationship with Barclays was about 72 months including businesses that closed and businesses that switched, compared with 85 months including only closures. It told us that this data was consistent with a substantial degree of switching behaviour. We note that this data is not inconsistent with the extent of switching shown in Table 3.52—about 5 per cent switching in the last year, about 12 per cent switching in the last three years and 23 per cent switching overall.

3.356. BMRB asked SMEs about switching. Table 3.52 shows the results for switching banks, ie SMEs switching all the banking services they had from their main bank to another bank or building society.

TABLE 3.52 **Switching banks**

percentage of SMEs

		Cumulative*
Within the last year	5.5	
Over 1 year and up to 2 years	3.3	8.8
Over 2 years and up to 3 years	2.8	11.6
Over 3 years and up to 5 years	2.1	13.6
Over 5 years	8.8	22.5
Don't know when switched	0.5	23.0
Ever switched	23.0	
Never switched	76.1	
Don't know if switched	0.9	
Total	100.0	
Sample size	1,211	

Source: BMRB survey.

*Totals may not sum because of rounding.

[1] Lloyds TSB told us that the figure would be an underestimate as its system under-recorded the year when a small number of existing Business Banking customers opened their accounts with Lloyds. However, it said that the figure would be an overestimate as it excluded customers with TSB which had not been providing banking services to businesses as long as Lloyds.

[2] Lloyds TSB told us that the figure would be an underestimate as its system under-recorded the year when a number of its existing Commercial Banking customers opened their accounts.

3.357. It emerges that 76 per cent of SMEs had never switched banks. 5 per cent had switched in the last year, 9 per cent had switched in the last two years and 12 per cent had switched in the last three years. BMRB asked those SMEs that had not switched banks during the last three years whether they had considered switching banks (88 per cent of the whole sample). Of these SMEs, 31 per cent had considered switching banks in that time.

3.358. Table 3.53 shows the results for switching banking services without switching banks completely.

TABLE 3.53 **Switching banking services**

percentage of SMEs

		Cumulative
Within the last year	4.8	
Over 1 year and up to 2 years	2.9	7.7
Over 2 years and up to 3 years	0.8	8.5
Over 3 years and up to 5 years	1.5	10.0
Over 5 years	2.7	12.7
Don't know when switched	0.7	13.4
Ever switched		13.4
Never switched		85.3
Don't know if switched		1.3
Total		100.0
Sample size		1,211

Source: BMRB survey.

3.359. 13 per cent of SMEs said that they had switched one or more of their banking services without switching banks completely. 5 per cent had switched some banking services in the last year, 8 per cent in the last two years and 9 per cent in the last three years. BMRB asked those SMEs that had not switched banking services during the last three years whether they had considered switching these services (91 per cent of the whole sample). Of these SMEs, 82 per cent had not considered switching banking services in that time. Thus 75 per cent of SMEs had neither switched banking services in the last three years nor considered doing so.

3.360. 31 per cent of SMEs that switched their banks in the last three years did so because of lower charges, fees or rates of interest at their new bank. 27 per cent did so because of poor relationships at their old bank and 20 per cent did so because of a better service at their new bank. These proportions can be set in the context of the whole sample of SMEs. Taking lower charges as an example, 4 per cent of SMEs switched banks in the last three years due to some combination of lower charges, fees and rates of interest at their new bank, equal on average to just over 1 per cent a year.

3.361. 84 per cent of SMEs that switched banks in the last three years said that they did not encounter any problems when switching.

3.362. BMRB asked SMEs that had switched banks during the last three years (12 per cent of the whole sample) whether they had obtained information from other banks or building societies before making their final decision to switch. 56 per cent said that they had obtained information and 41 per cent said that they had not. The SMEs that had obtained information from other banks and building societies were asked by BMRB to name these banks and building societies. The results are shown in Table 3.54.

TABLE 3.54 **Banks and building societies used by SMEs when deciding to switch banks**

Banks*	Percentage of SMEs
Lloyds TSB	34
Barclays	28
NatWest	24
RBS	24
HSBC	23
BoS	10
Halifax	10
Abbey National	5
Sample size	79

Source: BMRB survey.

*No other bank or building society was contacted by more than 4 per cent of SMEs.

3.363. Of those that obtained information, most did so from the four largest clearing groups (34 per cent used Lloyds TSB, 28 per cent used Barclays, 24 per cent used NatWest, 23 per cent used HSBC and 24 per cent used RBS). 10 per cent of SMEs obtained information from BoS. Very few SMEs obtained information from banks or building societies that the four largest clearing groups saw as having potential to grow their SME business. 10 per cent of SMEs obtained information from Halifax, 5 per cent from Abbey National, just under 4 per cent from Alliance & Leicester (including Girobank) and less than 2 per cent from Nationwide.

3.364. BMRB asked SMEs that had switched banks in the last three years what source of advice, other than banks or building societies, they had used when switching. The most frequent answer was accountants, given by 29 per cent of SMEs.

3.365. 39 per cent of SMEs that considered switching banks in the last three years but which did not switch banks or banking services (24 per cent of the sample) told their banks that they were considering switching. Of these SMEs, 38 per cent said that their banks reduced their prices, fees and charges, 29 per cent said their banks did nothing and 25 per cent said that their banks improved their services.

3.366. BMRB asked SMEs that considered switching banks in the last three years but did not switch banks or banking services during this time why they had considered switching banks. Table 3.55 shows the results.

TABLE 3.55 **Reasons why SMEs considered switching banks**

	Percentage of SMEs
Lower charges/fees at new bank	45
Better services at new bank	18
Poor relations/staff at old bank	11
Higher rates of interest at new bank	10
General lack of bank competency	7
Old bank refused to provide a service	6
Better location at new bank	3
Approached by another bank	2
Errors at old bank	2
Reduced overdraft/funding facility	1
Branch closed	1
Individual at old bank moved on	*
Other	8
Don't know	2
Sample size†	287

Source: BMRB survey.

*Less than 0.5 per cent.
†SMEs that considered switching banks but did not switch banks or banking services.

3.367. Table 3.55 shows that price features high in the reasons for SMEs considering changing banks—45 per cent gave a combination of lower charges and fees at the new bank, and 10 per cent gave higher rates of interest at the new bank. However, none of these SMEs switched banks or banking services, though 26 per cent are still considering whether to switch—the reasons why the SMEs have not switched are given in Table 3.56.

TABLE 3.56 **Reasons why SMEs considering switching banks have not switched banks nor banking services**

	Percentage of SMEs
Still considering/not decided yet	26
Did not find any better deals	22
Current bank offered better prices/fees/charges	14
Too much disruption to payments	10
Would take too long	8
Would cost too much	2
Financial penalty from current bank	1
Alternative no track record	1
N/A	*
Other	17
Don't know	4
Sample size†	287

Source: BMRB survey.

*Less than 0.5 per cent.
†SMEs that considered switching banks but did not switch banks or banking services.

3.368. As well as those SMEs still considering whether to switch, 22 per cent said that they did not find any better deals, 14 per cent said that their current bank offered them better prices, fees or charges and 10 per cent said that there would be too much disruption to payments.

4 Prices and service quality

Contents

Introduction

4.1. This chapter looks at prices and service quality. The prices section examines money transmission prices, interest on current accounts, margins on debt products, margins and rates of interest on deposit products and overall charges. The service quality section looks at overall satisfaction levels, satisfaction with overall service quality and at aspects of service quality. The chapter concludes by examining whether differences in pricing and service packages offered by the main clearing groups can explain their market shares.

Prices

4.2. We begin this section by summarizing the pricing packages of the four largest clearing banks for their money transmission services (see Table 4.1).

TABLE 4.1 **Charging packages for money transmission services for the four largest clearing banks, 2000**

	Category of SMEs	*Annual turnover*	*Charging packages*
NatWest	Start-ups		18 months' free banking and then 40 per cent off charges for the next two years
	Small Business tariff	Up to £100,000*	Published charges
	Standard Retail	£100,000 to £1 million	Published charges
	Corporate	Over £1 million	Negotiated charges
	Switchers		No
Barclays	Start-ups	Up to £100,000†	12 months' free banking or 18 months if have personal account
	Small Business tariff	Up to £100,000‡	Published charges
	Business tariff	Over £100,000	Published charges§
	Switchers	Up to £500,000	6-month free banking or 9 months if have personal account
HSBC	Start-ups		12 months' free banking or 24 months if have personal account¶
	Small SMEs	Up to £100,000	Published charges
	Large SMEs	Over £100,000	Negotiated charges
	Switchers		6 months' free banking—can be increased to 12 months at the branch manager's discretion¤
Lloyds TSB	Start-ups		12 months' free banking, 50% discount in year 2 and 25% in year 3
	Business Banking	Up to £2 million#	Published charges
	Commercial Banking	£2 and £100 million~	Negotiated charges
	Switchers		Offers free banking to Business Banking SMEs to win business but not a universal policy

Source: The banks.

---

*Also not available to SMEs with more than £10,000 cash handled (in and out) and/or more than 200 items collected (cheques paid in) per year.

†In credit or within agreed overdraft limit.

‡Excludes SMEs where cash paid in or out exceeds £10,000 per quarter or cheques paid in exceed 300 per quarter.

§Where businesses have a higher number of individual transactions and/or more complex requirements individual tariffs are negotiated.

¶Projected annual turnover of up to £1 million.

¤Annual turnover of up to £10 million.

#And borrowings up to £500,000. Prior to 1999 annual turnover of up to £1 million.

~And borrowings more than £500,000. Prior to 1999 lower annual turnover limit was over £1 million.

Pricing packages for start-ups and switchers

4.3. Table 4.1 shows that each of these banks offers free banking packages to new SMEs for the main money transmission services (for example, use of cheques, cash, direct debits and standing orders). New SMEs are still charged for non-core money transmission services such as banker's drafts or stopped cheques, and for some current account management items such as dealing with returned cheques, or recalled standing order payments. HSBC estimated that new SMEs paid [✂] per cent of the money transmission fees and [✂] per cent of the current account management fees of an equivalent customer on its Small Business tariff.

4.4. The free banking packages range from a number of months' free banking, for example 12 months with Barclays and HSBC, to a number of months' free banking plus a number of months with reduced prices for the main money transmission services, for example 18 months' free banking and then 40 per cent off charges for the next two years with NatWest and 12 months' free banking and a 50 per cent discount in year 2 and a 25 per cent discount in year 3 with Lloyds TSB. Barclays and HSBC extend their free banking offer if SMEs operate a personal account with them, for example from 12 to 18 months for Barclays and from 12 to 24 months for HSBC.

4.5. A number of other banks also offer free banking for start-ups: for example, in England and Wales Abbey National and Yorkshire offer 12 months' free banking; the same is offered in Scotland by the Scottish banks; and in Northern Ireland, Northern and Ulster Bank offer 12 months' free banking as standard. BoI told us that it had in place arrangements with individual businesses under which free banking was available for up to 18 months. First Trust does not offer free banking.

4.6. HSBC introduced its free banking for start-ups in 1986. Barclays introduced its free offering about ten years ago when it applied to new SMEs in credit. In March 1996 Barclays extended its free banking to SMEs that remained within an agreed overdraft limit. It was further extended to an 18-month offer for SMEs with a Barclays personal account.

4.7. Lloyds TSB's current package to new SMEs started in January 1998. Before this time, Lloyds TSB offered 12 months' free banking to new SMEs. Lloyds TSB told us that free banking by Lloyds started sometime prior to 1994.

4.8. Table 4.1 also shows that Barclays and HSBC have free banking packages for SMEs that switch banks. These packages offer six months' free banking for the main money transmission services. Barclays extends its package to nine months if the SMEs operate a personal account with Barclays. HSBC's package can be increased to 12 months at the discretion of the branch manager. Lloyds TSB told us that it sometimes offered free banking to SMEs switching their accounts to its banks. It said that this policy was used by its staff to win business and the availability of free banking for switchers and the period for which it was offered was a matter of discretion for the individual relationship manager. For money transmission customers switching to NatWest, NatWest charges normal rates but offers a refund amounting to twice the charges incurred if the customer is not satisfied after six months. BoS told us that SMEs that switched to BoS would receive a 50 per cent reduction on money transmission charges for the first year.

4.9. HSBC was the first bank to introduce free banking for switchers—in 1998.

4.10. HSBC said that its introductory offers were consistent with a competitive market and that such offers were a competitive outcome in situations where existing customers were less likely to shop around than new customers and where (consequently) customer relationships, once formed, lasted for a period of time. It stated that competition took place for the life cycle of the customer and that, over the life cycle as a whole, prices were competitive. HSBC gave the following reasons why its introductory offers were pro-competitive. The length of the introductory period was determined by the expected net revenues earned from customers over time. The new customer might close its account before positive net revenues were earned, for example. Many start-ups would prefer to pay no money transmission charges during the period in which they were establishing themselves and then pay charges once their businesses were more stable and once they knew more about their likely money transmission usage patterns. HSBC stated that, in any event, the scale of such offers was limited.

4.11. About 17 per cent of the number of all HSBC's SME current accounts receive the free banking package, and about one-third of its SMEs on its Small Business tariff (for SMEs with an annual turnover of up to £100,000). About 15 per cent of the number of all NatWest's SME current accounts receive the free banking package. The equivalent proportion for RBS is 5 per cent. Barclays told us that in any one year, about 13 per cent of its SMEs received its free banking offer. The proportion for Lloyds TSB was 14 per cent.

4.12. HSBC said that free banking customers still contributed to the costs of the bank in providing the services because: HSBC benefited from interest on credit balances, the customer still had to pay for non-core money transmission services and money transmission usage volumes tended to be less for start-ups than for established businesses. HSBC estimated that its overall cost recovery for SMEs in the free banking period was approximately [✂] per cent.[1] The [✂] per cent consists of [✂] percentage points from the revenue achieved on the value of credit balance and [✂] percentage points from the revenue on money transmission charges that fall outside the free banking package. HSBC told us that the costs of providing free banking to switchers was considerably higher than the cost of providing it to start-ups as switchers had a greater number of transactions.

4.13. RBSG told us that the cost of free banking (in terms of revenue forgone) as a proportion of total account management and money transmission fees from SMEs and other corporate customers was 3 per cent for RBS and 2 per cent for NatWest.

4.14. Barclays' free package for start-ups is restricted to SMEs with an annual turnover up to £100,000. By comparison, NatWest and HSBC both offer their free package to SMEs with an annual turnover of up to £1 million, and Lloyds TSB's free package is on offer to SMEs with an annual turnover up to £2 million.

4.15. Comparing the SME pricing packages to start-ups offered by the four largest clearing banks shows that NatWest offers the longest period of free banking with, in effect, just over two years' free banking (18 months' free banking and a reduction of 40 per cent in each of the next two years) and Barclays the shortest.

Money transmission charges

4.16. Banks tend to use published prices for smaller SMEs and unpublished prices for larger SMEs, the threshold varying between banks (see Table 4.1). Bank charges are published in *Business Money£acts*, *Business Money* and on the BBA/Business Money£acts web site. Excluding SMEs with free banking, 51 per cent of HSBC's SMEs are covered by its published tariff (ie SMEs with an annual turnover of up to £100,000). The equivalent proportions for Barclays, Lloyds TSB and NatWest are 100 per cent for Barclays (ie no turnover threshold), 92 per cent for Lloyds TSB (ie SMEs with an annual turnover of up to £2 million) and 89 per cent for NatWest (ie SMEs with an annual turnover of up to £1 million).

4.17. The four largest clearing groups said that the costs of current accounts were covered by revenue from money transmission charges and revenue from credit balances. Banks charge SMEs for a number of money transmission services ranging from frequently-used services such as withdrawing and depositing money by cheque to less frequently-used services such as providing copies of bank statements. Some also have a standing charge, sometimes referred to as an account maintenance fee.

4.18. We looked at the number of transactions by methods of payment (see Table 4.2) in order to decide which prices we should compare.

---

[1]

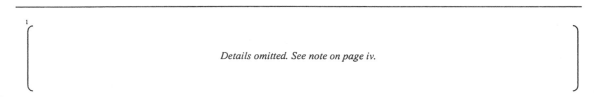

Details omitted. See note on page iv.

TABLE 4.2 Proportions of number of transactions by method of payment, 1999

per cent

	Barclays*	HSBC†	Lloyds TSB‡	NatWest§	BoS¶
Debits					
Cheque	64	76	58	62	64
Direct debit/standing order	26	21	20	22	21
Other	10	3	22	16	15
Total	100	100	100	100	100
Number (m)	170	173	149	175	37
Credits					
Cheque	15	N/A	60	64	36
Auto credits	50	N/A	15	13	59
Cash	5	N/A	N/A	N/A	N/A
Other	29	N/A	25	24	5
Total¤	100	N/A	100	100	100
Number (m)	85	31	168	244	19

Source: CC calculations on data provided by the banks.

*Statement entries which underestimate the number of cheque and cash transactions. Includes CACs.
†Excludes credits paid in at other banks and Head Office Collections.
‡Based on Lloyds Heritage account although Lloyds TSB said that this was representative of its other accounts.
§Based on SMEs with annual turnover up to £10 million. Includes CACs.
¶Year ended February 2000.
¤Totals may not sum because of rounding.

4.19. Cheques and direct debits/standing orders together account for by far the highest proportion of the number of debit transactions, ranging from 78 to 97 per cent. The same is true for cheques and auto credits with regard to the number of credit transactions, ranging from 65 to 95 per cent. Based on these proportions we decided to look at charges for using cheques (deposits and credits), standing orders and direct debits and auto credits.

4.20. Barclays provided actual volume data for cash handling. These showed that cash accounted for about 5 per cent of the number of credit transactions. This proportion varied with the size of the SME. For example, cash accounted for 6.5 per cent of the number of credit transactions for SMEs with an annual turnover of up to £1 million compared with 4 per cent with an annual turnover of between £10 million and £25 million. Barclays' data underestimated the number of cheque and cash transactions.[1] BMRB asked SMEs how their business made deposits and withdrawals and which was their main method for withdrawals and which was their method for deposits. 46 per cent of SMEs said that they made some deposits and withdrawals using cash. Cash was the main method of withdrawal and deposit for 10 and 16 per cent of SMEs respectively. The main method of payment was cheques.

4.21. For some SMEs, for example small retailers, cash will be very important. HSBC told us that many SMEs did not have cash requirements, but for some these requirements were important. It said that many SMEs (especially shops, pubs, taxi firms and restaurants) needed to obtain change and to deposit a mixture of cheques, notes and coins. HSBC stated that while SME customers accounted for around one-quarter of the visits to branches, they accounted for over 60 per cent of the work undertaken by cashiers and of their work for SMEs, and 79 per cent involved handling cash. It estimated that the cost to HSBC of providing this cashiering service was around £[✂] million a year, which excluded any costs for running the branches themselves.

4.22. As cash is an important method of payment for some SMEs we decided to compare prices for cash handling as well as for cheques, automated methods (direct debit, standing order and auto credit), non-auto credits (credit slips—as these are used when deposits are made by cheques and/or cash) and standing charges.

4.23. Before looking at the prices and then at the annual charges it is important to recognize that prices and charges will vary according to the circumstances of the SME, for example its turnover, its method of access (via a branch or direct), the number of its transactions, its credit balance and its use of cash. We look at each of these factors in turn.

---

[1]Barclays stated that its method only reflected the type of credit paid in and not the constituent parts of the credit paid in, for example an SME could pay in a credit with ten cheques but this would be counted as one cheque credit. The same could also be true of a cash credit, the SME could pay in as much or as little cash as they wished, but it would only be counted as one cash credit.

4.24. Barclays and NatWest have different published prices for smaller (annual turnover of up to £100,000) and larger (annual turnover of between £100,000 and £1 million for NatWest and over £100,000 for Barclays) SMEs. HSBC operates a similar type of pricing policy to Barclays and NatWest for its smaller SMEs (annual turnover of up to £100,000). It has no published tariffs for its larger SMEs. Lloyds TSB told us that its Small Business tariff was at one time only available to smaller SMEs but now it was available to its existing SMEs with an annual turnover of up to £2 million. It is no longer available to new SMEs, having been replaced with its current tariff package (Business Extra), a published tariff for SMEs with an annual turnover of up to £2 million. 51 per cent of HSBC's SMEs that pay its main money transmission prices (ie excluding those with free banking) are on its Small Business tariff. The equivalent proportions for Barclays and NatWest are 56 and 44 per cent respectively. Barclays and NatWest introduced their Small Business tariffs in 1987 and HSBC did so in 1988.

4.25. Smaller SMEs at these four banks[1] are normally charged by entry and not by item, for example a smaller SME paying in ten cheques on one credit slip would just be charged for the credit slip whereas a larger SME would be charged for the credit slip plus the ten cheques.[2] The same difference applies to paying in by cash: the smaller SME would pay only for the credit slip and not for the units of cash whereas the larger SME would pay for both. Similarly, when smaller SMEs withdraw cash by using a cheque they pay for the cheque and not the cash; larger SMEs pay for both. Yorkshire also has different published prices for its smaller and larger SMEs but both are charged by item. Barclays told us that smaller and larger SMEs paid different charges because the charges were set to take into account the scale of the customers' activity. Table 4.3 shows the differences in the published prices of the main money transmission services for Barclays, NatWest and Yorkshire.

TABLE 4.3 **Differences in published money transmission prices for smaller and larger SMEs, 2000**

	Pence per transaction						£ pa	Pence per £100	
	Direct debit	Standing order	Auto credit	Cheque in	Cheque out	Non-auto credit	Standing charges	Cash in	Cash out
Barclays									
Small SMEs*	45	45	45	0	64	64	30	0	0
Larger SMEs†	35	35	15	25	54	75	0	50	57
Small – large	10	10	30	–25	10	–11	30	–50	–57
NatWest									
Small SMEs*	40	40	40	0	67	67	30	0	0
Larger SMEs†	40	40	22	28	67	95	69	49	57
Small – large	0	0	18	–28	0	–28	–39	–49	–57
Yorkshire									
Small SMEs*	37	37	37	53	15	53	36	25	25
Larger SMEs†	35	35	20	75	28	75	0	50	50
Small – large	2	2	17	–22	–13	–22	36	–25	–25

Source: CC calculations on data provided by the banks.

*Annual turnover of up to £100,000.
†Annual turnover of between £100,000 and £1 million and over £100,000 for Barclays.

4.26. Smaller SMEs with Barclays and NatWest pay lower prices than larger SMEs because of the difference in the pricing per entry and per item—smaller SMEs not being charged for depositing cheques and cash and for withdrawing cash. They also have lower prices for credit slips. Smaller SMEs with NatWest also have a lower standing charge than larger SMEs. This is not the case at Barclays: it does not charge larger SMEs standing charges. Smaller SMEs incur higher prices than larger SMEs for automated transactions and cheque withdrawals at Barclays but for only auto credits at NatWest. Smaller SMEs incur lower prices than larger SMEs for paper transactions but higher prices for automated transactions at Yorkshire. Smaller SMEs incur a standing charge whereas larger ones do not.

[1]Including SMEs on Lloyds TSB's old tariff—Small Business tariff.
[2]HSBC told us that this was not necessarily the case for its larger SMEs as it would negotiate these arrangements with them. It said that even if they did pay per cheque, it was unlikely that they would be paying the same price per cheque as smaller SMEs as the number of cheques the larger businesses would be likely to pay in would be higher.

Method of access, number of transactions and credit balances

4.27. The differences in prices for these three factors can be illustrated by the Co-operative Bank's prices (see Table 4.4).

TABLE 4.4 **Published money transmission charges for the Co-operative Bank, 2000**

	Pence per transaction						£ pa	Pence per £100	
	Direct debit	Standing order	Auto credit	Cheque in	Cheque out	Non-auto credit	Standing charges	Cash in	Cash out
Business	40	40	20	28	60	70	60	55	55
Business Direct*	17	17	0	0	23	0	36	0	0
Direct – Business	–23	–23	–20	–28	–37	–70	–24	–55	–55

Source: CC calculations on data provided by the Co-operative Bank.

---

*Cheque withdrawals and auto debits are 70p each if balance is less than £2,000; after £4,000 per month (ie 40 entries per month) of cash deposited, cash is charged at 75p per £100 deposited; after 200 cheques per month, each cheque deposited is charged at 20p.

4.28. Table 4.4 shows that the Co-operative Bank's prices for its direct service, subject to the conditions of use which are discussed below, are lower than its prices for its branch-based service. Barclays told us that one of the reasons for direct services having lower prices than branch-based services was that direct services were generally stripped-down propositions compared with relationship-managed services. The conditions of use are the number of transactions and the value of credit balance. The number of transactions alters the price of depositing cash and cheques. Its price for depositing cash increases from zero to 75p after £4,000 (40 units of £100) has been deposited in a month and its price for depositing cheques increases from zero to 20p after 200 cheques have been deposited in a month. The credit balance alters the price of withdrawing cheques and using auto debits (direct debits and standing orders). Its price for withdrawing cheques increases from 23p to 70p per cheque and its price for auto debits increases from 17p to 70p if the value of the credit balance falls to less than £2,000.

4.29. The Co-operative Bank is not the only example where a pricing policy depends on these factors. Fleming's SME customers do not incur charges for the main money transmission items if the number of transactions per month is less than 20 or 200 depending on which account is used. The same is true for SMEs using Abbey National's service so long as they do not exceed its limit of 25 cheque withdrawals and 25 cheque deposits per month. BoS's direct account does not charge for the main money transmission services if the SME has a credit balance of £5,000 or over and it does not use more than 100 cheques per month. RBS's direct service, which offers free banking until the beginning of 2002, will offer sizeable savings over its branch-based service, savings ranging from about 20 to 69 per cent per transaction (see Table 3.6). Of the four largest clearing banks, Barclays and NatWest have a direct service. SMEs using NatWest's direct service do not pay standing charges (£30 and £69 a year for smaller and larger SMEs respectively using NatWest's branch-based services). Barclays' press release on its direct service, dated June 2001, states that there will be an average saving of 20 per cent on bank charges for its existing customers. HSBC plans to introduce a pilot Internet business banking service in 2001. Lloyds TSB told us that it had no plans to introduce direct services but these options were kept under constant review and it would respond to customer need and competitor action if required.

Use of cash

4.30. The differences in prices for this factor can be illustrated by Alliance & Leicester's prices (see Table 4.5).

TABLE 4.5 **Published money transmission charges for Alliance & Leicester, 2000**

	Pence per transaction						£ pa	Pence per £100	
	Direct debit	Standing order	Auto credit	Cheque in	Cheque out	Non-auto credit	Standing charges	Cash in	Cash out
High cash volumes	65	65	65	0	65	65	0	65	43
Low cash volumes	40	25	25	13	60	0	0	50	43
High – low cash	25	40	40	−13	5	65	0	15	0

Source: CC calculations on data provided by Alliance & Leicester.

4.31. Alliance & Leicester's prices for its high-volume cash account (formerly known as Girobank Direct) are higher for most items than its prices for its low-volume cash account. We now compare published money transmission prices between banks.

Comparison of published money transmission prices

4.32. In this section we look at the money transmission prices: in England and Wales, split into prices for smaller, larger and all SMEs; in Scotland and in Northern Ireland. Table 4.6 shows the published prices for the main money transmission items used by SMEs. As noted in Chapter 3 (see paragraph 3.175), some of Barclays' charges are higher in London and the South-East of England, although Barclays has now made the decision to abolish this premium. These differences are not included in Table 4.6.

4.33. Comparing the prices of the four largest clearing banks for smaller SMEs[1] shows HSBC with the lowest prices for all the main money transmission services. NatWest has the second lowest prices for automated transactions (14 per cent (5p) per transaction higher than HSBC) and Barclays has the second lowest prices for paper transaction (about 7 per cent (4p) per transaction higher than HSBC). Lloyds TSB has the highest prices, ranging from 10 (6p) to 89 (31p) per cent per transaction higher than HSBC. Although Lloyds TSB no longer offers this package to new SMEs, about one-quarter of its SMEs are charged under this tariff. Lloyds TSB told us that it was trying to encourage its existing SMEs that paid this tariff to transfer to its newer tariff—Business Extra. About one-quarter of Lloyds TSB's SMEs pay this tariff.[2] Business Extra has lower prices than Smaller Business tariff for automated transactions, cheque withdrawals and deposits, and standing charges but, unlike the old Small Business tariff, it charges for cash transactions. Yorkshire's prices are slightly higher than HSBC's for automated transactions, much lower for credit slips and cheque withdrawals but much higher for cheque deposits and cash transactions.

4.34. We have compared the pricing packages aimed at smaller SMEs with the more general packages offered by other banks and building societies. However, these price comparisons are only valid for SMEs with an annual turnover of £100,000 or less. Only Norwich & Peterborough offers a branch-based account that has lower prices for automated transactions (about 60 per cent (20p) per transaction lower than HSBC's prices). It also has a lower price for cheque withdrawal than HSBC (30p compared with 60p), although its price is higher than that offered by Yorkshire (15p). Norwich & Peterborough does charge for depositing cheques (20p) and cash (50p) but it does not have a standing charge. SMEs banking with Norwich & Peterborough cannot deposit coins, or cash exceeding £4,000 a day, and they cannot withdraw more than £500 a day from their own branch or £100 a day from another branch of Norwich & Peterborough. Overdrafts are allowed for SMEs with two years or more audited/certified accounts. Other branch-based accounts have lower prices than HSBC for some of the main money transmission items— Lloyds TSB's Business Extra (auto credit and cheque withdrawal), RBS (auto credit, cheque withdrawal and standing charge), BoS (direct debit, auto credit, cheque withdrawal, credit slips and standing charges) and the Co-operative Bank (auto credit). All these banks charge for cheque and cash withdrawal and cash deposits. Whether SMEs have lower charges for the main money transmission items overall at the four largest clearing banks or at other banks or building societies will depend on usage.

[1]Including SMEs on Lloyds TSB's Small Business tariff.
[2]Most of Lloyds TSB's other current accounts are no longer available to new SMEs, the largest of which (in terms of the proportion of the total number of Lloyds TSB's SME accounts) is its Itemised Business tariff which is still used by about 32 per cent of its SMEs.

TABLE 4.6 **Published money transmission charges, 2000**

| Company | Account name | Pence per transaction | | | | | | £ pa | Pence per £100 | |
		Direct debit	Standing order	Auto credit	Cheque in	Cheque out	Non-auto credit	Standing charges	Cash in	Cash out
England and Wales										
Smaller SMEs*										
Barclays	Small Business	45	45	45	0	64	64	30	0	0
HSBC		35	35	35	0	60	60	30	0	0
NatWest	Small Business	40	40	40	0	67	67	30	0	0
Lloyds TSB	Small Business†	66	66	66	0	66	66	42	0	0
Yorkshire		37	37	37	53	15	53	36	25	25
All SMEs										
Branch-based:										
Lloyds TSB‡	Business Extra	42	59	15	27	59	70	30	50	50
RBS		40	43	25	25	55	64	0	49	53
BoS		32	47	32	20	47	47	0	63	58
AIB (GB)		55	55	35	22	65	65	30	55	55
Co-operative Bank	Business	40	40	20	28	60	70	60	55	55
Norwich & Peterboro' Building Society§		15	15	15	20	30	0	0	50	0
Nationwide	BusinessInvestor	0	0	0	0	200¶	0	0	0	0
Larger SMEs										
Barclays	Business	35	35	15	25	54	75	0	50	57
NatWest	Business	40	40	22	28	67	95	69	49	57
Yorkshire		35	35	20	75	28	75	0	50	50
Direct:										
RBS	Direct	20	20	20	20	20	20	0	N/A	N/A
BoS	Direct	0	0	0	0	40#	0	0	N/A	N/A
Abbey National~		0	0	0	50	50	0	0	0	0
Co-operative Bank	Business Direct✳	17	17	0	0	23	0	36	0	0
Fleming	Corporate❖	50	50	50	50	50	50	0	0	0
Fleming	Investment✦	50	50	50	50	50	50	0	0	0
Alliance & Leicester	Direct	65	65	65	0	65	65	0	65	43
Alliance & Leicester	Business Plus	40	25	25	13	60	0	0	50	43
Alliance & Leicester	Flat Fee Account	0	0	0	0	0	0	120	0	0
Scotland										
RBS		31	45	27	19	46	46	0	61	59
BoS		32	47	32	20	47	47	0	63	58
Clydesdale		21	47	24	20	47	47	0	61	61
Lloyds TSB†	Business Extra	42	59	15	27	59	70	30	50	50
RBS	Direct	20	20	20	20	20	20	0	N/A	N/A
BoS	Direct	0	0	0	0	40#	0	0	N/A	N/A
Northern Ireland										
First Trust		37	50	37	33	50	50	26	63	63
Ulster Bank		38	49	38	33	49	49	24	60	60
BoI		38	49	32	33	49	47	24	60	60
Northern		38	49	38	33	49	49	24	58	58

Source: Companies and *Business Money£acts*.

---

*Turnover up to £100,000.

†Lloyds TSB told us that its Small Business tariff was at one time available only to smaller SMEs but now it was available to its existing SMEs with an annual turnover of up to £2 million. It is no longer available to new SMEs.

‡Turnover up to £2 million.

§Cannot deposit coins, or cash exceeding £4,000 per day, and cannot withdraw more than £500 per day from own branch or £100 a day from another branch of Norwich and Peterborough Building Society (Norwich & Peterborough).

¶First six transactions per month are free.

¤Turnover over £100,000 and up to £1 million for NatWest and over £100,000 for Barclays and Yorkshire.

#First 100 cheques are free per month if credit balance is greater than £5,000.

~First 25 cheque withdrawals and first 25 cheque deposits per month are free then each additional withdrawal/deposit costs 50p.

✳Cheque withdrawals and auto debits are 70p each if balance is less than £2,000; after £4,000 per month (ie 40 entries per month) of cash deposited, cash is charged at 75p per £100 deposited; after 200 cheques per month, each cheque deposited is charged at 20p.

❖200 free entries per month then 50p per entry. If the balance of the account is less than £5,000 when the monthly statement is prepared, there is a charge of 50p for each transaction.

✦20 free entries per month then 50p per entry.

4.35. Of the four largest clearing banks, only Barclays and NatWest have a published pricing package for larger SMEs. Lloyds TSB's current package covers SMEs with an annual turnover of up to £2 million and HSBC does not publish its prices for SMEs with an annual turnover of more than

£100,000. Except for cash transactions, where Barclays' and NatWest's prices are similar, Barclays' prices are lower than NatWest's, the difference ranging from 11 (3p) to 32 (7p) per cent. NatWest, unlike Barclays, also has a standing charge—£69 a year. Yorkshire also has published prices for larger SMEs. Its prices are lower than Barclays for cheque and cash withdrawals but higher than Barclays for auto credits and cheque deposits.

4.36. We have compared the pricing packages aimed at larger SMEs with the more general packages offered by other banks and building societies. However, these price comparisons are only valid for SMEs with an annual turnover of between £100,000 and £1 million.[1] Only Norwich & Peterborough offers a branch-based account that has lower prices for all the main money transmission items except cash deposits where its prices are in line with those of Barclays, NatWest and Yorkshire but, as described in paragraph 4.34, Norwich & Peterborough's account is subject to restrictions. Other branch-based accounts have lower prices than these three banks—Lloyds TSB's Business Extra, RBS, BoS, AIB (GB) and the Co-operative Bank for credit slips; and BoS for direct debits and cheque deposits (it also has lower prices than the two clearing banks for cheque withdrawals); and AIB (GB) for cheque deposits.

4.37. Prices for direct current accounts tend to be lower than prices for branch-based accounts. There may, however, be conditions attached to the direct accounts that alter their prices, for example maximum number of transactions and minimum value of credit balance (see paragraphs 4.27 to 4.29). Subject to SMEs keeping within the thresholds for the number of transactions and the value of credit balances, they would not incur prices for the main money transmission services if they banked with BoS, Abbey National or Fleming and they would incur lower prices at the Co-operative Bank and RBS than they would with branch-based services at the four largest clearing banks. Due to the different structure of one of its tariffs—a standing charge only—it is not possible to compare Alliance & Leicester's prices for this tariff with those of the other banks that have a pricing package for smaller SMEs. We compare Alliance & Leicester's tariff package with those of the other banks in the section on charges, where we take account of usage.

4.38. In Scotland, the Scottish banks' prices are broadly similar for standing orders, cheque and cash deposits, cheque and cash withdrawals and credit slips. For the other two main money transmission items—direct debit and auto credit—Clydesdale has the lower prices (about one-third (10p) lower for direct debits and about one-quarter (8p) lower for auto credits compared with BoS and 10 per cent (3p) lower compared with RBS). The prices of Lloyds TSB—the fourth largest provider in Scotland—for its current package—Business Extra—seem to be out of line with the prices of the Scottish banks. Lloyds TSB's prices are much higher for direct debits, standing orders, cheques and credit slips but much lower for auto credits and cash. Unlike the Scottish banks, Lloyds TSB's pricing package includes a standing charge. SMEs using the direct current accounts of RBS and BoS would have lower prices than those on offer with the branch-based accounts.

4.39. In Northern Ireland, the prices of the Northern Irish banks are broadly similar.

4.40. Table 4.7 shows the published prices for non-core money transmission services. The prices of these services do not tend to differ by size of SME or by method of access.[2]

4.41. Other banks and building societies charge lower prices than the four largest clearing banks for some of the non-core money transmission services but higher prices for others.

4.42. We now turn to charges based on the main money transmission items.

---

[1] Over £100,000 for Barclays.
[2] For an audit letter, BoS Direct charges £20 compared with £25 per hour (plus VAT) for its branch-based account.

TABLE 4.7 **Published prices for non-core money transmission items**

£

	Copy statement per sheet	Stop cheque	Unpaid cheque inwards	Unpaid cheque outwards	Special clearance	Status enquiry	CHAPS	Bankers draft	Audit letter*
England and Wales									
Barclays	5†	8	2	27.5	10	8	20	8.5‡	25§¶
HSBC	0¤	7.5#	4	28~	12	7.24§	17.5✶	10	25§
NatWest	2.5❖	10	0	30	15	8.5	21–23	12	10–27.5‡
Lloyds TSB	5	10	0	27.5	10	10	20◆	10	25§✳
RBS	5	10	4	30	15	10	20	10	25§▪
BoS	5✠	0	0	30**	12††	10	15‡‡	10	25§ §§
Abbey National	0	10	0	30	12	10	20	10	25§
AIB (GB)	5	8	5	25	10	8†§	17	10	25§¶¶
Alliance & Leicester	5	10	5¤¤	25	10	8	15	9	20§
Co-operative Bank	6	10	4.5	30	12	9	20	10	35§
Fleming	0##	6~~	0	25	N/A	10§	20	15★★	15
Norwich & Peterborough	5	6	4	27	15	10	17.5	N/A	25
Yorkshire	5	7.5	4	32	15	9	20	12	25§✳
Scotland									
RBS	5	10	4	30	15	10§	20	10	25§¶
BoS	5✠	0	0	30**	12††	10	15‡‡	10	25§ §§
Clydesdale	5	10	6	32	15	10§	20	12	27.5§¶
Lloyds TSB	5	10	0	27.5	10	10	20◆	10	25§✳
Northern Ireland									
First Trust	6	7	5	15–30	8	7.5§	25	6	20§❖❖
Ulster Bank	6	7	6	10–30	8–12	7.5§	5	5–10	25¶
BoI	6	7	5	30	8	7.5§	25	7	23¶
Northern	6	7.5	5	35	8–12.5	9.5§	25	7	25

Source: Business Money£acts.

---

*An audit letter is a reply to an auditor's request for information and is subject to VAT.

†First £5 then 95p. Duplicate statements produced at the same time as the original are 95p, if a duplicate statement must be manually prepared the charge is £5.

‡£15 if draft issued at branch other than customer's own, without prior arrangement.

§Plus VAT.

¶Minimum.

¤One set of copies free for most recent 12-month period, then variable charges agreed in advance.

#Free where as a result of theft or loss of blank cheque.

~Cheques of over £28, free for cheques under £10 and £10 for cheques between £10 and £28.

✶£20 interbank.

❖Minimum £5.

◆£5 for advice.

✳£25 per hour, minimum £25.

▪ Minimum £25.

✠Maximum £10.

**Maximum £90 per day.

††Plus expenses.

‡‡£12 if use electronic account.

§§£25 per hour, £20 for its direct service.

¶¶£5 per half hour.

¤¤At manager's discretion.

##First free then £5.

~~Nil if lost/stolen.

★★Plus registered postage if required.

❖❖£20 per hour, minimum £20.

Money transmission charges

4.43. In order to compare the overall money transmission charges for SMEs we asked the main clearing groups to provide us with their estimates of the number of transactions for the main money transmission items for an average SME. Some of the banks pointed out that estimates based on the average number of transactions could be misleading because of the diversity of SMEs. For example, Barclays told us that averaging across all SMEs failed to recognize the differing composition and sizes of businesses. It said that businesses in the retail sector usually had high volumes of cash and cheques. In other sectors there would be very few, if any, cash transactions. Larger businesses also tended to have higher transaction volumes than smaller ones. Data provided by the banks might reveal different average transaction volumes due to variations in their mix of SMEs. We accept that there will be variations around any estimates based upon average usage but we believe that these estimates are useful in comparing the charges of the different banks.

4.44. Table 4.8 shows the average number of main money transmission transactions for England and Wales, Scotland and Northern Ireland.

TABLE 4.8 **Average annual number of main money transmission items for SMEs**

	England and Wales	Scotland	Northern Ireland
Direct debit	49	63	40
Standing orders	10	10	7
Auto credit	59	90	34
Cheque out	182	205	156
Non-auto credit	70	55	40
Cheque in	228	184	162
Cash in (£100 units)	115	201	217
Cash out (£100 units)	44	103	95

Source: CC calculations on data provided by the banks.

4.45. We used the overall average number of transactions (as set out in Table 4.8) with the published prices (as set out in Table 4.6) to calculate average annual charges (see Table 4.9). We tested our results by calculating annual charges based on the average number of transactions provided by each bank separately. These two approaches produced very similar rankings of the banks. RBSG told us that while we had used the same average transaction volumes to compare the prices of different banks, it was clear that inclusion of data for SMEs up to £25 million annual turnover, or above, produced average volumes that were significantly higher than the majority of SMEs actually generated and, as a result, the prices quoted were significantly higher than most SMEs actually paid. It said that, for example, the actual average charge incurred by SME customers on NatWest's Small Business tariff (annual turnover of up to £100,000) was about £105, compared with £246 shown in Table 4.9 and the actual average charge incurred by all SME customers of NatWest Retail (annual turnover of up to £1 million) who paid charges was £280 (excluding those with free banking).

4.46. Comparing the average charges of the branch-based banks that have a tariff for smaller SMEs[1] shows that HSBC has the lowest average charge (£222). Its average charge is about 9 per cent lower than Barclays' and NatWest's. Lloyds TSB (with its Small Business tariff) has the highest average charge of the four largest clearing banks, 29 per cent higher than HSBC's. As noted in paragraph 4.33, although Lloyds TSB no longer offers this package to new SMEs, about one-quarter of its SMEs are charged under this tariff. The average charge of Lloyds TSB's current tariff—Business Extra—is 27 per cent higher than its old Small Business tariff package. Lloyds TSB's average charge based on its old Small Business tariff is slightly lower than Yorkshire's.

4.47. We have compared the average charges of pricing packages aimed at smaller SMEs with the more general packages offered by other banks and building societies. However, these comparisons are only valid for SMEs with an annual turnover of £100,000 or less. Only Norwich & Peterborough offers a branch-based account that has a sizeable lower average charge than HSBC's (over 20 per cent lower). Nationwide's average charge is slightly below HSBC's. The other branch-based accounts have higher average charges than the four largest clearing banks offering a tariff package for smaller SMEs only. Barclays told us that it was inappropriate to compare prices between other banks and building societies, and the four larger clearing banks as these other banks and building societies offered a more restrictive service than the four larger clearing banks.

---

[1]Including SMEs on Lloyds TSB's Small Business tariff.

TABLE 4.9 Annual charges based on published money transmission prices

	Tariff	£
England and Wales		
Smaller SMEs		
HSBC		222
Barclays	BSBT	244
NatWest		246
Lloyds TSB	Small Business	286
Yorkshire		305
All SMEs		
Branch-based:		
Norwich & Peterborough		175
Nationwide		220
BoS		301
RBS		320
Lloyds TSB	Business Extra	363
AIB (GB)		385
Co-operative Bank		405
Larger SMEs		
Barclays	BBT	320
Yorkshire		386
NatWest		439
Direct:		
Abbey National (25 free)		0
Fleming	Corporate	0
BoS	Business Direct	0
Co-operative Bank		88
RBS		120
Alliance & Leicester		120
Fleming	Investment	178
Alliance & Leicester	Business plus	252
Alliance & Leicester	Girobank direct	334
Scotland		
Clydesdale		384
RBS		386
BoS	Business Current	399
Lloyds TSB	Business Extra	437
BoS	Business Direct	0
RBS	Direct	121
Northern Ireland		
BoI		389
Northern		386
Ulster Bank		392
First Trust		405

Source: CC calculations based on data provided by the companies and in *Business Money£acts*.

Note: See Table 4.6 for footnotes.

4.48. Of the four largest clearing banks, only Barclays and NatWest have a separate published pricing package for larger SMEs. Lloyds TSB's current package covers SMEs with an annual turnover of up to £2 million and HSBC does not publish its prices for SMEs with an annual turnover of more than £100,000. Barclays' average charge is 27 per cent below NatWest's. The average charge of Yorkshire is higher than Barclays' (21 per cent) but below NatWest's (12 per cent).

4.49. We have compared the average charges of the pricing packages aimed at larger SMEs with the more general packages offered by other banks and building societies. However, these price comparisons are only valid for SMEs with an annual turnover of between £100,000 and £1 million.[1] Norwich & Peterborough, Nationwide and BoS have lower average charges than Barclays. All the branch-based accounts shown in Table 4.9 have lower average charges than NatWest.

[1]Over £100,000 for Barclays.

4.50. The average charges for direct current accounts tend to be lower than those for branch-based accounts. However, these average charges will change if the SMEs fail to meet the conditions attached to the direct accounts. Using our assumptions (see Table 4.8), SMEs would not incur charges for the main money transmission services if they used the direct accounts of BoS, Abbey National or Fleming (Corporate account). They would incur average charges lower than those of the four largest clearing banks for their branch-based services if they used the direct accounts of the Co-operative Bank, RBS, Alliance & Leicester (Flat Fee account) or Fleming (Investment account). Barclays told us that a direct service was different from a relationship-managed service in terms of the value that many customers would ascribe to it, and this was reflected in the price charged.

4.51. In Scotland, the average charges of the Scottish banks are broadly similar. The average charge of Lloyds TSB seems to be out of line with those of these three larger Scottish banks (between 10 and 14 per cent above those of these three larger Scottish banks). Using our assumptions (see Table 4.8), SMEs using the direct current account of BoS incur no charges, and those with RBS's direct account have much lower average charges than those on offer with the branch-based accounts (between 68 and 72 per cent lower).

4.52. In Northern Ireland, the average charges of the Northern Irish banks are very similar.

Changes in prices for money transmission services over time

4.53. On the whole, prices for the main money transmission items have not changed in nominal terms, thereby falling in real terms. Where prices have changed, on the whole they have fallen.

4.54. Bannock Consulting calculated price indices in real terms for bank charges for every quarter from June 1992 to August 1999. The indices were calculated as the sum of the published prices of cheques paid in, cheques issued, standing orders and direct debits on business accounts weighted by an estimate of each bank's market share and deflated by the RPI. Three indices were calculated: an all bank index,[1] an index for the 'Big Four' banks and an index for the 'non-Big Four'. The indices show real falls in bank charges, the 'Big Four' index falling by about 30 per cent in real terms between June 1992 and August 1999 and the 'non-Big Four' index falling by about 20 per cent over the same period. Barclays updated this analysis and included a more complete set of charges, and came to the same conclusion as Bannock Consulting.

4.55. HSBC stated that the average money transmission charge for its SME customers had fallen from about £298 to about £230 in nominal terms between 1995 and 1999. It said that the individual elements of its Small Business tariff had not increased in nominal terms since 1989 (and some elements had fallen); since 1992, charges on this tariff had fallen by about 20 per cent in real terms and the value of credit balances had also declined since that year.

4.56. Barclays said that it was important to recognize that innovation had resulted in new products and services being introduced at lower prices. It told us that it had introduced a number of new and improved services and at lower costs to the customer, for example the recent introduction of two new services for cash and cheque deposits. It stated that these services enabled businesses that paid in cash and/or cheques above certain volumes to retain the advantages of local depositing, while gaining the advantage of lower-cost central processing through Barclays cash and cheque processing centres. It said that it had also encouraged the use of alternative electronic payments products, at lower prices than their paper-based equivalents, for example the payment of salaries and/or suppliers through BACS in place of the issue of cheques or paper credit transfers.

4.57. In contrast to the findings that money transmission prices have been constant in nominal terms and falling in real terms, the FPB survey found that a majority of respondents claimed that their bank had increased money transmission charges[2] over the last three years. The FPB surveys asked businesses whether their banks had increased or decreased money transmission charges over the last three years. The results from the FPB's 1998 and 2000 surveys are shown in Table 4.10.

---

[1]Includes AIB (GB), BoS, Barclays, Clydesdale, Girobank, HSBC, Lloyds TSB and NatWest.
[2]The FPB survey used the term 'transaction charges'.

TABLE 4.10 **Proportions of businesses that claimed their banks had increased money transmission prices over the last three years**

	1998 %	2000 %	Change Percentage points
England and Wales			
Barclays	72.2	75.0	2.8
HSBC	64.0	66.3	2.3
Lloyds TSB	64.7	83.3	18.6
NatWest	64.3	73.3	9.0
Scotland			
RBS	65.4	66.1	0.7
BoS	75.2	66.9	−8.3
Clydesdale	73.6	89.5	15.9

Source: FPB surveys.

4.58. The proportions of businesses claiming an increase in money transmission charges range from two-thirds to 83 per cent in England and Wales in 2000 and from two-thirds to 90 per cent in Scotland in the same year. The results of the FPB's 1998 and 2000 surveys show that there has been a sizeable increase in the proportions claiming increases in money transmission prices for Lloyds TSB (19 percentage points), Clydesdale (16 percentage points) and NatWest (9 percentage points). The reverse is true for BoS—the proportion claiming increases in money transmission prices has fallen by eight percentage points. Barclays and HSBC criticized the FPB's results. HSBC told us that no weight should be attached to the FPB's findings. It said that the FPB's membership represented a small section of, and was not representative of, the overall business community, and it questioned some of the FPB's methodology. HSBC stated that the particular question behind the results in Table 4.10 was badly phrased and ambiguous; an SME whose bank had increased just one or two individual money transmission charges over the past three years, but which was actually paying less in overall charges than three years ago, might well have answered yes to the question. Barclays could not believe that 75 per cent of the FPB's members who were customers of Barclays in 2000 experienced increased money transmission prices. Barclays said that its nominal prices generally had not increased for at least six years and any increase in charges would be the result of increases in business volumes or base rates. It said that the wording of much of the FPB's research did not have a satisfactory level of objectivity. The question, whether bank charges had increased, was asked in such a way that it would include rises because of increases in base rates (as opposed to bank margins) and because of increases in the SME's volume of bank transactions (as opposed to bank tariffs). The FPB rejected these criticisms. It said that its members accounted for less than half (47 per cent) of the sample size (7,725) of its survey, over half (53 per cent) being the banks' own customers that were not members of the FPB. It said that the methodology of the survey had been consistent since 1988. The FPB did not believe that where elements of bank charging might have increased, but the overall charge decreased, respondents would have said that their charges increased. The FPB accepted that it could be argued that overall bank charges as a concept could include the necessity to apply mandatory base rate increases but it said that base rates had fallen in the period between its last two surveys. Lloyds TSB told us that the Bannock Consulting survey results should be given greater weight than the results of the FPB survey. It said that, in terms of reliability, the analysis of price changes over time (Bannock Consulting) was objectively verifiable whereas customer perceptions of changing prices (FPB) were likely to be flawed. Lloyds TSB stated that absolute charges (as covered by the FPB) would increase over time if a firm had grown over that period or if a customer had been enjoying free banking for a start-up period, and then moved on to pay tariff charges. Another possible explanation for the different findings on prices by Bannock Consulting/Barclays and the FPB is that neither Bannock Consulting nor Barclays included all the money transmission prices in their calculations, although Barclays did include more prices than Bannock Consulting.

4.59. BMRB asked SMEs whether the charges, fees and rates of interest at their main bank had changed over the last year. Those SMEs that said that their charges, fees and rates of interest had changed were asked whether these price changes alone resulted in them paying more or less or about the same overall to their main bank (see Table 4.11). Barclays told us that these questions provided no information on whether bank margins had changed and therefore whether banks had changed their prices as the changes referred to by BMRB could apply to increases in base rates just as much as to increases in bank margins, or to increases arising from increases in business volumes, or increases due to the maturing of the business, from start-up packages to tariffs for established businesses.

TABLE 4.11 **Proportions of SMEs experiencing changes in charges, fees and rates of interest over the previous year**

	%
Experiencing change:	
Increase overall	22
Decrease overall	10
No overall change	4
Don't know	1
Total with change	37
No overall change	51
Don't know	12
Total	100
Sample size	1,211

Source: BMRB survey.

4.60. The survey revealed that 37 per cent of SMEs said that their charges, fees and interest rate had changed over the last year. BMRB found that for 22 per cent of SMEs, price changes alone had resulted in them paying more to their main bank and for 10 per cent these changes resulted in them paying less to their main bank. 4 per cent of SMEs said that these price changes alone had resulted in them paying about the same to their main bank, suggesting that this group experienced increases in some prices and reductions in others which cancelled each other out.

Negotiated money transmission charges

4.61. HSBC told us that it negotiated money transmission prices with all SMEs with an annual turnover of greater than £100,000. It said that negotiating money transmission prices allowed the bank to tailor its charges according to the costs incurred by the bank. When entering negotiations to decide the appropriate level of money transmission charges on a current account, HSBC stated that its relationship manager would have in mind a cost recovery target on that account, and that costs would need to be covered by a combination of direct charges on money transmission usage and indirect charges arising from the value of credit balances on the account. It told us that the relationship manger would consider how to package up the charges according to the preferences of the customer.

4.62. RBSG told us that, excluding SMEs with free banking, 89 per cent of NatWest's SME customers with an annual turnover of less than £1 million paid NatWest's standard tariffs. It said that RBS had negotiable charges for SMEs with an annual turnover of more than £0.5 million. RBSG provided data that showed that 32 per cent of RBS's SMEs with an annual turnover of up to £0.25 million received negotiated charges. The equivalent proportions in 1998 and 1997 were 36 and 42 per cent respectively. RBSG told us that the majority of RBS's SMEs with an annual turnover of more than £1 million had negotiated charges.

4.63. Barclays provided us with data for its negotiated money transmission charges for each of the years 1997 to 1999. Table 4.12 compares these negotiated charges with Barclays' standard charges for 1999 for its main money transmission services.

TABLE 4.12 **Charges for Barclays' main money transmission services, 1999**

	Charges		Difference		% of SMEs with
	Standard*	Negotiated†			negotiated charges
	p	p	Pence	%	
Credit					
Auto credit	15				6
Cheque	25				4
Cash	50	*Figures omitted.*			7
		See note			
Debit		*on page iv.*			
Cheque	54				4
Cash	57				4

Source: CC calculations on data provided by Barclays.

*Business tariff.
†Simple average of Small Business and Business tariffs.

4.64. Table 4.12 shows that average negotiated charges for Barclays are between [✂] and [✂] per cent lower than its standard charges. Only a small proportion of SMEs that bank with Barclays receive these negotiated charges, ranging from 4 per cent (debit cheques) to 7 per cent (cash credits). Barclays provided us with data that showed that 7.5 per cent of its SMEs had negotiated money transmission charges.

4.65. HSBC provided us with data for 2000 that showed that 49 per cent of its SME accounts paid non-published tariffs. HSBC told us that, as a result of negotiation, [✂] per cent of these SMEs ([✂] per cent in all) did not pay charges for the main money transmission services but were required to hold minimum balances and [✂] per cent ([✂] per cent in all) had negotiated reductions in their main money transmission charges based on the value of their credit balances.

4.66. Lloyds TSB told us that most of its Business Banking customers paid its standard tariffs and that its Commercial Banking customers paid negotiated tariffs. Lloyds TSB stated that a little over [✂] Business Banking customers (less than 2 per cent) received a negotiated discount on money transmission service charges. The average discount was [✂] per cent. Lloyds TSB told us that the customers principally benefiting from this discount included a number of clubs, charities and societies, which, because they had high transaction volumes, did not qualify for the lower charges offered on accounts designed for these types of customer (ie permitting ten free debit items a month).

4.67. BoS said that about 5 per cent of its SME customers had negotiated their money transmission charges.

4.68. First Trust told us that, on average, SMEs received a [✂] per cent discount on its money transmission charges.

4.69. Non-tariff or negotiated prices clearly can affect revenue significantly. This is particularly so for HSBC that only has published money transmission prices for SMEs with an annual turnover of up to £100,000 (accounting for about [✂] of its SMEs). In order to take account of fees for money transmission services which are not published or which are negotiated, we have calculated average revenue from money transmission fees per SME current account (see Table 4.13).

TABLE 4.13 **Average revenue from money transmission fees, 1999**

	£
England and Wales	
Barclays	383
HSBC	232
Lloyds TSB	298
NatWest	384
Scotland	
RBS*	268
BoS	282
Clydesdale†	218
Northern Ireland	
First Trust	344
BoI	216
Northern	202
Ulster Bank	221

Source: CC calculations on data provided by the banks.

---

*Annual turnover of up to £10 million.
†Overestimate as it excludes SMEs with annual turnover of less than £100,000.

4.70. HSBC has lower average revenue for money transmission services (£232) than Lloyds TSB (£298), Barclays (£383) and NatWest (£384). Clydesdale has lower average revenue for money transmission services (£218) than RBS (£268) and BoS (£282). In Northern Ireland, Northern has lower average revenue (£202) than BoI (£216), Ulster Bank (£221) and First Trust (£344).

Negotiated charges for lending and deposits

4.71. There are few published rates of interest and other charges for lending products to SMEs. HSBC told us that this was because the lending risk, and therefore the prices, varied with the individual customer. The exception is unauthorized overdrafts, where more published information is available. Rates for lending products will depend on a range of factors and tend to be negotiated between the bank and the SME (see paragraphs 4.126 to 4.144 for information on margins associated with these products). HSBC said that negotiation was very common on its debt products. It told us that its commercial mortgage was a tariffed product and it did have guidelines for overdraft pricing, as well as a published rate of interest for one of its loan products—Small Business Loan—that covered loans up to £15,000. In 2000, this product accounted for about 3 per cent of HSBC's total lending book for SMEs with an annual turnover of less than £1 million and over one-third of the number of loans by these SMEs. As regards arrangement fees for lending, BoS said that about 53 per cent of its SMEs had negotiated these fees.

4.72. Rates of interest on deposit accounts tend to be published, although in some circumstances a small number of SMEs may be able to negotiate an improvement in rates. Unlike most of the rates of interest on deposit accounts, rates offered by banks on money market products are not published: they are usually set at a discount to the prevailing wholesale market rates.

4.73. 49 per cent of SMEs told BMRB that they had tried to negotiate charges, fees and interest rates with their main bank; 45 per cent said they had not tried. Responses varied by size of SMEs. For example, 31 per cent of SMEs with an annual turnover of up to £100,000 stated that they had tried to negotiate, compared with 78 per cent of SMEs with an annual turnover of between £5 and £25 million.

4.74. Table 4.14 shows the banking services SMEs tried to negotiate on and the proportions that were successful.

TABLE 4.14 **Proportion of SMEs that tried to negotiate on charges, fees and interest rates and those that succeeded**

per cent

Category*	Tried to negotiate	Successfully negotiated as a proportion of:	
		All SMEs	SMEs that tried to negotiate
Overdraft facility	21	17	79
Business deposit account	11	8	72
Overdraft	11	8	70
Business loan	11	9	79
Money transfer facility	11	8	78
Bank charges	8	5	66
Total that tried to negotiate	49		
Did not try to negotiate	45		
Bank will not negotiate	2		
Don't know	4		
Total	100		
Sample size	1,112	1,112	†

Source: BMRB survey.

*Only individual categories are shown where proportions for trying to negotiate are 5 per cent or more.
†Sample size is those that tried to negotiate, eg 21 per cent of SMEs tried to negotiate for an overdraft facility and of these, 79 per cent were successful.

4.75. Most of the negotiations were related to lending: 21 per cent for overdraft facilities, 11 per cent each for overdrafts and business loans. Others negotiating did so for business deposit accounts (11 per cent), money transfer facilities (11 per cent) and bank charges (8 per cent). There are two ways to analyse the proportions of SMEs that were successful in their negotiations: as a proportion of all SMEs, and as a proportion of SMEs that tried to negotiate. We look at each of these in turn. 17 per cent of SMEs successfully negotiated overdraft facilities. The proportions for deposit accounts, overdrafts, loans and money transfer facilities were about 8 to 9 per cent. The proportion for bank charges was lower: 5 per cent. In terms of SMEs that tried to negotiate, most were successful, ranging from nearly 80 per cent for overdraft facilities, business loans and money transfer facilities to 66 per cent for bank charges.

4.76. We tested whether the proportions of SMEs negotiating and those that were successful in negotiating differed between banks. We found very little difference between the banks. We were particularly interested in whether there was a difference in the proportions negotiating/successfully negotiating with HSBC and Barclays, Lloyds TSB and NatWest, due to HSBC's policy of only having published money transmission prices for SMEs with an annual turnover of up to £100,000—a much lower threshold than the other three largest clearing banks (see Table 4.1). We found very little difference in the proportions between HSBC and Barclays, Lloyds TSB and NatWest.

SMEs' knowledge of prices

4.77. BMRB asked those SMEs that had more than one banking service from their main bank (92 per cent of the whole sample) which were their most important banking services in terms of charges, fees and rates of interest. The most important was overdraft facility, given by 33 per cent of these SMEs; overdraft itself was given by 18 per cent of SMEs. Money transfers between accounts was given by 27 per cent of SMEs and business deposit accounts was given by 22 per cent of SMEs. Two other answers were given by 10 per cent or more SMEs: business loan (14 per cent) and business charging cards (10 per cent).

4.78. BMRB asked SMEs how they would describe their knowledge of their charges, fees and rates of interest for the banking services they considered to be the most and less important (see Table 4.15).

TABLE 4.15 **Proportion of SMEs that know about their charges, fees and rates of interest**

per cent

	Most important charges	Less important charges*
Know all of them	26	16
Know most of them	30	27
Know some of them	22	27
Know very few of them	13	20
Don't know any of them	7	9
Don't know	2	2
Total†	100	100
Sample size	999	920

Source: BMRB survey.

*Excluding no other charges.
†Total may not sum because of rounding.

4.79. Table 4.15 shows that 56 per cent of SMEs said that they knew all or most of their most important charges compared with 43 per cent which said the same for their less important charges. 42 per cent of SMEs said that they knew some, very few or none of their most important charges compared with 56 per cent which said the same for their less important charges.

Factors taken into account when setting money transmission charges

4.80. RBSG told us that the prices of its rivals were the main determinant of its prices. It said that cost was not a primary factor but that it was necessary to cover its incremental costs of providing services.

4.81. Barclays told us that its charges were based on costs, market conditions, competitive pressure, product life cycle, substitutability of alternative products and technological opportunities. It said that charges were higher to smaller SMEs because of their lower number of transactions.

4.82. HSBC said that when setting tariffs centrally or when negotiating prices at the local level, it would focus on the following key factors in its pricing decisions: the costs involved; the terms available on competing products; the terms available from competing suppliers; and the overall value of a customer to HSBC. It told us that its money transmission tariff was a package of charges, which, as a whole, was cost-reflective. It stated that the process of simplifying the tariff meant that item charges might or might not be above or below individual unit costs. HSBC said that the level of a negotiated tariff on a current account would reflect the same underlying cost drivers as for the standard tariff and that when negotiating prices the bank would attempt to achieve a price that properly reflected costs for that customer, based on the likely level of money transmission usage.

4.83. Lloyds TSB told us that its services, including the integral overdraft facility (see paragraphs 3.35 to 3.37), were packaged together to form an overall current account service, and that it looked at the costs of providing the package as a whole and set its prices in the light of these total costs. It said that in setting charges it would have regard to: the overall level of charges and charges per item levied by competitors with a view to winning new customers; changes in the cost of providing money transmission services; whether it wished to promote a particular money transmission service (Lloyds TSB told us that it had structured charges to promote the use of automated as opposed to paper money transmission services); and rationalizing the charging structure of Lloyds and TSB following the merger.

Interest on current accounts

4.84. On the whole, the main clearing groups do not pay interest on credit balances held in business current accounts. Lloyds TSB told us that while this was true, it and the other leading banks offered sweep facilities (see paragraphs 4.112 to 4.120), whereby an SME might arrange for any significant balance maintained on its account to be swept automatically into an interest-bearing account. Barclays said that it planned to introduce an interest-paying current account for businesses. Table 4.16 shows the banks that paid interest on current accounts as standard and those that paid interest on current accounts as a result of negotiation.

TABLE 4.16 **Interest-paying current accounts**

	Account name/characteristics	Proportion of number of SME current accounts (%)	Interest paid (%)
Accounts with standard rates of interest			
England and Wales			
Abbey National*	Business (direct account)	100	0.75–4.17
Alliance & Leicester	Flat fee current account	3.5	0.5–4.75
Alliance & Leicester	Where use Internet service	4.1	0.5–4.75
Co-operative Bank	Business Direct	46	1–4.62
Fleming	Corporate	100	1–3.15
	Investment	100	0.5–4.65
Lloyds TSB	Business Interest Cheque Account†	5.9‡	0.9–2.4
Nationwide	BusinessInvestor	100	1.8–3.6
Norwich & Peterborough	Business Gold	100	0.35–2.5
Scotland			
BoS	Direct Business Cheque	10	0.25–3.25
Negotiated rates of interest			*Average interest rates*
England and Wales			
Alliance & Leicester	Turnover greater than £500,000	2.4	1.25–4.95
Co-operative Bank	Business	3	4.6
HSBC	Business current account	1§	1.8
Lloyds TSB¶	Commercial Banking	0.4¤	4.0
Scotland			
BoS	Business Current Account	26	4–4.75
Northern Ireland			
First Trust	Current credit interest-bearing, Business Customers, Marketlink	5	4.2
Ulster Bank	Current—non-personal	#	4.7

Source: Companies and CC calculations based on data provided by the companies and in *Business Money£acts*.

---

*Also offered in Scotland and Northern Ireland.
†Available to ex-TSB Business Banking customers.
‡6.4 per cent of Business Banking customers.
§2 per cent of HSBC's SME customers on its unpublished tariffs.
¶Lloyds TSB also continues to provide High Interest Cheque Account to Lloyds Heritage customers, with rates of interest (0.9 to 1.4 per cent), accounting for 0.31 per cent of SME current accounts.
¤5 per cent of Commercial Banking customers.
#Less than 0.1 per cent.

4.85. None of the four largest clearing banks provides interest on current accounts as standard.[1] Only one of the six largest clearing banks does so: BoS with its direct account, which has a tiered interest rate of 0.25 to 3.25 per cent. BoS told us that the weighted average interest rate paid with this account was 2.75 per cent and the average balance was about £29,000. About 10 per cent of its SMEs have such an account. Most of the current accounts that offer interest as standard tend to be direct accounts. Norwich & Peterborough and Nationwide do offer branch-based current accounts that pay interest but their rates of interest tend to be lower than those paid with direct accounts.

4.86. Some banks, including some of the main clearing groups, do pay interest on current accounts as a result of negotiation. However, only a small proportion of SMEs receive this benefit. HSBC said that negotiation could result in other forms of benefit to the SME, for example no or reduced core money transmission charges (see paragraph 4.65).

4.87. Most of the four largest clearing groups said that they did not pay interest on credit balances in current accounts in order to minimize the money transmission charges on these accounts—the costs of current accounts being covered by revenue achieved from credit balances and revenue from money transmission charges. HSBC told us that there was always a balance to be struck between recovering the costs of providing the current account service through direct methods such as charges, or indirectly, through the value of credit balances—if interest were to be paid the level of charges would have to increase. This view was supported by Barclays, which told us that it would be uneconomic to serve significant proportions of the customer base if SME banks were obliged to pay interest on current accounts without adjustment to other charges. In HSBC's view, customers generally preferred the more visible element of charges to be minimized, and for costs to be recovered as much as possible through the value of credit balances. Its view was based on results from market research surveys[2] which, it said, showed that 60 per cent of customers stated that minimizing bank charges was a priority, compared with 8 per cent of customers who wanted to earn interest on credit balances. Barclays set its decision not to pay interest on credit balances in current accounts in the context of the liquidity management service. It said that the balance of pricing within the liquidity management service reflected customer preferences, which resulted in widely available cheaply priced credit and no interest on current accounts.

4.88. Table 4.17 shows the number and proportion of SMEs' current accounts that were in credit for all of 1999 and the total and average values held in these accounts for Barclays, NatWest, HSBC, Lloyds TSB, RBS, BoS, BoI and Ulster Bank. BoS and HSBC told us that their estimates of the average value held in these accounts were distorted by the inclusion of accounts that were part of a group arrangement where a group interest structure applied.

4.89. In broad terms about half of SMEs' current accounts were in credit for all of 1999. The average value ranged from about £[✂] (HSBC) to about £[✂] (Barclays). Barclays told us that Table 4.17 was misleading because it was based on one year. It said that it had evidence suggesting that only 13 per cent of new SME customers would reach the age of three years and would have remained in credit for the whole period and, of firms that would survive five years, only about 25 per cent would have remained in credit for the whole period.

---

[1]Lloyds TSB provides interest on current accounts but this is for ex-TSB Business Banking customers.
[2]HSBC's *Liability Research* (1999).

TABLE 4.17 **Total number of SME current accounts that remained in credit and their average values, 1999**

	Total
Barclays	
Accounts always in credit ('000)	(✂)
Accounts always in credit (%)	48
Total value in accounts in credit (£m)	[✂]
Average value in accounts in credit (£)*	
NatWest†	
Accounts always in credit ('000)	(✂)
Accounts always in credit (%)	49
Total value in accounts in credit (£m)	[✂]
Average value in accounts in credit (£)*	
HSBC‡	
Accounts always in credit ('000)	(✂)
Accounts always in credit (%)	51
Total value in accounts in credit (£m)	[✂]
Average value in accounts in credit (£)*	
Lloyds TSB†	
Accounts always in credit ('000)	(✂)
Accounts always in credit (%)	40
Total value in accounts in credit (£m)	[✂]
Average value in accounts in credit (£)*	
RBS†	
Accounts always in credit ('000)	(✂)
Accounts always in credit (%)	45
Total value in accounts in credit (£m)	[✂]
Average value in accounts in credit (£)*	
BoS§	
Accounts always in credit ('000)	(✂)
Accounts always in credit (%)	37
Total value in accounts in credit (£m)	[✂]
Average value in accounts in credit (£)*	
BoI	
Accounts always in credit ('000)	(✂)
Accounts always in credit (%)	55
Total value in accounts in credit (£m)	[✂]
Average value in accounts in credit (£)*	
Ulster Bank	
Accounts always in credit ('000)	(✂)
Accounts always in credit (%)	30
Total value in accounts in credit (£m)	[✂]
Average value in accounts in credit (£)	

Source: Banks and CC calculations on data provided by the banks.

---

*Calculated on unrounded data.
†Includes businesses with an annual turnover of up to £100 million.
‡Year ended August 2000. Includes accounts that are part of a group with a group interest structure applying.
§Year ended February 2000. Includes accounts that are part of a group with a group interest structure applying.

4.90. We have estimated the net interest income received by banks from current account credit balances and the average additional income SMEs would have received and the loss of income to the banks if SMEs had been paid interest on their current accounts. We used the estimates of net interest income from, and the value of, current account credit balances as set out in Chapter 6. In estimating the average value per SME account we have excluded those accounts that were overdrawn for the whole year. Our estimates are likely to be understated as they include SME accounts that were overdrawn for part of the year. Table 4.18 shows our results.

4.91. The net interest income margins for the four largest clearing banks are between just over 4.5 [✂] and just under 7 per cent [✂] with an average of just under 5.5 per cent. The margins for [*Details omitted. See note on page iv.*] with an average of 2.5 per cent, half the average for the four largest clearing banks. [*Details omitted. See note on page iv.*] In Northern Ireland, [✂] has a net interest income margin of about 3 per cent.

TABLE 4.18 Income to the banks from current account credit balances and possible loss to the banks and possible benefit to SMEs from interest being paid on current account credit balances, 1999

	(✂)	(✂)	(✂)*	(✂)†	(✂)‡	(✂)§	(✂)
Net interest income from credit balances (£m)							
Value of credit balances (£m)							
Net interest income margin (%)							
Lost income to the banks if following rates of interest were paid on current accounts (£m):¶							
1%							
2%							
3%			*Figures omitted. See note on page iv.*				
4%							
5%							
6%							
Average benefit to SME if following rates of interest were paid on current accounts (£):¶							
1%							
2%							
3%							
4%							
5%							
6%							
All of bank's net income margin							

Source: CC calculations based on data provided by the banks.

---

*[✂] said that it had not been able to establish the actual distribution of balances between interest tiers. We have shown a minimum figure, assuming existing interest paid was so distributed as to offset the requirement to pay interest on all accounts. Table 2.25 also shows a maximum figure assuming the distribution of interest paid is such that there would be no such offset.

†Annual turnover up to £1 million.

‡Annual turnover up to £10 million.

§[✂]

¶Deducts interest already paid.

4.92. Table 4.18 shows the lost income to the banks and the average benefits to SMEs if SMEs received one of a range of interest rates. The lost income to the banks is between just over £4 million and just under £195 million in England and Wales, between about £7 million and just over £40 million in Scotland and between about £1 million and about £2 million in Northern Ireland. The average benefits to SMEs are between just under £7 and just under £300 in England and Wales, between just under £40 and just over £350 in Scotland and between just over £30 and just over £60 in Northern Ireland. [

Details omitted. See note on page iv.

]

4.93. SMEs could reduce any income loss on their current accounts as a result of the non-payment of credit interest by making some use of their deposit accounts for transactions or by using set-off or sweep facilities. We deal with each of these in turn.

Use of deposit accounts for transactions

4.94. RBSG told us that deposit accounts for SMEs with its banks did not have the facility to generate transactions, ie cheque books, standing orders and direct debits were not permitted with such accounts. It said that this had always been the case.

4.95. Lloyds TSB provided us with data for May 2000, which showed that SMEs carried out about 3 per cent of their transactions from their business deposit accounts.

4.96. Barclays told us that deposit accounts were not typically used by SMEs to carry out transactions directly. Barclays provided us with data on the number of transactions carried out by its SMEs through deposit accounts. We combined this data with the number of SME transactions through current accounts. This showed that SMEs, excluding CACs, made very few transactions through their deposit accounts. CACs, on the other hand, made many transactions through their deposit accounts. In 1999 transactions through the deposit accounts held by SMEs (excluding those held by CACs) accounted for less than 5 per cent of all their transactions (through their deposit and current accounts). In the same year, deposit account transactions accounted for 62 and 56 per cent of all CACs' credit and debit transactions respectively. Barclays stated that it did not actively promote the use of deposit accounts for making transactions. It stated that it provided money transmission arrangements for SME depositors by linking the instant access Business Premium Account with the business current account.

4.97. HSBC said that deposit accounts were savings vehicles rather than a quasi-current (chequeing) account. It stated that this did not preclude the use of deposit account funds to carry out transactions—such as large, one-off purchases—on an occasional, rather than a day-to-day, basis. It told us that while it stated in its product material that standing orders and direct debits were not allowed on many deposit accounts, its systems did not currently preclude this, and there were cases in which direct debits from deposit accounts had been arranged by a branch.

4.98. BoS stated that very few of its SMEs used deposit accounts to carry out transactions. It told us that the use of deposit accounts for business transactions was contrary to the terms and conditions of the account and was therefore actively discouraged. BoS has rewritten its application form for these deposit accounts since 1997 to make more explicit mention of the purpose of the product.

Set-off facilities

4.99. Set-off facilities enable overdrawn accounts and accounts in credit to be grouped together, so that the SME only pays interest on any net overdrawn balance across the entire group of accounts. In this way the level of interest paid on debit balances is minimized. HSBC told us that set-offs were complicated facilities and were not suitable for many SMEs (particularly smaller SMEs).

4.100. Table 4.19 shows the proportion of SMEs with set-off facilities for the four largest clearing banks in 1999.

TABLE 4.19 **Proportion of SMEs with set-off facilities, 1999**

	Turnover bands of SMEs (£ million)						%
	0–1	Over 1–2	Over 2–5	Over 5–10	Over 10–25	Total	CACs
Barclays	0.4	4.6	8.5	12.9	18.6	1.0	0.7
HSBC	2.2	7.0	11.9	17.7	23.9	2.7	
NatWest	0.3			11.0*	36.2†	1.1	
RBS	0.7			10.4*	29.8†	2.0	0.3

Source: CC calculations based on data provided by the banks.

*Annual turnover of between £1 million and £10 million.
†Annual turnover of between £10 million and £100 million.

4.101. Table 4.19 shows that between 1 and 3 per cent of SMEs have set-off facilities. The proportions vary by size of SME. For example, for SMEs with an annual turnover of less than £1 million the proportion is less than 2.5 per cent whereas for those with an annual turnover of between £1 million and £10 million (RBS and NatWest) and between £10 million and £25 million (Barclays and HSBC) the proportions are 10, 11, 19 and 24 per cent respectively.

4.102. The proportions in Table 4.19 are based on the total number of current account relationships held by each of the banks. These proportions will underestimate the use of set-off facilities as they are designed for customers that are or might be overdrawn in one or more of their accounts. The main clearing groups provided us with data on the number of current accounts held by SMEs (not the number of relationships) that were overdrawn and that had overdraft facilities. The data showed that at the end of 1999 approximately 30 per cent of accounts had overdraft facilities and about 50 per cent of accounts were overdrawn at some point during 1999. On the basis of these proportions, between 2 and 9 per cent of SMEs with overdraft facilities or overdrafts had set-off facilities in 1999.

4.103. Lloyds TSB told us that its SMEs made very little use of set-off facilities. It told us that the relevant balances at any one time during the first six months of 2000 represented approximately 0.08 per cent of funds on deposit by its Business Banking customers. Lloyds TSB estimated that up to 5 per cent of its Commercial Banking customers (with annual turnover of between £2 million and £100 million) used deposit funds as set-off for interest rate purposes.

4.104. BoS told us that it had over 9,000 set-off arrangements—some 4.5 per cent of the number of its business current accounts. Set-off facilities were available without charge.

4.105. Anglia Business Associates Ltd (ABA) told us that group accounts for set-off purposes were not always straightforward. It said, for example, that if an SME had a credit balance of £10,000 and a debit balance of £25,000, the SME might expect the set-off arrangement to produce an interest charge based on the net balance of £15,000. This was not necessarily so. ABA quoted examples where these balances would result in an interest charge on £15,000 plus 2 per cent on £10,000, the charge on the credit balance (£10,000) being known as the 'turn'.

4.106. Barclays said that group facilities were relatively rare. Any turn arrangements were agreed with customers in advance and in recent cases clearly specified in facility letters. It was possible that the turn charge element in historic facility letters was open to interpretation, but Barclays said that its standard group arrangement facility letter, introduced in January 1999, clearly detailed the turn charges to be applied. Barclays stated that its practice was to review any disputed agreement in the light of the SME's understanding and available documentation. It said that it saw few such cases.

4.107. HSBC stated that there were different forms of set-off arrangements and they could be legally and administratively complex. It said that in its case, the exact form of the arrangement was always agreed with SMEs in advance, according to what was appropriate to their needs including whether or not it was subject to a turn. SMEs were always informed of the arrangements as the terms were contained in the letter of set-off and the facility letter.

4.108. Lloyds TSB said that it notified SMEs of the amount of any turn to be charged in its lending facility letter and it had not received any complaints about its turn component of its charges.

4.109. RBSG told us that since its banks provided their SMEs with written details of all terms and conditions and charges for each service, SMEs were fully informed of the fact that credit balances used in set-off arrangements were subject to a turn.

4.110. BoS said that where the debit balance exceeded the credit balance, interest would be charged on the net amount, but where the credit balance exceeded the debit balance, no interest would be charged nor paid to the SME. It stated that in normal circumstances a turn would be taken on the credit balance. BoS told us that such arrangements were invariably the subject of negotiation between the bank and the SME and therefore both parties were fully aware of the situation. In all cases, the arrangements were fully documented.

4.111. NAB stated that when Clydesdale entered into set-off arrangements with SMEs the details were documented and copied to the SMEs. It said that on the occasions where SMEs did not wish to enter into the documentation necessary to treat the net amount as one balance for the bank's regulatory balance sheet reporting, it was obliged to regard all account balances as discrete and was consequently obliged to apply regulatory capital and liquidity requirements to gross balances. In such circumstances, NAB said, Clydesdale applied a small interest margin to the credit balances, details of which were set out in the facility letter.

Sweep facilities

4.112. Sweep facilities (also known as auto transfers) are where a customer decides on a level of balance to be kept on an account. Often this will be a nil cleared balance on a non-interest-bearing current account. An auto transfer then operates to maintain the balance at the chosen level by transfer to and/or from another account, commonly a deposit-type account. This ensures that the customer makes optimum use of credit balances to earn interest, without having to arrange inter-account transfers itself. Some banks have a separate charge for this facility and some do not. For example, HSBC has a separate charge—£8 per month for weekly searches and £20 per month for daily searches but there is no separate charge for monthly searches—but RBS does not.

4.113. Table 4.20 shows the proportion of SMEs with auto transfers for Barclays and NatWest in 1999. The data behind Table 4.20 does not take into account circumstances where an SME undertakes its own cash management (via electronic and telephone banking) to transfer balances between its accounts.

TABLE 4.20 **Proportion of SME current accounts with auto transfers, 1999**

	Turnover bands of SMEs (£ million)						%
	0–1	Over 1–2	Over 2–5	Over 5–10	Over 10–25	Total	CACs
NatWest*	5.0	-	-	29.3†	46.0‡	6.6	-
Barclays§	7.7	24.9	29.0	30.7	33.2	10.7	27.5

Source: CC based on data provided by the banks.

---

*Proportion of relationships.
†Annual turnover of between £1 million and £10 million.
‡Annual turnover of between £10 million and £100 million.
§Assumes complete overlap between those SMEs with auto credit and auto debit facilities.

4.114. Table 4.20 shows that about 7 and 11 per cent of NatWest's and Barclays' SMEs respectively have auto transfers. These proportions vary by size of SME. For example, for SMEs with an annual turnover of less than £1 million the proportions are 5 (NatWest) and 8 per cent (Barclays) whereas for those with an annual turnover of between £1 million and £10 million (NatWest) and between £10 million and £25 million (Barclays) the proportions are 29 and 33 per cent respectively. Barclays said that it was not the case, as we had assumed, that there was complete overlap between its SMEs with auto credit and auto debit facilities. Taking this into account, Barclays estimated that about 12 per cent of its SMEs had auto transfers. This compares with our estimate of 11 per cent. Barclays and RBSG told us that the use of auto transfers had increased over the past few years.

4.115. Lloyds TSB provided us with data that showed that about 1 per cent of its Business Banking customers had automated sweep facilities in 1999. It said that some of its SMEs transferred funds between their accounts manually by using Lloyds TSB's electronic banking facilities. Lloyds TSB provided us with data that showed that just over 2 per cent of its Business Banking customers were registered to use such facilities as were 44 per cent of its Commercial Banking customers. It told us that there had been no significant change in the use of its automated sweep facilities since 1989.

4.116. HSBC said that only a minority of its SMEs (6.3 per cent of SMEs on its negotiated tariffs and about 0.7 per cent on its Small Business tariff—about 3.5 per cent in all) had sweep facilities and more significantly that relatively few of their transfers were made even from those accounts which had such facilities. It believed that this was due to the relatively inflexible nature of these automated transfers, and the facilities on many accounts being set up in such a way as to trigger a transfer only when the account had a relatively high credit balance—reflecting SMEs' preference for a substantial comfort zone of current account liquidity to deal with unexpected outgoings. It said that the low use of automated sweep facilities might also be due to the introduction of telephone, PC and Internet banking, which had made it much easier for SMEs to review balances of different accounts and to make transfers between them themselves. All of these facilities, according to HSBC, were more flexible than automated sweeps, both in terms of when the customer wanted to make the transfer and (particularly in the case of Internet banking) because they offered the prospect of moving money to a deposit account with another bank or building society. It stated that research suggested that one-fifth of customers reviewed their balances monthly or more frequently.

4.117. RBSG said that approximately 70 per cent of RBS's largest deposit accounts for SMEs with an annual turnover of less than £1 million were linked to a business current account by an automatic transfer. This proportion equates to about 18 per cent of RBS's SME current accounts with an annual turnover of less than £1 million. RBSG stated that these proportions did not take into account circumstances where SMEs undertook their own cash management via electronic banking.

4.118. BoS stated that it did not offer an automatic sweep facility. It said that manual sweeps were carried out by its staff on a very exceptional basis for certain high-valued SME relationships. It told us that in certain circumstances, it provided interest-bearing current accounts where the specific nature of the banking relationship justified the use of that product. It said that it promoted its PC banking where SMEs could transfer money between operating and investment accounts.

4.119. First Trust told us that offering a sweep facility was quite a common feature of banking relationships in Northern Ireland.

4.120. In contrast, Northern told us that about 1 per cent of its SMEs used sweep facilities on a daily basis.

Promotion of set-off and sweep facilities

4.121. We asked the main clearing groups to what extent they promoted set-off and sweep facilities. Barclays told us that it actively promoted them. HSBC stated that it did not actively promote these mechanisms at this time but it published details of these facilities in its Business Banking Charter, and also publicized the rates of interest on its deposit accounts. Lloyds TSB told us that it informed SMEs of the availability of sweep facilities. It said that information about the facility was available in branches and details of the associated charges were shown in tariff leaflets. RBSG stated that RBS had been actively promoting set-off and sweep facilities since 1998 but that NatWest did not systematically advise SMEs of the availability of these facilities. It said that neither NatWest nor RBS advised customers as a matter of course of the level of savings that might be achieved by using such facilities.

Margins and fees on debt products

4.122. 35 per cent of SMEs told BMRB that they had external funding (funding from outside the business, ie which does not come from retained profits or any personal sources). SMEs with a lower turnover had a smaller proportion of external funding than those with a larger turnover. For example, 26 per cent of SMEs with an annual turnover of up to £100,000 stated that they had external funding compared with 60 per cent for SMEs with an annual turnover of between £5 and £25 million.

4.123. 61 per cent of SMEs with external funding told BMRB that they used their main bank for some of this funding and 31 per cent did not use their main bank. The proportion of external funding from their main bank ranged from below 10 per cent of their external funding (12 per cent of SMEs) up to all of it (19 per cent of SMEs).

4.124. The difference between the rate of interest paid by SMEs to the banks and the interest cost of funds to the banks is what we refer to as the margin on lending. The interest cost to the banks may be the Bank Base Rate or LIBOR or some other measure of cost of funds. This margin does not take into account other costs associated with providing lending.

Comparing levels of margin in 1999

4.125. We now turn to examine the levels of average margins achieved by the main clearing groups on debt products in 1999.

Overdrafts

4.126. Table 4.21 shows the net interest income margins for overdrafts in 1999. The derivation of most of these margins is shown in Chapter 6.

TABLE 4.21 **Net interest income margins of overdrafts, 1999**

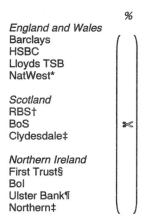

	%
England and Wales	
Barclays	
HSBC	
Lloyds TSB	
NatWest*	
Scotland	
RBS†	
BoS	✂
Clydesdale‡	
Northern Ireland	
First Trust§	
BoI	
Ulster Bank¶	
Northern‡	

Source: CC calculations on data provided by the banks.

*Annual turnover of up to £1 million.
†Annual turnover of up to £10 million. Net interest income is as shown in Chapter 6 (£[✂] million) but the value of outstanding overdrafts is £[✂] billion, which is an RBSG estimate.
‡Underestimate, as excludes SMEs with an annual turnover of less than £100,000.
§Loans and overdrafts.
¶Loans and overdrafts for all personal, SME and other corporate customers.

4.127. Table 4.21 shows that NatWest has a larger margin (just under [✂] per cent) than Lloyds TSB (just over [✂] per cent), HSBC (just over [✂] per cent) and Barclays (just over [✂] per cent). NatWest's margin is based on SMEs with an annual turnover of less than £1 million. We would expect its margin for SMEs with an annual turnover of less than £25 million to be lower than this: based on data from the other main clearing groups, we would expect a margin of just over [✂] per cent, slightly lower than that of Lloyds TSB. RBS's margin (just over [✂] per cent) is higher than Clydesdale's ([✂] per cent) and BoS's (just over [✂] per cent). The margins of the Northern Irish banks are in the range of [✂] per cent.

4.128. The margins in Table 4.21 are for all overdrafts—authorized and unauthorized. However, authorized overdrafts will account for by far the largest proportion of all the overdrafts. As a result, the margins in Table 4.21 will closely represent margins on authorized overdrafts. We now look at the margins on unauthorized overdrafts.

4.129. Unlike for authorized overdrafts, most banks publish their rates or margins for unauthorized overdrafts. Table 4.22 shows the margins for unauthorized overdrafts, which are based on published information.

4.130. Table 4.22 shows that margins on unauthorized overdrafts for the four largest clearing banks are between 15 and 24 per cent, with NatWest having the highest margin and Barclays having the lowest. Barclays told us that its actual margin on unauthorized overdrafts was just under 6 per cent. It said that the reason for the difference between its published and actual figures was that its relationship managers often did not apply the unauthorized rate to their customer's accounts. Barclays stated that this was usually the case when the relationship managers had satisfied themselves with the circumstances of the customer in question. The margins for the Scottish banks are between 21 and 24 per cent with RBS having a slightly higher margin than BoS which in turn has a higher margin than Clydesdale. BoS told us that its actual margin was much lower than its published margin. It said that its normal margin for unauthorized overdrafts was twice the agreed margin for authorized arrangements, the rate was included in its standard facility letter and in certain circumstances margins might be established by negotiation. Ulster Bank's margin (12 per cent) is lower than First Trust's (15 per cent).

TABLE 4.22 **Margins on unauthorized overdrafts**

	%
England and Wales	
NatWest	24
Barclays	15
Lloyds TSB*	19
HSBC	19
Scotland	
RBS	24
BoS	23
Clydesdale	21
Northern Ireland	
Ulster Bank†	12
BoI	Not published
Northern	Not published
First Trust	15

Source: CC calculations based on data in *Business Money£acts* and data published by the banks.

*Business Banking.
†Interest charges below £2 in any month are waived.

4.131. Margins for unauthorized overdrafts are much larger than margins for authorized overdrafts. Tables 4.21 and 4.22 show that margins for unauthorized overdrafts can be more than six times those for authorized overdrafts. Some of the four largest clearing groups told us that these higher rates were set to deter SMEs from taking out unauthorized overdrafts. HSBC said that unauthorized borrowing also imposed higher costs on the banks. The banks preferred to discuss with the SME its financial requirements and to arrange authorized funding. Barclays stated that the higher margins on unauthorized overdrafts reflected the extra costs and the risks incurred by the banks in relation to unauthorized borrowing.

4.132. Table 4.23 shows the types of fees that SMEs might incur when using authorized overdrafts. Most of these fees are not published.[1] The sizes of the fees shown are illustrative as they might be subject to negotiation.

TABLE 4.23 **Fees for overdrafts**

per cent

	Barclays	Lloyds TSB	NatWest	HSBC	BoS	RBS	NAB	BoI	Ulster Bank
Arrangement fee	0.6*	1.25†	Varies‡	1.25§	0.5–1	1¶	0.35–1¤	1#	Varies‡
Renewal/management fee	1	1.25†~	Varies‡	0.75~*		0.5¶	1	0.25#	

Source: The banks.

*Labelled as 'lending fees'.
†Business Banking. Minimum of £50.
‡Varies depending on the amount taken out.
§Minimum of £50.
¶Minimum of £100; average arrangement fee for new term loan was £205 (based on an average loan of £39,642).
¤Less than £50,000 is 1 per cent, minimum of £100; £50,000 to £1 million is 0.75 per cent; and over £1 million is 0.35 per cent.
#Minimum of £25.
~Separate management fee may be charged.
*Normally 0.75 per cent, with a minimum of £35.
Note: All percentages are the standard but may be negotiated.

4.133. Arrangement fees tend to lie between 0.35 and 1.25 per cent of the value of the overdraft. Renewal/management fees, which are usually paid every year, are between 0.25 and 1.25 per cent. SMEs might incur additional fees such as a commitment fee, an early termination fee, a non-utilization fee, a prepayment fee and an account control fee.

[1]HSBC publishes its charges for these fees in its Business Banking Charter.

4.134. Table 4.24 shows some of the fees that SMEs might incur when using unauthorized overdrafts. Most of these fees are published.

TABLE 4.24 **Additional fees with unauthorized overdrafts for the main clearing groups**

	Extra fee £	Unpaid cheque outwards £
England and Wales		
NatWest	3.50 per day	30
Barclays	12*	27.50
Lloyds TSB†	10*	27.50
HSBC	2 per working day	28‡
Scotland		
RBS	Discretional	30
BoS	0	30 to maximum 90 per day
Clydesdale	0	32
Northern Ireland		
Ulster Bank	9	10–30
BoI	0	30
Northern	0	35
First Trust	9	15–30 per item

Source: Business Money£acts.

*Charged whenever agreed facility exceeded by £50 or more and for each subsequent increase of £50 or more.
†Business Banking.
‡Cheques of over £28, free for cheques under £10 and £10 for cheques between £10 and £28.

4.135. Table 4.24 shows that the main clearing groups tend to charge extra fees, as do other banks (see Table 4.7).

Loans

4.136. Table 4.25 shows the net interest income margins for loans in 1999. The derivation of most of these margins is shown in Chapter 6.

TABLE 4.25 **Net interest income margins of loans, 1999**

	%
England and Wales	
Barclays	
HSBC*	
Lloyds TSB	
NatWest†	
Scotland	
RBS‡	
BoS	✂
Clydesdale§	
Northern Ireland	
First Trust¶	
BoI	
Ulster Bank¤	
Northern§	

Source: CC calculations on data provided by the banks.

*Based on an average value of £[✂] billion for loans outstanding.
†Annual turnover of up to £1 million.
‡Annual turnover of up to £10 million. Net interest income is as shown in Chapter 6 (£[✂] million) but the value of loans outstanding is £[✂] billion, which is an RBSG estimate.
§Underestimate, as excludes SMEs with an annual turnover of less than £100,000.
¶Loans and overdrafts.
¤Loans and overdrafts for all personal, SME and other corporate customers.

4.137. Table 4.25 shows that Barclays, HSBC and Lloyds TSB have a similar margin ([✂] per cent) which is slightly higher than that of NatWest ([✂] per cent). As is the case for overdrafts, NatWest's margin is based on SMEs with an annual turnover of less than £1 million. We would expect its margin for SMEs with an annual turnover of less than £25 million to be lower than this: based on data from other main clearing groups, we would expect a margin of just under [✂] per cent. RBS has a higher margin (just over [✂] per cent) than Clydesdale ([✂] per cent) and BoS (just under [✂] per cent). First Trust's margin ([✂] per cent) is a little higher than Ulster Bank's ([✂] per cent) (both margins are for loans and overdrafts but Ulster Bank's comprise loans and overdrafts for all personal, SME and other corporate customers), Northern's ([✂] per cent) and BoI's ([✂] per cent).

4.138.   Table 4.26 shows the arrangement fees for loans for the main clearing groups.

TABLE 4.26   **Arrangement fees for loans**

	%
England and Wales	
NatWest	1.6
Barclays	0.8
Lloyds TSB	1.25*
HSBC	1.25†
Scotland	
RBS	1‡
BoS	0.5–1
Clydesdale	0.35–1§
Northern Ireland	
Ulster Bank	Varies§
BoI	N/A
Northern	0.5–1¶
First Trust	Negotiated

Source: CC calculations based on data in *Business Money£acts*.

---

*Business Banking. Minimum of £50.
†Flexible Business Loan. There is no fee for Small Business Loan.
‡Minimum of £100.
§1 per cent for less than £50,000 with a minimum of £100, 0.75 per cent for £50,000 to £1 million and 0.35 per cent for over £1 million.
¶Tiered rates starting from £20 for loans of up to £1,999 up to 0.5 per cent for loans of £1 million or more.

4.139.   Arrangement fees for the four largest clearing banks are in the region of 0.8 to 1.6 per cent of the value of the loan. The Scottish banks have slightly lower arrangement fees—0.4 to 1 per cent—as does Northern. Other banks charge arrangement fees.

Asset finance

4.140.   Table 4.27 shows the margins for asset finance.

TABLE 4.27   **Average margins of asset finance, 1999**

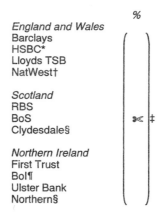

	%
England and Wales	
Barclays	
HSBC*	
Lloyds TSB	
NatWest†	
Scotland	
RBS	
BoS	✂ ‡
Clydesdale§	
Northern Ireland	
First Trust	
BoI¶	
Ulster Bank	
Northern§	

Source: CC calculations on data provided by the banks.

---

*[✂] per cent applies to HP and [✂] per cent applies to vehicle leases which may include personal customers.
†Annual turnover of up to £10 million.
‡Excludes motor business. Including motor business takes margin to [✂] per cent.
§NAB.
¶[✂] per cent applies to leasing and [✂] per cent applies to HP.

4.141. Average margins on asset finance tend to lie between 1 and 3 per cent. These margins are similar to those quoted to us by the FLA—it said that margins in the SME asset finance provisions were very tight, approximately 2 per cent over the relevant cost of funds.

4.142. Arrangement fees for asset finance are normally between £40 and £100. There can be other fees, for example a commitment fee and an option to purchase fee.

Sales finance

4.143. Table 4.28 shows the finance margins and service charges for factoring and invoice discounting.

TABLE 4.28 **Average margins and service charges for sales finance, 1999**

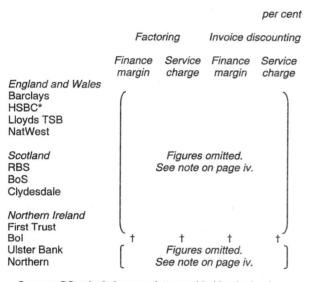

	Factoring		Invoice discounting	
	Finance margin	Service charge	Finance margin	Service charge
England and Wales				
Barclays				
HSBC*				
Lloyds TSB				
NatWest				
Scotland		Figures omitted.		
RBS		See note on page iv.		
BoS				
Clydesdale				
Northern Ireland				
First Trust				
BoI	†	†	†	†
Ulster Bank		Figures omitted.		
Northern		See note on page iv.		

Source: CC calculations on data provided by the banks.

*Factoring with credit protection and invoice discounting with credit protection.
†BoI was unable to split its data into factoring and invoice discounting but it was able to provide overall data for sales finance. For the year ended March 1999, its finance margin was [✂] per cent and its service charge was [✂] per cent.

4.144. Average finance margins for factoring are between 2 and 4 per cent compared with just under 1.5 to 3 per cent for invoice discounting. Service charges are higher for factoring—about 1 per cent—than for invoice discounting—about 0.2 per cent.

Trends in margins

Overdraft margins

4.145. We only have time series data on overdraft margins for three banks—Barclays, HSBC and Lloyds TSB—and their margins are shown in Figure 4.1. Lloyds TSB told us that its data should be treated with some caution because the data for 1995 and 1996 related to Lloyds whereas that after 1996 related to Lloyds TSB and the definition of some of the products had changed during the period covered. The trends in margins for Barclays and HSBC, but not their value, may be compared with those for Lloyds TSB. The margins for Lloyds TSB are for SMEs with an annual turnover of less than £2 million (Lloyds TSB's Business Banking division) whereas those for Barclays and HSBC are for SMEs with an annual turnover of up to £25 million. Banks tend to have lower margins for larger SMEs.

FIGURE 4.1

Net interest income margins for overdrafts, 1990 to 2000

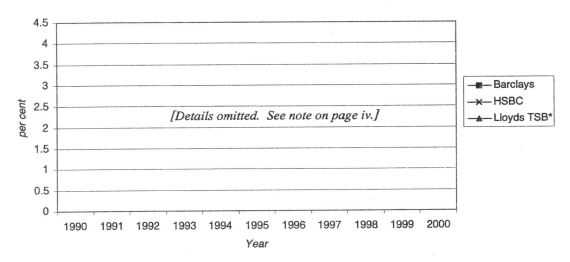

Source: CC calculations on data provided by the banks.

*Business Banking (annual turnover of up to £2 million). Only the trend in this margin can be compared with those of Barclays and HSBC (see paragraph 4.145).

4.146. Over the relevant periods, margins have been broadly constant (Barclays, although it fell in the early and late 1990s and rose in the mid-1990s) or risen slightly (HSBC and Lloyds TSB). Barclays told us that the fall in its margins at the onset of the recession was due to the pressure of high interest rates and low customer liquidity. It said that as the economy recovered and customer liquidity improved, there was some recovery of interest margins back to their pre-recession level. Barclays stated that the recent fall in its margins was a clear sign of competitive pressure. Lloyds TSB told us that the apparent rise in its margins was likely to be attributable, in part, to the larger number of low-value loans which had a proportionately higher set-up and operating cost, and to cover the proportionately higher commitment cost borne by Lloyds TSB as SMEs were using a smaller proportion of overdraft facilities.

Term loan margins

4.147. We have time series data on loan margins for two banks—Barclays and Lloyds TSB—and their margins are shown in Figure 4.2. Lloyds TSB had the same reservations about this data as it did for its data on overdrafts (see paragraph 4.145). Again, as with the data on overdrafts, the trends in margins for Barclays but not their value may be compared with those for Lloyds TSB as the latter are for smaller SMEs (Lloyds TSB's Business Banking division).

4.148. Barclays' margin has risen slightly over the period, increasing to 1995 and falling to 2000. Barclays told us that the changes in its loan margin were due to similar reasons as the changes in its overdraft margin (see paragraph 4.146). It added that the improvement in its loan margin after the recession was also due to the implementation of advanced risk assessment systems in the bank. Lloyds TSB's margin (for its Business Banking division) was broadly constant over the period. HSBC's margin on one of its loans—Small Business Loan—rose sharply between 1989 and 1990. HSBC told us that the margin on this product increased due to the higher perceived risk of bad debt. HSBC's Small Business Loan is its only non-mortgage debt product with a standard tariff. It does not account for a major proportion of HSBC's total business lending. In 2000 it accounted for about 3 per cent of HSBC's total lending book for SMEs with an annual turnover of less than £1 million and over one-third of the number of loans by these SMEs.

FIGURE 4.2

Net interest income margins for loans, 1990 to 2000

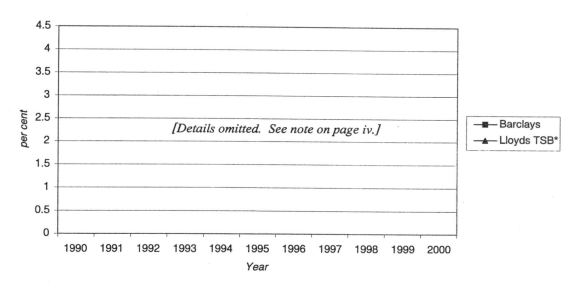

Source: CC calculations on data provided by the banks.

*Business Banking (annual turnover of up to £2 million). Only the trend in this margin can be compared with that of Barclays (see paragraph 4.147).

Margins on other debt products: sales finance and asset finance

4.149. We were provided with data on margins for asset finance products for Barclays from 1993 to 1999 and for sales finance products for Lloyds from 1989 to 1999 and for HSBC from 1991 to 1999 (see Figure 4.3).

FIGURE 4.3

Margins on asset and sales finance, 1989 to 1999

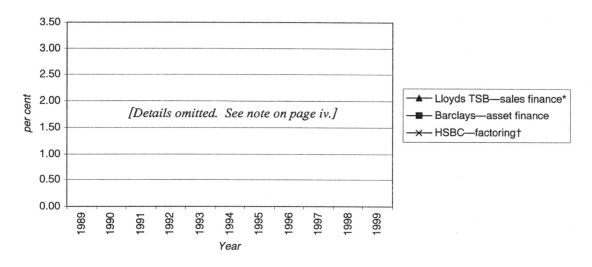

Source: CC calculations on data provided by the banks.

*All businesses.

†With credit protection.

4.150. Apart from a rise and subsequent fall in Lloyds' average margin between 1993 and 1995 and Barclays' average margin between 1995 and 1997, margins have been broadly constant over the period.

Factors affecting the level of margin

4.151. The main clearing groups told us that the level of margin varied depending on a range of factors, including:

(a) risk;

(b) the size of the SME;

(c) the size of the facility;

(d) costs;

(e) whether lending was authorized or unauthorized;

(f) security;

(g) the length of the term of the facility; and

(h) competitors' rates.

4.152. We look at each of these factors in turn.

Risk

4.153. All the main clearing groups told us that risk was a relevant factor in determining margins—higher risks required higher margins. Barclays said that the borrower's credit risk was the most important component of its pricing of SME debt. Lloyds TSB said that the cost of risk was the most variable element in the overall interest charge. HSBC told us that its perception of the degree of risk involved was the most important factor for it to consider in pricing debt finance, and that the cost to the bank in recovering or failing to recover bad debt was high.

Size of SME

4.154. Margins are generally lower for larger SMEs. The main clearing groups said that these differences in margins reflected their assessment that, as a proportion of total costs, the average costs of agreeing and monitoring advances were higher for smaller SMEs. Lloyds TSB told us that the reason for the lower margins for SMEs was because many of the costs incurred (such as administration costs) were fixed and not dependent on the size of the sum being borrowed/the size of the SME, hence average costs as a proportion of total costs would decline as the SME's size, and hence the amount of the total borrowing, increased. The main clearing groups also said that a range of additional factors which might be taken into account when negotiating rates of interest, such as competitor offers and other income earned from the SME, tended to have more influence for larger SMEs.

Size of the facility

4.155. This factor tends to be linked with larger SMEs—larger SMEs tend to have larger loans—and for the same reasons as for larger SMEs margins are generally smaller for larger loans.

Costs

4.156. Two cost factors were mentioned:

(a) first, in relation to fixed-rate products, the relevant cost of funds for the term of the debt product. This cost may be higher or lower than the existing base rate, depending on the market outlook for longer-term interest rates; and

(b) secondly, the ongoing cost of facilities, distinguishing term loans (which were relatively inexpensive to administer) from overdrafts (which required active monitoring).

Authorized or unauthorized lending

4.157. As discussed in paragraphs 4.129 to 4.131, banks generally publish rates for unauthorized borrowing which are significantly higher than would be agreed for authorized lending.

Security

4.158. Many SMEs taking out loans and overdrafts have to provide security and/or personal guarantees to their lenders (see paragraphs 3.244 to 3.256). Secured loans generally have lower margins than unsecured ones.

Length of term of loan

4.159. Barclays, BoI and Ulster Bank listed the term and maturity of facilities as a factor affecting the level of margin. Lloyds TSB said that, other things being equal, the risk of default was generally higher for loans of longer maturity than for loans of short maturity.

Competitors' rates

4.160. The main clearing groups told us that competitor rates affected their·pricing of debt products to SMEs. HSBC said that the prices of personal debt products were also an important factor.

Deposit products offered by the banks

4.161. The main clearing groups offer two types of deposit products: deposit accounts and money market products. We look at each of these in turn. A summary of the business deposit accounts and money market products offered by the main clearing groups is in Appendix 4.1.

Deposit accounts

4.162. The main clearing groups offer instant access deposit accounts and accounts with a notice or term period, for example 14-day notice and one-month notice, some of which require minimum credit balances. All the main clearing groups offer instant access deposit accounts. The four largest clearing banks offer 14-day notice accounts but the other main clearing groups do not. NatWest, Lloyds TSB, BoS and Ulster Bank offer one-month notice accounts while BoI offers a 90-day notice account. None of these accounts are designed for day-to-day transactions.

4.163. Banks also offer deposit accounts, known as Client Accounts, for professional businesses holding funds on behalf of third parties (for example, solicitors) and for charities. Most of these types of accounts incorporate a cheque-book facility and freedom to conduct transactions. Client accounts tend to offer higher rates of interest than equivalent deposit accounts for other SMEs.

4.164. RBSG said that many of NatWest's solicitor customers controlled large sums of money on behalf of their clients. The solicitor usually held these sums in separate accounts, but the rates paid by NatWest to the solicitor customer reflected the fact that an individual deposit was part of a larger pool of money deposited. It also stated that solicitors were valuable as a potential source of business introductions. Lloyds TSB told us that Clients' Call accounts tended to have high levels of transactions, but that they were typically electronic, undertaken by the solicitors and charged for separately.

Money market products

4.165. Apart from investing their funds in deposit accounts, some of the larger SMEs may invest their surplus monies direct on the money market, normally doing this via a bank. All the main clearing groups offer money market products. Unlike most of the rates of interest on deposit accounts which are published, rates offered by banks on money market products are not published—they are usually set at a discount to the prevailing wholesale market rates.

Different types of deposit products by notice or term period

4.166. Table 4.29 shows the breakdown of SME deposit products by type of product—deposit accounts and money market products—and by notice or term period—less than 30 days and 30 days or more.

TABLE 4.29 **Breakdown of deposit products by type of product and by notice/term period, 2000**

per cent*

| | Deposit accounts | | Money market products | |
	Less than 30 days	30 days or more	Less than 30 days	30 days or more
Proportion by number of accounts				
Breakdown within deposit accounts and within money market products				
NatWest—Retail†	99	1	-	-
NatWest—Corporate‡	95	5	-	-
Barclays	100	0	31	69
Lloyds TSB§	97	3	-	-
HSBC¶	99	1	37	63
RBS—Retail†	100	0	-	-
RBS—Corporate‡	100	0	49	51
BoS	96	4	29	71
Clydesdale	100	0	0	100
Ulster Bank	88	12	56	44
Northern	100	0	0	100
Breakdown within all deposit products				
Barclays	95	0	2	4
HSBC¶	90	1	3	6
RBS—Corporate‡	90	0	5	5
BoS	93	4	1	2
Ulster Bank	74	10	9	7
Clydesdale	91	0	0	9
Northern	89	0	0	11
Proportion by value of accounts				
Breakdown within deposit accounts and within money market products				
NatWest—Retail†	94	6	-	-
NatWest—Corporate‡	91	9	-	-
Barclays	100	0	39	61
Lloyds TSB§	95	5	-	-
HSBC¶	96	4	45	55
RBS—Retail†	100	0	-	-
RBS—Corporate‡	100	0	53	47
BoS	70	30	7	93
Clydesdale	100	0	0	100
Ulster Bank	79	21	50	50
Northern	100	0	0	100
Breakdown within all deposit products				
Barclays	49	0	20	31
HSBC¶	30	1	31	37
RBS—Corporate‡	68	0	17	15
BoS	43	18	3	36
Ulster Bank	25	7	34	34
Clydesdale	79	0	0	21
Northern	78	0	0	22

Source: CC calculations based on data provided by the banks.

*Totals may not sum because of rounding.
†Annual turnover of up to £1 million.
‡Annual turnover of up to £100 million.
§Annual turnover of up to £2 million.
¶Includes money market products held by businesses with an annual turnover of up to £100 million.

4.167. Table 4.29 shows that, based on number and value of accounts, deposit accounts with notice or term periods of less than 30 days account for most deposit accounts. For money market products, the split is more even. Deposit accounts of less than 30 days account for most of the number of all deposit products (deposit accounts and money market products). However, by value, the proportions are more evenly split between deposit accounts and money market products.

4.168. We have also calculated the average values of these different types of accounts (see Table 4.30).

TABLE 4.30 **Average value held in different types of deposit product by notice/term period, 2000**

£'000

	Deposit accounts		Money market products	
	Less than 30 days	30 days or more	Less than 30 days	30 days or more
NatWest—Retail*				
NatWest—Corporate†				
Barclays				
Lloyds TSB‡				
HSBC§		*Figures omitted.*		
RBS—Retail*		*See note on page iv.*		
RBS—Corporate†				
BoS				
Clydesdale				
Ulster Bank				
Northern				

Source: CC calculations based on data provided by the banks.

---

*Annual turnover of up to £1 million.
†Annual turnover of up to £100 million.
‡Annual turnover of up to £2 million.
§Includes money market products held by businesses with an annual turnover of up to £100 million.

4.169. Table 4.30 shows that the average value held in deposit accounts with a notice or term period of less than 30 days is, on the whole, much lower than the value held in accounts with a longer notice or term period. However, the average value held in these longer-term deposit accounts is much lower than the value held in money market products.

Business deposit accounts and personal deposit accounts

4.170. This description of business deposit accounts offered by banks has been limited to those products designed specifically for business. Banks tailor particular deposit products to their business customers and to their personal customers. Some of the main clearing groups have argued that personal customers and SMEs are part of the same economic market (see paragraphs 3.49 to 3.53).

4.171. Lloyds TSB told us that it designed and marketed personal deposit accounts for personal customers and business deposit accounts for business customers. It said that it priced the products differently based on its experience that SMEs tended to generate higher operating costs by making more frequent deposits and withdrawals from their deposit accounts than did personal customers.

4.172. RBSG told us that there was not a marked difference in the rates RBS and NatWest offered to business and personal deposits. It said that the overall margins on the personal savings book and on the business book of RBS and NatWest differed by only a few basis points. It stated that the average business savings account was very different from the average personal savings account because the business account generated much greater levels of activity that the personal account. RBSG provided us with data that showed that the annual number of transactions[1] per account on one of NatWest's personal deposit

---

[1]Includes the number of debits and credits (excluding standing orders and ATM withdrawals), items collected, BACS items and nightsafe wallets. The annual number of transactions per account for NatWest's one-month notice business account (Corporate Diamond Reserve) was 3.3.

accounts (First Reserve) was 16.1 compared with 24.9 on one of its business deposit accounts (Business Reserve). RBSG said that this difference would support rates for smaller balances on personal instant access accounts being marginally higher than the business rates. It told us that, for bigger balances, for example £250,000, a personal customer would be quoted the same rate as would a business customer.

4.173. Barclays said that, in general, its business gross rates of interest were higher than the comparable personal rates. It said that in the case of Treasury deposits, personal customers and business customers currently received the same rates.

4.174. HSBC said that it sometimes offered business customers a personal product if it suited their particular needs. It provided data on the rates paid on the two types of personal accounts that are generally offered to business: Instant Access Savings and High Interest Savings account. HSBC said that these two products accounted for around 3 per cent of the number of all business deposit accounts held by SMEs. It said that when setting its business deposit rates, it considered the rates it was offering on its personal products, reflecting that businesses could use personal products if they were more attractive. HSBC told us that any differential in rates between business and personal deposit products reflected the generally higher costs incurred in maintaining and operating business accounts (for example, activity levels on business accounts were much higher) (see paragraph 3.119).

4.175. Table 4.31 shows the differences in the rates of interest offered on personal and business deposit accounts. Negative numbers indicate that the rates on personal accounts are greater than rates on business accounts and positive numbers indicate the reverse (see Appendices 4.2 and 4.3 for rates on business accounts and Appendix 4.4 for rates on personal accounts).

4.176. Table 4.31 shows a mixed picture in relation to the difference in rates between personal and business deposit accounts.

4.177. NatWest's rates on its personal First Reserve account are on the whole higher than those on its Business deposit account whereas the reverse is true for its personal Reward Reserve. Rates on NatWest's 30-day notice account are higher for SMEs for credit balances between £10,000 and up to just under £50,000 and higher for personal customers with credit balances of £50,000 and over.

4.178. Rates for RBS's personal Instant Access account are higher than those for its business account for credit balances up to just under £2,000 and for £10,000 and over. Rates for RBS's personal Gold Deposit account are lower than those for its business account for all balances above £2,000.

4.179. On the whole the difference between the rates of interest on Barclays' personal and business instant access deposit accounts is less than 0.3 percentage points. This is not the case for Barclays' notice accounts (14-day for business and 30-day for personal), where rates for the business product are higher than those for the personal one for credit balances of £2,500 to just under £10,000 and for £25,000 and over.

4.180. Lloyds TSB's personal Instant Gold Savings account offers higher rates (between one and two percentage points) than those on its equivalent business account. The reverse is true for Lloyds TSB's personal Flexible Savings account, the differences being between about 0.5 and 1 percentage points.

4.181. The rates offered by HSBC on its Business No-Notice account were between one and two percentage points below those on its Instant Access personal account. HSBC told us that it discouraged businesses from depositing sums of more than £5,000 in its Business No-Notice account (see paragraph 4.214). It stated that its rates on the Business 14-day Notice account were designed to be roughly in line with the personal Instant Access Savings account for larger balances. As a general point, HSBC said that any differential in rates between business and personal deposit accounts reflected higher costs that it incurred on its business deposit accounts (see paragraph 4.174).

TABLE 4.31 **Difference* in rates of interest payable on business and personal deposit accounts, 2000**

percentage points

Amount invested

	£1	£500	£1k	£2.5k	£5k	£10k	£25k	£50k	£100k
NatWest									
Instant access branch-based†	−0.92	−0.06	−0.06	0.20	0.00	−0.51	−0.46	−0.72	−0.26
Instant access branch-based‡	-	-	-	0.46	0.46	−0.05	−0.01	−0.01	0.45
One-month notice	-	-	-	-	-	0.93	0.93	−0.21	−0.31
Barclays									
Instant access branch-based	0.60	−0.20	−0.20	0.00	−0.10	−0.20	0.20	0.20	0.35
Postal instant access	-	-	-	−0.13	−0.13	−0.13	−0.13	−0.13	0.25
Business 14-day and Personal 30-day	-	-	-	0.55	0.55	−0.05	0.46	0.06	0.22
Lloyds TSB									
Instant access branch-based§	-	-	-	−1.08	−1.08	−1.22	−1.57	−1.71	−1.71
Instant access branch-based¶	-	0.62	0.87	0.77	0.42	0.73	0.73	1.09	1.09
Business 30-day and Personal 90-day	-	-	-	-	-	0.02	0.19	−0.26	−0.35
HSBC									
Instant access branch-based	0.25	−1.25	−1.25	−1.35	−1.10	−1.35	−1.40	−1.85	−1.60
RBS									
Instant access branch-based¤	−0.85	−1.65	−1.65	0.26	0.06	−0.05	−0.25	−0.50	−0.20
Instant access branch-based#	−0.70	−0.70	−0.70	1.11	0.81	0.75	0.75	0.60	0.90
BoS									
Instant access branch-based	0.97	0.08	0.08	−0.67	−0.94	−1.78	−1.25	−1.59	−0.66
Instant access direct	0.00	0.00	0.00	0.00	0.00	0.00	0.00	0.00	0.00
30-day notice	2.24	2.24	2.24	1.94	1.64	0.84	0.44	0.19	0.15
Clydesdale									
Instant access branch-based~	−1.50	−1.50	−1.50	−2.10	−2.10	−2.05	−1.40	−1.50	−1.00
Instant access branch-based★	1.90	0.80	0.80	0.65	0.65	0.15	0.90	0.25	1.25
BoI									
Instant access branch-based	-	0.05	−0.15	0.15	−0.05	−0.65	−0.20	−0.25	0.20
90-day notice	-	0.00	0.00	0.00	0.00	0.00	0.00	0.00	0.00
Northern									
Instant access branch-based❖	-	-	-	−1.78	−1.78	−1.27	−1.80	−1.34	−1.49
Instant access branch-based◆	−0.69	−0.69	−0.69	−0.08	−0.08	0.43	0.05	0.51	0.51
Ulster Bank									
Instant access branch-based	-	-	0.00	0.90	2.40	1.25	2.00	2.50	2.50
30-day notice	-	-	−2.25	−3.25	−3.50	1.25	0.50	1.00	0.50

Source: CC calculations on data in *Business Money£acts* and *Money£acts* and on data supplied by the banks.

*Business rate less personal rate.
†Personal First Reserve.
‡Personal Reward Reserve.
§Personal Instant Gold Savings.
¶Personal Flexible Savings.
¤Personal Instant Access.
#Personal Gold Deposit.
~Personal Savings Account.
★Personal Instant Solutions.
❖Personal Summit Savings.
◆Personal Saver Plus.

4.182. On its branch-based instant access accounts, BoS generally offers higher rates on its personal account than on its equivalent business account; for some credit balances the difference is between 0.5 and just under 2 percentage points. BoS offers its electronic account (Home & Office Banking Service—HOBS) to both personal and business customers with the same rate of interest. Its business 30-day notice account pays much higher rates than its personal account for balances of less than £50,000 but BoS only advertises rates on its business product for credit balances of £50,000 or over.

4.183. Clydesdale's personal Savings Account offers higher rates (between one and two percentage points) than those on its equivalent business account. The reverse is true for its personal Instant Solutions account, the differences being between about 0.5 and 2 percentage points.

4.184. On the whole the difference between the rates of interest on BoI's personal and business deposit accounts is less than 0.3 percentage points. There is no difference for its 90-day notice accounts.

4.185. Northern's rates for its personal Summit Savings account are between one and two percentage points higher than its rates for its business account. For its personal Saver Plus account rates are higher for smaller credit balances (up to just under £10,000) but lower for larger credit balances (£10,000 and over).

4.186. Ulster Bank pays rates of interest between one and three percentage points higher on its business accounts than on its personal ones. First Trust told us that it paid the same rates of interest to SMEs and personal customers.

4.187. HSBC also provided us with data on its margins on business and personal money market products over the period from October 1995 to April 2000. Over this period, margins for business and personal accounts tended to move in line with each other, with business margins being slightly lower than personal margins between 1995 and 1998 (business margins were between about [✂] and [✂] per cent, compared with personal margins between [✂] and [✂] per cent) but slightly higher after 1998 (business margins were between about [✂] and [✂] per cent, compared with personal margins of between [✂] and [✂] per cent). The trend in both margins was relatively flat over the period, but increasing over 1999.

4.188. Barclays told us that it generally paid the same rates on its money market products to business and personal customers.

How are rates and margins determined?

4.189. Factors mentioned by the main clearing groups as influencing the rates of interest offered on their deposit products were as follows:

(a) the underlying cost of funds;

(b) competitor interest rates;

(c) the degree of liquidity associated with deposits;

(d) the size of the deposit;

(e) the access method employed, for example postal, counter;

(f) activity levels and associated costs;

(g) the bank's own liquidity position; and

(h) prudential regulation.

4.190. The main influencing factor for banks in setting interest rates on their deposit accounts is the relevant prevailing rate of interest at which the banks can invest funds. This may be the Bank Base Rate or LIBOR or some other measure of cost of funds.

4.191. HSBC said that the interest rates it paid on its business deposit accounts were heavily influenced by the Bank Base Rate, although they tended to follow the Bank Base Rate with a short lag. Rate changes were normally implemented only once a month.

4.192. RBSG said that the most important factors in setting deposit rates were competitive positioning and its need for funds.

4.193. Whether depositors are required to give banks notice before withdrawing funds from their deposit will affect the interest rate paid on that deposit. Higher interest rates are paid on notice accounts and in the case of fixed-term accounts, higher interest is paid the longer the term. RBSG told us that stable funds were more attractive, which resulted in higher rates being offered on longer-term deposits. HSBC said that this was its practice, which was in line with the structure of interest rates offered by its competitors. It stated that its customers expected this relationship and it was also in line with the term structure of interest rates and the conventional positive yield curve. It told us that there were also some cost advantages to having 14-day notice of withdrawal compared with the instant access accounts.

4.194. Higher rates are generally paid on individual products as the size of the deposit increases. RBSG said that it was usually more cost-effective to operate fewer large balance accounts rather than many small ones, resulting in higher rates being paid for larger deposits. HSBC told us that this was the case with its business deposits and was in line with the structure of interest rates offered by its competitors. It said that this structure was explained in part because consumers expected it. In addition, it stated that it incurred certain fixed costs in supplying a deposit account (for example, management and administration), which were recovered from the gross margin. Fixed costs spread over a larger deposit resulted in higher rates being paid.

4.195. Barclays stated that generally where a lower-cost access method was used, it paid higher rates of interest, for example on its Postal account.

4.196. Lloyds TSB listed the costs of establishing and operating the account as a factor that determined the level of interest rates offered. It said that banking liquidity regulations required it to have liquid assets to cover its wholesale deposit balances and 5 per cent of retail deposit balances that were repayable in five days. It told us that it was also required to place funds on non-interest-bearing deposit with the BoE according to the size of its deposits. It said that these regulations restricted its usage of deposited funds and reduced the returns that could be obtained from deposited funds. Lloyds TSB also stated that rates and margins were influenced by the frequency of calculation of interest on the sums held, the frequency of statement and the level of detail in the statement and whether the account was supported by a sweep facility.

4.197. A factor not listed in paragraph 4.189, but mentioned by HSBC, was a reluctance to reduce rates too far. HSBC said that this would discredit the product. It stated that when base rates fell in the second half of 1998 to an historic low, it did not reduce its deposit rates and thereby suffered a fall in margins. Base rates subsequently rose again in 1999.

Standard and negotiated rates

4.198. In general, banks offer standard rates on their deposit accounts. On their money market products, they generally quote rates when a customer enquires, by reference to prevailing wholesale market rates. The discount applied to the market rates was sometimes open to negotiation.

4.199. RBSG said that (excluding money market products) NatWest did not have negotiated rates of interest for its deposit accounts offered to SMEs. However, in 1998, the Corporate division (£1 million to £100 million annual turnover) introduced discretion for relationship managers to improve deposit rates by up to 0.25 per cent in certain cases. RBSG said that this occurred rarely. Approximately 3 per cent of SMEs using deposit products (4 per cent of balances) had discretionary interest benefits in 1999, the equivalent proportions by December 2000 were 3.5 and 6 per cent. It stated that, while the discretion limit had not changed since its introduction, the use of it had increased. It said that the reason for this was that NatWest's overall need for wholesale deposits was low, thereby reducing the competitiveness of the deposit rates NatWest was offering. RBSG stated that in order to retain valuable customers (when the whole banking relationship was examined) that might otherwise have switched suppliers, deposit rates could be improved. In these cases, RBSG said that negotiated rates did not reflect direct costs, but relationship values.

4.200. RBSG told us that RBS offered two main deposit products that had negotiable rates of interest: Client Deposit Service and Special Interest Bearing account. It provided us with numbers of SME accounts with RBS with a standard rate of interest and with a negotiated rate of interest. In 1999 about [✂] per cent of retail accounts had a standard rate of interest, while less than [✂] per cent of corporate accounts had a standard rate of interest.

4.201. Barclays stated that it did not actively promote its deposit accounts (apart from money market products) as having interest rates which were open to negotiation. It said that it would consider the value of the client relationship and the size and term of the deposit in negotiating an interest rate. It provided data on the proportion of two of its instant access deposit accounts (Business Premium and Clients Premium) used by SMEs with negotiated rates of interest at year-end 1999. Overall, only one-third of 1 per cent of Business Premium accounts to SMEs had negotiated rates. SMEs in the over £5 million to £10 million and over £10 million to £25 million turnover categories had proportions higher than this average, at about 1.2 per cent. A higher proportion (14 per cent) of Clients Premium accounts were subject to negotiated rates, with a proportion of about 25 per cent in the case of the two larger turnover categories. Overall, 2.3 per cent of SMEs with these deposit accounts in 1999 were subject to negotiated rates of interest. Barclays did not have data for its other deposit accounts but believed that negotiation was infrequent.

4.202. Lloyds TSB said that it did not negotiate variations to the standard rates of interest applicable to its accounts. It had offered a deposit account which had negotiated rates, but this was withdrawn in October 1998.

4.203. HSBC said that the only deposit products where individual managers could renegotiate centrally determined rates were money market products. For these deposits, standard rates are set centrally and advised to branches daily. However, branches would normally telephone their Regional Treasury Centre for every transaction to confirm current rates and could seek variances to the standard rates where they deemed it necessary either to attract monies or to protect a relationship. For money market overnight deposits, rates were not published, owing to their extreme volatility, and were advised to the customer at the time of lodging the deposit.

4.204. BoS said that standard rates of interest were paid on its Business Investment account and HOBS Investment account and that its policy was not to negotiate with SMEs where a product offered a standard interest rate. It said that it believed the number of non-standard rates on deposits was small.

Margins in 1999

4.205. Table 4.32 shows the net interest income margins for deposits in 1999. The derivation of these margins is shown in Chapter 6. As with lending, the margin is the difference between the interest income and interest cost to the banks. For deposits, it is the difference between rate of interest paid to SMEs by the banks and the interest income generated by the banks on the funds. The interest income to the banks may be the Bank Base Rate or LIBOR or some other rate. The margin does not take into account other costs associated with providing deposit products.

TABLE 4.32 **Net interest income margins of deposits, 1999**

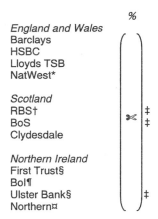

%

England and Wales
Barclays
HSBC
Lloyds TSB
NatWest*

Scotland
RBS†   ‡
BoS   ‡
Clydesdale

Northern Ireland
First Trust§
BoI¶
Ulster Bank§   ‡
Northern¤

Source: CC calculations on data provided by the banks.

*Annual turnover of up to £1 million.
†Annual turnover of up to £10 million.
‡Includes money market products.
§Deposit account and current account credit balances.
¶Year ending March 2000.
¤NAB told us that the margin for Northern was an overestimate as it included deposits with its global wholesale financial services division.

4.206. Table 4.32 shows that HSBC and NatWest have a larger margin ([✂] per cent) than Barclays (just over [✂] per cent) and Lloyds TSB ([✂] per cent). NatWest's margin is based on SMEs with an annual turnover of less than £1 million. We would expect its margin for SMEs with an annual turnover of less than £25 million to be lower than this: based on data from the other main clearing groups, we would expect a margin of just over [✂] per cent, similar to that of Barclays. RBS has a higher margin (just over [✂] per cent) than BoS (just under [✂] per cent). The margins in Northern Ireland are between [✂] per cent.

Trends in margins

4.207. We begin this section by examining the trends in the overall margins for all deposit products held by SMEs. We then look at the trends in specific products.

Overall margin

4.208. We have time series data for only three banks—Barclays, NatWest and HSBC. The trends for these three banks are shown in Figure 4.4. The trends in margins but not the value may be compared, because the margins for Barclays include money market deposits[1] whereas those for HSBC and NatWest do not. Banks tend to have lower margins on money market products.

FIGURE 4.4

Net interest income margins for deposits, 1990 to 2000

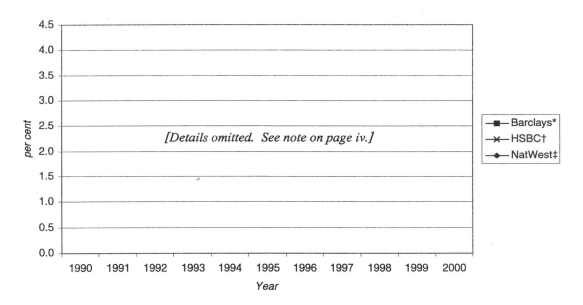

Source: CC calculations on data provided by the banks.
*Includes money market products. The trend in this margin but not the value can be compared with those of HSBC and NatWest (see paragraph 4.208).
†Excludes money market products. The value of deposits outstanding in 2000 (£3 billion) is a CC estimate.
‡Weighted average estimated by CC. Excludes money market products.

4.209. Figure 4.4 shows that Barclays' margin rose slightly between 1990 and 2000 with the main increase occurring in the first half of the period. NatWest's margin fell slightly between 1990 and 2000 with the main fall occurring in the first half of the period. HSBC's margin was broadly constant between

---

[1]The margin for Barclays in Table 4.32 excludes money market products.

1995 and 2000.[1] The trend in NatWest's margin is heavily influenced by one of its accounts (Deposit Account) which has much higher margins than its other main deposit accounts. Although this account comprised about one-fifth of NatWest's deposits in 1990, very few of NatWest's SMEs have held this account since the mid-1990s. NatWest's margin shows an increase between 1990 and 2000 when this account is excluded from the period. Barclays pointed out that its margin had fallen fairly consistently since 1993 (with the exception of a peak in 1996 which it said was distorted by the averaging of year-end balances). Barclays argued that the fall in its margin ([✀] per cent between 1993 and 2000) was clear evidence of the powerful impact of price competition in the market for SME deposits. The fall in Barclays' average margin between 1996 and 2000 (about [✀] per cent) occurred during the same period as its money market products—which have a lower margin than its deposit accounts ([✀] per cent compared with [✀] per cent in 1999 and 2000)—increased their proportion of the value of all Barclays deposit products held by SMEs from [✀] per cent. Barclays told us that it was this increase in the proportion of money market products and the shift in customer deposit balances to higher-interest products and accounts that led to the fall in its overall margin.

Specific products

4.210. We asked the four largest clearing banks to provide us with data on their margins on specific deposit account products supplied to SMEs for the period 1989 to 1999. We deal first with instant access accounts, then with notice accounts and finally with money market products.

Instant access accounts

4.211. Figure 4.5 shows margins achieved by these four banks over the period 1989 to 1999 on the banks' main SME instant access deposit accounts for deposits of £25,000 to just under £100,000. This value of deposits was chosen because the trend is broadly representative of the trends of other values of deposit and was the value for which the longest time series of data was provided. Barclays told us that the average balance on its instant access deposit accounts was lower than value range we had chosen. Differences in trends between different accounts and amounts of deposit are highlighted below.

4.212. Figure 4.5 shows that all four banks increased their margins over the period but that there was a difference between Lloyds TSB and the three other banks. Lloyds TSB increased its margin to a greater extent in the second part of the period (1996 to 1999—an annual average rate of increase of about [✀] per cent) than in the first (1990 to 1995—an annual average rate of increase of about [✀] per cent). The reverse is true for the three other banks, their margins in the first period increasing at a rate of about [✀] per cent a year compared with annual average rate of increase of about [✀] per cent for Barclays and NatWest and about [✀] per cent for HSBC. RSBG told us that the trend for NatWest should be seen as an illustration of NatWest's deposit margin as at the start of the period covered, NatWest did not have standard notice deposit products: instant access accounts therefore represented all of its deposit balances, compared with slightly more than 50 per cent in 1999.

4.213. One exception to the general trend illustrated in Figure 4.5 is for smaller balances in the earlier years. NatWest's margin on balances of £500 to just under £2,000 fell between 1990 and 1994. Barclays' margins did so between 1992 and 1995 for balances of up to just under £2,000. Similarly, Lloyds TSB's margins on deposits of up to just under £1,000 fell between 1992 and 1996.

---

[1]The margins for Barclays and HSBC are actual net interest income as a proportion of deposit balances whereas those for NatWest are weighted averages (by value) of its main deposit accounts where the margins for each account are average rates of interest less average base rates.

FIGURE 4.5

**Margins on Business No-Notice deposit accounts,
25,000 to £100,000, 1989 to 1999**

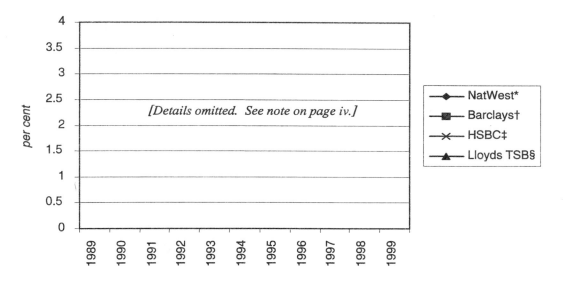

Source: The banks and CC calculations based on data provided by the banks.
*Business Reserve account.
†Business Premium account. Yearly average margins derived from daily margins provided.
‡Business No-Notice account (formerly MoneyMaster).
§Business Call account. £10,000 to £50,000.

4.214. HSBC said that its instant access deposit account was designed to accommodate low-value, short-term deposits with a high level of activity rather than the amounts covered in Figure 4.5. It stated that it discouraged SMEs from depositing more than £5,000 in its instant access account, higher rates being available for these larger balances on its 14-day notice account. It told us that this was particularly relevant to very large balances, such as £25,000 to just under £100,000—the band represented in Figure 4.5. HSBC said that one factor influencing its rates on the Business No-Notice account was its wish to discourage businesses with more than £5,000 from investing in that account. Until 1998 it also paid no interest on Business No-Notice balances below £5,000. It stated that it had started paying interest for fair-value pricing reasons. It told us that the low rate it paid to businesses for balances below £5,000 dated back to this previous policy, but also reflected the fact that business customers did not typically concern themselves with relatively modest balances.

4.215. However, HSBC also told us that the average balance in its instant access account as at 31 January 2000 was £22,000. As stated above (see paragraph 4.211), we used the value range of £25,000 to £100,000 because the trend is broadly representative of the trends of other values of deposit. HSBC disputed this. It provided us with data showing its margin on its instant access deposit account for values of less than £5,000. These margins increased from about [✂] per cent in 1989 to just under [✂] per cent in 2000, an increase of over [✂] per cent. Much of this increase occurred between 1989 and 1992 when margins rose from [✂] to just under [✂] per cent. They then fell to just over [✂] per cent in 1996 and rose to 2000 with a dip in 1999. The trend in the margin for HSBC's instant access account for the value range of £5,000 to just under £25,000 is the same as that for the value range of £25,000 to just under £100,000.

Notice accounts

4.216. Margins on Business 14-day Notice accounts for NatWest, Barclays, Lloyds TSB and HSBC, for deposits of £25,000 to £100,000, are displayed in Figure 4.6.

131

FIGURE 4.6

Margins on Business 14-day Notice accounts,
£25,000 to £100,000, 1991 to 1999

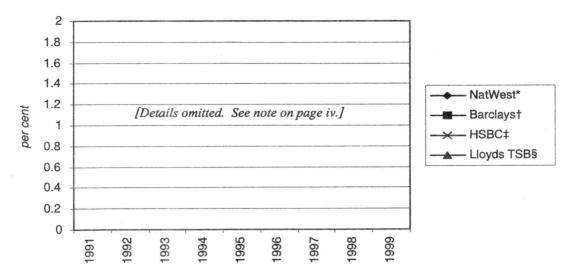

Source: The banks and CC calculations based on data provided by the banks.
*Capital Reserve account.
†HI Business account.
‡Business 14-day Notice account.
§Premier Interest account.

4.217. Figure 4.6 shows that all four banks increased their margins over the period, with all experiencing larger increases in the first part of the period (1992 to 1995) than in the second part (1996 to 1999). [✂] had the smallest increase—an annual average rate of increase of about [✂] per cent between 1992 and 1999; its margins fell by a rate of about [✂] per cent a year between 1996 and 1999. The three other banks experienced increases at rates of between [✂] and [✂] per cent a year in the first period and increases at rates of between [✂] and [✂] per cent a year in the second period.

4.218. Margins on NatWest's 30-day notice deposit account were provided for the period 1996 to 2000. These margins fell between 1996 and 1999 and increased in 2000.

4.219. We have not calculated the trend in margins for Lloyds TSB's 30-day notice account as it was only introduced in October 1998.

Trends in margins on money market products

4.220. Only HSBC provided us with margins on money market products over time—from October 1995 to May 2000. HSBC said that the margins were an average of all negotiated rates for each month for its business banking customers (ie not just SMEs). The cost of funds used in order to calculate the margin was the London Interbank Bid Rate (LIBID) at the time of the transaction. These margins are shown in Figure 4.7.

4.221. Figure 4.7 shows that the trend in margins on HSBC's money market products has been quite flat. The level of the margin is significantly lower than the margin on business deposit accounts (held by SMEs), at around [✂] per cent. HSBC said that the large size of such deposits, combined with a high proportion (81 per cent by value) of its money market accounts being notice period deposits rather than instant access, enabled higher rates to be paid on money market deposits. It told us that using the average margin for money market products to make a comparison with specific deposit products was meaningless, as the money market margin was not weighted for value or term. It said that it was more appropriate to compare the maximum margin on its 14-day notice money market product which was [✂] per cent between October 1999 and December 2000 and the margin on its 14-day notice deposit account which was [✂] per cent for the same period. However, while HSBC is comparing different products with the same term—14-day notice—it is comparing a maximum rate with what is in effect an average rate. In contrast with the view that the margins on these two types of products are comparable, HSBC also told us that the large average size of its money market balances relative to the costs led to its money market margins being substantially lower than those it achieved on standard deposit accounts. HSBC said that the large size of the customers, the wholesale and commodity nature of such deposits and the ease with which they could switch to alternative brokers of money market deposit products also contributed to the lower margins.

FIGURE 4.7

HSBC's margins on money market products for all business banking customers, 1995 to 2000

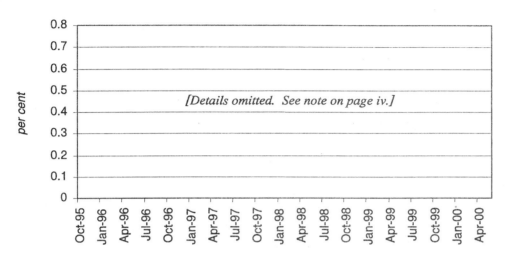

Source: HSBC.

4.222. Barclays said that it could not provide an analysis of margins on its Treasury Deposits over time because the duration and value of each contract was unique. However, Barclays did provide us with a list of current (provided on 24 November 2000) margins applied to its Treasury Deposits. The margins were based on LIBOR for term Treasury Deposits and on base rate for Call and 7 Day Notice Treasury Deposits.

4.223. Barclays' overall margin on money market products used by SMEs was [✂] per cent in 1999 and 2000. The margins provided fell as the level of deposit increased. For term Treasury Deposits, margins ranged from [✂] per cent for deposits of £1 million to less than £5 million for terms of between one and twelve months, to [✂] per cent for overnight deposits of between £250,000 and £499,999. Barclays said that for term Treasury Deposits (including overnight) over £5 million, the standard margin was [✂] per cent, using LIBOR as the comparable rate. Margins on call and seven-day notice accounts (based on base rate) varied from [✂] per cent for balances between £1 and £5 million, to [✂] per cent for smaller balances. Lloyds TSB provided us with data that showed that its margin on money market products attributable to SMEs was just under [✂] per cent in 2000. RBSG provided us with data that showed that NatWest's margin on money market products used by SMEs in NatWest's Retail business was [✂] per cent in 1999. BoI's data showed that its margin on money market products was [✂] per cent in the year ending March 2000.

Comparison of deposit interest rates in 2000

4.224. *Business MoneyEacts* publishes regular comparisons of deposit rates on offer in the UK. We examined the rates in the September 2000 edition. We checked the data in *Business MoneyEacts* against data provided to us by the main clearing groups and where these differed we used the data provided by the banks.

4.225. HSBC said that interest rates were only one feature of deposit accounts and that customers weighted up other factors such as notice period and minimum balance when deciding where to open an account. It told us that it competed on price, term, notice and access. HSBC stated that those accounts which offered higher rates generally imposed more restrictions on the SME and that rates could not be considered independently of access.

Branch-based instant access accounts

4.226. Table 4.33 shows the rates offered by the main clearing groups on their business deposit accounts in 2000 (see Appendix 4.2 for further details). It also shows the differences between the highest and lowest rates where the differences are expressed as a proportion of the interest rate.

TABLE 4.33 **Rates of interest on instant access branch-based business deposit products**

per cent

					Amount invested					
	£1	£500	£1k	£2.5k	£5k	£10k	£25k	£50k	£100k	£250k
England and Wales										
NatWest	1.10	1.96	1.96	2.22	2.22	2.22	2.57	2.57	3.03	3.17
Barclays	2.12	2.12	2.12	2.32	2.32	2.32	2.73	2.73	2.88	3.14
Lloyds TSB	1.97	1.97	2.22	2.22	2.22	2.53	2.53	2.89	2.89	3.09
HSBC	2.25	2.25	2.25	2.25	2.50	2.50	2.75	2.75	3.00	3.25
Difference of highest to lowest rate (%)	105	15	15	5	13	14	9	12	5	5
Number of other branch-based providers with higher rates*	1	10	11	13	14	15	17	17	15	14
Highest rates of branch-based providers	3.45	4.5	4.5	4.5	4.5	4.5	5.15	5.65	6	6
Increase compared with highest rate of large four (%)	53	100	100	94	80	78	87	96	98	85
Scotland										
RBS	0.25	0.25	0.25	2.26	2.26	2.40	2.65	2.65	2.95	3.17
BoS	2.63	2.63	2.63	2.63	2.63	2.63	3.51	3.51	4.65	4.65
Clydesdale	2.02	2.02	2.02	2.02	2.02	2.27	3.03	3.03	4.06	4.58
Lloyds TSB	1.97	1.97	2.22	2.22	2.22	2.53	2.53	2.89	2.89	3.09
Difference of highest to lowest rate (%)	952	952	952	30	30	16	39	32	61	50
Northern Ireland										
Northern	1.51	1.51	1.51	2.52	2.52	3.03	3.55	4.01	4.01	4.78
Bol†	-	2.15	2.15	2.45	2.70	2.70	3.60	4.00	4.70	4.70
First Trust	0.85	1.10	1.10	2.75	2.75	3.25	4.25	4.25	4.25	4.25
Ulster Bank	-	-	0.50	1.50	3.0	3.0	4.0	4.5	4.5	4.5
Difference of highest to lowest rate (%)	78	95	330	83	19	20	20	13	17	12

Source: Business Money£acts and data provided by the banks and CC calculations.

---

*Appendix 4.2 shows the rates of interest offered by other providers, some of which are lower than those offered by the four largest clearing banks.
†Gross rates for Premium Business Reserve.

4.227. The differences between the highest and lowest rates of the four largest clearing banks are between 5 and 15 per cent. However, for rates on credit balances of up to just under £500, the difference is 105 per cent as NatWest's rate is much lower than those of the other three banks. The average value held in deposit accounts with a notice or term period of less than 30 days is between £10,000 and £20,000 in England and Wales (see Table 4.30). For these values, NatWest offers the lowest rate of interest of these four banks and Lloyds TSB offers the highest, but the highest rate offered by other providers is 78 per cent higher than that offered by Lloyds TSB.

4.228. We have compared the rates of interest of the four largest clearing banks with those offered by other branch-based providers—mainly building societies. We identified 21 other branch-based providers from *Business Money£acts*.[1] Between 10 and 17 of them offer higher rates of interest than the

---

[1]BoS, Cheshire Building Society, Citibank, the Co-operative Bank, Coventry Building Society, Derbyshire Building Society, Ecology Building Society, Halifax, Loughborough Building Society, Manchester Building Society, Mansfield Building Society, Melton Mowbray Building Society, Nationwide, Newbury Building Society, Norwich & Peterborough, Nottingham Building Society, Skipton Building Society, Stafford Railway Building Society, Tipton & Coseley Building Society, Yorkshire and Yorkshire Building Society. Barclays told us that *Business Money£acts* showed 66 deposit account providers. These included the four largest clearing banks. The remainder included the following providers: those with notice accounts, those where savings are permitted from their local area only, those with direct accounts, those operating outside England and Wales and those that told us they did not provide banking services to SMEs.

highest rate offered by the four largest clearing banks. However, for credit balances up to just under £500 there is only one other branch-based provider that offers a higher rate than the highest rate offered by the four largest clearing banks. The rates offered by these other providers are between 50 and 100 per cent higher than the highest rates offered by the four largest clearing banks.

4.229. The differences between the highest and lowest rates of BoS, Clydesdale, Lloyd TSB and RBS are between 16 and 61 per cent. However, for the smaller credit balances (up to just under £2,000), the difference is over 950 per cent as RBS's rates are much lower than those of the other three banks. The average value held in deposit accounts with a notice or term period of less than 30 days is between £20,000 and £40,000 in Scotland (see Table 4.30). For these values, Clydesdale and Lloyds TSB offer lower rates of interest than BoS and RBS, and BoS offers the highest rates.

4.230. The differences between the highest and lowest rates of the Northern Irish banks are between 12 and 95 per cent. However, for rates on credit balances between £1,000 up to just under £2,500 the difference is 330 per cent, as Ulster Bank's rate is much lower than those of the other three banks. The average value held in deposit accounts with a notice or term period of less than 30 days is between £20,000 and £50,000 in Northern Ireland (see Table 4.30). For these values, BoI and Northern offer the lowest rate of interest and First Trust offers the highest.

Branch-based 14-day notice accounts

4.231. Table 4.34 shows the rates offered by the four largest clearing banks on their 14-day notice accounts in 2000 (see Appendix 4.2 for further details). It also shows the differences between the highest and lowest rates where the differences are expressed as a proportion of the interest rate. The other main clearing groups do not offer such accounts.

TABLE 4.34 **Rates of interest on branch-based 14-day notice deposit accounts**

per cent

	Amount invested									
	£1	£500	£1k	£2.5k	£5k	£10k	£25k	£50k	£100k	£250k
England and Wales										
NatWest*	-	-	-	3.39	3.39	3.39	4.06	4.06	4.42	4.68
Barclays*	-	-	-	3.55	3.55	3.55	4.06	4.06	4.42	4.68
Lloyds TSB	2.53	2.53	2.53	2.53	2.53	3.76	4.18	4.18	4.44	4.65
HSBC†	2.25	2.25	2.25	2.25	3.65	3.65	4.65	4.65	4.75	4.85
Difference of highest to lowest rate (%)	12	12	12	58	44	11	15	15	7	4
Number of other branch-based providers with higher rates (for instant access accounts)‡	1	8	8	4	4	6	2	3	3	3
Highest rates of branch-based providers	3.45	4.50	4.50	4.50	4.50	4.50	5.15	5.65	6	6
Increase compared with highest rate of large four (%)	36	78	78	27	23	20	11	22	26	24

Source: Business Money£acts and data provided by the banks and CC calculations.

*Minimum balance of £2,000 and rate for £2,500 applies to credit balance of £2,000.
†Minimum opening balance of £5,000.
‡Appendix 4.2 shows the rates of interest offered by other providers, some of which are lower than those offered by the four largest clearing banks.

4.232. Table 4.34 shows that only Lloyds TSB and HSBC offer rates of interest on credit balances of less than £2,000, although HSBC's account has a minimum balance of £5,000 so that it pays instant access rates on these lower amounts. The differences between the highest and lowest rates are between 4 and 15 per cent. However, for rates on credit balances between £2,500 and up to just under £5,000 and between £5,000 and up to just under £10,000, the differences are about 58 and over 40 per cent respectively. The average value held in deposit accounts with a notice or term period of less than 30 days is between £10,000 and £20,000 in England and Wales (see Table 4.30). For these values, Lloyds TSB offers a higher rate of interest than HSBC, Barclays and NatWest. The highest rate offered by other providers (for instant access accounts) is 20 per cent higher than that offered by Lloyds TSB.

4.233. As there are relatively few other providers that offer 14-day notice accounts, we have compared the rates of interest for 14-day notice accounts of the four largest clearing banks with those for instant access accounts offered by other branch-based providers. Between one and eight other branch-based providers offer higher rates of interest on instant access accounts than the highest rate offered by any of the four largest clearing banks on 14-day notice accounts. The rates offered by these other providers on instant access accounts are between 11 and 78 per cent higher than the highest rates offered by any of the four largest clearing banks on 14-day notice accounts.

30-day and more notice accounts

4.234. Table 4.35 shows the rates of interest offered by the main clearing groups in 2000 on their 30-day notice accounts and for BoI's 90-day notice account (see Appendix 4.3 for further details). It also shows the differences between the highest and lowest rates where the differences are expressed as a proportion of the interest rate. Only four of the main clearing groups—BoI, Lloyds TSB, NatWest and Ulster Bank—offer such accounts.

TABLE 4.35 **Rates of interest on branch-based 30-day or more notice deposit accounts**

per cent

					Amount invested					
	£1	£500	£1k	£2.5k	£5k	£10k	£25k	£50k	£100k	£250k
NatWest*						3.97	4.49	4.49	4.75	5.01
Lloyds TSB	1.00	1.00	1.00	1.00	1.00	3.92	4.44	4.44	4.75	4.80
Ulster Bank*	0.25	0.25	0.25	0.25	0.25	5.00	5.00	5.50	5.50	5.50
BoI†	-	1.70	1.70	3.05	4.30	4.65	5.25	5.35	5.50	5.50
Difference of highest to lowest rate (%)	300	580	580	1,120	1,620	28	18	24	16	15
Highest rates of branch-based providers (for instant access accounts)‡	3.45	4.50	4.50	4.50	4.50	4.50	5.15	5.65	6	6
Increase compared with NatWest (%)	-	-	-	-	-	13	15	26	26	20

Source: Business Money£acts and data provided by the banks and CC calculations.

*Minimum balance of £10,000.
†90-day. For Northern Ireland only.
‡Appendix 4.2 shows the rates of interest offered by other providers, some of which are lower than those offered by the above providers.

4.235. Of the main clearing groups that offer 30-day branch-based notice accounts, Lloyds TSB and Ulster Bank offer rates of interest on credit balances of less than £10,000, although Lloyds TSB offers a very low rate and RBSG told us that Ulster Bank's rate should be seen as a default rate under its £10,000 minimum balance. BoI offers interest on small credit balances for its 90-day notice account. Excluding Ulster Bank's default rates, the differences between the highest and lowest rates are between 15 and 28 per cent.

4.236. There are relatively few providers that offer branch-based 30-day notice accounts. Barclays said that this was not surprising as there was little need for these accounts to be branch-based as they were not closely related to the transaction needs of SMEs. Of those that do, Ulster Bank offers the highest rates of interest. There are other branch-based providers that offer longer notice accounts and some of these offer rates of interest higher than Ulster Bank for some credit balances. We have compared the rates of interest for NatWest's 30-day notice account for credit balances of £10,000 and over (it has slightly higher rates than Lloyds TSB) with those for instant access accounts offered by other branch-based providers. We found that some other providers offer higher rates of interest on instant access accounts than NatWest offers on its 30-day notice account. For credit balances of £10,000 or more, the highest rates offered on branch-based instant access accounts are between 13 and 26 per cent higher than NatWest's rates on its 30-day notice account.

4.237. Turning to direct business accounts, these accounts generally offer higher rates than branch-based accounts with comparable notice periods. Table 4.36 compares the rates of interest offered by Barclays, BoS and RBS on their direct and branch-based accounts and compares the rates on their direct accounts with the highest rates offered by other providers (see Appendix 4.2 for further details).

TABLE 4.36 **Rates of interest on direct and branch-based deposit accounts, 2000**

										per cent
					Amount saved					
	£1	£500	£1k	£2.5k	£5k	£10k	£25k	£50k	£100k	£250k
Barclays										
Direct	-	-	-	4.19	4.19	4.45	4.71	4.71	5.09	5.61
Branch-based	2.12	2.12	2.12	2.32	2.32	2.32	2.73	2.73	2.88	3.14
Difference (percentage points)	-	-	-	1.87	1.87	2.13	1.98	1.98	2.21	2.47
RBS										
Direct	-	4.30	4.30	4.30	4.30	4.30	4.55	4.55	5.15	5.50
Branch-based	0.25	0.25	0.25	2.26	2.26	2.40	2.65	2.65	2.95	3.17
Difference (percentage points)	-	4.05	4.05	2.04	2.04	1.90	1.90	1.90	2.20	2.33
BoS										
Direct	3.29	3.29	3.29	3.29	3.29	3.29	4.47	4.94	5.41	5.41
Branch-based	2.63	2.63	2.63	2.63	2.63	2.63	3.51	3.51	4.65	4.65
Difference (percentage points)	0.66	0.66	0.66	0.66	0.66	0.66	0.96	1.43	0.76	0.76
Maximum rate on direct accounts offered by other providers*	5.46	5.46	5.50	5.50	5.50	6.00	6.00	6.00	6.00	6.00
Increase compared with:										
Barclays	-	-	-	31	31	35	27	27	18	7
Highest of BoS/RBS	66	27	28	28	28	40	32	21	11	9

Source: CC calculations on data provided by the banks and from *Business Money£acts.*

*Appendix 4.2 shows the rates of interest offered by other providers, some of which are lower than those offered by the above providers.

4.238. The differences in the rates of interest between the direct and branch-based accounts of Barclays, BoS and RBS are mainly in the range of 0.7 and 2.5 percentage points. The difference is over four percentage points for RBS below its minimum balance of £2,000 on its branch-based account. RBSG told us that its rate for balances of less than £2,000 should be seen as a default rate. Some other providers offer much higher rates of interest on direct accounts than Barclays, BoS and RBS, for example Alliance & Leicester, Northern Rock plc, Scottish Widows Fund and Life Assurance Society and Standard Life Bank. The highest rates offered by these providers are between 7 and 35 per cent higher than the rates offered by Barclays and between 9 and 66 per cent higher than the highest rates offered by BoS or RBS.

Difference between rates of interest on retail and wholesale deposits

4.239. We compared the differences in the rates of interest between retail deposits (as given by the banks to SMEs) of different lengths of notice with the corresponding differences for wholesale deposits.[1] The results are shown in Table 4.37.

---

[1]We used LIBOR as the rate paid on wholesale deposits.

TABLE 4.37 **Differences in rates of interest on wholesale and retail deposit according to length of notice, 2000*†**

percentage points

Amount invested

	£1	£500	£1k	£2.5k	£5k	£10k	£25k	£50k	£100k	£250k
England and Wales										
Differences in rates on retail instant access and 14-day notice										
Barclays	-	-	-	1.23	1.23	1.23	1.33	1.33	1.54	1.54
NatWest	-	-	-	1.17	1.17	1.17	1.49	1.49	1.39	1.51
Lloyds TSB	0.56	0.56	0.31	0.31	0.31	1.23	1.65	1.29	1.55	1.56
HSBC	0.00	0.00	0.00	0.00	1.15	1.15	1.90	1.90	1.75	1.60
Difference in LIBOR	0.07	0.07	0.07	0.07	0.07	0.07	0.07	0.07	0.07	0.07
Differences in rates on retail 14-day and 30-day notice										
NatWest	-	-	-	-	-	0.58	0.43	0.43	0.33	0.33
Lloyds TSB	−1.53	−1.53	−1.53	−1.53	−1.53	0.16	0.26	0.26	0.31	0.15
Difference in LIBOR	0.06	0.06	0.06	0.06	0.06	0.06	0.06	0.06	0.06	0.06
Differences in rates on retail instant access and 30-day notice										
NatWest	-	-	-	-	-	1.75	1.92	1.92	1.72	1.84
Lloyds TSB	−0.97	−0.97	−1.22	−1.22	−1.22	1.39	1.91	1.55	1.86	1.71
Difference in LIBOR	0.12	0.12	0.12	0.12	0.12	0.12	0.12	0.12	0.12	0.12
Northern Ireland										
Differences in rates on retail instant access and 30-day notice										
Ulster Bank‡	-	-	-	-	-	2.00	1.00	1.00	1.00	1.00
Difference in LIBOR	0.12	0.12	0.12	0.12	0.12	0.12	0.12	0.12	0.12	0.12
Differences in rates on retail instant access and 90-day notice										
BoI	-	−0.45	−0.45	0.60	1.60	1.95	1.65	1.35	0.80	0.80
Difference in LIBOR	0.25	0.25	0.25	0.25	0.25	0.25	0.25	0.25	0.25	0.25

Source: CC calculations on data in *Business Money£acts* and provided by the banks and by the BoE.

*Average LIBOR rates used to represent wholesale rates.
†Longer-term rates minus shorter-term rates.
‡Excludes Ulster Bank's default rates on balances of less than £10,000.

4.240. Table 4.37 shows that on the whole, the differences in retail rates of interest are much larger than the differences in wholesale rates. The negative numbers in Table 4.37 arise because the retail rates of interest are higher on the shorter-term accounts than on the longer-term accounts.

Comparison of overall pricing

4.241. It is difficult to consolidate all the data on prices charged to SMEs by the main clearing groups for money transmission services, overdrafts, loans and deposit accounts, in order to say categorically that one bank is, overall, cheaper than another bank. The different products are priced differently, there are different pricing regimes depending on whether the SME is a start-up, a switcher, provides security, etc. Bearing this in mind, it is possible to make a broad assessment of how the banks compare on pricing.

4.242. In order to compare the overall prices of the main clearing groups we estimated illustrative overall charges paid by smaller and larger SMEs. For smaller SMEs, we assumed an overdraft of £2,000, a loan of £10,000 and a deposit account balance of £10,000. Our equivalent values for larger SMEs were £10,000 (overdraft), £50,000 (loan) and £30,000 (deposit). We received comments on our estimates from three of the four largest clearing groups. For example, HSBC and Lloyds TSB did not consider that these charges were typical of a representative SME—they should be seen as being for illustrative purposes only, as the actual charges paid would depend on the usage and requirements of the SME. NAB also made this point. We accept that there will be variations around our estimates but we believe that having compared charges of particular banking services—money transmission fees, margins on overdrafts, loans and deposits—it is useful to combine these services and compare overall charges. We used our estimates of average money transmission charges (see Table 4.9), of average margins for overdrafts and loans (see

138

Tables 4.21 and 4.25) and rates of interest paid on instant access deposits (see Table 4.33). We estimated these components for the banks where we did not have the required data. We compared overall prices for money transmission, overdrafts, loans and deposits using two different methods and for overall prices for money transmission, overdrafts, and deposits—the latter being broadly comparable with the liquidity management services market. In our first method we deducted the rates of interest paid on deposits from the charges for money transmission services and lending. In the second method, in order to take account of forgone income to SMEs, we added back the rates on deposits that SMEs would have received had they used the deposit accounts offering the highest rate of interest. For simplicity we used the highest rates offered on branch-based instant access accounts by the banks shown in Table 4.38 for the relevant countries. In order to compare overall prices in the liquidity management services market we deducted rates of interest paid on loans from our second method. Our illustrative charges will underestimate the charges paid by SMEs using these mixes of banking services. This is because we have used margins and not rates of interest for lending, we have excluded any fees for lending and we have excluded charges for non-core money transmission services. Our results are shown in Table 4.38.

TABLE 4.38 **Illustrative overall annual charges of the main clearing groups for larger and smaller SMEs**

£*

	Overall charges —method 1†			Overall charges —method 2‡			Overall charges in liquidity management services market§		
	Smaller SMEs¶	Larger SMEs¤	Simple average	Smaller SMEs¶	Larger SMEs¤	Simple average	Smaller SMEs¶	Larger SMEs¤	Simple average
England and Wales									
NatWest	280	930	600	530	1,750	1,140	340	800	570
Barclays	280	860	570	540	1,690	1,110	310	540	420
Lloyds TSB	330	1,080	710	580	1,910	1,250	350	760	560
HSBC	250	910	580	510	1,730	1,120	280	580	430
Scotland									
RBS	410	920	670	680	1,970	1,320	460	870	660
BoS	350	410	380	610	1,460	1,040	430	560	500
Clydesdale	400	680	540	660	1,730	1,190	460	730	590
Lloyds TSB	480	1,160	820	740	2,210	1,480	510	1,060	790
Northern Ireland									
Northern	300	400	350	620	1,680	1,150	450	830	640
BoI	310	270	290	640	1,540	1,090	500	840	670
First Trust	370	570	470	690	1,850	1,270	450	650	550
Ulster Bank	340	450	400	670	1,730	1,200	460	680	570

Source: CC calculations on data provided by the banks.

*Rounded to the nearest £10. Money transmission charges are as set out in Table 4.9. Margins for loans and overdrafts for the banks apart from NatWest are as set out in Tables 4.25 and 4.21. Margins for NatWest are lower than those shown in Tables 4.25 and 4.21 as those margins are for SMEs with an annual turnover of less than £1 million. Deposit rates are as set out in Table 4.33.

†Main money transmission charges plus net interest income on loans and overdrafts minus rate of interest paid on deposits.

‡As in note † plus rate of interest on deposits had SMEs used deposit accounts of other providers (see paragraph 4.242).

§As in note ‡ minus net interest income on loans.

¶Overdraft of £2,000, loan of £10,000 and deposit of £10,000.

¤Overdraft of £10,000, loan of £50,000 and deposit of £30,000.

4.243. Table 4.38 shows that irrespective of the method used and charges compared for all SMEs, Barclays and HSBC have cheaper overall average charges than Lloyds TSB and NatWest. The ranking of Lloyds TSB and NatWest change depending on the charges being compared: NatWest's overall average charges for all SMEs are cheaper than Lloyds TSB's when loans are included but slightly more expensive when loans are excluded.

4.244. The method used and charges compared makes no difference to the ranking of the banks in Scotland. BoS has the cheapest overall average charges followed by Clydesdale, RBS and Lloyds TSB.

4.245. The method used and charges compared make a difference to the ranking of the banks in Northern Ireland. BoI has the cheapest overall average charges followed by Northern, Ulster Bank and First Trust when loans are included but the rankings are reversed (First Trust is the cheapest bank followed by Ulster Bank, Northern and BoI) when loans are excluded.

Importance of prices to SMEs

4.246. BMRB asked SMEs why they had chosen the bank where they held their main business account. Only 9 per cent said that they had chosen their main bank because it offered the best prices. This was the third most popular answer. Another price reason, given by 2 per cent of SMEs, was the initial free banking period.

4.247. The main reason, given by 34 per cent of SMEs, was that they already had a personal account with the bank; 7 per cent said it was because they already had a previous relationship with the bank. BMRB asked the owners of the SMEs (20 per cent of the sample)[1] whether they had a personal account with the same bank that they used for their main business account. 64 per cent said that they did and 35 per cent said that they did not. The second most popular answer, given by 16 per cent of SMEs, was location/closest bank to business. A variety of service factors, including reputation, was mentioned by about 30 per cent of respondents as a reason for their choice of bank and recommendation by 8 per cent.

4.248. When asked which characteristics were important in a bank, price featured more prominently. 23 per cent of SMEs gave reasonable charges/fees/rates of interest. Similar proportions gave quality of relationship with bank manager (24 per cent) and efficiency (22 per cent). 10 per cent or more of SMEs gave the following reasons: convenient location (16 per cent), range of banking services offered (15 per cent), quality of service (14 per cent), quality of banking services (12 per cent) and competence (10 per cent).

4.249. RBSG provided us with data from various market research companies that showed the reasons why NatWest and other banks lost and gained SMEs. The survey of NatWest's corporate customers[2] showed that 41 per cent of corporate customers said that they joined NatWest because of better rates for lending and 25 per cent said they joined because of better prices for services generally. Non-price reasons were good/better relationship with manager (given by 36 per cent of respondents), quick decision-making (26 per cent) and inadequate service/errors/problems at previous bank (22 per cent). Price seemed to be less important in the reasons why NatWest lost corporate customers (14 per cent of respondents gave loan charges/rates). Non-price reasons were decision-making problems/slow decisions, not understand business and inflexible/bureaucratic/too conservative (each given by 46 per cent) and wanted to reduce the number of accounts (19 per cent).

4.250. The survey of start-ups[3] showed why these customers joined NatWest. The non-price reasons were that they had an existing relationship (59 per cent), convenient location and quality of staff (each given by 50 per cent), reputation (28 per cent) and willingness to lend (25 per cent). The price reasons were free banking (47 per cent) and preferential borrowing terms (16 per cent).

4.251. A series of market research surveys[4] showed the reasons why SMEs switched their main account. 21 per cent gave price as their reason. Non-price reasons were relationship (given by 27 per cent), lending (18 per cent) and service (12 per cent).

4.252. Barclays and Lloyds TSB provided us with data from a December 1999 market research survey (see Table 4.39).

---

[1]BMRB asked the respondents what their role was in the SMEs. 32 per cent said that they were directors/managing directors/chief executives, 21 per cent said that they were finance managers/directors and 20 per cent said that they owned the SME. The rest of the sample comprised accountants/bookkeepers/accounts persons (8 per cent), general manager/supervisory role (5 per cent), company secretary (3 per cent), administrator/general administration (2 per cent), secretary (1 per cent) and other (1 per cent).

[2]Includes companies with annual turnover of between £1 million and £100 million. Carried out between 27 September and 1 December 1999 with a sample size of 6,583 telephone respondents and 1,015 face-to-face respondents.

[3]Sample of 1,000 start-ups of less than 12 months old across all banks, March 2000.

[4]Undertaken between July 1998 and April 2000 with a sample size of 1,000. SMEs were defined as businesses with an annual turnover of up to £1 million and being up to seven years old.

TABLE 4.39 **Reasons for choosing first business bank account**

	per cent	
	Main reason	All reasons
Already had personal account there	34	40
Gave me good/better advice	11	17
Recommended	10	13
Convenient geographically/nearby	10	17
Best/good overall offer/package	6	13
Already had previous account there	6	10
Other partner's bank	4	5
Free banking offer	4	9
Bank specially helps new businesses	1	3
Low cost/free overdraft	1	3
Other	12	13

Source: Barclays and Lloyds TSB from a market research survey of start-ups, December 1999.

4.253. BMRB asked SMEs whether they would move their funding to another bank or financial institution if their main bank alone was to increase the cost of their funding by 5 and 10 per cent. 51 per cent said that they would move their funding in response to a 5 per cent price rise and a further 12 per cent said that they would do so in response to a 10 per cent price increase.[1]

Satisfaction with price

4.254. The BMRB survey asked SMEs if they were satisfied with the prices they paid for banking services. Table 4.40 shows the results.

TABLE 4.40 **Levels of satisfaction with price factors**

	Level of fees and charges (mean score*)	Rates of interest (mean score*)
All	57	59
England and Wales		
HSBC	61	64
Lloyds TSB	59	60
Barclays	56	58
NatWest	51	55
Other	56	56
Scotland		
BoS	69	72
RBS	61	63

Source: BMRB survey.

*Using very satisfied = 100, quite satisfied = 75, neither satisfied nor dissatisfied = 50, quite dissatisfied = 25 and very dissatisfied = 0.

4.255. The results of the BMRB survey indicated that the level of satisfaction with price factors (both rates of interest and fees and charges) was less than overall satisfaction levels. The average level of satisfaction with price factors was about 58, where a score of 50 represents being neither satisfied nor dissatisfied and 75 is quite satisfied. In contrast, the average overall level of satisfaction was 78 (see Table 4.42). This difference can be expressed in terms of the proportions saying that they were very satisfied or quite satisfied with these services. With regard to levels of fees and charges, 52 per cent of respondents said that they were very or quite satisfied and 55 per cent said the same for rates of interest on accounts and funding. However, 84 per cent of respondents said that overall they were very or quite satisfied with their bank.

---

[1] A 5 per cent price rise would be represented, for example, by an interest rate increase from 10 to 10.5 per cent.

4.256. The level of satisfaction with rates of interest on accounts and funding (59) was slightly higher than for fees and charges (57). Table 4.40 shows that the banks were ranked in the same order for the two price factors. In England and Wales, HSBC scored slightly higher than Lloyds TSB, which in turn scored slightly higher than Barclays, which in turn scored slightly higher than NatWest. In Scotland BoS scored higher than RBS.

Service quality

4.257. In this section, we examine the results from a market research report as well as various customer surveys. The surveys we examined include the BMRB survey which we commissioned and surveys by the FPB, the FSB, other market research companies and Barclays' small business survey.

4.258. In our analysis we have separated the banks into those that operate mainly in England and Wales, in Scotland and in Northern Ireland. While some of the surveys were separately carried out in different geographical areas, other surveys covered the whole of the UK. In the case of the latter surveys, the findings shown for particular countries will not be greatly affected by the wider geographical area covered by the survey because most of the banks' SME customers are based mainly in one particular country.

A market research report

4.259. The market research report's analysis of the services provided on business current accounts showed HSBC as the top-ranked bank. The report assessed the banks' current accounts on two different non-price factors: product services and access. Barclays told us that the evaluation of services undertaken by the report was unrepresentative of the array of service characteristics of a full service SME bank such as Barclays.

4.260. In assessing product services, the report examined the cash-card withdrawal limits of the account, whether a debit card was offered, whether the account had an overdraft facility and whether a charge card was offered. In assessing access to the account, the report analysed access by telephone, Internet, personal contact and PC access. The report's scores for these two features of current accounts are shown in Table 4.41, together with an unweighted average score for the two non-price features.

TABLE 4.41 **Scoring of non-price aspects of business current accounts offered to SMEs, 2000**

	Product services	Access	Average
England and Wales			
HSBC	91	65	78
Lloyds TSB	67	88	77.5
NatWest	67	82	74.5
Barclays	48	82	65
Abbey National	65	53	59
Co-operative Direct	78	24	51
Girobank	22	47	34.5
Co-operative Bank	35	18	26.5
Scotland			
BoS Direct	67	82	74.5
BoS	46	76	61
RBS	57	65	61
Highest possible score*	100	100	100

Source: A market research report and CC calculations.

---

*Applies to England and Wales and Scotland.

4.261. The report ranked HSBC first for product services, but it scored less well on access to the account. At the time of the report, HSBC, along with Abbey National and the Co-operative Bank, did not have Internet banking and BoS and BoS Direct had Internet banking but this service was restricted to viewing only. When the scores for product services and access are averaged, HSBC is still ranked first, but scored only marginally higher than Lloyds TSB, which scored highest for access.

4.262. NatWest had an average score slightly lower than Lloyds TSB and Barclays scored appreciably less for product services. Co-operative Direct scored second highest on product services but second lowest on access. Girobank and the Co-operative Bank received low scores on both measures. At the time of the report, Abbey National, Girobank and Co-operative Direct did not operate through branches nor offer overdraft facilities.

4.263. Of the Scottish banks, BoS Direct scored highest on both measures. BoS and RBS scored equally when the two measures were averaged, with RBS scoring higher on product services and BoS higher on access.

Customer satisfaction levels

4.264. Performance of the banks in general and relating to non-price and price factors can be assessed from customer satisfaction surveys, which provide information on how the banks' customers view their bank as performing on a wide range of issues. We look first at overall satisfaction and then at satisfaction with service. See paragraphs 4.254 to 4.256 for satisfaction on prices.

Overall satisfaction levels

4.265. A number of surveys have asked SMEs to say how satisfied they are with their bank overall. Answers to this type of question will therefore include satisfaction with price, quality and service. Table 4.42 shows results for various banks on overall satisfaction levels, from a number of recent surveys. Barclays told us that less weight should be attached to the surveys carried out by or on behalf of interest groups such as the FPB and the FSB and more weight should be attached to the BMRB survey and to the independent surveys carried out by market research companies, as these latter surveys seemed to be carried out to a much higher standard of objectivity and rigour.

TABLE 4.42 **Overall bank satisfaction levels**

	BMRB survey*	FPB†	Survey of small business‡	Survey of middle market§	FSB¶
All	78	-	69	-	63
England and Wales					
HSBC	81	58	74	73	67
Barclays	78	54	70	75	61
Lloyds TSB	78	54	69	70	64
NatWest	75	53	63	67	60
AIB (GB)	-	59	-	-	-
Fleming	-	58	-	-	-
Yorkshire	-	55	-	-	58
Co-operative Bank	-	54	-	-	68
Girobank	-	-	-	-	68
Abbey National	-	-	-	-	68
Halifax	-	-	-	-	63
Other banks	78	-	-	-	-
Scotland					
BoS	85	53	67	73	66
RBS	83	58	72	74	66
Clydesdale	-	48	59	65	57

Source: BMRB survey and other surveys.

*2000. Mean scores, where very satisfied = 100, quite satisfied = 75, neither satisfied nor dissatisfied = 50, quite dissatisfied = 25 and very dissatisfied = 0.

†2000. Bank Performance Index.

‡1999. Mean scores where excellent = 100, good = 67, not so good = 33 and poor = 0.

§1999. Overall quality of service rating, where excellent = 100, good = 67, not so good = 33 and poor = 0.

¶1998. We have applied the same scores used by BMRB to categories very high, high, medium, low and very low to obtain mean scores.

Levels of satisfaction

4.266. In the BMRB survey, overall satisfaction levels for HSBC, Barclays, Lloyds TSB, NatWest, BoS and RBS ranged from 75 to 85, where 75 was quite satisfied and 100 was very satisfied. BMRB asked SMEs that were not very satisfied with their bank why this was the case. Overall, 9 per cent answered that they would never be satisfied with their bank.

4.267. In the small business survey (covering businesses with annual turnover of up to £1 million), the average score was 69, where 67 represented good and 100 represented an excellent score. In the middle market survey (covering businesses with annual turnover between £1 million and £100 million), scores ranged from 65 to 75. We calculated an average level of satisfaction from the FSB survey of 63, which was between medium and high levels of satisfaction.

4.268. In Northern Ireland, the market research survey found that 83 per cent of businesses surveyed were satisfied with their main bank (27 per cent very satisfied; 56 per cent quite satisfied; 11 per cent neither; 4 per cent quite dissatisfied; 2 per cent very dissatisfied).

Rankings of the banks

4.269. From the BMRB survey, in England and Wales, HSBC is ranked slightly higher than Barclays and Lloyds TSB, which in turn are ranked slightly higher than NatWest.

4.270. There is a measure of consistency in the other surveys with these results. The FPB survey ranks these four banks in the same order, as does the small business survey. In the middle market survey, Barclays is ranked slightly higher than HSBC. In the FSB survey, Lloyds TSB is ranked slightly higher than Barclays.

4.271. Looking at the other banks in England and Wales, their average score in the BMRB survey was the same as that for Barclays and Lloyds TSB, slightly lower than HSBC and slightly higher than NatWest. In the FPB survey, AIB (GB) scored slightly higher than HSBC, whilst Fleming had the same score as HSBC. Yorkshire scored slightly higher than Barclays, Lloyds TSB and the Co-operative Bank. In the FSB survey, the Co-operative Bank, Girobank and Abbey National ranked slightly above HSBC, Halifax ranked slightly lower than Lloyds TSB, while Yorkshire ranked slightly lower than NatWest.

4.272. In Scotland, RBS is ranked ahead of BoS in the FPB, the small business and middle market surveys, slightly lower in the BMRB survey and equally in the FSB survey. Clydesdale generally ranks third out of these Scottish banks.

4.273. In Northern Ireland, First Trust had the highest score. Although Northern was nominated as the main institution of the majority of businesses surveyed, it was rated lowest across all the elements of customer service, compared with Ulster Bank, First Trust and BoI.

Trends in overall satisfaction levels over time

4.274. The FPB undertakes its survey of SMEs every two years. Barclays told us that the work by the FPB had a number of serious weaknesses. Barclays said that the work over-represented older and more established businesses; the questionnaires were completed by self-selecting respondents and returned to the FPB by post; and respondents were not given any opportunity to clarify the interpretation of any question. Figure 4.8 shows the performance indices (which include price factors) of the four largest clearing banks over the period 1990 to 2000 and Figure 4.9 shows the same for the Scottish banks. Other banks are not shown because they did not feature over the whole period.

FIGURE 4.8

FPB performance indices, 1990 to 2000

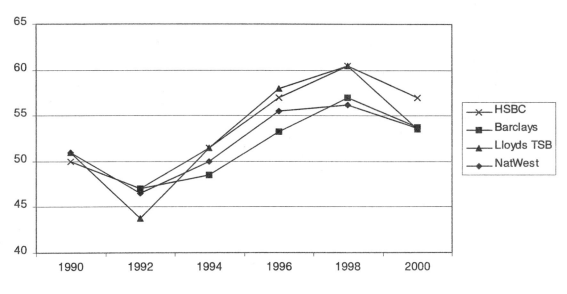

Source: FPB.

FIGURE 4.9

FPB performance indices, 1990 to 2000

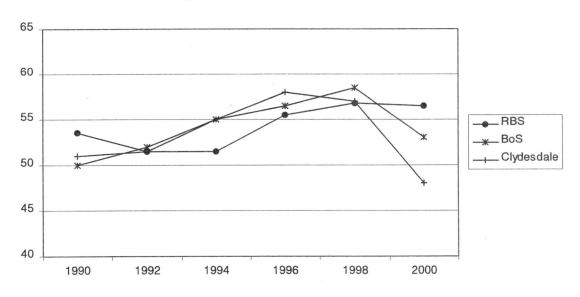

Source: FPB.

4.275. Figure 4.8 shows that the performance indices of HSBC, Barclays, Lloyds TSB and NatWest have moved broadly in line from 1990 to 2000. Between 1990 and 1992 the performance of these banks (as measured by the performance indices) fell; from 1992 to 1998 the trend in performance rose, before falling between 1998 and 2000. HSBC said that the results on overall bank satisfaction levels in the 2000 FPB survey were inconsistent with the previous biennial FPB surveys and all other evidence HSBC had seen. It said that this would appear to be confirmed by the BoE survey, *Finance for Small Firms*, published in January 2000, which stated that 'most recent indicators suggest that relationships between banks and small businesses have improved significantly over the last six years'. We note that the BoE report referred to by HSBC was published before the 2000 FPB survey. In its 2001 report, the BoE noted that the FPB's performance index fell by nine percentage points in 2000 compared with 1998, although it remained substantially higher than for the period prior to the 1996 survey.

4.276. The relative rankings of the banks changed over the ten-year period. HSBC improved its position, from being at about the same level as the other banks in 1990, to being close to or the top-ranked bank from 1994. By 2000 HSBC was the top-rated bank. On the other hand, Lloyds TSB's position fluctuated, falling to the lowest-ranked bank in 1992, then being close to or the top-rated bank between 1994 and 1998 and then falling again in 2000. The relative positions of NatWest (middle) and Barclays (bottom) remained fairly stable.

4.277. Figure 4.9 shows the performances of the Scottish banks following a broadly similar trend up until 1998. Performance levels were quite flat or falling (in the case of RBS) between 1990 and 1992, rising until 1998 and then falling or quite flat (in the case of RBS) to 2000. RBS was the only Scottish bank in the FPB survey that largely maintained its score between 1998 and 2000.[1] NAB told us that it had queried the fall in the performance of Clydesdale in the FPB's 2000 survey. NAB said that the sample used by the FPB was not representative of Clydesdale's customer base.

4.278. The relative position of Clydesdale declined over the ten-year period. It occupied a middle position between 1990 and 1994, improved to the top-ranked bank in 1996, before falling to the third-ranked bank by 2000. RBS's positioning fluctuated: from being the top-ranked Scottish bank in 1990, it fell to third position between 1994 and 1998, before improving to the top-ranked bank again in 2000. BoS's ranking improved from being the third-ranked bank in 1990 to the top-ranked bank in 1998, but fell to middle position in 2000.

4.279. Figure 4.10 shows the overall quality of service ratings (which include price factors) from the small business surveys from 1990 to 2000 for the four largest clearing banks. Results for BoS and RBS are also discussed.

FIGURE 4.10

Small business overall ratings, 1990 to 2000

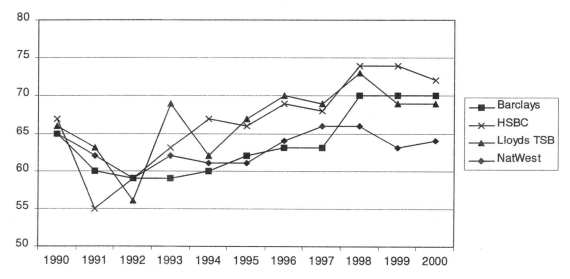

Source: Market research data provided by the banks.

4.280. Figure 4.10 shows a trend in the banks' ratings similar to that of the FPB performance indices. Broadly speaking, ratings fell between 1990 and 1992, increased to 1998 and then remained flat or fell to 2000.

4.281. HSBC's relative position improved over the ten-year period. After falling to fourth position in 1991, it then improved to become the top or close to top position from 1994 to 2000. Lloyds TSB's position fluctuated between 1990 and 1994, it was in top position from 1995 to 1997, before falling below HSBC and Barclays in 1999/2000. Barclays' position was at or close to fourth place until it improved in 1998, becoming the second highest rated bank from 1999. NatWest's position deteriorated steadily over the ten-year period, becoming the fourth-ranked bank from 1998.

---

[1]The Co-operative Bank also maintained its score between 1998 and 2000.

4.282. We were provided with data from the small business survey from 1997 to 1999 for RBS and BoS. In 1997 RBS scored higher than BoS (69 to 66). In 1998 that position was reversed, with BoS, at 73, being slightly better rated than RBS at 71. In 1999 the rankings changed once more, with RBS at 72 and BoS at 67.

4.283. Figure 4.11 shows the overall quality of service ratings (which include price factors) from the middle market surveys from 1989 to 1999 for the four largest clearing banks. Results of RBS from 1994 are also discussed.

FIGURE 4.11

Bank performance, middle market, 1989 to 1999

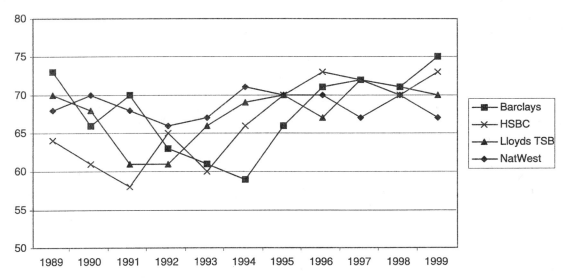

Source: Market research data provided by the banks.

4.284. The general trend in bank performance, as perceived by business customers with turnover between £1 million and £100 million, is similar to, although slightly flatter than, the trend in the small business survey. Broadly speaking, the trend in the banks' performance was falling between 1989 and the early 1990s, rising until the mid-1990s before falling again in the late 1990s.

4.285. Barclays was the top-rated bank in the middle market survey, both in 1989 and 1999, and in between that time, in 1994, it had fallen to being in fourth place. HSBC's ranking improved over time, from being ranked fourth to being in second place. From being ranked third in 1989, NatWest's position improved to being the top or equal top-ranked bank in 1990 and between 1992 and 1995, before falling to third place in 1996 and then to fourth or equal fourth-ranked bank between 1997 and 1999. Lloyds TSB's position deteriorated from 1989 to 1992, moving from second to fourth ranking. Between 1993 and 1995, it was ranked either second or equal first, fell to fourth place in 1996, equal first in 1997/98, before falling to third place in 1999.

4.286. RBS's performance in the middle market survey increased between 1994 and 1999, from 65 to 70. Over that period, it experienced an improvement between 1994 and 1995, a fall in the next year, followed by an improvement in 1997 and falls in 1998 and 1999.

Satisfaction with service

4.287. We begin this section by looking at satisfaction with overall service, then with the range of services provided and finally with relationship managers.

Overall service

4.288. Table 4.43 shows the results of two surveys that asked about overall service quality.

TABLE 4.43 **Satisfaction with service provided by the banks**

	FPB*	Barclays†
All	4.41	
England and Wales		
HSBC	4.72	✄
Barclays	4.45	
NatWest	4.34	
Lloyds TSB	4.29	
Scotland		
RBS	4.65	
BoS	4.26	
Clydesdale	4.04	

Source: FPB and Barclays.

---

*2000. One of the questions asked was 'Overall how do you feel about the service provided by your bank?' on a scale of 1 to 7, with 1 being very disappointed and 7 being delighted.
†1999. Barclays Small Business Competitor Benchmark Survey, satisfaction with overall service quality; mean scores out of 10.

4.289. Table 4.43 shows that in England and Wales, HSBC was ranked first for service in both the FPB and Barclays customer surveys, slightly above Barclays. Barclays in turn was ranked slightly higher than NatWest and Lloyds TSB, whose relative positions differed depending on the survey. Of the Scottish banks, in the FPB survey, RBS was ranked first, followed by BoS and then Clydesdale.

Range of services

4.290. Tables 4.44 and 4.45 show the results of surveys that asked respondents to rate their bank in terms of the range of services that it provided. Table 4.44 covers Great Britain while Table 4.45 covers Northern Ireland.

TABLE 4.44 **Ratings for range of services provided by the banks**

	Survey of small business*
England and Wales	
HSBC	62
Barclays	56
NatWest	55
Lloyds TSB	55
Scotland	
BoS	59
RBS	58
Clydesdale	50

Sources: The banks.

---

*1999. Mean scores where excellent = 100, good = 67, not so good = 33 and poor = 0.

4.291. In the small business survey, a score of 100 represented an excellent rating, 67 represented good, 33 represented not so good and a zero score was given for poor performance. Table 4.44 shows that the banks were rated between good and not so good in terms of supplying an appropriate range of products. HSBC was ranked above Barclays, which in turn was ranked slightly higher than NatWest and Lloyds TSB. BoS was ranked slightly higher than RBS, which in turn was ranked ahead of Clydesdale.

TABLE 4.45 **Ratings for range of services provided by the banks in Northern Ireland, 2000**

	Market research survey*
All	31
First Trust	37
BoI	32
Ulster Bank	32
Northern	26

Sources: Market research data provided by the banks.

---

*Percentage of very good ratings.

4.292. The results of the market research survey (see Table 4.45) shows the percentage of SMEs that rated the range of services provided by their bank in Northern Ireland as very good and as such it adopts a tougher criteria than that in Table 4.44. The survey showed that in the region of 30 per cent of respondents rated their bank as very good for the range of services offered. First Trust was ranked slightly higher than BoI and Ulster Bank, which in turn were ranked slightly higher than Northern.

Relationship management

4.293. The four largest clearing groups told us that relationship management was an important part of the service they provided to SMEs. This was confirmed by survey results. The BMRB survey showed that SMEs valued the quality of relationship they have with their bank manager slightly above other factors; 24 per cent of respondents considered it to be important (compared with 23 per cent nominating reasonable charges/fees/rates of interest and 22 per cent citing efficiency). [

Details omitted. See note on page iv.

]

4.294. Table 4.46 shows the results of a number of surveys that questioned business customers about their overall satisfaction with their relationship manager. Other survey results, focusing on specific aspects of relationship management, are contained in Appendix 4.5. Notable differences from the results shown in Table 4.46 are discussed in the text.

TABLE 4.46 **Ratings for relationship managers**

	Survey of small business*	Barclays†	FPB‡	Survey of middle market§
All	72		4.46	77
England and Wales				
HSBC	76		4.66	77
Barclays	74		4.68	80
Lloyds TSB	72		4.36	71
NatWest	65		4.58	76
Scotland				
RBS	79	-	4.64	74
BoS	69	-	3.93	-
Clydesdale	66	-	4.08	-

Sources: FPB and the banks.

---

*1999. Mean scores where excellent = 100, good = 67, not so good = 33 and poor = 0.
†1999. Barclays Small Business Competitor Benchmark Survey, mean scores out of 10.
‡2000. One of the questions asked respondents to rate their relationship with their bank manager, on a scale of 1 to 7, with 1 being very distant and 7 being very close.
§1999. Mean scores where excellent = 100, good = 67, not so good = 33 and poor = 0.

4.295. Table 4.46 shows that the average result from the survey of small businesses was 72, where 67 represented good and 100 was excellent. NatWest (65) and Clydesdale (66) scored slightly less than good. The average score in the middle market survey (77) was higher than the average for the small business survey. The average rating for relationship managers from the Barclays' survey was [✂]. The FPB survey used a scale of 1 to 7, where 1 was very distant and 7 was very close. The average score was about 4.5.

4.296. Ratings for some particular aspects of relationship management were somewhat lower than the overall satisfaction ratings. Barclays' survey results for frequency of contact, authority, availability and support (see Appendix 4.5, Part A) averaged about [✂], compared with [✂] for overall satisfaction. In the surveys, ratings for continuity of main contact (see Appendix 4.5, Part B) were slightly lower than those for overall satisfaction. The average rating from small businesses was 63 and from the middle market was 71, compared with 72 and 77, respectively for overall satisfaction.

4.297. For the overall ratings of relationship managers, shown in Table 4.46, the small business survey showed HSBC ranked slightly higher than Barclays, which in turn was ranked slightly higher than Lloyds TSB, which was ranked slightly higher than NatWest. [_Details omitted._ _See note on page iv._] and in both the FPB and middle market surveys, the positions of HSBC and Barclays were reversed, as were the positions of Lloyds TSB and NatWest.

4.298. In the FSB survey, respondents were asked to rank their relationship manager in terms of their understanding of the respondent's business (see Appendix 4.5, Part C). The rankings for the four largest clearing banks were similar to those of the Barclays survey for general ratings (see Table 4.46). Results for other banks in England and Wales were also provided. They all scored less than the four largest clearing banks. Yorkshire ranked slightly below NatWest, followed in turn by Girobank, Abbey National and the Co-operative Bank, Halifax and Alliance & Leicester.

4.299. In Scotland, the small business survey (see Table 4.46) showed that RBS ranked ten points higher than BoS, which in turn was ranked slightly higher than Clydesdale. The FPB survey (see Table 4.46) showed RBS as ranked higher than Clydesdale, which in turn was ranked slightly higher than BoS. A similar result is shown for continuity of main contact in the small business survey (see Appendix 4.5, Part B). Other results shown in Appendix 4.5 show RBS rated slightly higher than BoS. This was the case for the BMRB results for the relationship manager's understanding of business (see Appendix 4.5, Part C) and providing advice on funding alternatives (see Appendix 4.5, Part D). RBS and BoS were ranked equally in the BMRB survey in terms of local knowledge (see Appendix 4.5, Part E). In the FSB survey, RBS was ranked slightly higher than BoS, which was ranked slightly higher than Clydesdale on the understanding of business (see Appendix 4.5, Part C).

4.300. Results from the survey carried out in Northern Ireland for managers' understanding of business are shown in Appendix 4.5, Part C. First Trust and Ulster Bank were ranked ahead of BoI, which was ranked slightly higher than Northern.

Summary of customer satisfaction with non-price factors

4.301. In general, the survey results show that small business customers are satisfied with the performance of their banks. Given that the different surveys we have discussed have used different techniques and weightings in order to produce their rankings of the banks, there are some difficulties in consolidating this information. Bearing this in mind, we have attempted to provide a description of what the broad picture appears to be from the various surveys discussed.

4.302. In England and Wales, the rankings of the four largest clearing banks were quite close. However, the following ranking appeared to predominate: HSBC followed by Barclays, followed by Lloyds TSB, followed by NatWest. In terms of overall satisfaction levels (which will include price considerations), HSBC's relative performance improved over the ten years from 1990 to 2000. Lloyds TSB's relative ranking fluctuated, falling in the early 1990s, rising in the middle of the decade, before falling in the late 1990s, while the relative positions of Barclays and NatWest were more stable.

4.303. In Scotland, RBS appeared to be ranked higher than BoS, which in turn was ahead of Clydesdale. In terms of overall satisfaction levels (which will include price considerations), the relative performances of RBS and BoS fluctuated over time; with RBS's position improving in the late 1990s and BoS's falling, while the relative ranking of Clydesdale fell over the period 1990 to 2000.

4.304. In Northern Ireland, the rankings appeared to be: First Trust, Ulster Bank, BoI, followed by Northern.

Price and service combinations and market shares

4.305. In this section we examine whether the differences in the pricing and service packages offered by the main clearing groups can explain their market shares. We concentrate on those banks that have cheaper charges and a better quality of service as we would expect them to have more SME accounts than banks with more expensive charges and a lower quality of service.

4.306. Our work on overall average charges and service quality shows that in England and Wales, Barclays and HSBC have lower prices and higher service quality than Lloyds TSB and NatWest. We would therefore expect Barclays and HSBC to have more SME accounts than Lloyds TSB and NatWest. On the whole this is not the case. While Barclays has more SME accounts than Lloyds TSB, it does not have more accounts than NatWest, nor does HSBC have more accounts than NatWest or Lloyds TSB. Barclays, HSBC and RBSG told us that the issues were rather more complex than covered by our analysis. Barclays told us that we had ignored other critical factors including: the effectiveness of marketing and of price competition, the strategic focus of different banks at different times, their appetite for SME business and their overall skills, reputation and brand positioning, the quality of relationship managers, their approach to lending, regional coverage, branch network effects, the history and evolution of the banks, how they brought together competencies and strategic assets and so on. HSBC said that our analysis had not taken into account that, broadly, banks competed on a combination of service and price—some banks have better service and some were cheaper than others for particular SMEs. RBSG told us that our analysis failed to take into account several other key factors influencing SMEs' choice of bank, such as geographic convenience, quality of individual staff, recommendations (including by other SMEs, or professional advisers) and banks' reputations, all apparent from survey responses and all liable to variation over time.

4.307. In Scotland, BoS has cheaper overall average charges and higher service quality than Clydesdale. We would therefore expect BoS to have more SME accounts than Clydesdale. On the whole, this is the case, BoS having a greater share of the liquidity management services market than Clydesdale, although Clydesdale has a greater share of the general purpose business loans market.

4.308. In Northern Ireland, First Trust and Ulster Bank have lower prices (in the liquidity management services market) and higher service quality than BoI and Northern. We would therefore expect First Trust and Ulster Bank to have more SME accounts than BoI and Northern. This is true to some extent. Ulster Bank and First Trust have greater shares of the liquidity management services market in Northern Ireland than BoI but First Trust does not have a higher share than Northern and Ulster Bank has a lower share than Northern (by value of accounts) but a higher share of the number of accounts.

4.309. While there does not appear to be a strong relationship between the differences in the pricing and service packages of the main clearing groups and their market shares, their shares of SME accounts seem to resemble closely their shares of personal accounts. While Lloyds TSB has the largest share of personal accounts (22 per cent), it acquired about half of its personal accounts as a result of the merger between Lloyds and TSB. Taking this into account, it seems to be the case that Barclays and NatWest have higher shares of personal and SME accounts than Lloyds TSB and HSBC. This relationship between shares of personal accounts and shares of SME accounts seems to exist in Scotland and Northern Ireland. There is also little evidence of sizeable changes over time in the shares of SME accounts held by any of the main clearing groups.

5   The main suppliers of banking services to SMEs, their background, profitability, and capitalization

Contents

Introduction

5.1. This chapter provides financial information on the main banks serving SME customers in the UK, as well as information on the capital requirements placed on banks by the supervisory authorities to ensure that they maintain minimum levels of capital to meet their risks. The background to this inquiry was the Cruickshank review of banking services that was conducted on behalf of the Chancellor of the Exchequer, and resulted in the Cruickshank report issued in March 2000. The report recommended that a reference to the CC was necessary to investigate banking services to SMEs. Paragraph 59 of the report said:

> The Review recommends that: the Secretary of State should exercise his powers under section 51(1)(b) of the Fair Trading Act 1973 to refer the matter of the existence, or possible existence, of a complex monopoly situation in relation to the supply of money transmission services[1] and other related banking services (including the provision of debt and savings services) to small and medium sized business in the UK.

Appendix 5.1 summarizes the main points from the Cruickshank report on banks' services to SMEs. The chapters dealing with the views of the various banks include comments by some of them on the Cruickshank report.

5.2. This chapter concentrates on the six largest clearing groups that serve SME customers in the UK. We also provide information on further banks[2] that provide services to SMEs, plus Halifax, which recently announced its intention to enter the SME market, and Nationwide. This chapter reviews the banks' financial performance as a whole. Chapter 6 provides a detailed review of the banks' financial performance in serving SME customers.

5.3. For the six largest clearing groups, we asked for information from 1989 to 2000 so as to cover what had been considered to be a full economic cycle and to reflect the banks' long-term experience of bad debt. As discussed in the chapter, some banks were only able to provide information at the whole-bank level[3] over this period, and provided information for the SME banking business on a best endeavours basis for some of the more recent years only. For example, our definition of SMEs did not accord with the banks' internal definitions, and within each bank several separate business units serviced such SMEs. Therefore, to arrive at financial information relating to a bank's SME banking businesses, we and/or the banks had to make certain assumptions.

5.4. In this chapter we refer also to results for the banks' services to 'personal' customers. The banks noted, however, that this grouping also included SMEs that operated through personal rather than business bank accounts. In such circumstances, the SME benefited from the 'free' banking available to personal customers and did not pay account charges. In some cases the banks were not able to extract from the results for personal customers the usage of personal accounts by SMEs, or results from serving this sub-group, primarily because usage of personal accounts by SMEs is in many cases similar to usage by personal customers.

5.5. The presentation of the financial statements of banks is set out in statute[4] and can be distinguished from the accounts of a non-bank. For example, assets are shown in the order of liquidity with cash shown at the top of the list and prepayments and accrued income at the bottom. Liabilities are shown in order of timing of settlement with the shortest liabilities at the top of the list and the longest-term financing and the bank's share capital and reserves at the bottom.

5.6. The structure of a bank's balance sheet is also different from that of a non-bank trading business. As will be seen from the banks' balance sheets, fixed assets represent a small proportion of total assets, for example 1 per cent in the case of Barclays. Most of the assets and liabilities that were held within the banks' balance sheets consist of loans, deposits and other financial instruments. Total assets are large compared with shareholders' funds. It was apparent that banks do not require significant levels

---

[1]Generally in this report money transmission services is defined as including not only current accounts, but also overdrafts and short-term deposit accounts, which we have described as liquidity management services.

[2]These other banks are: NAB (including Clydesdale, Northern and Yorkshire), AIB (including First Trust), Ulster Bank, BoI, the Co-operative Bank, Alliance & Leicester and Abbey National.

[3]This means group results, or general results for a division that might have partially served SMEs within our definition.

[4]See Schedule 9, Companies Act 1985, and, in Northern Ireland, the Companies (NI) Order 1986.

of shareholders' capital to finance their assets but, consistent with any trading business, do require capital to protect themselves against risks specific to their trading activities. The minimum amount of capital required by the FSA is discussed in paragraphs 5.8 to 5.36.

5.7. In this chapter, we consider the capital structure of the banks, as reported to the supervisory authorities[1] and to their shareholders. In Chapters 6 and 7, we look at methods for *(a)* determining their capital base for the purpose of calculating economic returns; *(b)* allocating banks' capital to their respective activities; and *(c)* the outcome of applying these methodologies to specific banks.

The capital adequacy framework for UK banks

5.8. The FSA, in its role as banking supervisor (a role previously carried out by the BoE), requires all banks to hold a minimum level of capital at all times. This serves to protect the depositors from loss. The FSA applies an internationally agreed methodology, as outlined in the Basle Committee on Banking Supervision's 1988 Basle Capital Accord (the Basle Accord), for setting minimum capital charges against credit and market risk. In undertaking the prudential supervision of banks, the FSA also seeks to take account of other risks, including operational and liquidity risks, and the quality of a bank's management and systems; these areas are not governed by international standards. All of these factors are assessed in setting the capital adequacy targets and trigger ratios for individual banks. The FSA told us that it had a keen interest in the systemic risk implications of a bank's failure. But in setting capital ratios, its concerns extended beyond systemic risk. Its statutory objectives under the Financial Services and Markets Act 2001 include both market confidence and consumer protection. Therefore it applied capital ratios to all banks and building societies, including small institutions the failure of which would not have a material impact on the wider economy. In doing this, the FSA sought to ensure that banks have sufficient resources to safeguard depositors against the possibility of insolvency, although such protection cannot cover all eventualities. In addition there is a Deposit Protection Scheme for personal customers which is underwritten by all banks.

5.9. The four main categories of risk faced by banks are generally described as follows:

(a) Operational risk: this is inherent in all businesses and represents the potential for financial and reputational loss arising from failures in internal controls, operational processes or the systems that support them.

(b) Liquidity risk: this is the risk of loss arising from the failure of the bank to meet funding requirements, for example the replacement of existing funds as they mature or are withdrawn, or to satisfy the demands of customers for additional borrowings.

(c) Market risk: this is the risk of loss arising from adverse movements in the level of market prices, which can occur in the money, foreign exchange, equity and commodity markets.

(d) Credit risk: this is the risk that companies, financial institutions, individuals and other counterparties will be unable to meet their obligations to the bank.

5.10. The minimum level of capital required is determined by applying a capital adequacy risk-weighting framework under the 1988 Basle Accord to each bank's on- and off-balance-sheet exposures. The risk-weighting approach was designed to ensure that, within very broad parameters, capital requirements were matched to risk. As currently calculated, however, these parameters do not present a precise measure of probability of default and this is a major driver behind the Basle Committee's present efforts to revise the Accord. The capital adequacy risk-weighting rules are detailed and all UK-incorporated banks use the same set of rules to calculate their RWA ratios.

5.11. All the banks we approached said that they tended to maintain levels of capital in excess of the minimum level set by the FSA and that regulatory capital requirements served as only one of the constraints on a bank's capital base. The level of capital held within a bank was also linked to the rating given to the bank by credit rating agencies. If a bank reduced its level of capital to the regulatory level,

---

[1]The FSA or the BoE.

its credit rating was likely to be downgraded. This would increase the cost of the bank's debt and put it at a competitive disadvantage. The banks also said that a reduction in their capital base to the regulatory level would lead to an increase in their equity betas, which would in turn increase the cost of capital and their required rate of return. Finally, the banks said that sufficient capital was necessary to ensure that all strategic and business development objectives were met.

5.12. For 1998, 1999 and 2000, most banks provided us with data on total RWAs for the whole bank and the percentage attributable to the SME segment. This is considered and explained in greater detail in Chapter 7.

Comparison of capital adequacy requirements for the six largest clearing groups that serve SMEs in the UK

5.13. Table 5.1 shows a comparison of the group risk asset ratios (RARs) for the six largest clearing groups for the 2000 financial year. Other calculations of capital adequacy requirements are made such as the solus RAR (with all investments in subsidiaries and associated companies deducted from the bank's capital) and the solo-consolidated RAR (a consolidation of the bank and certain pre-agreed subsidiaries which meet specified FSA criteria). The chapter also shows details of the regulatory capital position of each of these banks between 1993 and 2000. We discuss some of the relevant terms used in the following paragraphs, for example the target and trigger ratios are covered in paragraphs 5.23 to 5.25. If the actual capital for a bank falls below the target ratio, it will have to take corrective action, or may face intervention by the FSA regarding its activities in the UK. We obtained details of the target and trigger ratios set by the FSA for each of the banks in Table 5.1 and of the capital required to meet them. The individual ratios are considered to be a confidential matter between the FSA and the bank concerned. Since we do not consider that information about the individual ratios is required for an understanding of our conclusions, we have not included it in the report.

TABLE 5.1 **Comparison of capital adequacy requirements for the six largest clearing groups serving the SME market in the UK for 2000**

£ billion

	Lloyds TSB	NatWest Group	Barclays	HSBC Bank	BoS	RBS
Capital base:						
Tier 1	7.7	6.9	10.5	7.0	4.9	5.9
Tier 2	7.6	6.5	6.6	5.2	3.3	4.1
Tier 3	0.0	0.2	0.3	0.0	0.0	0.0
Total eligible capital	15.3	13.6	17.4	12.2	8.2	10.0
Less: capital deductions	−6.9	−1.7	−1.3	−0.7	−0.2	−0.9
Total adjusted capital base	8.4	11.9	16.1	11.5	8.0	9.1
RWAs:						
Banking book	91.2	91.0	131.8	99.8	67.8	72.3
Trading book	3.0	7.3	15.2	7.5	1.1	5.1
Total	94.2	98.3	147.0	107.3	68.9	77.4
Published RAR (%)*	9.0	12.2	11.0	10.7	11.6	11.7

Source: FSA Form BSD3 for each bank.

*Published RAR is calculated as total adjusted capital base as a percentage of RWAs. For example, the published RAR for Lloyds TSB was 9.0 per cent, this being calculated from the total adjusted capital base of £8.4 billion as a percentage of RWAs of £94.2 billion (and taking account of rounding in the above table).

5.14. Some banks told us that if they anticipated that capital was likely to be required in the short term for investments such as acquisitions, additional capital (either in the form of equity or subordinated debt) would be held in the balance sheet.

Calculation of capital—Tiers 1, 2 and 3 capital

5.15. In calculating a bank's capital for supervisory purposes, the bank will identify three types of capital—Tier 1, Tier 2 and Tier 3—as well as specific items which result in a capital deduction.

5.16. Tier 1 capital forms a bank's core capital and will include:

(a) permanent share capital, which comprises ordinary shares and perpetual non-cumulative preference shares;

(b) reserves;

(c) retained profit and loss arising during the course of the current year net of tax (to the extent that it had been externally audited); proposed but unpaid dividends and other appropriations; and

(d) minority interests in Tier 1 items (on consolidation).

5.17. A bank is required under current supervisory rules to deduct from Tier 1:

(a) all holdings of its own shares;

(b) goodwill and other intangible assets; and

(c) current year's net losses.

The treatment of goodwill is an important issue for any bank making an acquisition that will generate a substantial level of purchased goodwill (that is, an acquisition where the consideration exceeds the fair value of the net chargeable assets acquired). In such a case, because of the need to deduct goodwill from Tier 1 capital in arriving at the capital base, the bank would need to build up its capital base for the acquisition or seek longer-term funding that can be classified as Tier 2 capital (see paragraphs 5.18 and 5.19). Additionally there are requirements to maintain a certain level of Tier 1 capital for various reasons and there are constraints on the amount of Tier 2 capital compared with Tier 1 capital.

5.18. Tier 2 capital is split into Upper Tier 2 and Lower Tier 2. Upper Tier 2 includes:

(a) reserves arising from the revaluation of tangible fixed assets and fixed asset investments;

(b) general provisions up to 1.25 per cent of RWAs; and

(c) hybrid capital instruments such as perpetual subordinated debt and cumulative preference shares.

5.19. Lower Tier 2 capital includes dated capital instruments with a maturity of at least five years and one day, such as term subordinated debt and dated preference shares.

5.20. Tier 3 capital is more short term than lower Tier 2 capital (though it still must have a minimum maturity of two years) and may only be used to support market risk in the trading book.

5.21. The following items, known as capital deductions, are deducted from total capital in order to obtain 'eligible' regulatory capital:

(a) investments in unconsolidated subsidiaries and associates;

(b) connected lending of a capital nature;

(c) all holdings of capital instruments issued by credit institutions and financial institutions held in the banking book and also in the trading book unless these are covered by a trading book exemption; and

(d) qualifying holdings in non-financial companies.

5.22. There are other capital restrictions that affect the calculation of eligible regulatory capital, for example:

(a) Tier 2 and 3 capital can only be included in eligible capital to the extent that the total of Tier 2 and 3 does not exceed Tier 1 capital.

(b) Lower Tier 2 capital (which is mainly dated subordinated debt) must not exceed 50 per cent of Tier 1 capital.

(c) In order to avoid a sudden diminution in the amount of capital available to a bank, Tier 2 dated capital must be amortized on a straight-line basis in its final four years to maturity.

Risk asset ratios, trigger ratios and target ratios

5.23. The RAR under current supervisory rules is defined as:

$$\frac{\text{Capital}}{\text{RWAs}}$$

5.24. The FSA sets the RAR, the target ratio and the trigger ratio for each bank. The trigger ratio is the capital ratio that the bank is required to maintain, failing which the FSA will take corrective action. The target ratio is usually set at around half a percentage point higher than the trigger ratio. Any bank that falls below its target ratio is required to report the breach to the FSA with an explanation as to its cause and a strategy to remedy the situation.

5.25. The FSA is obliged to set a minimum RAR of no less than 8 per cent under the Basle Accord, and under EC Directives[1] but in practice tends to set higher ratios depending upon the individual risk profile of the bank concerned. It is also noted that the banking book and trading book activities of the same bank (as discussed below) will have separate trigger ratios.

Calculation of RWAs

5.26. The first step in calculating a bank's RWAs is to divide all assets and commitments into banking book and trading book activities.

5.27. The banking book[2] is used to record loans, leases, investments and other assets that are not actively traded. The regulatory capital charges are based on credit risk measures and assume a longer hold period. The trading book consists of tradable instruments (securities and off-balance-sheet items) whose value is marked to market. The capital charges for securities take account of general market and issuer risk; those for off-balance-sheet items such as swaps also take account of counterparty default risk. Trading book capital charges are based on a ten-day hold period. The criteria for determining whether an asset is trading in nature are set out in each bank's trading book policy statement. Typically an asset will be classified as trading if:

(a) its value is marked to market daily and any gain or loss is recognized in the profit and loss account;

(b) it is subject to market risk limits and approvals; and

(c) the bank does not intend to hold the asset until maturity.

On-balance-sheet banking book assets and their relevant risk weightings

5.28. To calculate RWAs in the banking book each exposure is assigned a risk weight according to its counterparty or level of credit risk.

5.29. As a general guide, the weightings are as follows:

(a) cash, bullion and claims on OECD central governments—0 per cent risk weight;

---

[1]The 1988 Basle Accord was given statutory backing in the EC through the Solvency Ratio Directive (risk weighting and solvency ratio) and the Own Funds Directive (definition of capital). Both have subsequently been wrapped into a new consolidating measure, Directive 2000/12/EC (Article 47 of which states the 8 per cent minimum capital requirement).
[2]The FSA's Guide to Banking Supervisory Policy defines banking book and trading book assets.

(b) exposures to banks and public sector entities—20 per cent risk weight;

(c) loans secured by residential mortgages—50 per cent risk weight;

(d) OECD government securities—10 or 20 per cent risk weight;

(e) clearing house balances—20 per cent risk weight;

(f) goodwill and other intangible assets—incur a capital deduction; and

(g) all other balance sheet items including loans not included above, and fixed assets—100 per cent risk weight.

5.30. Where a loan or other exposure is secured, a lower risk weight may apply. Examples of reduced risk weightings include:

(a) a loan secured by cash or OECD government securities which would see a 0, 10 or 20 per cent risk weight apply to the extent of the security; or

(b) a finance lease secured by a bank guarantee that would be risk weighted at 20 per cent because the exposure has now become a bank risk.

Off-balance-sheet banking book items and their relevant risk weightings

5.31. Contingent liabilities and commitments (such as providing lending facilities to customers) are classified as off-balance-sheet items and are not included directly as a liability in a bank's balance sheet because the liability does not meet the recognition criteria prescribed by UK GAAP. However, the liability would be recognized once the criteria are satisfied. Banks can be required to set aside regulatory capital for contingent liabilities and commitments. The related costs, together with the administrative costs of providing the products, are recovered through fees charged by the banks.

5.32. Off-balance-sheet items include letters of credit, guarantees, indemnities, performance guarantees, undrawn overdraft facilities and other committed but undrawn loan facilities. The same counterparty risk weights apply as set out above. However, certain off-balance-sheet commitments are considered as being less risky than drawn amounts, and therefore the banking supervisory rules provide a credit conversion factor (CCF)—ie product weighting—to refine further the weighting of the exposure. The rates of CCF are noted below:

(a) standby letters of credit and guarantees—100 per cent CCF;

(b) indemnities and performance bonds—50 per cent CCF;

(c) undrawn loan commitments with an original maturity of greater than one year—50 per cent CCF;

(d) undrawn loan and overdraft commitments with a maturity of one year or less or unconditionally cancellable at any time—0 per cent CCF. This means that no capital needs to be held behind the undrawn portion of overdraft facilities so long as they are cancellable at any time or have a maturity of 365 days or less; and

(e) trade-related letters of credit—20 per cent CCF.

Trading book assets

5.33. Market risk[1] on trading book items is calculated either through a standardized approach or through the use of firm-specific value-at-risk models. The aim of the calculations is to measure the potential loss resulting from market movements in equities, interest rates, foreign exchange and commodity prices. Banks tend to build their own trading book risk models, which are then tested and approved by the FSA.

---

[1]The FSA's *Guide to Banking Supervisory Policy* covers these matters in greater detail.

5.34. In January 2001 the Basle Committee on Banking Supervision released the details of a draft new Capital Accord (Basle 2 proposals or draft new Accord), which is scheduled for implementation in 2004. It had been widely acknowledged that the requirements of the previous 1988 Basle Accord were crude and broad-brush measures of credit exposure and could distort a bank's lending profile. For example, loans to certain under-regulated overseas banks carried lower risk weights of 20 per cent and thus required less capital relative to loans to highly-rated corporates that carried higher risk weights of 100 per cent and thus required more capital.

5.35. The draft new Accord aims to refine the present rules by matching risks more closely with expected losses to determine an appropriate level of capital. This would be achieved by the derivation of a capital requirement based on a bank's own internal risk ratings where these were judged by the FSA to be robust. The new rules also propose separate capital in respect of operational risk such as direct or indirect losses from inadequate staff or systems or from unexpected events. Operational risk capital considerations are currently reflected in arriving at the trigger/target ratios. At present, these areas continue to be debated. The draft Accord is subject to amendment before its finalization.

5.36. It is envisaged that the new capital adequacy framework will be capital-neutral for banks with an average risk portfolio, but will require either more or less capital for banks with different risk profiles. We further discuss Basle 2 in paragraphs 5.483 to 5.530.

Performance of the banks serving SMEs in the UK

5.37. We now turn to a detailed description of the main banks that are involved in the provision of services to the SME segment in the UK, namely Barclays, Lloyds TSB, NatWest, HSBC Bank, RBS and BoS. We also provide a brief description of other banks in Great Britain and Northern Ireland with smaller SME banking businesses, namely NAB, AIB, Ulster Bank, BoI, the Co-operative Bank, Alliance & Leicester and Abbey National. We show the results of these banks, including the profitability and financial position of each bank as a whole, and the relative importance of the SME activities for each bank. We also note their overall bad debt record from lending, and review their capital adequacy ratios.

5.38. When considering the banks' financial returns and profitability we noted that banks derive earnings from interest on both their lending and their deposits. In terms of lending, banks earn net interest income directly by lending funds to customers at interest rates higher than their actual cost of funds. In terms of deposits, banks either pay no interest or pay interest at rates lower than that earned by the banks from investing the deposited funds. These points are considered in greater detail in Chapter 6.

5.39. In addition, we noted that banks enter into derivative agreements,[1] such as swaps, as part of their balance sheet management process to protect their income stream from movements in interest rates. The banks told us that depending on the type of derivative agreement entered into, net interest income in a particular year could be higher or lower than the level that would have applied had the banks not entered into such agreements.

5.40. Lloyds TSB said that it aimed to manage the volatility of net interest income over the course of the business cycle. This activity had been carried out by Group Balance Sheet Management (GBSM) since it was established as a unit in the Lloyds TSB group in 1996. The activities of GBSM would be expected to reduce net interest income in times of rising interest rates (relative to the group without GBSM) and to boost net interest income in a falling interest environment—the average net interest income over the cycle would remain broadly similar.

5.41. Most banks told us that they had a specialist central treasury unit for GBSM purposes that monitored and controlled internal interest rates receivable and payable on funds. The main objective of this unit is to remove the management of interest rate risk from the business units, thus enabling the business units to focus on product design and marketing and the provision of services/products to customers. The process is such that the units buy all the liabilities (ie customer deposits and accounts in credit) and fund all the assets associated with the business units' lending activities. Depending on their

---

[1]See glossary. Generally a financial instrument used to manage the risk of interest rate movements throughout the life of a transaction from the date a commitment is made to a customer to the date the transaction closes.

net funding requirements, business units pay or receive interest to or from the central group at an internal transfer price. The cost and benefit of funds is discussed in greater depth in Chapter 6, when we look at the results of the banks' services to SMEs.

5.42. Generally the banks said that they did not use a single rate such as LIBOR or LIBID or LIMEAN (London Interbank Mean Rate) for the internal transfer rates, and often a 90-day average rate was used to smooth out short-term market distortions. The rates used are intended to be reflective of the market rates and to match the interest rate repricing characteristics of each product in each business segment more closely than a single rate would do. The central unit sometimes operated on the policy that it was profit neutral and did not set rates with a bid or offer spread. In other cases, it was a profit centre, or a cost centre. The banks also used derivative instruments in order to smooth out the unpredictable extremes in their income, and would use special models to predict the money value-at-risk from particular instruments for a given level of exposure.

5.43. At the retail banking level, we noted that most of the six largest clearing groups had business units that served both the smaller SMEs and personal customers, but the banks had different tariff structures, depending on whether the customer was classified as personal or business. A feature of personal banking was that such customers did not pay charges for operating their current accounts in credit, but customers with business accounts were generally subject to charges for such money transmission services, irrespective of their size. Chapter 4 deals with such distinctions in greater detail.

5.44. Appendix 5.2 shows comments from the published financial statements of some of the largest clearing groups over the years 1989 to 1993 regarding their bad debt experience at the time. We noted that the banks indicated only to a limited extent in their financial statements that SMEs had been the predominant cause of concern to their long-term profitability over the recession years, 1990 to 1993.

5.45. The banks noted that the weakness of the UK economy over the recession years had an adverse effect on start-ups and in survival rates of small businesses and medium-sized corporates.

Barclays

History

5.46. Barclays is listed on the London Stock Exchange. On 29 June 2001 its market capitalization was £36 billion and its price:earnings ratio was 14.3. Barclays Bank, a wholly-owned subsidiary of Barclays, is the principal company in the group that provides banking services to SMEs within the UK.

5.47. The origins of Barclays can be traced back more than 300 years. The business that became Barclays commenced in 1690 in Lombard Street, London. The name Barclay became associated with the firm in 1736 when James Barclay became a partner. In 1896, 20 of the 100 or so private banks in London merged to form a joint stock bank named Barclay and Company. This bank continued to expand through mergers with other banks. In 1918 the company amalgamated with the London Provincial and South Western Bank and was called Barclays Bank Ltd. Barclays has continued to grow subsequently both organically and through acquisitions. In 1969 it merged with Martins Bank and in 2000 it merged with Woolwich. Barclays operates internationally, supplying services in over 60 countries, and its shares are traded on the New York and Tokyo Stock Exchanges as well as in London. As at 31 December 2000 group staff numbers worldwide were 75,300, of which 57,000 were in the UK. Since 1989 Barclays has disposed of equity shareholdings and assets in several companies that were engaged in the provision of banking services to SMEs in the UK. The larger disposals in the period were as follows:

(a) In February 1990 Barclays sold its 32 per cent holding of equity share capital in Yorkshire to NAB for £312 million.

(b) In June 2000 Barclays sold the Dial Group, a company that provided vehicle contract hire and fleet management services, to ABN AMRO Lease Holding NV for £269 million.

5.48. In October 2000 Barclays acquired Woolwich, a bank that at the time was not providing banking services to SME customers.

Business structure serving SMEs

5.49. Barclays told us that it reorganized its business structure in July 2000. Prior to the reorganization, banking services provided to UK SMEs fell within two different UK business units, Small Business Banking and Corporate Banking. Small Business Banking fell within a larger business unit, Retail Financial Services. This larger business unit covered Barclays' retail interests around the world and included both personal and small business customers. Corporate Banking was a separate unit in its own right.

5.50. Prior to the reorganization, Small Business Banking generally served business customers with annual turnover up to £0.5 million and Corporate Banking served business customers with turnover greater than £0.5 million. The reorganization led to the creation of a new business unit called Business Banking, which represented a merger of Small Business Banking and the medium-sized enterprise portion of business Corporate Banking.

5.51. The Business Banking unit currently provides lending, money transmission, liquidity management, deposit, invoice discounting, factoring and asset finance/leasing services to business customers with annual turnover up to £100 million. The main channels of banking service distribution are as follows:

(a) via relationship managers who operate from branches, corporate banking suites or on a mobile basis;

(b) via the branch network shared with retail personal customers; or

(c) via telephone banking, Internet and other e-commerce services (which are also shared with retail personal customers).

In certain cases Business Banking, through Barclays Ventures, provides equity finance to SMEs. Barclays told us that a total of 12,000 staff (FTEs) worked within Business Banking at the end of July 2000.

5.52. Barclays said that the only other business unit that provided banking services to SMEs was Barclaycard. Barclaycard provides merchant acquirer and charge-card services to SMEs. Barclays said that Barclaycard had a total headcount of some 4,500 employees at July 2000.

5.53. As the Business Banking unit was created only in July 2000, Barclays provided us with copies of its 1999 management accounts for Small Business Banking and Corporate Banking. In 1999 the management accounts of Small Business Banking reported average total balances over the year for loans to customers of £[✂] billion and customer deposits of £[✂] billion (of which about [✂] per cent, or £[✂] billion, was in non-interest-bearing current accounts). The management accounts for 1999 also reported total income of £[✂] million (of which a significant portion was earned on non-interest-bearing current accounts), total costs of £[✂] million, bad debts of £[✂] million and operating profit of £[✂] million.

5.54. In 1999 the management accounts of Corporate Banking reported average total balances over the year for loans to customers of £[✂] billion and customer deposits of £[✂] billion (of which [✂] per cent or £[✂] billion was in non-interest-bearing current accounts). The management accounts for 1999 also reported total income of £[✂] billion, total costs of £[✂], bad debts of £[✂] and operating profit of £[✂].

5.55. The 1999 cost:income ratio reported in the management accounts[1] was [✂] per cent for Small Business Banking and [✂] per cent for Corporate Banking. Table 5.8 provides further information on the performance of Retail Financial Services (of which Small Business Banking formed part) and Corporate Banking between 1997 and 2000.

Financial performance

Profit and loss accounts

5.56. Table 5.2 shows the profitability of Barclays from 1989 to 2000. Between 1989 and 2000 Barclays' operating income increased 75 per cent from £5.5 billion to £9.6 billion, the growth being achieved mainly in its personal customer and non-UK categories[2] (see paragraph 5.62). During the period, operating expenses increased 53 per cent from £3.6 billion to £5.5 billion. The level of bad debt charge ranged from £1.2 billion to £2.5 billion between 1989 and 1993, and has since fallen substantially into the range of £0.2 billion to £0.8 billion.

TABLE 5.2 **Barclays: consolidated profit and loss account, 1989 to 2000**

£ billion

Years ended 31 December

	1989	*1990*	*1991*	*1992*	*1993*	*1994*	*1995*	*1996*	*1997*	*1998*	*1999*	*2000*
Net interest income	3.4	3.5	3.6	3.7	3.9	3.7	3.8	3.9	4.0	4.3	4.6	5.2
Net fees and commissions	1.4	1.6	1.8	2.2	2.4	2.8	2.8	2.9	3.0	2.8	2.9	3.4
Other income	0.7	0.7	0.9	0.8	1.1	0.5	0.6	0.7	0.6	0.3	0.8	1.1
Operating income	5.5	5.7	6.3	6.7	7.4	7.0	7.2	7.5	7.6	7.4	8.4	9.6
Operating expenses	–3.6	–3.8	–4.3	–4.4	–4.8	–4.6	–5.0	–5.1	–5.2	–4.9	–5.1	–5.5
Operating profit before provisions	2.0	2.0	2.0	2.3	2.6	2.4	2.2	2.5	2.4	2.5	3.2	4.1
Bad debt charge	–1.4	–1.2	–1.5	–2.5	–1.9	–0.6	–0.4	–0.2	–0.2	–0.5	–0.6	–0.8
Other provisions	0.0	0.0	0.0	–0.1	0.0	0.0	0.0	0.0	0.0	–0.1	0.0	0.0
Operating profit after bad debt charge	0.6	0.7	0.5	–0.2	0.7	1.8	1.8	2.2	2.2	1.9	2.6	3.3
Exceptional and other items	0.0	0.2	0.0	0.0	0.0	0.0	0.2	0.1	–0.4	0.0	–0.1	0.2
Net profit before tax	0.6	1.0	0.5	–0.2	0.7	1.9	2.0	2.3	1.7	1.9	2.5	3.5
Tax	–0.2	–0.3	–0.2	0.0	–0.3	–0.6	–0.6	–0.6	–0.5	–0.5	–0.6	–0.9
Net profit after tax	0.4	0.6	0.3	–0.3	0.4	1.3	1.4	1.7	1.2	1.4	1.8	2.6
Minority interest	0.0	0.0	–0.1	–0.1	–0.1	–0.1	0.0	0.0	0.0	0.0	–0.1	–0.1
Profit for the financial year	0.4	0.6	0.2	–0.3	0.3	1.2	1.4	1.6	1.1	1.3	1.8	2.5
Dividends	–0.3	–0.3	–0.3	–0.2	–0.2	–0.3	–0.4	–0.5	–0.6	–0.6	–0.7	–0.9
Profit retained for the financial year	0.1	0.3	–0.1	–0.6	0.1	0.8	0.9	1.2	0.6	0.7	1.0	1.5
Number of employees* ('000)	117	111	115	107	99	95	92	87	84	80	77	77
Performance indicators												*per cent*
Tax charge as a percentage of profit before tax	33	35	44	–18	42	33	30	27	32	28	26	27
Percentage change in operating income	N/A	3	10	6	10	–5	3	5	1	–3	13	15
Change in number of employees	N/A	–6	4	–8	–8	–4	–3	–5	–3	–4	–3	-

Source: Barclays annual reports.

---

*Excludes agency staff and contractors.
Note: N/A = Not available.

---

[1]Cost:income ratios in the management accounts are calculated on a different basis from that used in the Barclays submission covering its SME business. The management accounts figures exclude a share of central costs, restructuring costs and long-term pension cost adjustments.

[2]These were categories under which we asked Barclays to analyse its overall financial performance, to compare with its analysis of results from services to SMEs. The personal category was services to personal customers, and the non-UK category was for the bank's services outside the UK.

5.57. Barclays reported an operating profit of £0.6 billion in 1989, an operating loss of £0.2 billion in 1992 (the first such loss in its history) and returned to an operating profit of £0.7 billion in 1993. Between 1994 and 2000 the level of operating profit increased year on year (except for 1998) from £1.8 billion to £3.3 billion. Barclays said that operating profit in 1998 was adversely affected by dealing losses reported by Barclays Capital.[1] Barclays said that its SME banking activities produced an operating profit of £[✂] in both 1999 and 2000.

5.58. Table 5.3 further analyses the overall performance of Barclays from 1989 to 2000 by comparing all items to operating income. Net interest income as a percentage of total income declined from 62 per cent in 1989 to 54 per cent in 2000, whilst net fees and commissions (which includes money transmission charges) as a percentage of total income increased from 26 per cent in 1989 to 35 per cent in 2000. Barclays said that movement in the 'other' income category (which was mainly dealing profits or losses from Barclays Capital) might affect the percentages shown in the table.

5.59. Operating expenses as a percentage of operating income (also referred to as the cost:income ratio) was in the range 64 to 70 per cent over the ten years to 1998 and for 2000 declined to 57 per cent. Barclays told us that the reduction in 1999 was due to the higher level of other income (mainly dealing profits from Barclays Capital) reported in that year. Barclays said that its cost:income ratio in 1999 was broadly in line with that of 1989 and that there were many factors that had affected the continuation of the level of the cost:income ratio over the period, especially changes in business mix, reductions in margins and prices, and reductions in costs.

TABLE 5.3 **Barclays: operating profit and loss items as a percentage of operating income, 1989 to 2000**

per cent

	1989	1990	1991	1992	1993	1994	1995	1996	1997	1998	1999	2000
Net interest income	62	61	57	55	53	53	53	52	53	58	55	54
Net fees and commissions	26	27	29	31	32	40	39	39	39	38	35	35
Other income	12	12	14	14	15	7	9	9	8	4	10	11
Operating income	100	100	100	100	100	100	100	100	100	100	100	100
Operating expenses	−64	−66	−68	−65	−65	−65	−70	−67	−68	−67	−62	−57
Operating profit before provisions	36	34	32	35	35	35	30	33	32	33	38	43
Bad debt charge	−25	−22	−24	−37	−25	−9	−6	−3	−3	−7	−7	−9
Other provisions	0	0	0	−2	0	0	0	0	0	−1	0	0
Operating profit after bad debt charge	11	13	8	−4	9	26	25	30	29	26	31	34
Exceptional and other items	0	4	–	0	0	1	3	1	−6	0	−2	2
Net profit before tax	11	17	8	−4	9	27	28	31	23	26	29	36

Source: Barclays.

5.60. The level of bad debt charge was a major factor influencing profits before tax, and fluctuated significantly between 1989 and 2000. The charge as a percentage of income was at its highest between 1989 and 1993 and peaked at around 37 per cent (or £2.5 billion) in 1992. Barclays said that the SME banking business had contributed significantly to the volatility and size of the overall bad debt charge (see Table 5.15 which shows bad debt charge by type of customer) and referred to the statement in the 1991 accounts that the bank had been losing £1 million a day in bad debts in the small business sector in that year (see Appendix 5.2). Since then, the percentage has declined and reached a low of around 3 per cent in 1996 and 1997 before increasing to around 7 to 9 per cent in 1998, 1999 and 2000. Barclays said that the 7 per cent in 1998 and 1999 should be seen in the context of benign economic conditions.

Analysis of performance by type of customer

5.61. We asked Barclays to divide further its UK activities into the following activities:

---

[1]Barclays Capital is Barclays' investment banking division and does not provide services to SMEs.

(a) personal customers;

(b) SME customers, which included business customers with turnover less than £25 million;

(c) corporate customers, which included business customers with turnover greater than £25 million; and

(d) 'other UK' customers, which included Barclays' investment banking and Barclaycard activities.

Most of these activities were not parts of Barclays' existing business structure and it had to adapt some of its internal data to meet our requests. Tables 5.4 to 5.7 provide an overview of Barclays' total income, costs and operating profits by type of customer for the 12 years to 2000.

5.62. Table 5.4 shows Barclays' operating income by type of customer from 1989 to 2000. During this period, income from personal customers increased [✂] per cent from £[✂] billion in 1989 to £[✂] billion in 2000, income from SME customers grew [✂] per cent from £[✂] billion in 1989 to £[✂] billion in 2000, and income from corporate customers showed no consistent pattern of growth. Barclays said that the higher rate of income growth within the personal customer activity was due to growth in consumer lending and personal loans, growth in personal mortgage lending, increased income from Barclaycard and new income streams such as the introduction of card protection insurance. Over the period, the contribution from personal customers to total income grew from [✂] per cent in 1989 to [✂] per cent in 1998 then fell back to [✂] per cent in 2000, whilst the contribution from the SME banking business declined from [✂] per cent in 1989 to [✂] per cent in 2000. Barclays told us that the reduction in the contribution from the SME banking business to overall group income was due to the higher rate of growth of the personal customer activity and strong income growth in recent years in investment banking.

TABLE 5.4 **Barclays: operating income by type of customer, 1989 to 2000***

| | £ billion | | | | | | | Proportion of total (%) | | | | | | |
Year	Per sonal	SME	Corp orate	Other UK	Total UK	Non- UK	Total	Per sonal	SME	Corp orate	Other UK	Total UK	Non- UK	Total
1989					4.5	1.1	5.6					80	20	100
1990					4.6	1.2	5.8					80	20	100
1991					5.0	1.4	6.4					79	21	100
1992					5.4	1.4	6.8					79	21	100
1993					6.0	1.4	7.4					81	19	100
1994	Figures omitted.				5.5	1.5	7.0	Figures omitted.				79	21	100
1995	See note on page iv.				6.0	1.3	7.3	See note on page iv.				82	18	100
1996					5.5	2.1	7.6					72	28	100
1997					5.7	1.9	7.6					75	25	100
1998					5.7	1.6	7.4					78	22	100
1999					6.4	1.9	8.4					77	23	100
2000					7.5	2.1	9.6					78	22	100

Source: Barclays.

***Operating income includes net interest income, net fees and commissions and other income.

5.63. Barclays clarified how it derived its income shown above, which it said was neutral of the capital used to support the various activities. This meant that when returns on capital were calculated an adjustment was necessary to take account of the notional interest that would be earned on such capital. It noted that based on its assessment of imputed capital of between £[✂] billion and £[✂] billion over the period for the SME banking business, the notional interest adjustment would be around £[✂] million in 1989 and 1990, around £[✂] million in 1991 and 1992, and some £[✂] million for each year thereafter, based on LIBOR rates. The high level of adjustment in the years 1989 to 1992 was because LIBOR rates were at very high levels, compared with later years. We deal with these adjustments for the SME banking business in greater detail in Chapters 6 and 7.

5.64. Table 5.5 shows Barclays' operating costs by type of customer from 1989 to 2000. During this period, operating costs within the personal customer activity increased [✂] per cent from £[✂] billion in 1989 to £[✂] billion in 2000 and operating costs within the other customers segment increased [✂] per cent from £[✂] in 1989 to £[✂] billion in 2000. Operating costs for the SME and corporate customers remained relatively unchanged at around £[✂] and £[✂] respectively. Overall in 2000, the personal, SME banking business and corporate activities accounted for [✂] per cent of total costs respectively. However, the proportion of costs for the SME banking business had fallen to [✂] per cent from [✂] per cent in 1989, which was consistent with the income proportion shown in Table 5.4 which fell from a proportion of [✂] per cent in 1989 to [✂] per cent in 2000.

TABLE 5.5 **Barclays: operating costs by type of customer, 1989 to 2000**

| | £ billion | | | | | | | Proportion of total (%) | | | | | | |
Year	Per-sonal	SME*	Corp-orate	Other UK	Total UK	Non-UK	Total	Per-sonal	SME*	Corp-orate	Other UK	Total UK	Non-UK	Total
1989					2.8	0.8	3.6					78	22	100
1990					3.0	0.8	3.8					79	21	100
1991					3.3	1.0	4.3					77	23	100
1992					3.3	1.0	4.3					77	23	100
1993					3.6	1.3	4.8					74	26	100
1994		Figures omitted.			3.4	1.2	4.6		Figures omitted.			74	26	100
1995		See note on page iv.			3.8	1.2	5.0		See note on page iv.			76	24	100
1996					3.3	1.8	5.1					64	36	100
1997					3.7	1.5	5.2					72	28	100
1998					3.7	1.2	4.9					76	24	100
1999					4.0	1.2	5.1					77	23	100
2000					4.2	1.3	5.5					76	24	100

Source: Barclays.

*The comparison of operating costs of the SME banking business with those of other activities is affected by the fact that the costs of the SME banking business include a share of group costs and pension cost adjustments which have not been included, for instance, in the costs of the personal customer activity.

5.65. Table 5.6 shows Barclays' cost:income ratio by type of customer from 1989 to 2000. During the period Barclays' cost:income ratio fluctuated within the different types of customer. From 1989 to 2000 the cost:income ratio for the personal customer activity declined from 93 to 55 per cent. Barclays told us that this was because of the very significant volume growth and change in business mix over the period; however, the position was also affected by variations in the method of presentation across types of customer. During this period, the cost:income ratio for the SME banking business ranged between 53 and 63 per cent and for the corporate customer activity between 42 and 64 per cent.

TABLE 5.6 **Barclays: cost:income ratios, 1989 to 2000***

per cent

Year	Personal	SME	Corporate	Other UK	Total UK	Non-UK	Total
1989	93	55	50	48	61	70	63
1990	84	57	56	58	65	68	65
1991	86	63	64	55	66	72	67
1992	70	59	61	59	62	70	64
1993	62	57	58	58	59	91	65
1994	64	55	56	64	61	81	65
1995	70	59	62	61	64	95	69
1996	69	61	59	45	59	88	67
1997	65	59	62	72	65	79	69
1998	62	61	54	80	65	71	66
1999	57	56	47	77	62	61	62
2000	55	53	42	62	56	62	57

Source: Barclays.

*The figures in this table are based on the actual income and cost data, rather than the rounded figures shown in Tables 5.4 and 5.5.

5.66. In 1998 and 1999 the personal and SME banking businesses reported similar cost:income ratios, with the ratios being higher than those of the corporate banking business. Barclays told us that the corporate banking business reported lower ratios because it was less labour intensive and involved more automated transactions. Barclays noted that it had programs that allocated costs to the constituent business units and it believed that its cost-allocation systems were fair and reasonable.

5.67. Table 5.7 shows Barclays' operating profits (after bad debt charge) by type of customer from 1989 to 2000. The level of bad debt charge was a major factor influencing operating profit before tax during the 11 years. Between 1990 and 1993 Barclays reported the lowest level of operating profits of the six largest clearing groups, with all banking businesses (except the 'other UK') reporting either zero operating profits or operating losses in one or more years. The 'other UK' customers activity reported trends that were different from those of the other banking businesses; in particular it reported high profits in 1991 due to the impact of very high market interest rates on the group's capital.

TABLE 5.7 **Barclays: operating profit by type of customer, 1989 to 2000**

£ billion

Year	Personal	SME	Corporate	Other UK	Total UK	Non UK	Total
1989				*	0.5	0.2	0.7
1990					0.7	0.1	0.8
1991					0.5	0.0	0.5
1992					−0.1	0.0	−0.1
1993					1.0	−0.3†	0.7
1994					1.8	0.1	1.8
1995		Figures omitted. See note on page iv.			1.9	0.0	1.9
1996					2.0	0.3	2.3
1997					1.7	0.4	2.2
1998					1.5	0.5	2.0
1999					1.9	0.7	2.6
2000					2.8	0.8	3.5

Source: Barclays.

*The operating loss for 1989 in the other UK activity was due to a large bad debt provision charge which was held centrally, rather than being charged to business groups.
†The operating loss in the non-UK activity for 1993 was mainly due to bad debt provisions in the USA.

5.68. Table 5.8 provides a further analysis of Barclays' business structure from 1997 to 2000, as reported in its published financial statements. During these years, the main business units were Retail Financial Services, Corporate Banking and Barclays Capital. Retail Financial Services consisted of all retail customers (defined as both personal customers and small business customers with turnover less than £0.5 million), wealth management and Barclaycard. Corporate Banking consisted of middle to large corporations and institutional customers with turnover greater than £0.5 million and Barclays Capital represented the investment banking business. Barclays said that the SME banking business as defined by us included parts of two business units, Retail Financial Services and Corporate Banking. For 2000, Retail Financial Services had a return on shareholders' funds of 29 per cent compared with Corporate Banking of 34 per cent, and Barclays Capital of 15 per cent. When we combined Retail Financial Services and Corporate, the return on equity was around 31 per cent.

5.69. In 2000 Retail Financial Services reported profit before tax of £2.1 billion, total assets of £89 billion and shareholders' funds of £7.2 billion. Corporate Banking reported profit before tax of £1.1 billion, total assets of £53 billion and shareholders' funds of £3.2 billion. In 2000 Retail Financial Services and Corporate Banking reported pre-tax return on shareholders' funds of 29 per cent and 34 per cent respectively. We noted, however, that the information provided by Barclays for its SME banking business, according to our definition, showed an estimated pre-tax return on equity as [✂] per cent in 2000 (see Table 6.3).

TABLE 5.8 Barclays: analysis by class of business, 1997 to 2000

£ billion

| | 1997 | | | | | 1998 | | | | |
	Retail Financial Services	Corporate Banking	Barclays Capital	Other	Total	Retail Financial Services	Corporate Banking	Barclays Capital	Other	Total
Net interest income	2.6	1.1	0.3	0.0	4.0	2.8	1.2	0.4	−0.1	4.3
Net fees and commissions	1.7	0.6	0.1	0.6	3.0	1.7	0.6	0.2	0.3	2.8
Other operating income	0.1	0.0	0.4	0.0	0.6	0.2	0.0	0.0	0.1	0.3
Total operating income	4.4	1.7	0.9	0.6	7.6	4.7	1.9	0.6	0.2	7.4
Total operating expenses	−2.8	−0.8	−0.6	−1.0	−5.2	−2.9	−0.9	−0.7	−0.5	−4.9
Operating profit before provisions	1.6	0.9	0.2	−0.4	2.4	1.9	1.0	−0.1	−0.3	2.5
Provisions for bad and doubtful debts	−0.4	0.0	0.0	0.2	−0.2	−0.4	0.0	−0.2	0.1	−0.5
Exceptional and other items	0.0	0.0	0.0	−0.4	−0.4	0.0	0.0	0.0	0.0	−0.1
Net profit before tax	1.3	0.9	0.2	−0.7	1.7	1.5	1.0	−0.3	−0.3	1.9
Total assets	41.7	39.0	132.2	19.5	232.4	46.2	45.3	114.7	13.3	219.5
Shareholders' funds*	2.3	2.1	2.2	1.2	7.9	2.5	2.4	2.4	0.8	8.2
					per cent					per cent
Net profit before tax as a percentage of shareholders' funds*	54	41	11	−5	22	58	39	−11	−31	23

| | 1999 | | | | | 2000 | | | | |
	Retail Financial Services	Corporate Banking	Barclays Capital	Other	Total	Retail Financial Services	Corporate Banking	Barclays Capital	Other	Total
Net interest income	3.0	1.3	0.4	0.0	4.6	3.3	1.3	0.5	0.0	5.2
Net fees and commissions	1.8	0.7	0.2	0.3	2.9	2.3	0.7	0.3	0.4	3.7
Other operating income	0.2	0.0	0.6	0.0	0.8	0.0	0.0	0.7	0.0	0.7
Total operating income	4.9	1.9	1.2	0.4	8.4	5.6	2.1	1.5	0.5	9.6
Total operating expenses	−2.7	−0.9	−0.8	−0.8	−5.1	−2.9	−0.9	−1.0	−0.7	−5.5
Operating profit before provisions	2.2	1.1	0.4	−0.4	3.2	2.7	1.2	0.5	-0.3	4.1
Provisions for bad and doubtful debts	−0.5	−0.1	0.0	0.0	−0.6	−0.6	−0.1	−0.1	0.0	−0.8
Exceptional and other items	0.0	0.0	0.0	−0.1	−0.1	-	-	-	0.2	0.2
Net profit before tax	1.7	0.9	0.3	−0.5	2.5	2.1	1.1	0.4	−0.1	3.5
Total assets	48.7	47.4	144.8	13.8	254.8	88.8	52.9	156.9	17.6	3,316.2
Shareholders' funds*	2.7	2.7	2.5	1.0	8.8	7.2	3.2	2.9	1.5	14.8
					per cent					per cent
Net profit before tax as a percentage of shareholders' funds*	64	36	12	−53	28	29	34	15	−7	24

Source: Barclays.

*Includes minority interests.
Note: Figures have been rounded and totals may not add exactly.

5.70. We asked Barclays to explain why the return calculated for the SME banking business of [✂] per cent in 1999 should be at the lower end of its published returns for Retail Financial Services and Corporate Banking of 64 and 36 per cent respectively. Barclays said that such comparisons of returns could be misleading as the analysis reported in the published accounts was primarily based on contributions to overall group RWAs and did not represent the usage of the group's capital. The bank's own calculation for the SME banking business showed returns of [✂] per cent and [✂] per cent for 1999 and 2000 respectively.

Balance sheets

5.71. Table 5.9 shows Barclays' balance sheets from 1993 to 2000.[1] Total assets have increased by £144 billion from £163 billion in 1993 to £307 billion in 2000. This was because of increases in the following category of assets:

(a) loans and advances to banks increased by £13 billion from £23 billion in 1993 to £36 billion in 2000;

(b) loans and advances to customers increased by £68 billion from £94 billion in 1993 to £162 billion in 2000;

(c) debt securities increased by £51 billion from £20 billion in 1993 to £71 billion in 2000; and

(d) other assets increased by £11 billion from £19 billion in 1993 to £30 billion in 2000.

5.72. Total liabilities increased from £157 billion in 1993 to £292 billion in 2000 and shareholders' funds increased from £6 billion in 1993 to close to £15 billion in 2000. During the period, Barclays acquired Woolwich, which resulted in the addition of £4.1 billion of goodwill to the balance sheet. Pre-tax profit as a percentage of average shareholders' funds has fluctuated, mainly reflecting the level of bad debt charge. The pre-tax return was at its lowest levels between 1990 and 1993, and was negative in 1992. Since 1994 the level of pre-tax return has ranged between 25 and 32 per cent (except for 1998, when pre-tax return fell to 23 per cent).

Summary of loans to customers, and customer accounts in credit

5.73. In common with other banks, the largest items within Barclays' balance sheet were loans and advances to customers, and customer accounts in credit. In all years fixed assets were around 1 per cent of total assets. In 2000 loans and advances to customers accounted for 53 per cent of total assets and customer deposit accounts accounted for 54 per cent of total liabilities.

---

[1]Financial figures for the years prior to 1993 were not comparable with later years because of a change in accounting policy. In addition certain presentations in the earlier years' balance sheets were different from those in later years.

TABLE 5.9 Barclays: consolidated balance sheet, 1993 to 2000

£ billion

As at 31 December

	1993	1994	1995	1996	1997	1998	1999	2000
Assets								
Treasury bills and other eligible bills	6	7	7	4	6	5	7	6
Loans and advances to banks	23	29	29	29	37	37	43	36
Loans and advances to customers*	94	84	82	89	100	96	114	162
Debt securities†	20	18	23	31	53	45	54	71
Fixed assets	2	2	2	2	2	2	2	2
Other assets‡	19	20	20	24	29	28	28	30
Total assets	163	159	164	180	226	212	247	307
Retail life-fund assets attributable to policy-holders	3	3	5	6	8	7	8	9
Total assets and retail life-fund assets	166	162	169	186	235	219	255	316
Liabilities								
Deposits by banks	31	27	30	34	44	34	44	50
Customer accounts in credit	90	89	88	97	108	109	124	159
Debt securities in issue§	12	9	7	12	20	18	23	31
Subordinated liabilities	4	4	4	3	3	4	5	6
Other liabilities¶	20	24	28	27	42	39	42	46
Total liabilities	157	153	157	173	219	204	238	292
Shareholders' funds and minority interest¤	6	6	7	8	8	8	9	15
Total liabilities and shareholders' funds	163	159	164	180	226	212	247	307
Retail life-fund liabilities attributable to policy-holders	3	3	5	6	8	7	8	9
Total liabilities, shareholders' funds and retail life-fund liabilities	166	162	169	186	235	219	255	316
Other information								
Cumulative goodwill written off to reserves	*	0.5	0.5	0.5	0.4	0.4	0.2	0.2
Repurchases of ordinary shares	0.0	0.0	0.2	0.7	0.3	0.5	0.5	0.3
Performance indicators								*per cent*
Pre-tax profit as a percentage of average shareholders' funds#	11	27	25	28	26	23	30	32
Loans and advances to customers as a percentage of total assets	58	53	50	50	44	45	46	53
Customer accounts in credit as a percentage of total liabilities	57	58	56	56	50	53	52	52
Shareholders' funds as a percentage of total assets	4	4	4	4	4	4	4	5
Fixed assets as a percentage of total assets	1	1	1	1	1	1	1	1

Source: Barclays.

---

*Loans and advances to customers reported are net of provisions for bad and doubtful debts and also include finance lease receivables.

†Debt securities can be classified as either investment securities or other securities. Investment securities (mainly bonds) are held as part of the group's treasury management portfolio for liquidity and regulatory purposes. Other securities comprise mainly short-term certificates of deposits.

‡In 2000 other assets consist mainly of balances arising from off-balance-sheet financial instruments, sundry debtors, goodwill and items in the course of collection from banks.

§Debt securities in issue consists mainly of short-term certificate of deposits.

¶In 2000 other liabilities consist mainly of balances arising from off-balance-sheet financial instruments, loan capital, short positions in securities and sundry creditors.

¤This includes minority interests. In 2000 minorities are £1.6 billion out of £14.8 billion.

#Average shareholders' funds includes capitalized goodwill.

5.74. Table 5.10 provides an overview of Barclays' total loans by type of customer from 1989 to 2000. During this period, loans to personal customers increased [✂] per cent from £[✂] billion in 1989 to £[✂] billion in 2000 and loans to SME customers decreased [✂] per cent from £[✂] billion in 1989 to £[✂] billion in 2000. Loans to corporate, 'other UK' and non-UK customers all increased during this period. Barclays said that the decline in loans to SME customers was due to improvements in the liquidity of SMEs, which led to a reduction in their borrowing requirement. In 2000, the personal, SME and corporate banking businesses accounted for [✂] per cent, [✂] per cent and [✂] per cent respectively of Barclays' total lending.

TABLE 5.10 **Barclays: analysis of loans to customers, 1989 to 2000**

| | £ billion | | | | | | | Proportion of total (%) | | | | | | |
Year	Per-sonal	SME	Corp-orate	Other UK	Total UK	Non-UK	Total	Per-sonal	SME	Corp-orate	Other UK	Total UK	Non-UK	Total
1989							77							100
1990							81							100
1991							83							100
1992							84							100
1993							94							100
1994			*Figures omitted.*				84			*Figures omitted.*				100
1995			*See note on page iv.*				82			*See note on page iv.*				100
1996							89							100
1997							100							100
1998							96							100
1999							114							100
2000							162							100

Source: Barclays.

5.75. Table 5.11 provides an overview of Barclays' total customer accounts in credit (ie customer deposits together with customer accounts in credit) by segment from 1989 to 2000. During this period, accounts in credit in the personal and SME banking businesses increased. Accounts in credit from the personal banking business increased [✂] per cent from £[✂] billion in 1989 to £[✂] billion in 2000, while accounts in credit from the SME banking business increased [✂] per cent from £[✂] billion in 1989 to £[✂] billion in 2000. In 2000, the personal, SME and corporate banking businesses accounted for [✂] per cent, [✂] per cent and [✂] per cent respectively of total customer accounts in credit with Barclays.

TABLE 5.11 **Barclays: analysis of customer accounts in credit, 1989 to 2000**

| | £ billion | | | | | | | Proportion of total (%) | | | | | | |
Year	Per-sonal	SME	Corp-orate	Other UK	Total UK	Non-UK	Total	Per-sonal	SME	Corp-orate	Other UK	Total UK	Non-UK	Total
1989							104							100
1990							111							100
1991							113							100
1992							117							100
1993							90							100
1994			*Figures omitted.*				89			*Figures omitted.*				100
1995			*See note on page iv.*				88			*See note on page iv.*				100
1996							97							100
1997							108							100
1998							109							100
1999							124							100
2000							159							100

Source: Barclays.

5.76. Appendix 5.3 shows the summarized average balance sheets for Barclays from 1993 to 2000, with the corresponding earnings of interest on assets, and payments of interest on liabilities in the respective years. In 2000 Barclays reported that it earned an average rate of 5.4 per cent on its assets (such as loans) and paid an average rate of 3.8 per cent on its liabilities (such as customer accounts in credit of which around £11 billion was interest free). In 2000 Barclays reported a net interest spread of around 1.7 per cent, which equated to net interest income of around £5.2 billion (as reported in its profit and loss statement—see Table 5.2). Barclays' net interest spread declined from 2.3 per cent in 1993 to 1.7 per cent in 2000.

Contingent liabilities and commitments

5.77. Table 5.12 shows an analysis of contingent liabilities and commitments for 1993 to 2000. Barclays' level of commitments increased from £42 billion in 1993 to £88 billion in 2000. Commitments to lend are agreements to lend to a customer in the future, subject to certain conditions. These off-balance-sheet items are significant to banks; for example, in 2000 Barclays reported total contingent liabilities of £23 billion and total commitments of £88 billion, compared with total on-balance-sheet liabilities of £292 billion.

TABLE 5.12 **Barclays: analysis of contingent liabilities and commitments, 1993 to 2000**

								£ billion
	1993	1994	1995	1996	1997	1998	1999	2000
Contingent liabilities								
Acceptances and endorsements	4	1	1	1	2	1	2	1
Guarantees and assets pledged as collateral security	7	6	6	5	7	9	12	15
Other contingent liabilities	6	5	5	5	5	5	5	7
	17	13	12	11	13	15	19	23
Commitments								
Standby facilities, credit lines and other	42	43	44	47	59	68	82	88

Source: Barclays.

Bad debts

5.78. Table 5.13 shows the level of year-end bad debt provision and the level of bad debt charge against profits for the financial years 1989 to 2000. The provision is divided into specific amounts (where the potential bad debt is attributable to a specific customer) and general provisions against the portfolio of lending. The level of bad debt provisions has fluctuated between 1989 and 2000 and reached a peak of £3.8 billion in 1993. Since 1993, the level of bad debt provisions has declined to around £2.4 billion in 2000. These levels of provisions equated to 4 per cent of loans at the peak (in the years 1992 to 1994) compared with 2 per cent at the end of the 1990s. Barclays said that the decline was due to improvements in the economy. The mix between general and specific provisions has also changed over this period. The level of general provisions has increased while the level of specific provisions has decreased. Appendix 5.2 shows comments from Barclays' annual reports on its bad debt experience over the recession years.

5.79. The level of bad debt charge against profits has fluctuated between 1989 and 2000, reaching a peak of around £2.5 billion or 4 per cent of total loans in 1992. Since 1993 the level of bad debt charge has declined to around £0.8 billion in 2000 or 0.5 per cent of total loans.

5.80. Barclays told us that the circumstances of its borrowing customers during the last UK recession (between 1990 and 1993) were exacerbated by high levels of customer gearing. As a result the levels of bad debt provision and bad debt charge were substantially higher during the period. Barclays added that there was an expectation from the Government for it to keep lending to small businesses, even if there were concerns over a recession.

TABLE 5.13 **Barclays: analysis of bad debt provision and charges to profit and loss, 1989 to 2000**

£ billion

	1989	1990	1991	1992	1993	1994	1995	1996	1997	1998	1999	2000
Analysis of movement in provision												
Balance at start of year	1.7	2.5	2.3	2.7	3.4	3.8	3.2	2.7	2.1	1.9	1.9	2.0
Charge against profits (analysed below)	1.4	1.2	1.5	2.5	1.9	0.6	0.4	0.2	0.2	0.5	0.6	0.8
Amounts written off	−0.7	−1.2	−1.2	−1.8	−1.6	−1.1	−0.9	−0.7	−0.5	−0.4	−0.6	−0.6
Other movements	0.2	−0.2	0.0	0.1	0.0	−0.1	0.0	−0.1	−0.1	0.0	0.0	0.1
Balance at end of year	2.5	2.3	2.7	3.4	3.8	3.2	2.7	2.1	1.9	1.9	2.0	2.4
Analysis of bad debt provision												
General provision	0.2	0.4	0.5	0.7	0.8	0.9	0.9	0.8	0.7	0.7	0.7	0.8
Specific provision	2.3	1.9	2.2	2.8	3.0	2.3	1.9	1.4	1.1	1.2	1.3	1.6
Closing bad debt provision	2.5	2.3	2.7	3.4	3.8	2.7	2.7	2.1	1.9	1.9	2.0	2.4
Analysis of bad debt charge to profit and loss												
New and additional provisions	1.5	1.3	1.6	2.6	2.2	1.2	0.9	0.8	0.6	0.8	0.9	1.0
Releases of provisions established in earlier years	-	-	-	-	−0.3	−0.5	−0.3	−0.4	−0.3	−0.2	−0.2	−0.1
Recoveries of advances written off in earlier years	−0.1	-	−0.1	−0.1	−0.1	−0.2	−0.2	−0.2	−0.1	−0.2	−0.1	−0.1
Other movements	-	-	-	-	0.1	-	-	−0.1	-	-	-	-
Bad debt charge to profit and loss	1.4	1.2	1.5	2.5	1.9	0.6	0.4	0.2	0.2	0.5	0.6	0.8
Performance indicators												*per cent*
Bad debt provision as a percentage of total loans	3	3	3	4	4	4	3	2	2	2	2	1
Bad debt charge as a percentage of total loans	1.8	1.5	1.9	3.0	2.0	0.7	0.5	0.2	0.2	0.5	0.5	0.5
Bad debt charge as a percentage of total income	25	22	24	38	25	9	6	3	3	7	7	9

Source: Barclays.

5.81. Table 5.14 shows Barclays' bad debt charge to profit and loss by type of customer from 1989 to 2000. The level of bad debt charge for Barclays was at its highest between 1989 and 1993 and peaked at £2.5 billion in 1992. Over the 12-year period to 2000, Barclays reported total bad debt charges of £12 billion, the analysis by segment being: personal £[✀] billion, SME £[✀] billion, corporate £[✀] billion, 'other UK' £[✀] billion and non-UK £[✀] billion.

TABLE 5.14 **Barclays: bad debt charge to profit and loss account by type of customer, 1989 to 2000**

£ million

Year	Personal*	SME	Corporate	Other UK*	Total UK	Non-UK*	Total
1989							1,397
1990							1,233
1991							1,547
1992							2,534
1993							1,869
1994							602
1995			*Figures omitted. See note on page iv.*				396
1996							215
1997							227
1998							492
1999							621
2000							817
Total							11,950
Average 1989–93							1,716
Average 1994–2000							481

Source: Barclays.

Note: Figures rounded. Totals may not therefore add up.

5.82. Barclays said that in the years since 1994 the level of bad debt charge for SMEs had improved because of the cyclicality of the SME banking business. Releases of provisions and recoveries from customers for loans regarded as bad in previous years were also a significant factor behind the low bad debt charges.

5.83. Table 5.15 shows Barclays' bad debt charge as a percentage of loans by type of customer from 1989 to 2000. During the period 1990 to 1993, the percentage within the personal banking business ranged from [✂] per cent, the percentage within the SME banking business ranged from [✂] per cent and the percentage within the corporate banking business ranged from [✂] per cent. Since 1993, the percentage in the SME and corporate banking businesses has declined and to a lesser extent in the personal banking business.

TABLE 5.15 **Barclays: bad debt charge as a percentage of loans to customers, 1989 to 2000**

per cent

Year	Personal	SME	Corporate	Other UK	Total UK	Non-UK	Total
1989							1.8
1990							1.5
1991							1.9
1992							3.0
1993							2.0
1994							0.7
1995							0.5
1996			Figures omitted. See note on page iv.				0.2
1997							0.2
1998							0.5
1999							0.5
2000							0.5
Average 1989–93							2.0
Average 1994–2000							0.5

Source: Barclays.

5.84. The bad debt charge as a percentage of loans for the non-UK activity was also at its highest between 1990 and 1993, where it ranged between [✂] per cent. Since then the percentage has also declined. The 'other UK' activity followed a different trend, the percentage being at its highest at [✂] per cent in 1989 reflecting the fact that a large provisions charge was held centrally, rather than being allocated out to the different businesses.

5.85. Over the five-year period, from 1989 to 1993, the SME banking business reported an average percentage of bad debt charge to loans of [✂] per cent. This compared to the personal banking business of [✂] per cent and the corporate banking business of [✂] per cent. Barclays said that the higher bad debt charge in the SME banking business highlighted its nature as a high-risk business. Over the same period, the 'other UK' activity and the non-UK activity reported average percentages of [✂] per cent respectively. Since 1993, the seven-year average of SME banking business bad debt charges to loans percentage fell to [✂] per cent, compared with [✂] per cent for the personal banking business.

5.86. Table 5.16 analyses Barclays' amounts written off for bad debts by sector between 1992 and 2000. The table also shows the relative significance of sectors to Barclays' overall bad debts experience; it compares later years' write-offs to the high level reached in 1992; and also shows bad debt write-offs as a percentage of lending to particular sectors for the relevant years. Over the period 1992 to 2000 business write-offs accounted for 47 per cent of the total, the personal sector accounted for 31 per cent, and the non-UK and sundry activities write-offs accounted for 22 per cent. In order of importance over the recession years 1992 to 1994, the property and construction sectors each accounted for annual write-offs around 5 per cent of lending; followed by wholesale, retail and leisure at 3.9 per cent; and then by business and other services at 2.8 per cent; which compared with the overall business bad debt average of 2.8 per cent. In the later 1990s Barclays' bad debt write-off levels as a percentage of lending to most business sectors declined and after 1994 only went above 1 per cent for isolated years with no obvious pattern. Overall for the portfolio of lending to business sectors, the average percentage bad debt write-off to lending ratio was 1.4 per cent in 1995, 1.1 per cent in 1996, 0.8 per cent in 1997, and 0.4 per cent in the years 1998, 1999 and 2000. These results compared with ratios of between 0.7 and 1.1 per cent for personal and home loans, and 0.3 and 1.1 per cent for non-UK lending.

TABLE 5.16 **Barclays: analysis of amounts written off* by sector, 1992 to 2000**

£ million

Bad debts written off* by sector	1992†	1993	1994	1995	1996	1997	1998	1999	2000
Banks and financial institutions	36	7	4	2	10	1	16	14	13
Agriculture, forestry and fishing	12	20	12	10	5	4	2	6	6
Manufacturing	107	95	83	33	22	20	28	20	30
Construction	147	122	76	47	38	12	12	12	8
Property	381	236	110	107	61	28	17	9	5
Energy and water	0	21	1	5	3	8	0	0	2
Wholesale, retail and leisure	285	254	203	102	74	48	25	35	34
Transport	29	12	7	22	17	63	2	4	3
Postal and communication	1	1	2	1	0	0	0	1	0
Business and other services	181	179	132	88	79	32	36	43	33
Total for business lending	1,179	947	630	417	309	216	138	144	134
Personal and home loans	388	349	164	260	281	212	262	366	450
Total UK	1,567	1,296	794	677	590	428	400	510	584
Non-UK and sundry items	283	318	356	246	232	143	165	141	96
Total amount written off for year	1,850	1,614	1,150	923	822	571	565	651	680

per cent

Summary of weighted amounts written off* as % of high write-off level in 1992	1992†	1993	1994	1995	1996	1997	1998	1999	2000	1992 to 2000 Cumulative total	Relative weighting
Banks and financial institutions	2	0	0	0	1	0	1	1	1	6	1
Agriculture, forestry and fishing	1	1	1	1	0	0	0	0	0	4	1
Manufacturing	6	5	4	2	1	1	2	1	2	24	5
Construction	8	7	4	3	2	1	1	1	0	26	5
Property	21	13	6	6	3	2	1	0	0	52	11
Energy and water	0	1	0	0	0	0	0	0	0	2	0
Wholesale, retail and leisure	15	14	11	6	4	3	1	2	2	57	12
Transport	2	1	0	1	1	3	0	0	0	9	2
Postal and communication	0	0	0	0	0	0	0	0	0	0	0
Business and other services	10	10	7	5	4	2	2	2	2	43	9
Total for business lending	64	51	34	23	17	12	7	8	7	222	47
Personal and home loans	21	19	9	14	15	11	14	20	24	147	31
Total UK	85	70	43	37	32	23	22	28	31	369	78
Non-UK and sundry items	15	17	19	13	13	8	9	8	5	105	22
Total written off for the year as a % of 1992 write-off	100	87	62	50	44	31	31	35	36	474	100

per cent

Bad debts written off as a % of total lending to the sector	1992†	1993	1994	1995	1996	1997	1998	1999	2000	Average 1992–94	Average 1992–2000
Banks and financial institutions	1.1	0.1	0.1	0.1	0.4	0.0	0.9	0.9	0.9	0.4	0.5
Agriculture, forestry and fishing	0.7	1.3	0.8	0.6	0.3	0.2	0.1	0.4	0.4	0.9	0.5
Manufacturing	1.7	1.7	1.6	0.6	0.4	0.4	0.4	0.3	0.4	1.7	0.8
Construction	5.4	5.8	5.1	3.3	3.1	1.1	1.0	0.9	0.5	5.4	2.9
Property	7.6	5.5	2.4	2.8	1.7	1.0	0.5	0.2	0.1	5.2	2.4
Energy and water	0.0	2.3	0.2	0.5	0.3	1.4	0.0	0.0	0.2	0.8	0.5
Wholesale, retail and leisure	4.1	4.3	3.4	1.8	1.3	0.8	0.4	0.5	0.5	3.9	1.9
Transport	2.9	1.2	0.6	1.9	1.3	7.2	0.2	0.3	0.2	1.6	1.8
Postal and communication	0.5	0.5	0.9	0.4	0.0	0.0	0.0	0.3	0.0	1.7	0.7
Business and other services	2.8	2.9	2.8	1.4	1.3	0.5	0.5	0.5	0.3	2.8	1.4
Total business lending	3.4	2.9	2.1	1.4	1.1	0.8	0.4	0.4	0.4	2.8	1.4
Personal and home loans	1.8	1.5	0.7	1.0	1.1	0.8	0.9	1.1	0.7	1.3	1.1
Non-UK and sundry items	0.9	1.0	1.3	1.1	1.2	0.7	0.8	0.5	0.3	1.1	0.9
Total for all activities	2.1	1.9	1.4	1.2	1.1	0.8	0.7	0.7	0.5	1.8	1.1

Source: Barclays.

---

*These are the amounts written off to the provisions account and will not equate to the bad debt charge, which took account of other movements, and recoveries.

†The amount written off in 1991 was £1,137 million, of which the business element was £599 million.

5.87. When we compared the nine-year simple average, the ratio of bad debt write-offs to lending was 1.4 per cent for business lending; 1.1 per cent for personal and home loans; 0.9 per cent for non-UK and sundry lending; and the average was 1.1 per cent across all the portfolios of lending.

5.88. Barclays told us that its guidance policy regarding debts written off said the following:

Debts should be written off immediately to the extent that there is no realistic prospect of a change in the customer's covenant and the whole or part of the debt is considered irrecoverable ... and the general rule is that there must be strong justification for a provision to remain outstanding for longer than 12 months or 6 months where the account is designated as non accrual.

Barclays added that an account would be designated 'non-accrual' when there was no expectation of receiving the repayment of the interest within a reasonable period. It noted that either subject to a legal or statutory bar or where it agreed specifically to forgive the debt written off or part thereof, the customer would continue to remain liable in full for all amounts written off and any interest accrued but not applied to those amounts written off.

Capital adequacy

5.89. Table 5.17 shows regulatory capital data for Barclays from 1993 to 2000. Between 1993 and 2000, Barclays Tier 1 ratio has ranged between 6 and 8 per cent and its RAR has ranged between 10 and 11 per cent. Barclays said that the level of capital required for regulatory purposes represented the absolute minimum level of capital and was significantly below the level of capital required by capital providers, debt holders and shareholders.

5.90. Barclays said that the level of capital held affected not only its credit rating (and hence its cost of debt), but also its cost of equity. It said that its equity beta was affected by a number of factors including level of capital held within the bank. If its level of capital reduced, its equity beta could increase, thus increasing its overall cost of capital.

TABLE 5.17 **Barclays: regulatory capital data, 1993 to 2000**

£ billion

As at 31 December

	1993	1994	1995	1996	1997	1998	1999	2000
RWAs	102.4	93.2	93.3	98.4	108.3	109.8	115.9	147.0
Tier 1 capital	6.0	6.5	7.1	7.4	7.9	8.0	8.7	10.5
Tier 2 capital	4.8	4.1	4.0	3.4	3.6	4.2	4.9	6.6
Tier 3 capital	0.0	0.0	0.0	0.0	0.0	0.3	0.3	0.3
Gross capital resources	10.8	10.6	11.1	10.9	11.5	12.5	13.9	17.4
Less: supervisory deductions	−0.9	−0.9	−1.0	−0.7	−0.6	−0.8	−0.9	−1.3
Total net capital resources	9.9	9.7	10.1	10.2	10.8	11.7	14.0	16.1

per cent

Ratios								
Tier 1 ratio	6	7	8	8	7	7	8	7
RAR*	10	10	11	10	10	11	11	11

Source: Barclays.

*The published RAR is calculated on the basis of the net capital resources divided by the RWAs and expressed as a percentage.

5.91. Barclays told us that it aimed to have a Tier 1 capital ratio of 7 per cent and a safety margin above the FSA minimum RAR. It said that this was appropriate to take account of commitments at any one time and exposure to credit losses, and was necessary to maintain a satisfactory credit rating.

Lloyds TSB

History

5.92. Lloyds is listed on the London Stock Exchange. On 29 June 2001 its market capitalization in the *Financial Times* was £39.1 billion and its price:earnings ratio was 14.0. All the material companies within Lloyds TSB that provided services to SMEs in the UK were directly or indirectly wholly-owned subsidiaries.

5.93. Lloyds began its history as a private bank in Birmingham in 1765. It converted into a joint stock bank in 1865 and thereafter grew by mergers in the Midlands and established a presence in London in the 1880s. In the twentieth century it continued its expansion across the UK and in 1911 began international banking. In 1988 the bank merged a number of its businesses with the Abbey Life insurance company to create Lloyds Abbey Life plc. Lloyds TSB was formed in 1995 from the merger of Lloyds Bank Plc (Lloyds) and the TSB Group plc (TSB). The merger of the two banks was seen by management as a good fit as Lloyds was strong in mortgages and in small business banking while TSB was strong as a savings institution and as a general insurer. The management also envisaged that the enlarged group would achieve improvements in revenue and reductions in operating costs. We discuss TSB as a stand-alone bank in paragraphs 5.134 to 5.145.

5.94. Since 1990 Lloyds TSB has made other significant acquisitions including:

(a) Cheltenham & Gloucester, a mortgage provider, for £1.8 billion in late 1995;

(b) Scottish Widows Fund and Life Assurance Society (Scottish Widows), a life assurance and pensions provider, for some £6 billion in March 2000; and

(c) Chartered Trust Group plc (Chartered Trust), which provides consumer credit, leasing and related services, for £614 million in September 2000.

5.95. The impact of these acquisitions on business with SMEs was limited, though Chartered Trust supplied services to SMEs. Lloyds TSB said that its SME banking business had been able to generate increased sales by offering its customers access to the Cheltenham & Gloucester and Scottish Widows product ranges. We noted that Lloyds TSB had derived a significant proportion of its group profits from insurance and investment activities (some 31 per cent in 2000); the Scottish Widows acquisition was likely to increase this proportion further, as well as increase the proportion of group income from fees. In January 2001 Lloyds TSB announced its intention to bid for Abbey National, subject to conditions. Abbey National was already providing services to SMEs (for example, mortgage loans, asset finance and current accounts with no overdraft) and had indicated its intention to increase its presence in the market. The proposed acquisition was referred to the CC for inquiry in February 2001. On 10 July 2001 the Secretary of State announced that the proposed bid would not be allowed to proceed.

Business structure serving SMEs

5.96. Lloyds TSB told us that the following five business units provided the majority of the group's SME banking business:

(a) *Business Banking* provided banking services such as lending, money transmission and deposit-taking to business customers with turnover less than £2 million.

(b) *Commercial Banking* provided banking services such as lending, money transmission and deposit-taking to business customers with turnover between £2 million and £100 million.

(c) *Agricultural Mortgage Corporation*[1] provided loan finance to businesses in the agricultural sector;

---

[1]The Agricultural Mortgage Corporation plc is a subsidiary of Lloyds TSB.

(d) Lloyds TSB Asset Finance provided asset finance products.

(e) Lloyds TSB Commercial Finance provided factoring and invoice discounting services.

We deal with the financial performance of Lloyds TSB's SME banking business in greater detail in Chapter 6, but discuss the two main business units involved, Business Banking and Commercial Banking, in the paragraphs below.

5.97. Lloyds TSB told us that prior to 1991 business customers were managed as part of the branch network. In late 1991 Lloyds Bank Commercial Services (of which Commercial Banking formed part) was established as a separate business unit to manage business customers with a turnover of more than £1 million a year, and/or those who borrowed more than £0.5 million. This led to the transfer of responsibility for business customer relationships from branches to dedicated relationship managers who were not based in the branches. At around the same time, Business Banking was also established as a separate business unit, with dedicated relationship managers, to manage business customers with a turnover of less than £1 million. Since that time, there have been no other significant changes to these business units providing banking services to business customers.

5.98. In 1999 the threshold for customers within Business Banking was increased from £1 million to £2 million of turnover. However, we were told that the turnover limits were not strictly observed in the allocation of customers between Business Banking and Commercial Banking. The main determinant was the complexity of the customer's banking needs.

5.99. The 2000 management accounts of Business Banking (serving business customers with turnover less than £2 million) reported average total balances over the year for loans to customers of £[✂] billion and customer deposits of £[✂] billion (of which about [✂] per cent or £[✂] billion was non-interest-bearing current accounts). The management accounts also reported total income of £[✂] million, total costs of £[✂] million, bad debt charges of £[✂] million, and a contribution of £[✂] million ([✂] per cent of income). Of the total income, we noted that some [✂] per cent was contributed by non-interest-bearing current accounts.

5.100. The 2000 management accounts of Commercial Banking (serving business customers with turnover between £2 million and £100 million) reported average total balances over the year for loans to customers of £[✂] billion and customer deposits of £[✂] billion (of which [✂] per cent or £[✂] was from non-interest-bearing current accounts). The management accounts also reported total income of £[✂] million, total costs of £[✂] million, a net bad debt credit of £[✂] million and contribution before tax of £[✂] million ([✂] per cent of income).

Financial performance

Profit and loss accounts

5.101. Table 5.18 shows the profitability of Lloyds TSB from 1989 to 2000. The figures reported from 1989 to 1994 were for Lloyds prior to its merger with TSB in December 1995. The figures reported for 1995 and thereafter were for the combined group. The results of the combined Lloyds TSB group for the 12 months to 31 December 1995 were prepared on a pro-forma basis for comparison with statutory results from 1996 onwards; these pro-forma accounts were unaudited. The table also includes the results from the group's insurance business, which became a significant source of profits after 1995. Between 1995 and 1999 the bank reduced its personnel numbers from 91,000 to 80,000, a fall of 12 per cent overall. The bank made a special charge of £1.5 billion for emerging markets debt in 1989, which was charged after operating profits and which created the only loss before tax in the period between 1989 and 2000. In Table 5.18, so as to show more clearly the trend in bad debt costs, we have included this in with the bad debt charge for the year, which therefore totalled £2.1 billion in 1989.

TABLE 5.18 Lloyds TSB: consolidated profit and loss account,* 1989 to 2000

£ billion

Years ended 31 December

	1989	1990	1991	1992	1993	1994	1995	1996	1997	1998	1999	2000
Net interest income	2.2	2.3	2.4	2.0	2.1	2.1	3.5	3.8	4.2	4.4	4.8	4.6
Net fees and commissions	†	†	†	1.2	1.3	1.4	1.8	1.9	2.0	2.0	2.1	2.3
Other income	1.4	1.5	1.6	0.5	0.5	0.4	0.9	1.1	1.1	0.7	1.0	1.6
Operating income	3.7	3.8	4.0	3.8	4.0	3.9	6.3	6.8	7.3	7.1	7.9	8.5
Operating expenses	−2.3	−2.5	−2.5	−2.4	−2.5	−2.5	−4.3	−4.0	−3.8	−3.6	−3.5	−4.1
Operating profit before provisions	1.3	1.4	1.5	1.4	1.5	1.4	2.0	2.8	3.5	3.5	4.3	4.4
Bad debt charge	−2.1‡	−0.8	−0.9	−0.6	−0.5	−0.1	−0.6	−0.3	−0.4	−0.5	−0.6	−0.5
Other provisions	0.1	0.0	0.0	0.0	0.0	0.0	0.0	0.0	−0.1	0.0	0.0	0.0
Operating profit after bad debt charge	−0.7	0.6	0.6	0.8	1.0	1.3	1.5	2.5	3.0	2.9	3.7	3.9
Exceptional, extraordinary and other items	0.0	0.1	0.0	0.0	0.0	0.0	0.2	0.0	0.2	0.1	−0.1	0.0
Net profit before tax	−0.7	0.7	0.7	0.8	1.0	1.3	1.7	2.5	3.2	3.0	3.6	3.9
Tax	0.2	−0.2	−0.2	−0.3	−0.3	−0.4	−0.6	−0.8	−0.8	−0.9	−1.1	−1.1
Net profit after tax	−0.5	0.5	0.5	0.5	0.7	0.9	1.1	1.7	2.3	2.1	2.5	2.8
Minority interest	−0.1	−0.1	−0.1	−0.1	−0.1	−0.1	−0.1	−0.1	0.0	0.0	0.0	0.0
Profit for the financial year	−0.6	0.4	0.4	0.4	0.6	0.8	1.0	1.6	2.3	2.1	2.5	2.7
Transfer to non-distributable reserve	−0.1	−0.1	0.0	0.0	0.0	0.0	0.0	0.0	0.0	0.0	0.0	0.0
Dividends	−0.2	−0.2	−0.2	−0.2	−0.3	−0.3	−1.6§	−0.7	−0.9	−1.2	−1.5	−1.7
Profit retained for the financial year	−0.8	0.2	0.2	0.2	0.3	0.5	−0.6	0.9	1.4	0.9	1.1	1.0
Number of employees ('000)¶	N/A	N/A	N/A	N/A	N/A	N/A	95	95	93	86	85	86
Performance indicators												*per cent*
Tax charge as a percentage of profit before tax	30	30	28	35	33	33	35	31	26	29	30	29
Percentage change in operating income	N/A	4.7	4.1	−4.8	4.9	−2.2	61.6	7.7	7.8	−2.4	10.7	7.6
Change in number of employees	N/A	N/A	N/A	N/A	N/A	N/A	33	0.	−2	−7	−1	1

Source: Lloyds TSB.

*Figures from 1989 to 1994 represent those of Lloyds before its merger with TSB. Figures from 1995 onwards represent those of the combined Lloyds TSB group. The figures for the year ended 31 December 1995 were prepared on a pro-forma basis to provide a prior year comparison with figures for the newly created Lloyds TSB from 1996 onwards. These 1995 results were unaudited.

†Separate data was not available. Net fees and commissions was included as part of 'other' income.

‡For 1989, the bad debt charge included provisions of £1.5 billion that related to emerging markets debt. This was shown in the accounts for the year as an exceptional item.

§As part of the terms of merger of Lloyds and TSB, a special cash dividend of £1 billion was paid to TSB shareholders in December 1995.

¶Calculated on a headcount basis and includes staff employed by the long-term assurance business.

Note: N/A = Not available.

5.102. Between 1989 and 1994 operating income for the bank remained relatively unchanged at around £4 billion. Following the merger with TSB, operating income increased 62 per cent from £3.9 billion in 1994 to £6.3 billion in 1995. Since then, operating income has increased a further 35 per cent to around £8.5 billion in 2000. During the same period, operating expenses decreased by 19 per cent from £4.3 billion in 1995 to £3.5 billion in 1999, but then rose to £4.1 billion in 2000. Operating profit after provisions increased 160 per cent from £1.5 billion in 1995 to £3.9 billion in 2000. Lloyds TSB told us that a key goal in the late 1990s was to make reductions in costs, and that it considered itself one of the most efficient UK retail banks. It noted that the reasons for the increase in operating profit included the effect of acquisitions (for example, Cheltenham & Gloucester and Scottish Widows) and benign economic conditions.

5.103. Table 5.19 further analyses the overall performance of Lloyds TSB from 1989 to 2000 as shown in Table 5.18 by showing all items as a percentage of operating income. Net interest income as a percentage of operating income declined from 60 per cent in 1989 to 55 per cent in 1994. Since the merger with TSB, it increased from 56 per cent in 1995 to 61 per cent in 1999, but then fell to 54 per cent in 2000. This income comes from both customer deposits and loans.

TABLE 5.19 **Lloyds TSB: operating profit and loss items as a percentage of operating income, 1989 to 2000**

per cent

	1989	1990	1991	1992	1993	1994	1995	1996	1997	1998	1999	2000
Net interest income	60	60	59	54	53	55	56	56	58	63	61	54
Net fees and commissions	*	*	*	32	33	35	29	29	28	28	26	27
Other income	40	40	41	14	14	9	15	16	14	10	13	19
Operating income	100	100	100	100	100	100	100	100	100	100	100	100
Operating expenses	−64	−64	−62	−64	−62	−64	−68	−59	−52	−51	−45	−48
Operating profit before provisions	36	36	38	36	38	36	32	41	48	49	55	52
Bad debt charge	−58†	−20	−23	−15	−13	−3	−9	−5	−6	−7	−8	−6
Other provisions	2	0	1	−1	0	0	0	0	0	−1	−1	0
Operating profit after bad debt charge	−20	15	16	20	25	33	23	36	41	41	47	46
Exceptional and other items	0	3	1	1	1	1	3	1	2	1	−1	0
Net profit before tax	−20	19	17	21	26	34	26	37	43	42	46	46

Source: Lloyds TSB.

*Net fees and commissions was included as part of other income.
†The 1989 figure included a provision for emerging markets debt, which amounted to 41 per cent of the total income for the year. This was shown in the accounts for the year as an exceptional item.

5.104. Operating expenses as a percentage of operating income (also referred to as the cost:income ratio) remained relatively static between 62 and 64 per cent in the six years to 1994. With the TSB merger in 1995, the percentage increased to a high of 68 per cent, as a result of a one-off restructuring cost of £425 million in that year for the integration and reorganization of the two banks. Since then, the percentage declined year on year until 1999 when the group's cost:income ratio was 45 per cent. However, this increased to 48 per cent in 2000 owing to higher investment spend.

5.105. In common with other banks, bad debt charge as a percentage of operating income was at its highest levels between 1989 and 1993. It was 58 per cent of income in 1989, of which 70 per cent (41 per cent of income) was because of losses on emerging markets lending, which the bank showed as an exceptional item in the year. The next peak was around 23 per cent of income (or £0.9 billion) in 1991. Since 1994, the bad debt charge has been below 10 per cent of income; in 2000 it was 6 per cent of income.

Analysis of performance by type of customer

5.106. We asked Lloyds TSB to analyse its UK activities from 1989 to 2000 into those serving the following types of customer:

(a) personal customers;

(b) SME customers, which included business customers with turnover less than £25 million;

(c) corporate customers, which included business customers with turnover greater than £25 million; and

(d) 'other' customers, which Lloyds TSB said included group treasury management, insurance and investments, private banking, group capital funds and group balance sheet management.

It noted, however, that the above categories of customer did not correspond with its existing business structure and that it was able to provide the data requested only from 1996 onwards and only on a 'best endeavours' basis. Tables 5.20 to 5.24 show the trends in operating income, operating costs and operating profits over the five years to 2000.

5.107. Table 5.20 shows operating income by type of customer from 1996 to 2000. During this period, operating income increased [✂] per cent from £[✂] billion to £[✂] billion. Over the period, operating income from personal, SME and corporate customers remained relatively unchanged; but their combined contribution to the group's operating income declined from [✂] per cent in 1996 to [✂] per cent in 2000. Much of the change in the income mix was accounted for by 'other' UK income, which increased from [✂] to [✂] per cent of total income over the period.

TABLE 5.20 Lloyds TSB: operating income by type of customer, 1996 to 2000*

			£ billion								Proportion of total (%)				
Year	Per-sonal	SME	Corp-orate	Other UK	Total UK	Non-UK	Total	Per-sonal	SME	Corp-orate	Other UK	Total UK	Non-UK	Total
Unadjusted for capital fund recharges														
1996					6.0	0.8	6.8					88	12	100
1997					6.3	1.0	7.3					86	14	100
1998	Figures omitted. See note on page iv.				6.1	1.0	7.1	Figures omitted. See note on page iv.				86	14	100
1999					6.9	1.0	7.9					87	13	100
2000					7.4	1.0	8.5					88	12	100

Source: Lloyds TSB.

*Operating income includes net interest income, net fees and commissions and other income.

5.108. Table 5.21 analyses the items covered by the 'other UK' category. Of the pre-tax profit of £[✂], £[✂] million was from Insurance and Investments, £[✂] million from Treasury and £[✂] million from Offshore Banking activities. The item shown as 'Group Capital' that had a surplus of £[✂] million included net fees and internal charges to the personal, corporate, SME banking businesses. Lloyds TSB explained that these internal charges were the notional capital charges (capital fund recharges) for investing equity in the form of share capital, reserves and fixed assets in its various business units.

TABLE 5.21 Lloyds TSB: summary of 'other UK' category for 1999

						£ million
	Insurance & Investments	Group Capital*	Treasury	Lloyds Development	Wealth Manage-ment	Sundry book entries†	Total
Income							
Costs							
Operating surplus/ deficit	Figures omitted. See note on page iv.						
Bad debt provisions							
Other provisions							
Pre-tax profit							

Source: Lloyds TSB.

*Includes a credit for the pension fund surplus in accordance with SSAP 24.
†These represent adjustments to reclassify items, for example to non-UK and international activities, and consolidation entries.

5.109. Table 5.22 shows operating costs by type of customer for Lloyds TSB from 1996 to 2000. Total operating costs increased by [✂] per cent from £[✂] billion in 1996 to £[✂] billion in 2000. During the same period, operating costs within the businesses also changed but at different rates. Comparing 2000 with 1996, personal, corporate and 'other UK' businesses remained fairly stable, though with increases between 1999 and 2000. The SME banking business showed an increase in costs from £[✂] in 1996 to £[✂] in 2000.

TABLE 5.22 **Lloyds TSB: operating costs by type of customer, 1996 to 2000**

	£ billion							Proportion of total (%)*						
Year	Per-sonal	SME	Corp-orate	Other UK*	Total UK*	Non-UK	Total*	Per-sonal	SME	Corp-orate	Other UK	Total UK	Non-UK	Total
Unadjusted for capital fund recharges														
1996					3.4	0.5	3.9					87	13	100
1997					3.2	0.5	3.7					86	14	100
1998	Figures omitted. See note on page iv.				2.9	0.5	3.5	Figures omitted. See note on page iv.				84	16	100
1999					2.9	0.5	3.4					85	15	100
2000					3.4	0.5	4.0					87	13	100

Source: Lloyds TSB.

*Operating costs exclude general insurance claims that are included in total costs shown in Table 5.18. General insurance claims arise in the Insurance and Investments business which forms part of 'other UK'. In 2000 such claims amounted to £[✂] million (1999, £[✂] million).

5.110. In terms of the proportions of costs by type of customer, the amount attributed to the personal customer business rose from [✂] per cent in 1996 to [✂] per cent in 2000. For the SME banking business, there was an increase from [✂] per cent in 1996 to [✂] per cent in 2000. However, for both corporate and 'other UK' customers, the proportions decreased over the same period. We deal with cost allocation issues in Chapter 6.

5.111. Table 5.23 shows the cost:income ratio for Lloyds TSB by type of customer from 1996 to 2000. The cost:income ratio for the bank decreased from 56 per cent in 1996 to 47 per cent in 2000, but at different rates for the various businesses. In 2000, the personal customer business reported the highest cost:income ratio of 61 per cent, compared with the SME, corporate and non-UK banking businesses, which reported ratios of 52, 48 and 51 per cent respectively.

TABLE 5.23 **Lloyds TSB: cost:income ratios, 1996 to 2000***

per cent

Year	Personal	SME	Corporate	Other UK	Total UK	Non-UK	Total
Unadjusted for capital fund recharges							
1996	65	57	63	37	56	62	56
1997	62	57	73	27	51	51	51
1998	59	59	58	14	48	55	49
1999	55	49	49	13	42	50	43
2000	61	52	48	20	46	51	47

Source: Lloyds TSB.

*The figures in this table are based on the actual income and cost data, rather than the rounded figures shown in Tables 5.20 and 5.22.

5.112. Lloyds TSB said that the fall in the cost:income ratio within the SME banking business from 59 to 49 per cent between 1998 and 1999 was due to higher operating costs in 1998. In 1998 the bank incurred a number of exceptional merger and IT-related costs, namely the integration of Lloyds and TSB processing systems, the 'towards one bank' restructuring and marketing programme, and costs for Year 2000 IT compliance issues. In 1999 the SME banking business was able to realize the cost benefits from the 1998 expenditure. In that year the business also pursued income growth strategies. For example, the benign economic conditions enabled the business to: grow its loan book (without unduly compromising the quality); grow the volume of pension and insurance products sold; attract and retain larger credit balances on deposit accounts; and benefit from operational gearing. Lloyds TSB said that overall the lower cost:income ratio in 1999 was due to operating cost efficiencies, increased sales and economies of scale. At the group level, the increase in 2000 was due to exceptional group restructuring costs of £188 million, increased costs following the acquisition of Scottish Widows and Chartered Trust of £117 million, and additional investments in revenue growth business and e-commerce of £224 million. If these were excluded, the costs only increased by £50 million, which was only 1 per cent and less than the underlying rate of inflation.

5.113. Table 5.24 shows Lloyds TSB's operating profits after bad debt charge by type of customer from 1996 to 2000. For 2000 the SME banking business contributed [✂] per cent of group profits, compared with [✂] per cent for the personal customers, [✂] per cent for corporate, [✂] per cent for 'other UK', and 12 per cent for non-UK activities.

TABLE 5.24 **Lloyds TSB: operating profit (after bad debt charges) by type of customer, 1996 to 2000**

	£ billion							Proportion of total (%)						
Year	Per-sonal	SME	Corp-orate	Other UK	Total UK	Non-UK	Total	Per-sonal	SME	Corp-orate	Other UK	Total UK	Non-UK	Total
1996					2.2	0.3	2.5					86	14	100
1997		Figures omitted.			2.7	0.4	3.2		Figures omitted.			86	14	100
1998		See note on page iv.			2.7	0.3	3.0		See note on page iv.			91	9	100
1999					3.2	0.4	3.6					88	12	100
2000					3.4	0.5	3.9					88	12	100

Source: Lloyds TSB.

5.114. Table 5.25 summarizes how Lloyds TSB reported its performance by class of business in its published accounts between 1996 and 2000. During this period, the main business classes were:

(a) UK Retail Banking, which provided banking and financial services to personal and small business customers;

(b) Mortgages, which represented the bank's total UK mortgage business and included Cheltenham & Gloucester;

(c) Insurance and Investments, which represented the bank's life, pensions and unit trust businesses;

(d) Wholesale Markets, which covered banking, treasury, factoring and invoice discounting and other related services for medium-sized UK businesses, major UK and multinational companies, banks and financial institutions; and

(e) International Banking, which provides banking and financial services in four main areas—the Americas, New Zealand, Europe and offshore banking—and deals with emerging markets debt.

Business Banking (which served business customers with turnover less than £2 million) was a separate unit within UK Retail Banking; and Commercial Banking (which served business customers with turnover greater than £2 million and under £100 million) was a separate unit within Wholesale Markets. Therefore the SME banking business as defined by us fell partly within UK Retail Banking and partly within Wholesale Markets. Lloyds TSB told us that the analysis by class of business in the statutory accounts was subject to regular revision to reflect the changing nature and internal management of the business streams. As a result the data was not on a consistent basis from year to year for each year from 1996 to 2000. In particular it was inappropriate to relate the disclosure of net assets (shareholders' funds) for a type of business directly to the profits for that business. We cover the issue of returns in greater detail in Chapters 6 and 7.

TABLE 5.25 **Lloyds TSB: analysis by class of business, 1996 to 2000**

£ billion

Class of business	1996	1997	1998	1999	2000
Net profit before tax					
UK Retail Banking*	0.7	0.8	0.7	0.8	†
Mortgages	0.5	0.7	0.7	0.9	1.6
Insurance and Investments	0.5	0.5	0.6	0.9	1.2
UK Retail Financial Services	1.8	2.1	2.0	2.6	2.8
Wholesale Markets*	0.6	0.7	0.6	0.8	1.2
International Banking	0.4	0.4	0.3	0.4	‡
Other	−0.2	0.0	0.0	−0.2	−0.1
Total	2.5	3.2	3.0	3.6	3.9
Shareholders' funds (equity)					
UK Retail Banking*	1.1	1.3	1.4	1.2	†
Mortgages	1.1	1.2	1.5	1.6	2.2
Insurance and Investments	1.7	2.1	2.5	2.8	6.5
UK Retail Financial Services	3.9	4.6	5.3	5.6	8.7
Wholesale Markets*	1.4	1.5	1.8	2.3	3.1
International Banking	0.2	0.3	0.4	0.9	‡
Other	−0.3	0.0	0.0	0.0	−2.1
Total	5.1	6.3	7.5	8.7	9.7
Assets					
UK Retail Banking*	22	22	22	17	†
Mortgages	43	42	45	48	71
Insurance and Investments	3	3	3	3	10
UK Retail Financial Services	68	67	69	68	81
Wholesale Markets*	46	54	57	65	85
International Banking	16	17	17	17	‡
Other	0	0	0	0	1
Total	129	138	144	150	167

Source: Lloyds TSB.

---

*The activities within these classes included business with SMEs, as defined by us, being customers with turnover to £25 million. We noted that the net profit for 2000 in respect of these two classes of activity, plus mortgages, showed a total profit of £2.8 billion, but in Table 5.24 the total profit for the personal, SME and corporate customers as reported to us was £1.7 billion. We also noted the difference between the 'other' income category which in the table above shows loss of £2.1 billion whereas in Table 5.24 the 'other' UK activities profit was shown as £1.7 billion. Lloyds TSB told us that the differences arose primarily from definitional differences between the classes of businesses identified by us and those applied for the statutory accounts.

†In the 2000 annual report and accounts, a combined total was shown for UK Retail Banking and Mortgages.

‡In the 2000 annual report and accounts, a combined total was shown for Wholesale Markets and International Banking.

Balance sheets

5.115. Table 5.26 shows the balance sheet for Lloyds TSB from 1992 to 2000.[1] The figures reported from 1992 to 1994 were for Lloyds prior to its merger with TSB in 1995. The figures reported for 1995 and thereafter were for the combined Lloyds TSB group. Total assets increased from £62 billion in 1992 to £72 billion in 1994, then increased to £130 billion in 1995 as a result of the merger with TSB and the acquisition of Cheltenham & Gloucester, and then increased to £161 billion in 2000. Total liabilities increased from £60 billion in 1992 to £157 billion in 2000, and shareholders' funds increased from £3 billion in 1992 to close to £10 billion in 2000. Over the nine years, Lloyds TSB did not make any share buy-backs because all surplus capital was needed to support acquisitions and organic growth within the business.

5.116. Between 1992 and 1995 operating profit as a percentage of average shareholders' funds (pre-tax returns) ranged between 25 and 29 per cent whereas in the years 1996 to 2000 pre-tax returns ranged between 41 and 52 per cent.

---

[1]Each year's balance sheet was prepared under the accounting standards and policies in effect at the time of preparation. Any changes in accounting policies over the period, such as the treatment of operating leases, will impact the comparability year on year.

TABLE 5.26 Lloyds TSB: consolidated balance sheet summary, 1992 to 2000

£ billion

As at 31 December*

	1992	1993	1994	1995	1996	1997	1998	1999	2000
Assets									
Cash and balances at central banks	2	2	2	3	3	3	3	3	3
Treasury bills and other eligible bills	3	3	3	4	3	4	3	2	2
Loans and advances to banks	6	13	12	17	15	21	18	17	15
Loans and advances to customers	39	39	39	79	86	88	96	103	115
Debt securities	3	6	7	14	11	13	12	14	14
Intangible fixed assets	0	0	0	0	0	0	0	0	3
Tangible fixed assets	2	2	2	2	2	2	2	2	3
Other assets	5	4	5	8	5	4	5	4	4
Prepayments and accrued income	1	1	1	2	2	2	2	3	3
Total assets	62	71	72	130	128	136	142	147	161
Retail life-fund assets attributable to policy-holders	7	9	9	18	20	22	26	29	58
Total assets and retail life-fund assets	69	80	81	148	147	158	168	176	218
Liabilities									
Deposits by banks	6	13	13	18	15	17	17	18	17
Customer accounts in credit	38	38	38	77	82	85	90	93	101
Debt securities in issue	5	7	7	11	11	12	12	12	18
Other liabilities	6	5	6	13	9	9	9	6	7
Accruals and deferred income	2	2	2	3	3	3	3	3	4
Other provisions	0	0	0	1	1	1	2	2	2
Subordinated liabilities	2	2	3	4	4	4	4	6	8
Total liabilities	60	68	69	127	124	132	137	141	157
Shareholders' funds†	3	4	4	5	5	6	8	9	10
Total liabilities and shareholders' funds	63	72	73	132	129	138	144	150	167
Retail life-fund liabilities attributable to policy-holders	6	8	8	16	18	20	24	27	51
Total liabilities, shareholders' funds and retail life-fund liabilities	69	80	81	148	147	158	168	176	218
Other information									
Cumulative goodwill written off to reserves	‡	‡	‡	2	1	3	2	2	2
Performance indicators									per cent
Operating profit as a percentage of average shareholders' funds§	25	29	26	27	49	52	42	46	41
Loans and advances to customers as a percentage of total assets	63	56	54	61	68	65	67	70	71
Customer accounts in credit as a percentage of total liabilities	64	56	55	61	66	65	66	66	64
Shareholders' funds as a percentage of total assets	5	5	6	4	4	5	5	6	6
Fixed assets as a percentage of total assets	3	3	2	2	2	1	1	1	2

Source: Lloyds TSB.

---

*Figures prior to 1995 represent those of Lloyds before its merger with TSB.

†This includes minority interests, which until 1999 was negligible. In 1999 minorities were £33 million out of shareholders' funds of £8,726 million, and in 2000 the figure was £552 million out of £10,289 million.

‡Figures below £1 billion.

§Average shareholders' funds includes any capitalized goodwill balances.

5.117. Over the period fixed assets declined from 3 to 2 per cent of total assets. In 2000 loans and advances to customers accounted for 71 per cent of total assets, and customer accounts in credit accounted for 64 per cent of total liabilities. In 2000 the bank reported loans to customers of £115 billion compared with customer accounts in credit of £101 billion.

5.118. Lloyds TSB's cumulative goodwill written off to reserves at the end of 1999 totalled £2.4 billion. Of the total, £0.7 billion was goodwill written off from the acquisition of Cheltenham & Gloucester in 1995 and a further £1 billion was goodwill written off from the purchase of a minority interest in Lloyds Abbey Life plc in 1996.

5.119. Lloyds TSB told us that the merger with TSB in 1995 could have been accounted for under either merger accounting rules,[1] where no goodwill would be shown as arising, or under acquisition

---

[1]In accordance with Statement of Standard Accounting Practice 23 (SSAP 23).

accounting rules. It decided to use merger accounting. Lloyds TSB told us that the goodwill that might have arisen from the transaction had it adopted acquisition accounting was around £[✂] billion and that we ought to take account of this when considering returns on equity for its SME banking business.

5.120. We further discuss adjustments to equity for the purpose of calculating returns on capital in Chapter 7.

Summary of loans to customers, and customer accounts in credit

5.121. Table 5.27 provides an overview of the total loans by type of customer for Lloyds TSB from 1996 to 2000. Total loans increased 33 per cent from £86 billion in 1996 to £115 billion in 2000. The largest percentage increases were in loans to corporate customers which increased [✂] per cent from £[✂] billion in 1996 to £[✂] billion in 2000; and loans to non-UK customers which increased 27 per cent from £11 billion in 1996 to £14 billion in 2000. Loans to personal customers increased [✂] per cent from £[✂] billion in 1996 to £[✂] billion in 2000, and loans to SMEs remained around £[✂] billion over the period.

TABLE 5.27 **Lloyds TSB: analysis of loans by type of customer, 1996 to 2000**

	£ billion							Proportion of total (%)						
Year	Per-sonal	SME	Corp-orate	Other UK	Total UK	Non-UK	Total	Per-sonal	SME	Corp-orate	Other UK	Total UK	Non-UK	Total
1996					75	11	86					87	13	100
1997					77	10	88					88	12	100
1998		Figures omitted.			83	12	96		Figures omitted.			87	13	100
1999		See note on page iv.			89	13	103		See note on page iv.			87	13	100
2000					100	14	115					87	13	100

Source: Lloyds TSB.

5.122. Comparing 2000 with 1996, loans to personal customers as a proportion of total loans declined from [✂] to [✂] per cent, and the proportion of loans to the SMEs also declined, from [✂] per cent in 1996 to [✂] per cent in 2000.

5.123. Table 5.28 provides an overview of total accounts in credit by type of customer from 1996 to 2000. Accounts in credit of personal customers increased [✂] per cent from £[✂] billion in 1996 to £[✂] billion in 2000, whereas accounts of SMEs in credit increased [✂] per cent from £[✂] billion in 1996 to £[✂] billion in 2000. In 2000 the personal, SME and corporate customers accounted for [✂] per cent, [✂] per cent and [✂] per cent respectively of total accounts in credit.

TABLE 5.28 **Lloyds TSB: customer accounts in credit, 1996 to 2000**

	£ billion							Proportion of total (%)						
Year	Per-sonal	SME	Corp-orate*	Other UK*	Total UK	Non-UK	Total	Per-sonal	SME	Corp-orate*	Other UK*	Total UK	Non-UK	Total
1996							82					90	10	100
1997							85					92	8	100
1998		Figures omitted.					90		Figures omitted.			91	9	100
1999		See note on page iv.					93		See note on page iv.			91	9	100
2000							101					91	9	100

Source: Lloyds TSB.

5.124. Lloyds TSB said that the loan:deposit ratio for the group increased from 1.06 in 1996 to 1.13 in 2000. This was largely explained by the increase in mortgage business within Cheltenham & Gloucester. The loan:deposit ratio for SME customers decreased from [✂] in 1996 to [✂] in 2000. Lloyds TSB said that the benign economic environment in recent years had resulted in SMEs generating more cash and depositing more funds into their accounts, which reduced their need for loan finance in the last few years.

5.125. UK banks, the shares of which are listed in the USA, are required by the Securities and Exchange Commission to publish details of interest payable and receivable over various categories of assets and liabilities. Lloyds TSB told us that it did not have a listing for its shares in the USA (though they were traded on the over-the-counter market in New York). In late 1999 it had reviewed the possibility of obtaining a listing in the USA, a registration statement had been filed with the Securities and Exchange Commission in October 2001 and dealings on the New York Stock Exchange were due to commence in November 2001. Lloyds TSB has provided similar information for 1996 to 2000 on the sources of net interest income and this is shown in Appendix 5.4. In 2000 Lloyds TSB earned a gross yield of [✂] per cent on the average banking book assets at a cost of [✂] per cent on average banking book liabilities.

Contingent liabilities and commitments

5.126. Table 5.29 shows an analysis of contingent liabilities and commitments for the bank from 1992 to 2000. The level of contingent liabilities remained relatively constant over the period at around £4 billion, compared with commitments which increased from £22 billion in 1994 to £43 billion in 2000. These off-balance-sheet items are significant; for example, in 2000 contingent liabilities and commitments were £48 billion, 31 per cent of liabilities of £157 billion (excluding shareholders' funds and life fund liabilities).

TABLE 5.29 **Lloyds TSB: analysis of contingent liabilities and commitments***

£ billion

	1992	1993	1994	1995	1996	1997	1998	1999	2000
Contingent liabilities:									
Acceptances and endorsements	1	1	1	1	1	0	0	0	0
Guarantees and assets pledged as collateral security	2	2	2	2	2	2	2	2	3
Other contingent liabilities	1	1	1	1	2	2	2	1	2
	4	4	4	4	4	4	4	4	5
Commitments:									
Standby facilities, credit lines and other	†	†	22	25	24	25	27	28	43

Source: Lloyds TSB.

*Data for 1992 to 1995 is for Lloyds only.
†Data not available.

Bad debts

5.127. Table 5.30 shows the level of closing bad debt provision and the level of bad debt charge against profits between 1989 and 2000. The level of closing bad debt provisions increased from £4.0 billion in 1989 to a peak of £5.0 billion in 1991, fell to around £3.2 billion by 1995, and then fell further to £2.2 billion by 2000. The level of provisions ranged from 6 to 9 per cent of loans over the period 1989 to 1994, compared with lower levels in later years that declined to 2 per cent in 2000. Lloyds TSB said that the decline was due to the benign economic conditions experienced between 1995 and 2000. Appendix 5.2 shows comments from Lloyds Bank Plc's annual reports on its bad debt experience over the recession years.

TABLE 5.30 **Lloyds TSB: analysis of bad debt provision and charges to profit and loss for whole bank, 1989 to 2000**

£ billion

	1989	1990	1991	1992	1993	1994	1995	1996	1997	1998	1999	2000
Analysis of movement in provision												
Balance at start of year	1.9	4.0	4.1	5.0	4.6	4.3	3.3	3.2	2.5	2.5	2.2	2.1
Charge against profits—P&L (analysed below)	2.2	1.0	1.6	1.2	0.8	0.3	0.6	0.3	0.4	0.5	0.6	0.5
Amounts written off	−0.3	−0.7	−0.8	−1.0	−1.0	−1.0	−0.8	−0.8	−0.7	−1.0	−0.7	−0.8
Recoveries	0.0	0.0	0.0	0.0	0.1	0.0	0.1	0.1	0.1	0.1	0.1	0.2
Other movements	0.1	−0.3	0.0	−0.6	−0.2	−0.3	0.0	−0.2	0.1	0.0	0.0	0.1
Balance at end of year	4.0	4.1	5.0	4.6	4.3	3.3	3.2	2.5	2.5	2.2	2.1	2.2
Analysis of bad debt provision												
General provision	*	*	*	*	*	0.4	0.5	0.5	0.4	0.4	0.4	0.4
Specific provision	*	*	*	*	*	2.9	2.7	2.1	2.1	1.8	1.8	1.8
Bad debt provision	4.0†	4.1	5.0	4.6	4.3	3.3	3.2	2.5	2.5	2.2	2.1	2.2
Analysis of bad debt charge to profit and loss account												
New and additional provisions	*	*	*	*	*	0.7	0.9	0.8	1.0	1.0	1.1	1.1
Releases of provisions established in earlier years	*	*	*	*	*	−0.5	−0.3	−0.4	−0.4	−0.3	−0.4	−0.5
Recoveries of advances written off in earlier years	*	*	*	*	*	0.0	−0.1	−0.1	−0.1	−0.1	−0.1	−0.1
Other movements	*	*	*	*	*	0.0	0.0	0.0	0.0	0.0	0.0	0.0
Bad debt charge to profit and loss	2.1†	0.8	0.9	0.6	0.5	0.1	0.6	0.3	0.4	0.5	0.6	0.5
												per cent
Performance indicators												
Bad debt provision as a percentage of total loans	7	7	9	8	8	6	4	3	3	2	2	2
Bad debt charge as a percentage of total loans	*	1.8	2.3	1.4	1.3	0.3	0.7	0.4	0.5	0.6	0.6	0.4
Bad debt charge as a percentage of total income	12	14	15	10	8	2	9	5	6	7	7	6

Source: Lloyds TSB.

*Information is unavailable.

†The bad debt charge for 1989 included a provision of £1.5 billion for emerging markets debt, which was shown in the 1989 accounts as an exceptional item. The provision has been regularly reviewed in subsequent years and at 31 December 2000 it stood at £0.8 billion.

5.128. Between 1989[1] and 2000 the level of bad debt charge against profits fluctuated from a peak at £2.1 billion in 1989, to around £0.5 billion a year in recent years. The charge was at its highest in 1989, mainly from provisions of £1.5 billion from lending to emerging markets countries. The next peak in bad debts was 1991 when the charge as a percentage of lending was 1.7 per cent, compared with levels from 0.4 to 0.7 per cent of loans from 1995 to 2000. When bad debt charges are shown as a percentage of total income, the peak figure in 1991 equates to 15 per cent of income compared with 6 per cent in 2000.

5.129. Table 5.31 shows the bad debt charge to profit and loss account for Lloyds TSB from 1989 to 1996 as prepared for the Cruickshank review analysed between 'small business' and 'other'. The table also shows a summary of bad debt information between 1996 and 2000 in accordance with our definition of SMEs. Lloyds TSB told us that it was unable to provide us with a full analysis, in accordance with our definition of SMEs, over the complete period. However, the general trend of small business bad debt charges to 1996 as provided to the Cruickshank review was the best available estimate of the trend which would have related to SMEs under our definition. Given the definitional differences in the businesses covered in each review, the absolute bad debt level would not have been directly comparable. Over the period 1989 to 1996 both the SME banking business and other activities showed significant bad debt charges. For the period 1996 to 2000 (for which Lloyds TSB was able to provide information under our definition of SMEs) the personal customer business showed annual bad debt charges between £[✄] and £[✄], and the SME banking business showed bad debt charges of roughly £[✄] a year. The relative significance of the bad debt charges for different categories of business can be ascertained by assessing the total amount of the charge in relation to the scale of that business and comparing the rates for different businesses (see paragraph 5.131).

[1]Lloyds TSB provided some £1.5 billion arising from emerging markets debt as an exceptional item in 1989, and this therefore did not form part of bad debt charge to profits in that year.

5.130. Using the information on bad debt charges by type of customer in accordance with our definitions, [✂] per cent of the total bad debt charge to the profit and loss in 1996 was attributable to SME customers. From 1996 the proportion represented by SME customers declined to [✂] per cent in 2000 when there was a small increase from the 1999 level of [✂] per cent.

TABLE 5.31 **Lloyds TSB: analysis of bad debt charge to profit and loss by type of customer, 1989 to 1996 as provided to the Cruickshank review, and 1996 to 2000 as provided to the CC**

	£ million			Proportion of total (%)		
Year	Small Business*	Other	Total	Small business*	Other	Total
1989			2,108			100
1990			778			100
1991			918		✂	100
1992			556			100
1993	Figures omitted.		503			100
1994	See note		135	†	†	†
1995	on page iv.		651			100
1996			327			100
Total			5,976			100
					✂	
Average 1989–93			972			100

	Per sonal	SME	Corp- orate	Other UK	Total UK	Non- UK	Total
1996					358	–31	327
1997					340	81	421
1998					363	165	528
1999	Figures omitted.				501	87	588
2000	See note on page iv.				426	49	475
Average 1996–2000					398	71	468

Source: Lloyds TSB.

*The figures shown were not exactly within the CC's definition of SMEs, which was enterprises with a turnover of £25 million or less. Lloyds TSB derived the figures from a special exercise for the Cruickshank review. In order to identify the magnitude of the difference in bad debt charge for SMEs when calculated on the Cruickshank basis compared with our definition, Lloyds TSB compared the available data for 1996. It indicated, using our definition of SMEs, that the bad debt charge was marginally higher under the Cruickshank basis (£[✂] million compared with £[✂] million).

†Calculations were not relevant as net credits were shown in 1994.

5.131. Table 5.32 shows the bad debt charge as a percentage of loans by type of customer for Lloyds TSB from 1996 to 2000. The bad debt charge as a percentage of loans for personal customers ranged from [✂] per cent; for SMEs between [✂] per cent; and for corporate customers at up to [✂] per cent. Lloyds TSB told us that the percentages were understated because they included releases of provisions made in previous years and recoveries from the customers. It said that to overcome the distortions it used a measure called 'asset quality ratio' for internal credit control purposes, which was calculated as the new bad debt provision charge as a percentage of average loans.

TABLE 5.32 **Lloyds TSB: bad debt charge as a percentage of loans to customers, 1996 to 2000***

						per cent	
Year	Personal	SME	Corporate	Other UK	Total UK	Non-UK	Total
1996					0.5	–0.3	0.4
1997					0.4	0.8	0.5
1998	Figures omitted.				0.4	1.3	0.6
1999	See note on page iv.				0.6	0.6	0.6
2000					0.4	0.3	0.4

Source: Lloyds TSB.

*Some figures are negative because of recoveries.

Capital adequacy

5.132. Table 5.33 shows the regulatory capital and RAR data for Lloyds TSB from 1993 to 2000. Over the period, its Tier 1 ratio ranged between 7 and 10 per cent, and its RAR ranged between 10 and 15 per cent. Lloyds TSB told us that the higher level of capital in 1999 had been due to the need to have sufficient capital to acquire Scottish Widows, which acquisition resulted in a significant element of purchased goodwill.

5.133. Lloyds TSB said that the level of capital required to run its business exceeded the minimum regulatory level of capital set by the FSA, which served merely to protect depositors. It said that additional capital was required to enable it to invest in projects designed to enable it to compete effectively (for example, by investing in innovation, and new product offerings) and to maintain a prudent buffer against major downturns.

TABLE 5.33 **Lloyds TSB: regulatory capital data, 1993 to 2000**

£ billion

	As at 31 December							
	1993	1994	1995	1996	1997	1998	1999	2000
RWAs	48.1	64.8	78.8	80.7	79.9	83.3	84.2	94.2
Tier 1	3.2	5.9	4.6	5.3	6.3	7.3	8.5	7.7
Tier 2	2.7	4.0	4.3	4.3	4.4	4.4	6.8	7.6
Tier 3	0.0	0.0	0.0	0.0	0.0	0.0	0.0	0.0
Gross capital resources	5.9	9.9	8.9	9.5	10.7	11.7	15.3	15.3
Less: supervisory deductions*	−0.8	−1.5	−1.3	−1.7	−2.0	−2.2	−2.6	−6.9
Total net capital resources	5.1	8.4	7.6	7.8	8.6	9.5	12.7	8.4
								per cent
Ratios								
Tier 1 ratio	7	9	6	7	8	9	10	8
RAR	11	13	10	10	11	11	15	9

Source: Lloyds TSB.

---

*Supervisory deductions relate mainly to the investment and insurance businesses.

TSB

History

5.134. In this section we briefly discuss the history of TSB and its services to SMEs which were integrated into Lloyds upon the merger in 1995. TSB has particular importance to our inquiry because it had been a new entrant to the market. TSB's origins were in the early nineteenth century when trustee savings banks were established in the UK to provide the poor with a safe place to deposit their savings. Later in the nineteenth century, the number of trustee savings banks reduced through transfers to the Post Office Savings Bank and amalgamations. In the late 1970s the trustee savings banks were freed from restrictions on their activities and were able change their structure and services in order to compete on a more equal footing with the clearing banks. Accordingly, the trustee savings banks saw the SME banking business as an opportunity to earn higher returns on their assets and gradually started to enter this market.

5.135. TSB was formed in 1982 from a collection of the remaining trustee savings banks at that time. TSB was listed on the London Stock Exchange in 1986. Later it acquired Hill Samuel plc (Hill Samuel) in 1987 for £777 million. At that time Hill Samuel had two main businesses: insurance and investments, and commercial banking. It was envisaged that Hill Samuel's strength in insurance, asset management and treasury would enable TSB to become a broad-based banking group. The commercial banking activity (also known as Hill Samuel Bank) was also complementary to that of TSB, as Hill Samuel had greater corporate activity whereas TSB had greater small business activity.

5.136. Lloyds TSB told us that the initial integration strategy between TSB and Hill Samuel's commercial banking activities was that:

(a) existing overlapping relationships with customers would be rationalized (with the customer's agreement) to the appropriate division; and

(b) new customers with turnover of between £0.5 million and £10 million would be targeted by TSB (although given the size of this market Hill Samuel would also continue to be active in it), and customers with turnover greater than £10 million would be mainly targeted by Hill Samuel.

5.137. In 1987 TSB allocated to Hill Samuel Bank funds of approximately £500 million to invest. At the height of the 1980s boom Hill Samuel Bank expanded its loan book and within several years had grown its loan book to about £5 billion. However, a large proportion comprised loans to property companies (and companies where the security provided was in the form of property) and Lloyds TSB told us that Hill Samuel Bank did not have the same credit control disciplines as the rest of TSB. As a result its loans were of poorer quality and when the UK moved into economic recession in the early 1990s a large proportion of Hill Samuel's loan book proved to be irrecoverable. As a result the group reported bad debt charges of £654 million in 1991, £597 million in 1992 and £335 million in 1993. Lloyds TSB told us that Hill Samuel primarily served larger businesses, many of which would have fallen outside our definition of SMEs, and that Hill Samuel had not had a material SME banking business.

5.138. In 1993 Hill Samuel Bank was restructured to focus on its core business of merchant banking. Its funding and liquidity management functions and its 12 branches were transferred to TSB.

Profit and loss performance to 1994

5.139. Table 5.34 shows the consolidated profit and loss account for TSB from 1989 to 1994. 1991 and 1992 were the two worst-performing years as TSB reported high bad debt charges of £654 million and £597 million respectively (see paragraph 5.137), which resulted in losses of £47 million in 1991, and a small profit of £40 million in 1992. Subsequently operating profits increased and the bank reported operating profits of £366 million in 1993 and £532 million in 1994.

TABLE 5.34 **TSB: consolidated profit and loss account, 1989 to 1994 (prior to merger with Lloyds)**

£ million

	1989*	1990	1991	1992	1993	1994
Net interest income	912	1,023	1,043	975	1,025	1,067
Other operating income	714	822	948	1,030	1,001	848
Operating income	1,626	1,845	1,991	2,005	2,026	1,915
Operating expenses	−1,178	−1,253	−1,313	−1,288	−1,245	−1,133
Profit before claims and charges	448	592	678	717	781	782
Claims costs in TSB General Insurance	*	−19	−71	−80	−79	−74
Profit before charges	448	573	607	637	702	708
Bad debt charge	−92	−261	−654	−597	−335	−173
Other charges	0	0	0	0	−1	−3
Operating profit/loss	356	312	−47	40	366	532
Exceptional items	−201	0	0	2	−70†	0
Profit/loss before businesses sold	155	312	−47	42	296	532
Profit/loss on businesses sold	*	−286	50	−37	5	−28
Profit before tax	*	26	3	5	301	504

Source: Lloyds TSB.

---

*Profit and loss data for 1989 was incomplete because of the change in the reporting format since that year.
†The group incurred £70 million in reorganization costs in respect of its announced policy of fundamentally reorganizing TSB's Retail Banking and Insurance divisions, and Hill Samuel Bank.

5.140. Table 5.35 shows TSB's profits by business unit from 1989 to 1994. The main cause of the group's poor performance in 1991 and 1992 was operating losses reported by Hill Samuel Bank of £40 million in 1990, and £422 million in 1991. In 1992 TSB established the Loan Administration Unit to manage the recovery of bad and doubtful debt transferred from Hill Samuel Bank. Following the transfer, the Loan Administration Unit reported a net deficit of £379 million in 1992, and £142 million in 1993. In 1994 the unit showed a small surplus of £4 million.

TABLE 5.35 **TSB: consolidated profit and loss account, 1989 to 1994 (prior to merger with Lloyds)**

£ million

	1989*	1990	1991	1992	1993	1994
TSB Retail Banking and Insurance:						
TSB Retail Banking	145	245	293	291	260	247
TSB Insurance	63	91	117	129	194	191
	208	336	410	420	454	438
Hill Samuel:						
Hill Samuel Bank	60	–40	–422	56	58	64
Hill Samuel Investment Management and Financial Services	18	23	13	27	38	21
	78	–17	–409	83	96	85
UDT	*	21	26	28	34	54
Loan Administration Unit†	-	-	-	–379	–142	4
Commercial activities	36	18	8	16	8	–2
Mortgage Express	11	–5	–24	–67	1	38
Central costs, including interest	*	–41	–58	–61	–85	–85
Operating profit/loss	*	312	–47	40	366	532

Source: Lloyds TSB.

---

*Profit and loss data for 1989 was incomplete because of the change in the reporting format since that year.
†The Loan Administration Unit was established to manage the recovery of bad and doubtful debts transferred from Hill Samuel Bank at the beginning of the 1992 financial year.

5.141. Profits from Hill Samuel Investment Management and Financial Services increased from £18 million in 1989 to a peak of £38 million in 1993, and decreased to £21 million in 1994.

5.142. Profits from TSB Retail Banking increased from £145 million in 1989 to a peak of £293 million in 1991, and then decreased to £247 million in 1994. Profits from TSB Insurance increased year on year from £63 million in 1989 to £191 million in 1994. However, when taking note of these profits, the unallocated central costs need to be deducted, which for 1994 totalled £85 million.

Balance sheets to 1994

5.143. Table 5.36 shows TSB's balance sheet extracts from 1989 to 1994. Total assets increased from £29 billion in 1989 to £35 billion in 1994. Loans to customers in the form of mortgages increased year on year from £6 billion in 1989 to £10 billion in 1994, while loans to corporate and commercial customers decreased from around £6 billion in 1991 to £4 billion in 1994.

TABLE 5.36 **TSB: balance sheet extracts, 1989 to 1994 (prior to the merger with Lloyds)**

£ billion

	1989	1990	1991	1992	1993	1994
Total assets	29	31	30	32	33	35
Total liabilities	27	29	28	31	31	33
Shareholders' funds	2	2	2	2	2	2
Loans to customers:						
Mortgages	6	7	7	8	9	10
Other personal	3	3	3	4	4	4
Corporate/commercial	5	6	6	5	5	4
Leased assets	1	2	2	1	1	1
Total loans	15	18	18	18	19	19
Provision for bad and doubtful debts	0	0	–1	–1	–1	–1
Net loans	14	17	17	16	17	18

Source: Lloyds TSB.

5.144. We asked Lloyds TSB to provide us with further information on the performance of TSB's SME banking business prior to the merger. Table 5.37 shows TSB's Commercial Banking performance[1] for the years 1992 to 1995, over which TSB made operating losses (before bad debt charges) in 1992 and 1993. After bad debt charges, it made losses in the three years to 1994, and a profit of only £4 million in 1995 compared with total income of £92 million. Loans and advances to customers fell by some 25 per cent, from around £1.6 billion in 1992 to £1.2 billion in 1995; whereas customer deposits increased from £1.16 billion in 1992 to £1.93 billion in 1995 (66 per cent). Lloyds TSB said that the figures represented a change from an asset-led strategy (ie lending to customers) to a liability strategy (ie taking deposits for investment) where the bank avoided risky lending, which resulted in reductions in lending levels. It added that the increase in total income in 1994 to £91 million, compared with £67 million in 1993, was after absorbing some of Hill Samuel's business into Commercial Banking.

TABLE 5.37 **TSB: Commercial Banking performance, 1992 to 1995**

				£ million
	1992	1993	1994	1995
Net interest income	29	31	46	47
Other operating income	38	36	45	45
	67	67	91	92
Total costs	−87	−71	−72	−74
Operating profit/loss before bad debts	−20	−4	19	18
Bad debt charges	−57	−36	−22	−14
	−77	−40	−3	4
Taxation	26	13	1	−2
Loss/profit after tax	−51	−27	−2	2
Balance sheet extracts:				
Loans and advances to customers	1,586	1,423	1,443	1,219
Customer deposits, ie liabilities	1,164	1,313	1,677	1,933
				per cent
Performance indicators				
Changes in lending	*	−10	1	−16
Changes in customer deposits	*	13	28	15

Source: Lloyds TSB.

*No information.

HSBC Bank

History

5.145. HSBC Holdings plc (HSBC) is listed on the London, Hong Kong, New York and Paris Stock Exchanges. On 29 June 2001 its market capitalization was £79 billion, and its price:earnings ratio was 14.5. HSBC Bank, a wholly-owned subsidiary of HSBC, is the principal company in the group that (together with its subsidiaries) provides banking services to SMEs within the UK. Until 1999, it operated as Midland (see below).

5.146. HSBC operates in 79 countries and territories worldwide through businesses in five regions: Europe; Hong Kong; the rest of the Asia-Pacific region (including the Middle East and Africa); North America; and Latin America.

---

[1]According to the marketing plan of TSB at 1994, customers were classified as: micro customers (turnover up to £100,000); small businesses (turnover between £100,000 and £1 million); middle market (turnover between £1 million and £50 million); and others, including professionals, solicitors, doctors, schools and charities.

5.147. HSBC's consolidated accounts for 2000 showed that its total operating income for the year was US$24.6 billion (approximately £16.4 billion) and its profit on ordinary activities before tax was US$9.8 billion (£6.5 billion). Total group assets were US$674 billion (£451 billion), and shareholders' funds were US$45.6 billion (£30.5 billion). Globally, the HSBC employed 172,000 FTE staff in 2000. HSBC's UK operations contributed US$3.1 billion (£2.0 billion) or 32 per cent to total group profits, and 41 per cent (£185 billion) to total group assets.

5.148. HSBC told us that, although its international subsidiaries are supervised by the banking regulators in their own countries, the FSA was the supervisor of HSBC as a whole, as well as of HSBC Bank. Accordingly, the FSA sets requirements for, and receives information on, the capital adequacy of HSBC. At December 2000 the Tier 1 ratio for HSBC was 9.0 per cent and the total capital ratio was 13.3 per cent.

5.149. Hongkong and Shanghai Banking Corporation Limited was established in Hong Kong and Shanghai in 1865. It also opened a London office in 1865, and the group has had a presence in the UK since that date. It purchased in 1987 a 14.9 per cent interest in Midland. Midland had been founded in 1836 in Birmingham and had grown during the nineteenth and twentieth centuries through a series of mergers and amalgamations. A cooperation agreement between Hongkong and Shanghai Banking Corporation Limited and Midland allowed the two banking groups to consolidate and rationalize their international activities by reciprocal transfers of business as, for example, the transfer of Midland Bank in Canada to Hongkong Bank of Canada in 1988.

5.150. In 1991 Hongkong and Shanghai Banking Corporation Limited and its subsidiaries were reorganized under a new holding company, HSBC, with shares listed on both the Hong Kong and London Stock Exchanges.

5.151. In 1992 HSBC purchased the remaining shares in Midland for which the fair value of the consideration was £3.7 billion. This resulted in the total assets of HSBC increasing from £86 billion at 31 December 1991 to over £170 billion at the end of 1992.

5.152. In January 1993 HSBC's head office was transferred from Hong Kong to London. Although the BoE now became the lead regulator for HSBC, the banking subsidiaries continued to be regulated locally in their respective countries of operation.

5.153. In 1998 HSBC Holdings announced the adoption of a unified brand using 'HSBC' and the Hexagon symbol everywhere it operated. This was effected in 1999. In the UK this resulted in a change of name from Midland Bank plc to HSBC Bank plc. In the UK HSBC Bank sets its own strategies, operating plan and business goals. Capital is allocated to HSBC Bank by HSBC in competition with other priorities and opportunities around the world. HSBC Bank has a UK network of 1,683 branches.

5.154. Since 1987 Midland/HSBC Bank has disposed of equity shareholdings in three companies that were engaged in the provision of banking services to SMEs in the UK. The disposals were as follows:

(a) In 1987 Midland sold its Scottish and Northern Irish subsidiaries, Clydesdale and Northern, to NAB (which we cover separately later in this chapter).

(b) In September 1992 Midland disposed of The Thomas Cook Group. The Thomas Cook Group provided foreign exchange services to SMEs in the UK, although its primary focus was on the travel and holiday market, providing retail services to the public.

5.155. In July 1993 Midland purchased Swan National Leasing Ltd for an aggregate consideration of £183 million. This business currently forms part of HSBC Vehicle Finance (UK) Limited.

Business structure serving SMEs

5.156. HSBC Bank and certain of its various HSBC-branded subsidiaries are engaged in the supply of banking services to SMEs in the UK. However, it told us that it was not organized into business units that directly covered our definition of SMEs. It also told us that it did not use our definition of SMEs for either operating or regulatory purposes. Its Commercial Banking business handled business accounts from the smallest SMEs to businesses broadly with borrowing facilities of less than US$100 million and provided lending, money transmission, deposit, invoice discounting, factoring and asset finance/leasing services. Corporate customers with borrowing facilities of at least US$100 million were, generally, managed within its Corporate and International Banking division.

5.157. HSBC Bank said that its banking services to SMEs were delivered primarily through its network of branch outlets, with support from regional or national teams of specialists in certain areas, such as agriculture and trade finance. However, it also provided telephone and electronic banking to businesses and would soon be launching its Internet banking service.

Financial performance

Profit and loss accounts

5.158. Table 5.38 shows the profitability of HSBC Bank from 1989 to 2000. Over the period HSBC Bank's operating income increased 69 per cent from £3.2 billion to £5.4 billion, whereas operating expenses rose less rapidly from £2.3 billion to £3.1 billion. The level of bad debt charge ranged between £0.7 billion and £0.9 billion between 1990 and 1993, and has since fallen substantially to between £0.1 billion and £0.3 billion. In 1989 HSBC Bank reported an exceptional loss of £0.8 billion, which was predominantly made up of a provision against loans to developing countries. As a result, HSBC Bank reported a net loss before tax of £0.3 billion in 1989, broke even in 1990 and 1991, and returned to an operating profit of £0.2 million in 1992. Since then, operating profits before tax have increased substantially, from £0.8 billion in 1993 to £2.0 billion in 2000.

TABLE 5.38 **HSBC Bank: consolidated profit and loss account, 1989 to 2000**

£ billion

Years ended 31 December

	1989	1990	1991	1992	1993	1994	1995	1996	1997	1998	1999	2000
Net interest income	1.9	1.6	1.8	1.6	1.8	1.8	1.9	2.1	2.2	2.2	2.4	2.7
Net fees and commissions	0.9	1.1	1.2	1.0	1.1	1.0	1.0	1.2	1.3	1.3	1.5	1.8
Other income	0.5	0.4	0.4	0.5	0.8	0.2	0.4	0.4	0.6	0.5	0.7	0.9
Operating income	3.2	3.1	3.3	3.2	3.6	3.1	3.4	3.6	4.0	4.0	4.5	5.4
Operating expenses	−2.3	−2.4	−2.4	−2.3	−2.2	−2.2	−2.3	−2.3	−2.3	−2.3	−2.5	−3.1
Operating profit before provisions	0.9	0.7	0.9	0.9	1.5	0.9	1.1	1.4	1.7	1.7	2.1	2.3
Bad debt charge	−1.2*	−0.7	−0.9	−0.6	−0.7	−0.1	−0.2	−0.2	−0.1	−0.2	−0.3	−0.2
Other provisions	0.0	0.0	0.0	−0.1	0.0	0.0	0.0	0.0	0.0	−0.1	−0.1	0.0
Operating profit after bad debts	−0.3	0.0	0.0	0.2	0.8	0.8	0.9	1.2	1.6	1.5	1.7	2.0
Exceptional and other items	0.0	0.0	0.0	0.0	0.1	0.1	0.1	0.1	0.0	0.0	0.0	0.0
Net profit/loss before tax	−0.3	0.0	0.0	0.2	0.8	0.9	1.0	1.3	1.6	1.5	1.7	2.0
Tax	0.1	−0.2	−0.1	−0.1	−0.2	−0.3	−0.4	−0.4	−0.6	−0.5	−0.5	0.6
Net profit/loss after tax	−0.2	−0.2	0.0	0.1	0.7	0.6	0.6	0.9	1.1	1.0	1.2	1.4
Dividends	−0.1	−0.1	0.0	0.0	−0.4	−0.4	−0.5	−0.5	−0.6	−0.7	−1.1	−1.2
Profit retained for the financial year	−0.3	−0.3	−0.1	0.1	0.2	0.2	0.1	0.3	0.4	0.3	0.1	0.1
FTE staff ('000)†	58	60	58	61	51	51	51	49	49	48	61	56
Performance indicators												per cent
Tax charge as a percentage of profit before tax	22	‡	‡	43	20	32	36	32	34	31	30	29
Percentage change in operating income	‡	−1	6	−4	14	−15	9	8	11	0	12	19

Source: Midland/HSBC Bank annual reports.

*Midland showed losses of £846 million as an exceptional item for the year, which arose from loans to developing countries.

†The details for Midland/HSBC Bank staff numbers for the years 1992 onwards include non-UK staff. All figures are averages for the year.

‡Not applicable as losses were incurred.

Note: Figures rounded and therefore may not sum to total shown.

5.159. HSBC Bank's accounts for 1994 reported that over the recession years, it had been able to increase its margins on lending from 2.65 per cent in 1992 to 2.86 per cent in 1994. The net interest figure for 1992 was based on income of £1.52 billion and average lending of £57.5 billion, and therefore the increased interest achieved of 0.21 percentage points equated to around £120 million. In terms of interest spread, HSBC Bank reported that the figure for 1994 was 2.32 per cent compared with 1.82 per cent for 1992, an increase of 0.5 percentage points over the two years. HSBC Bank was able to maintain its level of fees and commission at roughly constant levels over the recession years.

5.160. Table 5.39 restates the overall performance of HSBC Bank from 1989 to 2000 as shown in Table 5.38 by showing all items as a percentage of operating income. Net interest income as a percentage of total income declined from 58 per cent in 1989 to 50 per cent in 1993, then increased to 59 per cent in 1994, and since has fallen back to 50 per cent in 2000. Net fees and commissions as a percentage of total income increased from 27 per cent in 1989 to 37 per cent in 1991, and remained in the range 29 to 34 per cent thereafter. Other income fluctuated, peaking at 21 per cent in 1993, and dropping to its lowest level of 7 per cent in 1994. It has since increased to around 16 per cent in 2000. This peak was primarily caused by large dealing profits in 1993 (from securities and interest rate derivatives), which fell away in 1994, dealing profits being volatile by nature.

TABLE 5.39 **HSBC Bank: operating profit and loss items as a percentage of operating income, 1989 to 2000**

per cent

	1989	1990	1991	1992	1993	1994	1995	1996	1997	1998	1999	2000
Net interest income	58	52	53	51	50	59	57	56	55	55	53	50
Net fees and commissions	27	35	37	32	29	34	31	32	32	32	33	34
Other income	15	12	11	17	21	7	13	12	14	13	15	16
Operating income	100	100	100	100	100	100	100	100	100	100	100	100
Operating expenses	−72	−76	−72	−73	−60	−70	−67	−62	−57	−57	−54	−58
Operating profit before provisions	28	24	28	27	40	30	33	38	43	43	46	42
Bad debt charge	−36	−22	−27	−18	−19	−3	−6	−5	−3	−5	−6	−5
Other provisions	0	0	0	−2	−1	−1	0	−1	0	−1	−1	0
Operating profit after provisions	−8	1	1	7	21	25	27	32	39	37	38	38
Exceptional and other items	0	−1	0	−1	2	4	2	3	1	1	0	0
Net profit before tax	−8	0	1	6	23	29	30	35	40	38	38	38

Source: Midland/HSBC Bank.

5.161. Operating expenses as a percentage of operating income (also referred to as the cost:income ratio) reached high points of between 72 and 76 per cent over the four years to 1992, fell to around 62 per cent by 1996, and by 2000 had declined further to 58 per cent.

5.162. The level of bad debt charge fluctuated significantly between 1989 and 2000 and, as noted above, greatly affected reported net profits before tax in the period up to 1993. The bad debt charge as a percentage of income was at its highest between 1989 and 1993, at some 36 per cent in 1989, and around 27 per cent in 1991. Since then the percentage has declined, falling to a range between 3 and 6 per cent.

Analysis of performance by type of customer

5.163. While recognizing that HSBC Bank did not itself use our definition of SMEs, we asked HSBC Bank to analyse further its UK activities into the following activities:

(a) personal customers;

(b) SME customers which included business customers with less than £25 million turnover;

(c) corporate customers which included business customers with more than £25 million turnover; and

(d) other customers.

The categories as defined by us were not part of the bank's existing business structure and HSBC Bank had to adapt some of its internal data to meet our requests. Hence the information for the period 1990 to 2000 has been prepared on a 'best endeavours' basis for the purposes of our inquiry. Further, HSBC Bank said that, because of changes in its management information systems, it was not able to produce information prior to 1995 in the format that it used for subsequent years. The data provided for 1990 to 1994 was not strictly comparable with information for later years; for example, the 'SME' data derived to 1994 was prepared using a different cost-allocation system, and an alternative definition of SME. With these reservations, Tables 5.40 to 5.43 provide an overview of HSBC Bank's total income, costs, bad debt and operating profits by type of customer for the ten years to 2000.

5.164. Table 5.40 shows HSBC Bank's operating income by type of customer from 1995 to 2000. Only data for the SME banking business and the whole bank was available prior to 1995. Until 1993 the income from the SME banking business at around £[✂] million a year was significantly lower than income reported for later years, but (as noted in paragraph 5.163) the data for earlier and later years was prepared on different bases. Since 1995 income from the personal banking business has increased [✂] per cent from £[✂] billion to £[✂] billion, income from the SME banking business grew [✂] per cent from £[✂] to £[✂] billion, and income from the corporate banking business grew [✂] per cent from £[✂] to £[✂] billion. Over the same period the contribution from the personal banking business to total income increased marginally from [✂] per cent in 1995 to [✂] per cent in 1999 and decreased to [✂] per cent in 2000. Until 1999 contributions to income of the SME and corporate banking businesses remained relatively stable around [✂] and [✂] per cent respectively, but in 2000 the figure for the SME banking business fell to [✂] per cent.

TABLE 5.40 **HSBC Bank: operating income by type of customer, 1995 to 2000**

| | £ billion | | | | | | | Proportion of total (%) | | | | | | |
Year	Per-sonal	SME*	Corp-orate	Other UK	Total UK	Non-UK	Total	Per-sonal	SME*	Corp-orate	Other UK	Total UK	Non-UK	Total
1990	†	⎛⎞	†	†	†	†	3.1	†	⎛⎞	†	†	†	†	100
1991	†	⎜⎟	†	†	†	†	3.3	†	⎜⎟	†	†	†	†	100
1992	†	✂	†	†	†	†	3.2	†	✂	†	†	†	†	100
1993	†	⎜⎟	†	†	†	†	3.6	†	⎜⎟	†	†	†	†	100
1994	†	⎝⎠	†	†	†	†	3.1	†	⎝⎠	†	†	†	†	100
1995						2.8	0.5	3.4					84	16	100
1996						3.1	0.5	3.6					87	13	100
1997		Figures omitted.				3.6	0.5	4.0		Figures omitted.			89	11	100
1998		See note on page iv.				3.8	0.2	4.0		See note on page iv.			94	6	100
1999						4.2	0.4	4.5					92	8	100
2000						4.5	1.0	5.4					82	18	100

Source: Midland/HSBC Bank.

*Since a different cost-allocation system was employed prior to 1995, HSBC Bank provided only limited, indicative SME information for the period 1990 to 1994. This earlier data is not strictly comparable with the data from 1995 onwards and, aside from the cost-allocation system difference, is likely to exclude some of the larger-turnover 'SME' businesses, which were included in the 'corporate' portfolio at that time, rather than the commercial portfolio.
  †Not available.

5.165. Table 5.41 shows HSBC Bank's operating costs by type of customer from 1995 to 2000, and details for the SME banking business until 1994. Since 1995, operating costs within the personal banking business increased [✂] per cent from £[✂] to £[✂] billion in 2000. Over the same period, operating costs within the corporate and UK 'other' activities each increased from around £[✂] to £[✂] (around

[✂] per cent). In contrast, operating costs for the SME banking business grew at only [✂] per cent, from £[✂] million in 1995 to £[✂] million in 2000. In 2000 the personal, SME and corporate banking businesses accounted for [✂] per cent of total costs respectively. We look at HSBC Bank's costs in greater detail in Chapter 6.

TABLE 5.41 **HSBC Bank: operating costs by type of customer, 1995 to 2000**

	£ billion							Proportion of total (%)						
Year	Per-sonal	SME*	Corp-orate	Other UK	Total UK	Non-UK	Total	Per-sonal	SME*	Corp-orate	Other UK	Total UK	Non-UK	Total
1990	†	( )	†	†	†	†	2.4	†	( )	†	†	†	†	100
1991	†		†	†	†	†	2.4	†		†	†	†	†	100
1992	†	✂	†	†	†	†	2.3	†	✂	†	†	†	†	100
1993	†		†	†	†	†	2.2	†		†	†	†	†	100
1994	†	( )	†	†	†	†	2.2	†	( )	†	†	†	†	100
1995	(	‡		)	2.0	0.3	2.3	(			)	87	13	100
1996					2.0	0.3	2.3					87	13	100
1997		Figures omitted.			2.1	0.2	2.3		Figures omitted.			90	10	100
1998		See note on page iv.			2.2	0.1	2.3		See note on page iv.			96	4	100
1999		‡			2.3	0.1	2.5					94	6	100
2000	(			)	2.4	0.7	3.1	(			)	77	21	100

Source: Midland/HSBC Bank.

*Since a different cost-allocation system was employed prior to 1995, HSBC Bank provided only limited, indicative SME information for the period 1990 to 1994. This earlier data is not strictly comparable with the data from 1995 onwards and, aside from the cost-allocation system difference, is likely to exclude some of the larger-turnover 'SME' businesses, which were included in the 'corporate' portfolio at that time, rather than the commercial portfolio.
†Not available.
‡Actual for 1995 equals £[✂] million, and for 1999 equals £[✂] million.

5.166. Table 5.42 shows HSBC Bank's cost:income ratio by type of customer from 1995 to 2000, and details for the SME banking business until 1994. Since 1995 HSBC Bank's cost:income ratio fluctuated within the different banking businesses, although predominantly there was an overall downward trend. For example, the cost:income ratio within the personal banking business fell from 76 to 66 per cent. Within the SME banking business there was a similar reduction with the cost:income ratio falling from 75 to 61 per cent. In contrast, the corporate banking business cost:income ratio was relatively stable, increasing from 48 to 50 per cent between 1995 and 1997 and then decreasing to 44 per cent in 2000. The non-UK activity saw a large increase in its cost:income ratio, increasing from 56 per cent in 1995 to 68 per cent in 2000, after a low of 39 per cent in 1999 (reflecting the predominantly higher cost:income ratios of CCF and HSBC Republic). HSBC Republic and CCF were acquired from HSBC as part of a restructuring within HSBC. HSBC Bank told us that it believed its cost allocations to the respective segments had been fairly made (subject to the points made on the basis of preparation—see paragraph 5.163) and that servicing the SME banking business required a higher level of costs relative to the corporate banking business with the cost:income ratio of the bank overall of 58 per cent in 2000. HSBC Bank said that this was largely because of the bank's community banking strategy and the use of HSBC Bank's branch network by SMEs. HSBC Bank had concentrated customer-facing activity in the branches with relationship managers having a major role. In addition SMEs made proportionately more use of cash and cheque-processing facilities than did personal or corporate customers.

TABLE 5.42 **HSBC Bank: cost:income ratios by type of customer, 1990 to 2000***

per cent

Year	Personal	SME†	Corporate	Other UK	Total UK	Non-UK	Total
1990	‡	70	‡	‡	‡	‡	76
1991	‡	69	‡	‡	‡	‡	72
1992	‡	68	‡	‡	‡	‡	73
1993	‡	78	‡	‡	‡	‡	60
1994	‡	77	‡	‡	‡	‡	70
1995	76	75	48	68	69	56	67
1996	73	69	47	50	62	60	62
1997	67	63	50	45	58	51	57
1998	64	62	49	49	58	41	57
1999	60	63	46	48	56	39	54
2000§	66	61	44	40	56	68	58

Source: Midland/HSBC Bank.

*The figures in this table are based on the actual income and cost data, rather than the rounded figures shown in Tables 5.40 and 5.41.

†Since a different cost-allocation system was employed prior to 1995, HSBC Bank provided only limited, indicative SME information for the period 1990 to 1994. This earlier data is not strictly comparable with the data from 1995 onwards and, aside from the cost-allocation system difference, is likely to exclude some of the larger-turnover 'SME' businesses, which were included in the 'corporate' portfolio at that time, rather than the commercial portfolio.

‡Not available.

§The cost:income ratio of HSBC Bank in 2000 of 58 per cent included amortization of goodwill. The cost:income ratio excluding amortization of goodwill was 55.8 per cent.

5.167. Table 5.43 shows HSBC Bank's operating profits (after bad debts) by type of customer from 1995 to 2000, together with information for the SME banking business prior to 1995. The level of bad debt charge had a significant impact on profits before tax, especially in the period to 1993 when losses were incurred in the SME banking business. Since 1995 all UK activities experienced growth, although profit for the non-UK activity was more variable and contributed a smaller proportion to total profits. In 2000 the SME banking business contributed [✄] per cent of total profits, compared with [✄] per cent from the personal banking business and [✄] per cent from the corporate banking business.

TABLE 5.43 **HSBC Bank: operating profit by type of customer, 1995 to 2000**

Year	£ billion							Proportion of total (%)						
	Per-sonal	SME*	Corp-orate	Other UK	Total UK	Non-UK	Total	Per-sonal	SME	Corp-orate	Other UK	Total UK	Non-UK	Total
1990	†		†	†	†	†	0.0	†	†	†	†	†	†	100
1991	†		†	†	†	†	0.0	†	†	†	†	†	†	100
1992	†	✄	†	†	†	†	0.2	†	†	†	†	†	†	100
1993	†		†	†	†	†	0.8	†	†	†	†	†	†	100
1994	†		†	†	†	†	0.8	†	†	†	†	†	†	100
1995					0.7	0.2	0.9					77	23	100
1996					1.0	0.2	1.2					81	19	100
1997		Figures omitted.			1.3	0.3	1.6		Figures omitted.			81	19	100
1998		See note on page iv.			1.3	0.1	1.5		See note on page iv.			90	10	100
1999					1.5	0.2	1.7					86	14	100
2000					1.7	0.3	2.0					84	16	100

Source: Midland/HSBC Bank.

*Since a different cost-allocation system was employed prior to 1995, HSBC Bank provided only limited, indicative SME information for the period 1990 to 1994. This earlier data is not strictly comparable with the data from 1995 onwards and, aside from the cost-allocation system difference, is likely to exclude some of the larger-turnover 'SME' businesses, which were included in the 'corporate' portfolio at that time, rather than the commercial portfolio.

†Not available.

5.168. Appendix 5.5 provides a further analysis of HSBC Bank's business activities from 1996 to 2000, as reported in its published accounts. During these years the main business units were shown as

UK Banking, International Banking, Treasury and Capital Markets and Asset Finance (although from 1999 Asset Finance was combined with the UK Banking business). UK Banking consisted of personal, commercial and corporate banking and, from 1999, asset finance. The SME banking business as defined by the CC was included within the commercial banking unit, with some SMEs also making use of asset leasing, for example, and others of personal banking services. International Banking represented nearly all overseas operations. Treasury and Capital Markets was made up of foreign exchange, money market and capital markets activities.

5.169. In 2000 UK Banking was shown to have income of £4.1 billion, operating expenses of £2.3 billion (56 per cent), bad debt and other charges of £0.4 billion, and a profit before tax of £1.5 billion (which compared with total profits of £2.0 billion). Net assets or equity attributed to this segment was shown as £4.2 billion, and therefore the return on equity was 35 per cent. The return on equity for UK Banking was higher than that for International Banking at 4 per cent, and for Treasury and Capital Markets at 30 per cent. The UK Banking unit had total assets of £72.8 billion, out of total assets of £185.2 billion (39 per cent).

Balance sheets

5.170. Table 5.44 shows HSBC Bank's balance sheet summaries from 1992 to 2000. Total assets have increased from £71.5 billion in 1992 to £185 billion in 2000; total liabilities increased from £69.1 billion in 1992 to £169.8 billion in 2000, and shareholders' funds increased from £2.4 billion in 1992 to close to £15.4 billion in 2000.

5.171. Operating profit as a percentage of average shareholders' funds (pre-tax return) fluctuated in response to the level of bad debt charge, and was at its lowest in 1992 at 9 per cent. Since 1993 the level of pre-tax return has ranged between 20 and 38 per cent.

5.172. The increase in total assets reflected increases in the following categories of assets:

(a) loans and advances to banks increased from £8.3 billion in 1992 to £29.8 billion in 2000;

(b) loans and advances to customers increased from £42.5 billion in 1992 to £80.5 billion in 2000;

(c) debt securities increased from £5.9 billion in 1992 to £34.2 billion in 2000; and

(d) tangible fixed assets increased from £1.1 billion in 1992 to £4.4 billion in 2000.

5.173. In common with other banks, the largest items within the bank's balance sheet were loans and advances to customers, and customer deposit accounts. From 1992 to 1996 fixed assets fluctuated between 1.5 and 1.7 per cent of total assets, but increased to around 3 per cent of total assets from 1997. This largely reflected the acquisition in 1997 of Eversholt Holdings Ltd, a railway rolling stock leasing company that leases rolling stock which is presented as fixed assets in the accounts of HSBC Bank. In 2000, loans and advances to customers accounted for 43 per cent of total assets and customer deposits accounted for 60 per cent of total liabilities.

TABLE 5.44 HSBC Bank: consolidated balance sheet, 1992 to 2000

£ billion

As at 31 December

	1992*	1993	1994	1995	1996	1997	1998	1999	2000
Assets									
Cash and balances at central banks	0.5	0.4	0.5	0.5	0.6	0.6	0.5	1.3	1.6
Treasury bills and other eligible bills	2.9	1.7	2.5	4.6	1.6	3.0	2.6	4.0	5.7
Loans and advances to banks	8.3	10.8	12.9	12.4	14.9	13.4	11.5	12.2	29.8
Loans and advances to customers	42.5	37.5	37.8	42.5	45.4	50.1	52.4	57.6	80.5
Debt securities	5.9	13.0	12.4	13.6	16.9	17.4	18.7	14.8	34.2
Other investments	0.6	0.7	0.5	0.6	0.4	0.1	0.1	0.2	2.3
Intangible fixed assets†	0.0	0.0	0.0	0.0	0.0	0.0	0.0	0.1	8.2
Tangible fixed assets	1.1	1.3	1.4	1.4	1.5	2.8	3.3	3.3	4.4
Other assets	8.6	9.9	11.3	16.6	13.8	13.9	14.5	11.7	16.1
Prepayments and accrued income	1.1	1.1	1.0	1.4	1.1	0.9	1.3	1.2	2.4
Total assets	71.5	76.5	80.4	93.6	96.2	102.1	104.8	106.5	185.2
Liabilities									
Deposits by banks	12.2	16.8	13.7	15.2	12.4	12.3	11.9	11.8	29.1
Customer accounts in credit	41.9	40.5	44.6	49.6	53.9	57.9	60.3	66.1	102.2
Debt securities in issue	1.8	1.9	2.4	2.0	3.1	4.7	5.0	3.9	9.3
Other liabilities	9.5	10.7	12.7	18.9	18.0	17.6	17.6	14.3	19.8
Accruals and deferred income	1.1	1.0	1.2	1.3	1.0	1.1	1.1	1.1	2.8
Other provisions	0.4	0.4	0.4	0.4	0.5	0.7	0.8	1.0	1.3
Subordinated liabilities	2.2	2.3	2.5	2.8	3.2	3.3	3.4	3.4	5.2
Total liabilities	69.1	73.6	77.3	90.2	92.1	97.6	100.1	101.6	169.8
Shareholders' funds‡	2.4	2.8	3.1	3.4	4.1	4.4	4.8	4.9	15.4
	71.5	76.5	80.4	93.6	96.2	102.1	104.8	106.5	185.2
Cumulative goodwill written off to reserves	0.1	0.1	0.1	0.1	0.1	0.1	0.1	0.1	0.1
Performance indicators									per cent
Operating profit as a percentage of average shareholders' funds§	9	32	31	31	34	38	33	33	20
Post-tax operating profit as a percentage of average shareholders' funds	¤	26	21	20	23	25	23	22	14
Shareholders' funds as a percentage of total assets	3	4	4	4	4	4	5	5	8

Source: Midland/HSBC Bank.

---

*Financial figures for the years prior to 1992 were not comparable to later years because of a change in accounting policy. In addition the presentation in the earlier years' balance sheets is different from later years.

†In 2000 the increase in intangible fixed assets represents the goodwill associated with the acquisition of HSBC Republic Holdings (Luxembourg) SA (and its subsidiaries), Credit Commercial de France SA and HSBC Private Banking Holdings (Suisse) SA. Purchased goodwill was £7.9 billion. The remainder of the movement was due to exchange movements.

‡This includes minority interests which in 1999 were £41 million out of £4,909 million and in 2000 were £722 million out of £15.4 billion.

§Average shareholders' funds includes any capitalized goodwill balances.

¶This figure has been affected by the increase in average shareholders' funds attributable to new share capital subscribed in respect of subsidiary acquisitions during the year to the amount of £9.0 billion.

¤Not available.

5.174. HSBC told us that, net of goodwill on the disposal of The Thomas Cook Group Ltd, HSBC's accounts showed goodwill on the acquisition of Midland in 1992 of £1.9 billion. It further said that HSBC's average invested capital in Midland at 1999 was, in its view, some £6.6 billion, which represented the sum of the following:

(a) average shareholders' funds of £4,991 million in HSBC's accounts;

(b) less average preference share capital of £537 million;

(c) add average ordinary dividend not paid of £142 million;

(d) small adjustments of some £100 million; plus

(e) goodwill on acquisition of £1.9 billion in HSBC Holdings accounts.

5.175. In evaluating returns, HSBC proposed an increase to shareholders' equity for UK banks by approximately 200 per cent to determine a better estimate for the capital base. It noted that this was the average market to book equity ratio for US and Continental European banks between 1995 and 1999, which it considered was a reflection of the underlying value of intangible assets that were not reflected in the bank's accounts. We discuss the issue of returns on capital in greater detail in Chapters 6 and 7.

Summary of loans to customers, and customer accounts in credit

5.176. Table 5.45 provides an overview of HSBC Bank's total loans by type of customer. Since 1995 loans to personal customers have increased [✄] per cent from £[✄] billion to £[✄] billion in 2000. Loans to SMEs increased [✄] per cent from £[✄] billion in 1995 to £[✄] billion in 2000. Loans to corporate customers also increased, together with non-UK loans. In 2000, the personal, SME and corporate banking businesses accounted for [✄] per cent respectively of total loans.

TABLE 5.45 **HSBC Bank: analysis of loans by type of customer, 1995 to 2000**

	£ billion							Proportion of total (%)						
Year	Per-sonal	SME	Corp-orate	Other UK	Total UK	Non-UK	Total	Per-sonal	SME	Corp-orate	Other UK	Total UK	Non-UK	Total
1995					30.9	11.6	42.5					73	27	100
1996					35.2	10.1	45.4					78	22	100
1997		Figures omitted.			44.8	5.3	50.1		Figures omitted.			89	11	100
1998		See note on page iv.			46.4	6.0	52.4		See note on page iv.			89	11	100
1999					50.4	7.2	57.6					88	12	100
2000					54.8	25.7	80.5					68	32	100

Source: Midland/HSBC Bank.

5.177. Table 5.46 provides an analysis of HSBC Bank's customer accounts in credit by type of customer. Since 1995 the accounts in credit from personal customers increased by [✄] per cent, from £[✄] billion to £[✄] billion in 2000. Accounts in credit from SMEs increased [✄] per cent over the same period from £[✄] billion to £[✄] billion in 2000. In contrast corporate accounts in credit have been more variable, although there was a significant jump of [✄] per cent in one year between 1997 and 1998. In 2000 the personal, SME and corporate banking businesses accounted for [✄] per cent respectively of total customer accounts in credit.

TABLE 5.46 **HSBC Bank: analysis of customer accounts in credit by type of customer, 1995 to 2000**

	£ billion							Proportion of total (%)						
Year	Per-sonal	SME	Corp-orate	Other UK	Total UK	Non-UK	Total	Per-sonal	SME	Corp-orate	Other UK	Total UK	Non-UK	Total
1995					36.9	12.7	49.6					74	26	100
1996					43.8	10.2	53.9					81	19	100
1997		Figures omitted.			52.3	5.6	57.9		Figures omitted.			90	10	100
1998		See note on page iv.			53.8	6.5	60.3		See note on page iv.			89	11	100
1999					56.8	9.3	66.1					86	14	100
2000					62.7	39.5	102.2					61	39	100

Source: Midland/HSBC Bank.

5.178. Appendix 5.6 shows the summarized balance sheets for HSBC Bank over each of the years 1996 to 2000 (showing average balances), with the corresponding earnings of interest on assets and payments of interest on liabilities. In 2000 HSBC Bank reported that it earned an average rate of 7.6 per cent on its loans and advances to customers compared with an average rate of 5.6 per cent for total assets. Over the same period it paid an average rate of interest of 3.2 per cent on its interest-bearing demand deposits compared with 5.1 per cent for total interest-bearing liabilities. An additional £8.3 billion of customer deposits were interest-free. In 2000 HSBC Bank reported a net interest spread of around 2 per cent and this spread has been relatively constant over the past four years. In 2000 the net interest spread equated to net interest income of around £2.7 billion (see Table 5.38).

Contingent liabilities and commitments

5.179. Table 5.47 shows an analysis of contingent liabilities and commitments for 1992 to 2000. HSBC Bank's level of commitments increased from £25.1 billion in 1992 to £44.0 billion in 2000. Commitments to lend are agreements to lend to a customer in the future subject to certain conditions. These off-balance-sheet items are also significant to banks as a source of income, and in comparison with total on-balance-sheet assets/liabilities. For example, in 2000 HSBC Bank reported total contingent liabilities of £12.8 billion and total commitments of £44.0 billion, compared with total on-balance-sheet liabilities of £170 billion in that year.

TABLE 5.47   **HSBC Bank: contingent liabilities, 1992 to 2000**

£ billion

	1992	1993	1994	1995	1996	1997	1998	1999	2000
Acceptances and endorsements	0.5	0.4	0.3	0.8	0.8	1.2	1.2	1.2	1.4
Guarantees and assets pledged as collateral security	3.9	4.4	5.5	6.7	7.7	6.3	7.4	8.1	11.4
	4.4	4.8	5.8	7.5	8.4	7.6	8.6	9.2	12.8
Commitments	25.1	26.3	27.9	29.0	32.1	30.5	33.7	37.5	44.0

Source: Midland/HSBC Bank.

Bad debts

5.180. Table 5.48 shows the level of bad debt charge by type of customer from 1995 to 2000, and HSBC Bank's best estimates for the SME banking business between 1990 and 1994. The level of bad debt charge for HSBC Bank was at its highest between 1990 and 1993 and peaked at £903 million in 1991. HSBC Bank told us that the UK recession between 1990 and 1994 magnified bad debt charges because of the fall in the value of underlying securities, which included a high proportion of commercial and residential property. As a result, the levels of bad debt provision and bad debt charge were at exceptional levels during that period. Over the 11-year period, HSBC Bank reported a total bad debt charge of £4.2 billion, of which the total for SMEs was £1.4 billion. Appendix 5.2 shows comments from HSBC Bank's annual reports on its bad debt experience over the recession years.

TABLE 5.48   **HSBC Bank: analysis of bad debt charge to profit and loss by type of customer, 1990 to 2000**

£ million

Year	Personal	SME	Corp-orate	Other UK	Total UK	Non-UK	Total
1990	*	⎫	*	*	*	*	703
1991	*	⎪	*	*	*	*	903
1992	*	✂	*	*	*	*	582
1993	*	⎪	*	*	*	*	670
1994	*	⎭	*	*	*	*	98
1995		⎧			180	18	198
1996		⎪			204	−31	173
1997					212	−83	129
1998		Figures omitted.			204	−8	196
1999		See note on page iv			306	−25	281
2000		⎪			258	−14	244
Total		⎩			1,364	−143	4,177
Average 1990–1993	*	(✂)	*	*	*	*	*
Average 1994–2000	(	✂	)		227	−24	204

Source: Midland/HSBC Bank.

*Not available.

206

5.181. From 1997 to 1999 the personal banking business had a significant increase in its level of the bad debt charge. HSBC Bank told us that this largely reflected the contrasting growth in advances to the personal sector. Historically it noted that both new accounts and the 'youth' market have had higher than average levels of default, and that the trend was also consistent with the DTI's statistical press release which showed that personal bankruptcies had increased over 1997 to 1999.

5.182. Table 5.49 shows the level of closing bad debt provision and the level of bad debt charge against profits between 1989 and 2000. The level of bad debt provisions has fluctuated between 1989 and 2000 and reached a peak of £3.0 billion in 1991. Since 1993 the level of bad debt provisions has declined to around £1.2 billion in 1999, but rose again in 2000 to £2 billion. The main increase was in the specific provision for doubtful debts due to the acquisition of subsidiary undertakings. These levels of provisions over the 11-year period equated to 5.8 per cent of loans in 1992, compared with 2 per cent at the end of the 1990s and into 2000. HSBC Bank said that the decline was due to improvements in the economy.

TABLE 5.49 **HSBC Bank: analysis of bad debt provision and charges to profit and loss, 1989 to 2000**

£ billion

	1989	1990	1991	1992	1993	1994	1995	1996	1997	1998	1999	2000
Analysis of movement in provision												
Balance at start of year	1.9	2.8	2.7	2.4	2.5	2.1	1.5	1.4	1.3	1.1	1.0	1.2
Charge against profits—P&L (analysed below)	1.2	0.7	0.9	0.6	0.7	0.1	0.2	0.2	0.1	0.2	0.3	0.2
Amounts written off	–0.5	–0.5	–0.6	–0.7	–1.0	–0.8	–0.3	–0.3	–0.2	–0.3	–0.2	–0.3
Other movements	0.2	–0.4	0.1	0.2	0.0	0.0	0.0	–0.1	–0.1	0.0	0.0	0.8
Balance at end of year (analysed below)	2.8	2.7	3.0	2.5	2.1	1.5	1.4	1.3	1.1	1.0	1.2	2.0
Analysis of bad debt provision												
General provision	0.2	0.2	0.2	0.2	0.2	0.2	0.2	0.3	0.3	0.3	0.4	0.5
Specific provision	2.6	2.5	2.8	2.3	1.9	1.2	1.2	1.0	0.8	0.7	0.8	1.4
Closing bad debt provision	2.8	2.7	3.0	2.5	2.1	1.5	1.4	1.3	1.1	1.0	1.2	2.0
Analysis of bad debt charge to profit and loss												
New and additional provisions	*	*	*	*	*	*	*	*	*	*	*	*
Releases of provisions established in earlier years	*	*	*	*	*	*	*	*	*	*	*	*
Recoveries of advances written off in earlier years	*	*	*	*	*	*	*	*	*	*	*	*
Total bad debt charge	1.2†	0.7	0.9	0.6	0.7	0.1	0.2	0.2	0.1	0.2	0.3	0.2
Performance indicators												*per cent*
Bad debt provision as a percentage of total loans‡	*	*	*	5.8	5.5	3.8	3.4	2.8	2.2	2.0	2.0	2.4
Bad debt charge as a percentage of total loans‡	*	*	*	1.4	1.7	0.3	0.5	0.4	0.3	0.3	0.5	0.3
Bad debt charge as a percentage of total income‡	36.0	22.4	27.1	18.2	18.6	3.2	5.9	4.8	3.2	4.8	6.2	4.0

Source: Midland/HSBC Bank.

*Not available.
†£846 million, being in respect of loans to developing countries, was shown as an exceptional item in the year.
‡In 1993 the BBA's Statement of Recommended Accounting Practice on Advances was introduced, leading to a restatement of the 1992 specific bad debt provision.

5.183. The mix between general and specific provisions has also changed over this period, ie the level of general provisions increased while the level of specific provisions decreased. This movement was expected given that the general bad debt provision has been set at 0.6 per cent of customer loans outstanding, whereas specific bad debt charges are accrued in respect of individual loans when repayment is deemed unlikely. As the level of total customer lending increased, so too did the general bad debt provision. HSBC Bank said that the level of the general bad debt provision was set taking into account the structure and risk characteristics of HSBC Bank's loan portfolio and an evaluation of historic levels of latent risk. General provisions augmented specific provisions and provided cover for loans that were impaired at the balance sheet date but would not be identified as such until some time in the future.

5.184. The level of bad debt charge as a percentage of income has also fluctuated between 1989 and 2000, being at peak levels of around 36 per cent in 1989, and 27 per cent in 1991. Since 1994, the level of bad debt charge as a percentage of income remained between 3 and 6 per cent.

Capital adequacy

5.185. Table 5.50 shows regulatory capital data for HSBC Bank from 1990 to 2000. Between 1990 and 2000 HSBC Bank's Tier 1 ratio fluctuated between 5.4 and 6.8 per cent, while its total RAR ranged between 9.8 and 11.5 per cent. HSBC Bank said that it had very little surplus Tier 1 capital compared with other major banks in the UK, as any surplus capital was kept by its holding company, HSBC.

TABLE 5.50　**HSBC Bank: regulatory capital data, 1990 to 2000**

£ billion

As at 31 December

	1990	1991	1992	1993	1994	1995	1996	1997	1998	1999	2000
RWAs	43.8	41.5	41.9	45.4	48.2	57.4	63.8	66.8	71.1	71.6	107.3
Tier 1 capital	2.4	2.3	2.4	3.0	3.2	3.6	4.3	4.4	4.8	4.9	7.0
Tier 2 capital	1.9	2.0	2.1	2.2	2.4	2.6	3.3	3.5	3.4	3.7	5.2
Less: supervisory deductions	*	*	*	*	*	*	–0.3	–0.3	–0.3	–0.4	–0.7
Total net capital resources	4.3	4.3	4.5	5.1	5.5	6.2	7.3	7.6	7.9	8.1	11.5

per cent

Ratios											
Tier 1	5.4	5.5	5.7	6.5	6.6	6.3	6.7	6.7	6.8	6.8	6.5
Total	9.8	10.3	10.7	11.3	11.5	10.8	11.5	11.4	11.1	11.3	10.7

Source: Midland/HSBC Bank.

*Not available.

5.186. HSBC Bank told us that it needed to maintain a strong capital base, in excess of any regulatory minimum set by the FSA, for the following reasons:

(a) the FSA restricted the amount HSBC Bank can lend to any one counterparty or to a group of closely related counterparties (being members of the same group) to 25 per cent of capital base. In excess of this amount, credit proposals had to be pre-notified to the FSA;

(b) investors expected HSBC Bank to maintain a strong capital base (including the need to support the level of RWAs, including goodwill, for periods of the year when profits did not count towards the bank's capital base);

(c) changing the risk profile of returns to the bank's shareholders (as more risk-averse shareholders might prefer a bank to maintain a higher level of capital);

(d) minimizing the bank's overall cost of funds (as a higher level of capital might result in lower costs of debt capital);

(e) providing capital to invest in intangible assets, for example marketing, training and product development; and

(f) providing capital to finance acquisitions.

NatWest Group

History

5.187. NatWest Group[1] is engaged in the provision of a wide range of banking, financial and related activities in the UK and 22 other countries. Outside the UK, the USA was the only single territory accounting for more than 10 per cent of the group's total assets based on the published financial statements as at 31 December 1999. NatWest Group was incorporated in the UK in 1968 and was formed from the merger of National Provincial Bank Limited and Westminster Bank Limited.

5.188. In September 1999 BoS announced an offer to acquire NatWest Group. In the same month NatWest Group had agreed to acquire Legal and General Group Plc (Legal & General) and had raised £2.4 billion in subordinated debt to fund the acquisition. Following the offer from BoS, NatWest Group's offer for Legal & General lapsed. Subsequently, in November 1999 RBSG also announced an offer to acquire NatWest Group. The NatWest Group's board of directors advised its shareholders to reject the offers from both bidding banks. Competition between BoS and RBSG for control of NatWest Group led to both banks increasing their offers. Finally in March 2000 RBSG succeeded in gaining control of NatWest Group.

5.189. RBSG is listed on the London Stock Exchange and is now the holding company of NatWest Group. On 29 June 2001 its market capitalization was £42 billion and its price:earnings ratio was 17.3. Following the acquisition, RBSG comprises two main groups, RBS and NatWest Group. In this section we focus our discussion on NatWest Group and discuss RBS separately, the exception being the results for 2000 where we show the combined NatWest Group and RBS results in the separate section on RBS (see paragraph 5.231). However, our references to comments by NatWest Group in the following paragraphs relate to information and explanations that were provided by RBSG's management.

5.190. Between 1989 and 2000, apart from the unsuccessful attempt to acquire Legal & General, NatWest Group made no other material acquisitions of companies engaged in the provision of banking services to SMEs in the UK. However, NatWest Group did dispose of its shareholdings in several companies that provided banking services to SMEs in the UK. The main disposals were as follows:

(a) NatWest Group sold its 40 per cent shareholding in Yorkshire to the NAB group in 1990 for £389 million.

(b) Lombard North Central PLC (Lombard) (a subsidiary of NatWest Group) sold Lombard Business Equipment Leasing, a provider of point-of-sale vendor support finance to small businesses, in 1998.

(c) Lombard sold its 50 per cent shareholding in PSA Finance, a joint venture with Peugeot, in 1999 to First National Bank.

NatWest Group said that the Lombard disposals were made because it wanted to exit the point-of-sale market.

Business structure serving SMEs

5.191. NatWest Group said that in 1999, prior to its acquisition by RBSG, there were six main business units that provided banking services to business customers with turnover less than £25 million:

(a) Retail Banking—which consisted of two business units: Personal Banking Services, which provided banking services to personal customers, and Small Business Services, which provided banking services to business customers with turnover less than £1 million;

---

[1]NatWest Group is the term used in this report for National Westminster Bank plc and any of its subsidiaries that provide banking services to SMEs.

(b) Corporate Banking—which provided banking services to business customers with turnover greater than £1 million;

(c) Card Services—which issued a comprehensive range of credit, charge and debit cards to personal and business customers;

(d) Lombard—which provided asset finance services to business customers;

(e) Ulster Bank—which provided retail and wholesale financial services in Northern Ireland and the Republic of Ireland. We further discuss Ulster Bank in paragraphs 5.367 to 5.390; and

(f) Coutts—which provided services to wealthy individuals and to a small number of SMEs.

5.192. NatWest provided us with copies of its 1999 management accounts for Retail Banking and Corporate Banking, the two main business units that provided banking services to SME customers. RBSG told us that from May 2000 the board of RBSG would receive consolidated reports combining the management information on NatWest Group and RBS. We therefore include the performance of NatWest Group for 2000 with the results for RBSG in this chapter.

5.193. The 1999 management accounts of Small Business Services (which served business customers with turnover less than £1 million) reported total loans to customers of £[✂] billion and customer accounts in credit of £[✂] billion. The management accounts reported total income of £[✂] million but provided no information on total costs and contribution. NatWest Group said that total costs and contribution were reported only for Retail Banking (which included both Personal Banking Services and Small Business Services).

5.194. The 1999 management accounts of Corporate Banking (which served business customers with turnover greater than £1 million with no upper limit) reported total income of £[✂] billion, total costs of £[✂], bad debts of £[✂] million and contribution before tax of £[✂] ([✂] per cent of income).

5.195. In 1999 NatWest Group did not calculate a cost:income ratio for its Small Business Services, because NatWest Group did not allocate costs at this level, but the management accounts for Retail Banking (which included both personal and small business customers) showed this ratio as 75 per cent, and the management accounts showed the Corporate Banking ratio as 46 per cent. NatWest Group told us that the lower cost:income ratio for Corporate Banking reflected the lower costs of serving larger customers. We cover this issue in greater detail in Chapter 6.

5.196. NatWest Group said that it was unable to provide separate financial information for SME customers within Lombard and Coutts, but that only a small proportion of customers within each business unit were SME customers as defined by us. Appendix 5.7 shows a summary of Lombard's profit and loss accounts and balance sheets for the three years to 2000. For 2000 Lombard had total income of £0.7 billion, operating profits of £0.1 billion, total loans to customers of £7 billion, and shareholders' funds of £1 billion. Appendix 5.8 shows a summary of Coutts' profit and loss accounts and balance sheets for the three years to 2000. For 2000 it had total income of £210 million, operating profits of £25 million, total loans to customers of £2.0 billion, and shareholders' funds of £169 million.

Financial performance

Profit and loss accounts

5.197. Table 5.51 shows the profitability of NatWest Group from 1989 to 1999 (prior to its acquisition by RBSG) and for 2000. The profits for the enlarged RBSG for 2000 are shown in Table 5.65. Between 1989 and 2000 operating income for NatWest Group grew 39 per cent from £5.4 billion to

£7.5 billion. Much of the growth was in net fees and commissions, which grew 57 per cent from £1.4 billion to around £2.2 billion a year from 1992; although other income grew from £0.5 billion in 1989 to £1.0 billion in 1994, and further increased to around £1.5 billion in 2000. Net interest income remained relatively unchanged at around £3.7 billion a year over the period. Operating expenses increased from £3.6 billion in 1989 to a peak of £5.3 billion in 1997, fell to £4.8 billion in 1999 and increased to £5.3 billion in 2000. The increased expenses in 1997 were largely due to costs within NatWest Group's trading and capital markets businesses, which it said were unrelated to the SME banking business. NatWest Group added that the decline in costs over the two years to 1999 was largely due to divestment of businesses. Excluding divestments, operating expenses within NatWest Group would have increased from £4.6 billion in 1998 to £4.8 billion in 1999. Between 1999 and 2000 costs increased by £0.5 billion mainly because of due to an increase in restructuring costs incurred in respect of cost reductions and income enhancement targets.

TABLE 5.51 **NatWest Group: consolidated profit and loss account, 1989 to 2000**

£ billion

Years ended 31 December

	1989	1990	1991	1992	1993	1994	1995	1996	1997	1998	1999	2000
Net interest income	3.5	3.6	3.7	4.0	3.7	3.7	3.9	3.8	3.7	3.8	3.7	3.7
Net fees and commissions	1.4	1.6	2.1	2.3	2.3	2.3	2.2	2.4	2.3	2.2	2.2	2.3
Other income*	0.5	0.4	0.5	0.6	1.0	1.0	1.1	1.1	1.0	1.4	1.3	1.5
Operating income	5.4	5.6	6.2	6.9	7.0	6.9	7.2	7.3	7.0	7.4	7.2	7.5
Operating expenses	−3.6	−4.0	−4.2	−4.5	−4.6	−4.8	−4.9	−4.9	−5.3	−5.1	−4.8	−5.3
Operating profit before provisions	1.8	1.6	2.0	2.4	2.4	2.1	2.3	2.3	1.7	2.3	2.4	2.2
Bad debt charge	−1.4†	−1.2	−1.9	−1.9	−1.3	−0.6	−0.6	−0.6	−0.6	−0.5	−0.2	−0.4
Operating profit after bad debt charge	0.4	0.5	0.2	0.5	1.1	1.5	1.7	1.7	1.1	1.8	2.2	1.9
Exceptional, extraordinary and other items	0.0	0.2	0.0	−0.1	−0.1	0.1	0.1	−0.6	−0.1	0.4	0.1	1.0
Net profit before tax	0.4	0.7	0.1	0.4	1.0	1.6	1.8	1.1	1.0	2.1	2.3	2.9
Tax	−0.2	−0.3	−0.1	−0.2	−0.3	−0.5	−0.5	−0.7	−0.3	−0.5	−0.6	−0.7
Net profit after tax	0.2	0.4	0.1	0.2	0.6	1.1	1.2	0.5	0.7	1.6	1.7	2.2
Minority interests	0.0	0.0	0.0	0.0	0.0	0.0	0.0	0.0	0.0	0.0	0.0	0.0
Profit for the financial year	0.2	0.4	0.1	0.2	0.6	1.1	1.2	0.4	0.6	1.6	1.7	2.2
Dividends	−0.3	−0.3	−0.3	−0.3	−0.3	−0.4	−0.5	−0.5	−0.6	−0.7	−0.3	−4.6
Profit retained for the financial year	−0.1	0.1	−0.2	−0.1	0.3	0.7	0.7	−0.1	0.0	1.0	1.4	−2.4
Number of employees ('000)‡	§	§	§	95	91	87	82	71	70	64	62	52
Performance indicators												*per cent*
Tax charge as a percentage of profit before tax	44	44	81	41	35	29	29	58	32	23	26	24
Percentage change in operating income	N/A	5	11	10	2	−1	4	0	−4	6	−2	4
Change in number of employees	N/A	N/A	N/A	N/A	−4	−4	−5	−11	−1	−6	−2	−10

Source: NatWest Group.

*Dividend income, dealing profits and other operating income.
†Of which £1 billion related to problem country debt.
‡FTE permanent staff.
§Not available.

5.198. The bad debt charge was at its highest level between 1989 and 1993, when it ranged between £1.2 billion and £1.9 billion because of depressed economic conditions in the UK and also in other parts of the world where NatWest Group had operations. NatWest Group said that of the £1.4 billion bad debt charge in 1989, £1 billion was related to problem country debt; and that there was a bad debt charge of £1.4 billion over the three years 1991 to 1993 (27 per cent of the total bad debt charge in the period) which related to small SMEs with turnover below £1 million. Since 1994 the bad debt charge has reduced, and has ranged between £0.2 billion and £0.6 billion.

5.199. As a result, operating profit after bad debt charges was at its lowest level between 1989 and 1993, when it ranged between £0.2 billion and £1.1 billion. Since 1994 these profits increased year on year (except in 1997) and reached £2.2 billion in 1999, decreasing again in 2000 to £1.9 billion. In 1997 NatWest Group incurred losses in its trading and capital markets business of £292 million as a result of terminating its equity operations, a charge £85 million for the mispricing of interest rate options and swaps, and a £106 million charge to write down the bank's finance lease receivables.

5.200. Table 5.52 further analyses the overall performance of NatWest Group from 1989 to 2000 by showing all items as a percentage of operating income. Between 1989 and 2000 net interest income as a percentage of operating income declined from 65 to 49 per cent. Comparatively, fee and commissions increased from 26 to 31 per cent. Other income rose from 9 to 20 per cent. During the years 1989 to 1993 the proportion of operating income provided by net interest income decreased from 65 to 53 per cent, compared with increases in the proportions of fees and other income.

TABLE 5.52 **NatWest Group: operating profit and loss items as a percentage of operating income, 1989 to 2000**

per cent

	1989	1990	1991	1992	1993	1994	1995	1996	1997	1998	1999	2000
Net interest income	65	64	59	57	53	53	54	53	53	52	51	49
Net fees and commissions	26	29	33	33	33	33	31	33	33	30	31	31
Other income	9	7	8	9	14	14	15	14	14	19	18	20
Operating income	100	100	100	100	100	100	100	100	100	100	100	100
Operating expenses	−67	−71	−68	−65	−66	−69	−68	−68	−76	−69	−66	−70
Operating profit before provisions	33	29	32	35	34	31	32	32	24	31	34	30
Bad debt charge	−27	−20	−30	−28	−18	−9	−9	−8	−8	−7	−3	−5
Other provisions	0	0	0	0	0	0	0	−1	0	0	−1	0
Operating profit after bad debt charge	7	9	2	8	16	22	23	24	16	24	30	25
Exceptional and other items	0	3	0	−2	−2	1	1	−8	−2	5	1	14
Net profit before tax	7	12	2	6	14	23	24	15	14	29	31	39

Source: NatWest Group.

5.201. Over the period, operating expenses as a percentage of operating income (also referred to as the cost:income ratio) fluctuated between 65 and 76 per cent. The ratio peaked at 76 per cent in 1997 because of special losses or charges in the year as discussed above. Then the ratio declined to 66 per cent in 1999 and then increased to 70 per cent in 2000. NatWest Group noted that it had a higher cost:income ratio than its peer group of commercial banks (and considered that Lloyds TSB's low ratio was not comparable because it had a different business mix and risk profile). RBSG said that NatWest Group's high cost base limited its earnings growth and this had adversely affected its share price performance, which in turn made it vulnerable to takeover.

5.202. Bad debt charges as a percentage of operating income were at their highest levels between 1989 and 1993, when charges ranged between 18 and 30 per cent of income. Since 1994 the percentage declined from 9 to 3 per cent in 1999 and rose to 5 per cent in 2000.

Future cost savings

5.203. In 1999 NatWest Group's defence document noted that it expected to make cost savings of some £525 million a year in the future. However, RBSG told us that its current estimates were that it could achieve cost savings for the enlarged group, NatWest Group and RBS, of up to £1.3 billion a year by 2003. RBSG estimated that it would achieve cost savings of £0.3 billion in 2000, £0.7 billion in 2001, £1.1 billion in 2002, and £1.3 billion from 2003 onwards. The cost saving estimates for 2003 included removal of £0.6 billion duplicated costs (mainly in IT and head offices), and a further £0.6 billion from efficiency improvements. RBSG told us that to achieve the long-term cost savings proposed the group would incur one-off costs of around £1.5 billion a year between 2000 and 2003. RBSG said that the combined cost:income ratio, based on a combination of income growth and cost savings, was in its view likely to fall to less than 50 per cent by 2004. Accordingly the payback period for the investment to achieve the savings would be a few years and, RBSG being a bank, there was no difficulty in financing the investment. RBSG noted that such investment involved a funding cost.

5.204. RBSG added that only a portion of the proposed cost savings would relate to activities serving SMEs. However, as the SME banking business was not a defined business unit within its business structure, it was unable to quantify the extent of this portion.

Analysis of performance by type of customer

5.205. We asked NatWest Group to analyse its UK activities from 1989 to 2000 into the following activities:

(a) personal customers;

(b) SME customers (business customers with turnover less than £25 million);

(c) corporate customers (business customers with turnover greater than £25 million); and

(d) 'other' customers, which NatWest Group said included overseas customers and customers of trading and wealth management businesses.

This required the bank to allocate operating costs, operating income and bad debt charges to the respective businesses in order to derive operating profits over the period. RBSG told us, however, that the above segments were not part of its business structure and therefore (as explained in paragraph 5.206), it was unable to provide the data requested except for 1999 where it could only provide figures for operating income and bad debts. For 1997 and 1998 NatWest Group noted its inability to allocate income according to our definition of SMEs, ie it was only able to provide operating income for personal and business customers with turnover less than £1 million, and it was unable to extract from its Corporate Banking division's activities an estimate of the income from corporate customers having turnover between £1 million and £25 million.

5.206. NatWest Group emphasized its inability to allocate cost for any year by type of customer. RBSG told us that the group (including NatWest Group) was organized into customer-facing divisions, responsible solely for growing income and controlling direct costs (such as salaries of customer-facing staff). The bank monitored the contributions from these units, which taken together were set against shared costs, which were a large portion of the group's costs. It added that the shared costs were controlled by a separate central unit called the 'Manufacturing' division. RBSG said that its approach in no way undermined its ability to know the overall costs of its business, and its emphasis was to measure costs at the point of incidence and it put enormous efforts into ensuring that the group ran as efficiently as possible. It added that it did not need to allocate costs because it actively managed both its income and costs, and the level of reporting reflected the degree of control. The Managing Directors of the customer-facing divisions were responsible for their income, their income growth, and their direct costs; whereas the Managing Director of the Manufacturing division was tasked with ensuring that the costs associated with technology and processing supported the bank's activities. It therefore believed that this division of functions avoided fruitless debates about transfer charges by aligning reporting with responsibility.

5.207. We discuss further RBSG's views on cost allocations in paragraph 5.246. In Chapter 6 we show our estimates of profitability for NatWest Group's SME banking business based on information provided to us.

5.208. Table 5.53 shows operating income by type of customer for 1999 and 2000. In 1999 operating income for the SME banking business was £[✂] billion and represented [✂] per cent of the NatWest Group's operating income which remained constant during 2000. NatWest Group's other activities represented [✂] per cent of income in 1999 and [✂] per cent of income in 2000.

TABLE 5.53 **NatWest Group: operating income by type of customer, 1999 and 2000**

	£ billion					Proportion of total (%)				
Year	Per-sonal	SME†	Corp-orate	Other	Total	Per-sonal	SME†	Corp-orate	Other	Total
1999	Figures omitted. See note on page iv.				7.2	Figures omitted. See note on page iv.				100
2000					7.5					100

Source: NatWest Group.

*Operating income includes net interest income, net fees and commissions and other income.
†The SME banking business figure excludes income from Lombard and Coutts, which is shown in the 'other' segment. NatWest Group said that it was unable to identify how much of the income from these subsidiaries related to its SME banking business.

5.209. Table 5.54 summarizes how NatWest Group reported the performance of its various activities in its published financial statements between 1997 and 1999. Comparable information for 2000 was not available as the information for that year was collected on the new RBSG organization. During this period, the main business classes were:

(a) NatWest UK, which covered:

   (i)   Retail Banking, which provided banking services to personal and small business customers and was responsible for the branch network;

   (ii) Corporate Banking, which provided banking services to mid-sized and large corporate customer; and

   (iii) Card Services, which provided credit, charge and debit cards to personal and business customers;

(b) Ulster Bank, which provided retail and wholesale financial services in Northern Ireland and the Republic of Ireland;

(c) NatWest Wealth Management, which provided wealth management services to customers;

(d) Global Financial Markets, which provided specialist services in a range of foreign exchange and interest rate management products to corporate and institutional clients;

(e) Group Head Office, which comprised group-wide functions such as audit, compliance, corporate affairs, finance, human resources, IT and operations, legal and risk; and

(f) Other, which mainly comprised Greenwich NatWest, a trading and capital markets business.

TABLE 5.54 **NatWest Group: analysis by business units, 1997 to 1999**

£ billion

Business units	1997	1998	1999	1997	1998	1999
	Operating income			Profit before tax		
NatWest UK	4.2	4.4	4.7	1.1	1.2	1.4
Ulster Bank	0.4	0.4	0.4	0.1	0.2	0.2
NatWest Wealth Management	0.8	0.9	0.9	0.2	0.4	0.3
Global Financial Markets	0.5	0.6	0.5	0.2	0.4	0.3
Group Head Office	-	-	-	−0.2	−0.2	−0.2
Other	1.1	1.1	0.7	−0.6	0.2	0.2
Total	7.0	7.4	7.2	0.9	2.1	2.2
Discontinued operations				0.1	0.1	0.1
Total				1.0	2.1	2.3
	Net assets (equity)			Average total assets		
NatWest UK	2.6	3.6	5.5	61	70	80
Ulster Bank	0.5	0.6	0.7	9	9	9
NatWest Wealth Management	0.8	0.8	0.8	9	8	8
Global Financial Markets	0.5	0.5	0.6	41	40	44
Group Head Office	0.2	0.3	0.3	−1	1	−1
Other	3.4	2.6	1.4	88	69	49
Total	8.0	8.5	9.3	207	197	190

	1997	1998	1999
		per cent	
Cost:income ratios*			
NatWest UK	67	68	66
Ulster Bank	57	56	56
NatWest Wealth Management	69	63	65
Global Financial Markets	48	38	43
Other	132	101	100
Total for all units	76	69	66
Return on average net assets (equity)†			
NatWest UK		38	30
Ulster Bank		27	25
NatWest Wealth Management		43	36
Global Financial Markets		79	53
Other		5	11
Total for all units		25	24

Source: NatWest Group.

---

*The operating cost figures to compute these ratios are not shown in the table. Such costs for the business units exclude allocations of group head office costs of some £200 million a year, but such costs are included in the total figures for all units.

†This is profit before tax as a percentage of average net assets. The profit before tax for the business units excludes allocations of group head office costs of some £200 million a year, but such costs are included in the total figures for all units.

5.210. The main business unit within NatWest Group that served SME customers was NatWest UK. Between 1997 and 1999 NatWest UK reported that operating income increased 12 per cent from £4.2 billion to £4.7 billion, and that profit before tax increased 27 per cent from £1.1 billion to £1.4 billion. The cost:income ratio for the business unit remained relatively unchanged at between 66 and 68 per cent. Over the same period, the business unit reported that average total assets increased 31 per cent from £61 billion to £80 billion and shareholders' funds (or equity) attributed to this unit increased 112 per cent from £2.6 billion to £5.5 billion. NatWest Group said that the increase in assets and shareholders' funds was due to the transfer to NatWest UK of Lombard. Between 1998 and 1999 the return on average shareholders' funds fell from 38 to 30 per cent.

5.211. Another business unit that served SME customers was Ulster Bank, a provider of financial services in Northern Ireland and the Republic of Ireland. We separately discuss Ulster Bank's financial performance in paragraphs 5.372 to 5.390.

Balance sheets

5.212. Table 5.55 shows balance sheet summaries for NatWest Group from 1992 to 2000.[1] During the period NatWest Group's structure underwent significant changes as a result of acquisitions and disposals. Total assets (excluding insurance assets) increased from £153 billion in 1992 to £182 billion in 1996, and fell slightly to £177 billion by 1999. In 2000 they rose to £186 billion. Total liabilities increased from £148 billion in 1992 to around £179 billion in 2000, and shareholders' funds increased from £6 billion in 1992 to close to £9 billion in 1999, only to reduce again in

5.213. Between 1993 and 2000 the pre-tax returns on average shareholders' funds ranged between 20 and 24 per cent (except in 1997 when it fell to 14 per cent for the reasons 2000 to £7 billion. NatWest Group spent some £1.4 billion on share buy-backs between 1996 and 1999.discussed above). We noted that, over the period to 1999, pre-tax returns reported by NatWest Group were generally lower than those reported by the other three largest clearing groups, and RBSG noted that this factor made NatWest Group vulnerable to takeover. Between 1993 and 1999 the bank reduced its personnel numbers from 95,000 to 62,000, a reduction of 35 per cent overall, partially as a result of disposals such as Bancorp and parts of Lombard and equity securities business.

5.214. Over the period fixed assets ranged between 1 and 2 per cent of total assets. In 2000, loans and advances to customers of £99 billion accounted for 53 per cent of total assets; and customer accounts in credit of £110 billion accounted for 61 per cent of total liabilities. In 2000 the bank reported loans to customers of £99 billion in comparison with customer accounts in credit of £110 billion.

5.215. NatWest Group said that, prior to 1996, its policy for goodwill was to deduct all purchased goodwill from its profit and loss reserve. In 1996 the bank changed its policy such that all purchased goodwill might be either deducted from its profit or loss account or capitalized as an asset and amortized over its useful economic life. Therefore in 1996 NatWest Group capitalized £0.7 billion of purchased goodwill.

5.216. NatWest Group's accounting policy for goodwill changed again in 1998, in response to changes in accounting standards[2] related to goodwill, such that all purchased goodwill was to be capitalized as an asset and amortized over its useful economic life. Therefore in 1998 NatWest Group reinstated £0.3 billion of purchased goodwill back on to its balance sheet as an asset.

---

[1]Financial figures for the years prior to 1992 were not comparable with later years because of a change in accounting policy. In addition certain presentations in the earlier years' balance sheets were different from those in later years.
[2]FRS 10: *Goodwill and Intangible Assets*.

TABLE 5.55 **NatWest Group: consolidated balance sheet summary, 1992 to 2000**

£ billion

As at 31 December

	1992	1993	1994	1995	1996	1997	1998	1999	2000
Assets									
Cash and balances at central banks	1	1	1	2	1	1	1	2	1
Treasury bills and other eligible bills	8	8	9	10	5	6	6	3	3
Loans and advances to banks	29	30	32	29	35	32	32	29	35
Loans and advances to customers	86	80	80	87	81	84	79	89	99
Debt securities	9	12	13	16	33	30	38	40	34
Other investments	1	2	2	3	4	4	0	0	1
Intangible fixed assets	0	0	0	0	1	1	1	1	0
Tangible fixed assets	3	3	3	3	3	3	2	2	3
Other assets	14	13	14	15	18	18	16	11	8
Prepayments and accrued income	1	1	2	2	2	2	2	2	2
Total assets	153	152	157	166	182	182	179	177	186
Retail life-fund assets attributable to policy-holders	0	1	1	2	3	4	7	8	0
Total assets and retail life-fund assets	153	153	158	168	185	185	186	185	186
Liabilities									
Deposits by banks	33	33	33	32	36	28	27	27	30
Customer accounts in credit	86	84	84	88	84	90	96	98	110
Debt securities in issue	9	8	11	15	18	18	16	12	9
Other liabilities	12	13	14	16	28	28	23	20	19
Accruals and deferred income	2	2	2	2	2	3	3	2	3
Other provisions	1	1	1	1	1	2	1	1	1
Subordinated liabilities	5	5	5	5	5	5	5	8	7
Total liabilities	148	146	150	159	175	174	170	168	179
Shareholders' funds*	6	6	6	7	8	8	9	9	7
Total liabilities and shareholders' funds	153	152	157	166	182	182	179	177	186
Retail life-fund assets attributable to policy-holders	0	1	1	2	3	4	7	8	0
Total liabilities, shareholders' funds and retail life-fund liabilities	153	153	158	168	185	185	186	185	186
Other information									
Cumulative goodwill written off to reserves†	1.0	0.7	1.0	1.2	0.3	0.3	-	-	-
Repurchases of ordinary shares	-	-	-	-	0.5	0.0	0.4	0.6	-

per cent

	1992	1993	1994	1995	1996	1997	1998	1999	2000
Performance indicators									
Operating profit as a percentage of average shareholders' funds‡	10	20	24	24	23	14	22	24	22
Loans and advances to customers as a percentage of total assets	56	52	51	53	43	46	44	48	53
Customer accounts in credit as a percentage of total liabilities	58	57	56	56	48	52	57	58	61
Shareholders' funds as a percentage of total assets	4	4	4	4	4	4	5	5	4
Fixed assets as a percentage of total assets	2	2	2	2	1	2	1	1	2

Source: NatWest Group.

*This is after write-off of goodwill until 1997.

†£0.7 billion of purchased goodwill in 1996 and a further £0.3 billion in 1998 was reinstated as assets in the balance sheet.

‡Average shareholders' funds includes any capitalized goodwill balances.

Summary of loans to customers, and customer accounts in credit

5.217. Table 5.56 shows an analysis of NatWest Group's total loans by type of customer for the three years to 2000. The bank was not able to provide this information for earlier years. Total loans increased 24 per cent, from £80 billion in 1998 to £99 billion in 2000. The largest increases were in loans to corporate customers, which increased from £[✄] billion in 1998 to £[✄] billion in 1999 before falling to £[✄] billion in 2000; and loans to the 'other' customers, which increased from £[✄] billion in 1998 to £[✄] billion in 2000. In 2000 loans to personal customers were £[✄] billion, and loans to SMEs were £[✄] billion, which accounted for [✄] per cent and [✄] per cent respectively of the bank's lending.

217

TABLE 5.56 **NatWest Group: analysis of loans by type of customer, 1998 to 2000**

Year	£ billion Per-sonal	SME	Corp-orate	Other	Total	Proportion of total (%) Per-sonal	SME	Corp-orate	Other	Total
1998					80					100
1999	Figures omitted. See note on page iv.				90	Figures omitted. See note on page iv.				100
2000					99					100

Source: NatWest Group.

5.218. Table 5.57 analyses customer accounts in credit (ie customer deposits) by type of customer for the three years to 2000. In 2000 accounts in credit from its SME banking business totalled around £[✂] billion and accounted for [✂] per cent of total deposits. Accordingly (for both its SME banking business and for the bank as a whole), customer accounts in credit, in effect, financed the total level of lending, subject to the need of the bank to manage its funding to cover interest rate exposures and differences in maturity profiles between customer accounts and lending. The personal and corporate banking businesses accounted for [✂] per cent and [✂] per cent respectively of total accounts in credit in 2000. NatWest Group said that the 'loans:customer accounts in credit' ratio for the group increased from [✂] in 1998 to [✂] in 1999.

TABLE 5.57 **NatWest Group: analysis of customer accounts in credit, 1998 to 2000**

Year	£ billion Per-sonal	SME	Corp-orate	Other	Total	Proportion of total (%) Per-sonal	SME	Corp-orate	Other	Total
1998					96					100
1999	Figures omitted. See note on page iv.				98	Figures omitted. See note on page iv.				100
2000					110					100

Source: NatWest Group.

5.219. Appendix 5.9 shows the summary balance sheets for NatWest Group from 1993 to 2000, with the corresponding earnings of interest on assets, and payments of interest on liabilities. In 2000 NatWest Group reported that it earned an average rate of 6.1 per cent on its assets and paid an average rate of 4.0 per cent on its liabilities (such as customer accounts in credit, of which around £17 billion was interest free). In 2000 NatWest Group had a net interest spread of around 2.1 per cent, which equated to net interest income of around £4.0 billion; and compared with higher spreads in earlier years, such as 2.4 per cent in 1993, and a low point of 1.8 per cent in 1997.

Contingent liabilities and commitments

5.220. Table 5.58 shows an analysis of contingent liabilities and commitments for the bank from 1992 to 2000. NatWest Group's level of contingent liabilities declined from £15 billion in 1992 to £8 billion in 2000, and the level of commitments increased from £47 billion in 1992 to £62 billion in 2000. These off-balance-sheet items are significant relative to on-balance-sheet items. For example, in 2000 contingent liabilities and commitments amounted to £70 billion, compared with total liabilities of £179 billion (39 per cent).

TABLE 5.58 **NatWest Group: analysis of contingent liabilities and commitments, 1992 to 2000**

£ billion

	1992	1993	1994	1995	1996	1997	1998	1999	2000
Contingent liabilities:									
Acceptances and endorsements	2	1	1	1	1	1	1	1	1
Guarantees and assets pledged as collateral security	14	12	10	9	10	10	10	7	7
	15	13	11	10	11	11	11	8	8
Commitments:									
Standby facilities, credit lines and other	47	50	52	57	50	53	48	56	62

Source: NatWest.

Bad debts

5.221. Table 5.59 shows the level of closing bad debt provision and the level of bad debt charge against profits between 1989 and 2000. The level of closing bad debt provisions was £2.1 billion in 1989, peaked at £2.4 billion in 1992, and declined to a low of £1.1 billion in 1999. This increased in 2000 to £2.2 billion reflecting a reinstatement of both provisions and losses written off, following a change in accounting policy to bring NatWest Group in line with RBS. Loans and advances are classified as bad debts and written off in part or in whole when there is no reasonable prospect of recovery. Over the period, the level of provisions generally ranged between 2 and 3 per cent of loans. Appendix 5.2 shows comments from NatWest Group's annual reports on its bad debt experience over the recession years.

TABLE 5.59 **NatWest Group: analysis of bad debt provision and charges to profit and loss for whole bank, 1989 to 2000**

£ billion

	1989	1990	1991	1992	1993	1994	1995	1996	1997	1998	1999	2000
Analysis of movement in provision												
Balance at start of year	*	*	*	*	2.4	*	*	*	*	*	*	1.1
Restatement†	*	*	*	*	–0.1	*	*	*	*	*	*	1.1
Balance at start of year	1.6	2.1	1.6	2.0	2.3	2.1	1.8	1.7	1.5	1.4	1.4	2.2
Charge against profits— P&L (analysed below)	1.4	1.2	1.9	1.9	1.3	0.6	0.6	0.6	0.6	0.5	0.2	0.4
Amounts written off	–1.1	–1.5	–1.6	–1.6	–1.6	–1.2	–1.0	–0.8	–0.8	–0.6	–0.7	–0.6
Recoveries	*	*	*	*	0.2	0.3	0.2	0.2	0.2	0.2	0.2	0.2
Other movements	0.2	–0.1	0.1	0.1	0.0	0.0	0.0	–0.2	0.0	0.0	0.0	0.0
Balance at end of year	2.1	1.6	2.0	2.4	2.1	1.8	1.7	1.5	1.4	1.4	1.1	2.2
Analysis of bad debt provision												
General provision	0.3	0.4	0.4	0.5	0.4	0.3	0.4	0.3	0.4	0.4	0.4	0.4
Specific provision	1.8	1.2	1.5	1.9	1.8	1.5	1.3	1.2	1.0	1.0	0.7	1.7
Bad debt provision	2.1	1.6	2.0	2.4	2.1	1.8	1.7	1.5	1.4	1.4	1.1	2.1
Analysis of bad debt charge to profit and loss												
New and additional provisions	*	*	*	*	*	1.1	1.1	1.0	0.9	0.8	0.6	0.6
Releases of provisions established in earlier years	*	*	*	*	*	–0.3	–0.2	–0.2	–0.1	–0.1	–0.1	–0.1
Recoveries of advances written off in earlier years	*	*	*	*	*	–0.3	–0.2	–0.2	–0.2	–0.2	–0.2	–0.2
Bad debt charge to profit and loss	1.4	1.2	1.9	1.9	1.3	0.6	0.6	0.6	0.6	0.5	0.2	0.4
Performance indicators												per cent
Bad debt provision as a percentage of total loans	3	2	2	3	3	2	2	2	2	2	1	2
Bad debt charge as a percentage of total loans	1.8	1.4	2.3	2.2	1.5	0.8	0.7	0.7	0.7	0.6	0.3	0.4
Bad debt charge as a percentage of total income	27	20	30	28	18	9	9	8	8	7	3	5

Source: NatWest Group.

*Information is unavailable.
†Provisions were reinstated in 1993 and 2000 to reflect changes in accounting policy.

5.222. Closing bad debt provisions consists of general and specific provisions. Over the period, the level of general provisions remained relatively unchanged at £0.4 billion while the level of specific provisions declined from £1.8 billion in 1999 to £0.7 billion in 1999. This increased to £1.7 billion in 2000. NatWest Group said that the decline in specific provisions up to 1999 was due to changes in its portfolio, particularly problem country debt and certain country exposures. In 1989 NatWest Group held specific provisions of £1.2 billion against problem country debt, and by 1997 such provisions had reduced to £6 million. We also noted that prior to 2000 and a change in accounting policy for bad debts specific provisions were at their highest between 1991 and 1994.

5.223. Over the 12-year period the level of bad debt charge against profits fluctuated from a peak of £1.9 billion in both 1991 and 1992 to around £0.6 billion between 1994 and 1998, and a low charge of £0.2 billion in 1999. The charge equated to about 2.3 per cent of loans at the peak in 1991 and 1992, to about 0.7 per cent between 1994 and 1998, and in 1999 fell to a low of 0.3 per cent. When bad debt charges are compared with total income, the peak figure in 1991 and 1992 equated to around 30 per cent of income, compared with 3 per cent in 1999.

5.224. Table 5.60 shows an analysis by type of customer of NatWest Group's bad debt charge to the profit and loss account from 1997 to 2000, which was the only period for which it could provide this form of analysis. It was unable to provide bad debt charges figures for the SME and corporate banking businesses, but made estimates for the bad debt charges in respect of SMEs, as we discuss in the following paragraphs.

TABLE 5.60 **NatWest Group: analysis of bad debt charge to profit and loss account by type of customer, 1997 to 2000**

£ million

Year	Personal	SME	Corporate	Other	Total
1997		*	*		562
1998		*	*		499
1999		*	*		237
2000	✂	*	*	✂	359
Average 1997–2000		*	*		414

Source: NatWest Group.

*Not available—see Table 5.63 for NatWest Group's estimates.

5.225. Table 5.61 shows NatWest Group's bad debt charge as a percentage of loans by type of customer for 1998 and 2000. In 1998 the percentage was [✂] for the personal banking business, compared with [✂] per cent for the 'other' activity, and [✂] per cent for the SME banking business. In 2000 the proportions were [✂] per cent respectively. NatWest Group was unable to split out from the 'other' segment the bad debt charge that related to the SME banking business.

TABLE 5.61 **NatWest Group: bad debt charge as a percentage of loans to customers, 1998 to 2000**

per cent

Year	Personal	SME	Corporate	Other	Total
1998		Figures omitted.			0.6
1999		See note on page iv.			0.3
2000					0.6

Source: NatWest Group.

5.226. Because of the limited data on SME banking shown in the above tables for the analysis of NatWest Group's bad debt charges, it undertook special exercises for this purpose, first to assist the Cruickshank review by providing details of bad debts on lending to SMEs with turnover under £1 million; and second, for this inquiry by showing estimates of bad debts on lending to SMEs with turnover between £1 million and £25 million. Table 5.62 shows a summary of the results of this analysis. For customers with turnover less than £1 million, NatWest Group's lending was between £[✂] billion and £[✂] billion between 1989 and 1993, and fell significantly to around £[✂] billion in the three years to 1999 as NatWest Group told us that it feared the onset of a recession in the three years to 1999 and therefore was selective in its lending. The bad debt charge:lending ratio in this category reached a high of [✂] per cent in 1992, but was [✂] per cent in 1999. For customers with turnover from £1 million to £25 million, NatWest Group's lending increased from £[✂] billion in 1989 to around £[✂] billion after 1995, but NatWest Group was unable to say exactly what was the level of bad debt charge. It estimated the charges over the 11-year period as a cumulative low estimate of £[✂] million, or a more realistic level of £[✂], which equated to an estimated average bad debt charge:lending ratio of [✂] per cent or [✂] per cent respectively.

TABLE 5.62 **NatWest Group: analysis of lending and bad debt charges to customers with turnover less than £25 million, 1989 to 1999**

| | Customers with turnover less than £1m* | | | Customers with turnover between £1m and £25m | | | | |
| | | | | | Lower estimate | | Higher estimate | |
Year	Lending £bn	Bad debt charge £m	Charge: lending ratio %	Lending £bn	Bad debt charge £m	Charge: lending ratio %	Bad debt charge £m	Charge: lending ratio %
1989								
1990								
1991								
1992								
1993								
1994								
1995			Figures omitted. See note on page iv.					
1996								
1997								
1998								
1999								
Cumulative total								
Average								

Summary of lending to SMEs with turnover to £25 million

| | | Lower estimate | Higher estimate | Lower estimate | Higher estimate |
Year	Total lending £bn	Bad debt charge £m	Bad debt charge £m	Charge: lending ratio %	Charge: lending ratio %
1989					
1990					
1991					
1992					
1993					
1994					
1995		Figures omitted. See note on page iv.			
1996					
1997					
1998					
1999					
11-year total					
Average					

Source: NatWest Group.

*Information provided to the Cruickshank review.

5.227. Table 5.62 also shows that NatWest Group's lending to SMEs fell from around £[✂] billion in 1990 to some £[✂] billion since 1996. NatWest Group's lower estimate for its cumulative bad debt charges on lending to SMEs totalled £[✂] billion for the 11 years, which equated to an average annual bad debt:lending ratio of 1.6 per cent. This compared with NatWest Group's higher estimate of £[✂] billion on lending to SMEs, and a cumulative bad debt:lending ratio of [✂] per cent. Based on NatWest Group's higher estimate, the SME banking business bad debt charge:lending ratio reached a peak of [✂] per cent in 1992.

5.228. Table 5.63 compares NatWest Group's higher estimate for bad debt charges from its SME banking business to its overall bad debt charge for the 11 years to 1999. The SME banking business proportion was between [✂] and [✂] per cent of the total charge over the recession years 1991 to 1994, and over the 11-year period the SME banking business bad debt charge of some £[✂] billion was [✂] per cent of the overall charge of some £[✂] billion. Using the lower estimate of £[✂] billion, the SME banking business proportion of total bad debts would decrease to [✂] per cent.

TABLE 5.63 **NatWest Group: comparison of SME banking business bad debt charges to whole bank charges, 1989 to 1999**

	£ million			Proportion of total (%)		
Year	SME higher estimate for bad debt charge	Other activities	Total charge	SME	Other activities	Total
1989			1,435			100
1990			1,153			100
1991			1,875			100
1992			1,903			100
1993			1,262			100
1994			616			100
1995			639			100
1996			574			100
1997	✂		562	✂		100
1998			499			100
1999			237			100
11-year total	*		10,755			100
Average 1989–93			1,525			100
Average 1994–99			521			100

Source: NatWest Group.

*The lower estimate was £[✂].

Capital adequacy

5.229. Table 5.64 shows regulatory capital data for NatWest Group from 1993 to 2000. Over the period, its Tier 1 ratio increased from 6 per cent in 1993 to 9 per cent in 1999 and back to 7 per cent in 2000. Its RAR increased from 11 per cent in 1993 to 16 per cent in 1999, falling to 12 per cent in 2000.

TABLE 5.64 **NatWest Group: regulatory capital data, 1993 to 2000**

£ billion

	As at 31 December							
	1993	1994	1995	1996	1997	1998	1999	2000
RWAs	103.4	103.4	110.0	104.7	103.2	96.4	97.2	98.3
Tier 1	5.9	6.6	7.4	7.0	7.5	8.0	8.9	6.9
Tier 2	5.7	5.4	5.1	4.7	5.2	5.2	7.3	6.5
Tier 3	0.0	0.0	0.0	0.0	0.0	0.0	0.2	0.2
Gross capital resources	11.6	12.0	12.5	11.7	12.6	13.3	16.4	13.6
Less: supervisory deductions	−0.4	−0.6	−0.8	−0.4	−0.6	−0.6	−0.6	−1.7
Total net capital resources	11.2	11.3	11.8	11.3	12.1	12.7	15.7	11.9
								per cent
Ratios								
Tier 1 ratio	6	6	7	7	7	8	9	7
RAR	11	11	11	11	12	13	16	12

Source: NatWest Group.

5.230. Between 1998 and 1999, NatWest Group reported that its Tier 2 capital (which consisted of subordinated debt) had increased from £5.2 billion to £7.3 billion. Consequently its RAR increased from

13 per cent in 1998 to 16 per cent in 1999. It said that the capital increase was in anticipation of its acquisition of Legal & General in September 1999, and it had raised £2.4 billion in subordinated debt for this purpose. The offer for Legal & General, however, lapsed following the offers by BoS and subsequently RBSG to acquire NatWest Group.

RBS

History

5.231. RBSG, which is the parent company of RBS, is a diversified financial services group engaged in a wide range of banking, financial and finance-related activities in the UK and internationally. In March 2000 it acquired NatWest Group and thereby increased significantly in size. It is listed on the London Stock Exchange and at 29 June 2001 its market capitalization was £42 billion and its price: earnings ratio was 17.3.

5.232. Outside the UK, the USA was the only single territory accounting for more than 10 per cent of the group's total assets, based on the published financial statutory accounts at 30 September 1999.

5.233. The acquisition of NatWest Group in 2000 has enabled RBSG to create one of the largest business and financial services groups in Europe.

Business structure serving SMEs

5.234. Prior to RBSG's acquisition of NatWest Group in March 2000, the main business within the group that provided services to SMEs was its UK Bank (RBS), which consisted of three main business units:

(a) Retail Banking, which provided banking services to personal and small business customers with turnover less than £1 million;

(b) Corporate and Institutional Banking, which provided banking services to mid and large corporations with turnover greater than £1 million; and

(c) Cards, which provided credit and debit card services to personal and business customers.

5.235. Other significant businesses within RBS were as follows:

(a) Direct Line Insurance, which sells and underwrites its own automobile and domestic household insurance policies;

(b) Citizens, which is RBS's US subsidiary that engages in retail and corporate banking activities in the USA;

(c) Angel Trains, which acquires rolling stock from manufacturers, leases such assets to train operating companies and contracts to manage and maintain the assets; and

(d) various new Retail Financial Services Businesses in which RBS was a partner (such as Tesco Personal Finance and Virgin Direct Personal Finance).

5.236. After RBSG acquired NatWest Group, it integrated its businesses (predominantly RBS) with NatWest Group to form a new structure, which consisted of six business units that provide services to SMEs:

(a) Retail Banking, for servicing personal customers and business customers with turnover less than £1 million;

(b) CBFM, for providing banking services to business and institutional customers with turnover greater than £1 million;

(c) Card Businesses & E-commerce within the Retail Direct division, which comprised the Card and E-commerce businesses of NatWest Group and RBS;

(d) Coutts, for providing private banking services to high net worth clients;

(e) Ulster Bank, for providing retail and wholesale financial services in Northern Ireland and the Republic of Ireland; and

(f) Manufacturing division, which comprised operations, support services and technology.

5.237. RBS provided us with copies of its 1999 management accounts for the two main business units that provided banking services to SME customers, Retail Banking and Corporate and Institutional Banking.

5.238. Retail Banking's management accounts for 1999 showed that loans to business customers totalled £[✂] billion and customers' deposits £[✂] billion (of which about [✂] per cent or £[✂] was in non-interest-bearing current accounts). The management accounts also showed total income of £[✂] million (of which [✂] per cent or £[✂] million was interest earned on non-interest-bearing current accounts).

5.239. The management accounts reported operating costs for Retail Banking but did not separate operating cost between personal and business customers. The cost:income ratio reported for Retail Banking was 60 per cent, but RBS considered that this understated the ratio because of the embedded value accounting treatment of Royal Scottish Assurance (RSA), and the £5.3 million gain on the sale of a business. RSA is accounted for by taking the movement in embedded value through non-interest income in the profit and loss account (in line with standard industry practice), rather than by recognizing the costs on an accruals basis.

5.240. Within Corporate and Institutional Banking, business customers were segmented into three categories:

(a) Commercial, which was loosely defined as business customers with turnover between £1 million and £10 million. In 1999 Commercial reported operating profit of £[✂] million and a direct cost:income ratio of 28 per cent.

(b) Mid Corporate, which was loosely defined as business customers with turnover between £10 million and £100 million. In 1999 Mid Corporate reported operating profit of £[✂] million and a direct cost:income ratio of 16 per cent.

(c) Large Corporate, which was loosely defined as business customers with turnover greater than £100 million. In 1999 Large Corporate reported operating profit of £[✂] million and a direct cost:income ratio of 14 per cent.

We noted that the profit and cost:income ratios quoted above were over- and understated respectively, as there were certain additional shared costs that were not allocated to the categories.

Financial performance

Profit and loss accounts

5.241. Table 5.65 shows the summarized profit and loss accounts of RBS from 1993 to 2000. The figures reported from 1993 to 1999 are for RBS prior to its acquisition of NatWest Group, whereas those for 2000 are for RBSG plus consolidation adjustments for the 15 months ended 31 December 2000. The table also separately shows net income from the group's Direct Line Insurance business. Between 1993 and 1999 (2000 was a 15-month period) operating income grew 167 per cent from £1.5 billion to £3.4 billion. Over this period, net interest income doubled from £0.9 billion to £1.8 billion, net fees and commissions also doubled from £0.5 billion to £1.0 billion, and other income grew 250 per cent from £0.2 billion to £0.7 billion. Over the same period operating expenses doubled from £1 billion in 1993 to £2.0 billion in 1999; and the bad debt charge ranged between £0.1 billion and £0.3 billion. As a result operating profit after bad debt charge grew from £0.3 billion in 1993 to £1.2 billion in 1999.

TABLE 5.65 RBS: consolidated profit and loss account, 1993 to 2000

£ billion

	1993	1994	1995	1996	1997	1998	1999	15 months to 31.12.00
				Years ended 30 September*				
Net interest income	0.9	1.0	1.1	1.2	1.4	1.6	1.8	5.8
Net fees and commissions	0.5	0.5	0.6	0.6	0.7	0.8	1.0	3.1
Other income	0.2	0.1	0.2	0.2	0.3	0.7	0.7	2.0
Operating income	1.5	1.7	1.8	2.0	2.4	3.1	3.4	10.9
Operating expenses	−1.0	−1.1	−1.2	−1.3	−1.6	−1.9	−2.0	−7.3
Operating profit (excluding insurance)	0.5	0.5	0.6	0.7	0.8	1.2	1.4	3.6
Net income from insurance activity†	0.1	0.2	0.2	0.0	0.0	0.1	0.1	0.3
Operating profit before provisions	0.6	0.7	0.7	0.7	0.9	1.3	1.5	3.9
Bad debt charge	−0.3	−0.2	−0.1	−0.1	−0.1	−0.2	−0.3	−0.6
Other provisions	0.0	0.0	0.0	0.0	0.0	0.0	0.0	0.0
Operating profit after bad debt charge	0.3	0.5	0.6	0.6	0.7	1.1	1.2	3.3
Exceptional, extraordinary and other items	0.0	0.0	0.0	0.1	0.1	−0.1	0.0	0.1
Net profit before tax	0.3	0.5	0.6	0.7	0.8	1.0	1.2	3.4
Tax	−0.1	−0.1	−0.2	−0.2	−0.2	−0.3	−0.4	−1.2
Net profit after tax	0.2	0.4	0.4	0.5	0.5	0.7	0.9	2.2
Minority interest	0.0	0.0	0.0	0.0	0.0	0.0	0.0	0.0
Profit for the financial year	0.2	0.4	0.4	0.5	0.5	0.7	0.9	2.2
Dividends	−0.1	−0.2	−0.2	−0.2	−0.2	−0.3	−0.3	−1.2
Profit retained for the financial year	0.0	0.2	0.2	0.3	0.3	0.4	0.5	1.0
Number of employees ('000)‡	§	§	§	27	31	32	32	94
Performance indicators								per cent
Tax charge as a percentage of profit before tax	31	27	34	27	29	29	30	35
Percentage change in operating income	N/A	9	9	12	19	29	10	220
Change in the number of employees	§	§	§	§	14	3	3	187

Source: RBS.

---

*Figures from 1993 to 1999 represent those prior to the acquisition of NatWest Group. Figures for 2000 represent those of the enlarged RBSG. Following the merger in 2000, the financial year end was changed from 30 September to 31 December, and therefore the final year period shown as 2000 is for 15 months.

†This predominantly relates to the Direct Line business and excludes the operating costs of the insurance activities. RBS told us that the latter were not significant.

‡Excluding temporary staff.

§Not provided.

5.242. Table 5.66 further analyses the overall performance of RBS from 1993 to 2000 by showing all items as a percentage of operating income.

TABLE 5.66 RBS: operating profit and loss items as a percentage of operating income, 1993 to 2000

per cent

	1993	1994	1995	1996	1997	1998	1999	15 months to 31.12.00
Net interest income	57	58	60	59	59	51	51	53
Net fees and commissions	33	33	31	30	30	27	29	28
Other income	10	9	9	10	11	22	20	18
Operating income	100	100	100	100	100	100	100	100
Operating expenses	−67	−69	−69	−66	−65	−60	−60	−67
Operating profit (excluding insurance)	33	31	31	34	35	40	40	33
Profit from insurance activity	6	10	9	2	2	3	4	3
Operating profit before provisions	39	41	40	36	37	42	44	36
Bad debt charge	−19	−11	−6	−6	−6	−6	−8	−6
Other provisions	−1	0	0	0	−2	−1	0	0
Operating profit after bad debt charge	19	30	33	31	29	35	35	30
Exceptional and other items	−2	2	0	4	3	−2	0	1
Net profit before tax	17	32	33	34	31	32	35	31

Source: RBS.

5.243. Over the five years to 1997 operating expenses as a percentage of operating income (also referred to as the cost:income ratio) ranged between 65 and 69 per cent. In 1998 and 1999 the ratio fell to 60 per cent (including costs from the Direct Line activity), but increased to 67 per cent in 2000. RBSG told us that the enlarged group (including NatWest Group) was planning to achieve cost savings of up to around £1.5 billion by 2003 (as noted in paragraph 5.203) and that this, coupled with income growth, would be likely to reduce the group's cost:income ratio below 50 per cent by 2004.

5.244. Table 5.67 shows the profitability of the UK Banking division, which provided banking services to personal and business customers, between 1995 and 2000. Over the period, profit before tax increased from £0.4 billion in 1995 to £1.3 billion in the 15 months ended 31 December 2000. Following the reorganization of the group after the acquisition of NatWest Group, the UK Banking division had ceased to exist at 31 December 2000. The figures for 2000 in the table represent the results of certain businesses only and are not comparable with the figures for earlier years.

TABLE 5.67 **RBS: consolidated profit and loss account for the UK Banking division, 1995 to 2000**

£ billion

	1995	1996	1997	1998	1999	15 months to 31.12.00
Net interest income	0.8	0.9	1.0	1.0	1.1	1.7
Non-interest income	0.6	0.7	0.7	0.7	0.8	1.7
Operating income	1.5	1.6	1.7	1.7	1.9	3.4
Operating costs	−0.9	−1.0	−1.0	−0.9	−1.0	−1.7
Profit before provisions	0.5	0.6	0.7	0.8	0.9	1.7
Bad debt charge	−0.1	−0.1	−0.1	−0.1	−0.2	−0.4
Profit before tax	0.4	0.5	0.6	0.6	0.7	1.3
Total assets	40	45	51	52	58	149
Shareholders' funds	1.7	1.8	2.2	2.2	2.5	5.1

per cent

	1995	1996	1997	1998	1999	15 months to 31.12.00
Cost:income ratio	65	60	58	55	52	49
Pre-tax return on average shareholders' funds	*	31	29	29	32	35

Source: RBS.

*Not provided.

Analysis of performance by type of customer

5.245. We asked RBS to analyse its UK activities from 1997 to 2000 into the following segments:

(a) personal customers;

(b) SME customers, which included business customers with turnover less than £25 million;

(c) corporate customers, which included business customers with turnover greater than £25 million; and

(d) 'other' activities, for example Treasury and Capital markets, Structured Finance, Royal Bank Leasing, Citizens (USA), Royal Bank of Scotland International (Offshore), Angel Trains, Investor Services and non-insurance income from Direct Line.

RBS noted that the above segments were not part of its business structure and therefore, as explained more fully below, it was unable to provide the data requested except on a 'best endeavours' basis. It was unable to separate its business customers into an SME banking business as defined by us, and it could show business customers' income only in the following turnover bands: less than £10 million, £10 million to £100 million, and greater than £100 million.

5.246. RBS was also unable to allocate cost, and hence profits, across types of customer. It said that the group was organized into customer-facing divisions, responsible only for growing income and controlling direct costs (such as salaries of customer-facing staff). It said that our definition of SMEs covered customers in three business units: Retail Banking, CBFM, and Retail Direct. However, over 40 per cent of the costs of these three business units were shared or indirect costs covering operational technology, account processing and management, and money transmission, which were managed by either its Manufacturing division or its Group central functions. It did not allocate any indirect costs to its business units for its management accounting purposes, and made similar arguments as NatWest Group in paragraph 5.206 on why such cost allocations were not relevant to its management of the business.

5.247. RBS said that any method of cost allocation would not only be complex but would also produce a variety of outcomes, depending on the assumptions employed. Therefore it believed that no meaningful information could be obtained from such an exercise. In Chapter 6 we show an estimate of the profitability of RBS's SME banking business for 1998 to 2000, which we prepared from its submissions.

5.248. Table 5.68 shows RBS's allocation of operating income (excluding its Direct Line Insurance activity) by type of customer from 1997 to 2000. The business customer income figures were according to its own allocation with customers having turnover less than £10 million, from £10 million to £100 million, and greater than £100 million. Between 1997 and 2000 operating income from the personal banking business increased from £0.6 billion in 1997 to £0.8 billion in 1999 and then to £1.1 billion in the 15-months to 31 December 2000. Operating income from business customers increased to £0.9 billion for the 15 month period to 31 December 2000. Between 1997 and 2000 the personal banking business typically accounted for around 24 per cent, and all business customers for around 18 per cent, of total operating income. For 2000 business customers with turnover up to £100 million accounted for 13 per cent of total income. RBS suggested that 25 per cent of the £10 million to £100 million turnover band might be representative in determining the amount of income and assets in the £10 million to £25 million turnover band.

TABLE 5.68 **RBS: operating income (excluding insurance activity) by customer segment, 1997 to 2000***

| | | £ billion | | | | | Proportion of total (%) | | | | | |
| | Per- | Business customer turnovers | | | | | Per- | Business customer turnovers | | | | |
Year†	sonal	(<£10m)	(£10–£100m)	(>£100m)	Other‡	Total	sonal	(<£10m)	(£10–£100m)	(>£100m)	Other‡	Total
1997	0.6	0.3	0.1	0.1	1.3	2.4	26	13	4	3	53	100
1998	0.7	0.3	0.1	0.1	1.8	3.0	24	11	4	3	59	100
1999	0.8	0.4	0.1	0.1	2.0	3.4	24	10	3	4	59	100
2000	1.1	0.4	0.2	0.3	2.9	4.8	23	9	4	5	59	100

Source: RBS.

*Operating income includes net interest income, net fees and commissions and other income.
†2000 was a 15-month period.
‡This includes Corporate and Institutional Banking business, which does not fall into the SME category as defined for the reference. It consists of Treasury and Capital Markets, Structured Finance and Royal Bank Leasing activities. It is shown in 'other' as these activities did not fit within the definition of personal, SME or Corporate Banking business. Corporate and Institutional Banking had income of £733 million in 1999 and CBFM had income of £1,389 million in 2000. The remaining activities represented by 'other' included the Citizens business which contributed £549 million of income in 1999 and £1,071 million in 2000; Angel Trains, Wealth Management, Direct Line Insurance and the Cards business.

5.249. Table 5.69 summarizes how RBS reported its segmental performance in its published accounts between 1997 and 1999. Data for 2000 is unavailable for the UK Bank on a comparable basis as the organizational structure changed during the year. During the period, the main classes of business were UK Bank (as discussed above), Direct Line Insurance, Citizens Bank and 'Other' (mainly Angel Trains and New Retail Financial Services Businesses). Between 1997 and 1999, profit before tax for Direct Line Insurance and Citizens Bank remained relatively unchanged at £0.1 billion and £0.2 billion respectively. In 1999 return on average shareholders' funds was 30 per cent for both Direct Line Insurance and Citizens Bank. This compared with 32 per cent reported for the UK Bank and 35 per cent for the bank as a whole. For 1999, the UK Bank accounted for 53 per cent of total profits before tax, but only 41 per cent of income (as shown in Table 5.68).

TABLE 5.69 **RBS: segmental analysis by class of business, 1997 to 1999**

Class of business	1997	1998	1999
Profit before tax:			
UK Bank	0.5	0.6	0.7
Direct Line Insurance	0.0	0.1	0.1
Citizens Bank	0.2	0.2	0.2
Other*	−0.1	0.3	0.2
Total	0.7	1.2	1.3
Shareholders' funds (equity):			
UK Bank	2.2	2.2	2.5
Direct Line Insurance	0.3	0.3	0.4
Citizens Bank	0.6	0.7	0.9
Other	0.1	−0.2	0.6
Total	3.2	3.0	4.3
Total assets:			
UK Bank	50.7	51.8	57.9
Direct Line Insurance	1.1	1.2	1.4
Citizens Bank	9.6	9.7	11.8
Other	11.2	17.0	17.7
Total	72.6	79.7	88.9
			per cent
Profit before tax as percentage of average shareholders' funds:			
UK Bank		29	32
Direct Line Insurance		19	30
Citizens Bank		39	30
Other		†	†
Total		38	35

Source: RBS.

*'Other' for the purposes of this analysis does not include the same components shown in the segmental analysis in Tables 5.68. For this analysis, the Corporate and Institutional Banking business is included within the UK Banking division as represented in the annual reports of RBS.

†Not applicable as shareholders' funds were negative for 1998.

Balance sheets

5.250. Table 5.70 shows the summary of RBS's balance sheets from 1993 to 2000,[1] with 2000 showing the effect of the NatWest Group acquisition on the enlarged group. Total assets increased from £37 billion in 1993 to £309 billion in 2000. Total liabilities increased from £36 billion in 1993 to £286 billion in 2000, and shareholders' funds increased from £2 billion in 1993 to £23 billion in 2000. Over the period fixed assets ranged between 1 and 3 per cent of total assets. Between 1993 and 2000 loans and advances to customers increased 630 per cent from £23 billion to £168 billion, and customer accounts in credit increased 580 per cent from £26 billion to £177 billion. RBS said that the increase in loans and customer accounts in credit was achieved through organic growth and acquisitions. In 2000 loans and advances to customers accounted for 54 per cent of total assets, and customer accounts in credit accounted for 62 per cent of total liabilities. Between 1993 and 2000 operating profit after bad debt charge as a percentage of average shareholders' funds (pre-tax returns) ranged between 16 and 34 per cent.

[1]Financial figures for the years prior to 1992 were not comparable with later years because of a change in accounting policy. In addition the presentation in the earlier years' balance sheets were different from later years.

TABLE 5.70 **RBS: consolidated balance sheet summary, 1993 to 2000**

£ billion

As at 30 September*

	1993	1994	1995	1996	1997	1998	1999	As at 31.12.00
Assets								
Cash and balances at central banks	1	1	1	1	1	1	1	3
Items in course of collection	0	0	0	0	0	0	0	3
Treasury bills and other eligible bills	0	0	1	1	1	1	1	3
Loans and advances to banks	7	9	9	12	14	12	10	32
Loans and advances to customers	23	26	29	33	39	41	49	168
Debt securities	2	4	5	7	10	13	15	58
Other investments	0	0	0	0	1	1	1	2
Intangible fixed assets†	0	0	0	0	0	0	0	12
Tangible fixed assets	1	1	1	1	1	2	3	6
Other assets	3	3	4	4	6	8	7	18
Prepayments and accrued income	0	1	1	1	1	1	1	4
Total assets	37	45	51	61	73	80	89	309
Long-term assurance assets								11
Total assets including long-term insurance assets								320
Liabilities								
Deposits by banks	3	4	5	5	5	4	6	35
Items in course of transmission	0	0	0	0	0	0	0	2
Customer accounts in credit	26	29	33	38	48	51	55	177
Debt securities in issue	1	3	3	6	5	7	9	19
Other liabilities	3	4	5	5	7	9	8	33
Accruals and deferred income	1	1	1	2	2	2	3	7
Other provisions	0	0	0	0	0	0	0	2
Subordinated liabilities	2	2	2	2	3	3	3	10
Total liabilities	36	43	49	58	69	77	85	286
Shareholders' funds‡	2	2	2	3	3	3	4	23
Total liabilities and shareholders' funds	37	45	51	61	73	80	89	309
Long-term assurance assets								11
Total assets including long-term assurance assets								320
Other information								
Cumulative goodwill written off to reserves	0.2	0.4	0.4	0.4	0.5	1.2	1.1	1.1
Performance indicators								per cent
Operating profit as a percentage of average shareholders' funds§	16	26	29	26	24	34	33	N/A
Loans and advances to customers as a percentage of total assets	61	57	57	55	53	51	56	54
Customer accounts in credit as a percentage of total liabilities	73	68	67	65	69	66	65	62
Shareholders' funds as a percentage of total assets	5	4	4	5	4	4	4	7
Fixed assets as a percentage of total assets	2	2	2	2	1	3	3	2

Source: RBS.

*Figures between 1993 and 1999 are prior to the acquisition of NatWest Group. Figures for 2000 represent those of the enlarged group (and include NatWest Group).
†This is goodwill relating to the NatWest Group acquisition.
‡This is after write-offs to reserves, for example £1.2 billion for 1999 as shown in the table.
§Average shareholders' funds includes capitalized goodwill balances.

5.251. Over the period to 1998, RBS wrote off £1.2 billion in purchased goodwill to reserves, of which £0.6 billion related to several acquisitions made by Citizens between 1993 and 1999, and £0.4 billion related to the acquisition of Angel Trains in 1998.

5.252. RBSG said that the total consideration paid for NatWest Group in March 2000 was £21 billion and the purchased goodwill generated was £11.4 billion, which it accounted for as an asset in RBSG's balance sheet. RBSG planned to amortize the purchased goodwill over an estimated useful life of 20 years, and this would result in a goodwill amortization charge of £570 million a year for the next 20 years.

5.253. In evaluating returns for NatWest Group, RBSG said that the best estimate of its capital base was the replacement cost for its assets and that this was best approximated by market value, which it considered reflected both the value of shareholders' funds but also the value of intangibles. We discuss the issue of returns on capital in greater detail in Chapters 6 and 7.

5.254. RBSG said that shareholders' funds as reported in its balance sheet of £23 billion in 2000 was understated as it did not take into account the following items:

(a) adjustment to allow for the impact of inflation;

(b) internally generated goodwill;

(c) goodwill purchased in the past but written off; and

(d) other intangibles such as brands and intellectual property in relation to IT, the costs of recruiting and retaining staff and the costs of customer acquisition.

RBSG said that on a conservative basis, to take account of the above factors, it considered that the capital value estimated by such an approach would be much greater than shareholders' funds, and possibly around three times for most UK banks, and around twice shareholders' funds for RBSG assuming that its shareholders' funds included capitalized goodwill from the acquisition of NatWest Group. We further discuss any adjustments to equity for the purpose of calculating returns on capital in Chapters 6 and 7.

Summary of loans to customers, and customer accounts in credit

5.255. Table 5.71 analyses RBS's loans to customers in accordance with the type of customer for which it had data between 1997 and 2000. Total loans increased 78 per cent from £39 billion in 1997 to £69 billion in 2000. The largest percentage increases were in loans to business customers with turnover greater than £100 million from £6 billion in 1997 to £17 billion in 2000; and in loans to the 'other' segment from £16 billion in 1997 to £29 billion in 2000. In 2000 loans to customers with turnover less than £100 million accounted for 15 per cent of total lending, compared with 19 per cent to personal customers, and 42 per cent to 'other' customers.

TABLE 5.71 **RBS: analysis of loans to customers, 1997 to 2000**

| | £ billion | | | | | | Proportion of total (%) | | | | | |
| | Per- | Business customer turnovers | | | | | Per- | Business customer turnovers | | | | |
Year	sonal	(<£10m)	(£10–100m)	(>£100m)	Other*	Total	sonal	(<£10m)	(£10–£100m)	(>£100m)	Other	Total
1997	8	5	3	6	16	39	21	12	9	17	42	100
1998	9	5	4	7	16	41	23	12	9	18	38	100
1999	10	5	3	9	21	49	21	11	7	19	42	100
2000	13	6	4	17	29†	69	19	9	6	25	42	100

Source: RBS.

*This includes Corporate and Institutional Banking business (CBFM for 2000), which does not fall into the SME category. It consists of Treasury and Capital Markets, Structured Finance and Royal Bank Leasing activities. It is shown in 'other' as these activities did not fit within the definition of personal, SME or Corporate Banking business. The remaining activities represented by 'other' included the Citizens business; Angel Trains, Wealth Management, Direct Line Insurance and the Cards business.
†Corporate Banking and Financial Markets includes £10 billion, Citizens £11.7 billion, Retail Direct £6.4 billion.

5.256. Table 5.72 shows the analysis of customer accounts in credit from 1997 to 2000 over the main types of customer. Total accounts in credit increased by 42 per cent from £48 billion in 1997 to £68 billion in 2000. Customer accounts in credit from business customers with turnover less than £10 million increased 61 per cent from around £4 billion in 1997 to £7 billion in 2000; and accounts in credit from the 'other' segment increased 34 per cent from £26 billion in 1997 to £35 billion in 2000. In 2000 loans to the 'other' segment accounted for 52 per cent of total customer accounts in credit, and the proportion for customers with turnover less than £100 million accounted for 19 per cent of total accounts in credit.

TABLE 5.72 **RBS: analysis of customer accounts in credit, 1997 to 2000**

| | | £ billion | | | | | | Proportion of total (%) | | | | |
| | Per- | Business customer turnovers | | | | | Per- | Business customer turnovers | | | | |
Year	sonal	(<£10m)	(£10–£100m)	(>£100m)	Other*	Total	sonal	(<£10m)	(£10–£100m)	(>£100m)	Other	Total
1997	8	4	4	5	26	48	16	9	8	11	56	100
1998	9	5	4	5	28	51	17	10	8	10	55	100
1999	9	6	4	6	30	55	17	11	7	11	55	100
2000	10	7	6	9	35†	68	15	10	9	14	52	100

Source: RBS.

*This includes the Corporate and Institutional Banking business (Corporate Banking and Financial Markets in 2000), which does not fall into the SME category. It consists of Treasury and Capital Markets, Structured Finance and Royal Bank Leasing activities. It is shown in 'other' as these activities did not fit within the definition of personal, SME or corporate business. The remaining activities represented by 'other' included the Citizens business; Angel Trains, Wealth Management, Direct Line Insurance and the Cards business.
†This included £8.7 billion from Corporate Banking and Financial Markets customers, £17 billion for Citizens, £9 billion for Wealth Management, £2 billion for Retail Direct, £1.6 billion for Retail, and contras of around £3 billion.

5.257. RBS said that the 'loans:customer accounts in credit' ratio for the group increased from 0.81 in 1997 to 1.02 in 2000. The 'loans:customer accounts in credit' ratio for business customers with turnover less than £10 million decreased from 1.08 in 1997 to 0.92 in 2000.

5.258. Appendix 5.10 shows the summary balance sheets for RBS from 1993 to 1999, with the corresponding figures for interest earned on assets, and interest paid on liabilities. RBS told us that there was no longer an appropriate level for which data for 2000 could be extracted. In 1999 RBS reported that it earned an average rate of 5.9 per cent on its assets, and paid an average rate of 3.8 per cent on its liabilities, of which around £3 billion was interest free. In 1999 RBS reported a net interest spread of around 2.1 per cent, which equated to net interest income of around £1.8 billion.

5.259. RBS's net interest spread in 1993 and 1994 was 2.4 per cent and it fell to 2.1 per cent for 1996 to 1999.

Contingent liabilities and commitments

5.260. Table 5.73 shows an analysis of contingent liabilities and commitments for the bank from 1993 to 2000. Paragraph 5.31 discusses contingent liabilities and commitments generally as an important source of income for banks. RBS's level of contingent liabilities increased from £1.9 billion in 1993 to £3.5 billion in 2000, and the level of commitments increased from £9 billion in 1993 to £32 billion in 2000. These off-balance-sheet items are significant, for example in 1999 contingent liabilities and commitments of £24 billion, compared with total liabilities of £85 billion (28 per cent).

TABLE 5.73 **RBS: analysis of contingent liabilities and commitments**

								£ billion
	1993	1994	1995	1996	1997	1998	1999	2000
Contingent liabilities:								
Acceptances and endorsements	0.7	0.6	0.7	0.9	0.9	1.0	0.9	0.4
Guarantees and assets pledged as collateral security	0.7	0.7	0.7	0.9	1.0	0.9	1.0	1.7
Other contingent liabilities	0.5	0.5	0.6	0.5	0.8	0.9	0.9	1.4
	1.9	1.9	2.0	2.4	2.6	2.8	2.7	3.5
Commitments:								
Standby facilities, credit lines and other	9	11	12	14	17	16	21	32

Source: RBS.

Bad debts

5.261. Table 5.74 shows the level of closing bad debt provision from 1989 to 2000 and the level of bad debt charge against profits between 1989 and 2000. From 1989 to 2000 the level of closing bad debt provisions ranged between £0.5 billion and £1.1 billion (and equated to between 1 and 3 per cent of loans). From 1989 to 2000, the level of bad debt charge ranged between £0.1 billion and £0.5 billion (which equated to between 0.3 and 1.3 per cent of loans). The bad debt charge was £0.4 billion in 1991 and 1992. After 1995 the bad debt charge declined and ranged between 0.3 and 0.7 per cent of loans. In terms of bad debt charges as a percentage of total income, the percentage fell from 19 per cent in 1993 to 9 per cent in 2000. Appendix 5.2 shows comments from RBS's annual reports on its bad debt experience over the recession years.

TABLE 5.74 **RBS: analysis of bad debt provision and charges to profit and loss for whole bank, 1989 to 2000**

£ billion

	1989	1990	1991	1992	1993	1994	1995	1996	1997	1998	1999	2000
Analysis of movement in provision												
Balance at start of year	0.4	0.6	0.5	0.5	0.7	0.6	0.6	0.5	0.5	0.5	0.6	0.7
Charge against profits—P&L (analysed below)	0.1	0.2	0.4	0.4	0.3	0.2	0.1	0.1	0.1	0.2	0.3	0.5
Amounts written off	−0.1	−0.2	−0.3	−0.3	−0.3	−0.3	−0.2	−0.2	−0.2	−0.2	−0.2	−0.3
Recoveries	0.0	0.0	0.0	0.0	0.0	0.0	0.0	0.0	0.0	0.0	0.1	0.1
Other movements	0.1	0.0	0.0	0.0	0.0	0.1	0.0	0.0	0.0	0.1	0.0	0.1
Balance at end of year	0.6	0.5	0.5	0.7	0.6	0.6	0.5	0.5	0.5	0.6	0.7	1.1
Analysis of bad debt provision												
General provision	0.1	0.1	0.1	0.1	0.1	0.1	0.1	0.1	0.1	0.2	0.2	0.2
Specific provision	0.5	0.4	0.5	0.6	0.6	0.5	0.4	0.4	0.4	0.5	0.6	0.9
Bad debt provision	0.6	0.5	0.5	0.7	0.6	0.6	0.5	0.5	0.5	0.6	0.7	1.1
Analysis of bad debt charge to profit and loss												
New and additional provisions	0.1	0.3	0.4	0.4	0.3	0.3	0.2	0.2	0.2	0.3	0.4	0.6
Releases of provisions established in earlier years	0.0	−0.1	−0.1	0.0	0.0	0.0	0.0	0.0	0.0	0.0	0.0	0.0
Recoveries of advances written off in earlier years	0.0	0.0	0.0	0.0	0.0	0.0	0.0	0.0	0.0	0.0	0.0	0.0
Other movements	0.0	0.0	0.0	0.0	0.0	0.0	0.0	0.0	0.0	0.0	0.0	0.0
Bad debt charge to profit and loss	0.1	0.2	0.4	0.4	0.3	0.2	0.1	0.1	0.1	0.2	0.3	0.5
Performance indicators												per cent
Bad debt provision as a percentage of total loans	*	*	*	*	3	2	2	1	1	2	1	2
Bad debt charge as a percentage of total loans	*	*	*	*	1.3	0.7	0.4	0.3	0.4	0.5	0.6	0.7
Bad debt charge as a percentage of total income	*	*	*	*	19	11	6	6	6	6	8	9

Source: RBS.

*Not provided, or information is not available in this form.

5.262. Table 5.75 shows RBS's bad debt charge to profit and loss account by categories between 1991 and 2000. RBS was not able to provide the analysis within our definition of SME banking business and, for example, the 'business' category referred to customers with turnover less than £100 million. The business activity incurred its highest level of bad debt charge between 1991 and 1994, in the range £[✂] million to £[✂] million. Since then the level has declined and reached a low of £[✂] million in 2000. Bad debt charges for the personal category were also high in the early 1990s at around £[✂] million.

TABLE 5.75 **RBS: bad debt charge to profit and loss account by segment, 1991 to 2000**

£ million

Year	Personal	Business*	Other	Total
1991				351
1992				401
1993				293
1994				182
1995				112
1996				113
1997		*Figures omitted.*		146
1998		*See note on page iv.*		200
1999				276
2000				467
Average 1991–93				348
Average 1994–2000				214

Source: RBS.

*Business customers comprise those with turnover up to £100 million. Customers with turnover over £100 million are included in 'other'.

5.263. Table 5.76 shows RBS's bad debt charge as a percentage of loans by category from 1992 to 2000. RBS said that in the early 1990s the bad debt percentage for business customers with turnover less than £100 million was higher than that of the other categories at around [✂] per cent. The percentage fell after 1994 and has since remained at around [✂] per cent a year. In terms of the personal category, the percentage was also high in the early 1990s, at a high of [✂] per cent in 1992. Between 1994 and 1997 the percentage declined and ranged between [✂] and [✂] per cent, but in 1998 it increased to [✂] per cent, and then to [✂] per cent in 2000. The 'other' category also had a high percentage of [✂] per cent in 1992.

TABLE 5.76 **RBS: bad debt charge as a percentage of loans to customers, 1992 to 2000**

per cent

Year	Personal	Business*	Other	Total
1992				1.9
1993				1.3
1994				0.7
1995		*Figures omitted.*		0.4
1996		*See note on page iv.*		0.3
1997				0.4
1998				0.5
1999				0.6
2000				0.7

Source: RBS.

*Business customers include those with turnover up to £100 million. Customers with turnover over £100 million are included in 'other'.

Capital adequacy

5.264. Table 5.77 shows regulatory capital data for RBS from 1993 to 2000. Between 1993 and 1999, its Tier 1 ratio ranged between 6 and 8 per cent and its RAR ranged between 10 and 12 per cent. RBS noted that the minimum level of regulatory capital was designed to protect depositors, and was not a measure of the capital invested in the business by shareholders for the purpose of evaluating economic returns. RBSG said that following its acquisition of NatWest Group in March 2000 its targeted Tier 1 ratio was between 6.5 and 7 per cent.

TABLE 5.77 **RBS: regulatory capital data, 1993 to 2000**

£ billion

| | | | As at 30 September | | | | | At 31 Dec |
	1993	1994	1995	1996	1997	1998	1999	2000
RWAs	25.9	28.9	33.3	37.5	45.8	49.1	56.8	77.4
Tier 1	1.8	1.9	2.1	2.5	3.1	3.2	4.6	5.9
Tier 2	1.6	1.8	1.9	2.4	2.7	3.0	3.3	4.1
Tier 3	0.0	0.0	0.0	0.0	0.0	0.0	0.0	0.0
Gross capital resources	3.4	3.6	4.0	4.9	5.8	6.2	7.9	10.0
Less: supervisory deductions	−0.2	−0.5	−0.6	−0.8	−0.5	−0.7	−1.0	−0.9
Total net capital resources	3.2	3.1	3.4	4.1	5.3	5.5	6.9	9.1

per cent

Ratios								
Tier 1 ratio	7	6	6	7	7	7	8	8
RAR	12	11	10	11	12	11	12	12

Source: RBS.

BoS

History

5.265. Until September 2001, BoS was listed on the London Stock Exchange, and on 29 June 2001 its market capitalization was £10.4 billion and its price:earnings ratio was 17.3. In September 2001 it merged with Halifax under a new holding company, HBOS plc. From September 2001 the shares of HBOS plc have been listed on the London Stock Exchange (see paragraph 5.271).

5.266. BoS was established by an Act of the Parliament of Scotland, in 1695, 'for the Carrying-on and Managing of a Public Bank'. Since then it has grown through a series of amalgamations and acquisitions. The most important of these were with the Glasgow-based Union Bank of Scotland in 1955, and with the British Linen Bank in 1971. In 1977 the British Linen Bank was revived as the bank's merchant banking subsidiary. Bank of Wales was established as a regional bank in 1986. In 1995 the Bank of Western Australia Limited, a full service bank based in Western Australia, was acquired. The BoS shareholding now stands at 55.8 per cent (2001).

5.267. Until January 1999, the bank internally reported to management along legal entity lines, these being Bank of Scotland, Bank of Scotland Treasury Services PLC, Capital Bank plc, the British Linen Bank Limited, Bank of Wales PLC, and the Bank of Western Australia.

5.268. In January 1999 BoS restructured its UK business and established three customer-facing divisions. These are:

(a) Personal Banking, which provides personal customers with consumer products and services through a variety of delivery channels;

(b) Business Banking, which provides direct services to SMEs with turnover up to £10 million; and

(c) Corporate Banking, which focuses on larger businesses, that require customized financial services.

5.269. These divisions are in turn supported by the following divisions:

(a) Services Division, which provides centralized support services including processing and IT;

(b) Group office, which provides strategic and policy support including accounting and finance, risk, compliance and human resources; and

(c) Bank of Scotland Treasury Services PLC, which also operates as a separate division within the group.

5.270. The operations of the UK subsidiaries, including Capital Bank, British Linen Bank and Bank of Wales, were realigned to fit the new structure. Bank of Western Australia was excluded from the restructuring.

5.271. BoS and Abbey National had held talks during July and August 2000 with a view to a combination. The talks were terminated by Abbey National in November 2000 as it wished to concentrate on organic growth. Talks were later reopened, but were again terminated in February 2001. On 4 May 2001 BoS and Halifax announced that they had agreed to merge subject to shareholder, regulatory and court approvals. Halifax has a negligible presence in the UK SME banking business. BoS and Halifax have emphasized that the proposed merger was pro-competitive by the creation of a new force to challenge the high SME banking business shares held by Barclays, HSBC, Lloyds TSB, NatWest and RBS. The transaction was approved by both sets of shareholders and dealings in a new holding company, HBOS plc, commenced on 10 September 2001.

Business structure serving SMEs

5.272. The Business Banking division was formed as an amalgamation of the banking services and the asset finance business. It currently provides a range of services to SME customers including:

(a) core banking services through a network of business locations throughout Scotland, England and Wales;

(b) electronic banking and other direct banking facilities;

(c) cash flow finance including invoice discounting and factoring services;

(d) extended purchase and lease facilities in the agriculture, construction, engineering, marine, printing, transport and asset finance sectors;

(e) vehicle management and contract hire facilities;

(f) tailored banking for the healthcare, property investment and leisure markets;

(g) motor sector finance products through franchised and non-franchised dealers, and joint ventures with distributors, manufacturers and large dealer groups; and

(h) merchant acquiring services.

5.273. BoS has announced a strategic alliance with British Telecommunications plc. This will offer Internet banking and a range of other business services to SMEs. BoS has over 300 branches throughout Scotland, 24 offices in England, and a number of offices around the world.

Financial performance

Profit and loss accounts

5.274. Table 5.78 shows the profitability of BoS for years ended 28 February from 1994 to 2001. Between 1994 and 2001 BoS's operating income increased 145 per cent, from £1.1 billion to £2.7 billion. During the period operating expenses doubled from £0.6 billion to £1.2 billion. The level of bad debt charge was in the range £0.2 billion and £0.4 billion over the period. As a result, BoS's profit before tax steadily increased from £0.3 billion in 1994 to £1 billion in 2001.

TABLE 5.78 BoS: consolidated profit and loss account, 1994 to 2001

£ billion

Years ended 28 February

	1994	1995	1996	1997	1998	1999	2000	2001
Net interest income	0.8	0.9	1.0	1.2	1.3	1.5	1.7	1.8
Net fees and commissions	0.3	0.4	0.4	0.5	0.5	0.5	0.6	0.7
Other income	0.0	0.0	0.0	0.1	0.1	0.1	0.1	0.2
Operating income	1.1	1.3	1.4	1.8	1.9	2.2	2.4	2.7
Operating expenses	−0.6	−0.6	−0.8	−0.9	−1.0	−1.1	−1.1	−1.2
Operating profit before provisions	0.6	0.7	0.7	0.8	0.9	1.1	1.3	1.5
Bad and doubtful debts charge	−0.3	−0.2	−0.2	−0.2	−0.2	−0.3	−0.3	−0.4
Other provisions	0.0	0.0	0.0	0.0	0.0	0.0	0.0	0.0
Operating profit	0.3	0.4	0.5	0.7	0.7	0.8	1.0	1.1
Exceptional and other items	0.0	0.0	0.1	0.0	0.0	0.2	−0.1	−0.1
Net profit before tax	0.3	0.4	0.5	0.7	0.7	1.0	0.9	1.0
Tax	−0.1	−0.2	−0.2	−0.2	−0.2	−0.4†	−0.3	−0.3
Net profit after tax	0.2	0.3	0.3	0.4	0.5	0.6	0.6	0.7
Minority interests	0.0	0.0	0.0	0.0	0.0	0.0	0.0	−0.1
Profit for the financial year	0.2	0.3	0.3	0.4	0.5	0.6	0.6	0.6
Dividends	−0.1	−0.1	−0.1	−0.1	−0.2	−0.2	−0.2	−0.2
Profit retained for the financial year	0.1	0.2	0.2	0.3	0.4	0.4	0.4	0.4
Cumulative goodwill written off against reserves	0.1	0.1	0.2	0.2	0.3	0.2	0.2	0.2
Number of FTE employees ('000)	15.0	15.6	18.8	19.4	20.8	20.4	19.8	19.2

per cent

	1994	1995	1996	1997	1998	1999	2000	2001
Performance indicators Percentage change in operating income	*	14	11	23	8	14	10	11

Source: BoS.

---

*Not available.

†The relatively large tax charge in 1999 was a result of a non-recurring charge of £80 million that arose from a change in the level of provisioning in respect of deferred tax.

5.275. BoS's operating profit as a percentage of average shareholders' funds (pre-tax return) remained relatively steady at between 28 and 32 per cent until 1999, but dropped to 26 per cent in 2000 and in 2001 to 22 per cent (see Table 5.81).

5.276. Table 5.79 further analyses the overall performance of BoS from 1994 to 2001 by comparing all items with operating income. Net interest income as a percentage of total income remained between 67 and 71 per cent in the period, while the net fees and commissions proportion fell from 30 per cent in 1994 to 26 per cent in 2001. The 'other' income proportion remained relatively constant at around 3 to 5 per cent over the period. BoS said that, because it had a relatively small Treasury division, 'other' income was not greatly affected by large swings in dealing profits or losses.

TABLE 5.79 BoS: operating profit and loss items as a percentage of operating income, 1994 to 2001

per cent

	1994	1995	1996	1997	1998	1999	2000	2001
Net interest income	67	69	69	69	70	71	70	69
Net fees and commissions	30	29	28	27	27	25	27	26
Other income	3	2	2	4	3	4	3	5
Operating income	100	100	100	100	100	100	100	100
Operating expenses	−48	−50	−54	−52	−52	−49	−47	−45
Operating profit before provisions	52	50	46	48	48	51	53	55
Bad and doubtful debts charge	−27	−17	−12	−10	−12	−12	−13	−15
Other provisions	−2	0	0	−1	0	0	0	0
Operating profit after provisions	22	33	34	37	37	38	39	40
Exceptional and other items	1	2	4	1	2	8	−1	−3
Net profit before tax	24	35	38	38	39	47	38	37

Source: BoS.

5.277. Operating expenses as a percentage of operating income (also referred to as the cost:income ratio) fluctuated from 48 per cent in 1994, up to 54 per cent in 1996 and then fell to 45 per cent in 2001. The increase in 1996 was a result of greater expenditure on infrastructure and systems in the clearing bank and substantial investment in systems, new products, staff and training in the finance subsidiary.

5.278. The level of bad debt charge as a percentage of income fell significantly from its 1994 level of 27 per cent to 15 per cent in 2001.

Analysis of performance by type of customer

5.279. We asked BoS to segment further its UK activities into the following categories:

(a) personal customers;

(b) SME customers, which included business customers with less than £25 million turnover;

(c) corporate customers, which included business customers with more than £25 million turnover; and

(d) other customers.

BoS said that it was unable to provide the historical data we had requested because, until March 2000, it analysed its business activities by legal entity rather than by customer-facing sectors. It was able to provide segmented data only on a 'best endeavours' basis for the financial year to 28 February 2001. BoS had two business units that served SMEs according to our definition: Business Banking, which had a customer cut-off at turnover up to £10 million, and Corporate Banking. Table 5.80 summarizes the information provided by BoS on its SME banking business for the year to February 2001.

TABLE 5.80 **BoS: summary of analysed results for 2001**

| | | SME banking customers | | | £ million |
	Personal	'Business'*	'Corporate't	Other‡	Total
Income	1,027	697	587	317	2628
Operating costs	−562	−370	−118	−152	−1,202
Operating profit before bad debts	465	327	469	165	1426
Bad debt charge	−169	−80	−126	−10	−385
Operating profit after bad debts and before other items	296	247	343	155	1,041
					per cent
Cost:income ratio	55	53	20	48	46

Source: BoS.

*Includes customers with turnover to £10 million.
†Includes customers with turnover above £10 million.
‡Includes Other UK business and the Australian subsidiary.

5.280. In the year to February 2001, income from personal customers totalled £1,027 million. This represented 39 per cent of income for the total banking group. Income from the 'business' unit totalled £697 million, and income for the 'corporate' unit was £587 million, which were 27 per cent and 22 per cent respectively of total group income.

5.281. In the year to February 2001 operating costs (excluding bad debts) attributable to the personal sector totalled £562 million (46 per cent of total operating costs). The 'business' unit's operating costs totalled £370 million, and costs attributable to the 'corporate' unit were £118 million, which represented 31 per cent and 10 per cent respectively of total operating costs.

5.282. During the year to February 2001, the cost:income ratio of the personal segment was 55 per cent. For the business and corporate units, the cost:income ratios were 53 per cent and 20 per cent respectively, and the ratio for the whole bank was 46 per cent.

5.283. For the year to February 2001, the bad debt charge attributable to the personal segment was £169 million (44 per cent of the total bad debt charge). This compared with £80 million for the 'business' unit, and £126 million for the 'corporate' unit, which were, respectively, 21 per cent and 33 per cent of total group bad debt charge.

Balance sheets

5.284. Table 5.81 shows BoS's balance sheets at 28 February from 1994 to 2001. Total assets have increased from £30.7 billion in 1994 to 86.1 in 2001. This was because of increases in the following categories of assets:

(a) loans and advances to banks from £2.7 billion in 1994 to £5.3 billion in 2001;

(b) loans and advances to customers from £22.6 billion in 1994 to £66.7 billion in 2001 (ie an increase of 195 per cent);

(c) debt securities from £2.7 billion in 1994 to £9.0 billion in 2001; and

(d) 'other' from £2.7 billion in 1994 to £5.1 billion in 2001.

TABLE 5.81 **BoS: consolidated balance sheet, 1994 to 2001**

£ billion

As at 28 February

	1994	1995	1996	1997	1998	1999	2000	2001
Assets								
Cash and balances at central banks	0.4	0.4	0.5	0.6	0.6	0.6	0.6	0.8
Items in the course of collection	0.4	0.4	0.4	0.4	0.4	0.4	0.5	0.5
Treasury bills and other eligible bills	0.9	0.7	0.9	0.5	0.9	0.4	0.5	0.4
Loans and advances to banks	2.7	2.9	3.6	3.1	4.7	4.8	4.0	5.3
Loans and advances to customers	22.6	24.8	32.6	37.1	42.9	46.6	55.5	66.7
Debt securities	2.7	3.8	4.8	4.0	3.2	4.6	8.0	9.0
Other investments	0.0	0.1	0.1	0.1	0.1	0.2	0.2	0.3
Intangible fixed assets	0.0	0.0	0.0	0.0	0.0	0.0	0.1	0.2
Tangible fixed assets	0.4	0.4	0.6	0.6	0.6	0.6	0.6	0.6
Other assets	0.2	0.1	0.2	0.4	0.6	0.9	1.1	1.4
Prepayments and accrued income	0.4	0.5	0.6	0.6	0.6	0.6	0.7	0.9
Total assets	30.7	34.1	44.1	47.3	54.7	59.8	71.8	86.1
Liabilities								
Deposits by banks	5.6	6.2	6.4	4.2	5.9	6.2	7.9	8.0
Customer accounts in credit	17.8	19.9	25.4	27.1	29.9	28.6	30.0	35.9
Debt securities in issue	3.3	3.5	6.6	9.6	11.7	16.7	24.2	30.0
Other liabilities	0.9	1.0	1.2	1.4	1.6	2.2	2.4	2.6
Accruals and deferred income	0.5	0.5	0.7	0.8	0.8	0.9	0.9	1.3
Other provisions	0.2	0.2	0.2	0.3	0.3	0.4	0.5	0.5
Subordinated liabilities	1.1	1.2	1.7	1.7	1.8	1.8	2.3	2.9
Total liabilities	29.4	32.6	42.2	45.1	52.0	56.7	68.3	81.2
Shareholders' funds*	1.3	1.5	1.9	2.2	2.7	3.1	3.5	4.9
Total liabilities and shareholders' funds	30.7	34.1	44.1	47.3	54.7	59.8	71.8	86.1
Performance indicators								per cent
Operating profit as a percentage of average shareholders' funds	*	30	28	32	29	29	26	22
Loans and advances to customers as a percentage of total assets	74	73	74	79	78	78	77	77
Customer accounts in credit as a percentage of total liabilities	60	61	60	60	57	50	44	44
Shareholders' funds as a percentage of total assets	4	4	4	5	5	5	5	6
Fixed assets as a percentage of total assets	1	1	1	1	1	1	1	1

Source: BoS.

*Includes minority interest which is negligible, for example in 2001 minorities were £566 million out of £4,958 million.

5.285. Total liabilities increased from £29.4 billion in 1994 to £81.2 billion in 2001. This was because of increases in customer accounts from £17.8 billion to £35.9 billion (102 per cent), and increases in debt securities in issue from £3.3 billion to £30.0 billion. Shareholders' funds increased from £1.3 billion in 1994 to £4.9 billion in 2001.

Loans to customers, and accounts in credit

5.286. In common with other banks, the largest items within the bank's balance sheet were loans and advances to customers, and customer deposit accounts. In contrast with some of the other banks, the level of debt securities in issue in 2001 was nearly as large as the funding from customer deposit accounts. This showed that BoS has not been able to grow its customer deposit base at the same rate as its loan book and had therefore funded the growth in the loan book through debt issues in the wholesale market. It told us that a factor that affected its returns was its limited income from customer accounts in credit.

5.287. At 28 February 2001 loans and advances to customers accounted for 77 per cent of total assets and customer accounts in credit accounted for 44 per cent of total liabilities. At 28 February 2001 loans and advances to personal customers totalled £20 billion, compared with £19 billion to the business unit's customers, and £22 billion to the corporate unit's customers. This represented 30 per cent, 28 per cent and 33 per cent respectively of total loans outstanding for the whole bank. BoS stated that even though its SME banking business was heavily reliant on customers in Scotland, its overall lending levels appeared significant when compared with the four largest clearing groups that operated in England and Wales. BoS noted that unlike the banks its asset finance lending fell within its Business Banking division and was therefore included in these figures as it was a major aspect of its activities across the UK. It added that the inconsistency of this approach was further demonstrated by the fact that BoS held only 1 per cent of the SME banking activity in the UK.

5.288. As at 28 February 2001 customer accounts in credit totalled £12 billion from the personal segment, £10 billion from the 'business' unit's customers, and £8 billion from the corporate unit's customers. This represented 33 per cent, 28 per cent and 22 per cent respectively of total customer accounts in credit for the whole bank.

Contingent liabilities and commitments

5.289. Table 5.82 shows an analysis of contingent liabilities and commitments for 1994 to 2001. BoS's level of commitments increased from £3.9 billion in 1994 to £10.2 billion in 2001. In 2001 BoS reported total contingent liabilities of £2.0 billion and total commitments of £10.2 billion, compared with total on-balance-sheet liabilities of £81.2 billion.

TABLE 5.82 **BoS: contingent liabilities and commitments, 1994 to 2001**

£ billion

	1994	1995	1996	1997	1998	1999	2000	2001
Acceptances and endorsements	0.2	0.2	0.4	0.3	0.2	0.2	0.2	0.2
Guarantees and assets pledged as collateral security	0.9	0.9	1.0	1.1	1.2	1.4	1.6	1.8
	1.1	1.0	1.5	1.4	1.4	1.6	1.7	2.0
Commitments	3.9	4.7	4.6	5.2	5.7	7.2	7.4	10.2

Source: BoS.

Bad debts

5.290. Table 5.83 shows the level of closing bad debt provision and the level of bad debt charges against profits between 1994 and 2001. The level of bad debt provisions ranged between a low of £661 million in 1997 and a high level of around £1,039 million in 2001. In 1994, the level of provision equated to 3.3 per cent of the total loan book. The level of provision at 2001 represented only 1.6 per cent of the total loan book. The mix between general and specific provisions also changed over the period: the level of general provisions increased while the level of specific provisions was generally lower. This movement is expected given that the general bad debt provision is based on formulae applied to RWAs whereas specific bad debt charges are formulae driven in respect of individual loans when repayment is deemed unlikely.

TABLE 5.83   **BoS (total group): analysis of bad debt provision and charges to profit and loss, 1994 to 2001**

£ million

	1994	1995	1996	1997	1998	1999	2000	2001
Analysis of bad debt provision:								
General provision	146	180	239	271	308	338	372	412
Specific provision	604	514	441	390	369	370	513	627
Closing bad debt provision	750	694	680	661	677	708	885	1,039
Analysis of bad debt charge to profit and loss:								
New provisions less releases	323	236	194	197	240	292	365	404
Recoveries of advances written off in earlier years	–9	–14	–17	–21	–21	–24	–48	–19
Total bad debt charge	314	222	177	175	219	268	317	385
Performance indicators								*per cent*
Bad debt provision as a percentage of total loans	3.3	2.8	2.1	1.8	1.6	1.5	1.6	1.6
Bad debt charge as a percentage of total loans*	1.4	0.9	0.5	0.5	0.5	0.6	0.6	0.6
Bad debt charge as a percentage of total income	27.5	17.1	12.3	9.9	11.5	12.4	13.4	14.6

Source: BoS.

*BoS noted ratios for 1991 as 1.2 per cent, 1992 as 1.4 per cent, and 1993 as 1.8 per cent.

5.291.   The level of bad debt charge as a percentage of income was 27.5 per cent in 1994. Since 1996 the level of bad debt charge as a percentage of income has remained between 10 and 15 per cent. The percentage increase in the bad debt charge is broadly in line with the percentage increase in advances to customers over the period.

Capital adequacy

5.292.   Table 5.84 shows regulatory capital data for BoS from 1994 to 2001. Between 1994 and 2001 BoS's Tier 1 ratio fluctuated between 5.9 and 7.1 per cent, while its total RAR ranged between 10.7 and 11.9 per cent. BoS confirmed to us that its capital ratio was now at the lower end of its peer group, and claimed that it was 'working the capital that bit harder'.

TABLE 5.84   **BoS: regulatory capital data, 1994 to 2001**

£ billion

As at 28 February

	1994	1995	1996	1997	1998	1999	2000	2001
RWAs	22.4	24.8	31.4	34.6	40.3	46.7	55.4	68.9
Tier 1 capital	1.3	1.5	1.9	2.2	2.7	3.2	3.6	4.9
Tier 2 capital	1.2	1.3	1.8	1.9	2.0	2.0	2.4	3.3
Total net capital resources	2.6	2.8	3.7	4.1	4.7	5.2	6.0	8.2
								per cent
Ratios								
Tier 1	5.9	6.1	6.1	6.4	6.8	6.8	6.4	7.1
Total	11.4	11.4	11.8	11.8	11.7	11.1	10.7	11.9

Source: BoS.

Further banks serving SMEs

5.293. In the paragraphs below we provide information on further banks[1] that provided services to SMEs, plus Halifax which recently announced its intention to enter the SME banking business. We have shown information to 1999, which was the main year where full information was available during the inquiry. We have updated this to 2000 only where this was relevant to our conclusions.

NAB

History

5.294. NAB is an international financial services group providing a range of services across four continents and 15 countries. It is ranked as one of the 50 largest banks in the world. In Australia, NAB is one of the three largest companies listed on the Australian Stock Exchange. At 29 June 2001 its market capitalization was £19.4 billion.

5.295. The company was established in the Australian state of Victoria in 1858 as The National Bank of Australasia. After its early growth in the urban and rural areas of Victoria, supplemented through the absorption of a number of regional banks, the National Bank of Australasia merged with the Commercial Banking Company of Sydney in 1981 to form what is now NAB.

5.296. The accounts of NAB for the year ended 30 September 2000 show that total operating income was A$12.3 billion (£4.4 billion), operating profit before tax was A$4.9 billion (£1.8 billion), and total assets were A$344 billion (£123 billion).

5.297. NAB's operations in the UK consist of Northern, acquired in 1987; Clydesdale, acquired in 1987; and Yorkshire, acquired in 1990. Each of these is discussed in further detail below. NAB has other operations in Europe and has a European holding company, National Australia Group Europe Ltd.

NAB

Financial performance

5.298. NAB was unable to provide profit and loss and balance sheet figures by segment for any of the banks (Clydesdale, Northern and Yorkshire). However, it was able to produce consolidated information for the three banks, as shown in Table 5.86.

5.299. Table 5.85 shows the profit and loss account of NAB's UK operations for 1999/2000 which include the results of Clydesdale, Northern and Yorkshire. The operating income for the year was £1.2 billion and operating expenses were £559 million, which resulted in an operating profit before bad debt charges of £599 million. The cost:income ratio was 48 per cent.

---

[1]These other banks are NAB (including Clydesdale, Northern and Yorkshire), AIB (including First Trust), Ulster Bank, BoI, the Co-operative Bank, Alliance & Leicester, Abbey National and Halifax, together with Nationwide.

TABLE 5.85   **NAB: UK consolidated profit and loss account,* year ended 30 September 2000**

	£m
Net interest income	740
Net fees and commissions	396
Other income	22
Operating income	1,158
Operating expenses	−559
Operating profit before bad debts	599
Bad debt charge	−108
Net profit before tax	491
Tax	−150
Net profit after tax	341
	%
Performance indicator	
Cost:income ratio	48

Source: NAB.

---

*Incorporates results of Clydesdale, Northern and Yorkshire.

5.300.   Table 5.86 further analyses the above profit and loss account of NAB for 1999/2000 by type of customer. During the year, income from personal customers totalled £[✂] million, which represented [✂] per cent of total income for NAB. Income from the SME banking business totalled £[✂] million compared with income of £[✂] million from the 'other' activity, which included corporate customers. These represented [✂] per cent and [✂] per cent respectively of total group income. NAB noted that its cost:income ratio for the SME banking business of [✂] per cent was similar to that of the whole of NAB of 48 per cent. The cost:income ratio for the 'other' segment was comparatively high at [✂] per cent. NAB told us that this was because the 'other' segment contained a number of business units, such as Payments, the cost:income ratios of which were high, and a number of centrally-held costs that were not allocated to the personal banking business in 2000.

TABLE 5.86   **NAB: UK summary of segmental results, 2000**

	Personal	SME	Other*	£ million Total
Income				1,158
Operating costs				−559
Operating profit before bad debts				599
Bad debt charge				−108
Operating profit after bad debts and before other items		Figures omitted. See note on page iv.		491
				per cent
Cost:income ratio				48
Income as proportion of total income				100
Profit as a proportion of total operating profit after bad debt charge				100

Source: NAB.

---

*Includes corporate customers.

5.301.   Table 5.87 shows the consolidated balance sheet for the UK operations of NAB as at 30 September 2000. Loans and advances to customers totalled £[✂] billion, compared with customer accounts in credit of £[✂] billion, leaving a difference that was funded by loans from other entities within the NAB group.

TABLE 5.87 **NAB: UK consolidated balance sheet* as at 30 September 2000**

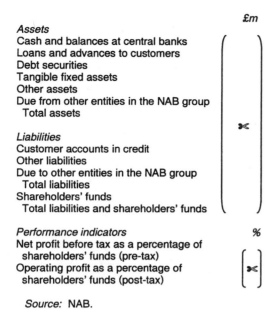

£m

Assets
Cash and balances at central banks
Loans and advances to customers
Debt securities
Tangible fixed assets
Other assets
Due from other entities in the NAB group
  Total assets

Liabilities
Customer accounts in credit
Other liabilities
Due to other entities in the NAB group
  Total liabilities
Shareholders' funds
  Total liabilities and shareholders' funds

Performance indicators   %
Net profit before tax as a percentage of
  shareholders' funds (pre-tax)
Operating profit as a percentage of
  shareholders' funds (post-tax)

Source: NAB.

*Incorporates results of Clydesdale, Northern and Yorkshire.

5.302. We now provide general information on each of the three banks, Clydesdale, Northern and Yorkshire, in the following paragraphs, outlining financial performance and balance sheet information for the years 1995 to 2000.

Clydesdale

5.303. Clydesdale was established in 1838 as the Clydesdale Banking Company with its Head Office in Glasgow and a single branch in Edinburgh. By a series of mergers and acquisitions it grew from a local Glasgow bank to one of the major Scottish banks with 274 branches across Scotland, in London, and the North of England.

Financial performance

5.304. Table 5.88 shows the profitability of Clydesdale from 1995 to 2000. Between 1995 and 2000 the bank's operating income increased from £331 million to £469 million (42 per cent). Operating expenses increased at a much lower rate from £201 million to £234 million (16 per cent). The level of bad debt charge increased from £17 million in 1995 to £43 million in 1998, and then to £77 million in 1999 (although this latter increase partly reflected a change in methodology of calculating the provision). Profit before tax increased by 64 per cent, from £113 million in 1995 to £185 million in 2000.

TABLE 5.88 Clydesdale: consolidated profit and loss account, 1995 to 2000

£ million

	1995	1996	1997	1998	1999	2000
Net interest income	217	223	227	246	278	287
Net fees and commissions	105	109	118	135	150	166
Other income	9	14	18	21	21	16
Operating income	331	347	363	401	448	469
Operating expenses	−201	−197	−193	−207	−209	−234
Operating profit before provisions	130	149	170	194	239	235
Bad debt charge	−17	−23	−24	−43	−77	−50
Operating profit after provisions	113	126	146	150	162	185
Exceptional and other items	-	−1	1	−1	−4	*
Net profit before tax	114	125	146	149	158	185
Tax	−37	−44	−47	−45	−55	−56
Net profit after tax	77	81	99	105	102	129
Dividends	−67	−53	−44	−76	−57	−100
Retained profits	10	28	55	29	45	29

Source: Clydesdale.

*Not provided.

5.305. Table 5.89 further analyses the overall performance of Clydesdale from 1995 to 2000, by comparing all items with operating income. Net interest income as a percentage of total income decreased from 65 per cent in 1995 to 61 per cent in 2000. At the same time, net fees and commissions rose from 32 per cent in 1995 to 35 per cent in 2000.

5.306. Operating expenses as a percentage of operating income (also referred to as the cost:income ratio) fell from 61 per cent in 1995 to 47 per cent in 1999, then rose to 50 per cent in 2000. Clydesdale said that this improvement was due to organizational restructuring and a continued focus on cost management.

TABLE 5.89 Clydesdale: operating profit as a percentage of operating income, 1995 to 2000

per cent

	1995	1996	1997	1998	1999	2000
Net interest income	65	64	63	61	62	61
Net fees and commissions	32	32	33	34	33	35
Other income	3	4	5	5	5	3
Operating income	100	100	100	100	100	100
Operating expenses	−61	−57	−53	−52	−47	−50
Operating profit before provisions	39	43	47	48	53	50
Bad debt charge	−5	−7	−7	−11	−17	−11
Operating profit before provisions	34	36	40	37	36	39
Exceptional and other items	*	*	*	*	−1	*
Net profit before tax	34	36	40	37	35	39

Source: Clydesdale.

*Clydesdale had negligible exceptional and other items in 1995,1996,1997 and 1998.

Balance sheets

5.307. Table 5.90 shows Clydesdale's balance sheets from 1995 to 2000. Total assets increased from £6.7 billion in 1995 to £8.9 billion in 2000. This was mostly because of increases in loans and advances to customers from £4.7 billion in 1995 to £7.0 billion in 2000 (a 49 per cent increase).

TABLE 5.90 Clydesdale: consolidated balance sheet, 1995 to 2000

£ million

As at 30 September

	1995	1996	1997	1998	1999	2000
Assets						
Cash and balances at central banks	380	217	221	48	59	475
Items in the course of collection from other banks	214	201	160	167	153	186
Treasury bills and other eligible bills	-	-	30	-	-	-
Loans and advances to banks	1,016	935	1,238	1,261	868	838
Loans and advances to customers	4,716	5,407	5,860	6,282	6,674	7,041
Debt securities	230	582	125	61	14	10
Other investments	6	10	11	15	12	3
Tangible fixed assets	115	108	114	103	96	91
Other assets	8	8	13	23	91	97
Prepayments and accrued income	64	62	107	130	114	130
Total assets	6,748	7,529	7,878	8,089	8,081	8,869
Liabilities						
Deposits by banks	1,136	1,092	1,536	995	1,139	1,462
Customer accounts in credit	4,200	4,618	5,005	5,603	5,214	5,542
Items in the course of transmission to other banks	117	155	122	33	31	29
Notes in circulation	337	358	368	391	405	442
Debt securities in issue	316	606	16	9	3	3
Other liabilities	55	53	61	218	394	440
Accruals and deferred income	64	66	114	134	123	154
Other provisions	19	25	25	27	21	18
Subordinated liabilities	138	169	188	206	230	230
Total liabilities	6,381	7,141	7,434	7,616	7,560	8,320
Shareholders' funds	367	388	444	473	521	550
Total liabilities and shareholders' funds	6,748	7,529	7,878	8,090	8,081	8,869
Performance indicators						per cent
Net profit before tax as a percentage of average shareholders' funds	*	33	35	33	32	35
Net profit after tax as a percentage of average shareholders' funds	*	21	24	23	21	24

Source: Clydesdale.

*Not applicable or not available.

5.308. Clydesdale's net profit before tax as a percentage of average shareholders' funds increased from 33 per cent in 1996 to 35 per cent in 2000.

5.309. Total liabilities increased from £6.4 billion in 1995 to £8.3 billion in 2000. This was because of increases in customer accounts in credit from £4.2 billion to £5.5 billion (31 per cent), and increases in deposits by banks from £1.1 billion to £1.5 billion. Shareholders' funds increased from £367 million to £550 million.

5.310. In common with other banks, the largest items within the bank's balance sheet were loans and advances to customers, and customer accounts in credit (deposit and savings accounts). In 2000 loans and advances to customers accounted for 79 per cent of Clydesdale's total balance sheet assets.

5.311. Table 5.91 shows an analysis of contingent liabilities and commitments for 1995 to 2000. Clydesdale's level of commitments increased from £2.0 billion in 1995 to £2.9 billion in 2000. In 2000 Clydesdale reported total contingent liabilities of £424 million and total commitments of £2.9 billion, compared with total on-balance-sheet liabilities of £8.3 billion.

TABLE 5.91 Clydesdale: contingent liabilities and commitments, 1995 to 2000

£ million

	1995	1996	1997	1998	1999	2000
Acceptances and endorsements	259	247	161	184	205	234
Guarantees and assets pledged as collateral security	306	329	300	304	270	190
	565	575	461	488	475	424
Commitments	2,035	2,176	2,607	2,234	2,457	2,878

Source: Clydesdale.

Bad debts

5.312. Table 5.92 shows Clydesdale's level of closing bad debt provision, and the level of bad debt charge against profits between 1995 and 2000. The level of bad debt provisions fluctuated during the period, between £52 million in 1995 and £96 million in 2000. The provision rose sharply in 1999 from £55 million to £94 million because of a change in methodology with regard to calculation of the provision. The bank adopted a new methodology for the calculation of the general provision, developed by its parent group. In 1995 the level of the provision equated to 0.9 per cent of the total loan book. This ratio fell to 0.8 per cent in 1997 and increased to 1.3 per cent in 2000. Over the period the level of specific provisions fluctuated between a low of £23 million in 1997 and 1998 and a peak of £40 million in 1999. In 2000 the specific provision was £39 million.

TABLE 5.92 Clydesdale: analysis of bad debt provision and charges to profit and loss, 1995 to 2000

£ million

	1995	1996	1997	1998	1999	2000
Analysis of bad debt provision:						
General provision	24	27	29	32	54	57
Specific provision	28	28	23	23	40	39
Closing bad debt provision	52	55	52	55	94	96
Bad debt charge to profit and loss account	17	23	24	43	77	50
Performance indicators						per cent
Bad debt provision as a percentage of total loans	0.9	0.9	0.8	0.9	1.4	1.3
Bad debt charge as a percentage of total loans	0.3	0.4	0.4	0.7	1.1	0.7
Bad debt charge as a percentage of total income	5	7	15	13	17	11

Source: Clydesdale.

5.313. The bad debt charge as a percentage of total loans was 0.3 per cent in 1995 and rose to 1.1 per cent in 1999. In 2000 the percentage fell to 0.7. Clydesdale noted that the most recent increases were due to a move to a statistical approach to bad debt provision in 1999, as described in its annual report and accounts.

Capital adequacy

5.314. Table 5.93 shows Clydesdale's capital adequacy ratios for 1999 and 2000. In 1999 its Tier 1 ratio was 7.83 per cent and its total capital ratio was 12.22 per cent. In 2000 the ratios were 8.31 per cent and 12.62 per cent respectively.

TABLE 5.93 **Clydesdale: capital adequacy data, 1999 and 2000**

per cent

As at 30 September

	1999	*2000*
Ratios		
Tier 1	7.83	8.31
Total	12.22	12.62

Source: Clydesdale.

Northern

5.315. Northern was established in 1824. It told us that it was the largest retail bank in Northern Ireland with a network of 96 branches and 12 business centres spread across the province.

Financial performance

5.316. Table 5.94 shows the profitability of Northern from 1995 to 2000. Between 1995 and 2000 the bank's operating income increased from £159 million to £202 million (27 per cent). Operating expenses increased at a much slower rate from £98 million to £104 million (6 per cent). The level of bad debt charge fluctuated throughout the period between £3 million in 1997 and £6 million in 2000. Profit before tax also fluctuated throughout the period but predominantly increased, ranging between £57 million in 1995 and £100 million in 1999, but fell to £92 million in 2000.

TABLE 5.94 **Northern: consolidated profit and loss account, 1995 to 2000**

£ million

	1995	*1996*	*1997*	*1998*	*1999*	*2000*
Net interest income	113	119	127	133	133	133
Net fees and commissions	40	42	49	51	55	60
Other income	6	12	6	6	10	10
Operating income	159	173	182	190	199	202
Operating expenses	−98	−91	−96	−104	−92	−104
Operating profit	61	82	86	86	107	99
Bad debt charge	−5	−6	−3	−4	−6	−6
Net profit before tax	57	76	83	82	100	92
Tax	−19	−25	−27	−25	−32	−29
Net profit after tax	37	51	56	57	69	64
Dividends	−33	−32	−43	−25	−52	−62
Profit retained for the financial year	4	19	13	32	17	2

Source: Northern.

5.317. Table 5.95 further analyses the overall performance of Northern from 1995 to 2000, by comparing all items with operating income. Net interest income as a percentage of total income remained relatively stable, between 66 and 71 per cent. At the same time, net fees and commissions rose from 25 per cent in 1995 to 30 per cent in 2000.

5.318. Operating expenses as a percentage of operating income (also referred to as the cost:income ratio) was 61 per cent in 1995 and fell to around 51 per cent by 2000. Northern said that this improvement was due to the benefits of organizational restructuring and a continued focus on cost management.

TABLE 5.95 **Northern: operating profit as a percentage of operating income, 1995 to 2000**

						per cent
	1995	1996	1997	1998	1999	2000
Net interest income	71	69	70	70	67	66
Net fees and commissions	25	24	27	27	28	30
Other income	4	7	3	3	5	5
Operating income	100	100	100	100	100	100
Operating expenses	−61	−53	−53	−55	−46	−51
Operating profit before provisions	39	47	47	45	54	49
Bad debt charge	−3	−3	−2	−2	−3	−3
Net profit before tax	36	44	46	43	51	46

Source: Northern.

Balance sheets

5.319. Table 5.96 shows Northern's balance sheets from 1995 to 2000. Total assets increased from £2.8 billion in 1995 to £3.8 billion in 2000. This was mainly because of increases in loans and advances to customers from £1.8 billion in 1995 to £2.8 billion in 2000 (55 per cent increase).

TABLE 5.96 **Northern: consolidated balance sheet, 1995 to 2000**

						£ million
			As at 30 September			
	1995	1996	1997	1998	1999	2000
Assets						
Cash and balances at central banks			Figures omitted.			
Items in the course of collection from other banks			See note on page iv.			
Loans and advances to banks	502	732	736	743	719	398
Loans and advances to customers	1,840	1,971	2,216	2,512	2,543	2,808
Debt securities						
Tangible fixed assets			Figures omitted.			
Other assets			See note on page iv.			
Prepayments and accrued income						
Total assets	2,816	3,053	3,325	3,580	3,536	3,758
Liabilities						
Deposits by banks	103	18	67	50	57	220
Customer accounts in credit	2,197	2,440	2,630	2,822	2,786	2,783
Items in the course of transmission to other banks						
Notes in circulation						
Other liabilities			Figures omitted.			
Accruals and deferred income			See note on page iv.			
Other provisions						
Subordinated liabilities						
Total liabilities	2,641	2,858	3,115	3,336	3,275	3,494
Shareholders' funds	175	195	210	244	261	264
Total liabilities and shareholders' funds	2,816	3,053	3,325	3,580	3,536	3,758
Performance indicators						per cent
Net profit before tax as a percentage of average shareholders' funds (pre-tax)	33	41	41	36	40	35
Operating profit as a percentage of average shareholders' funds (post-tax)	22	28	28	25	27	24

Source: Northern.

5.320. Northern's net profit before tax as a percentage of average shareholders' funds ranged between 33 and 41 per cent over the five years to 30 September 2000.

5.321. Total liabilities increased from £2.6 billion in 1995 to £3.5 billion in 2000. This was largely because of increases in customer accounts in credit from £2.2 billion to £2.8 billion (27 per cent).

Shareholders' funds increased from £175 million to £264 million. Overall in 2000 lending to customers at £2.8 billion was close to customer accounts in credit, and in 2000 loans and advances to customers accounted for 75 per cent of Northern's total balance sheet assets.

5.322. In common with other banks, the largest items within the bank's balance sheet were loans and advances to customers, and customer accounts in credit (deposit and savings accounts).

5.323. Table 5.97 shows an analysis of contingent liabilities and commitments for 1995 to 2000. Northern's level of commitments increased from £[✂] billion in 1995 to £[✂] billion in 2000. In 2000, Northern reported total contingent liabilities of £[✂] million and total commitments of £[✂] billion, compared with total on-balance-sheet liabilities of £3.5 billion (excluding shareholders' funds).

TABLE 5.97 **Northern: contingent liabilities and commitments, 1995 to 2000**

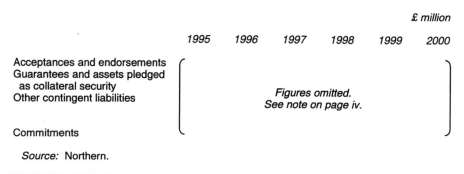

						£ million
	1995	1996	1997	1998	1999	2000
Acceptances and endorsements						
Guarantees and assets pledged as collateral security						
Other contingent liabilities			Figures omitted. See note on page iv.			
Commitments						

Source: Northern.

Bad debts

5.324. Table 5.98 shows Northern's level of closing bad debt provision, and the level of bad debt charge against profits between 1995 and 2000. The level of bad debt provisions steadily increased during the period from £[✂] million in 1995 to £[✂] million in 2000. In the period the level of the provision as a percentage of loans varied between [✂] and [✂] per cent. The bad debt charge as a percentage of total loans was [✂] per cent in 1995 and 1996, [✂] per cent in 1997 and [✂] per cent between 1998 and 2000.

TABLE 5.98 **Northern: analysis of bad debt provision and charges to profit and loss, 1995 to 2000**

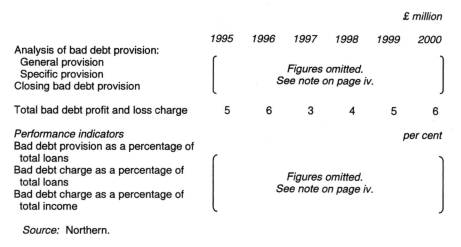

						£ million
	1995	1996	1997	1998	1999	2000
Analysis of bad debt provision:						
General provision						
Specific provision			Figures omitted. See note on page iv.			
Closing bad debt provision						
Total bad debt profit and loss charge	5	6	3	4	5	6
Performance indicators						per cent
Bad debt provision as a percentage of total loans						
Bad debt charge as a percentage of total loans			Figures omitted. See note on page iv.			
Bad debt charge as a percentage of total income						

Source: Northern.

Capital adequacy

5.325. Table 5.99 shows Northern's capital adequacy ratios for 1999 and 2000. In 1999 its Tier 1 ratio was 9.21 per cent and its total capital ratio was 13.65 per cent, while in 2000 the ratios were 8.83 and 13.59 per cent respectively.

TABLE 5.99 Northern: capital adequacy data, 1999 and 2000

per cent

As at 30 September

	1999	2000
Ratios		
Tier 1	9.21	8.83
Total	13.65	13.49

Source: Northern.

Yorkshire

5.326. Yorkshire was founded in 1859 in Halifax, West Yorkshire, as a philanthropic organization aimed at providing a means of saving for the working classes. During the late nineteenth century it became known as the Yorkshire Penny Bank. In 1990 NAB acquired Yorkshire for a consideration of £1 billion. Its Head Office is based at Leeds, and some 4,037 people are employed at 257 branches and regional business centres.

Financial performance

5.327. Table 5.100 shows the profitability of Yorkshire from 1995 to 2000. Between 1995 and 2000 the bank's operating income increased 26 per cent, from £386 million to £485 million. Operating expenses increased at a much slower rate from £212 million to £223 million. The level of bad debt charge has been quite volatile, ranging from £27 million to £78 million over the six years to 2000, and included a change in methodology for calculating the provision in 1999. This resulted in an additional £37 million one-off charge to the profit and loss account in that year. The bad debt charge for the year 2000 was £44 million. Profit before tax increased by 58 per cent, from £138 million in 1995 to £218 million in 2000.

TABLE 5.100 **Yorkshire: consolidated profit and loss account, 1995 to 2000**

£ million

	1995	1996	1997	1998	1999	2000
Net interest income	266	277	291	292	301	320
Net fees and commissions	111	128	127	127	136	150
Other income	9	11	3	10	12	15
Operating income	386	416	421	428	449	485
Operating expenses	−212	−219	−210	−244	−219	−223
Operating profit before provisions	175	197	211	184	230	262
Bad debt charge	−36	−78	−56	−27	−65*	−44
Operating profit after provisions	138	119	155	156	165	218
Exceptional and other items	-	−1	†	1	-	-
Net profit before tax	138	118	155	157	165	218
Tax	−50	−38	−51	−48	−64	−71
Net profit after tax	89	79	104	109	101	146
Minority interest	†	†	†	−1	†	-
Profit for the financial year	89	79	104	108	101	146
Dividends	−29	−56	−77	−98	−96	−67
Profit retained for the financial year	60	23	27	10	5	80

Source: Yorkshire.

---

*Includes £37 million owing to change in methodology to calculate provision.
†Negligible amount.

5.328. Table 5.101 further analyses the overall performance of Yorkshire from 1995 to 2000, by comparing all items with operating income. Net interest income as a percentage of total income remained quite steady, ranging between 66 and 69 per cent over the six years to 2000. At the same time, net fees and commissions rose from 29 to 31 per cent over the same period.

5.329. Operating expenses as a percentage of operating income (also referred to as the cost:income ratio) remained relatively constant at around 55 per cent between 1995 and 1998, and then fell to 46 per cent in 2000. Yorkshire said that this improvement was due to organizational restructuring and continued focus on cost management.

TABLE 5.101 **Yorkshire: operating profit as a percentage of operating income, 1995 to 2000**

						per cent
	1995	1996	1997	1998	1999	2000
Net interest income	69	67	69	68	67	66
Net fees and commissions	29	31	30	30	30	31
Other income	2	3	1	2	3	3
Operating income	100	100	100	100	100	100
Operating expenses	−55	−53	−50	−57	−49	−46
Operating profit before provisions	45	47	50	43	51	54
Bad debt charge*	−9	−19	−13	−6	−14	−9
Operating profit before provisions	36	29	37	37	37	45
Exceptional and other items	−	†	†	†	†	−
Net profit before tax	36	28	37	37	37	45

Source: Yorkshire.

*The 1999 bad debt charge has been increased by £37 million (8 per cent of operational income) because of a change in methodology to calculate the provision.
†Negligible amount.

Balance sheets

5.330. Table 5.102 shows Yorkshire's balance sheets from 1995 to 2000. Total assets increased from £4.7 billion in 1995 to £7.0 billion in 2000. This was because of an increase in loans and advances to customers from £3.7 billion in 1995 to £6.0 billion in 2000 (62 per cent increase).

TABLE 5.102 **Yorkshire: consolidated balance sheet, 1995 to 2000**

						£ million
			As at 30 September			
	1995	1996	1997	1998	1999	2000
Assets						
Cash and balances at central banks	45	46	59	53	48	62
Items in the course of collection from other banks	171	214	169	131	120	146
Loans and advances to banks	287	337	464	731	896	570
Loans and advances to customers	3,703	3,963	4,111	4,346	4,977	5,992
Debt securities	257	86	21	*	*	-
Tangible fixed assets	125	123	119	123	112	96
Other assets	74	87	190	128	138	56
Prepayments and accrued income	22	41	34	39	34	58
Total assets	4,685	4,897	5,147	5,551	6,326	6,981
Liabilities						
Deposits by banks	432	662	473	657	1,270	1,496
Customer accounts in credit	3,142	3,471	3,779	3,981	4,083	4,393
Items in the course of transmission to other banks	73	74	56	49	44	46
Debt securities in issue	471	88	58	58	112	111
Other liabilities	77	76	205	181	179	202
Accruals and deferred income	40	37	50	76	84	89
Other provisions	9	13	12	24	22	13
Subordinated liabilities	128	140	152	152	152	172
Total liabilities	4,373	4,561	4,784	5,177	5,947	6,523
Minority interests	-	-	-	1	-	-
Shareholders' funds	312	336	363	373	379	459
Total liabilities and shareholders' funds	4,685	4,897	5,147	5,551	6,326	6,981
Performance indicators						per cent
Net profit before tax as a percentage of average shareholders' funds	-	36	44	43	44	52
Operating profit as a percentage of average shareholders' funds (post-tax)	-	25	30	30	27	35

Source: Yorkshire.

*Balance negligible.

251

5.331. Yorkshire's net profit before tax as a percentage of average shareholders' funds increased from 36 per cent in 1996 to 52 per cent in 2000.

5.332. Total liabilities increased from £4.4 billion in 1995 to £6.5 billion in 2000, within which customer accounts in credit increased from £3.1 billion to £4.4 billion (42 per cent). In addition, deposits by banks increased from £0.4 billion to £1.5 billion. Shareholders' funds increased from £312 million in 1995 to £459 million in 2000 as a result of profits retained by Yorkshire to support balance sheet growth.

5.333. In common with other banks, the largest items within the bank's balance sheet were loans and advances to customers, and customer accounts in credit (deposit and savings accounts). In 2000 Yorkshire had lent more to customers (around £6 billion) than it had customer accounts in credit (£4.4 billion). The loans and advances to customers accounted for 86 per cent of Yorkshire's total balance sheet assets.

5.334. Table 5.103 shows that Yorkshire's level of commitments increased from £1.4 billion in 1995 to £3.1 billion in 2000. In 2000 it reported total contingent liabilities of £271 million and total commitments of £3.1 billion, compared with total on-balance-sheet liabilities of £6.5 billion.

TABLE 5.103 **Yorkshire: contingent liabilities and commitments, 1995 to 2000**

						£ million
	1995	1996	1997	1998	1999	2000
Acceptances and endorsements	23	44	161	124	69	61
Guarantees and assets pledged as collateral security	129	143	84	179	165	204
Other contingent liabilities	-	5	5	7	7	7
	152	192	250	309	240	271
Commitments	1,364	1,624	2,086	2,248	3,189	3,128

Source: Yorkshire.

Bad debts

5.335. Table 5.104 shows Yorkshire's level of closing bad debt provision, and the level of bad debt charge against profits between 1995 and 2000. The bad debt provisions increased year on year from 1995 to 1997. The provision rose sharply in 1999 from £42 million to £76 million due to a change in methodology with regard to the calculation of the provision. The bank adopted a new methodology for the calculation of the general provision, developed by its parent group. In 1995 the level of the provision equated to 0.9 per cent of the total loan book, and has since increased to 1.4 per cent in 2000. Over the period the general provision remained relatively constant until 1999 when it increased by 170 per cent.

TABLE 5.104 **Yorkshire: analysis of bad debt provision and charges to profit and loss, 1995 to 2000**

						£ million
	1995	1996	1997	1998	1999	2000
Analysis of bad debt provision:						
General provision	19	21	22	23	62	76
Specific provision	15	36	40	19	14	12
Closing bad debt provision	34	57	62	42	76	88
Total bad debt profit and loss charge	36	78	56	27	65*	44
Performance indicators						*per cent*
Bad debt provision as a percentage of total loans	0.9	1.4	1.4	0.9	1.5	1.4
Bad debt charge as a percentage of total loans	1.0	1.9	1.3	0.6	1.3	0.7
Bad debt charge as a percentage of total income	9	19	13	6	13	9

Source: Yorkshire.

*Includes effect of change in methodology of £37 million.

5.336. The bad debt charge as a percentage of total loans was 1.0 per cent in 1995 and fluctuated over the six years to 2000 between 0.6 per cent in 1998 and 1.9 per cent in 1996. In 2000 it was 0.7 per cent, which Yorkshire said was owing to a move to statistical provisioning in 1999, as indicated in its report and accounts.

Capital adequacy

5.337. Table 5.105 shows Yorkshire's capital adequacy ratios for 1999 and 2000. In 1999 its Tier 1 ratio was 7.52 per cent and its total capital ratio was 11.80 per cent; in 2000 the ratios were 7.71 per cent and 11.86 per cent respectively.

TABLE 5.105 **Yorkshire: capital adequacy data, 1999 and 2000**

per cent

As at 30 September

RARs	1999	2000
Tier 1	7.52	7.71
Total	11.80	11.86

Source: Yorkshire.

AIB including First Trust

History

5.338. Allied Irish Banks plc, originally named Allied Irish Banks Limited, was incorporated in the Republic of Ireland in 1966 upon the amalgamation of three long-established banks. In 1970 it commenced the expansion of its network of branches in Great Britain. That 'branch' business was expanded alongside the establishment of investment banking and finance house activities through the 1970s and 1980s. The UK activities in the late 1980s were characterized by lending-led growth, particularly commercial mortgage lending to SMEs by its finance house operation. As a result, during the late 1980s and early 1990s UK recession, the business in Great Britain suffered bad debt losses that threatened its viability and necessitated the implementation of a downsizing and recovery operation.

5.339. The accounts of Allied Irish Banks plc for 1999 show that its total operating income was €2.8 billion (£1.7 billion), total group profit before tax was €1.1 billion (£0.7 billion) and total assets were €67 billion (£42 billion). Allied Irish Banks plc operates internationally with offices in the USA, controlling interests in two Polish banks, and a strategic alliance with the Singapore Bank, Keppel TatLee. Internationally the group has over 31,000 employees.

5.340. In July 1991 Allied Irish Banks plc acquired TSB Bank Northern Ireland plc, a bank with 56 branches in Northern Ireland. In 1994 the businesses in Northern Ireland of Allied Irish Banks plc and TSB Bank Northern Ireland plc were integrated and the combined operations traded under the name First Trust Bank. Currently, First Trust operates through nearly 70 branches in Northern Ireland and employs over 1,500 people.

5.341. On 1 October 1996 Allied Irish Bank (GB), which was the trading name for the retail banking operation of Allied Irish Banks plc in Great Britain, was amalgamated with the business in Northern Ireland and the enlarged entity was incorporated in the UK as AIB Group (UK) plc (AIB).

5.342. The business of AIB is managed and coordinated under a divisional structure, comprising First Trust and AIB (GB). While there are certain over-arching high level controls, the company covers two distinctly separate regions of the UK.

Business structure serving the SMEs

5.343. In Northern Ireland, First Trust operates from around 70 branches and serves both business and personal customers. In recent years it has been prominent in many of the commercial and residential redevelopment projects that aim to improve the Northern Ireland infrastructure. First Trust noted that it had made heavy investment in technology with the introduction of online real-time banking for all customers and that this has facilitated strong growth in all sectors.

5.344. In Great Britain AIB (GB) operates from 34 branches and outlets (12 of which are in the Greater London area). It provides a core range of banking services including current accounts, overdraft and loan facilities, mortgage lending, deposits and investment services. In 1997 AIB (GB) decided to concentrate on the business and professional markets, rather than the mass market, and further to grow the business through a relationship approach. It therefore focused on providing specialized banking services to business customers, mainly in the small and medium sector, and to high net worth personal customers. There was also significant growth in the higher education sector.

5.345. In both regions, the Corporate and Commercial Banking units are responsible for supporting and controlling all lending to business customers, principally SMEs. Within these units there are corporate banking teams whose role is to service the loan business, particularly in their chosen niche markets, and to support the branch network in larger more complex transactions which have a branch relationship.

5.346. In Northern Ireland, First Trust has created a specialist business banking team in Belfast to support branches and business units in their dealings with SMEs.

Financial performance

5.347. Table 5.106 shows the profitability of AIB from 1997 to 1999. Between 1997 and 1999 the bank's operating income increased, from £229 million to £281 million (23 per cent), compared with a smaller increase in operating expenses from £127 million to £147 million (16 per cent). The level of bad debt charge was around £13 million in 1997 and fell to £10 million in 1999. As a result, AIB's profit before tax increased from £89 million in 1997 to £125 million in 1999.

TABLE 5.106 **AIB: consolidated profit and loss account, 1997 to 1999**

£ million

Years ended 31 December

	1997	1998	1999
Net interest income	165	184	200
Net fees and commissions	60	66	72
Other income	5	9	10
Operating income	229	259	281
Operating expenses	−127	−135	−147
Operating profit before provisions	102	124	135
Bad and doubtful debts charge	−13	−14	−10
Operating profit before tax	89	110	125
Tax	−25	−30	−30
Net profit after tax	64	80	95
Dividends	−3	−27	−38
Profit retained for the financial year	61	53	57
Number of employees ('000)	2	2	2
Performance indicators			*per cent*
Tax charge as a percentage of profit before tax	28	27	24
Percentage change in operating income	65*	13	9

Source: AIB.

*The 65 per cent change in operating income in 1997 was a result of the amalgamation in 1996 of AIB (GB)'s business with that of First Trust to form AIB.

5.348. Table 5.107 further analyses the overall performance of AIB from 1997 to 1999, by comparing all items with operating income. Net interest income as a percentage of total income fell slightly from 72 per cent in 1997 to 71 per cent in 1999. At the same time, net fees and commissions remained steady at around 26 per cent. Operating expenses as a percentage of operating income (also referred to as the cost:income ratio) fell from 55 per cent in 1997 to 52 per cent in 1999. AIB noted that the downward trend in this ratio was due to a number of factors including the inclusion in 1997 of one-off costs associated with the reorganization and rebranding of the AIB (GB) business, and additional income from the increased capital base required for the enlarged UK operation, while maintaining strong cost containment.

TABLE 5.107 **AIB: profit and loss items as a percentage of operating income, 1997 to 1999**

	per cent		
	1997	1998	1999
Net interest income	72	71	71
Net fees and commissions	26	26	25
Other income	2	4	3
Operating income	100	100	100
Operating expenses	−55	−52	−52
Operating profit before provisions	45	48	48
Bad and doubtful debts charge	−6	−6	−3
Operating profit after provisions	39	42	44
Exceptional and other items	0	0	0
Net profit before tax	39	42	44

Source: AIB.

5.349. Table 5.108 breaks down the performance of AIB into First Trust and AIB (GB) for 1999. Operating income for First Trust in 1999 was £[✂] million compared with AIB (GB)'s income of £[✂] million. Similarly, operating expenses for First Trust were greater than for AIB (GB) at £[✂] million compared with £[✂] million. The bad and doubtful debts charge for First Trust was £[✂] million, and for AIB (GB) £[✂] million. This resulted in operating profit before tax for First Trust being £[✂] million compared with AIB (GB)'s operating profit of £[✂] million. The cost:income ratios for First Trust and AIB (GB) were [✂] per cent and [✂] per cent respectively. First Trust told us that its cost:income ratio increased in 1999 because of higher staff numbers supporting a new sales structure for the personal market and a general slowdown in income growth due to margin compression.

TABLE 5.108 **First Trust and AIB (GB): operating profit and loss, 1999**

	£ million		
	First Trust	AIB (GB)	Total*
Net interest income			
Net fees and commissions			
Other income			
Operating income		*Figures omitted.*	
Operating expenses		*See note on page iv.*	
Operating profit before provisions			
Bad and doubtful debts charge			
Operating profit before tax			
	per cent		
Performance indicators			
Cost:income ratio			
Net interest income as a percentage of total income		*Figures omitted.*	
Net fees and commissions as a percentage of total income		*See note on page iv.*	

Source: AIB.

*First Trust and AIB (GB)'s data was provided by each organization separately. Total operating profit before tax is £2 million different from published AIB accounts. This amount is not considered material for further inquiry.

5.350. We asked both First Trust and AIB (GB) to provide an analysis of performance by type of customer. First Trust noted that the Northern Ireland economy was essentially a small business economy, with research data suggesting that 91 per cent of businesses in Northern Ireland had a turnover of less than £1 million a year. Therefore all but a very small number of First Trust's corporate customers fell within our definition of an SME. First Trust did not provide cost data for the SME banking business but made an estimate of [✂] per cent for the cost:income ratio for services to SMEs.

5.351. AIB (GB) provided data on the SME banking business that is in accordance with our definition of SMEs as businesses with turnover up to £25 million. It noted that clubs, charities and associates were excluded from the data because AIB (GB)'s involvement in this subsector was immaterial. AIB (GB) did not provide cost data for the SME banking business. However, we derived these figures from AIB (GB)'s estimate of a [✂] per cent cost:income ratio for the SME banking business.

5.352. Table 5.109 analyses the performance of First Trust by type of customer for 1999. Income from the personal banking business totalled £[✂] million, while income from the SME banking business totalled £[✂] million. This represented [✂] per cent and [✂] per cent of First Trust's total income respectively.

TABLE 5.109　**First Trust: summary of results by type of customer, 1999**

£ million

	Personal	SME	Total
Operating income			
Operating costs			
Operating profit before bad debts	*Figures omitted.*		
Bad debt charge	*See note on page iv.*		
Operating profit after bad debts and before other items			

per cent

Performance indicators			
Cost:income ratio			
Proportion of total income	*Figures omitted.*		
Proportion of total operating profit after bad debts	*See note on page iv.*		

Source: AIB.

5.353. First Trust noted that its cost:income ratio for the SME banking business was approximately [✂] per cent, much higher than for the personal banking business of [✂] per cent. Operating costs attributable to the SME banking business were £[✂] million ([✂] per cent of total operating costs), compared with £[✂] million for services to personal customers.

5.354. Table 5.110 analyses the performance of AIB (GB) by SME banking business and 'other' for 1999. Income from the SME banking business totalled £[✂] million, which was [✂] per cent of AIB (GB)'s total income. The 'other' grouping, which included personal, corporate and non-customer income, totalled £[✂] million ([✂] per cent of AIB (GB)'s total income). AIB (GB) told us that non-customer income arose from the investment of the bank's own funds and the results of a number of strategic hedging operations. It also contained other income derived from the bank's own assets such as rent received from the bank's properties occupied by third parties.

TABLE 5.110 **AIB (GB): summary of results by type of customer, 1999**

£ million

	SME	Other	Total
Income			
Operating costs			
Operating profit before bad debts			
Bad debt charge	*Figures omitted.*		
Operating profit after bad debts and before other items	*See note on page iv.*		

per cent

Performance indicators			
Cost:income ratio			
Proportion of total income	*Figures omitted.*		
Proportion of total operating profit after bad debts	*See note on page iv.*		

Source: AIB.

5.355. AIB (GB) said that its cost:income ratio for services to SMEs was approximately [✄] per cent. Operating costs attributable to the SME banking business were £[✄] million ([✄] per cent of total operating costs).

Balance sheets

5.356. Table 5.111 shows AIB's balance sheets from 1997 to 1999. Total assets increased from £4.7 billion in 1997 to £5.7 billion in 1999. Most of this related to a £0.8 billion or 25 per cent increase in loans and advances to customers.

5.357. In 1999 loans and advances to customers accounted for 67 per cent of AIB's total balance sheet assets, and loans to banks for 23 per cent.

TABLE 5.111 **AIB: balance sheet, 1997 to 1999**

£ million

As at 31 December

	1997	1998	1999
Assets			
Cash and balances at central banks	37	37	54
Loans and advances to banks	1,267	1,651	1,302
Loans and advances to customers	3,040	3,316	3,809
Debt securities	115	207	303
Other investments	13	0	10
Tangible fixed assets	59	65	59
Other assets	107	116	142
Prepayments and accrued income	22	25	25
Total assets	4,661	5,418	5,704
Liabilities			
Deposits by banks	1,081	1,279	1,231
Customer accounts in credit	2,836	3,290	3,548
Other liabilities	288	333	352
Accruals and deferred income	32	35	38
Other provisions	9	6	5
Debenture stock	56	56	56
Total liabilities	4,302	5,000	5,229
Shareholders' funds	358	418	475
	4,661	5,418	5,704
Performance indicators			per cent
Pre-tax operating profit as a percentage of average shareholders' funds*	28	28	28

Source: AIB.

*Average shareholders' funds includes any capitalized goodwill balances.

5.358. Total liabilities increased from £4.3 billion in 1997 to £5.2 billion in 1999. This was because of increases in customer accounts in credit from £2.8 billion to £3.5 billion (25 per cent), and increases in deposits by banks from £1.0 billion to £1.2 billion. Customer accounts in credit, at £3.5 billion in 1999, accounted for 68 per cent of AIB's total balance sheet liabilities. Shareholders' funds increased from £358 million to £475 million, mostly as a result of accumulated retained earnings.

5.359. AIB's pre-tax operating profit as a percentage of average shareholders' funds (pre-tax return) remained steady from 1997 to 1999 at 28 per cent.

5.360. Table 5.112 shows the balance sheets for both AIB (GB) and First Trust for 1999 and the combined total. In common with other banks, the largest items within both AIB (GB)'s and First Trust's balance sheets (excluding intra-company loans) were loans and advances to customers, and customer accounts in credit (current accounts and savings accounts).

TABLE 5.112 **First Trust and AIB (GB): balance sheets, 1999**

£ million

As at 31 December

	First Trust	AIB (GB)	Inter-company	Total*
Assets				
Cash and balances at central banks				
Loans and advances to banks				
Loans and advances to customers†				
Items in the course of collection				
Debt securities				
Other investments				
Tangible fixed assets				
Other assets				
Prepayments and accrued income				
Total assets				
Liabilities				
Deposits by banks		*Figures omitted.*		
Customer accounts in credit‡		*See note on page iv.*		
Other liabilities				
Accruals and deferred income				
Other provisions				
Debenture stock				
Total liabilities				
Shareholders' funds				
Further analysis				
SME loans to customers				
SME customer accounts in credit				

Source: AIB.

*First Trust and AIB (GB) data was provided by each organization separately. [
Details omitted. See note on page iv.

]

†For First Trust [✄] per cent to SME banking business, and for AIB (GB) [✄] per cent to SME banking business.
‡For First Trust [✄] per cent from SME business, and for AIB (GB) [✄] per cent from SME business.

5.361. In 1999 First Trust had loans and advances to customers of £[✄] billion, of which £[✄] million ([✄] per cent) related to loans to SMEs. At the same date, AIB (GB)'s loans to customers were £[✄] billion, of which AIB (GB) said that £[✄] billion ([✄] per cent) was to SME banking business.

5.362. In 1999 First Trust's customer accounts in credit totalled £[✄] billion. First Trust told us that, of this balance, £[✄] million or [✄] per cent related to the SME business. In the same period, AIB (GB) had customer accounts in credit of some £[✄] billion, which it said included £[✄] million ([✄] per cent) from the SME banking business.

5.363. Table 5.113 shows an analysis of contingent liabilities and commitments for 1997 to 1999. AIB's level of commitments increased from £502 million in 1997 to £565 million in 1999. In 1999 AIB reported total contingent liabilities of £297 million and total commitments of £565 million, compared with total on-balance-sheet liabilities of £5.2 billion.

TABLE 5.113 **AIB: contingent liabilities and commitments, 1997 to 1999**

	£ million		
	1997	1998	1999
Acceptances and endorsements	9	4	9
Guarantees and assets pledged			
as collateral security	144	178	230
Other contingent liabilities	46	43	58
	198	225	297
Commitments	502	513	565

Source: AIB.

Bad debts

5.364. Table 5.114 shows AIB's level of closing bad debt provision, and the level of bad debt charge against profits between 1997 and 1999. The level of bad debt provisions remained relatively constant between 1997 and 1999 at around £65 million. In 1997, the level of the provision equated to 2.1 per cent of the total loan book, and fell to 1.7 per cent in 1999. Over the period the general provision fell slightly from £36.7 million to £34.5 million, while the level of specific provisions increased from £28.3 million to £30.4 million.

TABLE 5.114 **AIB: analysis of bad debt provision and charges to profit and loss, 1997 to 1999**

	£ million		
	1997	1998	1999
Analysis of bad debt provision:			
General provision	36.7	34.7	34.5
Specific provision	28.3	29.5	30.4
Closing bad debt provision	65.0	64.2	64.9
Total bad debt charge to profit and loss account	13	14	10
			per cent
Performance indicators			
Bad debt provision as a percentage of total loans	2.1	1.9	1.7
Bad debt charge as a percentage of total loans	0.4	0.4	0.3
Bad debt charge as a percentage of total income	6	6	3

Source: AIB.

5.365. The bad debt charge as a percentage of total loans has remained constant at around 0.4 per cent over the three years to 1999.

Capital adequacy

5.366. First Trust and AIB (GB) do not report separate capital adequacy ratios to the FSA. AIB's capital adequacy ratio as reported at 31 December 1999 was 11.4 per cent, which was above AIB's own internal target ratio of 11 per cent.

Ulster Bank

History

5.367. Ulster Bank was established in 1836 and together with its subsidiaries provides banking and financial services to customers in Northern Ireland and the Republic of Ireland. It is part of the NatWest Group, which was acquired by RBSG in March 2000, and therefore RBSG is now the ultimate holding company of Ulster Bank. Ulster Bank's results, which formed part of NatWest's results until 1999, are shown in detail below.

Business structure serving the SME banking business

5.368. Ulster Bank said that overall trends in the Northern Ireland economy were closely linked to those in the UK generally. The growth in manufacturing output for Northern Ireland followed the UK average closely with the major exception of the two years 1989 and 1990, when Northern Ireland avoided the worst effects of the recession. However, Northern Ireland's growth subsequently converged to the UK trend path.

5.369. Ulster Bank said that there were two main business units within the group, Retail and Business Banking, and Capital Markets. The main divisions within Retail and Business Banking that provided services to SME customers were:

(a) Retail Banking, which provides services to personal and small SME customers via a branch network of 95 outlets in Northern Ireland, complemented by telephone, ATM, Internet and postal delivery channels;

(b) Business Banking, which provides services (including invoice discounting) to small business and mid corporate customers;

(c) Cards, which provides merchant acquiring services to business customers;

(d) Lombard & Ulster Limited, which provides asset finance services in Northern Ireland; and

(e) JCB Finance Limited, which provides asset finance services.

5.370. Capital Markets provides a range of financial products and services to corporate, institutional and personal customers. Products and services offered are as follows: treasury and currency products (including euro facilities), domestic and international corporate lending, specialized finance, fund management and administration services, stockbroking and corporate finance.

5.371. Ulster Bank provided us with copies of its 1999 management accounts for its Retail and Business Banking divisions. In 1999 profit before tax for its Northern Ireland operations was £[✂] million, average total loans were £[✂] billion and average total deposits were £[✂] billion. The results for the Northern Ireland operations are further analysed in Table 5.119.

Financial performance

5.372. Table 5.115 shows the profitability of Ulster Bank from 1992 to 2000. Over the period, the bank's operating income increased 102 per cent, from £229 million to £464 million, which compared with the increase in its operating expenses of 71 per cent, from £148 million to £253 million. The level of bad debt charge was at its highest level in 1992 and 1993, at around £20 million, and declined significantly between 1994 and 1997, before increasing again to around £19 million in 2000. Overall profit before tax increased by 164 per cent, from £58 million in 1992 to £153 million in 2000.

TABLE 5.115 **Ulster Bank: consolidated profit and loss account, 1992 to 2000**

£ million

Years ended 31 December

	1992	1993	1994	1995	1996	1997	1998	1999	2000
Net interest income	169	183	188	212	229	243	255	272	294
Net fees and commissions	36	44	48	62	72	73	89	111	119
Other income	24	37	38	43	49	52	46	30	51
Operating income	229	264	273	317	350	369	391	412	464
Operating expenses	−148	−151	−162	−192	−207	−213	−222	−232	−253
Operating profit before provisions	81	114	111	125	143	156	169	180	211
Bad debt charge	−22	−20	−8	−5	−8	−12	−16	−17	−19
Operating profit after bad debt charge	58	93	103	120	136	144	153	163	192
Exceptional, extraordinary and other items	0	0	0	0	0	0	0	0	61
Net profit before tax	58	93	103	120	136	144	153	163	253
Tax	−17	−32	−34	−31	−41	−37	−41	−40	−63
Net profit after tax	41	61	68	89	95	107	112	123	190
Minority interest	0	0	0	−1	−1	−1	−1	−1	−1
Profit for the financial year	40	61	68	88	94	106	111	122	189
Dividends	−103	−20	−22	−24	−26	−28	−56	−50	−59
Profit retained for the financial year	−63	41	46	64	68	78	55	72	131
Number of employees ('000)	4	4	4	4	4	5	5	5	*
Performance indicators									*per cent*
Tax charge as a percentage of profit before tax	30	35	33	25	30	26	27	25	25
Percentage change in operating income	*	15	3	16	10	5	6	5	13

Source: Ulster Bank.

*Not provided.

5.373. Table 5.116 further analyses the overall performance of Ulster Bank from 1992 to 2000, by comparing all items with operating income.

TABLE 5.116 **Ulster Bank: operating profit and loss items as a percentage of operating income, 1992 to 2000**

per cent

	1992	1993	1994	1995	1996	1997	1998	1999	2000
Net interest income	74	69	69	67	65	66	65	66	63
Net fees and commissions	16	17	17	19	21	20	23	27	26
Other income	11	14	14	14	14	14	12	7	11
Operating income	100	100	100	100	100	100	100	100	100
Operating expenses	−65	−57	−59	−61	−59	−58	−57	−56	−55
Operating profit before provisions	35	43	41	39	41	42	43	44	45
Bad and doubtful debts charge	−10	−8	−3	−2	−2	−3	−4	−4	−4
Operating profit after provisions	25	35	38	38	39	39	39	40	41
Exceptional and other items	0	0	0	0	0	0	0	0	0
Net profit before tax	25	35	38	38	39	39	39	40	42

Source: Ulster Bank.

5.374. Net interest income as a percentage of total income decreased from 74 per cent in 1992 to 63 per cent in 2000. Other income also decreased from 11 per cent of total income in 1992 to 7 per cent of total income in 1999 but rose to 11 per cent in 2000. Net fees and commissions increased from 16 per cent of total income in 1992 to 26 per cent of total income in 2000.

5.375. Operating expenses as a percentage of operating income (also referred to as the cost:income ratio) declined from 65 per cent in 1992 to 55 per cent in 2000. Ulster Bank said that this improvement was due to growth in business volume and improved operational efficiency.

Analysis of performance by type of customer

5.376. We asked Ulster Bank to analyse its UK activities into four categories: personal, SME, corporate and 'other' customers. It said that these categories were not part of its existing business structure and that it was unable to provide much of the data we requested.

5.377. In particular Ulster Bank said that it was unable to estimate revenue, costs or bad debts for the SME banking business. However, it did provide combined profitability data for those business units that provided services to SME customers in Northern Ireland. We were unable to draw conclusions from the combined profitability data as the business units also provided services to other types of customer.

5.378. Table 5.117 summarizes how Ulster Bank reported its performance by class of business in its published accounts for 1998 to 2000. As stated above, there are two main business units, Retail and Business Banking, and Capital Markets. The amounts shown include the operations of Ulster Bank in the Republic of Ireland.

TABLE 5.117 **Ulster Bank: segmental analysis by class of business, 1998 to 2000**

Class of business	£ million			Proportion of total (%)		
	1998	1999	2000	1998	1999	2000
Profit before tax:						
Retail and Business Banking	110	100	125	72	61	49
Capital Markets	43	63	128*	28	39	51
Total	153	163	253	100	100	100
Total assets:						
Retail and Business Banking	4,923	4,268	5,153	49	46	46
Capital Markets	5,028	5,074	6,092	51	54	54
Total	9,951	9,342	11,244	100	100	100
Net assets:†						
Retail and Business Banking	387	357	470	59	49	53
Capital Markets	269	376	420	41	51	47
Total	656	733	891	100	100	100
	per cent					
Profit before tax as a percentage of average net assets:						
Retail and Business Banking	31	28	27			
Capital Markets	16	17	30			
Total	25	22	28			

Source: Ulster Bank.

*Includes an exceptional profit of £60.6 million form the sale of investment management subsidiaries.
†Net assets comprise shareholders' funds, loan capital and minority interests.

5.379. Profit before tax for Retail and Business Banking increased from £110 million in 1998 to £125 million in 2000. However, as a percentage of Ulster Bank's profits, the contribution from Retail and Business Banking decreased from 72 per cent in 1998 to 49 per cent in 2000. Profit before tax as a percentage of average shareholders' funds for Retail and Business Banking was 27 per cent in 2000, compared with 30 per cent for Capital Markets. The increase in profits in 2000 for Capital Markets is due to £60.6 million of exceptional profit from the sale of investment management subsidiaries.

5.380. Table 5.118 summarizes how Ulster Bank reported its performance by geographical area (UK and Republic of Ireland) in its published accounts for 1998 to 2000. Profit before tax from its operations in the UK in 1998 to 2000 was £58 million, £63 million and £73 million respectively. In 1998 and 1999, UK operations accounted for around 39 per cent of the bank's profit before tax. In 2000 this decreased to 29 per cent. This was owing to the inclusion of £60.6 million of extraordinary profit in the results of the Republic of Ireland from the sale of investment management subsidiaries during the year. The profit before tax as a percentage of average shareholders' funds in 1998 and 1999 was 41 per cent and 37 per cent respectively for the UK operations. This compared with 25 per cent in 1998 and 24 per cent in 1999 for the bank as a whole. In 2000, this percentage was also effected by the extraordinary profit reported by the Republic of Ireland operations, and the profit before tax as a percentage of average shareholders' funds for the UK operations subsequently fell to 33 per cent.

TABLE 5.118 **Ulster Bank: segmental analysis by geographical segments, 1998 to 2000**

	£ million			Proportion of total (%)		
Class of business	1998	1999	2000	1998	1999	2000
Profit before tax:						
UK	58	63	73	38	39	29
Republic of Ireland	95	100	181*	62	61	72
Total	153	163	253	100	100	100
Total assets:						
UK	3,417	3,352	3,573	34	36	32
Republic of Ireland	6,535	5,990	7,672	66	64	68
Total	9,952	9,342	11,244	100	100	100
Net assets:†						
UK	131	215	218	20	29	24
Republic of Ireland	525	518	672	80	71	75
Total	656	733	891	100	100	100
		per cent				
Profit before tax as a percentage of average net assets:						
UK	41	37	33			
Republic of Ireland	20	19	27			
Total	25	24	28			

Source: Ulster Bank.

*Includes an exceptional profit of £60.6 million form the sale of investment management subsidiaries.
†Net assets comprise shareholders' funds, loan capital and minority interests.

5.381. Table 5.119 provides a further analysis of Ulster Bank's Retail and Business Banking operations in Northern Ireland for 1999. The three main divisions were Retail, Lombard & Ulster and Business Banking. Ulster Bank told us that it used borrowing requirements as the primary indicator of the range and complexity of services that an SME was likely to require. Therefore SMEs with a borrowing requirement of £1 million or more were serviced by the Business Banking division, while SME customers borrowing up to £1 million were serviced by the Retail division. All non-personal asset finance provided by Lombard & Ulster was almost exclusively to SMEs.

TABLE 5.119 Ulster Bank: analysis of Retail and Business Banking in Northern Ireland by division, 1999*

£ million

Class of business	Retail Banking	Lombard & Ulster	Business Banking	Other	Total
Net interest income					
Non-interest income					
Total operating income					
Direct costs:					
Staff costs					
Other administration costs					
Depreciation and amortization		*Figures omitted.*			
Other operating costs		*See note on page iv.*			
Total direct costs					
Allocated costs					
Total costs					
Trading surplus					
Bad debt charge					
Profit before tax					

per cent

Cost:income ratio	(	✄		)	

Source: Ulster Bank.

---

*The Northern Ireland business is a subset of total UK business, the results of which are reported in Table 5.118.

5.382. In 1999 the Northern Ireland Retail and Business Banking unit reported operating income of £[✄] million, operating costs of £[✄] million, bad debt charge of £[✄] million and profit before tax of £[✄] million. It also reported a cost:income ratio of [✄] per cent in 1999, which was higher than the 56 per cent reported by the whole bank. The Retail Banking sub-unit had the highest cost:income ratio of [✄] per cent, while the Lombard & Ulster and Business Banking sub-units had ratios of [✄] per cent and [✄] per cent respectively.

Balance sheets

5.383. Table 5.120 shows a summary of Ulster Bank's balance sheets from 1992 to 2000. Total assets increased from £6 billion in 1992 to £11.2 billion in 2000. Total liabilities increased from £6 billion in 1992 to £10.4 billion in 2000 and shareholders' funds increased from £0.3 billion in 1992 to £0.8 billion in 2000. Over the period fixed assets ranged between 1 and 2 per cent of total assets.

264

TABLE 5.120 **Ulster Bank: consolidated balance sheet, 1992 to 2000**

£ billion

As at 31 December

	1992	1993	1994	1995	1996	1997	1998	1999	2000
Assets									
Cash and balances at central banks	0.1	0.2	0.2	0.2	0.1	0.1	0.3	0.3	0.3
Loans and advances to banks	2.0	1.7	1.8	1.7	2.5	2.7	2.2	1.1	1.2
Loans and advances to customers	2.7	2.8	3.2	3.7	4.2	4.8	5.5	6.3	7.6
Debt securities	0.6	0.6	0.8	1.1	1.0	0.9	0.9	0.8	1.1
Tangible fixed assets	0.1	0.1	0.1	0.1	0.1	0.1	0.1	0.2	0.2
Other assets	0.4	0.6	0.3	0.8	0.8	0.7	0.8	0.6	0.7
Prepayments and accrued income	0.1	0.1	0.1	0.1	0.1	0.1	0.1	0.1	0.1
Total assets	6.0	6.0	6.4	7.7	8.7	9.4	10.0	9.3	11.2
Liabilities									
Deposits by banks	1.9	1.6	1.9	1.9	2.4	2.8	1.6	1.0	1.6
Customer accounts in credit	3.0	3.3	3.6	4.3	4.5	4.8	6.3	6.3	7.3
Debt securities in issue	0.1	0.0	0.1	0.0	0.1	0.1	0.2	0.4	0.3
Other liabilities	0.5	0.3	0.4	0.9	1.0	0.9	1.0	0.8*	1.1
Accruals and deferred income	0.1	0.0	0.0	0.1	0.1	0.1	0.1	0.1	0.1
Total liabilities	5.7	5.3	6.1	7.3	8.2	8.8	9.3	8.7	10.4
Shareholders' funds	0.3	0.3	0.4	0.4	0.5	0.5	0.6	0.7	0.8
Total liabilities and shareholders' funds	6.0	5.6	6.4	7.7	8.7	9.4	10.0	9.3	11.2
Performance indicators									per cent
Profit before tax as a percentage of average shareholders' funds†	21	30	30	30	29	28	26	25	26

Source: Ulster Bank.

*Includes £0.1 million of subordinated liabilities.
†Average shareholders' funds includes any capitalized goodwill.

5.384. In common with other banks, the largest items within the bank's balance sheet were loans and advances to customers (68 per cent of total assets in 2000), and customer accounts in credit (70 per cent of total liabilities in 2000). Between 1992 and 2000 loans and advances to customers increased from £2.7 billion to £7.6 billion, and customer accounts in credit from £3.0 billion to £7.3 billion.

5.385. For the year ended 1999, Ulster Bank said that its loans and advances of £6.3 billion could be segmented along geographic lines such that [✂] per cent (£[✂] billion) related to its UK operations and the remaining [✂] per cent (£[✂] billion) to its non-UK operations. It analysed its UK loans and advances as follows: personal customers accounted for £[✂] ([✂] per cent), SMEs £[✂] billion ([✂] per cent), and the 'other' activity £[✂] ([✂] per cent).

5.386. Ulster Bank's operating profit as a percentage of average shareholders' funds (pre-tax return) fluctuated from a low of 21 per cent in 1992 to a high of 30 per cent between 1993 and 1995, and then declined to 26 per cent in 2000.

5.387. Table 5.121 shows an analysis of contingent liabilities and commitments for 1992 to 2000. Ulster Bank's level of commitments increased from £1.0 billion in 1992 to £1.9 billion in 1999. In 1999, it reported total contingent liabilities of £0.4 billion and total commitments of £1.9 billion, compared with total on-balance-sheet liabilities of £8.7 billion. The commitments for 2000 were not provided; however, the contingent liability balances were relatively unchanged from 1999.

TABLE 5.121 **Ulster Bank: contingent liabilities and commitments, 1992 to 2000**

£ billion

	1992	1993	1994	1995	1996	1997	1998	1999	2000
Guarantees and assets pledged as collateral security	0.2	0.1	0.1	0.1	0.1	0.1	0.1	0.1	0.1
Other contingent liabilities	0.3	0.2	0.2	0.2	0.2	0.2	0.3	0.3	0.3
Total contingent liabilities	0.5	0.4	0.4	0.3	0.3	0.4	0.4	0.4	0.4
Commitments	1.0	1.0	1.3	1.5	1.8	1.8	1.8	1.9	*

Source: Ulster Bank.

*Not provided.

Bad debts

5.388. Table 5.122 shows Ulster Bank's level of closing bad debt provision, and the level of bad debt charge against profits between 1992 and 2000. During this period, bad debt provisions as a percentage of loans declined from around 2.1 per cent in 1992 and 1993 to 0.9 per cent in 2000. Over the period, general provision increased from £3 million in 1992 to £22 million in 2000 while specific provisions declined from £54 million in 1992 to £41 million in 2000.

TABLE 5.122 **Ulster Bank: analysis of bad debt provision and charges to profit and loss, 1992 to 2000**

£ million

	1992	1993	1994	1995	1996	1997	1998	1999	2000
Analysis of bad debt provision:									
General provision	3	3	3	4	7	9	12	17	22
Specific provision	54	57	53	53	46	42	42	39	41
Closing bad debt provision	58	60	57	57	53	51	54	56	63
Total bad debt profit and loss charge	22	20	8	5	8	12	16	17	19
Performance indicators									*per cent*
Bad debt provision as a percentage of total loans	2.1	2.2	1.8	1.6	1.3	1.1	1.0	0.9	0.9
Bad debt charge as a percentage of total loans	0.8	0.7	0.3	0.1	0.2	0.2	0.3	0.3	0.3
Bad debt charge as a percentage of total income	10	8	3	2	2	3	4	4	4

Source: Ulster Bank.

5.389. The bad debt charge as a percentage of total loans was 0.8 per cent in 1992, and reached a low of 0.1 per cent in 1995 before it increased to 0.3 per cent in 2000. The bad debt charge as a percentage of total income was 10 per cent in 1992, and reached a low of 2 per cent in 1995 and 1996 before it increased to 4 per cent in 2000. Ulster Bank told us that this reflected a trend towards a more normal level of loss following exceptionally low figures between 1994 and 1997.

Capital adequacy

5.390. Table 5.123 shows Ulster Bank's capital adequacy ratios for 1999. Its Tier 1 ratio was 9.1 per cent and its total capital ratio was 10.8 per cent.

TABLE 5.123 Ulster Bank: capital adequacy data, as at 31 December 1999

	%
Ratios	
Tier 1	9.1
Total	10.8

Source: Ulster Bank.

BoI

History

5.391. BoI was incorporated in 1783 under Royal Charter in what is now the Republic of Ireland. Entry into what is now Northern Ireland was in 1825, with the first branches set up in that year. BoI told us that it sought to play the role in Northern Ireland of a universal bank, having coverage throughout the island for both personal and business banking.

5.392. BoI's accounts for 1999 showed that its total operating income was IR£1.5 billion (£1.3 billion), total group profit before tax was IR£0.8 billion (£0.7 billion) and total assets were IR£42.8 billion (£36.2 billion). Internationally the group has 15,618 employees. The bank is based in the Republic of Ireland, but maintains 47 branches and 7 business centres in Northern Ireland. The Northern Ireland operation (referred to below as BoI NI) does not operate as a separate legal entity but rather as a business unit of BoI. The data provided in this section relates to the Northern Ireland operations only. As BoI is not a UK clearing bank (ie it is not a member of CCCC), and also does not have a significant presence in Great Britain, we did not obtain from BoI data on its Great Britain activities. BoI told us that its business in Great Britain was roughly half the size of the Northern Ireland business.

Business structure serving the SME banking business

5.393. BoI told us that it did not have a standard definition of SME. The nature of the Northern Ireland economy was such that all businesses were 'small'. Therefore it divided its business customers by the size of the debt finance facility they required and this determined the business unit of BoI that handled the customer relationship. These business units were:

— Corporate Banking: this unit was responsible for management of relationships with a debt facility in excess of £1 million;

— Business Centres (seven in Northern Ireland): these managed relationships with a debt facility between £25,000 and £1 million; and

— Branches (47 in Northern Ireland): these managed relationships with a borrowing requirement less than £25,000.

5.394. Business relationships not requiring a debt finance facility were managed by the account-holding branch, although in some cases, for example where foreign exchange or treasury services are required, other business units could share responsibility for management of the customer relationship. Banking services provided to SMEs included money transmission, debt finance and deposit facilities. There were no restrictions on the use of these services and all business customers had access to the complete range of services.

Financial performance

5.395. Table 5.124 shows the profitability of BoI NI from 1998 to 2000. Between 1998 and 2000 the bank's operating income increased by [✂] per cent, from £[✂] million to £[✂] million. Operating costs increased by [✂] per cent, from £[✂] million to £[✂] million. The level of bad debt charge was halved from £[✂] million in 1998 to £[✂] million in 1999, then increased to £[✂] million in 2000. As a result, profit before tax increased by [✂] per cent, from £[✂] million in 1998 to £[✂] million in 2000.

TABLE 5.124 **BoI NI: profit and loss account, 1998 to 2000**

£ million

Years ended 31 March

	1998	1999	2000
Net interest income			
Net fees and commissions			
Operating income			
Operating costs			
Operating profit before bad debts	*Figures omitted.*		
Bad debt charge	*See note on*		
Operating profit after provisions	*page iv.*		
Tax			
Net profit after tax			

per cent

Performance indicators			
Percentage change in operating income	(	✂	)

Source: BoI.

5.396. Table 5.125 further analyses the overall performance of BoI NI from 1998 to 2000, by comparing all items with operating income. Net interest income as a percentage of total income was around [✂] per cent compared with net fees and commissions of [✂] per cent.

5.397. Operating expenses as a percentage of operating income (also referred to as the cost:income ratio) reduced from [✂] per cent in 1998 to [✂] per cent in 2000. BoI NI said that this improvement was due to a substantial increase in income from higher business volume and effective cost management.

TABLE 5.125 **BoI NI: operating profit and loss items as a percentage of operating income, 1998 to 2000**

per cent

	1998	1999	2000
Net interest income			
Net fees and commissions			
Total income			
Operating expenses	*Figures omitted.*		
Operating profit before bad debts	*See note on*		
Bad debt charge	*page iv.*		
Net profit before tax			

Source: BoI.

Analysis of performance by type of customer

5.398. BoI used three broad groupings to segregate its business:

(a) Business—including those relationships managed by its Corporate and Business Banking units. It included a few (about 10 to 12) relationships that exceeded the £25 million SME definition threshold;

(b) Retail—represented personal banking; and

(c) Other—included public sector, churches and charities and non-resident accounts. It included incomes and costs arising from BoI's own 'Note Issue' business.

Table 5.126 analyses the performance of BoI NI for 2000 by type of customer. Income from personal customers totalled £[✂] million and represented [✂] per cent of total income. Income from the business customers totalled £[✂] million, and income from other customers was £[✂] million, representing

[✂] per cent and [✂] per cent respectively of total income. BoI NI's cost:income ratios were different according to the type of customer. The overall cost:income ratio was [✂] per cent.

TABLE 5.126 **BoI NI: summary of analysed results, 2000**

£ million

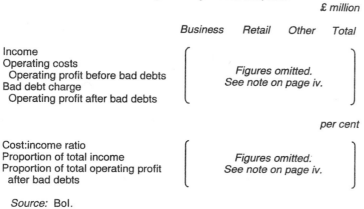

	Business	Retail	Other	Total
Income				
Operating costs				
Operating profit before bad debts	*Figures omitted.*			
Bad debt charge	*See note on page iv.*			
Operating profit after bad debts				

per cent

Cost:income ratio				
Proportion of total income	*Figures omitted.*			
Proportion of total operating profit	*See note on page iv.*			
after bad debts				

Source: BoI.

Balance sheets

5.399. Table 5.127 shows BoI NI's balance sheets from 1998 to 2000. Total assets increased from £[✂] billion in 1998 to £[✂] billion in 2000. This was mainly because of an increase of [✂] per cent in loans and advances to customers from £[✂] billion in 1998 to £[✂] billion in 2000.

5.400. BoI NI's operating profit as a percentage of average shareholders' funds (pre-tax return) fell from [✂] per cent in 1999 to [✂] per cent in 2000. This was largely a result of a [✂] per cent increase in shareholders' funds (including a £[✂] million increase in equity and a £[✂] million increase in loan stocks). The change resulted from the increase in the level of advances to customers and the revised methodology for the allocation of capital adopted by BoI. Total liabilities increased from £[✂] billion in 1998 to £[✂] billion in 2000. This was because of increases in customer accounts in credit from £[✂] billion to £[✂] billion ([✂] per cent). Shareholders' funds increased from £[✂] million to £[✂] million.

TABLE 5.127 **BoI NI: balance sheet, 1998 to 2000**

£ million

As at 31 March

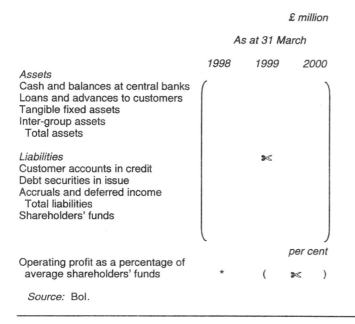

	1998	1999	2000
Assets			
Cash and balances at central banks			
Loans and advances to customers			
Tangible fixed assets			
Inter-group assets			
Total assets			
Liabilities		✂	
Customer accounts in credit			
Debt securities in issue			
Accruals and deferred income			
Total liabilities			
Shareholders' funds			

per cent

Operating profit as a percentage of average shareholders' funds	*	(	✂	)

Source: BoI.

*Data not available.

5.401. BoI NI lent [✄] to customers as was held in credit. In 2000 loans and advances to customers accounted for [✄] per cent of total balance sheet assets. It reported to us loans and advances to business customers of £[✄] billion, compared with £[✄] million to retail customers, and £[✄] million to the 'other' segment.

5.402. Table 5.128 shows an analysis of contingent liabilities and commitments for 1998 to 2000. BoI NI's level of commitments increased from £[✄] million in 1998 to £[✄] million in 2000. In 2000, it reported total contingent liabilities of £[✄] million and total commitments of £[✄] million, compared with total on-balance-sheet liabilities of £[✄] billion.

TABLE 5.128 **BoI NI: contingent liabilities and commitments, 1998 to 2000**

£ million

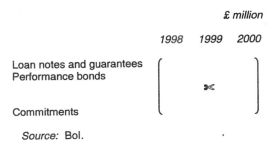

	1998	1999	2000
Loan notes and guarantees			
Performance bonds		✄	
Commitments			

Source: BoI.

Bad debts

5.403. Table 5.129 shows BoI NI's level of closing bad debt provision, and the level of bad debt charge against profits between 1998 and 2000.

5.404. The bad debt charge as a percentage of total loans was [✄] per cent in 1998 and fell to [✄] per cent in 2000.

TABLE 5.129 **BoI NI: analysis of bad debt provision and charges to profit and loss, 1998 to 2000**

£ million

	1998	1999	2000
Analysis of bad debt provision:			
General provision			
Specific provision			
Closing bad debt provision	*	*	*
Total bad debt profit and loss charge	(	✄	)
Performance indicators		*per cent*	
Bad debt provision as a percentage of total loans	*	*	*
Bad debt charge as a percentage of total loans			
Bad debt charge as a percentage of total income		✄	

Source: BoI.

*Not available.

Capital adequacy

5.405. BoI told us that the bank in the UK was treated for statutory and regulatory purposes as a 'branch' of BoI. As such, its regulator was the Central Bank of Ireland, and the Northern Ireland business was included in an aggregated return for the group. Table 5.130 shows BoI capital adequacy ratios for 1999 and 2000 for the bank as a whole.

TABLE 5.130 **BoI: capital adequacy data, 1999 and 2000**

per cent

	As at 31 March	
	1999	2000
Ratios		
Tier 1	9.0	7.4
Total	13.0	11.8

Source: BoI.

The Co-operative Bank

History

5.406. The Co-operative Bank was founded in 1872 as the Loans and Deposits Department of the Co-operative Wholesale Society in order to provide banking services for the Co-operative movement. It was not until 1972 that the Co-operative Bank was established in its present form and in 1975 it achieved clearing bank status. In the late 1970s the bank went through rapid expansion, opening new branches and expanding into the personal banking products market.

5.407. To be a clearing bank, the Co-operative Bank is required to be a plc. However, the plc is wholly owned by the Co-operative Wholesale Society, which has recently been renamed Co-operative Group (CWS) Ltd (the Co-operative Group). The Co-operative Group is governed by the Industrial and Provident Societies Acts 1965–1978. The Co-operative Group is owned and controlled by its members comprising both Co-operative Societies and approximately 1.5 million members.

5.408. The Co-operative Group is a large family of businesses which includes 1,000 retail stores. Its businesses include community stores, travel agencies (Travel Care), insurance (CIS), funeral services, farming, pharmacies, department stores and opticians.

5.409. As a co-operative any profits are reinvested in its business, directed to social purposes, or distributed to its members in the form of dividends. The motivation for profit does not derive from external shareholders and the bank does not have the stock market pressures that apply to listed plcs. Owing to the uniqueness of the ownership structure, the bank has limited access to capital and cannot raise share capital in the normal way. Accordingly the Co-operative Bank's current capital base was achieved from reinvested profits, organic growth, an issue of preference shares in 1988 and subsequent issues of subordinated loan notes.

5.410. The Co-operative Bank told us that it operated a 'Partnership Approach'. The goal of the bank was to deliver value to all its 'partners', which included customers, staff, suppliers, the community and society at large. The bank emphasized its strong public ethical stance, which was documented and which defined with whom the bank did business. The bank said that it appealed to like-minded individuals and businesses for customer support and this influenced its customer base. For example, the Co-operative Bank noted that its ethical stance attracted a large number of charities as customers.

Business structure serving the SME banking business

5.411. The Co-operative Bank told us that it had a share of about 1 per cent of the non-personal market. It noted that the SME business had never been a defined target market for the bank, but it provided them with a full banking service via relationship managers who were regionally located across the country. Because the Co-operative Bank operated as a niche player, it had concentrated its strengths in certain sectors and developed specialist teams to service them, for example local authorities where it had 30 per cent of the market, and credit unions where it had a market penetration of some 60 per cent.

Financial performance

5.412. Table 5.131 shows the profitability of the Co-operative Bank from 1993 to 1999. Between 1993 and 1999 the bank's operating income increased from £228 million to £403 million. Operating expenses increased at a slower rate, from £172 million to £262 million. The level of bad debt charge was £38 million and £32 million in 1993 and 1994 respectively, and then dipped to between £23 million and £26 million from 1995 to 1997. In 1998 and 1999 the bad debt charge rose sharply again to £42 million and £53 million respectively. As a result, profit before tax increased by nearly 400 per cent, from £18 million in 1993 to £89 million in 1999. The Co-operative Bank paid ordinary dividends of £2.5 million in 1993, £3.0 million in 1994, £4.0 million in 1995 and £5.0 million in 1996. A preference dividend of £5.5 million was paid every year.

TABLE 5.131 **The Co-operative Bank: consolidated profit and loss account, 1993 to 1999***

£ million

	1993	1994	1995	1996	1997	1998	1999
Net interest income	130	139	146	180	209	241	279
Net fees and commissions	93	100	102	103	105	111	119
Other income	5	−1	2	3	2	3	6
Operating income	228	238	250	287	316	354	403
Operating expenses	−172	−179	−190	−218	−237	−241	−262
Operating profit before provisions	55	59	60	68	80	113	142
Bad and doubtful debts charge	−38	−32	−23	−24	−26	−42	−53
Other provisions	0	0	−1	0	0	0	0
Operating profit	17	27	37	44	53	72	88
Exceptional and other items	1	0	0	1	2	2	0
Net profit before tax	18	28	37	46	55	74	89
Tax	−7	−9	−13	−17	−18	−23	−27
Net profit after tax	11	18	24	29	37	51	61
Minority interest	0	0	0	0	−1	−1	−1
Profit for the financial year	11	18	23	28	36	50	60
Dividends	−8	−9	−10	−11	−6	−6	−6
Profit retained for the financial year	3	9	14	18	31	44	54
Number of employees ('000)	3.9	3.8	4.0	4.2	4.2	4.0	4.0
Performance indicators							per cent
Tax charge as a percentage of profit before tax	38	34	36	37	33	31	31
Percentage change in operating income	†	5	5	15	10	12	14

Source: The Co-operative Bank.

*Year ended early January subsequent year.
†Not available.

5.413. Table 5.132 further analyses the overall performance of the Co-operative Bank from 1993 to 1999, by comparing all items with operating income. Net interest income as a percentage of total income increased from 57 per cent in 1993 to 69 per cent in 1999. At the same time, net fees and commissions fell from 41 per cent in 1993 to 30 per cent in 1999.

5.414. Operating expenses as a percentage of operating income (also referred to as the cost:income ratio) remained constant at around 75 per cent between 1993 and 1997, and fell to 65 per cent in 1999. The Co-operative Bank said that this improvement was due to cost efficiency and productivity improvements.

TABLE 5.132 **The Co-operative Bank: operating profit and loss items as a percentage of operating income, 1993 to 1999**

							per cent
	1993	1994	1995	1996	1997	1998	1999
Net interest income	57	58	58	63	66	68	69
Net fees and commissions	41	42	41	36	33	31	30
Other income	2	−1	1	1	1	1	1
Operating income	100	100	100	100	100	100	100
Operating expenses	−76	−75	−76	−76	−75	−68	−65
Operating profit before provisions	24	25	24	24	25	32	35
Bad and doubtful debts charge	−17	−13	−9	−8	−8	−12	−13
Other provisions	0	0	0	0	0	0	0
Operating profit after provisions	7	11	15	16	17	20	22
Exceptional and other items	0	0	0	0	1	1	0
Net profit before tax	8	12	15	16	17	21	22

Source: The Co-operative Bank.

Analysis of performance by type of customer

5.415. Table 5.133 analyses the performance of the Co-operative Bank in 1999 by type of customer. In 1999 income from personal customers totalled £[✂] million. This represented [✂] per cent of income for the total banking group. Income from SMEs totalled £[✂] million, and income from corporate customers was £[✂] million, representing [✂] per cent and [✂] per cent respectively of total group income. These results were not significantly different from those for 1998.

TABLE 5.133 **The Co-operative Bank: summary of analysed results, 1999**

	Personal	SME	Corporate	Other	Total
					£ million
Income					404
Operating costs					−262
Operating profit before bad debts					142
Bad debt charge					−53
Operating profit after bad debts and before other items		*Figures omitted. See note on page iv.*			89
					per cent
Cost:income ratio					65
Proportion of total income					100
Proportion of total operating profit after bad debts					100

Source: The Co-operative Bank.

5.416. Overall, the Co-operative Bank said that its cost ratios were similar across all segments. In 1999 operating costs (excluding bad debts) attributable to the personal sector totalled £[✂] million ([✂] per cent of total operating costs). Operating costs of the SME banking business totalled £[✂] million, and costs attributable to corporate clients were £[✂] million, which represented [✂] per cent and [✂] per cent respectively of total operating costs.

Balance sheets

5.417. Table 5.134 shows the Co-operative Bank's balance sheets from 1993 to 1999. Total assets increased from £3.4 billion in 1993 to £6.2 billion in 1999. This was due mostly to increases in loans and advances to customers and debt securities, offset by a fall in loans and advances to banks.

TABLE 5.134 **The Co-operative Bank: consolidated balance sheet, 1993 to 1999***

£ million

	1993	1994	1995	1996	1997	1998	1999
Assets							
Cash and balances at central banks	32	38	33	35	34	48	75
Treasury bills and other eligible bills	0	0	56	1	13	0	36
Loans and advances to banks	1,019	699	906	614	508	431	494
Loans and advances to customers	1,721	1,790	1,974	2,197	2,503	2,784	2,978
Debt securities	383	564	712	1,380	1,926	1,978	2,340
Other investments	1	1	1	1	2	2	2
Tangible fixed assets	40	45	52	63	64	61	65
Other assets	170	119	137	148	148	158	168
Prepayments and accrued income	32	39	52	58	76	78	77
Total assets	3,399	3,294	3,924	4,497	5,272	5,539	6,234
Liabilities							
Deposits by banks	572	602	404	564	576	599	912
Customer accounts in credit	2,411	2,273	2,891	3,334	3,913	4,196	4,533
Debt securities in issue	67	50	107	84	167	57	62
Other liabilities	74	60	52	67	72	108	91
Accruals and deferred income	30	54	66	69	100	87	86
Other provisions	7	8	17	13	12	15	17
Subordinated liabilities	81	81	205	168	198	198	193
Total liabilities	3,242	3,128	3,743	4,299	5,037	5,260	5,894
Shareholders' funds	157	166	180	198	235	280	340
	3,399	3,294	3,924	4,497	5,272	5,539	6,234
Performance indicators							
Operating profit as a percentage of average shareholders' funds†	‡	17	21	23	25	28	28

Source: The Co-operative Bank.

---

*As at early January subsequent year.
†Average shareholders' funds includes any capitalized goodwill.
‡Not available.

5.418. Total liabilities increased from £3.2 billion in 1993 to £5.9 billion in 1999. This was mostly because of increases in customer accounts in credit from £2.4 billion to £4.5 billion (88 per cent). Shareholders' funds increased from £157 million to £340 million, the growth representing accumulated retained earnings.

5.419. In common with other banks, the largest items within the bank's balance sheet were loans and advances to customers, and customer accounts in credit (deposit and savings accounts). The Co-operative Bank has consistently had more customer deposits than it has lent to customers, and the excess funds were invested in debt securities.

5.420. In 1999 loans and advances to customers accounted for 48 per cent of the Co-operative Bank's total balance sheet assets, and debt securities for 38 per cent. The bank analysed loans and advances to the personal segment at £[✂] billion, compared with £[✂] to SMEs (businesses with a turnover up to £25 million), and £[✂] to corporate customers. This represented [✂] per cent, [✂] per cent and [✂] per cent respectively of total loans outstanding for the whole bank.

5.421. The Co-operative Bank's operating profit as a percentage of average shareholders' funds (pre-tax return) increased from 17 per cent in 1993 to 28 per cent in 1998 and 1999.

5.422. Table 5.135 shows an analysis of contingent liabilities and commitments for 1993 to 1999. The Co-operative Bank's level of commitments increased from £1.8 billion in 1993 to £4.2 billion in 1999. In 1999 Co-operative Bank reported total contingent liabilities of £106 million and total commitments of £4.2 billion, compared with total on-balance-sheet liabilities of £5.9 billion.

TABLE 5.135 **The Co-operative Bank: contingent liabilities and commitments, 1993 to 1999**

						£ million	
	1993	1994	1995	1996	1997	1998	1999
Acceptances and endorsements	42	81	44	31	30	42	53
Guarantees and assets pledged as collateral security	70	67	62	64	75	46	53
	112	149	106	95	105	88	106
Commitments	1,813	1,750	2,023	2,287	2,725	3,281	4,176

Source: The Co-operative Bank.

Bad debts

5.423. Table 5.136 shows the Co-operative Bank's level of closing bad debt provision, and the level of bad debt charge against profits between 1993 and 1999. The level of bad debt provisions fluctuated during the period, between £148 million in 1993 and £76 million in 1996, the balance at the end of 1999 being £118 million. In 1993, the level of the provision equated to 8.6 per cent of the total loan book. This ratio fell to 3.2 per cent in 1997 and increased to 4 per cent in 1999. Over the period the general provision remained constant at £5 million, but the level of specific provisions fluctuated, and was the main constituent of the provision.

TABLE 5.136 **The Co-operative Bank: analysis of bad debt provision and charges to profit and loss, 1993 to 1999**

						£ million	
	1993	1994	1995	1996	1997	1998	1999
Analysis of bad debt provision:							
General provision	5	5	5	5	5	5	5
Specific provision	143	139	104	71	75	85	113
Closing bad debt provision	148	144	109	76	80	90	118
Total bad debt profit and loss charge*	38	32	23	24	26	42	53
Performance indicators						*per cent*	
Bad debt provision as a percentage of total loans	8.6	8.0	5.5	3.5	3.2	3.2	4.0
Bad debt charge as a percentage of total loans	2.2	1.8	1.2	1.1	1.0	1.5	1.8
Bad debt charge as a percentage of total income	17	13	9	8	8	12	13

Source: The Co-operative Bank.

*This figure is a net figure following write-backs and recoveries.

5.424. The bad debt charge as a percentage of total loans was 2.2 per cent in 1993 and fell to 1.0 per cent in 1997. In 1998 and 1999 the charge increased to 1.5 per cent and 1.8 per cent respectively. The Co-operative Bank said that the most recent increases were due to planned growth in personal sector lending. Personal bad debt charges were driven mainly by standard formulae based on the ageing of overdue accounts. Credit and behavioural scoring techniques were used to project bad debt rates and ensure that growth in operating income more than offset increases in bad debt charges. New products generated low bad debt charges in their first year and progressively increased to their projected level thereafter. This characteristic contributed to the increase in bad debt charge and the charge as a percentage of loan balances. The bad debt:loan ratio had been high in recent years because of the high proportion of unsecured personal lending in the overall loan book.

Capital adequacy

5.425. Table 5.137 shows the Co-operative Bank's capital adequacy ratios from 1993 to 1999. From 1995 to 1998 its Tier 1 ratio remained relatively constant, and fluctuated between 7.1 and 7.8 per cent, but increased to 8.6 per cent in 1999. The total capital ratio was 11.5 per cent in 1993, increased to 13.3 per cent in 1995 and fluctuated between 12.5 and 13 per cent between 1996 and 1999.

TABLE 5.137 **The Co-operative Bank: capital adequacy data, 1993 to 1999***

| | | | | | | | per cent |
	1993	1994	1995	1996	1997	1998	1999
Ratios							
Tier 1	7.5	7.7	7.4	7.1	7.1	7.8	8.6
Total	11.5	11.7	13.3	12.5	12.8	12.9	13.0

Source: The Co-operative Bank.

*As at early January subsequent year.

5.426. The Co-operative Bank told us that the target capital ratios it aimed to work within over the next few years was around 13 per cent. It told us that a higher capital ratio highlighted a prudent approach to management and reassured note-holders and depositors. It said that this was appropriate for the current business climate.

Alliance & Leicester

5.427. The business now carried on by Alliance & Leicester was established by the merger in October 1985 of the Alliance Building Society and the Leicester Building Society.

5.428. Following the vote in favour of conversion at a special general meeting in December 1996, Alliance & Leicester became a public company on 21 April 1997 and shortly after obtained a listing on the London Stock Exchange, and joined the FTSE 100. This conversion to public company status ended 144 years of mutuality. At 29 June 2001 Alliance & Leicester had a market capitalization of £4.2 billion and a price:earnings ratio of 13.4.

5.429. Alliance & Leicester's service to SMEs is carried out through a wholly-owned subsidiary, Girobank. Girobank was privatized in 1990 having previously been owned by the Post Office, and Alliance & Leicester told us that the Government's intention was that its ownership did not pass into the control of the large UK banks. The Alliance & Leicester Building Society acquired Girobank upon its privatization and it is a wholly-owned subsidiary of Alliance & Leicester.

5.430. Because Girobank was acquired by a building society that at the time was not empowered to make non-property loans, Alliance & Leicester was required to go through a complex restructuring which removed loans to commercial businesses from its balance sheet. When Alliance & Leicester became a public company in 1997 it began to provide the full range of services expected from retail banks of its size. Girobank is a member of APACS, BACS and CCCC (although only modest use is made of the credit clearing element), but is not a member of CHAPS.

Girobank and its relationship with the Post Office

5.431. Girobank uses the Post Office network to provide counter service to both personal and business customers. [

Details omitted. See note on page iv.

] The Girobank relationship with the Post Office is discussed further in paragraph 3.212.

Business structure serving the SME banking business

5.432. Alliance & Leicester told us that it did not have a specific business segment that served SME customers within our definition. It defined its commercial customers as either small businesses or large corporates; small businesses were those with a business turnover up to £1 million. In terms of service offerings, a further distinction was made between small businesses with turnovers above and below £500,000. Large corporates were classified as any company with a turnover above £1 million. Small business service offerings were rebranded as Alliance Business Banking and the Girobank brand was phased out of use within the small business sector at the end of 2000. Alliance & Leicester stated that its aim was to acquire a 10 per cent share of the small business market by 2005.

Financial performance

5.433. Table 5.138 shows Alliance & Leicester's profit and loss account (including Girobank results) for the four years to 1999. Operating income increased from £1,077 million in 1996 to £1,173 million in 1999 (an increase of around 9 per cent). Operating expenses decreased from £752 million in 1996 to £632 million in 1999 (a decrease of around 16 per cent). Bad debt charges increased by just over 100 per cent, from £20 million to £41 million between 1996 and 1999.

TABLE 5.138 **Alliance & Leicester: consolidated profit and loss account, 1996 to 1999**

£ million

Years ended 31 December

	1996	1997	1998	1999
Net interest income	644	693	740	753
Net fees and commissions	369	353	377	376
Other income	64	71	73	44
Operating income	1,077	1,118	1,189	1,173
Operating expenses	−752	−694	−695	−632
Operating profit before provisions	325	424	494	542
Bad debt charge	−20	−29	−39	−41
Net profit before tax	306	395	455	500
Tax	−120	−134	−137	−146
Net profit after tax	186	261	318	354
Dividends	-	−121	−143	−163
Profit retained for the financial year	186	140	175	191

Source: Alliance & Leicester.

5.434. Table 5.139 further analyses the overall performance of Alliance & Leicester from 1996 to 1999, by comparing all items with operating income. The net interest proportion of income increased from 60 per cent in 1996 to 64 per cent in 1999. The net fees and commissions proportion of total income decreased from 34 per cent in 1996 to 32 per cent in 1999. Operating expenses as a percentage of operating income (cost:income ratio) decreased significantly from 70 per cent in 1996 to 54 per cent in 1999, which Alliance & Leicester said was the effect of its focus on cost reduction and efficiency since its demutualization in 1997.

TABLE 5.139 **Alliance & Leicester: operating profit as a percentage of operating income, 1996 to 1999**

per cent

	1996	1997	1998	1999
Net interest income	60	62	62	64
Net fees and commissions	34	32	32	32
Other income	6	6	6	4
Operating income	100	100	100	100
Operating expenses	−70	−62	−58	−54
Operating profit before provisions	30	38	42	46
Provisions for bad and doubtful debts	−2	−3	−3	−4
Net profit before tax	28	35	38	43

Source: Alliance & Leicester.

5.435. Table 5.140 shows the financial performance of Girobank for 1998 and 1999. Net interest income was £61 million in both years, compared with net fees and commissions of £272 million in 1998 and £200 million in 1999. Total income fell from £381 million in 1998 to £261 million in 1999, while operating expenses decreased from £325 million in 1998 to £203 million in 1999 (a decrease of around 38 per cent). Alliance & Leicester explained that the reason for these movements was twofold. [

Details omitted. See note on page iv.

] Secondly, the accounting treatment of inter-group recharges was altered, and approximately £70 million was reclassified from fee income in 1998 to a negative cost adjustment in 1999.

TABLE 5.140 **Girobank: consolidated profit and loss account, 1998 and 1999**

	£ million	
	1998	*1999*
Net interest income	61	61
Net fees and commissions	272	200
Other income	48	-
Operating income	381	261
Operating expenses	−325	−203
Operating profit before provisions	56	58
Bad debt charge	-	−1
Net profit before tax	56	57
Tax	−18	−18
Net profit after tax	39	39

Source: Alliance & Leicester.

5.436. Table 5.141 further analyses Girobank's operating profit as a percentage of income in 1998 and 1999. Net fees and commissions were 71 and 77 per cent of operating income in 1998 and 1999 respectively. Girobank's cost:income ratio dropped from 85 per cent in 1998 to 78 per cent in 1999, which resulted in its net profit before tax to operating income margin improving from 15 per cent in 1998 to 22 per cent in 1999.

TABLE 5.141 **Girobank: operating profit as a percentage of operating income, 1998 and 1999**

	per cent	
	1998	*1999*
Net interest income	16	23
Net fees and commissions	71	77
Other income	13	-
Operating income	100	100
Operating expenses	−85	−78
Operating profit before provisions (pre-tax)	15	22
Provisions for bad and doubtful debts	*	*
Net profit before tax	15	22

Source: Alliance & Leicester.

*Girobank had negligible bad debt charges in 1998 and 1999.

Analysis of performance by type of customer

5.437. Table 5.142 analyses the performance of Alliance & Leicester by type of customer for 1999. The income from personal customers totalled £[✂] million, which represented [✂] per cent of Alliance & Leicester's income. Income from the SMEs totalled £[✂] million or [✂] per cent of total income; and 'other commercial' customers contributed [✂] per cent of total income. These results were not significantly different from those for 1998.

TABLE 5.142 **Alliance & Leicester: summary of analysed results, 1999**

	Personal	SME	Other commercial	Other	Total
					£ million
Income					1,173
Operating expenses*					−632
Operating profit before bad debts					541
Bad debt charge					−41
Operating profit after bad debts and before other items		Figures omitted. See note on page iv.			500
					per cent
Cost:income ratio					54
Proportion of total income					100
Proportion of total operating profit after bad debts					100

Source: CC based on information from Alliance & Leicester.

*No fixed costs were allocated among segments by Alliance & Leicester. Therefore we made allocations based on respective proportions of turnover.

5.438. The cost:income ratios between the segments differed considerably. In 1999 the ratio of the SME banking business was [✂] per cent compared with [✂] per cent for 'other commercial' and [✂] per cent for the personal banking business. The personal banking business contributed [✂] per cent of group operating profit after bad debts, followed by 'other commercial' at [✂] per cent, and then the SME banking business with [✂] per cent.

Balance sheets

5.439. Table 5.143 shows the consolidated balance sheets of Alliance & Leicester for the four years to 1999. Total assets increased from £24.1 billion in 1996 to £30.5 billion in 1999 mainly as a result of increases in loans and advances to customers of some £18.3 billion to £23.7 billion. The other significant increase was in debt securities, which increased over the period by around £500 million to £3.7 billion in 1999. However, these increases were offset by a decrease in loans and advances to banks from £1.7 billion in 1996 to £1.2 billion in 1999.

5.440. Total liabilities increased from £22.5 billion in 1993 to £28.4 billion in 1999 and reflected increases in customer accounts in credit from £18.2 billion in 1996 to £20.1 billion in 1999, and increases in debt securities in issue from £2.3 billion in 1996 to £5.8 billion in 1999. Shareholders' funds increased from £1.6 billion to £1.8 billion, as a result of accumulated retained earnings.

5.441. In common with other banks, the largest items within the bank's balance sheet were loans and advances to customers, and customer accounts in credit (deposit and savings accounts). In 1999 Alliance & Leicester had lent some £3.6 billion more than it received from customer accounts in credit, and funded the difference mainly by the issue of debt securities. In 1999 lending to small business customers was on a very small scale, £127 million or 0.5 per cent of Alliance & Leicester's loans and advances to customers of £23.7 billion.

5.442. Pre-tax returns as a percentage of average shareholders' funds increased from 24 per cent in 1996 to 28 per cent in 1999.

TABLE 5.143   Alliance & Leicester: consolidated balance sheet, 1996 to 1999

£ million

| | As at 31 December | | | |
	1996	1997	1998	1999
Assets				
Cash and balances at central banks	101	85	67	156
Treasury bills and other eligible bills	85	203	455	280
Loans and advances to banks	1,676	1,842	2,061	1,231
Items in the course of collection from other banks	156	118	129	102
Loans and advances to customers	18,261	19,134	21,475	23,732
Debt securities	3,196	2,307	2,275	3,744
Tangible fixed assets	322	356	441	517
Other assets	80	60	172	171
Prepayments and accrued income	108	173	269	238
Long-term assurance business attributable to shareholders	28	33	56	65
	24,013	24,309	27,399	30,234
Long-term assurance business attributable to policy-holders	65	95	180	258
Total assets	24,078	24,404	27,579	30,492
Liabilities				
Deposits by banks	235	89	721	1,024
Items in the course of transmission to other banks	207	201	142	198
Customer accounts in credit	18,201	18,948	19,892	20,125
Debt securities in issue	2,341	1,821	3,407	5,751
Other liabilities	383	350	345	352
Accruals and deferred income	502	629	712	659
Other provisions	13	18	54	100
Subordinated liabilities	575	575	273	274
Total liabilities	22,457	22,631	25,546	28,483
Shareholders' funds	1,556	1,678	1,853	1,752
	24,013	24,309	27,399	30,234
Long-term assurance liabilities to policy-holders	65	95	180	258
	24,078	24,404	27,579	30,492
Performance indicators				per cent
Operating profit as a percentage of average shareholders' funds*	*	24	26	28

Source: Alliance & Leicester.

---

*Average shareholders' funds includes any capitalized goodwill.

5.443.   Table 5.144 shows the contingent liabilities and commitments of Alliance & Leicester from 1996 to 1999. Alliance & Leicester's level of contingencies and commitments increased from £35 million in 1996 to £442 million in 1999. The reported total contingent liabilities and capital commitments in 1999 were £442 million, compared with total on-balance-sheet liabilities of £28.5 billion.

TABLE 5.144   Alliance & Leicester: contingent liabilities and commitments,* 1996 to 1999

£ million

	1996	1997	1998	1999
Contingent liabilities	-	-	31	31
Commitments	35	199	306	411
	35	199	337	442

Source: Alliance & Leicester.

---

*Includes Girobank.

5.444. Table 5.145 shows the balance sheets of Girobank in 1998 and 1999. Girobank's total assets increased from £1.8 billion in 1998 to £2.5 billion in 1999. The largest proportion of Girobank's assets were loans and advances to banks at around 64 per cent of total assets in 1999. These comprised loans to its parent company Alliance & Leicester, which we note used the funds for lending to personal and mortgage customers.

TABLE 5.145 **Girobank: consolidated balance sheet, 1998 and 1999**

	£ million	
	1998	1999
Assets		
Cash and balances at central banks	13	33
Loans and advances to banks	1,014	1,577
Items in the course of collection from other banks	129	101
Loans and advances to customers	216	305
Tangible fixed assets	45	41
Interest in associated undertakings	227	228
Other assets	158	155
Prepayments and accrued income	37	38
Total assets	1,839	2,478
Liabilities		
Deposits by banks	63	98
Items in the course of transmission to other banks	105	187
Customer accounts in credit	1,299	1,783
Other liabilities	104	111
Accruals and deferred income	44	37
Other provisions	4	3
Total liabilities	1,619	2,219
Shareholders' funds	220	259
	1,839	2,478

Source: Alliance & Leicester.

5.445. Total liabilities increased from £1.6 billion in 1998 to £2.2 billion in 1999. This increase was primarily driven by increases in customer accounts in credit, which increased by some £500 million between 1998 and 1999 as a result of business growth and slightly differing year-end days.

5.446. Table 5.146 shows the contingent liabilities and commitments of Girobank in 1998 and 1999. Contingent liabilities and contingencies increased from £176 million in 1998 to £219 million in 1999.

TABLE 5.146 **Girobank: contingent liabilities and commitments, 1998 and 1999**

	£ million	
	1998	1999
Contingent liabilities	31	52
Commitments	145	167
	176	219

Source: Alliance & Leicester.

Capital adequacy

5.447. Table 5.147 shows Alliance & Leicester's capital adequacy ratios from 1996 to 1999. In 1996 its Tier 1 and total ratios were 13.2 and 17.7 per cent respectively, which by 1999 had decreased to 11.2 and 12.8 per cent respectively.

TABLE 5.147 Alliance & Leicester: capital adequacy data, 1996 to 1999

£ million

As at 31 December

	1996	1997	1998	1999
Ratios				
Tier 1	13.2	13.9	13.4	11.2
Total (for Tiers 1, 2 and 3)	17.7	18.4	15.1	12.8

Source: Alliance & Leicester.

Abbey National

History

5.448. Abbey National is listed on the London Stock Exchange. At 29 June 2001 its market capitalization was £17.8 billion and its price:earnings ratio was 14.2.

5.449. The roots of Abbey National were in personal mortgage banking, its predecessor—the National Freehold Land and Building Society—having been founded in 1849. The Abbey National Building Society was founded in 1944, when the National Building Society merged with the Abbey Road Building Society (founded in 1874 as the Abbey Road & St John's Wood Permanent Building Society). The Abbey National Building Society demutualized in 1989, thereby becoming a bank that was then listed on the Stock Exchange. It has over the past few years sought to diversify away from mortgage banking and savings products and has a target of achieving 65 per cent of profits from businesses, other than mortgages and savings.

5.450. In 1997 Abbey National decided to extend its core activity of providing financial services to people by providing new banking services to businesses in local and regional communities. Initially, the obvious candidates for this service were Abbey National's personal customers. In 1998 it decided to extend the range of activities of its subsidiary, First National Bank, a consumer finance operation acquired in 1995, to business asset financing. A number of business asset finance units have since been acquired or established within First National Bank.

5.451. In 1999 management responsibility for Abbey National Business and Professional Banking was transferred to First National Bank. This step was taken to facilitate the provision of a range of banking and asset finance services under one management structure. As a result of these developments, the main business units within First National Bank that now offer services to business customers are as follows:

(a) First National Vehicle Holdings, which provides vehicle contract hire;

(b) First National Invoice Finance, which provides factoring/invoice discounting services;

(c) First National Commercial Banking, which provides commercial mortgages through intermediaries/brokers;

(d) First National Business Equipment Leasing, which offers finance for equipment leasing; and

(e) Abbey National Business and Professional Banking, which offers certain banking facilities (for example, current and deposit accounts) to business customers.

At present the totality of Abbey National's involvement with all types of business is relatively small. Abbey National estimated its share of the SME business banking at around 1 per cent. However, it also said that it was keen to expand its presence in the market and in June 2000 announced its intention to capture some 4 to 5 per cent of business banking customers within the next five years. Abbey National is a member of APACS, BACS and CCCC.

Financial performance

5.452. Table 5.148 shows the profitability of Abbey National from 1994 to 1999. Between 1994 and 1999, Abbey National's operating income more than doubled, from £1.8 billion to £3.8 billion. During the period, operating expenses increased from £0.8 billion to £1.6 billion. The level of bad debt charge remained constant from 1994 through to 1997 at around £100 million; however, it increased to £201 million in 1998, and increased again to £303 million in 1999. When compared with lending levels, these bad debt charges are low (see paragraph 5.463). As a result, Abbey National's profit before tax doubled from £0.9 billion in 1994 to £1.8 billion in 1999.

TABLE 5.148 **Abbey National: consolidated profit and loss account, 1994 to 1999**

						£ billion
	Years ended 31 December					
	1994	1995	1996	1997	1998	1999
Net interest income	1.4	1.6	1.8	1.9	2.2	2.7
Net fees and commissions	0.2	0.2	0.3	0.5	0.5	0.5
Other income	0.2	0.2	0.2	0.3	0.4	0.6
Operating income	1.8	2.0	2.3	2.6	3.1	3.8
Operating expenses	−0.8	−0.9	−1.0	−1.2	−1.3	−1.6
Operating profit before provisions	1.0	1.1	1.3	1.4	1.8	2.1
Bad and doubtful debts charge	−0.1	−0.1	−0.1	−0.1	−0.2	−0.3
Net profit before tax	0.9	1.0	1.2	1.3	1.5	1.8
Tax	−0.3	−0.3	−0.4	−0.3	−0.5	−0.5
Net profit after tax	0.6	0.7	0.8	1.0	1.1	1.2
Dividends	−0.2	−0.3	−0.4	−0.5	−0.5	−0.6
Transfer to non-distributable reserve	−0.1	−0.1	−0.1	−0.1	−0.1	0.0
Profit retained for the financial year	0.3	0.3	0.3	0.4	0.4	0.6
Number of employees ('000)	15	20	22	25	28	28
Performance indicators						*per cent*
Tax charge as a percentage of profit before tax	35	34	35	25	30	30
Percentage change in operating income	*	13	18	11	19	21

Source: Abbey National.

*Not available.

5.453. Table 5.149 further analyses the overall performance of Abbey National from 1994 to 1999, by comparing all items with operating income. Net interest income as a percentage of total income declined from its peak of 80 per cent in 1995 to 71 per cent in 1999. At the same time net fees and commissions fluctuated from 10 per cent of income in 1994, up to 17 per cent in 1997, and then back to 13 per cent in 1999. This is a much smaller percentage than that reported by the six largest clearing groups that provide a full banking service. 'Other' income steadily increased from around 8 per cent in 1995 to 16 per cent in 1999. The increase has come from a number of sources including dealing activities and profit on disposal of equity shares.

TABLE 5.149 **Abbey National: operating profit and loss items as a percentage of operating income, 1994 to 1999**

per cent

	1994	1995	1996	1997	1998	1999
Net interest income	79	80	76	72	72	71
Net fees and commissions	10	12	14	17	16	13
Other income	11	8	9	10	12	16
Operating income	100	100	100	100	100	100
Operating expenses	−43	−44	−44	−46	−42	−43
Operating profit before provisions	57	56	56	54	58	57
Bad and doubtful debts charge	−4	−4	−5	−5	−6	−8
Other provisions	0	−1	−1	−1	−1	−1
Operating profit after provisions	53	52	50	49	51	48
Exceptional and other items	0	0	0	0	−2	−1
Net profit before tax	53	52	50	49	49	47

Source: Abbey National.

5.454. Operating expenses as a percentage of operating income (also referred to as the cost:income ratio) remained relatively constant, ranging between 42 and 46 per cent. The ratio was considerably lower than for the other large banks that offered a full service to SMEs and corporate customers as discussed above, and reflected Abbey National's concentration towards the personal mortgage business.

5.455. The level of bad debt charge as a percentage of income increased, rising from 4 per cent in 1994 to 6 per cent in 1998, and then to 8 per cent in 1999. As Abbey National was predominantly in the mortgage market, its bad debt experience in the early 1990s was relatively better than that of the retail banks that lent to a wider spectrum of customers.

5.456. As outlined in Chapter 6, we estimated that Abbey National's total income from its SME banking business in 1999 was £[✂] million, or [✂] per cent of total Abbey National income, while net profit before tax and before allocation of central overheads was £[✂] million, or [✂] per cent of total Abbey National profit before tax. This was negligible compared with its total activities, but Abbey National noted its intention of increasing its SME banking business (see paragraph 5.451).

Balance sheets

5.457. Table 5.150 shows Abbey National's balance sheets from 1994 to 1999. Total assets (including long-term assurance assets) increased from £94.5 billion in 1994 to £181 billion in 1999. This was mainly because of increases in the following categories of assets:

(a) loans and advances to customers from £48.5 billion in 1994 to £75.2 billion in 1999 (55 per cent increase);

(b) debt securities from £32.3 billion to £59.4 billion in 1999; and

(c) assets of long-term assurance business from £4.2 billion in 1994 to £17.4 billion in 1999.

5.458. Total liabilities increased from £86.5 billion in 1994 to £157.2 billion in 1999. This was because of increases in customer accounts in credit from £38.1 billion to £59.9 billion, and increases in debt securities in issue from £23.9 billion to £51.4 billion. Shareholders' funds increased from £3.7 billion to £6.1 billion.

5.459. In common with other banks, the largest items within the bank's balance sheet were loans and advances to customers, and customers' accounts in credit (deposit and savings accounts). The level of debt securities assets in 1999 at £59 billion compared with debt securities in issue of £51 billion.

TABLE 5.150 **Abbey National: consolidated balance sheet, 1994 to 1999**

£ billion

As at 31 December

	1994	1995	1996	1997	1998	1999
Assets						
Cash and balances at central banks	0.2	0.1	0.2	0.3	0.3	0.7
Treasury bills and other eligible bills	0.4	0.2	0.1	1.6	2.1	1.1
Loans and advances to banks	2.9	3.6	2.8	8.3	7.4	11.5
Loans and advances to customers	48.5	51.1	64.2	66.9	72.3	75.2
Debt securities	32.3	35.2	39.7	46.5	54.2	59.4
Other investments	0.0	0.1	0.1	0.1	0.1	0.4
Intangible fixed assets	0.0	0.0	0.0	0.0	0.2	0.2
Tangible fixed assets	0.5	0.6	0.7	0.7	0.7	0.8
Net investment in finance leases	2.3	2.8	4.3	4.7	5.3	5.4
Assets under stock borrowing and lending agreements	0.0	0.0	0.0	6.7	15.0	0.0
Other assets	1.4	2.1	2.1	3.0	4.3	5.9
Prepayments and accrued income	1.6	1.8	1.9	2.0	2.4	2.7
	90.2	97.6	116.1	140.7	164.4	163.3
Assets of long-term assurance business	4.2	5.5	7.9	10.1	13.4	17.4
Total assets	94.5	103.1	124.0	150.8	177.8	180.7
Liabilities						
Deposits by banks	17.8	19.4	17.7	23.8	35.6	29.8
Customer accounts in credit	38.1	41.0	49.7	55.7	52.9	59.9
Debt securities in issue	23.9	26.1	35.2	40.2	43.0	51.4
Liabilities under stock borrowing and lending agreements	0.0	0.0	0.0	6.7	15.0	0.0
Other liabilities	2.2	2.1	3.2	3.0	4.9	7.3
Accruals and deferred income	2.6	2.4	2.6	2.8	3.0	2.9
Other provisions	0.5	0.6	1.0	1.1	1.2	1.3
Subordinated liabilities	1.5	2.1	2.4	2.5	3.3	4.6
Total liabilities	86.5	93.7	111.7	135.8	159.0	157.2
Shareholders' funds	3.7	3.9	4.4	4.9	5.4	6.1
	90.2	97.6	116.1	140.7	164.4	163.3
Retail life-fund assets attributable to policy-holders	4.2	5.5	7.9	10.1	13.4	17.4
Total liabilities and shareholders' funds	94.5	103.1	124.0	150.8	177.8	180.7
Performance indicators						*per cent*
Operating profit as a percentage of average shareholders' funds*	*	29	31	31	35	37

Source: Abbey National.

---

*Average shareholders' funds includes any capitalized goodwill.

5.460. In 1999 loans and advances to customers accounted for 42 per cent of total balance sheet assets, debt securities for 33 per cent, and loans and advances to banks of 6 per cent. Of the total loans and advances to customers, 86 per cent were mortgage loans, showing Abbey National's concentration in this activity. It estimated that less than 1 per cent of total loans and advances were to SME customers in 1999. Abbey National also estimated that in 1999 less than 1 per cent of total customer deposits were from SMEs.

5.461. Abbey National's operating profit as a percentage of average shareholders' funds (pre-tax return) increased from 29 per cent in 1995 to 37 per cent in 1999.

Bad debts

5.462. Table 5.151 shows Abbey National's level of closing bad debt provision, and the level of bad debt charges against profits between 1994 and 1999. The level of provision fluctuated over this period. In 1994 the provision was £361 million, then increased to £534 million by 1996, fell to £457 million in 1997 and then increased in 1998 and 1999 to £561 million and £529 million respectively. In 1994 the level of the provision equated to 0.7 per cent of Abbey National's total loan book, and this ratio has remained relatively constant to date. The mix between general and specific provisions has, however, changed over the period: the level of general provisions has increased while the level of specific provisions has generally decreased.

TABLE 5.151 **Abbey National: analysis of bad debt provision and charges to profit and loss, 1994 to 1999**

£ million

	1994	1995	1996	1997	1998	1999
Analysis of bad debt provision:						
General provision	71	66	95	117	199	193
Specific provision	290	417	439	340	362	336
Closing bad debt provision	361	483	534	457	561	529
Total bad debt charges	74	72	127	121	201	303
Performance indicators						per cent
Bad debt provision as a percentage of total loans	0.7	0.9	0.8	0.7	0.8	0.7
Bad debt charge as a percentage of total loans	0.2	0.1	0.2	0.2	0.3	0.4
Bad debt charge as a percentage of total income	4	4	5	5	6	8

Source: Abbey National.

5.463. The level of bad debt charge as a percentage of total loans has remained low compared with other banks, at around 0.2 per cent since 1994, only increasing to 0.3 per cent and then 0.4 per cent in 1998 and 1999. The low bad debt rate was consistent with Abbey National's focus as a mortgage lender on the security of property. Abbey National told us that the increase in the bad debt charge from 1997 to 1998 was due to asset growth and an increase in mortgage and unsecured lending arrears. The increase from 1998 to 1999 was a result of the acquisition of two point-of-sale businesses and a sales aid leasing business.

Capital adequacy

5.464. Table 5.152 shows capital adequacy data for Abbey National from 1995 to 1999. Between 1995 and 1997, Abbey National's Tier 1 ratio remained relatively constant at around 8.4 per cent. In 1998 and 1999, the ratio decreased to 7.3 and 7.7 per cent respectively. The total capital ratio was 11.7 per cent in 1995 and 1996, dropped down to 10.2 per cent in 1998, but increased again to 11.6 per cent in 1999.

TABLE 5.152 **Abbey National: capital adequacy data, 1995 to 1999**

£ billion

As at 31 December

	1995	1996	1997	1998	1999
RWAs	47.0	51.9	58.0	71.3	75.9
Tier 1 capital	3.9	4.4	4.9	5.2	5.9
Tier 2 capital	1.5	1.7	1.6	2.0	2.9
Total net capital resources	5.5	6.1	6.4	7.2	8.8
					per cent
Ratios					
Tier 1	8.4	8.5	8.4	7.3	7.7
Total	11.7	11.7	11.1	10.2	11.6

Source: Abbey National.

Halifax

History

5.465. Until September 2001, Halifax was listed on the London Stock Exchange. At 29 June 2001 its market capitalization was £18.5 billion and its price:earnings ratio was 14.8. In September 2001 Halifax merged with BoS and shares in a new holding company, HBOS plc, are now listed (see paragraph 5.271).

5.466. Halifax was established in 1853, as The Halifax Permanent Benefit Building and Investment Society. It converted to plc status in June 1997 and listed on the London Stock Exchange. It is currently focused on providing personal financial services including mortgages, long-term savings, home, motor and creditor insurance, retail banking mainly to personal customers, consumer credit and share dealing. Halifax operates only in the UK and has almost 900 branches and over 600 agencies.

5.467. Halifax is a member of APACS and BACS but not CCCC. Cheque clearing for Halifax is performed under an agency arrangement with Barclays.

Business structure serving the SME banking business

5.468. Halifax does not currently offer banking services to SMEs. However, it told us that it potentially could serve the SME banking business, if not in total then in part, and it was currently considering these options. Halifax's initial thoughts were that it could focus on deposit-based activity, which, it believed, could be provided more competitively for some SMEs.

5.469. Halifax told us that it had announced plans to merge with BoS, to form a new banking group to be called HBOS plc. Halifax noted that BoS currently provided a full range of banking services to SMEs, with a strong customer base in Scotland. It was of the view that the new group would be in a position to use the skills and experience of BoS to increase its presence in the SME banking business throughout the whole of the UK.

Financial performance

5.470. Table 5.153 shows the profitability of Halifax in 1998 and 1999. The bank's operating income in 1999 was £3.3 billion, operating expenses were £1.6 billion, and the level of bad debt charge was £123 million. As a result, profit before tax was £1.6 billion (48 per cent of income). Halifax's cost:income ratio in 1999 was 48 per cent.

TABLE 5.153 **Halifax: consolidated profit and loss account, 1998 and 1999**

£ billion

Years ended 31 December

	1998	1999
Net interest income	2.4	2.5
Net fees and commissions	0.6	0.6
Other income	0.2	0.2
Operating income	3.2	3.3
Operating expenses	−1.4	−1.6
Operating profit before provisions	1.8	1.7
Bad and doubtful debts charge	−0.1	−0.1
Operating profit before tax and other items	1.7	1.6
Other Items	0.0	0.0
Operating profit before tax	1.7	1.6
Tax	−0.5	−0.5
Net profit after tax	1.2	1.1
Minority interests (non-equity)	0.0	0.0
Profit attributable to shareholders	1.2	1.1
Dividends	−0.5	−0.5
Profit retained for the financial year	0.7	0.5
Number of employees (full-time)	26,506	26,583
Number of employees (part-time)	9,872	10,645
Performance indicators		*per cent*
Tax charge as a percentage of profit before tax	31	34
Cost:income ratio	43	48

Source: Halifax.

Balance sheets

5.471. Table 5.154 shows Halifax's balance sheets for 1998 and 1999. Total assets in 1999 were £162 billion. The largest category of asset was loans and advances to customers at £97 billion, including £90 billion of loans fully secured on residential property, £5 billion of other secured advances, and £2 billion of other unsecured loans. Halifax's tangible fixed assets were around £900 million or 0.6 per cent of total assets.

TABLE 5.154 **Halifax: consolidated balance sheet, 1998 and 1999**

£ billion

As at 31 December

	1998	1999
Assets		
Cash and balances at central banks	0.2	0.4
Treasury bills and other eligible bills	2.0	2.8
Loans and advances to banks	10.8	10.8
Loans and advances to customers	85.1	96.6
Debt securities	23.8	22.8
Other investments	0.2	0.2
Intangible fixed assets	0.0	0.4
Tangible fixed assets	0.9	0.9
Other assets	0.3	0.3
Prepayments and accrued income	1.2	1.1
Long-term assurance business attributable to shareholders	0.9	1.7
Long-term assurance assets attributable to shareholders	19.1	24.2
Total assets	144.6	162.1
Liabilities		
Amount owed to credit institutions	9.4	11.9
Customer accounts in credit	85.0	87.9
Debt securities in issue	16.4	23.5
Other liabilities	1.4	1.3
Accruals and deferred income	4.2	3.4
Other provisions	0.1	0.1
Subordinated liabilities	1.9	2.9
Total liabilities	118.3	130.9
Minority interests	0.0	0.7
Equity shareholders' funds	7.1	6.3
Long-term assurance liabilities attributable to policy-holders	19.1	24.2
	144.6	162.1
Contingent liabilities		
Contingent liabilities	0.6	0.0
Commitments	4.5	5.5

Source: Halifax.

5.472. Total liabilities in 1999 were £131 billion, which included £88 billion of customer accounts in credit, and £23 billion of debt securities. Shareholders' funds in 1999 were £6.3 billion. At the end of 1999 Halifax reported total commitments of £5.5 billion.

Bad debts

5.473. Table 5.155 shows Halifax's level of closing bad debt provision, and the level of bad debt charge against profits for 1998 and 1999. The level of bad debt provisions in 1999 was £555 million, which equated to 0.6 per cent of the total loan book. The bad debt charge was 0.1 per cent of total loans for both 1998 and 1999. The low bad debt rate was consistent with Halifax's focus as a mortgage lender on secured property.

TABLE 5.155 **Halifax: analysis of bad debt provision and charges to profit and loss account, 1998 and 1999**

£ million

	1998	1999
Analysis of bad debt provision:		
General provision	203	221
Specific provision	351	334
Closing bad debt provision	554	555
Total bad debt profit and loss charge	96	123

Performance indicators	per cent	
Bad debt provision as a percentage of total loans	0.7	0.6
Bad debt charge as a percentage of total loans	0.1	0.1
Bad debt charge as a percentage of total income	3.0	4.0

Source: Halifax.

Nationwide Building Society

History

5.474. Nationwide is the UK's fourth largest mortgage lender and has its origins in regional building societies dating back to the mid-1800s. Like all building societies, Nationwide is regulated by the Building Societies Commission.

5.475. Nationwide has a mutual status, which means that it is owned by its members (both depositors and borrowers) and is run day to day by an executive management team overseen by an elected board of directors. In its financial accounts, Nationwide stated that it aimed to earn only enough profit to finance the growth in its business and to return anything extra to its members in the form of better borrowing and savings rates and other benefits.

Business structure serving the SME banking business

5.476. Nationwide provides limited banking services to certain classes of SMEs in the UK. It offers an interest-paying savings account called BusinessInvestor with cheque-book access and it also lends to small businesses when the advance can be secured by commercial property. Nationwide told us that its core focus has been on the provision of financial services for the private customer. It also told us that it had not ruled out future developments to its banking services and business current account offering for SMEs. However, Nationwide believed that at present it could not contribute a truly credible alternative to the competitor offerings, stating that its branch network, head offices and staff were not properly established to meet the cash-handling or relationship management (business advice) needs that it regarded as crucial to SMEs. Nationwide is a member of APACS, CCCC, BACS and LINK Interchange Ltd and is responsible for its own cheque clearance processes. It told us that it considered its systems in this area were efficient.

Financial performance

5.477. Table 5.156 shows the profitability of Nationwide for 1999 and 2000. The bank's operating income in 2000 was £1.1 billion, operating expenses were £663 million, and the level of bad debt charge was £38 million. As a result, profit before tax was £424 million.

£ million

Years ended 4 April

	1999	2000
Net interest income	853	970
Net fees and commissions	137	86
Other income	61	69
Operating income	1,051	1,125
Operating expenses	−584	−663
Operating profit before provisions	468	462
Bad and doubtful debts charge	−60	−38
Operating profit before tax	408	424
Tax	−136	−136
Net profit after tax	272	288
Number of employees (full-time)	9,313	9,741
Number of employees (part-time)	2,897	3,167

Performance indicators		*per cent*
Tax charge as a percentage of profit before tax	33	32
Cost:income ratio	56	59

Source: Nationwide.

5.478. Nationwide's cost:income ratio in 2000 was 59 per cent. This ratio is high compared with that of similar, but not mutual, mortgage-based institutions such as Abbey National with a cost:income ratio in the same period of 43 per cent (see paragraphs 5.453 and 5.454), and the excess is equivalent to approximately £416 million of income for Nationwide. As mentioned previously, Nationwide is a mutual, and profits of the organization are returned to members in the form of lower prices. The lower prices resulted in a lower income for the building society and therefore a higher cost:income ratio.

Balance sheets

5.479. Table 5.157 shows Nationwide's balance sheets for 1999 and 2000. Total assets in 2000 were £64 billion. The largest category of asset was loans and advances to customers at £48 billion, including £42 billion of loans fully secured on residential property, £5 billion of loans fully secured on land, and £1 billion of 'other' loans, which includes loans secured by commercial property.

5.480. Total liabilities in 2000 were £64 billion which included £41.6 billion of share account balances (ie members' accounts in credit) and £5.7 billion of customer accounts in credit. Nationwide's subscribed capital of £296 million is made up of two tranches of unsecured 'All Permanent Interest Bearing Shares' that were issued in March 2000. The first tranche expires in March 2015, or any fifth anniversary thereafter, and the second tranche expires on March 2030, or any fifth anniversary thereafter. Nationwide stated in its Year 2000 financial report that the debt raising would ensure that its capital ratios remained satisfactory even if growth continued at a rapid pace. The general reserve balance of £3.2 billion represented accumulated retained profits.

5.481. In 2000 Nationwide reported total commitments of £1.6 billion, which was nearly double the amount for the previous year.

TABLE 5.157 **Nationwide: consolidated balance sheet, 1999 and 2000**

£ million

As at 4 April

	1999	2000
Assets		
Cash and balances at central banks	161	200
Loans and advances to credit institutions	790	1,528
Loans and advances to customers	41,497	47,818
Debt securities	8,520	11,879
Other investments	4	4
Intangible fixed assets	32	21
Tangible fixed assets	664	696
Other assets	1,018	1,539
Prepayments and accrued income	269	325
Total assets	52,953	64,010
Liabilities		
Shares	37,442	41,646
Amount owed to credit institutions	806	2,316
Amounts owed to other customers	4,621	5,698
Debt securities in issue	5,269	8,476
Other liabilities	1,309	1,722
Accruals and deferred income	306	340
Other provisions	26	26
Subordinated liabilities	237	233
Subscribed capital	0	296
Revaluation reserve	71	102
General reserve	2,867	3,155
Total liabilities	52,953	64,010
Contingent liabilities		
Commitments	843	1,611

Source: Nationwide.

Bad debts

5.482. Table 5.158 shows Nationwide's level of closing bad debt provision, and the level of bad debt charge against profits for 1999 and 2000. The level of bad debt provisions in 1999 was £190 million, which equated to 0.4 per cent of the total loan book. The bad debt charge was 0.1 per cent of total loans for both 1998 and 1999. The low bad debt rate was consistent with Nationwide's focus as a mortgage lender on secured property.

TABLE 5.158 **Nationwide: analysis of bad debt provision and charges to profit and loss account, 1999 and 2000**

£ million

	1999	2000
Analysis of bad debt provision:		
General provision	72	105
Specific provision	122	85
Closing bad debt provision	194	190
Total bad debt profit and loss charge	60	38
Performance indicators	per cent	
Bad debt provision as a percentage of total loans	0.5	0.4
Bad debt charge as a percentage of total loans	0.1	0.1
Bad debt charge as a percentage of total income	5.7	3.4

Source: Nationwide.

Basle 2 proposals

Overview

5.483. On 15 January 2001 the Basle Committee on Banking Supervision released a detailed proposal for the replacement of the 1988 Capital Accord with a more risk-sensitive capital adequacy framework. The Committee sought comments on the new Accord by 31 May 2001 and expected a final version to be published around the end of 2001 for implementation in 2004. In June 2001, the Committee announced that it had received over 250 comments on its January 2001 proposals. In order to review and consider all the comments received, the Committee decided to modify the timetable for completion and implementation of the new Accord. The Committee said that it would release a complete and fully specified proposal for an additional round of consultation in early 2002 and would finalize the new Accord during 2002. The Committee envisaged an implementation date of 2005 for the new Accord. The outline of the proposed new Accord in this chapter reflects the Committee's January 2001 consultative document. As indicated, the Committee will be releasing a further consultative document early in 2002 and this could incorporate material changes from the January 2001 proposals. The Committee referred to a number of specific points in its June 2001 statement (see paragraph 5.530).

5.484. The intent of the new framework is to improve safety and soundness in the financial system by placing more emphasis on banks' own internal control and management, the supervisory review process and market discipline. Whereas the 1988 Accord provided essentially only one option for measuring a bank's appropriate capital level, the new framework provides a spectrum of approaches from simple to advanced methodologies for the measurement of both credit risk and operational risk in determining capital levels. Banks adopt those approaches that best fit their level of sophistication and risk profile. The framework also deliberately builds in incentives for stronger and more accurate risk measurement.

5.485. The new framework is less prescriptive than the original Accord but potentially more complex. It offers a range of approaches for banks to use, if capable of using more risk-sensitive analytical methodologies.

Structure of the new Accord

5.486. The new Accord consists of three mutually reinforcing pillars:

(a) first pillar: minimum capital requirement;

(b) second pillar: supervisory review process—see paragraph 5.497; and

(c) third pillar: market discipline—see paragraph 5.498.

5.487. The Basle Committee stressed the need for rigorous application of all three pillars and noted that it planned to work actively with supervisors to achieve the effective implementation of all aspects of the Accord.

The first pillar: minimum capital requirement

5.488. The new framework maintains both the current definition of capital and the minimum requirement of 8 per cent of capital to RWAs. The revision focuses on improvements in the measurement of risks, ie the calculation of the denominator in the capital ratio or RWAs. New approaches to the measurement of credit and risk have been proposed. A new capital adequacy requirement for operational risk has been proposed. There is no change to the current calculation of market risk.

Credit risk

5.489. The credit risk measurement methods are more complex than those in the current Accord. Two principal options are being proposed. The first is the standardized approach and the second the 'internal ratings based' (IRB) approach. There are also two variants of the IRB approach, 'foundati and 'advanced'. The use of either IRB approach will be subject to approval by the relevant banki supervisor.

5.490. The standardized approach is conceptually the same approach as that contained in the Accord, but it is intended better to reflect the risk of an exposure. The bank allocates a risk weight to each of its on- and off-balance-sheet exposures and produces a sum of RWA values. Individual risk weights currently depend upon the broad category of borrower, ie governments, banks or corporates. Under the new Accord, the risk weights are to be refined by reference to a rating provided by an external credit assessment institution (such as an independent ratings agency) that meets strict standards. For example, for non-bank corporate lending the existing Accord provides only one risk weight category of 100 per cent, but the new Accord will provide four categories of 20 per cent, 50 per cent, 100 per cent and 150 per cent depending on the ratings of the corporate (if a corporate is unrated, the risk weight will be 100 per cent). The introduction of a 150 per cent risk weight is a new concept. It is to be used for lowly-rated corporates (below B–), and effectively means that capital of at least 12 per cent of the exposure will be required in support, rather than the previous minimum of 8 per cent.

5.491. Under the IRB approach, banks will be allowed to use their internal view of borrower credit-worthiness, to assess credit risk in their portfolios. Distinct analytical frameworks will be provided for different types of loan exposure, for example corporate and retail lending, where each can have different loss characteristics. It is currently uncertain as to what extent small business lending should fall within the retail portfolios, since *(a)* there are similar credit assessment techniques in the two sectors, and *(b)* it is argued that there is a lower volatility of loss for a given expected loss in the SME book than in cor-porate lending more generally.

5.492. Under the IRB approach, a bank assesses each borrower's creditworthiness, and the results are translated into estimates of a potential future loss amount, which forms the basis of capital require-ments. The framework allows for both a foundation method and more advanced methodologies for cor-porate, government and bank exposures (see paragraphs 5.511 to 5.520 for retail exposures). In the 'foundation' methodology, banks estimate the probability of default associated with each borrower and the banking supervisors will supply the other inputs to the risk-weighting calculation (see paragraph 5.506). In the 'advanced' methodology, a bank with sufficiently developed internal capital allocation processes will be permitted to supply other inputs, such as estimates of 'exposure at default'. Under both the foundation and advanced IRB approaches, the range of risk weights will be wider than those in the standardized approach, resulting in a greater risk sensitivity.

5.493. The new framework also introduces more risk-sensitive approaches to the treatment of collat-eral, guarantees, credit derivatives and asset securitization, under both the standard and IRB approaches, although the details have still to be decided.

Operational risk

5.494. The current Accord set a capital requirement in terms of credit and market risk. In addition to its efforts to introduce greater credit risk sensitivity, the Basle Committee has been working with banks to develop a suitable capital charge for operational risk (for example, the risk of loss from inadequate or failed processes, people and systems, or from external events such as computer failures, poor documen-tation, or fraud). Operational risk considerations are currently reflected in arriving at the target/trigger ratios.

5.495. The Basle Committee noted that the work on operational risk is in a developmental stage, but three different approaches of increasing sophistication have been identified: basic indicator, standardized and internal measurement. The basic indicator approach specifies one indicator, for example gross income, as the driver of operational risk for a bank's total activity. The standardized approach identifies different risk indicators for different business lines (see paragraph 5.502). The internal measurement approach requires banks to utilize their internal loss data in the estimation of required capital for oper-ational risk. Based on work to date, the Committee suggested that operational risk on average would con-stitute approximately 20 per cent of the overall capital requirements under the new framework.

sle Committee has stressed that its goal is neither to raise nor lower the regulatory
of operational risk, for internationally-active banks using the standardized approach.
the standardized approach, the Committee's goal with the IRB approach is to ensure that
capital requirement is sufficient to address underlying risks. However, the IRB approach
incentives for banks to migrate from the standardized approach to the IRB approach,
nould be recognized that the criteria to be satisfied are challenging.

econd pillar: supervisory review process

5.497. The supervisory review process requires banking supervisors to ensure that each bank has
sound internal processes in place to assess the adequacy of its capital based on a thorough evaluation of
its risks. The new framework stresses the importance of a bank's management developing an internal
capital assessment process and setting targets for capital that are commensurate with the bank's particular risk profiles and control environment. Supervisors would be responsible for evaluating how well
banks are assessing their capital adequacy needs relative to their risks. This internal process would then
be subject to supervisory review and intervention where appropriate.

The third pillar: market discipline

5.498. The third pillar of the new framework aims to bolster market discipline through enhanced disclosure by banks. Effective disclosure is essential to ensure that market participants can better understand
a bank's risk profile and the adequacy of its capital position. The new framework sets out disclosure
requirements and recommendations in several areas, including the way a bank calculates its capital
requirements and determines its risk assessment methods. The core set of disclosure recommendations
applies to all banks, with more detailed requirements for supervisory recognition of internal methodologies for credit risk, credit risk mitigation techniques and asset securitization.

The effect of the new Accord on the calculation of RWAs for SME banking business

5.499. At this stage the effect of the Accord on the calculation of RWAs generated by activities to
serve SMEs will be twofold. First, changes in the measurement of credit risk for regulatory purposes are
likely to apply to many SMEs. Secondly, the new operational risk measurements will require capital to
be held in relation to the operational risk inherent in all aspects of a bank's business including its SME
banking business. The FSA noted that it already took account of operational risk in setting firm specific
capital ratios and that therefore UK banks already faced an implicit 'capital charge' in respect of operational risk. The FSA told us that to the extent that Basle/EC widen the scope of the international rules to
bring in an operational risk charge, it will have to recalibrate its trigger and target ratios.

Credit risk

5.500. Under the old accord, the risk-weighted measure for SME exposures was straightforward.
Except where the exposure was guaranteed by an OECD bank or cash-collateralized, on-balance-sheet
exposures were treated as exposures to corporate counterparties and were risk-weighted at 100 per cent.
For off-balance-sheet exposures, the risk weight will reflect the appropriate credit conversion factor
(being 0, 20, 50 or 100 per cent) and therefore the exposure's risk weight could be below 100 per cent.

5.501. Under the new accord, RWAs resulting from SME banking business are to be calculated in
one of three ways: the standardized approach, the foundation IRB approach or the advanced IRB
approach, as discussed below.

Standardized approach

5.502. This approach is similar in application to the old accord. However, exposures to corporate counterparties are now assigned risk weights based on credit assessments by ratings agencies. The new risk weights for corporate counterparties are as follows:

Credit assessment	AAA to AA–	A+ to A–	BBB+ to BB–	Below BB–	Unrated
Proposed risk weights	20%	50%	100%	150%	100%

5.503. As SME businesses would predominantly be unrated, the 100 per cent risk weight would continue to apply to most of the SME counterparties. However, a 150 per cent risk weight could potentially apply if the company was rated below BB–.

5.504. We note that the 100 per cent risk weight for unrated corporates represents a floor and the Basle Committee is encouraging Banking Supervisors to increase this standard risk weight when warranted by the overall default experience in their jurisdiction. The FSA told us that it did not envisage applying a higher than 100 per cent weight for unrated corporate exposures that would not otherwise fall in the 150 per cent weighting band.

5.505. The FSA told us that unrated exposures varied in quality from those that were effectively prime investment grade to those that were impaired or carried expected losses of 20 per cent or more. The concern was to avoid the implication that a minimum 8 per cent capital requirement was economically the correct figure if a bank's unrated exposures were biased heavily towards speculative corporate debt, private equity or certain emerging market exposures. The 8 per cent figure was intended as a reasonable minimum capital level against a diversified portfolio of bankable[1] assets, without large concentrations to speculative sectors. To the extent that UK banks already had concentrations of high-risk exposure, the FSA aimed to capture this in the trigger ratio that it set. The FSA added that for any well-run bank, the appropriate action to take in respect of impaired debt was for the institution to set up a provision, rather than for banking supervisors to adjust the appropriate capital target. In order to carry a provision in respect of an impairment, however, it would be necessary for the bank to be able to demonstrate that the debt was impaired, ie based upon current information and events the creditworthiness of the borrower has undergone a deterioration such that the debt is no longer expected to be recoverable in full.

Foundation internal ratings-based approach

5.506. The Foundation IRB approach is available to those banks whose internal ratings systems meet robust supervisory standards. Under this approach, RWA values for corporate exposures are calculated using the following formulae:

RWA = EAD x RWc

where EAD is the exposure level at time of default and RWc is the exposure's risk weight.

RWc is calculated as the smaller of

LGD/50 x BRWc(PD), or 12.50 × LGD

where PD is the probability of default, LGD is the loss incurred given a default event and BRWc is benchmark risk weight provided by banking supervisors, which is a function of the probability of default.

5.507. The banks provide the probability of default rate from their own internal credit rating systems. This must represent a conservative view of a long-run average probability of default for each borrower grade and must be based upon historical experience and empirical evidence. The other risk factors will be standardized estimates provided by the banking supervisor.

---

[1]In the sense that these are performing and would continue to meet reasonable underwriting standards.

5.508. The Basle Committee also proposed that a 'granularity' adjustment should be made to the above formulae, which would benefit those lenders that had numerous exposures as compared with lenders with more concentrated portfolios. This would result in a capital incentive for a bank to lend money to a number of SMEs rather than lend the same money to a single large corporate borrower. In other words, a more diverse portfolio of lending could lead to a lower capital requirement to take account of the reduced risk of large unexpected losses.

5.509. We performed some worked examples below:

(a) Where a loan is outstanding to an SME for £100 and where the probability of default for that counterparty is calculated by the bank to be 0.7 per cent. Per the Basle Committee's suggested risk-weight matrix, the BRWc for a PD of 0.7 is 100 per cent. The Committee also recommended that the LGD of a senior claim on a corporate without specifically recognized collateral should be 50 per cent. Therefore the RWA value in this example will be:

$$£100 * ((50/50) * 100\%) = £100$$

(b) If the same loan as described in (a) was now a subordinated facility, then the LGD would change. The Committee recommended a figure of 75 per cent for subordinated loans. Hence the RWA calculation would be:

$$£100 * ((75/50) * 100\%) = £150$$

(c) If the same loan as described in (a) was made to a lower-rated counterparty with a PD of 2 per cent, then, as the Committee recommended a BRWc of 192 per cent for a PD of 2 per cent, the RWA value would be:

$$£100 * ((50/50) * 192\%) = £192$$

Advanced internal ratings-based approach

5.510. The advanced IRB approach will only be available for banking organizations that meet more rigorous supervisory standards. Under this approach, the same formulae as outlined above will still be used to calculate RWA values, but the risk components, LGD and EAD factors will be assessed internally by the bank. Banks using the advanced IRB approach will also be required to include a maturity factor for the loan portfolio in their calculations. Long-term loans will be considered riskier than short-term loans and will generate a larger capital requirement.

Treatment of retail exposures that may potentially include services to SMEs

5.511. The Basle Committee is proposing an IRB approach for retail exposures that is distinct from that for the corporate portfolio. It will build on the basic framework outlined above, but also reflect the particular characteristics of retail exposures. The Committee noted that one of the most significant differences between corporate and retail portfolios lay in the way that banks differentiated their various risks. For retail exposures, the use of a fixed rating scale and the assignment of borrower ratings is much less common. Rather on the basis of borrower, transaction/product and other characteristics, banks commonly divide the portfolio into segments made up of exposures with similar risk characteristics.

5.512. Banks will be required for IRB purposes to group retail exposures into internally-determined segments in accordance with a set of minimum requirements. The assessment of risk components will be made at the segment level rather than at the rating grade level, as is the case for corporate exposures. Banks will provide their own estimates of EAD, PD/LGD, or EL (being 'expected loss'). This is because many banks have large amounts of detailed data on risk and borrower performance in their retail portfolios.

5.513. The separation of retail exposures from corporate exposures has arisen because preliminary research by the Basle Committee has indicated that retail exposures are less risky than corporate exposures. It said the following: 'One of the industry surveys indicated that retail risk weights should be approximately half of the magnitude of the corporate risk weights for given PD/LGD pairs. They further suggest that this rough 50 per cent rule would hold regardless of product type or country. There was some limited degree of support on an individual bank basis.'

5.514. The Committee used the above supposition as a basis for deriving a risk-weight framework for retail exposures. However, it stressed that the risk weights provided should be treated with caution and were subject to further discussion.

5.515. It is currently unclear as to what extent a bank's SME banking business will fall within the definition of retail. The Committee proposed a definition, which sought to capture homogeneous portfolios comprising a large number of low-value loans with either a consumer or business focus, and where the incremental risk of any single exposure was small. This could therefore include smaller SMEs within this grouping.

5.516. The Committee noted that there were some advantages to classifying small business lending as part of the retail portfolio, since many banks treated such exposures on a pooled basis. Also in some cases it was difficult to separate lending to businesses from personal lending. On the other hand, the Committee was concerned that some small business lending had more volatile loss patterns than other retail portfolios. To the extent that there were capital differences between retail and corporate portfolios, it would be undesirable for all such lending to be classified as retail regardless of risk. The Basle Committee was therefore considering whether further criteria were appropriate to distinguish between these cases. This could include global limits on the size of small business loans that could be classified as retail or other criteria such as requiring a connection between lending to the small business enterprise and lending to the principals of the business as individuals.

5.517. The FSA told us that as it understood the discussion in Basle, the intention was to allow banks that used the same scorecard techniques for small businesses as for personal customers to use the IRB approach. But it was felt inappropriate by a number of countries to extend the definition of retail to those SMEs that were incorporated and had significant tangible assets or turnover and would be assessed by banks as corporate banking customers. The required capital levels proposed for retail exposures were significantly lower than those proposed to support general corporate lending. The reason for this, as suggested by the FSA, was the much greater volatility of corporate banking losses from year to year compared with retail banking where, for a given 'expected loss', the variation (or unexpected loss) around this number was generally much lower.

5.518. There has been much comment in the media on the Basle 2 proposals. In particular there has been mention of the pro-cyclicality of the new system, and the fact that banks may need more capital in bad times, for example recessions. There was concern that this might discourage banks from lending in the bad times and encourage them to lend imprudently in the good, with the effect of making economic cycles more severe. In the *Financial Times* of 17 January 2001, a commentator noted:

> The framework proposed by the Basle Committee risks making this pro-cyclicality sharper. Not only will banks' capital vary up and down with the cycle; the RWAs will vary too—in the opposite direction. The proposals will mean that risks are assessed on the basis of a more realistic view of the probability of default. In an economic upswing, the risks are likely to fall, while in a downswing they will rise. So the ratio of capital to RWAs will change in both the numerator and the denominator. In good times, the ratios will look healthier than under the existing framework and in bad times they will look worse.

5.519. The FSA responded to the above concerns by noting that it was concerned to ensure that while the new Accord was risk sensitive, it did not generate excessive volatility in bank behaviour. The FSA noted that the Basle Committee had a group looking at this issue, and in the context of the IRB approach it believed that there was a good case for basing the estimates of probability of default and recovery rates (for the advanced approach) in long-term estimates.

5.520. The FSA also commented that one advantage of the internal ratings was that it gave those running the bank better management information about the composition and credit quality of the bank's book. It said that there should be less scope for senior management being 'surprised' by the impact of changes in the risk composition of their portfolio. It had been argued that one of the issues in connection with the early 1990s recession was that banks had less appreciation of the structure of their lending in the late 1980s and were taken by surprise by the extent of their losses and the need to subsequently provision (1990 to 1992). This might have contributed to the rapid reassessment of underwriting and credit quality standards at the time.

Operational risk

5.521. Operational risk is defined by the Basle Committee as 'the risk of direct or indirect loss resulting from inadequate or failed internal processes, people and systems, or from external events'. This definition includes legal risk. Work on operational risk is in a development stage and current proposals are therefore subject to change (see paragraph 5.495).

5.522. The Committee proposed three methods for calculating operational risk capital requirements in a continuum of increasing sophistication and risk sensitivity: the basic indicator approach, the standard approach and the internal measurement approach. Banks are encouraged to move along the spectrum of available approaches as they develop more sophisticated operational risk measurement systems and practices. Banks will be permitted to use the standardized approach for some business lines and the internal measurement approach for others. Banks will not be allowed to choose to revert to simpler approaches once they have been approved for more advanced approaches.

5.523. The Basic Indicator Approach requires banks to hold capital for operational risk equal to a fixed percentage (denoted Alpha) of gross income.

5.524. The standardized approach requires banks to divide their activities into standardized business units and business lines. Within each business line, there is a specified broad indicator that reflects the size or volume of banks' activities in that area. The indicator serves as a rough proxy for the amount of operational risk within each of these business lines. Table 5.159 shows the proposed business units, business lines and indicators.

TABLE 5.159 **Basle 2 proposals: business units and proposed operational risk indicators under the standardized approach**

Business units	Business lines	Indicators	'Capital' beta factors
Investment Banking	Corporate finance	Gross income	B_1
	Trading and sales	Gross income or VAR	B_2
Banking	Retail banking	Annual average assets	B_3
	Commercial banking	Annual average assets	B_4
	Payment and Settlement	Annual settlement throughput	B_5
Others	Retail brokerage	Gross income	B_6
Others	Asset management	Total funds under management	B_7

Source: Basle Committee.

5.525. Within each business line, the capital required is calculated by multiplying the indicator by a capital factor assigned to it. The betas will be set by the banking supervisor and will serve as a rough proxy for the industry-wide relationship between the operational risk loss experience for a given business line and the indicator for that business line. The total operational risk capital requirement is calculated as the simple summation of the regulatory capital values across each of the business lines.

5.526. The internal measurement approach derives a capital requirement for the operational risk of banks by reference to the following procedures:

(a) A bank's activities are categorized into the same business lines as in the standardized approach. A broad set of operational risk types is defined and applied across business lines.

(b) Within each business line, the banking supervisor specifies an exposure indicator (EI) which is the proxy for the size of each business line's operational risk exposure to each risk type.

(c) For each business line banks use their internal loss data to determine a parameter representing the probability of loss event (PE), and a parameter representing the loss given that event (LGE). The product of EI, PE and LGE is used to calculate the expected loss (EL).

(d) The banking supervisor supplies a factor (denoted gamma) for each business line. Gamma translates the expected loss into a capital requirement and is determined by the supervisor, based on industry-wide data. The capital charge for each business line is the product of gamma and the expected loss.

(e) The overall operational risk capital requirement for a bank is the sum of all the resulting products of gamma and expected loss.

5.527. There has been much comment in the press over the Basle Committee's attempt to measure operational risk. In an article in the *Financial Times* on 23 January 2001 a commentator wrote:

> Is a capital cushion the correct protection against the errors of inadequate people? And who can quantify the risk of employees' catastrophic mistakes or define the correct amount of capital to provide against them. Risks traditionally covered by bank capital—market and credit risk—are quantifiable because they result from recorded contracts and commitments. Catastrophic operational failures of the kind that bring banks down are typically unknown ones. They tick away undetected in the records until they explode. Banks that are clever enough to enumerate their errors and quantify their risks do not protect themselves with a capital cushion: they strengthen their weak processes.

5.528. The FSA told us that although Basle 2 would require operational risk capital to be held for the first time against banks' SME banking business, the SME banking business had not been singled out for special treatment. The cited business lines included 'commercial banking' and 'retail banking'. In addition the FSA said that it set individual capital ratios (trigger ratios) at or above the Basle/EC minimum 8 per cent requirement. One of the reasons for doing this had been to capture various operational and managerial risks that were not adequately addressed by the current standardized approach (which was based on credit risk). When the FSA comes to implement the Basle/EC rules, it will need to recalibrate banks' trigger ratios to ensure that it does not 'double count' operational risk.

5.529. Finally the FSA said that the IRB approach would oblige banks suddenly to discriminate against SMEs. It said that banks (in an unscientific way) had always charged SMEs higher margins than most other corporate borrowers, and the larger banks had sought to become more scientific in their approach to lending through the use of grading systems and economic capital models to supplement a branch manager's judgement. The FSA said that the IRB approach followed this trend and that even if the amount of regulatory capital allocated to certain SME exposures increased, this might have no impact on pricing if this was not a binding constraint. In addition, the Basle proposals included a widening of recognized collateral and guarantors. Within the corporate foundation IRB approach, eligible commercial and residential real estate would be recognized for the purpose of reducing the loss-given default. The FSA noted that this might be of particular importance to SMEs. A number of the banks disagreed with the position of the FSA on the implications of Basle 2 for the pricing of services to SMEs. One bank told us that it would price to reflect perceived risk. If capital against an SME exposure increased to reflect the inherent riskiness of the exposure, there would be a related cost of that capital. Pricing on a cost-reflective basis therefore, prima facie, the bank would have to change prices to customers, in the same way as if there was a change in the costs of its other inputs.

Possible further changes to the Basle 2 proposals

5.530. When announcing the revised timetable for introduction of the new Accord (paragraph 5.483), the Committee said that, in the light of the comments received, the target proportion (of 20 per cent) of regulatory capital attributed to cover operational risk would be reduced in line with the view that this reflected too large an allocation of regulatory capital to this risk as the Committee had defined it. The Committee said that it was considering numerous other comments and suggestions related to operational risk. In addition the Committee said that it believed further efforts were needed to ensure appropriate treatment of credit exposures relating to SMEs, which was likely to lead to lower capital for SME banking business lending compared with the proposals in the January 2001 consultative paper.

6 The profitability of the banks' services to SMEs

Contents

Introduction

6.1. In this chapter, we present the financial information prepared for the banks primarily involved in the SME market to show the performance of their SME banking business. Chapter 5 covered the overall financial performance of the banks and showed the relative importance of their services to SMEs and any special issues regarding their capital structure and the supervisory regime to protect depositors from loss. Chapter 7 will deal with comparison of banks' returns with cost of capital to consider whether returns are at a level more than necessary to finance the banks' services to SMEs.

6.2. We asked the four largest clearing groups in the UK, namely Barclays, HSBC, Lloyds TSB, NatWest and RBS, to provide us with financial information for SME banking business over the period 1989 to 2000. We also asked BoS to provide us with similar financial information over the period 1997 to 2000, as well as information on its bad debts record since 1989. These six clearing groups account for most of the current SME market in England, Wales and Scotland. We also asked smaller banks serving particular regions, for example Northern Ireland, to give us relevant information from 1997 to 2000 as well as information covering a longer period for their bad debt record with SMEs.

6.3. The six largest clearing groups in the UK told us that they did not have a business unit within their existing organizational structure that matched our definition of SME banking business. Some banks were able to give detailed financial information only for recent years and in some cases we had to make best estimates, based on information contained in published accounts or management accounts. For the smaller banks, most of their business services were to SMEs within our definition, as they did not have many customers with turnover greater than £25 million.

6.4. As appropriate, we note information from the banks' services to SMEs on bad debts; product development costs; forward plans and cost savings; and advertising and marketing.

6.5. In Chapter 7 we look at the arguments put to us relating to *(a)* determination of the banks' capital base for the purpose of calculating economic returns; *(b)* allocation of banks' capital to their respective activities; and *(c)* the assessment of the effect of these methodologies on the results for specific banks. These issues included considerations of the replacement cost of assets, the treatment of brands and other intangible assets in the capital base, goodwill on acquisitions, the need for capital to cover a bank's risks, and determining the cost of capital. We then compare profits from SME banking business with the cost of capital and examine cost:income ratios and efficiency; margins from specific banking products; bad debts; and other factors.

6.6. When considering SME banking business, we recognized that a balance sheet for the business units that served this market would need to reflect the fact that all the banks collected deposits from various activities (for example, from both business and personal customers), and pooled these funds in order to direct them to activities that the banks wished to fund. Therefore, a balance sheet for SME banking business would show lending and deposit balances that might not be in balance, and the imbalance could be made up from other activities or by positions in the wholesale markets. Overall, a bank would balance its funds in accordance with its assessment of risks across all the business units, and fund the overall position by long-term borrowings or capital. We have summarized this in Chapter 5 where the group balance sheets for the respective banks are shown. Where banks were able to give us figures for lending, customer deposits and fixed assets attributable to their SME banking business, we used this information in the following analysis.

6.7. We have also observed that some banks, even though they had a significant share of the SME market, were unable to provide detailed performance information for this business, for example because their business was not organized to show the information we needed, or because they were unable to allocate indirect costs to this business. Where this occurred we have noted the banks' reasons, and made our own estimates so as to assess the profitability of the respective bank's services to SMEs. In such cases, we have only been able to make estimates of profitability for 1999 or 2000, but as appropriate looked at longer-term trends for the relevant variables.

6.8. For much of the course of this inquiry, 1999 was the latest year for which the banks had full-year information to discuss with us. We have, however, updated our findings for 2000 results for the six largest clearing groups, as such information became available while we were concluding our report. For the smaller banks which provide SME banking services in the UK, data for 2000 was reviewed and included within this report for those that had a significant regional presence (England and Wales, Northern Ireland or Scotland) as well as substantial SME banking business relative to their total business. For the remaining smaller banks, data has been presented up to the end of 1999.

The suppliers of services to SMEs

6.9. We now turn to the results of the six largest clearing groups that are the main suppliers of services to SMEs, namely Barclays, Lloyds TSB, HSBC, NatWest, RBS and BoS; as well as the smaller players in the market: Ulster Bank, BoI, NAB (Yorkshire, Clydesdale and Northern), AIB, Alliance & Leicester, the Co-operative Bank and Abbey National.

6.10. As explained in paragraph 6.3, none of the banks had a specific business unit that matched our definition of SMEs. To overcome some of the problems of consistency of data we asked the banks to complete a number of standard tables of income and costs. We asked all the banks to provide their information for direct and indirect costs under specific cost categories. We found, however, that all the banks provided information within their own categorization of costs, such that line-by-line comparisons were not possible, and neither was a direct comparison possible of the way in which banks allocated direct and indirect costs to the SME banking business. In such circumstances we used comparison of ratio (as we discuss further) to address these difficulties.

Barclays

Overview of its business in serving SMEs

6.11. Chapter 5 deals in detail with Barclays group position and business generally. The sections below deal with its SME banking business. Barclays told us that since 1989 there had been a number of distinct phases in its provision of banking services to SMEs. It summarized the phases as follows: from 1989 to 1990—the end of the boom; from 1991 to 1993—the recession; from 1994 to 1998—the recovery; and from 1999 to 2000—the new economy. Barclays said that during the recession of the early 1990s its market share of SME banking declined. The decline was reversed following the recovery of the mid-1990s.

6.12. Barclays described the latter half of the 1980s as a period of growth in the economy in general and SME banking business in particular. One of Barclays' objectives during this 'boom' phase was to become the leading business bank in the UK. The bank raised almost £1 billion to strengthen the group's balance sheet in support of business expansion in a number of areas, both in the UK and overseas. During this period, Barclays launched Business Centres (which were dedicated centres of expertise for business customers) and Business Bankers, who were dedicated to service business customers.

6.13. Barclays told us that the timing and severity of the recession of the early 1990s was unexpected and led to many SMEs defaulting on their loan obligations. Hence, Barclays experienced an increase in the level of provision for bad debts due to SMEs (as shown in Table 6.14). In an effort to reduce losses from its SME banking business, Barclays focused on reducing cost and limiting new risk exposure. The bank also concentrated on improving the quality of its risk assessment tools, techniques and expertise.[1]

6.14. Barclays said that the policies adopted during the recession led to a decline in its market share. Therefore, during the recovery phase, Barclays introduced new programmes to rebuild its SME banking business. The thrust of the new programmes was to differentiate Barclays in the market and win business from its competitors, by emphasizing a distinctive relationship-banking proposition. Internally, Barclays also had improved risk processes (Lending Advisor, RAP and SFPP) to support its new programmes. Barclays told us that the programmes were successful and led to increased levels of customer satisfaction and, as a result, recovery in its market share.

6.15. Barclays said that in recent years its strategy had continued to focus on customer relationships, risk management, pricing and distribution channels. Barclays believed that by continuing to focus on customer relationships and providing customers with a full range of banking products, it could differentiate itself from its competitors. [*Details omitted. See note on page iv.*] As for its pricing strategy, Barclays aimed to keep its products and prices competitive. Barclays told us that its pricing policy in respect of lending was such that lower-risk customers benefited from lower cost of lending while higher-risk customers incurred higher cost of lending. Barclays said that its distribution channel strategy was to detach the management of customer relationships with SMEs from the actual branch network, by introducing mobile work practices, equipping relationship managers with laptop computers and developing programs and tools. It stated that this would enable them to meet customer needs more quickly, at the customer's premises and without recourse to branches or business centres. In recent years Barclays had also introduced electronic, online and telephone banking channels to supplement and substitute for the traditional branch-based services.

Financial performance of the SME banking business

6.16. We asked Barclays to provide us with profitability data on its SME banking business for the period between 1989 and 2000. Barclays said that the SME banking business was not a defined business unit within its existing organizational structure, and since its reorganization in July 2000, the SME banking business largely fell within its newly-created business grouping called Business Banking, which served business customers with turnover up to £100 million. However, the Merchant Services division was part of another Barclays business—Barclaycard. But the information required for this aspect of the SME banking business could be extracted for our purposes.

6.17. Table 6.1 shows more detail of the profitability of Barclays' SME banking business from 1989 to 2000, continuing the analysis in Chapter 5 which showed the SME banking business in the context of the whole bank. During this period, operating income increased [✁] per cent from £[✁] billion in 1989 to £[✁] billion in 2000, and operating cost increased [✁] per cent from £[✁] million in 1989 to £[✁] million in 2000, having risen to £[✁] million in 1998. Barclays stated that these growth rates were less than the increase in prices of [✁] per cent over the period (as measured by the GDP deflator) implying falls of [✁] per cent in income and [✁] per cent in operating costs in real terms. The level of bad debt charge fluctuated over the period and was at its highest between 1990 and 1993 when it ranged between £[✁] million and £[✁] million. From 1993 bad debt charges after the benefit of recoveries of bad debts previously provided for declined, to around £[✁] million in 2000, and were [✁] in 1998. As a result of this performance, Barclays showed an operating profit of £[✁] million in 1989, and £[✁] million in 1990, but operating losses of £[✁] million and £[✁] million in 1991 and 1992. These losses fell to almost [✁] in 1993. From 1994 operating profits [✁] and between 1994 and 1999 ranged between £[✁] million and £[✁] million a year. In 2000 operating profit was £[✁] million.

---

[1]The bank introduced Lending Advisor, Risk Adjusted Pricing model (RAP) and Small Firms Pricing Policy (SFPP), some of which included off-the-shelf software that was customized to the bank's requirements.

TABLE 6.1 Barclays: profit and loss account from SME banking business, 1989 to 2000*

£ million

Years ended 31 December

	1989	1990	1991	1992	1993	1994	1995	1996	1997	1998	1999	2000
Current accounts (benefit of funds)												
Deposit accounts												
Loans and overdrafts												
Other—clubs and charities												
Net interest income												
Net fees and commissions												
Other income												
Total operating income						*Figures omitted. See note on page iv.*						
Operating expenses												
Operating profit before provisions												
Bad debt charge												
Operating profit/loss												
Long-term pension costs†												
Restructuring costs‡												
Net profit/loss before tax§												

Source: Barclays.

*See also Table 6.2, which shows the items in this table as a percentage of total operating income.

†These costs represent a notional charge for staff pension benefits as they accrued. They were charged to the SME banking business at the contribution rate defined by the scheme actuaries. These costs were not paid in cash as Barclays had a pension surplus.

‡Shown as exceptional costs in financial statements.

§As requested by us, these figures were calculated on the basis that all lending is financed from borrowing in wholesale markets. In fact, a proportion will be financed by the bank's equity, and it is therefore necessary to make an adjustment for this (see Table 6.3) before comparing returns on capital derived from these profit figures with the bank's cost of capital.

6.18. Table 6.2 further analyses the overall performance of Barclays' SME banking business from 1989 to 2000 by showing all items as a percentage of operating income. Net interest income as a percentage of operating income declined from [✂] per cent in 1989 to [✂] per cent in 1993, and since increased as a proportion to around [✂] per cent. Conversely income from net fees and commission charges as a percentage of operating income was at its highest level during the recession years. This reflected both lower net interest income and increased fees and commissions during this period.

6.19. Barclays said that when assessing its profitability from SME banking business, we should reduce profits to take account of its pension costs and restructuring costs as noted in Table 6.1 below the operating profit line. We noted that the pension adjustment of £[✂] million in 1999 was some [✂] per cent of employment costs, which was the contribution rate defined by the scheme's actuaries. This represented the true economic costs of staff pension benefits as they accrued based on the actuary's calculation. In addition, it considered that recoveries of earlier bad debts should be excluded from profits, if any period shorter than the economic cycle was considered (see Table 6.14), which over the six years from 1994 to 1999 ranged between £[✂] million and £[✂] million. It also proposed that profits from structural hedging transactions should be disregarded. These profits had ranged between £[✂] million and £[✂] million a year between 1994 and 1999. Barclays did not accept that the structural hedge profits were part of its normal SME banking business and an aspect of prudential banking. It rather noted that the structural hedges were designed to stabilize its income stream, ie to remove volatility from movements in market interest rates. It said that a bank could not be expected to profit systematically through the use of structural hedges. Consequently it felt that the SME income had been increased artificially by such hedges by up to £[✂] million a year and that these exceptional profits should be deducted in a fair assessment of the profitability of SME banking business in the long run. Barclays considered that there was no certainty that these hedging profits would continue and that in effect they arose from swapping short-term market interest rates for longer-term fixed rates.

TABLE 6.2 **Barclays: operating profit and loss items as a percentage of operating income from SME banking business, 1989 to 2000**

per cent

	1989	1990	1991	1992	1993	1994	1995	1996	1997	1998	1999	2000
Current accounts (benefit of funds)												
Deposit accounts												
Loans and overdrafts												
Other—clubs and charities												
Net interest income												
Net fees and commissions												
Other income												
Total operating income												
Operating expenses												
Operating profit before provisions												
Provisions for bad and doubtful debts												
Operating profit/loss												
Long-term pension costs												
Restructuring costs*												
Net profit/loss before tax†												

Figures omitted. See note on page iv.

Source: Barclays.

---

*Shown as exceptional costs in the financial statements.

†As requested by us, these figures were calculated on the basis that all lending is financed from borrowing in wholesale markets. In fact, a proportion will be financed by the bank's equity, and it is therefore necessary to make an adjustment for this (see Table 6.3) before comparing returns on capital derived from these profit figures with the bank's cost of capital.

6.20. The SME banking business cost:income ratio fluctuated between 1989 and 2000 in the range 53 to 63 per cent. The ratio was at a high point of 63 per cent in 1991 and then stabilized at close to 60 per cent between 1995 and 1998. In 1999 it fell to 56 per cent, which Barclays said was due to the fact that Barclays was able to cut its costs slightly faster than prices were driven down by the market. In particular, in 1999 the bank undertook a wide-ranging restructuring programme to reduce costs. Barclays emphasized that cost:income ratios could only illustrate the relativities of costs and income, and was not a measure of cost efficiency. The SME ratio in 2000 was 53 per cent compared with that of the whole bank at 57 per cent (see Chapter 5).

Attributable capital to support the SME banking business and potential returns

6.21. Tables 6.1 and 6.2 show the trends in Barclays' profits from its SME banking business. In order to form a view on the significance of such profits, we also consider Barclays' capital base. We look at this subject in greater detail in Chapter 7 for all the main suppliers.

6.22. In determining the attributable capital to support Barclays' services to SMEs for the years 1998 to 2000, our methodology, as discussed later, was in broad terms as follows:

(a) We initially calculated the RWAs for the SME banking business, and for the bank as a whole.

(b) Next, we calculated the proportion of SME RWAs, relative to the bank as a whole—this proportion showed the relative importance of the SME banking business to the overall bank in terms of weighting its overall capital.

(c) We then used this proportion to allocate the whole bank's shareholders' funds to derive the capital attributable to the SME banking business.

Barclays objected to the methodology based on RWAs, and put forward an alternative approach, as is discussed in Chapter 7.

6.23. The risk weightings used were as presently covered by FSA regulations, and reflected credit risk in particular. We noted that credit risk (among others) was a key factor in the variability of banks' profitability over a long-term economic period, as shown by the variability of bad debt levels. Barclays, however, said that RWAs should not be used to give any credence to the use of RWAs in the allocation of capital, as RWAs relied on a very simplistic assessment of credit risk.

6.24. Applying our methodology, we put to Barclays our initial assessment that its attributable capital to support its SME banking business (based on an apportionment of its closing balance sheet capital for 1998 to 2000) would be £[✂] for 1998, £[✂] for 1999, and £[✂] for 2000. In Table 6.1 we noted that Barclays' profits from SME banking business were based on its calculation of net income from lending as if wholly financed from wholesale markets at LIBOR. However, in identifying the rate of return to compare with the cost of capital, an adjustment must be made to reflect that a proportion of lending was funded by capital and not from the wholesale markets. This is necessary to avoid an overestimation of interest costs, ie double counting, and the appropriate adjustment is attributable capital times the average three-month LIBOR. The rates used for each of the years 1998, 1999 and 2000 were 7.3 per cent, 5.45 per cent and 6.1 per cent respectively.[1]

6.25. Table 6.3 incorporates this adjustment, together with the information shown in Table 6.1 on profitability, and shows estimates of returns (subject to further adjustments discussed in Chapter 7). For 1999, which was a year with relatively low bad debt levels, the initial estimate for Barclays' pre-tax return on capital was [✂] per cent, based on closing capital. Barclays emphasized that on its own workings as covered in Chapter 7, its average post-tax return on capital before any adjustments was [✂] per cent over the 11 years of the economic cycle to 1999 (see Table 7.53). In Chapter 7 we consider Barclays' appropriate cost of capital, and what adjustments are necessary regarding these returns. In Chapter 2 we give our conclusions on this issue.

TABLE 6.3 **Barclays: summary of profits, capital and returns from Barclays services to SMEs, 1998 to 2000**

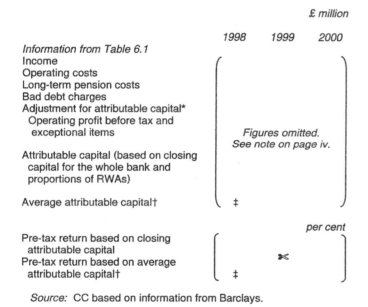

£ million

	1998	1999	2000
Information from Table 6.1			
Income			
Operating costs			
Long-term pension costs			
Bad debt charges			
Adjustment for attributable capital*			
Operating profit before tax and exceptional items			
		Figures omitted. See note on page iv.	
Attributable capital (based on closing capital for the whole bank and proportions of RWAs)			
Average attributable capital†	‡		

		per cent	
Pre-tax return based on closing attributable capital		✂	
Pre-tax return based on average attributable capital†	‡		

Source: CC based on information from Barclays.

---

*At 7.3 per cent for 1998, 5.45 per cent for 1999, and 6.10 per cent for 2000, based on three-month LIBOR.
†The attributable capital for 1999, which is shown as based on the closing capital level for Barclays, could alternatively be based on the average of the closing attributable capital figures for each year. For 2000, the resultant figure would therefore be £[✂], and the pre-tax return, based on this average attributable capital, would be [✂] per cent, ie an increase of [✂] percentage points.
‡Not calculated.

6.26. A further alternative in considering the above returns would be to use an average capital figure, for example the average of the opening and closing capital base, rather than a return based on the closing figure. For 2000 we calculated that the effect on the pre-tax return would be an increase of [✂] percentage points to [✂] per cent. However, this approach was not practicable for some banks because data was not available. Barclays added that the average opening and closing capital base of the SME banking business was not an accurate representation of the capital base throughout the year.

---

[1]The rate Barclays used to calculate the adjustment for 1996 to 2000 was the average three-year government rate for the year (measured monthly) and for 1989 to 1995 the average three-month Treasury rate for the year (measured monthly) .

6.27. Barclays told us that its view of its capital attributable to its SME banking business was £[✄] for 1998, and £[✄] for 1999, which we cover further in Chapter 7, and accordingly reduced its returns to the amounts as shown in Table 7.53 (29 per cent in 1998 and 27 per cent in 1999). In noting the returns for 1998 to 2000 Barclays said that the SME banking business was particularly exposed to the economic cycle and, as Tables 6.1 and 6.2 highlight, the business had tended to make losses in economic downturns and profits in growth/benign stages of the economic cycle. It added that no sensible or rational assessment of returns on capital for the business or whether this did or might be expected to operate against the public interest could be made by looking at profits and losses in just one stage of the economic cycle.

Further analysis of income and expenses

6.28. Table 6.4 provides an analysis of operating income by type of banking service to SME banking business customers from 1998 to 2000. In 2000 the four main types of banking relationships from which Barclays earned income were loans, current accounts with overdrafts, current accounts with no overdraft facilities, and deposits. In aggregate in 2000, they contributed [✄] per cent of the £[✄] billion operating income from the SME banking business.

TABLE 6.4 **Barclays: analysis of net income* by type of banking service to SME banking business customers, 1998 to 2000**

Years ended 31 December

	£ million			Income share (%)		
	1998	*1999*	*2000*	*1998*	*1999*	*2000*
Net income* from:						
Loans						
Current accounts with overdrafts						
Current accounts (with no overdraft facilities)		*Figures omitted.*				
Deposits		*See note on page iv.*				
Subtotal						
Merchant acquiring						
Other income						
Charities and clubs						
Total						

Source: Barclays.

*Includes net interest income and net fees and commissions. Operational costs and bad debt charges are then deducted from this income to derive net operating profit.

6.29. Table 6.5 provides a breakdown of net operating income from the SME banking business into net interest income, net fees and commission, and 'other' income from 1998 to 2000. Barclays derived interest income, not only from loans and overdrafts to SME banking business customers, but also from the use of money held on deposit and current accounts of the SMEs. The table also shows the net interest margin earned by the bank from different types of banking relationships with SMEs. The table shows the income earned, as well as the notional cost of funds to finance lending, and the benefit of funds deposited by SMEs. For 2000 the average total value of deposits from SMEs totalled £[✄] billion, which in effect Barclays was able to use in financing its lending to SMEs and other customers. Overall for 2000, in terms of the average balance values, Barclays' SME banking business had:

— £[✄] of funds deposited from SMEs, ie deposits of £[✄] and current accounts in credit of £[✄]; and

— lending of £[✄] to SMEs, made up of loans of £[✄] and overdrafts of £[✄].

This provided almost £[✄] for lending/investment on non-SME banking business. Barclays, however, stated that in the 1990s the position was opposite with SME banking business being a net user of funds; see also Table 6.13.

TABLE 6.5 **Barclays: analysis of operating income by type of service to SMEs, 1998 to 2000**

Years ended 31 December

	£ million			Margin and lending balances		
	1998	*1999*	*2000*	*1998*	*1999*	*2000*
Loans						
Iinterest income						
Allocated cost of funds						
Net interest income						
Account management fees						
Other						
Net income*						
Average lending balance on balance sheet (£m)						
Annualized net interest (%)†						
Current accounts utilizing overdraft facility						
Interest income						
Cost of funds						
Net interest income						
Account management fees						
Money transmission						
Net income*						
Average overdraft balance in balance sheet (£m)‡						
Annualized net interest (%)†						
Other current accounts§						
Benefit of funds from SMEs						
Interest income (unapproved)						
Allocated cost of funds						
Net interest income						
Account management fees						
Money transmission						
Net income¶						
Average balance on balance sheet (£m)‡						
Annualized net interest (%)†						
Deposits						
Benefit of funds from SMEs						
Interest paid						
Net interest income						
Other income						
Net interest income§						
Average deposit balance on balance sheet (£m)						
Annualized net interest (%)†						
Other net income from						
Merchant acquiring						
Sundry other services						
Charities and clubs						
Total net income from SMEs						

Figures omitted.
See note on page iv.

Source: Barclays.

*Before deducting operational costs and bad debt charges, to derive the net operating profit from this service to customers.

†Net interest as percentages of average balances. For the current accounts this is only an approximate measure as there will be interest from some accounts categorized as having utilized their overdraft facility that at some point in the year may have been in credit. Similarly other current accounts may have been in overdraft at some point over the year.

‡These balances are approximate as some accounts will have changed their classification as well as their balance during the year.

§Includes current accounts without an overdraft facility and current accounts with an overdraft facility that has not been utilized. Of the current accounts without an overdraft facility, this classification will include those accounts that have an unauthorized overdraft. The related interest charged on these balances has also been accounted for under this classification.

¶Before deducting operational costs to derive the net operating profit from this service to customers.

6.30. Barclays said that, for loans and overdrafts, interest income reflected actual interest earned from customers and the cost of funds was calculated using 'transfer LIBOR' (30-day rolling average one-month LIBOR) for variable rate balances or appropriate market rates for fixed-rate balances. As for deposits and current accounts (with no overdraft facilities), the benefit of funds reflected the value of funds to the bank and included benefits from structural hedges. As current accounts were non-interest-bearing, there was no interest paid to customers. We refer in paragraph 6.19 to Barclays' use of structural hedges to protect its interest income earned from customer balances.

6.31. Table 6.5 shows that in 2000 Barclays earned SME income of £[✄] million from loans to SME banking business customers (of which £[✄] million was net interest income, £[✄] million was account management fees, and £[✄] million was 'other' income). It also earned income of £[✄] million from customer deposits (of which £[✄] million was the imputed net interest benefit of the customer deposits, and £[✄] million was earned as fees).

6.32. In 2000 Barclays' SME banking business also earned income of £[✄] million from overdrafts (of which £[✄] million was net interest income, £[✄] million was from account management fees and £[✄] million from money transmission fees), ie a proportion of [✄] between interest and charges. Barclays said that the reason for the concentration of fees compared with interest income was because the income identified did not relate to just overdrafts, it related to current accounts with an agreed over-draft facility, and hence a significant proportion of the non-interest income identified related to money transmission charges. It also earned income of £[✄] million from customer current accounts with no approved overdraft facilities (of which £[✄] million was mostly the imputed net interest benefit of the funds, and £[✄] million was fees from the provision of money transmission services).

6.33. Among the various income-earning categories for 1998 to 2000, current accounts (with no overdraft facilities) reported the highest net interest margins[1] at [✄] per cent for 2000. The reason for this margin was that the bank earned interest on the current account balances but paid no interest for the use of the funds. Barclays said that the interest income from current account balances was necessary to pay for the costs of money transmission transactions not covered by charges in the context of an overall liquidity management servic . Loans and overdrafts showed similar net interest margins over 1998 to 2000 at around [✄] per cent, compared with lower margins on deposit balances of around [✄] per cent. However, Barclays said that even though the margin on deposits was relatively small, it accounted for around [✄] per cent of its SME income (see Table 6.4). Barclays told us that the pricing of its components of the liquidity management service—current accounts, short-term deposit accounts and short-term borrowing (particularly overdrafts)—were closely linked.

6.34. Barclays said that between 1994 and 2000 it had experienced significant declines in prices and margins on all product areas: current account charges fell by [✄] per cent (per account in real terms), current account margins by [✄] per cent, deposit margins [✄] per cent, overdraft margins [✄] per cent, and loan margins by [✄] per cent:

  (a) for loan and overdraft margins, the decline reflected competitive pressures from a wide range of finance providers;

  (b) for current account margins, the decline reflected a fall in base rates; and

  (c) for deposits margins, the decline reflected growth in deposit balances and the movement in balances to accounts and products that paid higher rates of interest.

It added that its current account charges had fallen in real terms, which it considered reflected customer and competitor pressures prohibiting banks from increasing nominal charges in line with inflation.

6.35. Table 6.6 provides a further analysis of operating profits[2] for the SME banking business by types of banking service from 1998 to 2000. Table 6.9 summarizes these results in terms of cost:income ratios. For 2000:

  (a) lending activity showed net income of £[✄] million and operating profit (before bad debt charges) of £[✄] million ([✄] per cent of net income);

  (b) current accounts utilizing an overdraft facility showed net income of £[✄] million, and operating profit before bad debt charges of £[✄] million ([✄] per cent);

---

[1]This is net interest income divided by average current account balances.
[2]Profit before restructuring charges and long-term pension costs.

(c) other current accounts (with no overdraft facility or where the facility is not utilized) showed net income of £[✂] million and profit of £[✂] million ([✂] per cent);

(d) deposit activities showed net income of £[✂] million and operating profit of £[✂] million ([✂] per cent);

(e) merchant acquiring and 'other' income activities showed combined income of £[✂] million and profit of £[✂] million ([✂] per cent); and

(f) CACs showed income of £[✂] million and a loss of £[✂] million.

TABLE 6.6 **Barclays: analysis of operating profit by type of service to SMEs, 1998 to 2000**

Years ended 31 December

	£ million			Proportion of net income (%)		
	1998	1999	2000	1998	1999	2000
Loans						
Net income*						
Costs						
Bad debt charge						
Profit						
Current accounts utilizing overdraft facility						
Net income*						
Costs						
Bad debt charge						
Profit						
Other current accounts†						
Net income*						
Costs						
Profit						
Deposits						
Net income*						
Costs						
Profit						
Merchant acquiring						
Net income*						
Costs						
Profit						
Other income						
Income						
Costs						
Profit						
Clubs and charities						
Income						
Costs						
Profit						
Operating profit from SMEs before provision for doubtful debts‡						
Operating profit from SMEs after provision for doubtful debts§						

Figures omitted. See note on page iv.

Source: Barclays.

---

*Net interest income plus fees and commissions.

†Includes current accounts without an overdraft facility and current accounts with an overdraft facility that has not been utilized. Of the current accounts without an overdraft facility this classification will include those accounts that have an unauthorized overdraft. The related interest charged on these balances has also been accounted for under this classification.

‡For information purposes.

§Profit before restructuring charges and pension costs.

313

6.36. Table 6.7 provides a further analysis of operating profits for the SME banking business using 1999 profits for each main service category, both before and after allowing for bad debt charges. These profits have been presented as a proportion of both total profits and as a return on equity. The equity figures used as the denominator of the return on equity calculation were provided by Barclays and represent its internally calculated economic capital figures. The basis of calculation of these capital figures is discussed in Chapter 7.

6.37. Loans and current accounts utilizing an overdraft facility are the two areas of service which have been allocated the highest amount of equity by Barclays. Together they have been allocated [✂] per cent of the equity base. The returns proportionate to this allocation of equity, however, are the lowest of each of the service areas, being [✂] per cent and [✂] per cent respectively, after bad debts. Other current accounts and deposits show a return on their equity allocation after bad debts of [✂] per cent and [✂] per cent respectively. By way of contrast their equity allocation represents [✂] per cent of the total equity base.

TABLE 6.7 **Barclays: comparison of sources of profits and returns by type of service to SMEs, 1999**

	Profit before bad debts* £m	Profit after bad debts* £m	Profit before bad debts as a proportion of total profit before bad debts %	Profit after bad debts as a proportion of total profit after bad debts %	Barclays' economic equity† £m	Profit before bad debts as a proportion of equity %	Profit after bad debts as a proportion of equity %
Loans							
Current accounts utilizing an overdraft facility							
Other current accounts							
Deposits			Figures omitted. See note on page iv.				
Merchant acquiring							
CACs							
Other							
Total							

Source: CC based on information provided by Barclays.

*Figures per Table 6.5.
†Equity figures used as the denominator of these percentages were provided by Barclays as part of the original submissions to the CC. These are unadjusted by the CC.
Note: N/A = not applicable.

6.38. Table 6.8 shows the return on equity per type of service as calculated by Barclays. In its calculation Barclays made some adjustments to the profit figures used in Table 6.7. First, an adjustment has been made which reduces profit for the amount of restructuring costs which is attributable to the services of the SME banking business and the allocated cost of the pension surplus. Secondly, there has been an adjustment for the attributable capital adjustment discussed in paragraph 6.24 which has the effect of increasing profit. These adjustments have been shown as an aggregate adjustment figure for each service in Table 6.8. In addition, the resultant profit figure has been tax effected at a rate of [✂] per cent. A return on equity using the adjusted profit figure after tax has then been calculated using the same equity allocation as discussed in Table 6.7.

6.39. The return on equity from loans and current accounts utilizing an overdraft facility still significantly produces the lowest returns on equity while being allocated a significantly higher amount of capital than the other service areas. Deposits and other current accounts provide a return of around [✂] per cent of the equity base they have been allocated. In providing this information, Barclays said that it felt it was inappropriate to consider the rates of return on narrow product groups in isolation. It suggested that it was more appropriate to look at the return of the SME banking business as a whole, which was [✂] per cent in 1999.

314

TABLE 6.8 **Barclays: calculation of return on equity by type of service to SMEs for 1999.**

	Profit before bad debts* £m	Profit after bad debts* £m	Adjust-ment† £m	Adjusted profit after bad debts £m	Adjusted profit after bad debts and after tax‡ £m	Barclays' economic equity £m	Return on capital using adjusted profit after bad debts and tax %
Loans							
Current accounts utilizing an over-draft facility							
Other current accounts			*Figures omitted. See note on page iv.*				
Deposits							
Merchant acquiring							
CACs							
Other							
Total							

Source: Barclays.

---

*As per Table 6.5.

†Represents the aggregate of additional costs for pensions (£[✂] million for the SME banking business) and restructuring (£[✂] million for the SME banking business) and the addition to income for the attributable capital adjustment. The attributable capital adjustment has been calculated by applying a rate of 5.45 per cent to the allocated capital figure for the service being provided, ie loans. The rationale for the attributable capital adjustment is discussed in paragraph 6.24.

‡The tax rate applied was 30 per cent.

§The calculation of this capital figure is discussed in detail in Chapter 7.

Note: N/A = not applicable.

6.40. Table 6.9 further analyses Barclays' costs for 1999 and 2000 into direct and indirect costs by type of service, and shows the cost:income ratios for such services for the three years to 2000. Around [✂] per cent of costs were direct, and [✂] per cent were indirect for both years. Barclays stated that indirect costs were allocated costs controlled by other parts of the group. Barclays emphasized that its costs were allocated by detailed costing systems and it believed its cost allocations to services in the SME banking business were fair and reasonable.

6.41. The cost:income ratios varied according to the different types of banking activities within the SME banking business. Deposits had the [✂] cost:income ratio of [✂] per cent in 1999 and [✂] per cent in 2000. Other types of banking services such as other current accounts (with no overdraft facility or where facility is not utilized) had cost:income ratios of [✂] per cent in 2000, but [✂] per cent for over-drawn current accounts. We noted that a reason for the difference was that current accounts in credit gave the bank an extra source of revenue that was, on average, better than the margin from lending on overdrafts. Lending had cost:income ratios of [✂] per cent in 1999 and [✂] per cent in 2000.

6.42. All the banks told us that the mix of banking activities and services they provided influenced their overall cost:income ratios, such that a bank with a higher proportion of deposits relative to lending would generate a lower cost:income ratio, compared with a similar bank of equal efficiency, that had a relatively lower level of average deposits. In addition, cost:income ratios were affected by a whole range of pricing, costing and other strategic decisions on the part of the banks. We discuss this issue of business mix further in Chapter 7.

TABLE 6.9 **Barclays: analysis of income and costs from services to SMEs by product category, and summary of cost:income ratios by type of service, 1999 and 2000**

| | | | £ million | | per cent | |
| | | | Operating costs | | Cost proportion | |
	Income	Costs	Direct	Indirect	Direct	Indirect
1999						
Lending						
Current accounts utilizing overdraft facility						
Other current accounts						
Deposits						
Merchant acquiring						
Other						
Charities and clubs						
Bad debt charges						
Total costs*						
2000						
Lending						
Current accounts utilizing an overdraft facility						
Other current accounts						
Deposits						
Merchant acquiring						
Other						
Charities and clubs						
Bad debt charge						
Total costs*						

Figures omitted. See note on page iv.

	1999	2000
Summary of cost:income ratios†		
Lending		
Current accounts utilizing overdraft facility		
Other current accounts		
Deposits	✂	
Merchant acquiring		
Other income		
Charities and clubs		
Overall		

Source: Barclays.

---

*As identified in Table 6.1, but excludes notional long-term pension costs of £[✂] million, and restructuring costs of £[✂] million.
†Cost component excludes restructuring costs and long-term pension costs.

6.43. Table 6.10 provides a further analysis of operating costs for Barclays' SME banking business by activity from 1998 to 2000. Within the SME banking business local operations and centralized processing-based activities accounted for around [✂] per cent of total costs in each of the three years. Barclays stated that most of the local operations expenditure represented the cost of staff dedicated to corporate customers while some of the central processing units served only the corporate customer base. Included within local operations costs were direct costs such as business centres and relationship managers, and recharged costs such as branch counter staff and cash handling. Included within central processing costs were direct costs such as the staff cost of processing loans (producing letters of credit, etc), factoring and invoice discounting, and recharged costs such as cheque-clearing services. Barclays said that costs allocated to local operations and central processing were part of a wider group of costs termed Customer Service and Delivery costs. The proportion of these costs which related to the SME banking business was around 30 per cent for each of the three years 1998, 1999 and 2000. Costs were split between tariffed costs, variable costs and shares of fixed costs; however, the way in which these costs were allocated to the SME banking business was not specified.

TABLE 6.10 **Barclays: analysis of SME banking business operating cost by activity, 1998 to 2000**

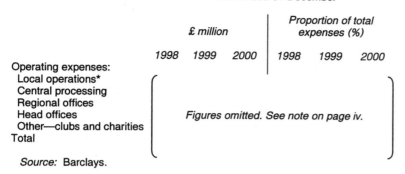

Years ended 31 December

| | £ million | | | Proportion of total expenses (%) | | |
	1998	1999	2000	1998	1999	2000
Operating expenses:						
Local operations*						
Central processing						
Regional offices		*Figures omitted. See note on page iv.*				
Head offices						
Other—clubs and charities						
Total						

Source: Barclays.

*Includes branches, business centres, cash centres and relationship managers.

6.44. Table 6.11 shows the analysis of Barclays' direct personnel serving SME banking business customers in 1999 and 2000 by location and function, in terms of FTE personnel. Of the total of 9,000 in 2000, some 5,100 were wholly dedicated to SME banking business (57 per cent). The balance had partial responsibilities and therefore their costs were recoverable over several activities. Some [✂] people operated from branches, [✂] were in central processing activities, and [✂] were operating from the head office. In terms of functions, [✂] people were in selling and marketing, [✂] were in servicing and processing activities, some [✂] were in credit risk activities, and [✂] were in administration and support functions (which includes a range of activities such as systems development). Overall, the cost of personnel serving SME banking business customers was £[✂] million at an average annual cost per employee of £[✂], but Barclays overall had a higher average cost at some £[✂]. Barclays, however, added that it had a large number of staff in other parts of the bank who indirectly served SME banking business customers, for example in branches as cashiers, and in clearing processes. It was unable to quantify these numbers and they were charged to the SME banking business as allocated costs.

6.45. Based on total income of £[✂] billion, each direct FTE employee generated income of £[✂] in 2000, which compared with £[✂] in 1996. Barclays, however, considered that the average revenue per FTE employee could not be used as a measure of performance because it was dependent upon the organizational structure of business, ie the extent to which services were provided by direct staff or those in service units outside Business Banking. It felt that a distinction was needed between support staff and relationship management personnel, as the latter had sales performance targets to achieve and were generators of revenue.

6.46. Barclays told us that the majority of its marketing and promotion activity was undertaken by way of person-to-person contact by relationship managers and customer service staff around the UK. It added that it was unable to identify the precise cost of this customer-facing recruitment and marketing activity but this was a significant proportion of the network costs of relationship managers and customer service staff who cost some £[✂] million in 1999. In addition, Barclays said that it undertook a wide range of advertising, marketing and promotion through external suppliers, and this accounted for £[✂] million in 2000 for the whole bank, of which it estimated that corporate banking (including SME banking business) accounted for £[✂] million of the costs ([✂] per cent).

TABLE 6.11 **Barclays: summary of personnel serving SME banking business customers analysed by location of duties, and by function, 1999 and 2000**

	Number of persons 100% serving SMEs	FTE of persons with partial involvement	Total personnel
1999			
Analysis of direct personnel by location			
Branches			
Central processing	Figures omitted.		
Regional offices	See note on page iv.		
Head Office			
	<u>5,474</u>	<u>4,259</u>	9,733*
Other personnel some of which indirectly serve SME customers			<u>67,267</u>† <u>77,000</u>
Analysis of personnel by function			
Selling and marketing			
Servicing and processing	Figures omitted.		
Credit risk	See note on page iv.		
Administration and support			
Management			
	<u>5,474</u>	<u>4,259</u>	9,733*
Other personnel some of which indirectly serve SME customers			<u>67,267</u>† <u>77,000</u>
2000			
Analysis of direct personnel by location			
Branches			
Central processing	Figures omitted.		
Regional offices	See note on page iv.		
Head Office			
	<u>5,118</u>	<u>3,971</u>	9,089
Other personnel some of which indirectly serve SME customers			<u>65,595</u> <u>74,684</u>
Analysis of personnel by function			
Selling and marketing			
Servicing and processing	Figures omitted.		
Credit risk	See note on page iv.		
Administration and support			
Management			
	<u>5,118</u>	<u>3,971</u>	9,089
Other personnel some of which indirectly serve SME customers			<u>65,595</u> <u>74,684</u>

Source: Barclays.

*For 2000 total employment costs for SME banking business was £[✂] million, which equated to an average cost of £[✂].

†For 2000 total employment costs for non-SME banking business were £[✂], which equated to an average cost of £[✂].

6.47. Having considered the costs and income by type of activity in paragraph 6.44 from Barclays' services to SME banking business, Table 6.12 summarizes such operating profits from 1998 to 2000. The deposit accounts, and other current accounts, made the largest contributions to overall operating profits. This result derived from the benefit of the funds deposited with the bank and relatively lower costs for such activities compared with lending. In 2000 operating profit from deposits was £[✂] million, and operating profit from other current accounts was £[✂] million, which together accounted for [✂] per cent of operating profits in 2000 of £[✂] million.

TABLE 6.12 **Barclays: summary of SME banking business operating profit (after bad debt charges) by type of banking relationship, 1998 to 2000**

Years ended 31 December

	£ million			Proportion of total profit %		
	1998	1999	2000	1998	1999	2000
Operating profit* arising from						
Lending						
Current accounts utilizing overdraft facility						
Other current accounts						
Deposits		*Figures omitted. See note on page iv.*				
Merchant acquiring						
Other income						
Clubs and charities						
Total						
Operating profit as a percentage of operating income		*per cent*				
Lending*						
Current accounts utilizing overdraft facility						
Other current accounts						
Deposits		*Figures omitted. See note on page iv.*				
Merchant acquiring						
Other activities						
Clubs and charities						
Total						

Source: Barclays.

*Calculated after bad debt charges but before pension costs and exceptional items. For 1999 the bad debt charge from lending was £[✂] million ([✂] per cent of income), and £[✂] million from overdrawn current accounts ([✂] per cent of operating income)—see Table 6.6.

6.48. In 2000, SME banking business operating profit as a percentage of operating income was [✂] per cent for deposits, and [✂] per cent for other current accounts (with no overdraft facility or where the facility is not being utilized). However, lending and current accounts utilizing overdraft facility reported much lower percentages of [✂] and [✂] per cent. Bad debt charges were deducted in arriving at the lending and current account operating profits for the purpose of making these calculations. For the lending activity, the bad debt charge was £[✂] million ([✂] per cent of operating income), and for overdrawn current accounts £[✂] million ([✂] per cent of operating income). Barclays noted that, in a future downturn, higher bad debt levels could further erode its lending and overdraft profitability; and in addition, [*Details omitted. See note on page iv.*]. It illustrated this by noting that 'corporate income gearing'[1] in the period 1970 to 2000 reached peaks between [✂] and [✂] per cent at three points around 1975, 1981 and 1991. By 1995 this had reduced to around [✂] per cent, but has since risen to around [✂] per cent at present and Barclays said would increase further in a recession.

Balance sheet items

6.49. Table 6.13 shows loans, fixed assets and customer accounts in credit for Barclays' SME banking business between 1989 and 2000. Barclays said that the SME banking business did not correspond directly to a business unit within its business structure. It therefore had to construct a balance sheet for the SME banking business from the relevant areas of the bank's business, which it successfully did for a full 12 years. We noted that constructing a balance sheet for the SME banking business would be inconclusive because Barclays collected deposits from its various activities with both business and personal customers, and pooled these funds in order to determine where it should make its lending. Therefore, a balance sheet for SME banking business would show lending and deposit balances that might not be in balance; where there was more lending than deposits, there would be a need to receive funds from other activities. Barclays was, however, able to give us figures for lending, customer deposits, and fixed assets attributable to the SME banking business.

[1]Defined as gross interest paid as a percentage of post-tax income.

Years ended 31 December

	1989	1990	1991	1992	1993	1994	1995	1996	1997	1998	1999	2000
Loans and overdrawn current accounts												
Customer accounts in credit*					Figures omitted. See note on page iv.							
Funds required (+) or available (–)												

Source: Barclays.

*Includes both deposit accounts, and current accounts in credit.

6.50. From Table 6.13 it can be seen that the level of loans to SME banking business customers was at its highest between 1989 and 1992 when it ranged around £[✂] billion. Since 1992 the level of loans has declined and was £[✂] billion in 2000. Barclays noted that the benign conditions in the late 1990s resulted in customers not needing to borrow, rather than it having avoided lending to classes of SME banking business. Regarding the level of customer accounts in credit, the balances increased [✂] per cent from £[✂] billion in 1989 to £[✂] billion in 2000. As a result the loan:deposit ratio declined from [✂] in 1989 to [✂] in 2000. Barclays said that the situation could change in the future as economic conditions altered. The surpluses of deposit balances nevertheless gave Barclays income from the benefit of such funds (that were invested elsewhere), and such income contributed to improvements in the cost:income ratio in recent years.

Capital expenditure and development costs

6.51. Banks generally do not have significant tangible fixed assets in relation to their total assets, and write off what they term as investment costs as they are incurred. Barclays told us that its investment expenditure took two forms: it was either capitalized or expensed through the profit and loss account. For 2000 it noted that capitalized expenditure excluding goodwill for the whole was around £350 million compared with £242 million in 1999 and £305 million in 1998. Investment expenditure written off to the profit and loss account included £440 million of strategic investment costs in 2000 and £229 in 1999. Further investment costs were incurred in sustaining the current level of business which were estimated at £[✂] million in 2000 for the SME banking business. Barclays said that it planned further capital expenditure of £[✂] million for the two years to 2001.

6.52. Barclays' business development expenditure for the whole bank was expensed through the profit and loss account, and for 2000 was estimated at £[✂] million, and £[✂] billion for each of the two years to 2002. The Business Banking division estimated that its annual development expenditure planned for the three years to 2003 was in the region of £[✂] million.

Bad debts

6.53. Table 6.14 shows the level of bad debt provision at the year end, and bad debt charges to the profit and loss account between 1989 and 2000 relating to its SME banking business. Between 1991 and 1995 bad debt provisions were at their highest levels and ranged between £[✂] and £[✂]. Since 1995 the level declined to around £[✂]. The levels of closing provision equated to [✂] per cent of loans at the peak in 1994, compared with [✂] per cent at the end of the 1990s and [✂] per cent in 2000. Barclays said that the decline was due to benign economic conditions since the severe recession in the early 1990s.

TABLE 6.14 **Barclays: analysis of bad debt provision and charges to profit and loss account from services to SME banking business, 1989 to 2000**

£ million

	1989	1990	1991	1992	1993	1994	1995	1996	1997	1998	1999	2000
Analysis of bad debt provision												
General provision												
Specific provision												
Bad debt provision												
Analysis of bad debt charge to profit and loss												
New and additional provisions net of releases												
Recoveries of advances written off in earlier years												
Bad debt charge to profit and loss												

Figures omitted. See note on page iv.

per cent

	Average*
Performance indicators	
Bad debt provision as a percentage of total loans	
Bad debt charge as a percentage of total loans†	
Bad debt charge as a percentage of total income	

Figures omitted. See note on page iv.

Source: Barclays.

*Arithmetic average.

†The simple average for the bad debt charge to lending ratio for the five years to 1993 was [✂] per cent, and [✂] per cent for the six years to 2000.

6.54. The level of bad debt charge (after recoveries) also fluctuated between 1989 and 2000 with a peak of [✂] per cent of loans and [✂] per cent of income in 1992. Subsequently the level of bad debt charge declined and was [✂] per cent of loans and [✂] per cent of income, in 2000. Over the 12 years between 1989 and 2000 the SME banking business showed an average annual bad debt charge of [✂] per cent of loans and [✂] per cent of total income. Over the six years to 2000 the simple average of the bad debt charge as a percentage of lending was [✂] per cent. Barclays suggested that we should disregard recoveries when calculating the above ratios, which would mean that the peak ratio of [✂] per cent in 1992 would increase to [✂] per cent and [✂] per cent of income.

6.55. Barclays added that its internal model for pricing loans assumed a long-term bad debt charge to lending ratio of [✂] per cent for loans to businesses with turnover up to £250,000, [✂] per cent for loans to customers in the next band to £1 million turnover, and [✂] per cent for loans to customers in the next band to £20 million turnover which it believed was consistent with the historical bad debt rate after recoveries of [✂] per cent for lending, or [✂] per cent inclusive of recoveries. It therefore considered that we should treat the [✂] per cent experience as a good indicator of its bad debt rate when we considered possible excess profits from its services to SME banking business.

6.56. Barclays also gave us its assessment of the economic cycles over the long term, which it noted was based more on art than science. It said that looking back over the past 50 years, two developments were apparent:

(a) The underlying rate of corporate insolvency had risen through each business cycle. The recent experience in the late 1990s, even though benign, was of a higher corporate insolvency rate than at any time except in the late 1980s. It illustrated this by noting that the corporate default rate (percentage of companies going into liquidation/receivership) was around 0.5 per cent in the 1950s, between 0.5 and 0.8 per cent in the 1960s, rose to around 1.6 per cent between 1980 and 1984 and then fell back to 1.1 per cent around 1987. It then increased to a peak of 2.5 per cent in 1990 and by 1993 fell back to around 1.2 per cent, a level that had been unchanged to date.

(b) The volatility of the bad debt cycle had increased. The volatility of defaults, as measured by the standard deviation of corporate defaults, increased steadily: 0.05 per cent in the 1950s, 0.10 per cent in the 1960s, 0.18 per cent in the 1970s, 0.30 per cent in the 1980s and 0.47 per cent in the 1990s. The length of business cycles had increased, for example it believed that in the 1960s/early 1970s the cycle was around six years, but the two cycles since had lengthened to around ten years each.

6.57. When assessing its profitability, Barclays told us that we should exclude bad debt recoveries from profits if individual years were considered in isolation or if averages were considered for periods less than the whole cycle, in considering whether it had earned excess profits from serving the SME market. Barclays' view was that bad debt recoveries were expected to be very small in the future, as the impact of the early 1990s recession tailed off, and therefore profits for future years would be lower because such benefits from recoveries would not arise. Equally, its view was that its profits since 1995 should exclude bad debt recoveries in determining whether it had made excess profits, and only included if a longer cycle was used.

6.58. Table 6.15 provides an analysis of the average net interest margin and bad debt charge by size of loans to SME banking business for 1998 and 1999. As stated earlier, average net interest spread decreased as the size of loans to SME banking business customers increased, such that in 1999, for loans below £50,000, the average net interest spread was [✄] per cent, but [✄] per cent for loans greater than £250,000. The level of bad debt charge as a percentage of loans remained fairly similar, irrespective of the size of loans. For example, in 1999 the bad debt percentage for loans below £50,000 and for loans greater than £250,000 were both around [✄] per cent, and were both [✄] in 1998. Barclays added that the cost of serving customers of different sizes and of providing loans of different sizes also varied.

TABLE 6.15 **Barclays: analysis of loans and overdrafts to SME banking business, 1998 and 1999**

	1998				1999			
Loans to SMEs	<£50k	£50k–£250k	>£250k	Total	<£50k	£50k–£250k	>£250k	Total
Total loans (£bn)								
Net interest income (£m)								
Bad debt charge (£m)								
Average net interest spread (%)								
Bad debt charge as a percentage of loans (%)*								
Overdrafts to SMEs Total overdrafts (£bn)								
Net interest income (£m)								
Bad debt charge (£m)								
Average net interest spread (%)								
Bad debt charge as a percentage of overdrafts (%)								

Figures omitted. See note on page iv.

Source: Barclays.

*For 1998, the figures were negligible.

6.59. Appendix 6.1 analyses the information for loans and overdrafts so that the trend in net spread, bad debts and levels of lending can be seen from 1994 for loans below £50,000, those between £50,000 and £250,000, and those greater than £250,000. Table 6.16 summarizes the average results from such activities for the five years to 1999. The table shows:

(a) For loans up to £50,000 the average bad debt charge as a percentage of lending was [✄] per cent, compared with overdrafts where the average bad debt rate was [✄] per cent. However, the average interest spread was [*Details omitted. See note on page iv.*], at [✄] per cent for loans and [✄] per cent for overdrafts.

(b) For loans between £50,000 and £250,000, the average bad debt charge as a percentage of lending was [✂] per cent, compared with overdrafts where the average bad debt rate was [✂] per cent. The average interest spread was [✂] per cent for both loans and overdrafts.

(c) For loans greater than £50,000, the average bad debt charge as a percentage of lending was [✂] per cent, compared with overdrafts where the average bad debt rate was [✂] per cent. The average interest spread was [✂] per cent for loans and [✂] per cent for overdrafts.

TABLE 6.16 **Barclays: summary of average performance from loans and overdrafts for the five years 1995 to 1999**

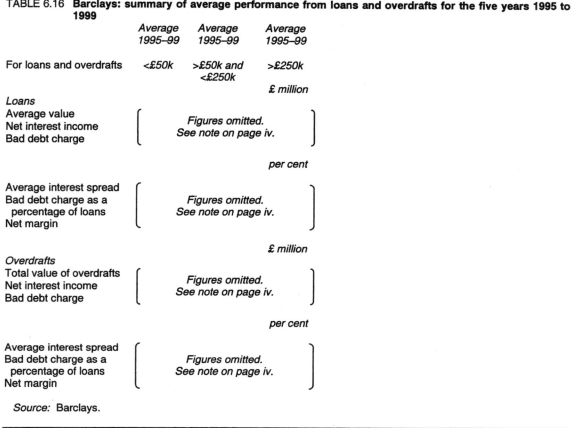

For loans and overdrafts	Average 1995–99 <£50k	Average 1995–99 >£50k and <£250k	Average 1995–99 >£250k
			£ million
Loans			
Average value			
Net interest income	*Figures omitted. See note on page iv.*		
Bad debt charge			
			per cent
Average interest spread			
Bad debt charge as a percentage of loans	*Figures omitted. See note on page iv.*		
Net margin			
			£ million
Overdrafts			
Total value of overdrafts			
Net interest income	*Figures omitted. See note on page iv.*		
Bad debt charge			
			per cent
Average interest spread			
Bad debt charge as a percentage of loans	*Figures omitted. See note on page iv.*		
Net margin			

Source: Barclays.

Future strategy in serving the SME banking business

6.60. [

Details omitted. See note on page iv.

]

6.61. [

Details omitted. See note on page iv.

]

6.62. [

]

6.63. [

]

6.64. [

]

6.65. [

]

6.66. [

]

Lloyds TSB

Overview of its business in serving SMEs

6.67. Chapter 5 deals in detail with the Lloyds TSB group position and business generally. The sections below deal with its SME banking business. Until 1991 Lloyds managed SME banking business customers out of its Retail Banking business unit. This reflected the fact that SME banking business customers were served out of the branch network. Regional directors managed a network of regional branches, with responsibility for all the business undertaken by those branches.

6.68. In late 1991 Lloyds Bank Commercial Services (of which the business known today as Commercial Banking formed part) was established as a separate business unit to manage customers with an annual turnover of more than £1 million and less than £100 million. This led to a policy of transferring the management of the SME relationships (at least for larger customers) from bank branches to dedicated relationship managers based in locations such as business parks. At around the same time, the Business Banking unit was also established to manage SME banking business customers with a turnover of up to £1 million. Once again, dedicated relationship managers took on responsibility for managing the relationship with Business Banking customers. This arrangement continues.

6.69. In 1999 the threshold for customers within Business Banking was increased from £1 million of turnover to £2 million of turnover. However, Lloyds TSB told us that the turnover limits were not strictly observed in the allocation of customers between Business Banking and Commercial Banking. The main determinant was the complexity of the customer's banking needs.

6.70. Traditionally TSB had principally served individual customers but, in the ten years prior to the 1995 merger with Lloyds, it had started to provide banking services to SMEs. In 1987 TSB had purchased Hill Samuel to enable TSB to become a broad-based banking group as it would bring greater strengths in insurance, asset management and treasury to TSB. The commercial banking business of Hill Samuel was considered to be complementary to that of TSB as Hill Samuel had greater corporate activity where TSB had greater small business activity. As a result, TSB (including Hill Samuel) had some 75,000 business customers by the time of the merger with Lloyds Bank in 1995.

6.71. The activities of TSB have not yet been fully integrated with the equivalent activities of Lloyds. Lloyds TSB said that it had not been possible to effect that integration until the enactment of the Lloyds TSB Act 1998, which provided for the formal merger of the two banks. Indeed, Lloyds TSB told us that it might, in certain circumstances, continue to serve ex-TSB customers on a different basis from that applicable to ex-Lloyds customers. This primarily reflected the different existing contractual arrangements entered into by Lloyds TSB with customers and, in the short term, the complexities of integrating IT systems or other practical restraints.

Financial performance of the SME banking business

6.72. We asked Lloyds TSB to provide us with profitability data on its SME banking business for the period between 1989 and 2000. It responded that the SME banking business was not a defined business unit within its existing organizational structure and that the SME banking business fell predominantly within five of its existing business units: Business Banking, Commercial Banking, Agricultural Mortgage Corporation plc (AMC), Lloyds TSB Asset Finance and Lloyds TSB Commercial Finance. Moreover, some of these business units served both SMEs and non-SME banking business customers. Lloyds TSB explained that it did not maintain separate accounts for the SME portions of those business units and there was no straightforward basis on which to extract financial data in respect of SMEs from a particular business unit, therefore the provision of data on the basis requested by the CC raised difficulties both in terms of principle and in terms of extraction of the relevant data.

6.73. Table 6.17 shows the profitability of Lloyds TSB's SME banking business from 1989 to 1996, which was produced as a special exercise for the Cruickshank report. Lloyds TSB said that the profitability table was not produced on the same basis as that provided to us. However, the table provided a good indicator of the bank's profitability from services to SME banking business customers over the period, particularly the bad debt charges incurred as a consequence of the recession of the early 1990s and the resultant impact on earnings. In 1992 and 1993, as a result of high bad debt charges, it reported operating losses of £[✕] million and £[✕] million respectively in respect of its SME banking business.

TABLE 6.17 **Lloyds TSB: profit and loss account from SME banking business, 1989 to 1996, as submitted for the purposes of the Cruickshank report**

£ million

Years ended 31 December

	1989	1990	1991	1992	1993	1994	1995	1996
Total operating income								
Operating expenses								
Operating profit before bad debt charge				*Figures omitted. See note on page iv.*				
Bad debt charge								
Operating profit								

Source: Lloyds TSB.

---

*Differs from operating income of £[✀] reported to us.
†Differs from operating costs of £[✀] million reported to us.

6.74. Lloyds TSB said that the difference between the 1996 operating income reported to the Cruickshank review of £[✀] million and that reported to us of £[✀] was mainly because of the inclusion of Lloyds TSB Asset Finance in the income figures reported to us. The difference between the 1996 operating costs reported to the review of £[✀] million and those reported to us of £[✀] million was also due to the additional costs associated with Lloyds TSB Asset Finance.

6.75. Table 6.18 shows the profitability of Lloyds TSB's SME banking business from 1996 to 2000 continuing the analysis in Table 6.17. Operating income increased [✀] per cent from £[✀] billion in 1996 to £[✀] billion in 2000. Operating expenses were £[✀] million in 1996, increased to a high of £[✀] million in 1998, and fell to £[✀] million in 1999. In 2000 they were £[✀] million. The level of bad debt charge fluctuated over the period, from a high of £[✀] million in 1996 to a low of £[✀] million in 1999. In 2000 it increased by [✀] per cent from 1999 to £[✀] million. Operating profit (before long-term pension costs) was £[✀] million in 1996, increased to £[✀] million in 1997, fell to £[✀] million in 1998 and increased to £[✀] million in 2000. Lloyds TSB said that the fall in 1998 was due to increased operating costs from exceptional merger and IT-related costs, namely the integration of Lloyds and TSB processing systems, the 'towards one bank' restructuring and marketing programme, and the costs of Year 2000 IT compliance issues.

TABLE 6.18 **Lloyds TSB: profit and loss account from SME banking business, 1996 to 2000**

£ million

Years ended 31 December

	1996	1997	1998	1999	2000
Current accounts (benefit of funds)	*				
Deposit accounts	*				
Loans and overdrafts	*				
Other—clubs and charities	*				
Net interest income†	*				
Net fees and commissions	*	✀	*Figures omitted. See note on page iv.*		
Other income	*				
Total operating income					
Operating expenses					
Operating profit before provisions	✀				
Bad debt charge					
Operating profit					
Long-term pension costs	‡	‡			
Net profit before tax§	(✀)				

Source: Lloyds TSB.

---

*Not provided.
†See also Table 6.19, which shows the items in this table as a percentage of total operating income.
‡The charge that would have arisen if Lloyds TSB's current pension scheme was not in surplus. Data for this adjustment was provided only for 1998, 1999 and 2000.
§As requested by us, these figures were calculated on the basis that all lending is financed from borrowing in wholesale markets. In fact a proportion will be financed by the bank's equity, and it is therefore necessary to make an adjustment for this (see Table 6.20) before comparing returns on capital derived from these profit figures with the bank's cost of capital.

6.76. Table 6.19 further analyses the overall performance of Lloyds TSB's SME banking business from 1996 to 2000 by showing all items as a percentage of operating income. Between 1997 and 2000 net interest income was around [✁] per cent of operating income compared with net fees and commissions at around [✁] per cent of operating income.

TABLE 6.19 **Lloyds TSB: operating profit and loss items as a percentage of operating income from SME banking business, 1996 to 2000**

per cent

	1996	1997	1998	1999*	2000

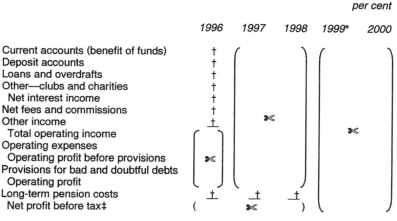

Current accounts (benefit of funds)
Deposit accounts
Loans and overdrafts
Other—clubs and charities
 Net interest income
Net fees and commissions
Other income
 Total operating income
Operating expenses
 Operating profit before provisions
Provisions for bad and doubtful debts
 Operating profit
Long-term pension costs
 Net profit before tax‡

Source: Lloyds TSB.

---

*Excluding bad debt charge, the cost:income ratio would be [✁] per cent (ie income remains unchanged at £[✁], costs increase from £[✁] million to £[✁] million, as a result of a long-term pension charge of £[✁] million) shown in Table 6.18.

†Not provided.

‡As requested by us, these figures were calculated on the basis that all lending is financed from borrowing in wholesale markets. In fact a proportion will be financed by the bank's equity, and it is therefore necessary to make an adjustment for this (see Table 6.18) before comparing returns on capital derived from these profit figures with the bank's cost of capital.

6.77. The SME banking business cost:income ratio (before including long-term pension costs) between 1996 and 2000 was at its highest level (between 57 and 59 per cent) in 1997 and 1998, fell to 49 per cent in 1999, and since increased to 52 per cent in 2000. Lloyds TSB said that in 1999, the SME banking business realized the benefits from its investment expenditures in 1998 (discussed in paragraph 6.75) and also pursued income growth strategies. For example, the benign economic conditions enabled the SME banking business to grow its loan book, without unduly compromising the quality; grow the volume of pension and insurance products sold; attract and retain larger credit balances on deposit accounts; and benefit from operational gearing. Lloyds TSB said that overall the lower cost:income ratio in 1999 of 49 per cent (before including long-term pension costs) was due to operating cost efficiencies, increased sales and economies of scale. We noted that the SME banking business cost:income ratio in 1999 of 49 per cent was higher than that of the whole bank at 46 per cent, as shown in Chapter 5. Lloyds TSB said that the increase in the cost:income ratio from 49 per cent in 1999 to 52 per cent in 2000 primarily reflected the presentational change in the accounting for operating leases. This increased both the depreciation charge and the operating income while reducing the net interest income. In addition there was a higher level of investment costs in 2000 compared with 1999, particularly in business banking.

6.78. Lloyds TSB said that, when assessing its profitability from SME banking business, we should reduce profits for its notional pension costs, which in 1999 were estimated at £[✁] million. Accordingly the revised true costs of its SME banking business in 1999 were £[✁] million against income of £[✁], resulting in a revised cost:income ratio of 51 per cent.

Attributable capital to support the SME banking business and potential returns

6.79. Tables 6.17 to 6.19 consider the trends in Lloyds TSB's profits from its SME banking business. In order to form a view on the significance of such profits we also consider Lloyds TSB's capital

327

base. We look at this subject in greater detail in Chapter 7 for all the main suppliers. In our discussion with Lloyds TSB on determining the attributable capital to support its services to SMEs, we made a number of calculations for the years 1998 to 2000, based on our methodology discussed in paragraphs 6.22 and 6.23.

6.80. Applying our methodology we estimated that the capital requirement of the SME banking business (based on an apportionment of its closing balance sheet capital for 1998 to 2000) was £[✂] for 1998, £[✂] for 1999, and £[✂] for 2000. In Table 6.18 we noted that Lloyds TSB's profits from SME banking business were based on its calculation of net income from lending as if wholly financed from wholesale markets at LIBOR. However, in identifying the rate of return to compare with the cost of capital, an adjustment must be made to reflect that a proportion of lending was funded by capital and not from the wholesale markets. This is necessary to avoid an overestimation of interest costs (ie double counting), and the appropriate adjustment is attributable capital times the average three-month LIBOR. The rates used for each of the years 1998, 1999 and 2000 were 7.3 per cent, 5.45 per cent and 6.1 per cent respectively.

6.81. Table 6.20 incorporates this adjustment together with the information shown in Table 6.18 on profitability, and shows estimates of returns (subject to further adjustments discussed in Chapter 7). For 1999, which was a year with relatively low bad debt levels, Lloyds TSB's pre-tax return on capital (derived using the methodology above) was [✂] per cent. In Chapter 7 we consider Lloyds TSB's appropriate cost of capital, and what adjustments are necessary regarding these returns. In Chapter 2 we give our conclusions on this issue.

6.82. An alternative method of calculating the capital allocated to the SME banking business would be to use an average capital figure, for example a simple average of the opening and closing capital base, rather than a return based on the closing figure. For 1999, we calculated that the effect on the pre-tax return of using a simple average would be an increase of four percentage points to [✂] per cent.

TABLE 6.20 **Lloyds TSB: summary of profits, capital and returns from Lloyds TSB services to SMEs, 1998 to 2000**

£ million

	1998	1999	2000
Information from Table 6.19			
Income			
Operating costs			
Long-term pension costs*		✂	
Bad debt charge			
Adjustment for attributable capital†			
Operating profit before tax and exceptional items			
Attributable capital (based on closing capital for the whole bank and proportions of RWAs)	(✂)	(✂)‡	(✂)
Average attributable capital	§	(✂)	

per cent

Pre-tax return based on closing attributable capital	(	✂	)
Pre-tax return based on average attributable capital	§	(✂)‡	(✂)

Source: CC based on information from Lloyds TSB.

*We have assumed similar figures in 1998 for pension costs and the capital fund recharges, based on information supplied by Lloyds TSB for 1999 and 2000.

†7.3 per cent for 1998, 5.45 per cent for 1999 and 6.1 per cent for 2000, based on three-month LIBOR.

‡The attributable capital for 1999, which is shown as based on the closing capital level for Lloyds TSB, could alternatively be based on the average of the closing attributable capital figures for 1998 and 1999. The resultant figure would therefore be £[✂], and the pre-tax return, based on this average attributable capital, would be [✂] per cent, ie an increase of [✂] percentage points.

§Not estimated.

6.83. Lloyds TSB told us that since January 2001 it had adopted an equity attribution model as its principal method for imputing equity requirements to each business unit. Until 1999 it had relied on the regulatory capital rules to impute equity requirements to each business unit. In 2000 it continued to use the regulatory capital rules as the basis for imputing equity but also used the equity attribution model as a 'shadow' system.

6.84. The equity attribution model measured equity for each business unit based on a bottom-up approach and not an allocation of regulatory capital. Lloyds TSB said that the level of equity attributed to the business units took into account five types of risk: credit, market, insurance, business and operational. It concluded that the equity attribution model measured an absolute minimum of required capital, without making an allowance for the additional capital that a business would in practice require. For this reason, any capital figure derived from the equity attribution model would understate the full capital requirements of any business.

6.85. To this end, Lloyds proposed an uplift to the equity attribution figures to reflect full capital requirements. An illustration of how this works is detailed in Chapter 7. The minimum capital requirement for the SME banking business in 1999 to cover the identified risks was an estimated £[✂] using the equity attribution model. This was lower than the figure based on the risk-weighted basis. For 2000 Lloyds TSB's estimate of the minimum capital requirement for the SME banking business was £[✂].

6.86. Lloyds TSB said that its budgeted post-tax return on economic equity in 2000 was around [✂] per cent for Business Banking (which serviced business customers with turnover up to £2 million) and around [✂] per cent for Commercial Banking (which serviced business customers with turnover greater than £2 million and less than £100 million).

Further analysis of income and expenses

6.87. Table 6.21 provides an analysis of operating income by type of banking service to SME banking business customers from 1998 to 2000. During 1998 to 2000 the five main types of banking services from which the bank earned income were loans, asset finance, current accounts with overdrafts, deposits and current accounts with no overdrafts. In aggregate for 2000, these services contributed [✂] per cent of the £[✂] billion operating income from the bank's services to SME banking business customers. Current accounts with no overdrafts were the largest source of operating income and contributed [✂] per cent of operating income. This compared with loans that contributed [✂] per cent of operating income, current accounts with overdrafts that contributed [✂] per cent of operating income and deposits that contributed [✂] per cent of operating income.

TABLE 6.21 **Lloyds TSB: analysis of income by type of banking service to SME banking business customers, 1998 to 2000**

Years ended 31 December

	£ million			Income share (%)		
	1998	*1999*	*2000*	*1998*	*1999*	*2000*
Net income from:*						
Loans	†			†		
Current accounts utilizing an overdraft facility	†			†		
Other current accounts	†			†		
Deposits	†			†		
Asset finance	†		[✂]	†		[✂]
Subtotal	†			†		
Merchant acquiring	†			†		
Other income	†			†		
Clubs and charities	†			†		
Total	([✂])			([✂])		

Source: Lloyds TSB.

*Includes net interest income. Operational costs and bad debt charges are then deducted from this income to derive net operating profit.
†Not available.

6.88. Table 6.22 provides a further breakdown of net operating income from the SME banking business into net interest income and 'other' income for 1999 and 2000. The table shows the actual income earned, as well as the notional cost of funds to finance the lending, and the benefit of funds deposited by SMEs. Lloyds TSB derived considerable interest income, not only from loans and overdrafts made to SME banking business customers, but also from money in deposit and current accounts of the SMEs. The table also shows the net interest margin earned by the bank from different types of banking relationships with the SMEs. For 1999 the average value of deposits from SMEs totalled £[✂] billion, which in effect Lloyds was able to use in financing its lending to SMEs. In 2000 the average value of deposits increased to £[✂] billion.

6.89. Lloyds TSB said that net interest income for loans, asset finance and current accounts utilizing an overdraft facility was made up of actual interest earned less the cost of funds as determined by its Group Balance Sheet Management division. It added that net interest income from customers' deposits and other current accounts (no overdraft facility or where a facility was not being utilized) was the benefit of funds to the bank less the actual interest paid to customers. As other current accounts were non-interest-bearing, there was no interest paid to customers.

6.90. In 1999 and 2000 other current accounts (no overdraft facility or where a facility was not being utilized) had the highest net interest margin at [✂] and [✂] per cent respectively. Net interest margins for the other types of services in 2000 were as follows: [✂] per cent for loans, [✂] per cent for deposits and [✂] per cent for overdrafts.

6.91. Table 6.23 provides a further analysis of operating profits by type of service to SME banking business customers for 1999 and 2000. However, Lloyds TSB told us that it was unable to analyse operating profit between loans and current accounts utilizing overdraft facilities, and we have therefore shown combined operating profit for both types of banking services. Effectively for 2000:

(a) loans and overdraft services showed net income of £[✂] million, and operating profit (after bad debt charges) of £[✂] million ([✂] per cent of net income);

(b) other current accounts (no overdraft facility or where a facility was not being utilized) showed net income of £[✂] million, and operating profit of £[✂] million ([✂] per cent);

(c) deposit services showed net income of £[✂] million, no bad debt charges and operating profit of £[✂] million ([✂] per cent);

(d) asset finance showed net income of £[✂] million, and operating losses (after bad debt charges) of £[✂] million;

TABLE 6.22 **Lloyds TSB: analysis of operating income by type of service to SMEs, 1999 and to 2000**

Years ended 31 December

	£ million		Margin and lending balances	
	1999	*2000*	*1999*	*2000*
Loans				
Interest income				
Allocated cost of funds				
Net interest income				
Account management fees				
Other				
Net income*				
Average balance of loans on balance sheet (£m)			[✂]	
Annualized net interest (%)†				
Current accounts utilizing overdraft facility				
Interest income				
Allocated cost of funds				
Net interest income				
Fees for lending‡				
Net income*				
Average overdraft balance on balance sheet (£m)§			[✂]	
Annualized net interest (%)†				
Other current accounts¶				
Interest income				
Benefit of funds from SMEs				
Interest paid				
Net interest income				
Fees (including money transmission)				
Other				
Net income¤				
Average balance on balance sheet (£m)§	Figures omitted.		[✂]	
Annualized net interest (%)†	See note			
	on page iv.			
Deposits				
Benefit of funds from SMEs				
Interest paid				
Net interest income				
Other income				
Net income¤				
Average deposit balance on balance sheet (£m)			[✂]	
Annualized net interest (%)†				
Asset finance				
Interest income				
Allocated cost of funds				
Net interest income				
Fees				
Other#				
Net income*				
Average account balance on balance sheet (£m)				~
Annualized net interest (%)†			(✂)	~
Other net income from				
Merchant acquiring				
Sundry other services✶				
Clubs and charities				
Total net income from SMEs				

Source: Lloyds TSB.

---

*Operational costs and bad debt charges are deducted from this income to derive the net operating profit from this service to customers.

†Net interest as percentages of average balances. For the current accounts this is only an approximate measure as there will be interest from some accounts categorized as having utilized their overdraft facility that at some point in the year may have been in credit. Similarly other current accounts may have been in overdraft at some point over the year.

‡This represents account management fees only. All money transmission fees earned on current accounts, whether they have an overdraft or not, are captured by the one fee income account. This is presented under the classification of fee income for current accounts with no overdrafts.

§These balances are approximate as some individual accounts will have changed their classification, as well as their balance during the year.

¶Includes current accounts without an overdraft facility and current accounts with an overdraft facility that has not been utilized. Of the current accounts without an overdraft facility, this classification will include those accounts that have an unauthorized overdraft. The related interest charged on these balances has also been accounted for under this classification.

¤Before deducting operational costs, to derive the net operating profit from the services to customers.

#The £[✂] million debit balance for 1999 relates to commissions paid by the Asset Finance business. In 2000 the debit is partly offset by the impact of the change in accounting policy for operating leases.

~Data not provided.

✶Mainly represents fees associated with the provision of factoring services to SMEs.

(e) merchant acquiring and 'other' services (mainly factoring services) showed combined net income of £[✂] million, and operating profit (after bad debt charges) of £[✂] million; and

(f) clubs and charities showed income of £[✂] million and operating profit of £[✂] million ([✂] per cent).

TABLE 6.23 **Lloyds TSB: analysis of operating profit by type of service to SMEs, 1999 and 2000**

Years ended 31 December

	£ million		Proportion of total net income (%)	
	1999	*2000*	*1999*	*2000*
Loans and overdrafts*				
Net income†				
Costs				
Bad debt charge				
Operating profit				
Other current accounts‡				
Net income†				
Costs				
Operating profit				
Deposits				
Net income†				
Costs				
Operating profit				
Asset finance				
Net income†				
Costs				
Bad debt charge				
Operating profit				
Merchant acquiring				
Net income†				
Costs				
Bad debt charge				
Operating profit				
Other income				
Income				
Costs				
Bad debt charge				
Operating profit				
Clubs and charities				
Income				
Costs				
Operating profit				
Total operating profit from SMEs before providing for doubtful debts				
Total operating profit from SMEs after providing for doubtful debts				

Figures omitted. See note on page iv.

Source: Lloyds TSB.

*Lloyds TSB was unable to analyse operating profit between loans and overdrafts.
†Net interest income plus fees and commissions. Table 6.22 shows how net interest income was derived.
‡Includes current accounts without an overdraft facility and current accounts with an overdraft facility that has not been utilized. Of the current accounts without an overdraft facility, this classification will include those accounts that have an unauthorized overdraft. The related interest charged on these balances has also been accounted for under this classification.

6.92. Table 6.24 provides a further analysis of operating profits for the SME banking business using 1999 profits for each main service category, both before and after allowing for bad debt charges. These profits have been presented as a proportion of total profits both before and after bad debt charges. Loans and current accounts show the highest contributions to profit with [✂] per cent of profits before allowing for bad debts and [✂] per cent of profits after allowing for bad debts being represented by these services. Deposits were the next highest contributor to profits before and after allowing for bad debts with [✂] per cent and [✂] per cent respectively.

TABLE 6.24 **Lloyds TSB: comparison of profit by type of service to SMEs, 1999**

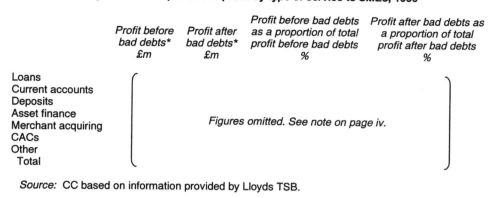

	Profit before bad debts* £m	Profit after bad debts* £m	Profit before bad debts as a proportion of total profit before bad debts %	Profit after bad debts as a proportion of total profit after bad debts %
Loans				
Current accounts				
Deposits				
Asset finance				
Merchant acquiring	*Figures omitted. See note on page iv.*			
CACs				
Other				
Total				

Source: CC based on information provided by Lloyds TSB.

---

*Per Table 6.23.

6.93. Operating profit from lending on loans and overdrafts, and asset finance were further reduced by bad debt charges. Bad debt charges in respect of lending on loans and overdrafts were £[✂] million and on asset finance were £[✂] million in 2000.

6.94. Other current accounts with no overdraft facility or where the facility was not utilized had no bad debt costs and were the largest contributor to operating profit for the SME banking business, at £[✂] million in 2000. As shown in Table 6.22, this source of operating profits had benefits of funds of £[✂] million, against which interest costs were offset, leaving a net interest benefit of £[✂] million that contributed significantly to this result.

6.95. Table 6.25 further analyses Lloyds TSB's costs for 1999 and 2000 between direct and indirect costs by type of service, and shows the cost:income ratios for such services for these years. The percentage of costs that were direct or indirect varied between the service categories, and overall in 2000 [✂] per cent of total costs were direct and [✂] per cent were indirect compared with [✂] and [✂] in 1999 respectively. For deposits and other current accounts (no overdraft facility or where the facility was not being utilized), for both 1999 and 2000, over [✂] per cent of costs were indirect, which Lloyds TSB said reflected the use of centralized group-wide functions, such as the branch network, in servicing customers with these products. Lloyds TSB said that the branch network was a distinct management unit which incurred direct costs through its activities and recharged these costs to the business unit responsible for the customer relationship, hence giving rise to indirect costs.

TABLE 6.25 Lloyds TSB: analysis of 1999 and 2000 income and costs from services to SMEs by product category, and summary of cost:income ratios by type of service

| | | | £ million | | per cent | |
| | | | Operating costs | | Cost proportion | |
	Income	Costs	Direct	Indirect	Direct	Indirect
1999						
Loans and overdrafts						
Other current accounts						
Deposits						
Asset finance						
Merchant acquiring						
Other						
Clubs and charities						
Total operating costs as per Table 6.16		*				
Bad debt charge as per Table 6.16						
Total costs						
2000						
Loans and overdrafts						
Other current accounts						
Deposits						
Asset finance						
Merchant acquiring						
Other						
Clubs and charities						
Total operating costs as per Table 6.16		*				
Bad debt charge as per Table 6.16						
Total costs						

Figures omitted. See note on page iv.

	1999	2000
Cost:income ratios		
Loans and overdrafts		
Deposits		
Current accounts (with no overdrafts)		
Asset finance		
Merchant acquiring	✂	
Other income		
Charities and clubs		
Overall		

Source: Lloyds TSB.

*As identified in Table 6.18 but excludes notional long-term pension costs of £[✄] million.

6.96. Lloyds TSB emphasized that its costs were allocated by detailed costing systems and it believed its cost allocations to services and the SME banking business were fair and reasonable. Its methodology for allocating indirect costs was called 'cost transfer pricing'. Where the operation was volume driven, costs were recharged on a unit cost basis multiplied by volume, and where the operation was non-volume driven, other bases were used.

6.97. [

Details omitted. See note on page iv.

]

6.98. Table 6.26 provides a further analysis of operating cost for services to SME banking business customers by cost category from 1997 to 2000. Within direct costs, staff cost was the largest cost category and in 2000 was £[✄] million (or [✄] per cent of total costs). Within indirect costs, centralized IT and network services cost was the largest category, and in 2000 was £[✄] million (or [✄] per cent of total costs).

TABLE 6.26 Lloyds TSB: analysis of SME banking business operating cost by category, 1997 to 2000

Years ended 31 December

	£ million				Proportion of total (%)			
	1997	1998	1999	2000	1997	1998	1999	2000
Direct costs								
Staff costs								
Premises and equipment								
Depreciation*								
Other costs								
Charities and clubs								
Total								
Indirect costs								
Centralized IT and network services								
Selling and marketing								
Central costs								
Transmission services								
Other								
Clubs and charities								
Total								
Total operating costs								

Figures omitted. See note on page iv.

Source: Lloyds TSB.

---

*In 2000, Lloyds TSB treated operating lease assets as fixed assets rather than as part of loans and advances. Accordingly, the depreciation charge for 2000 has increased significantly.

6.99. Lloyds TSB said that centralized IT and network services included the costs of branch networks and relationship managers, and that the main cost categories were staff, property occupation and shared IT systems. Central costs included the cost of sustaining the business, which was predominantly related to strategy, the costs of integrating the bank 'towards one bank' and the cost associated with other one-off projects such as EMU and Year 2000 issues.

6.100. In 2000 other indirect costs totalled £[✄] million and consisted of costs allocated to Business Banking and Commercial Banking. For Business Banking, this included the cost of planning and developing the retail network, specific IT projects, marketing and premises. For Commercial Banking, this included premises costs and risk management.

6.101. We showed in Chapter 5 the five primary business units within Lloyds TSB that provide services to the SME banking business. Table 6.27 separates 1999 indirect cost for the SME banking business between Business Banking, which serviced business customers with turnover of up to £2 million, and the other four business units. We show the analysis of indirect costs at £[✄] million for Business Banking separately in 1999, as it accounted for [✄] per cent of the total indirect costs of £[✄] million allocated to the SME banking business. Lloyds TSB said that Business Banking had relatively higher allocated costs than personal banking due to the complex nature of its activities, which required business managers with more expertise in a wide range of business fields and more face-to-face customer relationships. The table also shows a further analysis of the indirect costs allocated to Business Banking by type of activity.

TABLE 6.27 Lloyds TSB: further analysis of 1999 indirect costs for services to SMEs

£ million

	Business Banking £0–£2m	Other*	Total SME £0–£25m
Indirect costs			
Centralized IT and network services			
Selling and marketing			
Central costs			
Transmission services			
Other			
Charities and clubs			
Total†		*Figures omitted.*	
		See note on page iv.	
Indirect costs by activity			
Branch network			
Distribution			
Central money transmission			
IT			
Other			
Total			

Source: Lloyds TSB.

*Includes Commercial Banking (SME customers with turnover greater than £2 million), AMC, Lloyds TSB Asset Finance and Lloyds TSB Commercial Finance.
†Total indirect costs as per Table 6.26.

6.102. Of the £[✀] million indirect costs allocated to Business Banking in 1999, [✀] per cent (£[✀] million) was for branch network costs and included the costs of opening new accounts, managing existing accounts and branch transaction costs. We provide a further analysis of branch network costs in Table 6.28.

6.103. The other types of activities that contributed to indirect costs for Business Banking were as follows:

(a) Distribution costs of £[✀] million: this included the cost of support services for 1999 branch closures and relocations, and operational service centres that provided telephony services.

(b) Central money transmission costs of £[✀] million: this included the cost of processing and supporting UK and international transactions, covering paper and electronic/automated payments.

(c) IT costs of £[✀] million: this included the cost (including depreciation) of maintaining and supporting the core banking system, PCs and projects.

(d) Other costs of £[✀] million: this included the provision of finance and human resources support, selling and marketing costs, purchasing, mail and distribution and property.

6.104. Table 6.28 provides a further analysis of 1999 branch network costs allocated to Business Banking of £[✀] million. The cost of opening new accounts for existing and new customers, ie loans, overdrafts and current accounts, was £[✀] million ([✀] per cent of total branch network costs), and the cost of managing existing accounts was £[✀] million ([✀] per cent of the total). Branch transaction costs were £[✀] million ([✀] per cent of the total), of which credits (cash and cheques) paid in at branches accounted for £[✀] million.

TABLE 6.28 Lloyds TSB: analysis of branch network costs for Business Banking, 1999

	£m	Proportion of total %	Number of accounts '000	Average cost per account £
Opening new accounts for existing and new customers				
Managing existing accounts		*Figures omitted. See note on page iv.*		
Total account costs				
Branch transaction costs	*			
Total branch network costs				

Source: Lloyds TSB.

*Credits (cash and cheques) paid in at branches accounted for costs of £[✄] million.

6.105. Lloyds said that the high branch network costs of £[✄] million in 1999 reflected recent customer growth and greater use of accounts by business customers when compared with personal customers. In addition, it was also due to the complexity of its relationship with the business customer, which required more face-to-face managerial input and was often at customers' premises. For example, each of its Business Banking managers had, on average, [✄] customers compared with [✄] customers for its Personal Banking managers. Lloyds TSB said that the level of service offered by a relationship manager of an SME banking business customer was, at an absolute minimum, an annual consultation. From there, as dictated by the needs of the customer, more extensive and frequent contact was maintained. The level of care required greatly depended on the nature of the business of the customer. Some relationship managers deal with a much lesser number of customers than the average quoted above, with the greater proportion of this customer portfolio requiring more regular, intensive contact.

6.106. Table 6.28 also shows that in 1999 the average cost of opening a new account was £[✄], compared with an average annual cost of £[✄] for maintaining an existing account. [
Details omitted. See note on page iv.

]

6.107. Table 6.29 shows an analysis of Lloyds TSB's personnel serving SMEs in 1999 and 2000 by location and function, in terms of FTE personnel.

6.108. In 2000 there were the equivalent of 6,545 personnel involved in the provision of services to SME banking business customers, of which [✄] directly served SME banking business customers and [✄] were part of the indirect cost base of the business units. Further, 5,154 personnel were wholly dedicated to the SME banking business (79 per cent), of which [✄] people operated from branches. Those personnel who had partial responsibilities in serving SME banking business customers numbered 1,391 and were located in central processing centres, regional and head offices.

6.109. In terms of functions, [✄] personnel were in selling and marketing, [✄] were in administration, [✄] were in operations and [✄] were in management. Overall, the cost of personnel serving SMEs was £[✄] million at an average cost of £[✄], which compared with the whole bank's average cost of around £[✄] (ie [✄   ]). Based on total income from SME banking business customers of £[✄] billion in 2000, each FTE person generated income of around £[✄].

TABLE 6.29 Lloyds TSB: summary of direct personnel serving SME banking business customers analysed by location of duties and by function, 1999 and 2000

	Number of persons 100% serving SMEs	FTE of persons with partial involvement	Total direct personnel
1999			
Analysis of direct personnel by location			
Branch			
Central processing centres			
Regional offices			
Head Office	*Figures omitted. See note on page iv.*		
Other—Business service centres			
Asset finance			
AMC			
Total direct personnel in SME banking business	4,564	1,183	5,747*
Personnel in non-SME banking business			70,310†
			76,057
Analysis of direct personnel by function			
Selling and marketing			
Management			
Administration	*Figures omitted. See note on page iv.*		
Operations staff			
Other			
Total number	4,564	1,183	5,747*
Personnel in non-SME banking business			70,310†
			76,057
2000			
Analysis of direct personnel by location			
Branch			
Central processing centres			
Regional Offices			
Head Office	*Figures omitted. See note on page iv.*		
Other—Business service centres			
Asset Finance			
AMC			
Total direct personnel in SME banking business	5,154	1,391	6,545*
Personnel in non-SME banking business			70,995†
			77,540
Analysis of direct personnel by function			
Selling and marketing			
Management			
Administration	*Figures omitted. See note on page iv.*		
Operations staff			
Other			
Total number	5,154	1,391	6,545*
Personnel in non-SME banking business			70,995†
			77,540

Source: Lloyds TSB.

---

*In 1999 total employment costs for SME banking business was £[✂] million, which equated to an average cost of £[✂] per employee. In 2000 total employment costs for SME banking business was £[✂] million, which equated to an average cost of £[✂] per employee (after making an allowance for a full year of Chartered Trust which was acquired on 1 September 2000).

†In 1999 total employment costs for non-SME banking business were £[✂], which equated to an average cost of £[✂] per employee. In 2000, total employment costs for non-SME banking business were £[✂], which equated to an average cost of £[✂] per employee. Lloyds TSB told us that the year-on-year increase in staff costs arose from the impact of acquisitions (Scottish Widows and the non-SME part of Chartered Trust); increased severance payments; millennium-related overtime; an additional provision in respect of employee share schemes; higher levels of performance-related sales force and senior management bonuses; a change in mix of staff towards higher grades; and group e-commerce activities.

6.110. Lloyds TSB told us that in 2000 the group spent £[✂] million on marketing and advertising ([✂] per cent of total income). It estimated that its business units serving SME banking business customers incurred £[✂] million in the form of direct advertising, marketing and promotions and a further £[✂] million in the form of indirect costs allocated from Group Customer Marketing. It said that the estimate of direct and indirect costs at £[✂] million was overstated as the relevant business units also provided services to non-SME banking business customers, but it was not able to estimate the proportion that related to SME banking business.

6.111. Lloyds TSB said that its business units used different approaches to marketing. Business Banking, which focused on smaller SME banking business customers, was involved in mass-market retention and attraction of customers. In contrast, Commercial Banking, which provided services to larger SME banking business customers, focused on particular customers and prospective customers; hence it relied more on relationship managers as a means of marketing. It added that relationship and business development managers within Commercial Banking and Business Banking included an element of marketing-type activity but such activities were classified as staff costs.

6.112. Having considered the costs and income by type of activity in paragraph 6.88 from Lloyds TSB's services to SMEs, Table 6.30 summarizes such operating profits from 1998 to 2000. It shows an analysis of operating profit (after bad debt charge) by type of service provided to SME banking business customers from 1998 to 2000. The SME banking business achieved operating profits of £[✂] million in 1998, £[✂] million in 1999 and £[✂] million in 2000. In 2000 operating profit from current accounts with no overdrafts was £[✂] million ([✂] per cent of operating profit) and was derived mainly from the benefit of the funds deposited by SME banking business customers with Lloyds TSB. The operating profit from loans and overdrafts was £[✂] million and from deposits was £[✂] million, which represented [✂] per cent and [✂] per cent of operating profit respectively.

TABLE 6.30 **Lloyds TSB: summary of SME banking business operating profit (after bad debt charges) by type of banking services, 1998 to 2000**

Years ended 31 December

	£ million			Proportion of total profit %		
	1998	1999	2000	1998	1999	2000
Operating profit arising from						
Loans and current accounts with overdrafts*	†			†		
Other current accounts	†			†		
Deposits	†			†		
Asset finance†*	†	✂		†	✂	
Merchant acquiring	†			†		
Other income	†			†		
Clubs and charities						
Total	(✂)			(✂)		
Operating profit as a percentage of operating income	per cent					
Loans and overdrafts†	†					
Other current accounts	†					
Deposits	†					
Asset finance†	†	✂				
Merchant acquiring	†					
Other activities	†					
Clubs and charities						
Total	(✂)					

Source: Lloyds TSB.

*Operating profit is calculated after bad debt charges but before pension costs. For 1999, the bad debt charge from loans and overdrafts was £[✂] million ([✂] per cent of income) and £[✂] million from asset finance ([✂] per cent of income). In 2000 the Asset Finance division had a loss of £[✂] million which Lloyds TSB explained as arising from incurring restructuring costs arising from the acquisition of Chartered Trust, and from lower levels of new business particularly in motor finance and plant and equipment leasing.
†Not available.

6.113. In 2000 operating profit as a percentage of operating income was [✂] per cent for deposits, and [✂] per cent for other current accounts. Loans and current accounts with overdrafts had a percentage of [✂], while asset finance had losses of £[✂] million, giving a negative percentage of [✂] per cent. All profits analysed were after bad debt charges.

Balance sheet items

6.114. Table 6.31 shows total loans/advances to customers, and total customer accounts in credit for Lloyds TSB's SME banking business between 1996 and 2000. Lloyds TSB said that the SME banking business as defined by us was not a separately identifiable business unit within its business structure, and therefore that it was unable to produce a full balance sheet for the business. However, we noted that constructing a balance sheet for this business would be inconclusive, as discussed in paragraph 6.49.

TABLE 6.31 **Lloyds TSB: loans, and customer accounts in credit from services to SME banking business customers, 1996 to 2000**

£ billion

As at 31 December

	1996	1997	1998	1999	2000
Loans, asset finance, advances to customers and overdrawn current accounts					
Customer accounts in credit*		*Figures omitted. See note on page iv.*			
Funds required					

Source: Lloyds TSB

*Includes both deposit accounts, and current accounts in credit.

6.115. Between 1996 and 2000 the level of loans, asset finance and overdrafts provided to SME banking business customers remained relatively constant at around £[✂] billion and £[✂] billion. Over the same period the level of SME customer accounts in credit increased from £[✂] billion in 1996 to £[✂] billion in 2000. [*Details omitted. See note on page iv.*]

Capital expenditure and development costs

6.116. Lloyds TSB told us that its capital expenditure levels for the bank over the three years to 2002 were around £[✂] million to £[✂] million a year. The main costs would be [*Details omitted. See note on page iv.*], which account for more than [✂] per cent of the planned expenditure. The business units that serve SME banking business customers had total capital expenditure forecast at around £[✂] million, but much of this related to non-SME banking business of those business units which carried on both SME and non-SME banking business. Lloyds TSB noted that there was an additional element of capital costs, that it could not directly attribute to the business units concerned, relating to capital projects that benefited the whole bank, such as expenditure on IT, the branch network and central money transmission operations.

6.117. Regarding product development initiatives, it noted that cost estimates and net benefit estimates were developed for each project aimed at meeting customer needs. The totals were then compared with investment funds and resources available to the group, and where too many projects required approval, a prioritization process was applied.

Bad debts

6.118. Table 6.32 shows the level of bad debt provision at the year end, and bad debt charge to the profit and loss account between 1989 and 2000 relating to its SME banking business. Lloyds TSB was not able to provide us with a series of its bad debt charges for services to SMEs over the 12 years to 2000 as it did not have the detailed data from earlier years from which to extract the SME data for the asset finance businesses. It was able to provide this data only for the year ended 31 December 1997 onwards.

TABLE 6.32 **Lloyds TSB: analysis of bad debt provision and charges to profit and loss account from services to SMEs**

£ million

Analysis of bad debt provision	1989	1990	1991	1992	1993	1994	1995	1996	1997	1998	1999	2000
General provision	*	*	*	*	*	*	*	*	*	*	*	*
Specific provision	*	*	*	*	*	*	*	*	*	*	*	*
Bad debt provision	*	*	*	*	*	*	*	*	*	*	*	*
Analysis of bad debt charge to profit and loss												
New and additional provisions	*	*	*	*	*	*	*	*	*	*	*	*
Releases of provisions established in earlier years	*	*	*	*	*	*	*	*	*	*	*	*
Recoveries of advances written off in earlier years	*	*	*	*	*	*	*	*	*	*	*	*
Bad debt charge to profit and loss	*	*	*	*	*	*	*	*	*	*	*	*

Performance indicators per cent

	1989	1990	1991	1992	1993	1994	1995	1996	1997	1998	1999	2000
Bad debt provision as a percentage of total loans	*	*	*	*	*	*	*	*	*	*	*	*
Bad debt charge as a percentage of total loans	*	*	*	*	*	*	*	Figures omitted. See note on page iv.				
Bad debt charge as a percentage of total income	*	*	*	*	*	*	*					

Source: Lloyds TSB.

*Lloyds TSB was unable to provide.

6.119. Table 6.33 shows the level of bad debt provision net of releases and recoveries, compared with lending over the 11 years to 1999 for services to Business Banking and Corporate Service customers, but excluding bad debts from asset finance and AMC activities. Lloyds TSB told us it felt that because these two areas provided specialist business services and the bad debts experience of these two areas was so different from that of Business Banking and Commercial Banking, to include them would distort this information. It said that the bad debt charge to profit and loss account was understated as it was after accounting for recoveries in some years. It therefore used a measure called 'asset quality ratio' (AQR) for internal credit control purposes, which was calculated as the net charge to the profit and loss account divided by average customer balances. Included within the net charge were the new provisions, provision releases and provision recoveries.

TABLE 6.33 **Lloyds TSB: summary of new bad debt provisions compared with lending for services to SME provided by its Business Banking and Commercial Banking units, 1989 to 2000**

	1989	1990	1991	1992	1993	1994	1995	1996	1997	1998	1999	2000	Average
New charges* (£m)													
Lending balance† (£bn)					Figures omitted. See note on page iv.								
New provisions as a percentage of lending (%)													

Source: Lloyds TSB.

*Lloyds TSB said that the bad debt charge for the total SME banking business was £[✂] million for 1996, £[✂] million for 1997, £[✂] million for 1998 and £[✂] million for 1999. The differences were not significant and were due to recoveries and other adjustments.

†Lloyds TSB reported to us lending levels between 1996 and 1999 of £[✂] billion, £[✂] billion, £[✂] billion and £[✂] billion. It told us that the difference in lending figures related to its asset finance and AMC activities, which accordingly accounted for roughly [✂] per cent of SME lending in 1999.

‡Lloyds TSB was unable to separate TSB data from Lloyds Bank Plc for 1994 and 1995.

6.120. Over the 12-year period to 2000, Lloyds TSB's AQR from services to SMEs was [✂] per cent of lending, excluding AMC and asset finance lending. New bad debt provisions were at their highest levels between 1990 and 1995, and peaked at £[✂] million in 1992. Since 1992 the provisions declined to £[✂] million in 1999 and £[✂] million in 2000. They peaked at [✂] per cent of lending in 1992 before they declined to a low of [✂] per cent in 2000. Lloyds TSB said that the lower level of AQRs in recent years were due to a more stable economic environment and improved lending controls.

6.121. In terms of the future, Lloyds TSB envisaged that the AQRs for its Business Banking and Commercial Banking business units would average out to around [✂] per cent and [✂] per cent respectively. Lloyds TSB said that while neither the Business Banking nor Commercial Banking divisions on their own or in combination were a direct proxy for the SME banking business, some weighted combination of the two divisions would be. Therefore the future AQR estimates for these two divisions could be indicative of a range of future results of Lloyds TSB's SME banking business. Lloyds TSB told us that it intended to continue to monitor and support SME banking business customers who displayed symptoms of business deterioration. To some extent, control over bad debt charge would be offset by increased operating costs in managing SME relationships. Lloyds TSB also noted that its low cost:income ratio was not a reason for its long-term bad debt rate to be potentially higher than its sector. It noted that it had striven to achieve an appropriate balance between operational expenditure and bad debt management.

6.122. Lloyds TSB suggested that lending on SME banking business was more risky than normal banking activities, and defined riskiness as the possibility of incurring an unexpected loss. It added that although all businesses expected a bad debt loss and such could be built into product prices, the risk of a business depended on the certainty of the level of losses, and the more uncertain and volatile the loss level, the more risky was the business. [

Details omitted. See note on page iv.

]

Future strategy in serving the SME banking business

6.123. [

Details omitted. See note on page iv.

]

6.124. [*Details omitted. See note on page iv.*

]

6.125. [

Details omitted. See note on page iv.

]

6.126. [

Details omitted. See note on page iv.

]

TABLE 6.34 **Lloyds TSB: comparison of Business and Commercial Banking plans for 2002 with 1999 results**

	Actual 1999 £m	Plan 2002 £m	Average annual change %
Business Banking			
Income			
Costs			
Profit before bad debt charge			
Bad debt charge:			
Gross charges before recoveries			
Recoveries of past charges			
Operating profit before tax			
Commercial Banking			
Income			
Costs			
Profit before bad debt charge			
Bad debt charge:	*Figures omitted.*		
Gross charges before recoveries	*See note on page iv.*		
Recoveries of past charges			
Operating profit before tax			
Business and Commercial Banking			
Income			
Costs			
Profit before bad debt charge			
Bad debt charge:			
Gross charges before recoveries			
Recoveries of past charges			
Operating profit before tax			

	per cent
*Cost:income ratio**	
Business Banking	
Commercial Banking	✂
Combined	

Source: Lloyds TSB.

---

*Excluding adjustment for pension costs.

HSBC

Overview of its business in serving SMEs

6.128. Chapter 5 describes HSBC's group position and business generally between personal, SME, corporate and other businesses. This section deals in greater depth with its financial performance in providing services to SMEs. Until 1999 HSBC operated in the UK as Midland but then rebranded its business as HSBC to accord with its worldwide name.

Financial performance of the SME banking business

6.129. We asked HSBC to provide us with profitability data on the SME banking business as defined by us for the period between 1989 and 2000. HSBC said that it was not organized along business definitions that provided a breakdown for the SME banking business. Rather, a Commercial Banking business existed that handled business accounts broadly, with borrowing facilities less than

US$100 million. HSBC used best efforts to separate the Commercial Banking business for the purpose of this inquiry into SME banking business and all other corporate banking. HSBC was able to provide information for the period 1990 to 2000 on a 'best endeavours' basis and only for the purpose of the CC's investigation, in order to provide an illustration of the position regarding the SME banking business. Further, it was noted by HSBC that there was limited reliable data available before 1995. The information reflects certain underlying assumptions by HSBC—for example, the same basis for pro-rating income for core banking products has been used for each year in the period 1995 to 2000 and the same cost:income ratios associated with a particular product sale have been used for all customer business. HSBC also assumed a consistent mix of customer business activity and income streams over the period 1995 to 2000. It stated that, from 1995, a new management information system was adopted that allocated costs between types of customer based on the transactions per product that they utilized. Each product had a charge associated with it that allowed a cost base to be estimated subject to the assumptions referred to above. Since a different cost-allocation system was employed prior to 1995, HSBC provided only limited, indicative SME banking business information for the period 1990 to 1994. This earlier data is not strictly comparable with the data from 1995 onwards and, aside from the cost-allocation system difference, is likely to exclude some of the larger-turnover SME banking business customers, which were included in the corporate portfolio at that time, rather than the commercial portfolio. The earlier data also excluded balances for CACs, which we have included for the later years.

6.130. Table 6.35 shows details of the profitability of HSBC's SME banking business from 1990 to 2000, continuing the analysis in Chapter 5 which showed the SME banking business in the context of the whole bank. In 1990, operating income was £[✕] million. It fell to around £[✕] million for the years 1991 to 1993, and then rose to £[✕] million in 1994. Operating expenses fell from £[✕] million in 1990 to around £[✕] million in 1991 and 1992, then rose to £[✕] million in 1994. Over the period from 1990 to 1993 HSBC incurred significant bad debt charges, in respect of SMEs, which peaked at £[✕] million and £[✕] million in 1991 and 1992 respectively (see Chapter 5). In 1994 the bad debt charge for SMEs fell to £[✕] million. As a result of the above movements, SME banking business generated a loss of £[✕] million in 1990 which increased to £[✕] million and £[✕] million in 1991 and 1992 respectively and fell to £[✕] million in 1993. In 1994 the SME banking business made a profit of £[✕] million.

6.131. From 1995 to 2000 operating income in respect of SMEs increased [✕] per cent from £[✕] million in 1995 to £[✕] million in 2000, and operating cost increased by [✕] per cent from £[✕] million in 1995 to £[✕] million in 2000. The level of bad debt charge was lower in 1995 and 1996, at around £[✕] million, than from 1997 to 1999, when the bad debt expense ranged between £[✕] million and £[✕] million. In 2000 the bad debt charge had reduced to £[✕] million. As a result of the above movements, operating profits from HSBC's SME banking business increased from £[✕] million in 1995 to £[✕] million in 2000.

TABLE 6.35 **HSBC: profit and loss account from SME banking business, 1990 to 2000*†**

£ million

Years ended 31 December

	1990†	1991†	1992†	1993†	1994†	1995	1996	1997	1998	1999	2000
Net interest income	‡	‡	‡	‡	‡						
Net fees and commissions	‡	‡	‡	‡	‡						
Other income	‡	‡	‡	‡	‡						
Total operating income											
Operating expenses			Figures omitted.					Figures omitted.			
Operating profit before provisions			See note on page iv.					See note on page iv.			
Bad debt charge											
Net profit before tax§											

Source: HSBC.

*See also Table 6.36, which shows the items in this table as a percentage of total operating income.

†Data from 1990 to 1994 is not strictly comparable with that from 1995 onwards because of changes to the cost-allocation systems. The earlier data is also likely to exclude some of the larger turnover 'SME' businesses, which were included in the 'corporate' portfolio at that time, rather than the commercial portfolio, and does exclude clubs, associates and charities which has been manually added to the data from 1995 to 2000.

‡Not available.

§As requested by us, these figures were calculated on the basis that all lending is financed from borrowing in wholesale markets. In fact, a proportion will be financed by the bank's equity, and it is therefore necessary to make an adjustment for this (see Table 6.37) before comparing returns on capital derived from these profit figures with the bank's cost of capital.

6.132. Table 6.36 further analyses the overall performance of HSBC's SME banking business from 1990 to 2000 by showing all items as a percentage of operating income. Net interest income as a percentage of operating income declined from [✂] per cent in 1995 to [✂] per cent in 2000. Net fees and commissions as a percentage of operating income also fell over the period from [✂] per cent. In contrast, 'other' income increased from [✂] per cent of total income.

TABLE 6.36 **HSBC: operating profit and loss items as a percentage of operating income from SME banking business, 1990 to 2000***

per cent

	1990*	1991*	1992*	1993*	1994*	1995	1996	1997	1998	1999	2000
Net interest income	†	†	†	†	†						
Net fees and commissions	†	†	†	†	†						
Other income	†	†	†	†	†						
Total operating income											
Operating expenses											
Operating profit before provisions			*Figures omitted.*					*Figures omitted.*			
Provisions for bad and doubtful debts			*See note on page iv.*					*See note on page iv.*			
Net profit before tax‡											

Source: HSBC.

*Data from 1990 to 1994 is not strictly comparable with the data from 1995 onwards because of changes to the cost-allocation systems. The earlier data is also likely to exclude some of the larger turnover 'SME' businesses, which were included in the 'corporate' portfolio at that time, rather than the commercial portfolio, and does exclude clubs, associates and charities which has been manually added to the data from 1995 to 2000.

†Not available.

‡As requested by us, these figures are calculated on the basis that all lending is financed from borrowing in wholesale markets. In fact, a proportion will be financed by the bank's equity, and it is therefore necessary to make an adjustment for this (see Table 6.37) before comparing returns on capital derived from these profit figures with the bank's cost of capital.

6.133. From 1990 to 1994 the SME banking business's cost:income ratio increased from around 69 per cent between 1990 and 1992 to 78 and 77 per cent in 1993 and 1994 respectively.

6.134. The SME banking business cost:income ratio fell from 75 per cent in 1995 to 61 per cent in 2000. HSBC noted that the improvement was in line with a bank-wide reduction in the cost:income ratio. This had been achieved by tight cost control and improved operational efficiency, and increased income, as a result of improved customer service and new product development. We noted that the SME banking business cost:income ratio in 2000 of 61 per cent was higher than that of the whole bank at 58 per cent, as shown in Chapter 5. It is noted that HSBC's published cost:income ratio in 2000 was 56 per cent. HSBC said that the higher cost:income ratio for the SME banking business compared with that of the whole bank was largely because of its community banking strategy and the use of HSBC's branch network by SMEs. HSBC's community banking meant that HSBC had concentrated customer-facing activities in the branches with relationship managers having a high degree of responsibility. HSBC said that this provided a high level of service and SMEs used HSBC's local branch relationship managers extensively for advice and sorting out problems. Businesses larger than SMEs, on the other hand, made more use of automated products like Hexagon (HSBC's electronic banking product), with the largest of these managed centrally by HSBC's Corporate and Institutional Banking division.

6.135. HSBC told us that its allocation of costs was likely to underestimate the costs created by high-volume low-value businesses, such as personal business and SME banking business, and overstate the costs of low-volume high-value businesses, such as corporate. This was because its cost-allocation system, a cost-per-product approach, assumed a constant cost allocation for each product while the reality is that economies of scale would exist.

Attributable capital to support the SME banking business and potential returns

6.136. Tables 6.35 and 6.36 consider the trends in HSBC's profits from its SME banking business. In order to form a view on the significance of such profits, we also consider HSBC's capital base. We look at this subject in greater detail in Chapter 7 for all the main suppliers. In our discussion with HSBC on determining the attributable capital to support its services to SMEs, we made a number of calculations for the years 1998 to 2000, based on our methodology as discussed in paragraphs 6.22 and 6.23.

6.137. Applying our methodology, we put to HSBC our initial assessment that its attributable capital to support its SME banking business, recognizing that HSBC does not specifically attribute capital to the SME banking business. The attributable capital calculated, based on an apportionment of its closing balance sheet capital for 1998 to 2000, was £[✁] million for 1998, £[✁] million for 1999 and £[✁] for 2000. For 2000, the large increase in capital reflects the effect of acquisitions during the year. HSBC said that the approach was not unreasonable, but it was only one of a number of possible ways to identify capital.

6.138. In Table 6.35 we also noted that HSBC's profits from SME banking business were based on its calculation of net income from lending as if wholly financed from wholesale markets at LIMEAN. However, in identifying the rate of return to compare with the cost of capital, an adjustment must be made to reflect that a proportion of lending was funded by capital and not from the wholesale markets. This is necessary to avoid double counting and the appropriate adjustment is attributable capital times the average three-month LIBOR. The rates used for each of the years 1998, 1999 and 2000 were 7.3 per cent, 5.45 per cent and 6.1 per cent respectively.

6.139. Table 6.37 incorporates this adjustment together with the information shown in Table 6.35 on profitability, and shows estimates of returns (subject to adjustments discussed in Chapter 7). For 1999, which was a year with relatively low bad debt levels, the initial estimate for HSBC's pre-tax return on capital was [✁] per cent, based on closing attributable capital. In Chapter 7 we consider HSBC's appropriate cost of capital, and what adjustments are necessary regarding these returns. In Chapter 2 we give our conclusions on this issue.

TABLE 6.37 **HSBC: summary of profits, capital and returns from HSBC services to SMEs, 1998 to 2000**

£ million

	1998	1999	2000
Information from Table 6.35			
Income			
Operating costs			
Bad debt charge		Figures omitted.	
Adjustment for attributable capital*		See note on page iv.	
Operating profit before tax and exceptional items			
Attributable capital (based on closing capital for the whole bank and proportions of RWAs)	(✁)	(✁)†	(✁)
Average attributable capital	‡	(✁)	(✁)
			per cent
Pre-tax return based on closing attributable capital	(✁)	(✁)†	(✁)
Pre-tax return based on average attributable capital	‡	(✁)	(✁)

Source: CC based on information from HSBC.

*At 7.3 per cent for 1998, 5.45 per cent for 1999, and 6.10 per cent for 2000, based on three-month LIBOR.
†The attributable capital for 1999, which is shown as based on the closing capital level for HSBC, could alternatively be based on the average of the closing attributable capital figures for 1998 and 1999. The resultant figure would therefore be £[✁] million, and the pre-tax return, based on this average attributable capital, would be [✁] per cent, ie an increase of one percentage point.
‡Not estimated.

6.140. A further alternative in considering the above returns would be to use an average capital figure, for example the average of the opening and closing capital base, rather than a return based on the closing figure. For 1999 we calculated that the effect on the pre-tax return would be an increase of one percentage point to [✂] per cent. However, this approach was not practicable for some banks because data was not available.

6.141. HSBC told us that it did not calculate economic capital for all business. It noted that required capital was the amount considered necessary by management to enable a line of business to operate and must be at least equal to the minimum regulatory requirement. It agreed that our methodology of allocating regulatory capital on the basis of RWAs was not unreasonable and noted that this was the main basis it used for allocation of capital to its commercial business.

6.142. HSBC told us that for the purposes of calculating economic profit, which it used in strategic evaluation, an allocated or regulated minimum was used at the business unit/plan level. At legal entity level, economic profit was reported on actual invested capital. 'Actual invested capital' was defined as:

Ordinary shareholders' funds
 − revaluation reserves
 + goodwill written off or amortized
 + minority interests
 + intra-group loan capital and preference shares treated as invested capital
 − intra-group lending treated as invested capital
 − investment in subsidiaries
 + ordinary dividends declared but not paid

6.143. HSBC viewed the difference between actual invested capital and the minimum required under regulatory regimes as surplus capital to meet other needs. At entity level, a return still needed to be generated on 'surplus' equity not allocated at business unit level.

6.144. HSBC noted that HSBC Bank had very little, if any, 'surplus' compared with other banks, as 'surplus' capital was generally paid as a dividend to its parent, HSBC Holdings plc, and that consequently HSBC considered that HSBC Bank's return on equity might appear higher than competitors because of a lower actual capital base than its competitors.

Further analysis of income and expenses

6.145. Subject to the bases of preparation described in paragraph 6.129, Table 6.38 provides an analysis of operating income by type of banking service to SME banking business customers from 1998 to 2000. In 1998 to 2000 the five main types of banking relationships from which the bank earned income were loans, current accounts utilizing an overdraft facility, other current accounts, deposits, and asset finance. In aggregate, they contributed [✂] per cent of the £[✂] million operating income from the SME banking business for 2000.

TABLE 6.38 HSBC: analysis of net income* by type of banking service to SME banking business customers, 1998 to 2000

Years ended 31 December

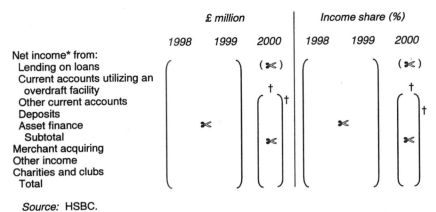

	£ million			Income share (%)		
Net income* from:	1998	1999	2000	1998	1999	2000
Lending on loans			(✂)			(✂)
Current accounts utilizing an overdraft facility			†			†
Other current accounts			†			†
Deposits	✂			✂		
Asset finance						
Subtotal			✂			✂
Merchant acquiring						
Other income						
Charities and clubs						
Total						

Source: HSBC.

---

*Includes net interest income and net fees and commissions. Operational costs and bad debt charges are then deducted from this income to derive net operating profit.

†For 2000 HSBC was not able to provide the split between current accounts with authorized overdrafts and current accounts without authorized overdraft facilities. The aggregate for current account overdraft facilities takes into account both categories.

6.146. Table 6.39 provides a further breakdown of net operating income from the SME banking business into net interest income, net fees and commission, and 'other' income from 1998 to 2000. HSBC derived considerable interest income, not only from loans, asset financing and overdrafts made to SME banking business customers, but also from money held in deposit and current accounts of the SMEs. The table also shows the net interest margin as a percentage of related balances earned by the bank from different types of banking relationships with the SMEs. It shows the income earned, as well as the cost of funds to finance the lending, and the benefit of funds deposited by SMEs. At year-end 1999 the total value of customer accounts in credit (both deposits and other current accounts) from SMEs totalled £[✂] billion, which HSBC was able to use to partly finance its lending to SMEs.

6.147. HSBC said that for loans and overdrafts, interest income reflected actual interest earned from customers and the cost of funds was calculated using LIMEAN (mid-market rates) for variable rate balances or appropriate market rates for fixed-rate balances. As for deposits and current accounts (with and without overdraft facilities), the benefit of funds reflected the value of funds to the bank. Its current accounts were paying small amounts of interest, and for 1999 HSBC obtained the benefit of SME funds at £[✂] million on which it paid interest of £[✂] million, the value of the current accounts being used to recover costs incurred in administering the accounts.

6.148. Table 6.39 shows that in 1999 HSBC earned income of £[✂] million from loans to SME banking business customers (of which £[✂] million was net interest income, and £[✂] million was 'other' income). It also earned £[✂] million income from asset finance (of which £[✂] million was net interest income, £[✂] million was from asset finance fees, and £[✂] million was operating lease income).

6.149. HSBC's customer deposit income in 1999 was £[✂] million, all of which represented the net interest benefit arising from holding SME deposits. HSBC also earned income of £[✂] million from customer current accounts and overdrafts, of which £[✂] million was the imputed net interest benefit of the funds, and £[✂] million was net interest income from overdrafts.

6.150. In 1999 HSBC also earned fee income of £[✂] million from current accounts and overdrafts.

6.151. Among the various income-earning categories for 1998 and 1999, other current accounts with no overdraft facility, or where a facility was not being utilized, reported the highest net interest margin at [✂] per cent for 1999. The reason for this margin was that HSBC earned interest on the current account balances in overdraft but paid small levels of interest for the use of the funds in credit, together with the need to cover related administrative costs of the customer using the account. The net interest margin for loans and asset finance was around [✂] per cent in both 1998 and 1999. Overdrafts showed a similar margin in 1998, but this increased to [✂] per cent in 1999. Interest margins on deposit balances were also around [✂] per cent for both 1998 and 1999.

TABLE 6.39 HSBC: analysis of operating income by type of service to SMEs, 1998 to 2000

Years ended 31 December

	£ million			Margin and lending balances		
	1998	*1999*	*2000*	*1998*	*1999*	*2000*
Loans						
Interest income						
Allocated cost of funds						
Net interest income						
Other						
Net income*						
Current accounts utilizing overdraft facility						
Interest income						
Cost of funds						
Net interest income						
Fees for lending						
Net income*						
Year-end overdraft balance (£m)‡						§
Annual net interest (%)¶						§
Other current accounts¤						
Benefit of funds from SME						
Interest paid						
Net interest income						
Fees (money transmission)						
Other charges						
Net income#						
Year-end other current account balance (£m)‡						§
Annual net interest (%)¶						§
Deposits						
Benefit of funds from SMEs						
Interest paid						
Net interest income#						
Year-end deposit balance (£m)‡						§
Annualized net interest (%)¶						§
Asset finance						
Interest income						
Allocated cost of funds to finance asset financing						
Net interest income						
Fees						
Other						
Net income*						
Year-end lending and asset finance balance (£m)‡						§
Annual net interest (%)¶						§
Net income total of above groupings						
Other net income from						
Merchant acquiring						
Sundry other services						
Charities and clubs						
Total net income from SMEs						

Source: HSBC.

*Operational costs and bad debt charges are deducted from this income to derive the net operating profit from this service to customers.

†The split of fee income for 2000 between current accounts utilizing overdraft facilities and other current accounts has not been provided by HSBC.

‡HSBC said that it was unable to provide average balances so we have used spot year-end balances instead. This may slightly distort the percentage margins calculated. In the case of the asset finance figures, the balance is the aggregate of loans and asset finance as HSBC was not able to separate the balances.

§Not provided.

¶Net interest as percentages of average balances. For the current accounts this is only an approximate measure as there will be interest from some accounts categorized as having utilized their overdraft facility that at some point in the year may have been in credit. Similarly other current accounts may have been in overdraft at some point over the year.

¤Includes current accounts without an overdraft facility and current accounts with an overdraft facility that has not been utilized. Of the current accounts without an overdraft facility this classification will include those accounts that have an unauthorized overdraft. The related interest charged on these balances has also been accounted for under this classification.

#Before deducting operational costs, to derive the net operating profit from this service to customers.

6.152. Table 6.40 provides a further analysis of operating profits for the SME banking business by types of banking service from 1998 to 2000. Table 6.42 summarizes these results in terms of cost:income ratios. HSBC suggested that the costs of servicing current accounts was running at [✂] per cent in 1999, which was almost [✂] its cost levels for lending and asset finance activities. We consider the issue of cost levels between the banks, and the appropriateness of cost allocations, in Chapter 7. HSBC told us that its costs were allocated to individual customers by multiplying customer-specific transaction volumes by transaction unit costs. Costs were allocated to product types by multiplying income by the relevant cost:income ratio. The transaction unit costs were calculated within their product profitability reporting model which allocated all costs incurred within HSBC to the relevant cost drivers for each product. Each transaction unit cost was a 'fully absorbed' cost and therefore included an allocation of Head Office costs in addition to the direct costs of processing. Since a standard methodology was used for all business activities and products, HSBC considered the resulting cost allocations to the SME banking business to be fair and reasonable subject to comments made in relation to the basis of preparation in paragraph 6.129 and the fact that the cost:income ratio of a product would be the same irrespective of the customer. We, however, told HSBC that its [✂] per cent estimate for current accounts seemed high and could reflect overallocation of costs to this grouping. HSBC's view was that this high figure could be explained by HSBC's community banking strategy and could also be due to HSBC's full cost absorption methodology. It noted that more than half its SME banking business was concentrated on smaller customers (with up to £1 million turnover) who were heavy users of money transmission services requiring much manual processing.

TABLE 6.40 **HSBC: analysis of operating profit by type of service to SMEs, 1998 to 2000**

Years ended 31 December

	£ million			Proportion of income (%)		
	1998	*1999*	*2000*	*1998*	*1999*	*2000*
Lending and asset finance						
Net income*						
Costs†						
Bad debt charge						
Profit						
Current accounts and overdrafts						
Net income*						
Costs						
Bad debt charge‡						
Profit						
Deposits						
Net income*						
Costs						
Profit						
Merchant acquiring						
Net income*	Figures omitted. See note on page iv.					
Costs						
Profit						
Other income§						
Income						
Costs						
Bad debt charge						
Profit						
Clubs and charities						
Income						
Costs						
Profit						
Total profit from SMEs before providing for doubtful debts						
Total profit from SMEs after providing for doubtful debts						

Source: HSBC.

*Net interest income plus fees and commissions.
†HSBC could provide its estimate of costs only for the combined loans and asset finance grouping.
‡HSBC said that bad debt charges, other than in relation to asset finance, had not been allocated to products.
§Includes income from regional treasury centres and card issuing.

6.153. Table 6.41 provides a further analysis of operating profits for the SME banking business using 1999 profits for each main service category, both before and after allowing for bad debt charges. These profits have been presented as a proportion of total profits both before and after bad debt charges. Loans, including asset finance, and current accounts show the highest contributions to profit with [✂] per cent of profits before allowing for bad debts and [✂] per cent of profits after allowing for bad debts being represented by these services. Deposits were the next highest contributor to profits before and after allowing for bad debts with [✂] per cent and [✂] per cent respectively.

TABLE 6.41 **HSBC: comparison of profits by type of service to SMEs, 1999**

	Profit before bad debts* £m	Profit after bad debts* £m	Profit before bad debts as a proportion of total profit before bad debts %	Profit after bad debts as a proportion of total profit after bad debts %
Loans and asset finance				
Current accounts				
Deposits				
Merchant acquiring		*Figures omitted. See note on page iv.*		
CACs				
Other				
Total				

Source: CC based on information provided by HSBC.

*Per Table 6.40.

6.154. Table 6.42 further analyses HSBC's costs for 1999 and 2000 into direct and indirect costs by type of service, and the cost:income ratios for such services for the three years to 2000. The cost:income ratios varied according to the different types of banking activities with SME banking business customers. Deposits had the lowest ratio of between [✂] and [✂] per cent, however. Lending and asset finance had ratios between [✂] and [✂] per cent. Current accounts both with and without overdraft facilities were noted as having a much higher cost:income ratio at [✂] per cent, as discussed above. Given the basis of preparation of the financial information, the cost:income ratios set out below are at best illustrative.

6.155. All banks told us that their mix of banking services with customers, together with the way in which banks decided to deliver those products, determined their overall cost:income ratios, such that a bank with a higher proportion of deposits would be able to benefit from this income and so would report a lower cost:income ratio, to the extent that costs of administering those deposits are significantly lower, compared with a similar bank of equal costs, that had customers having a lower level of average deposits. We discuss this issue of business mix further in Chapter 7.

TABLE 6.42 HSBC: summary of 1999 income and costs from services to SMEs by product category, and summary of cost; income ratios by type of service, 1998 to 2000

			£ million		per cent	
			Costs		Cost proportion	
	Income	Costs	Direct*‡	Indirect	Direct	Indirect
1999						
Lending and asset finance‡			(✂)		(✂)	
Current accounts					†	†
Deposits			†		†	†
Merchant acquiring			†		†	†
Other			†	✂	†	†
Charities and clubs			†		†	†
Total costs in Table 6.35			‡		†	†
Bad debt charge			†			
2000	✂					
Lending and asset finance‡			(✂)		(✂)	
Current accounts			†		†	†
Deposits			†		†	†
Merchant acquiring			†		†	†
Other			†	✂	†	†
Charities and clubs			†		†	†
Total costs in Table 6.35			†		†	†
Bad debt charge			‡			
			*			

Cost:income ratios	1998	1999	2000
Lending and asset finance‡			
Current accounts			
Deposits		*Figures omitted.*	
Merchant acquiring		*See note on page iv.*	
Other income			
Charities and clubs			
Overall			

Source: HSBC.

*Data not provided by HSBC.
†Direct costs relate to asset finance only.
‡HSBC could only provide its estimate of costs for the combined loans and asset finance grouping.

6.156. Table 6.43 provides a further analysis of operating cost for the SME banking business by activity for 1999 and 2000. Branches and central processing were the two main activities within HSBC's SME banking business, and together accounted for [✂] per cent of total costs in 1999 and [✂] per cent in 2000. They represented large blocks of costs that were shared between activities that served both business and personal customers. Included within branch costs were direct costs such as business centres and relationship managers, and recharged costs such as branch counter staff and cash handling. Included within central processing costs were direct costs such as the cost of staff processing loans (producing letters of credit, etc).

TABLE 6.43 HSBC: analysis of SME banking business operating cost by activity, 1999 and 2000

	Years ended 31 December			
	£ million		Proportion of total (%)	
	1999	2000	1999	2000
Operating expenses:				
Branches				
Central processing and support		*		*
Asset finance				
Cards		*Figures omitted.*		
Other		*See note on page iv.*		
Clubs and charities				
Total				

Source: HSBC.

*In 2000, the split of costs between branches and central processing and support could not be performed. Therefore the value shown for branches in 2000 is an aggregate for these two cost categories.

6.157. HSBC estimated that in 1999 it had approximately 12,000 FTE staff servicing the SME banking business, with around 1,352 staff 100 per cent involved in servicing SMEs. Total employee costs attributable to the SME banking business were approximately £[✂] million. [

Details omitted. See note on page iv.

]

6.158. Table 6.44 analyses HSBC's advertising, marketing and promotion expenditure for 1999 and 2000, split into SME banking business and non-SME banking business. In 2000 HSBC's Retail and Corporate division spent £[✂] million on advertising and promotion, of which the portion attributable to the SME banking business was £[✂] million or [✂] per cent. This compared with £[✂] million in total in 1999 of which £[✂] million or [✂] per cent was attributable to SME banking business. Bank-wide, £[✂] million was spent on advertising and promotion, of which [✂] per cent was attributable to SME banking business. [*Details omitted. See note on page iv.*

]

TABLE 6.44 **HSBC: analysis of advertising, marketing and promotion expenditure, 1999 and 2000**

£ million

	Advertising SME	Advertising non-SME	Promotion SME	Promotion non-SME	Total SME	Total non-SME
1999						
Retail and corporate						
First direct						
Central						
HSBC asset finance						
Treasury						
International						
Total						
2000		*Figures omitted. See note on page iv.*				
Retail and corporate						
First direct						
Central						
HSBC asset finance						
Treasury						
International						
Total						

Source: HSBC.

6.159. [

Details omitted. See note on page iv.

]

6.160. Subject to the basis of preparation set out in paragraph 6.129, Table 6.45 shows an analysis of operating profit for the SME banking business by type of banking relationship from 1998 to 2000. In 1998 and 1999 the SME banking business achieved operating profits of £[✂] million and £[✂] million respectively. In 2000 this increased by [✂] per cent to £[✂] million. Lending and asset finance, and current accounts and overdrafts, were the two largest contributors to operating profit from SME banking business. Together they contributed £[✂] million or [✂] per cent to total profit from SME banking business. In 2000 operating profit from deposits was £[✂] million, and operating profit from clubs and charities was £[✂] million.

6.161. In 2000 operating profit as a percentage of operating income was [✂] per cent for deposits and [✂] per cent for lending and asset finance. However, current accounts and overdrafts reported a much lower percentage of [✂] per cent. The bad debt charges were deducted in arriving at the lending operating profits for the purpose of making these calculations. For the lending activity, the bad debt charge was £[✂] million.

TABLE 6.45 **HSBC: analysis of SME banking business operating profit (after bad debt charges) by type of banking relationship, 1998 to 2000**

Years ended 31 December

	£ million			Proportion of total profit (%)		
	1998	1999	2000	1998	1999	2000
Operating profit* arising from						
Lending and asset finance†						
Current accounts with and without overdrafts						
Deposits						
Merchant acquiring	*Figures omitted. See note on page iv.*					
Other income						
Clubs and charities						
Total						

	per cent					
Operating profit as a percentage of operating income						
Lending and asset finance†						
Current accounts with and without overdraft						
Deposits	*Figures omitted. See note on page iv.*					
Merchant acquiring						
Other activities						
Clubs and charities						
Total						

Source: HSBC.

*Calculated after bad debt charges but before pension costs and exceptional items.
†HSBC could only provide its estimate of costs for the combined loans and asset finance grouping.

Balance sheet items

6.162. Table 6.46 shows loans, and customer accounts in credit, for HSBC's SME banking business between 1990 and 2000. We note that producing a balance sheet for HSBC's services to SMEs was not relevant as assets and liabilities are managed on a pooled basis across the bank, in accordance with policies on interest rate risk and liquidity. Therefore, a balance sheet for SME banking business would show lending and deposit balances that may not be in balance; where there was more lending than deposits, there would be a need to receive funds from other activities, or issue long-term debt instruments. HSBC said that the growth in SME loans in 1993 and 1994 reflects the redefinition of amounts classified as such, together with the result of increased investment in marketing and improvement of the overall service proposition leading to the acquisition of more customers.

TABLE 6.46 **HSBC: SME banking business loans, and customer accounts in credit, 1990 to 2000***

£ billion

Years ended 31 December

	1990	1991	1992	1993	1994	1995	1996	1997	1998	1999	2000
Loans and advances to customers											
Overdrafts											
Other											
Total loans and advances to customers											
Deposits	*Figures omitted. See note on page iv.*										
Current accounts											
Other											
Total customer accounts in credit											
Funds required (+), or available (–)											

Source: HSBC/Midland.

*Data from 1990 to 1994 is not strictly comparable with that from 1995 onwards because of changes to the cost-allocation systems. The earlier data is also likely to exclude some of the larger turnover 'SME' businesses, which were included in the 'corporate' portfolio at that time, rather than the commercial portfolio, and does exclude clubs, associates and charities which has been manually added to the data from 1995 to 2000.

6.163. From Table 6.46 it can be seen that the level of loans to SME banking business customers was at its lowest between 1990 and 1993 when the balance hovered at around £[✕] billion. Between 1993 and 1999 loans and advances to SME banking business customers increased and at the end of 2000 was £[✕] billion. Overdrafts also increased, although not on the same scale, from lows of around £[✕] in the early 1990s to £[✕] billion in 2000. Regarding the level of total customer accounts in credit, including both current accounts and overdrafts, the balances increased [✕] per cent from £[✕] billion in 1990 to £[✕] billion in 2000. As a result the ratio of 'loans:customer accounts in credit' increased from [✕] in 1990 to [✕] in 2000, which indicated that HSBC was lending much more than it had received from SME banking business customers.

Capital expenditure and development costs

6.164. We note that banks generally do not have significant tangible fixed assets in relation to their total fixed assets, and write off what they term as investment costs as they are incurred. HSBC, however, considered that a proportion of its revenue expenditure should be treated as if capitalized and depreciated for the purpose of calculating its returns because it suggested that such costs had economic benefits of up to several years. We cover this point in greater detail in Chapter 7.

6.165. HSBC told us that over the last three years in the UK the estimated cost of development and running the combination of Hexagon (electronic banking), Internet and telephone banking was £[✕] million. If this cost was apportioned to customer business by the number of customers, approximately £[✕] million or [✕] per cent would be attributable to the SME banking business. HSBC said that, while difficult to assess and subject to change in the rate of technological advances, [

Details omitted. See note on page iv.

].

Bad debts

6.166. Table 6.47 shows the level of bad debt provision and bad debt charges to profit and loss between 1990 and 2000 relating to HSBC's SME banking business. The level of bad debt provision was £[✕] million in 1995 and fell to £[✕] million in 2000. The levels of closing provision equated to [✕] per cent of loans in 1995, compared with [✕] per cent in 2000. During the years from 1990 to 1993 HSBC incurred significant bad debt charges arising from Midland's business, which peaked at £[✕] million in 1991. This represented [✕] per cent of total loans outstanding or over [✕] per cent of operating income for that year. HSBC said that this was attributable to the fact that this coincided with the lowest point of the deepest and longest recession experienced in the UK for generations. The SME banking business was particularly badly affected. Not only was SME banking business trading adversely affected but the whole supply chain deteriorated so that late payment and SME banking business bad debts were commonplace. HSBC added that prior to this period, it had expanded its lending to the SME banking business aggressively, using remotely-based relationship managers. Property lending was a particular growth area and this industry was badly hit in the recession, together with associated construction and contract lending. HSBC said that the value of underlying security was also seriously undermined as property prices fell significantly, particularly in London, the South-East and East Anglia. The net result was high bad debt provisions, significant management time spent on 'intensive care' lending, a drop in operating income and the announcement of bank-level losses of £0.3 billion in 1989, breaking even in 1990 and 1991.

TABLE 6.47   **HSBC: analysis of bad debt provision and charges to profit and loss account from services to SMEs**

£ million

	1990*	1991*	1992*	1993*	1994*	1995	1996	1997	1998	1999	2000
Analysis of bad debt provision											
General provision	†	†	†	†	†						
Specific provision	‡	‡	‡	‡	‡			Figures omitted. See note on page iv.			
Bad debt provision	‡	‡	‡	‡	‡						
Analysis of bad debt charge to profit and loss											
New and additional provisions	†	†	†	†	†	†	†	†	†	†	†
Releases of provisions established in earlier years	†	†	†	†	†	†	†	†	†	†	†
Recoveries of advances written off in earlier years	†	†	†	†	†			Figures omitted. See note on page iv.			
Bad debt charge to profit and loss	(		✂		)						

per cent

											Average‡
Performance indicators											
Bad debt provision as a percentage of total loans	†	†	†	†	†						
Bad debt charge as a percentage of total loans*			Figures omitted. See note on page iv.					Figures omitted. See note on page iv.			
Bad debt charge as a percentage of total income											

Source: HSBC.

---

*Data from 1990 to 1994 is not strictly comparable with that from 1995 onwards because of changes to the cost-allocation systems. It also excludes the larger-turnover SMEs as they were included in the corporate classification. The abnormally high figures to 1993 reflected special problems at Midland, as discussed in the above paragraph.

†Not available.

‡Arithmetic average. The simple average for the bad debt charge to lending ratio for the five years to 1994 was [✂] per cent and for the five years to 1999 was [✂] per cent.

6.167. HSBC told us that during the economic recession from 1990 to 1994 all industry group sectors showed a significant increase in provisioning levels. It added that the large losses incurred in the early 1990s were a result, not only of the economic downturn at that time, but also because Midland had adopted an inappropriate strategy in terms of the way that it serviced its SME banking business customers. It had introduced regional centralization of delivery of its services to SMEs through a network of business banking, which its customers did not like. Instead Midland/HSBC's customers preferred to have a local relationship with a business banking manager and Midland/HSBC therefore reversed its delivery strategy in favour of a local service. HSBC said that it also incurred additional management and executive resource costs in tackling the large number of problem accounts and developing recovery strategies with customers. It estimated its market share of business current accounts was about 16 per cent, excluding personal current accounts. HSBC's view was that it would be more appropriate to estimate market share by including personal current accounts, which would give an estimate of about 13.6 per cent. Nevertheless on the basis that our method is used, HSBC noted that its market share in the business current account market, a high proportion of which related to SMEs, dipped from 14 to 12 per cent during the early 1990s but had since increased to 16 per cent.

6.168. In 1995 and 1996 the bad debt charges fell to £[✂] million and £[✂] million respectively. HSBC told us that these figures were influenced by recoveries of bad debts written off in prior years. Between 1997 and 1999 the level of bad debt charge has remained relatively constant at between £[✂] million and £[✂] million, which represented between [✂] per cent of loans, and in 2000 the charge fell to £[✂] million, representing around [✂] per cent of loans. Over the 11 years between 1990 and 2000 the SME banking business showed an average bad debt charge of [✂] per cent of loans, which on average was [✂] per cent of total income. Over the five years to 1999 the simple average of the bad debt charge as a percentage of lending was [✂] per cent.

6.169. HSBC noted that between 1995 and 1999 a return to economic stability saw a reduction in bad debt figures. Manufacturing was the major source of bad debts during this period, with key factors including the continued strength of the pound sterling, intensively competitive global markets and significant structural change. It noted that during this period SMEs in some regions were particularly hard hit by declines in sectors concentrated in those regions; there was also a regional bias in the performance of industry business and the interdependency of SMEs who acted as local suppliers to larger players. Examples were the automotive sector in the West Midlands, the steel industry in the North and Scotland and the textile industry in the East Midlands and Yorkshire areas. The agricultural sector has deteriorated over the latter part of this period, with a rise particularly in SME banking business debts (see paragraph 6.176 for comments on the foot and mouth outbreak). This sector had a very heavy regional bias in Wales, East Anglia and the North of England.

6.170. HSBC considered that lending on SME banking business was more risky than normal banking activities, and reflected the following factors:

— Credit risk.

— Legal risk—ie the need to ensure that the documentation was appropriate and enforceable to recover non-performing loans, or to charge for services.

— Reputational risk—ie aiming to encourage an enterprise culture and to support businesses tempered by the objective to protect the bank's reputation and its desire not to be involved with any businesses which were illegal or which would generate adverse publicity.

— Risk of fraud in the SME banking business sector.

— 'Chargeback' risk in relation to, for example, merchant acquiring (where HSBC carried the risk of meeting the costs of faulty goods/services purchased using credit cards to the extent that the costs could not be met by the relevant supplier).

6.171. In addition HSBC added that SME banking business, when compared with larger corporates, generally experienced:

(a)   greater volatility in earnings;

(b)   greater reliance on a smaller population of customers and sometimes reliance on a few major customers;

(c)   more susceptibility to effects of the economic cycle; a lower survival rate;

(d)   greater reliance on a smaller number of products;

(e)   'weaker' corporate governance, ie more likely to function without a corporate infrastructure of professionals with specialist and dedicated functions who could deal with issues on a timely basis;

(f)   weaker capital structure and less ability to absorb 'one-off' hits and trade out of trading problems; and

(g)   greater susceptibility to the effects of late payment (although this last factor was becoming less important).

6.172. HSBC noted that, as well as the crystallizing of credit risk, the effect of the above characteristics could be to put at risk the volume of 'sales' that HSBC could make to the SME market and therefore it carried the risk that its fixed-cost overhead base would not be fully recovered. HSBC said that it invested for the long term based on enduring benefit and therefore this was clearly an exposure.

6.173. In terms of the future economic outlook, HSBC noted that the pattern of deep recessions had been about seven to ten years apart in recent economic history (1973 to 1975, 1979 to 1981 and 1990 to 1992). However, it had become apparent over the last three to four years that a more stable period of macroeconomic growth had emerged in the UK and other countries—more bumps and dips than 'boom and bust'. The reasons for this were many, but the targeting of low inflation by the BoE was one, particularly as it influenced expectations of stable inflation and stable growth.

6.174. HSBC added that fluctuations around trend growth were thus becoming less pronounced at the macroeconomic level, with one to two years of slightly above trend (3 per cent) growth followed by one to two years of slightly below trend growth (1 to 2 per cent). The volatility of the economic cycle had thus diminished, as well as its length becoming shorter.

6.175. HSBC noted that as the macroeconomic cycle became less pronounced, there were nevertheless underlying sectoral variations, which it thought were becoming more important in business planning. A growth forecast of 2.5 per cent a year for GDP might well encompass some sectors growing at 10 per cent (for example, until recently telecommunications services and electronic manufacturing) and others declining slightly (for example, agriculture and heavy engineering).

6.176. HSBC also commented on the foot and mouth problem that faced the UK in 2001. It estimated that almost [✂] per cent of its SME banking business lending book (£[✂] billion) was in sectors likely to be affected, directly or indirectly, by the commercial impact of the disease. It suggested that the customers affected would include the following:

— farmers;

— hotels, retailers, and leisure sites serving tourists in affected areas;

— hauliers and distributors of livestock; and

— food processors, packagers and handlers.

6.177. It considered that its lending risks would increase, and the bank could suffer loss of income from other sources. HSBC said that it had given a commitment to the Government that all reasonable requests for financial assistance would be sympathetically received, and its managers were communicating this message to the regions affected. It believed its approach of working with customers in good and bad times out of its desire for long-term relationships was both morally and commercially sensible. It noted, however, that temporary financial solutions could only be considered for customers where there was a realistic prospect of repayment, be it from subsidies, compensation or an eventual recovery.

Future strategy in serving the SME banking business

6.178. HSBC provided us with its medium-term forecast for the commercial banking business unit from 2001 to 2003 (ie broadly serving business customers with borrowing facilities below US$100 million). It pointed out its commitment to being a full service provider for the UK commercial banking market, providing a comprehensive financial service across the full range of channels (face to face, telephone and screen). It stated that the key objectives of its commercial business unit were:

(a) to broaden and deepen existing relationships by increasing penetration of value-added products into the existing customer base;

(b) to grow the customer base, in a limited and controlled manner, through targeted and selective recruitment and reduction in avoidable attrition; and

(c) to manage down unit processing costs through a combination of rationalization, centralization, global processing, selective outsourcing, automation, straight through processing and optimization of the channel mix.

6.179. [

Details omitted. See note on page iv.

]

358

6.180. HSBC also said that it planned to make greater use of new technology, including the use of new channels, telephone and electronic communication to deliver products. [

Details omitted. See note on page iv.   ]

6.181. [

Details omitted. See note on page iv.

                                                                                   ]

TABLE 6.48 **HSBC: comparison of forecast Commercial Banking income and expenditure for 2003 with 1998 actual results and 2000 estimates**

		£ million		per cent
	1998 actual	2000 estimate	2003 plan	Change 2000–2003
Net income				
Total variable costs				
Allocated costs				
Other allocated costs				
Net profit before provisions				
Bad debt charge	*Figures omitted.*			
Net profit before tax	*See note on page iv.*			
Cost:income ratio (excluding Head Office costs)				
Cost:income ratio (including allocated costs)				

Source: HSBC.

6.182. [

Details omitted. See note on page iv.

                                                                                   ]

NatWest

6.183. Chapter 5 deals in detail with the position of NatWest and of its activities generally. The sections below deal with its services to SMEs. It was acquired by RBSG in 2000, and from a management perspective has now been fully integrated with RBS's operations. However, NatWest continues to be used as a brand by both Retail and Corporate Banking divisions of RBSG. We comment separately on RBS's activities in the SME market later in this chapter.

6.184. RBSG as the new parent of NatWest informed us that NatWest was unable to provide complete segmental financial performance information according to our definition of SME banking business for any of the years (1989 to 2000), as it did not have a division within its structure that matched our definition. The only figures that NatWest was able to provide on a 'best estimates' basis for its SME banking business were operating income (ie net interest and fees and commissions) and bad debts for the three years 1998, 1999 and 2000. It estimated the operating costs for its SME banking business for 1999, being the only year where a reasonable estimate was possible. We therefore made further estimates of operating costs for 1998 and 2000 as discussed below.

Financial performance of the SME banking business

6.185. NatWest told us that until its integration within the management structure of RBSG in 2000, the SME banking business was part of NatWest UK. The business units within NatWest UK were as follows:

(a) Retail Banking—this provided services to personal customers and business customers with turnover less than £1 million.

(b) Mortgages—this offered mortgages to personal customers for the purchase of residential properties.

(c) Corporate Banking—this provided services to mid-sized and large corporate customers.

(d) Cards—this provided credit, charge and debit card services to personal and corporate customers.

(e) 'Other', which consisted mainly of insurance and life insurance businesses.

6.186. Table 6.49 shows NatWest UK's analysis of performance in 1999 by business unit, as shown in its management accounts. The Retail Banking, Corporate Banking and Cards units provided services to SMEs. As noted in Chapter 5, NatWest said that actual cost allocations were not appropriate because the group was organized into customer-facing divisions, responsible solely for growing income and controlling direct costs (such as salaries of customer-facing staff). It was only able, therefore, to allocate costs between businesses on a best estimates basis. The bank monitored the contributions from the business units, which taken together were set against shared costs that were a large portion of the group's costs. It added that a separate central unit called the 'Manufacturing' division controlled the shared costs. RBSG (as the new owner of NatWest) stressed that this approach in no way undermined the bank's ability to know the overall costs of its business; the emphasis was to measure costs at the point of incidence and enormous efforts were put into ensuring that the group ran as efficiently as possible.

TABLE 6.49 **NatWest: summary of NatWest UK's performance by business unit, 1999**

£ million

Year ended 31 December 1999

	Business units					Other, such as insurance	Total for NatWest UK*
	Retail Banking	Mortgages	Corporate Banking	Cards	Subtotal		
Operating income						(✂)	
Direct costs (including restructuring)†						‡	‡
Allocated costs						‡	‡
Transferred costs		Figures omitted. See note on page iv.					
Total operating costs							
Trading surplus						✂	
Bad debt charge							
Other items							
Profit before tax§							
							per cent
Direct cost as a percentage of operating income		Figures omitted. See note on page iv.				‡	‡
Cost:income ratio						(✂)	

Source: CC based on information from NatWest.

*Reconciled to published accounts.
†Based on information in management accounts.
‡Unavailable.
§As requested by us, these figures are calculated on the basis that all lending is financed from borrowing in wholesale markets. In addition, NatWest said that the benefit of deposits was determined assuming that they were placed in the wholesale markets. In fact, a proportion of lending will be financed by the bank's equity, and it is therefore necessary to make an adjustment for this (see Table 6.52) before comparing returns on capital derived from these profit figures with the bank's cost of capital.

6.187. NatWest used the information in its management accounts to estimate the costs and profits of its SME banking business for 1999. Table 6.49 shows that direct costs as a percentage of income for the Retail Banking unit was [✂] per cent, [✂] per cent for Corporate Banking, and [✂] per cent for the Cards unit. In addition, the bank had allocated costs of £[✂] million, which were described by NatWest as those costs incurred in the general furtherance of the business, including overall management and some business and system development expenses. These costs, which amounted to [✂] per cent of income, were allocated to each unit pro rata to income. The bank also included 'transferred costs' of £[✂] million to reflect internal transfer charges between units for costs incurred, such as:

(a) IT resources supplied for most of NatWest UK's businesses by the Retail Banking unit; and

(b) charges to the units for support costs, principally premises and human resources.

After taking account of these indirect costs, its overall cost:income ratio increased to [✂] per cent for Retail Banking, and to [✂] per cent for Corporate Banking.

6.188. Table 6.50 shows the estimate of the profitability of NatWest's services to SMEs for 1999, based on NatWest's analysis of its income from SMEs of £[✂] with the three business units shown in the table. NatWest was able to give us its bad debt charges for SMEs from its Retail Banking business, and an estimate for its Corporate Banking business. In order to estimate the operating costs for the respective units, it used the cost:income ratios as shown in Table 6.50. This resulted in a weighted average cost:income ratio of 68 per cent. The estimated operating profit for services to SMEs in 1999 was £[✂] million. NatWest informed us that in 2000 its income from services to SMEs increased to £[✂], an increase of around [✂] per cent over the previous year. For 1998 we estimated that the equivalent income was £[✂].

TABLE 6.50 **NatWest: estimate of the profitability of NatWest's services to SMEs, 1999**

£ million

Year ended 31 December 1999

	Retail/Corporate Banking — customers with turnover from £0–£1m	Corporate Banking — customers with turnover from £1–£25m	Cards — customers with turnover from £0–£25m	Total for customers with turnover from £0–£25m
Net interest income				
Net fees and commission				
Operating income				
Operating costs*	✂ †	*Figures omitted. See note on page iv.*		
Operating profit				
Bad debt charge				
Profit before tax‡				

				per cent
Performance indicators				
Cost:income ratio	(✂)§	(✂)		68

Source: CC based on information from NatWest.

*We estimated operating costs, in accordance with the cost:income ratios shown on Table 6.49.
†Includes direct costs which are further analysed in Table 6.55.
‡As requested by us, these figures are calculated on the basis that all lending is financed from borrowing in wholesale markets. In addition, NatWest said that the benefit of deposits was determined assuming that they were placed in the wholesale markets. In fact, a proportion of lending will be financed by the bank's equity, and it is therefore necessary to make an adjustment for this (see Table 6.52) before comparing returns on capital derived from these profit figures with the bank's cost of capital.
§This is a percentage based on a [✂] per cent cost:income ratio for income from small business customers, and [✂] per cent for income from corporate customers with turnover to £1 million.

6.189. From Table 6.50, the operating income from the SME banking business in 1999 of £[✂] billion was analysed as follows:

(a) £[✂] million from business customers with turnover less than £1 million (£[✂] for Retail Banking and £[✂] for Corporate Banking, accounting for [✂] per cent of total operating income from the Retail Banking unit);

(b) £[✂] million from business customers with turnover of between £1 million and £25 million (accounting for [✂] per cent of total operating income from the Corporate Banking unit); and

(c) £[✂] million from Cards (accounting for [✂] per cent of total operating income from the Cards unit).

6.190. Table 6.51 further analyses the overall performance of NatWest's SME banking business for 1999 by showing all items as a percentage of operating income. In 1999 net interest income was [✂] per cent of operating income, and net fees and commissions accounted for the remaining [✂] per cent. Net interest income as a percentage of operating income was higher for both Retail Banking and Corporate Banking, and was around [✂] per cent.

TABLE 6.51 **NatWest: SME operating profit and loss items as a percentage of operating income, 1999**

per cent

Year ended 31 December 1999

	Retail Corporate Banking — customers with turnover from £0–£1m	Corporate Banking — customers with turnover from £1–£25m	Cards — customers with turnover from £0–£25m	Total for customers with turnover from £0–£25m
Net interest income				
Net fees and commission				
Operating income		*Figures omitted. See note on page iv.*		
Operating costs				
Operating profit before bad debt charge				

Source: CC based on information from NatWest.

6.191. NatWest was not able to provide us with estimates of its operating costs for 1998 and 2000 for services to SMEs. However, following discussion with RBSG we did the following:

(a) for 1998 we used an estimated operating income figure of £[✂   ], and applied the 1999 cost:income ratio of 68 per cent to impute an operating cost figure of £[✂] million; and

(b) for 2000, we estimated that the operating cost figure for 1999 of £[✂] million would remain unchanged on the assumption that after the acquisition by RBSG, such costs would not increase. When applied to the NatWest income figure for the year of £[✂   ], the 2000 cost:income ratio was estimated at 64 per cent.

Attributable capital to support the SME banking business and potential returns

6.192. Table 6.52 shows the profit from NatWest's SME activity for 1999. In order to form a view on the significance of such profits, we also considered NatWest's capital base. We look at this subject in greater detail in Chapter 7 for all the main suppliers. In our discussion with NatWest on determining the attributable capital to support its services to SMEs, we made a number of calculations for the years 1998 to 2000, based on our methodology as discussed in paragraphs 6.22 and 6.23.

6.193. Applying our methodology, we put to NatWest our initial assessment that its attributable capital to support its SME banking business (based on an apportionment of its closing balance sheet capital for 1998, 1999 and 2000) would be £[✂   ] for 1998, £[✂   ] for 1999 and £[✂   ] for

2000. In Table 6.50 NatWest's profits from SME banking business were based on it calculating net income from lending as if wholly financed from wholesale markets at LIBOR. However, in identifying the rate of return to compare with the cost of capital, an adjustment must be made to reflect that a proportion of lending was funded by capital and not from the wholesale markets. This is necessary to avoid double counting, and the appropriate adjustment for 1999 is attributable capital times the average three-month LIBOR. The rates used for 1998, 1999 and 2000 were 7.3 per cent, 5.45 per cent and 6.1 per cent respectively.

6.194. NatWest said that when assessing its profitability from SME banking business, we should make an adjustment to take into account the amortization of its pension surplus, which had accumulated to over £1 billion. These adjustments were £[✂] million for both 1998 and 1999 and £[✂] million for 2000.

6.195. Table 6.52 incorporates these adjustments, together with the information shown in Table 6.50 on profitability, and shows estimates of returns (subject to adjustments discussed later in Chapter 7). For 1999 NatWest's pre-tax return on closing capital was [✂] per cent. In Chapter 7 we consider NatWest's appropriate cost of capital, and what adjustments are necessary regarding these returns. In Chapter 2 we give our conclusions on this issue.

6.196. For 2000, it was noted that the share of RBS group's capital base allocated to NatWest according to its submissions was £[✂] billion. [*Details omitted. See note on page iv.*] When we calculated the capital attributable to SME banking business under the methodology discussed above, the figure was £[✂] billion, well below the figure of £[✂] billion for 1999. We have used this capital figure together with the other information in Table 6.52 to show an estimate of returns for 1998, 1999 and 2000 (subject to further adjustments in Chapter 7).

TABLE 6.52 **NatWest: summary of profits, capital and returns from NatWest services to SMEs, 1998 to 2000**

£ million

	1998	1999	2000
Information from Table 6.50			
Income			
Operating costs*			
Adjustment for attributable capital†			
Bad debt charge		Figures omitted.	
Operating profit before tax		See note on page iv.	
Pension costs			
Net profit before tax			
Attributable capital (based on closing capital for the whole bank and proportions of RWAs)			
Average attributable capital	‡	(✂	)

per cent

	1998	1999	2000
Pre-tax return based on closing attributable capital	(	✂	)
Pre-tax return based on average attributable capital	‡	(✂	)

Source: CC based on information from NatWest.

---

*NatWest was unable to provide an allocation of costs for the SME banking business for 2000. Therefore the figure for 1999 has been used as a proxy, on the assumption that after the acquisition by RBS, such costs would not increase.
†At 7.30 per cent for 1998, 5.45 per cent for 1999 and 6.10 per cent for 2000, based on three-month LIBOR.
‡Not provided.

6.197. An alternative in considering the above returns would be to use an average capital figure, for example the average of the opening and closing capital base, rather than a return based on the closing figure. For 2000 we calculated that the effect on the pre-tax return would be a decrease of four percentage points.

6.198. NatWest told us that, in its view, the capital attributable to its SME banking business should be significantly higher and approximately two to three times the level of attributable shareholders' funds to reflect the value of intangible assets associated with the business. We consider this argument later in Chapter 7.

Further analysis of income and expenses

6.199. Table 6.53 provides an analysis of operating income by type of banking service to SME customers for 1999 and 2000. The four main sources of revenue were loans, current accounts utilizing an overdraft facility, other current accounts, and deposits. In aggregate, these sources contributed [✄] per cent of NatWest's £[✄] billion operating income from services to SMEs in 1999 and [✄] per cent of its £[✄] billion operating income from services to SMEs in 2000.

TABLE 6.53 **NatWest: analysis of operating income from SME customers, by type of banking service, 1999 and 2000**

	Year ended 31 December 1999		Year ended 31 December 2000	
	£m	Income share (%)	£m	Income share (%)
Operating income* (before bad debt charges and operating costs) from:				
Lending on loans				
Current accounts utilizing an overdraft facility				
Other current accounts		Figures omitted.		
Deposits		See note on page iv.		
Subtotal				
Merchant acquiring				
Other income				
Clubs and charities				
Total				

Source: CC based on information from NatWest.

*Includes net interest income and net fees and commissions.

6.200. Table 6.54 provides a further breakdown of the 1999 operating income for the SME banking business into the following categories: net interest income, account management fees, and 'other'. The table also shows net interest margins for NatWest's services to SME customers with turnover less than £1 million, but NatWest told us that it was not able to provide the equivalent information for customers with turnover between £1 million and £25 million. We estimated that the average credit balance for 1999 for customers with turnover from £1 million to £25 million was some £[✄] billion, and for 2000 was some £[✄] billion. NatWest also confirmed that it has not to date paid any interest to customers on current accounts for their balances in credit.

6.201. Banks derive net interest income not only from loans and overdrafts made to SME customers but also from the value of deposits and current account balances in credit. NatWest said that for loans and overdrafts, net interest income reflected actual interest earned from customers after deducting the cost of funds as calculated by its 'Gross Funds Transfer Pricing' (GFTP) model. When calculating the cost of funds for loans, the GFTP model took into account the following factors: maturity, profile and whether interest rates were fixed or variable. For deposits and current accounts in credit, the benefit of funds reflected the value to the bank as calculated by its GFTP model, and included not only interest earned by investing such funds in the money market, but also interest earned from hedging/interest swap operations. As current accounts in credit were non-interest-bearing, there was no interest cost on such funds.

TABLE 6.54 **NatWest: analysis of SME operating income by type of banking relationship with SMEs, 1999 and 2000**

£ million

	Year ended 31 December 1999			Year ended 31 December 2000		
	£0–£1m turnover	£1–£25m turnover	Total	£0–£1m turnover	£1–£25m turnover	Total
Loans						
Interest income						
Allocated cost of funds						
Net interest income						
Account management fees		✂			✂	
Other						
Contribution						
Average lending balance on balance sheet (£m)		*	*		*	*
Annualized net interest (%)†		*	*		*	*
Current accounts utilizing overdraft facility						
Interest income		*	*		*	*
Allocated cost of funds		*	*		*	*
Net interest income		*	*		*	*
Fees for lending		*	*		*	*
Contribution		*	*		*	*
Average overdraft balance in balance sheet (£m)‡		*	*		*	*
Annualized net interest (%)†	✂	*	*	✂	*	*
Other current accounts§						
Benefit of SME funds						
Fees (money transmission)						
Contribution		✂			✂	
Average credit balance (£m)‡						
Annualized net interest (%)†						
Deposits						
Benefit of SME funds						
Interest paid						
Net interest income						
Average deposit balance on balance sheet (£m)		*	*		*	*
Annualized net interest (%)†		*	*		*	*
Subtotal of above income		(✂)			(✂)	
Other contribution						
Merchant acquiring						
Other income		✂			✂	
Charities and clubs						
Total operating income from SMEs						

Source: CC based on information from NatWest.

*Not provided.

†Net interest as percentages of average balances. For the current accounts this is only an approximate measure as there will be interest from some accounts categorized as having utilized their overdraft facility that at some point in the year may have been in credit. Similarly other current accounts may have been in overdraft at some point over the year.

‡These balances are approximate as some accounts will have changed their classification as well as their balance during the year.

§Includes current accounts without an overdraft facility and current accounts with an overdraft facility that has not been utilized. Of the current accounts without an overdraft facility this classification will include those accounts that have an unauthorized overdraft. The related interest charged on these balances has also been accounted for under this classification.

6.202. Total income for 2000 was £[✂] compared with £[✂] in 1999, an increase of £[✂] million. The main components of the change were:

(a) loans income which increased by £[✂] million to £[✂] million in 2000;

(b) current accounts with overdrafts income which increased by £[✂] million to £[✂] million in 2000;

(c) deposits income which increased by £[✂] million to £[✂] million in 2000; and

(d) an increase in 'other' income of £[✂] million from £[✂] million in 1999 to £[✂] million in 2000.

6.203. For 1999 and 2000 NatWest was able to provide net interest margins only for SME customers with turnover less than £1 million. Other current accounts reported the highest net interest margins, at [✂] per cent for 1999 and [✂] per cent in 2000. These higher net interest margins on current accounts arose as NatWest benefited from the current account balances but paid no interest to customers. The net interest margin on deposit accounts was [✂] per cent in 1999 and [✂] per cent in 2000. In addition:

(a) loans showed a net interest margin of [✂] and [✂] per cent; and

(b) overdrafts showed a net interest margin of [✂] and [✂] per cent.

6.204. Table 6.55 analyses the direct costs by type of activity for Retail Banking services in 1999. SME customers with turnover less than £1 million formed part of Retail Banking; we estimated the direct costs for services to them at £[✂] million for the year, based on [✂] per cent of total direct costs (the relative proportion of income from SMEs to total income for this unit).

TABLE 6.55 **NatWest: analysis of Retail Banking direct costs by type of activity, 1999**

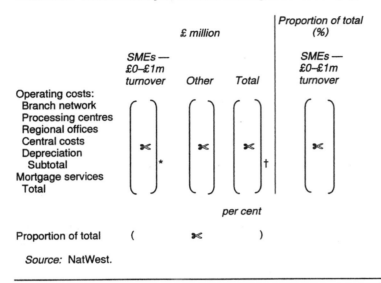

Source: NatWest.

---

*These costs are [✂] per cent of the total costs, being the proportion of income from customers with turnover up to £1 million of £[✂] million, to total income of £[✂] from the Retail Banking unit as shown in Tables 6.49 and 6.50.
†Total as shown in Table 6.49.

6.205. In 1999 central costs accounted for [✂] per cent of total operating costs, branch network costs accounted for [✂] per cent, and processing centres accounted for [✂] per cent. NatWest explained the costs shown in Table 6.55 as covering the following:

(a) Branch network costs—these included the costs of traditional branches, business centres and the ATM network across the UK.

(b) Processing centre costs—these included the costs of specialized units that processed large volumes of transactions that were generated by the customer and the bank, primarily from the branch network. The costs also included voucher processing, bulk cash processing, lending and security centres, and account management centres (dealing with opening/closing accounts and various aspects of customer records and transactions).

(c) Regional offices costs—these were the costs of overseeing the branch network and the operation of semi-centralized functions (for example, higher level sanctioning decisions, or monitoring performance). NatWest noted that relationship managers are included within the branch network costs. For corporate banks they are in the regional offices.

(d) Central costs—which included all IT expenditure (which accounted for [✂] per cent of Head Office costs), and all central functions such as executive, finance, credit, marketing and human resources.

6.206. Table 6.56 analyses Corporate Banking's direct costs for 1999 by type of activity. For 1999, we estimated £[✄] million as the costs associated with services to SME customers with turnover between £1 million and £25 million. This was [✄] per cent of total direct costs for Corporate Banking, based on the relative proportion of income.

TABLE 6.56 **NatWest: analysis of Corporate Banking operating costs by activity, 1999**

| | £ million | | | Proportion of total (%) |
	SMEs — £1–£25m turnover	Other	Total	Total
Operating costs:				
Processing centres	*	*		
Regional offices	*	*		
Head Office costs	*	*	✄	✄
Lombard Asset Finance Group	*	*		
Total	(✄)†	(✄)		

per cent

Proportion of total (✄)

Source: CC based on information from NatWest.

*Not available.

†These costs are [✄] per cent of the total costs, being the proportion of income from customers with turnover from £1 million to £25 million of £[✄] million, to total income of £[✄] from the Corporate Banking unit as shown in Tables 6.49 and 6.50.

6.207. NatWest told us that it currently had 977 people employed fully in supplying services to small businesses, within its Retail Banking unit. The employment costs were £[✄] million (an average cost of £[✄]). Of these, [✄] people were in marketing (relationship management), [✄] were in credit sanctioning and problem management, and the balance of [✄] in management and administration. In addition, it had 780 people in the Corporate Banking unit who were fully involved in serving the small business market, of which [✄] were in selling and marketing, and the balance in management and administration. Employment costs were £[✄] million (an average cost of £[✄]).

6.208. NatWest also said that it had a significant number of personnel who, as part of their duties, provided services to SMEs, but it was unable to quantify such numbers or their costs. It added that the majority of its selling and marketing staff were located in branches across the UK, reflecting customer need. The bank's credit staff were located in Edinburgh and Manchester.

6.209. NatWest told us that most of its marketing expenditure was not aimed specifically at the SME banking business as it was not recognized as a specific business unit. Its total group advertising and marketing expenditure for 1999 was £[✄] million, of which only £[✄] million was identified as being specifically for SMEs and corporate customers. The balance was for literature to personal/retail customers at the branches of around £[✄] million, £[✄] million for card services, £[✄] million was spent on other businesses not covered above, and £[✄] million on central costs including television and sponsorship. The cost to support the relationship managers' role was £[✄] million for 1999. NatWest reported that the advertising and marketing cost as a percentage of revenue in 1999 was [✄] per cent for Retail Banking, and [✄] per cent for Corporate Banking. It commented that in a mature market there was not necessarily a market correlation between levels of advertising expenditure and income. NatWest's Corporate Banking unit had put considerable emphasis on sustaining its market share through the development of relationships and the consequent investment in relationship managers.

6.210. [

Details omitted. See note on page iv.

]

Balance sheet extracts

6.211. Table 6.57 shows loans, overdrafts and customer accounts in credit for NatWest's SME banking business from 1989 to 2000. NatWest said that the SME banking business, as defined by us, was not an isolated business unit within its business structure and therefore it was unable to produce all the information requested. As discussed in the introduction to this chapter, it said that producing a balance sheet for the bank's services to SMEs is not relevant as assets and liabilities were managed on a pooled basis across the bank in accordance with policies on interest rate risk and liquidity.

TABLE 6.57 **NatWest: SME loans, overdrafts and customer accounts in credit, 1989 to 2000**

£ billion

Years ended 31 December

	1989	1990	1991	1992	1993	1994	1995	1996	1997	1998	1999	2000
Loans:												
SME customers with turnover to £1m												
SME customers with turnover from £1m to £25m			*Figures omitted. See note on page iv.*								✂	
Total loans to SME customers												
Customer accounts in credit*	†	†	†	†	†	†	†	†	†			
Funds required (+) or available (−)	†	†	†	†	†	†	†	†	†			

Source: NatWest.

*Includes deposits and current accounts in credit.
†Not available.

6.212. Over the period total loans to SME customers declined from £[✂] billion in 1989 to £[✂] billion in 1998 but recovered to £[✂] billion in 2000. The decrease over the period to 1999 was mainly due to a reduction in loans to the smaller SME customers (ie those with turnover less than £1 million), where total loans declined from £[✂] billion in 1989 to £[✂] billion in 2000. NatWest said that the decline in loans to the smaller SMEs up to 2000 was due to its decision to reduce lending to this customer type because of fears of a recession. Over the same period loans to SME customers with turnover between £1 million and £25 million remained relatively unchanged. At 1998 the level of customer accounts in credit was £[✂] billion, which fell to £[✂] billion in 1999, and exceeded the total lent to SMEs by some £[✂] billion. In effect, deposits received from SMEs have fully funded NatWest's lending to the business.

Bad debts

6.213. Table 6.58 shows the level of bad debt charge to profit and loss account for the SME banking business between 1989 and 2000. The average bad debt charge as a percentage of loans over the period for the smaller end of SME customers (ie those with turnover less than £1 million) was [✂] per cent. However, for the remaining SME customers (ie those with turnover between £1 million and £25 million) NatWest provided a range for the average bad debt charge as a percentage of lending to SMEs for the 11 years to 1999 of [✂] per cent as a lower estimate, or [✂] per cent as a higher estimate. Over the six years 1994 to 1999, the average charge for bad debt (both higher and lower estimates) was [✂] per cent of lending.

6.214. The bad debt charge was at its highest level between 1990 and 1993, and the higher estimate peaked at £[✂] million or [✂] per cent of lending in 1992. Since 1993 the bad debt charge declined, and was around [✂] per cent of lending in 1999. Until 1998 bad debt charge was higher at the smaller end of SME customers (ie those with turnover less than £1 million) compared with SME customers with turnover between £1 million and £25 million.

TABLE 6.58   NatWest: analysis of estimated bad debt charge to profit and loss from services to SMEs, 1989 to 2000

£ million

	1989	1990	1991	1992	1993	1994	1995	1996	1997	1998	1999	2000

Lower estimate of bad debt charge to profit and loss account
SMEs with up to £1m turnover
SMEs with £1m to £25m turnover
 Total SME customers

Higher estimate of bad debt charge to profit and loss account
SMEs with up to £1m turnover
SMEs with £1m to £25m turnover
 Total SME customers

Figures omitted. See note on page iv.

per cent

Performance indicators
Lower estimated bad debt charge as a percentage of total loans
SMEs with up to £1m turnover
SMEs with £1m to £25m turnover
 Weighted average for SME
 customers

Higher estimated bad debt charge as a percentage of total loans*
SMEs with up to £1m turnover
SMEs with £1m to £25m turnover
 Weighted average for SME
 customers

Average ratio

Figures omitted. See note on page iv.

Source: NatWest.

*Based on the higher estimate of SME bad debt charges, the simple average for the bad debt charge to lending ratio for the five years to 1993 was [✀] per cent, and [✀] per cent for the six years to 1999.

Future strategy in serving the SME banking business

6.215. [

Details omitted. See note on page iv.

]

369

6.216. NatWest noted that expenditure on new product developments, advertising and marketing was expensed when incurred, even though it was likely to have economic benefits in later periods. It also noted that such expenditure, although not giving rise to a separate intangible asset on the balance sheet, contributed to the Group's internally generated goodwill.

6.217. NatWest required capital expenditure of around £[✂] million in both 1997 and 1998, and this fell to £[✂] million in 1999. The capital expenditure expected for the combined NatWest/RBS groups would be around £[✂] million a year for the three years to 2003.

6.218. [

Details omitted. See note on page iv.

]

RBS

Overview of its activities in serving the SME market

6.219. Chapter 5 deals in detail with the RBS position and activities generally. The sections below deal with its services to SMEs. RBS said that it separated business customers into four categories:

(a) Retail, which included firms with annual turnover less than £1 million, serviced by its Retail Banking business unit;

(b) Commercial, which included firms with annual turnover between £1 million and £10 million, and Mid-Corporate, which included firms with annual turnover between £10 million and £100 million. Both these categories are serviced by its Corporate & Commercial Banking sub-unit, within the CBFM business unit; and

(c) Large Corporate, which included firms with annual turnover greater than £100 million, serviced by its Corporate & Institutional sub-unit, within the CBFM business unit.

Hence SME customers fell within three of the four categories listed above, Retail, Commercial and Mid-Corporate.

Financial performance of the SME banking business

6.220. We asked RBS to provide us with profitability data on its SME banking business (defined by us as business customers with turnover up to £25 million) for the period between 1997 and 2000. Due to its current business structure, RBS could provide income data only for customers with the following turnover bands: up to £1 million, £1 million to £10 million, and £10 million to £100 million (the Mid-Corporate sub-unit). It said that it was unable to estimate an income figure for services to SME customers with turnover to £25 million, as this would require estimation of income for customers with turnover in the range £10 million to £25 million. We, however, made our own estimates for 1998 and 1999 in discussion with RBS, using information in its management accounts.

6.221. RBS suggested that [✂] per cent of the Mid-Corporate (customers with £10 million to £100 million turnover) sub-unit's operating income, costs and bad debt charges was likely to fall within the £10 million to £25 million turnover band. This information is shown in Table 6.59.

6.222. RBS provided us with estimates of operating costs for its services to SME customers for the years 1998 and 1999. RBS's management accounts allocated costs (both direct and central recharges) into the various units of the bank, such as Retail, Cards, Commercial and Other. We discussed the issue of cost allocation in Chapter 5. Cost:income ratios were then calculated for each of the business units, and these were used to calculate operating costs for each of the sub-groups that made up the SME banking business according to our definition. Direct costs for the Cards and Corporate units were determined directly from the management accounts.

6.223. Table 6.59 shows the estimated profitability of RBS's SME banking business in 1998 and 1999, based on allocation of costs from its management accounts. Operating profit for its SME banking business (after allowing for central costs and bad debt charges) was £[✂] million in 1998, and £[✂] million in 1999. The table also shows the profitability of RBS's Mid-Corporate sub-unit (customers with turnover from £10 to £100 million) for 1998 and 1999. RBS said that the Cards business unit formed part of its SME banking business. The table shows that the overall cost:income ratio for 1998 was [✂] per cent, and for 1999 was [✂] per cent. This includes an additional allocation of central costs, advised to us by RBS towards the end of the inquiry as £[✂] million in 1998 and £[✂] million in 1999, which amounted to some [✂] per cent of income.

TABLE 6.59 RBS: profit and loss account from SME banking business, 1998 and 1999

£ million

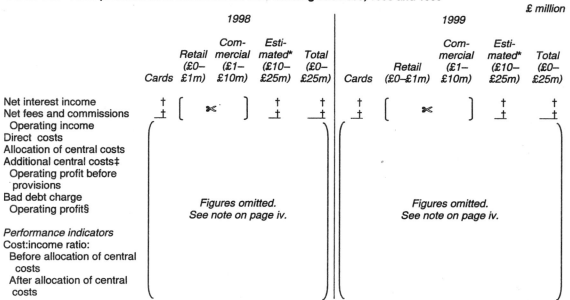

| | | 1998 | | | | | 1999 | | | |
	Cards	Retail (£0–£1m)	Com-mercial (£1–£10m)	Esti-mated* (£10–£25m)	Total (£0–£25m)	Cards	Retail (£0–£1m)	Com-mercial (£1–£10m)	Esti-mated* (£10–£25m)	Total (£0–£25m)
Net interest income	†	[✂]		†	†	†	[✂]		†	†
Net fees and commissions	‡			‡	‡	‡			‡	‡
Operating income										
Direct costs										
Allocation of central costs										
Additional central costs‡										
Operating profit before provisions										
Bad debt charge		Figures omitted. See note on page iv.					Figures omitted. See note on page iv.			
Operating profit§										
Performance indicators										
Cost:income ratio:										
Before allocation of central costs										
After allocation of central costs										

Profit and loss account for Mid-Corporate (£10–£100 million) from which we obtained information to derive results for the £10–£25 grouping (see paragraph 6.221)

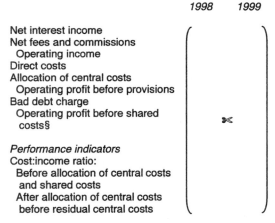

	1998	1999
Net interest income		
Net fees and commissions		
Operating income		
Direct costs		
Allocation of central costs		
Operating profit before provisions		
Bad debt charge	✂	
Operating profit before shared costs§		
Performance indicators		
Cost:income ratio:		
Before allocation of central costs and shared costs		
After allocation of central costs before residual central costs		

Source: CC based this on information from RBS.

---

*RBS estimated that [✂] per cent of the Mid-Corporate sub-unit (£10m–£100m) fell within the £10m–£25m turnover band.

†Not available.

‡Residual costs, which RBS identified as costs that were not charged to business units. They have been allocated according to income.

§As requested by us, these figures are calculated on the basis that all lending is financed from borrowing in whole-sale markets. In addition NatWest noted that the benefit of deposits was determined assuming that they were placed in the wholesale markets. In fact, a proportion will be financed by the bank's equity, and it is therefore necessary to make an adjustment for this (see Table 6.60) before comparing returns on capital derived from these profit figures with the bank's cost of capital.

6.224. In both years, a large proportion of operating income and profit was derived from the two sub-units serving the smaller end of SME customers, Retail (ie customers with turnover to £1 million) and Commercial (customers with turnover from £1 to £10 million). The Retail sub-unit reported operating income of £[✂] million in 1998 and £[✂] million in 1999, and contributed operating profit of £[✂] million in 1998 and £[✂] million in 1999. The Commercial sub-unit reported operating income of £[✂] million in 1998 and £[✂] million in 1999, and produced operating profits of £[✂] million in 1998 and £[✂] million in 1999.

6.225. The Mid-Corporate sub-unit (£10 million to £100 million) reported operating income of £[✂] million in 1998 and £[✂] million in 1999, and operating profit of £[✂] million in 1998 and £[✂] million in 1999, the improvement being mainly due to low bad debt charges in 1999. We estimated [✂] per cent as the portion of the Mid-Corporate sub-unit that related to SME customers with turnover between £10 million and £25 million, and accordingly, estimated this operating income at around £[✂] million for 1998 and £[✂] million for 1999, and operating profit as £[✂] million and £[✂] million respectively.

6.226. For 2000, RBS was able to provide us only with overall SME income data, without any cost allocations. Because of this lack of detailed data and the effect of its acquisition of NatWest during the year, we had to make a number of assumptions to arrive at a profit for the former RBS business from its SME banking business in 2000, as we discuss in paragraph 6.229.

Attributable capital to support the SME banking business and potential returns

6.227. The above tables estimated the profitability of RBS's SME banking business. In order to form a view on the significance of such profits we considered its capital base. We look at this subject in greater detail in Chapter 7 for all the main suppliers. In our discussion with RBS on determining the attributable capital to support its services to SMEs, we made a number of calculations for the years 1998 to 2000, based on our methodology as discussed in paragraphs 6.22 and 6.23.

6.228. In order to apply a similar methodology for capital allocation as that applied to other banks, we had to make a number of assumptions. RBS did not provide RWAs for its SME banking business in 1998, 1999 or 2000. We assumed that its total loans to SME customers were risk weighted at 100 per cent. Total estimated loans to SMEs (and thus RWAs) were £[✂] in 1998, £[✂] in 1999 and £[✂] in 2000. In 1998, 1999 and 2000 the RWAs for the bank as a whole were £49,090 million in 1998, £56,755 million in 1999 and £76,900 million in 2000. We calculated the percentage of SME RWAs to that of the whole bank at [✂] per cent for 1998, and this fell to [✂] per cent for 1999 and to [✂] per cent in 2000.

6.229. As discussed in paragraph 6.342, RBS provided us only with data on income from its services to SMEs for 2000, but no information on profitability. It told us that income from services to SMEs for the 15 months to 31 December 2000 was £[✂] million and therefore on a time-apportionment basis we calculated its income for the year 2000 at around £[✂] million. This compared with income for the 1999 year of £[✂] million and £[✂] million for 1998. For the purpose of calculating a return for 2000 we assumed that costs for 2000 were no more than the level for 1999, on the assumption that RBS would institute cost reduction and de-duplication programmes arising from its acquisition of NatWest. RBSG, however, did not accept this and considered that costs should be increased, but without suggesting a figure.

6.230. In addition, when determining the return to compare with the cost of capital, an adjustment had to be made to reflect the fact that a proportion of lending was funded by capital. This was necessary to avoid double counting, and for our purposes the appropriate adjustment is attributable capital times the average three-month LIBOR. The rates used were 7.3 per cent for 1998, 5.45 per cent for 1999 and 6.1 per cent for 2000.

6.231. RBS said that when assessing its profitability from SME banking business, we should make an adjustment to take into account the amortization of its pension surplus, which had accumulated to over £320 million. These adjustments were £[✂] million for both 1998 and 1999 and £[✂] million for 2000.

6.232. Table 6.60 incorporates these adjustments, our initial estimates of attributable capital, and the information shown in Table 6.59 on profitability, and shows estimates of returns (subject to adjustments discussed in Chapter 7). For 1998 and 1999, which were years with relatively low bad debt levels, RBS's pre-tax return on capital was [✂] per cent and [✂] per cent respectively. As discussed in Chapter 3, we noted that RBS's number of current accounts in 2000 from its original business was split roughly in the ratio [✂] for England and Wales, compared with Scotland.

TABLE 6.60 **RBS: summary of profits, capital and returns from services to SMEs, 1998 to 2000**

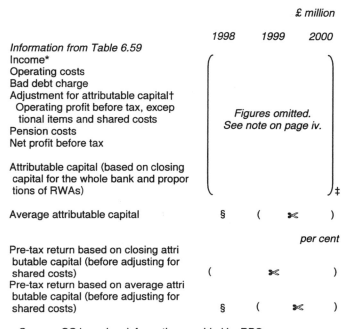

£ million

	1998	1999	2000
Information from Table 6.59			
Income*			
Operating costs			
Bad debt charge			
Adjustment for attributable capital†			
Operating profit before tax, exceptional items and shared costs		*Figures omitted. See note on page iv.*	
Pension costs			
Net profit before tax			
Attributable capital (based on closing capital for the whole bank and proportions of RWAs)			‡
Average attributable capital	§	(✂	)
			per cent
Pre-tax return based on closing attributable capital (before adjusting for shared costs)	(	✂	)
Pre-tax return based on average attributable capital (before adjusting for shared costs)	§	(✂	)

Source: CC based on information provided by RBS.

---

*RBS provided income figures for customers with turnover up to £10 million and we estimated income for customers with turnover from £10 million to £25 million. These estimates were £[✂] million in 1998, £[✂] million in 1999 and £[✂] million in 2000. The income figure for 2000 is a 12-month figure as RBS provided data for 15 months to 31 December 2000. The following tables in this chapter which show income for RBS for year ended 31 December 2000 are for 15 months.

†At 7.3 per cent for 1998, 5.45 per cent for 1999, and 6.10 per cent for 2000, based on three-month LIBOR.

‡Attributable capital increased by [✂] per cent from the 1999 figure due to RBS's acquisition of NatWest. This figure includes goodwill from the acquisition and is deducted in Chapter 7 in the calculation of what we term baseline capital. Chapter 2 gives our conclusions on the capital that we attribute to the SME banking business.

§Not calculated.

6.233. A further alternative of calculating the capital allocated to the SME banking business would be to use an average capital figure, for example the average of the opening and closing capital base, rather than a return based on the closing figure. For 1999 we calculated that the effect on the pre-tax return would be an increase of five percentage points.

Further analysis of income and expenses

6.234. As previously stated, RBS was unable to provide any financial data for SME customers with turnover between £10 million and £25 million. It was able to provide some of the financial data requested for SME customers with turnover less than £10 million and between £10 million and £100 million, which we present in the tables below.

6.235. Table 6.61 provides an analysis of operating income by type of banking service to SME customers with turnover less than £10 million, from 1998 to 2000, and our estimate for those customers with turnover from £10 million to £25 million. In 1998 and 1999 the four main types of banking services from which the bank earned income were loans, deposits, current accounts utilizing an overdraft facility, and other current accounts (no overdraft facility or where facility is not utilized). In aggregate, for customers with turnover to £10 million, these services contributed [✂] per cent of the £[✂] million, and £[✂] million operating income from the bank's services to SME customers with turnover less than £10 million, in 1998 and 1999 respectively.

TABLE 6.61 **RBS: analysis of income by type of banking service to SME customers with turnover less than £10 million, 1998 to 2000***

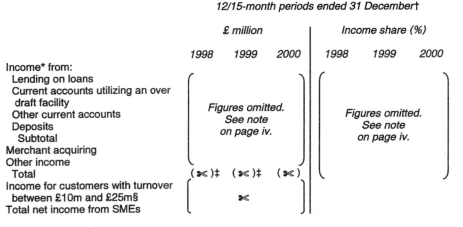

12/15-month periods ended 31 December†

Source: RBS.

---

*Net income includes net interest income and net fees and commissions. Operational costs and bad debt charges are then deducted from this income to derive net operating profit. For 2000 the figures reflect a 12-month period to 31 December 2000.
†Years ended 30 September 1998 and 1999, and 15 months ended 31 December 2000. The data in the table shows information for SMEs with turnover to £10 million, and our estimates for income from SMEs with turnover £10 million to £25 million.
‡As per Table 6.59 for SME customers with turnover less than £10 million.
§Estimated by the CC.

6.236. Table 6.62 provides a further breakdown of net operating income from SME customers with turnover less than £10 million into net interest income, net fees and commission, and 'other' income from 1998 to 2000. In common with other banks, RBS derived considerable interest income, not only from loans and overdrafts made to SME customers, but also money held in deposit and current accounts of the SMEs. The table also shows the estimated net interest margin earned by the bank from different types of banking relationships with the SMEs. For 1999, the average total value of deposits in current accounts and deposit accounts from SMEs was £[✂] billion, which in effect RBS was able to use in financing most of its lending to SMEs (loans and overdrafts) of £[✂] billion. RBS said that it used a system called 'funds transfer pricing' (FTP) to charge or reward divisions for the use or deployment of funds.

6.237. Each division was seen as both a provider and user of funds and in effect sells its liabilities (for example, customers' deposits) and buys the funds required to support its assets (for example, loans), at appropriate transfer prices. [

Details omitted. See note on page iv.

]

6.238. RBS said that in 1998 and 1999 the average total balances for loans and overdrafts combined were £[✂] and £[✂] respectively. It was unable to separate the average total balances between loans and overdrafts. The combined net interest margins for both loans and overdrafts were [✂] per cent in 1998 and [✂] per cent in 1999. Similarly for deposits and current accounts in credits, RBS said that the total average balances for both services combined were £[✂] in 1998 and £[✂] in 1999. We estimated that the net interest margins for deposits and current accounts in credit taken together were [✂] per cent in 1998 and [✂] per cent in 1999.

TABLE 6.62 RBS: analysis of operating income by type of service to SME customers, 1998 to 2000*

£ million

	12/15-month periods ended*			Margin and lending balances		
	1998	1999	2000	1998	1999	2000
Loans						
Interest income						
Allocated cost of funds						
Net interest income						
Other						
Net income†						
Current accounts utilizing an overdraft facility						
Interest income						
Allocated cost of funds						
Net interest income						
Fees for lending						
Net income†						
Average loans and overdraft balance on balance sheet (£m)						‡
Annualized net interest for loans and overdrafts(%)§¶						‡
Other current accounts¤						
Benefit of funds from SMEs						
Fees (money transmission)						
Net income#		Figures omitted.				
Average current account balance on balance sheet (£m)		See note on page iv.		✂		‡
Annualized net interest (%)¶						‡
Deposits						
Benefit of funds from SMEs						
Interest paid						
Net income#						
Average deposit balance on balance sheet (£m)						‡
Annualized net interest (%)¶						‡
Other net income from						
Merchant acquiring						
Sundry other services						
Total for SME customers with turnover to £10m						
Income for customers with turnover between £10m and £25m~						
Total income from SMEs						

Source: RBS.

*Years ended 30 September 1998 and 1999, and 15 months ended 31 December 2000. The data in the table shows information for SMEs with turnover to £10 million, and our estimates for income from SMEs with turnover £10 million to £25 million.

†Operational costs and bad debt charges are deducted from this income to derive the net operating profit from this service to customers.

‡RBS did not provide for 2000.

§RBS said that the average total lending balance (both loans and overdrafts) was £[✂] in 1998 and £[✂] in 1999. Hence we were unable to estimate the net interest margin for both loans and overdrafts, but in Chapter 4 an estimate is shown for illustrative purposes.

¶Net interest as percentages of average balances. For the current accounts this is only an approximate measure as there will be interest from some accounts categorized as having utilized their overdraft facility that at some point in the year may have been in credit. Similarly other current accounts may have been in overdraft at some point over the year.

¤Includes current accounts without an overdraft facility and current accounts with an overdraft facility that has not been utilized. Of the current accounts without an overdraft facility this classification will include those accounts that have an unauthorized overdraft. The related interest charged on these balances has also been accounted for under this classification.

#Operational costs are deducted from this income to derive the net operating profit from this service to customers.

~Estimated by the CC.

6.239. As stated earlier, RBS was able to provide estimates of operating costs for 1998 and 1999 and hence profits to the SME banking business. Table 6.63 shows a further analysis of operating costs for the Retail Banking division for 1999, which is split between SME customers with turnover up to £1 million and other activities. Operating costs for SME customers with turnover up to £1 million were £[✂] million in 1999, of which £[✂] million or [✂] per cent represented direct costs, and £[✂] million recharged costs ([✂] per cent). RBS said that the bulk of direct costs were staff costs and that the bulk of allocated costs were branch network costs.

TABLE 6.63 **RBS: analysis of operating cost for the Retail Banking division, 1999**

| | Year ended 31 December 1999 | | | | |
| | £ million | | | Proportion of total operating costs (%) | |
	SME £0–£1m	Other	Total	SME £0–£1m	
Operating income					
Operating expenses:					
Staff					
Property and equipment					
Other					
Total direct costs		Figures omitted.			
Recharges		See note on page iv.			
Total operating costs					
Operating profit before bad debt charge					
Bad debt charge					
Operating profit after bad debt charge					
Cost:income ratio (%)					

Source: RBS.

6.240. RBS said that there were 1,837 FTE staff who were devoted 100 per cent to providing services to SME customers. In addition, there were significant numbers of staff, either within the divisions or within the shared services operations, who were involved in providing or supporting the provision of services to SME customers.

6.241. In terms of marketing and advertising, RBS said that the bank as a whole spent £[✂] million in 1999, which equated to [✂] per cent of operating income. It was unable to provide the amount spent on marketing and advertising to SME customers as these customers were not an identifiable unit within the bank.

Balance sheet extracts

6.242. Table 6.64 shows loans and customer accounts in credit for RBS's business customers, separated between those with turnover less than £10 million and those with turnover between £10 million and £100 million, from 1997 to 2000. RBS said that the SME banking business, as defined by us, was not an isolated business unit within its business structure and hence it was unable to provide any financial information for that business. RBS estimated that 25 per cent of loans to SME customers with turnover between £10 million and £100 million fell into the £10 million to £25 million turnover band.

6.243. Between 1997 and 2000, for business customers with turnover less than £10 million total loans were around £[✂] billion and customer accounts in credit ranged from £[✂] billion to £[✂] billion. For business customers with turnover between £25 million and £100 million, total loans were around £[✂] billion and customer accounts in credit ranged from £[✂] billion to £[✂] billion. We estimated that total loans were around £[✂] billion for business customers with turnover between £10 million and £25 million.

TABLE 6.64 **RBS: loans and customer accounts in credit for business customers with turnover to £100 million, 1997 to 2000**

£ billion

As at 31 December

	1997	1998	1999	2000
Loans*				
Business customers (turnover):				
— to £10m				
— from £10m to £25m (estimated)†				
— total (SME customers <£25m)				
— from £25m to £100m†				
Customer accounts in credit‡		*Figures omitted.*		
Business customers (turnover):		*See note on page iv.*		
— to £10m				
— from £10m to £100m				
Funds required (+), or available (−)				

Source: RBS.

---

*Includes overdrafts.

†RBS estimated that [✂] per cent of loans to SME customers with turnover between £10 million and £100 million fell into the £10 million to £25 million turnover band.

‡Includes customer balances held in deposits and current accounts.

Bad debts

6.244. Table 6.65 shows the level of bad debt charge to profit and loss between 1991 and 2000 for RBS's business customers with turnover to £100 million. Between 1997 and 2000, RBS separated bad debt charges between those business customers with turnover less than £10 million and those with turnover between £10 million and £100 million. The level of bad debt charge was high between 1991 and 1994, and peaked at £[✂] million or [✂] per cent of loans in 1992. Since that year, the level has declined to £[✂] million or [✂] per cent of loans in 1999. However, the level increased to £[✂] million or [✂] per cent in 2000, predominantly from lending to larger business customers with turnover greater than £10 million. RBSG believed that based upon the figures for NatWest, which showed a longer-term perspective, the bad debt to asset ratio should be in the order of [✂] per cent.

TABLE 6.65 **RBS: analysis of bad debt charge to profit and loss for business customers with turnover less than £100 million, 1991 to 2000**

£ million

Years ended 31 December

	1991	1992	1993	1994	1995	1996	1997	1998	1999	2000
Analysis of bad debt charge to profit and loss account for business customers with turnover:										
— to £10m	*	*	*	*	*	*				
— from £10m to £100m	*	*	*	*	*	*		✂		
Total	(		✂			)				
										per cent
Bad debt charge as a percentage of total loans for business customers with turnover:										
— to £10m	*	*	*	*	*	*				
— from £10m to £100m	*	*	*	*	*	*		✂		
Total	*	(✂)†	(✂)†	(✂)†	(	✂	)			
Bad debt charge as a percentage of total income for business customers with turnover:										
— to £10m	*	*	*	*	*	*				
— from £10m to £100m	*	*	*	*	*	*		✂		
Total	*	(		✂			)			

Source: RBS.

---

*Not provided.

†RBSG stated that it incurred £[✂] of bad debts over a three-year period, which caused profits to fall significantly. It added that if this situation had continued then the group's future would have been materially affected.

6.245. RBS was unable to provide information on bad debt charge by size of loans and overdrafts to business customers for any of the other years under review.

Capital expenditure, development costs and future outlook for the SME banking business

6.246. Paragraphs 6.215 to 6.218 discussed capital expenditure and development costs for both RBS and NatWest, and the future strategy for the combined group to achieve substantial cost savings.

BoS

Overview of its business in serving SMEs

6.247. Chapter 5 deals with the position of BoS and its activities generally. The sections below deal with its services to SMEs.

6.248. Although BoS has long provided services to the SME market in Scotland, it did not enter the market in England until the 1980s, when it began to develop a reputation for facilitating management buyouts and providing other specialist banking products. At that time, BoS was not aiming to provide a full range of banking services to all types of SME customer. In the mid-1990s BoS changed its strategy and decided to expand into the more general banking market in England. It did this in two ways: first, by developing business through its existing offices, and secondly, through the establishment of a direct banking operation based in Edinburgh. The direct banking operation was initially designed purely to gather deposits. It offered interest-bearing current accounts and free banking.

6.249. BoS told us that it served SME customers through both its Business Banking business unit (customers with up to £10 million turnover) and its Corporate Banking business unit (customers with greater than £10 million turnover). Business Banking included all of the Asset Finance business, irrespective of customer size, and thus included some 'big ticket' leasing business.

Financial performance of the SME banking business

6.250. We asked BoS to provide us with profitability data on the SME banking business for the period between 1997 and 2000. It responded that the availability of historical data on SME banking business was limited as the UK group had been restructured in 1999/2000. Prior to the restructuring, the business was managed and reported on a legal entity basis with management information largely based on product rather than customer groupings. Changes to BoS source systems had been implemented to facilitate reporting on the new structure but these only provided data by customer groupings from the date of the change.

6.251. BoS said that its definition of 'Business Banking' activity differed from our definition of SMEs. It had therefore made estimates of SME banking business profitability for the years ended February 2000 and 2001. In obtaining its estimate for SME profitability, BoS took the Business Banking published profit and loss balances, subtracted overseas activities and 'big ticket' leasing balances and then added an amount for corporate banking customers the turnover of which fell between £10 million and £25 million.

6.252. Table 6.66 shows the estimated profitability of BoS's SME banking business for the years ended February 2000 and 2001. Operating income for the year ended February 2001 (before the benefit of funding from capital) was estimated at £[✂] million, while over the same period operating expenses were £[✂] million. The level of bad debt charge was £[✂] million and the share of profits from associates was £[✂] million. As a result, operating profit before tax was £[✂] million. As requested by us, these results were before BoS took account of lending that was funded by capital.

TABLE 6.66 **BoS: estimated profit and loss account from SME banking business, years ended February 2000 and 2001**

£ million

	Year ended 29 February 2000	Year ended 28 February 2001
Net interest income*	(✂)	
Net fees and commissions	(✂)†	
Other income	†	
Total operating income		
Operating costs		
Operating profit before provisions		✂
Bad debt charge	✂	
Profit from associates		
Operating profit adjusted to basis for calculating returns‡		

Source: BoS.

*See also Table 6.67 which shows the items in this table as a percentage of total operating income.
†BoS was able to provide only total non-interest income for 2000 of £[✂] million, and was not able to split this between fees and commissions, and other income.
‡As requested by us, these figures are calculated on the basis that all lending is financed from borrowing in wholesale markets. In fact, a proportion will be financed by the bank's equity, and it is therefore necessary to make an adjustment for this (see Table 6.68) before comparing returns on capital derived from these profit figures with the bank's cost of capital.

6.253. Table 6.67 further analyses the overall performance of BoS's SME banking business for the years ended February 2000 and 2001, by showing all items as a percentage of operating income. Adjusted net interest income was around [✂] per cent of operating income for 2000/01. Total non-interest income was [✂] and [✂] per cent respectively for the two years.

TABLE 6.67 **BoS: operating profit and loss items as a percentage of operating income from SME banking business, years ended February 2000 and 2001**

per cent

	Year ended 29 February 2000	Year ended 28 February 2001
Net interest income		
Net fees, commission and other income		
Total operating income		
Operating costs	*Figures omitted.*	
Operating profit before provisions	*See note*	
Bad debt charge	*on page iv.*	
Profit for associates		
Operating profit*		

Source: BoS.

*As requested by us, these figures are calculated on the basis that all lending is financed from borrowing in wholesale markets. In fact, a proportion will be financed by the bank's equity, and it is therefore necessary to make an adjustment for this (see Table 6.68) before comparing returns on capital derived from these profit figures with the bank's cost of capital.

6.254. The SME banking business cost:income ratio was [⊁] per cent for both years, and was higher than that of the whole bank at around [⊁] per cent as shown in Chapter 5. BoS said that its internal aim was to reduce the group-wide cost:income ratio to below [⊁] per cent. Each of the bank's divisions would contribute to the overall improvement but no specific level had been set as a target for the SME banking business.

Attributable capital to support the SME banking business and potential returns

6.255. Tables 6.66 and 6.67 show BoS's profits from its SME banking business. In order to form a view on the significance of such profits, we also need to consider BoS's capital base. We consider this subject in greater detail in Chapter 7 for all the main suppliers. In our discussion with BoS on determining the attributable capital to support its services to SMEs, we made a number of calculations for the years 1998 to 2000, based on our methodology as discussed in paragraphs 6.22 and 6.23.

6.256. Based on our methodology, we put to BoS our initial assessment that its attributable capital to support its SME banking business (based on an apportionment of its closing balance sheet capital for the year ended February 2000) would be £[⊁] million. For 2000/01, BoS estimated that the equivalent figure should be £[⊁], an increase of [⊁] per cent. BoS noted that this reflected the increase in its overall capital in the year, and that it had also increased proportionately its RWAs from lending to SME customers.

6.257. Table 6.66 shows that BoS's profits from SME banking business were based on its calculation of net income from lending as if wholly financed from wholesale markets at LIBOR. However, in identifying the rate of return to compare with the cost of capital, an adjustment must be made to reflect the fact that a proportion of lending was funded by capital and not from the wholesale markets. This is necessary to avoid overstating the interest costs (ie double counting). The appropriate adjustment is calculated as attributable capital times the average three-month LIBOR for 2000 of some 6.10 per cent.

6.258. Table 6.68 incorporates this adjustment, together with the information shown in Table 6.66 on profitability, and shows estimates of returns (subject to further adjustments discussed in Chapter 7). For the year ended February 2000, which was a year with relatively significant bad debt levels, the initial estimate for BoS's pre-tax return on closing capital was [⊁] per cent; the equivalent return for the year to February 2001 was [⊁] per cent. Using the average capital value of £[⊁] for 2000/01, the pre-tax return for the year increased by one percentage point to [⊁] per cent. We noted that:

(a) BoS paid significant sums of interest on current accounts in 2000, which we consider further in paragraph 6.382. These reduced profits for 2000/01 compared with banks that did not pay interest on current accounts.

(b) BoS stated in its annual report for 2001 (page 8) that there was pressure on SME lending margins during the year, which eased during the second half. BoS told us that this was the main reason why the increase in operating income ([⊁] per cent) was significantly lower than the increase in the capital attributable to SME banking business ([⊁] per cent).

6.259. BoS told us that it expected the benefit of its increased capital in its SME banking business to materialize in future years. In Chapter 7 we consider BoS's appropriate cost of capital, and what adjustments are necessary regarding these returns. In Chapter 2 we give our conclusions on this issue.

£ million

	Year ended 29 February 2000	Year ended 28 February 2001
Information from Table 6.66		
Income		
Operating costs		
Profit from associates		
Bad debt charge	*Figures omitted.*	
Adjustment for attributable capital	*See note*	
Operating profit before tax	*on page iv.*	
Attributable capital (based on closing capital for the whole bank and proportions of RWAs)		
Average attributable capital (see paragraph above)†	*	(✂)
		per cent
Pre-tax return (based on closing attributable capital)	(✂)	
Pre-tax return (based on average attributable capital)	*	(✂)

Source: BoS.

---

*Not applicable.

†The simple average of these closing estimates for attributable capital in 2000 and 2001 was £[✂], which BoS suggested would be less than a figure derived based on a more precise timing of the changes to overall capital. It computed a figure of £[✂] for the purposes of calculating returns.

Further analysis of income and expenses

6.260. Table 6.69 provides an analysis of total operating income of the SME banking business for the year ended February 2001 by type of banking service. In this period, the five main types of banking services from which the bank earned income were loans, loans utilizing an overdraft facility, overdrafts, other current accounts, deposits and asset finance. Other financing activities were mainly factoring and invoice discounting, hire purchase and vehicle management products. In aggregate, these services contributed [✂] per cent of the £[✂] million operating income from the bank's services to SME customers. Asset finance (including motor vehicle finance) was the largest source of operating income and contrib.-uted [✂] per cent of operating income. This compared with loans, which contributed [✂] per cent, current accounts (with no overdraft facilities) of [✂] per cent, and overdrafts of [✂] per cent. Deposits contributed only [✂] per cent of operating income.

TABLE 6.69 **BoS: analysis of income by type of banking service to SME customers for the year ended February 2001**

	£m	Income share (%)
Income* from:		
Lending on loans		
Current accounts utilizing an overdraft facility		
Current accounts†		
Deposits		
Asset finance	✂	
Other financing		
Subtotal		
Merchant acquiring		
Other income		
Total		

Source: BoS.

---

*Includes net interest income and net fees and commissions. Operational costs and bad debt charges are then deducted from this income to derive operating profit.

†Includes money transmission income.

6.261. Table 6.70 provides a further breakdown of BoS's operating income from the SME banking business for the year ended February 2001 by type of banking service into net interest income, net fees and commission, and 'other' income. The table shows the actual income earned, as well as the notional cost of funds to finance the lending, and the benefit of funds deposited by SMEs. BoS derived considerable interest income from its Asset Finance business, and from lending to SME customers. It also earned income from money in deposit and current accounts of the SMEs. Unlike some other banks, BoS pays interest on its 'Direct Banking' and other current accounts, which significantly offsets the net interest earned on these balances.

6.262. Table 6.70 also shows the net interest margin as a percentage of average balances generated by different types of banking relationships with the SMEs. For the year to February 2001, the average value of deposits and current accounts in credit from SMEs totalled £[✂] billion. This was roughly half the level of average lending on loans, overdrafts and asset financing to SMEs of £[✂] billion over the same period.

6.263. BoS said that net interest income from loans, asset finance and current accounts utilizing an overdraft facility, represented the actual interest earned less the cost of funds. Cost of funds comprised matched funding and non-matched items were funded at a rolling average of daily three-month LIBOR. Net interest income for customers' deposits and current accounts with no overdrafts was the benefit of funds to the bank, less the actual interest paid to customers. BoS paid significant levels of interest on its current accounts in the year ended July 2001. The benefit of current account balances was £[✂] million and the interest paid was £[✂] million, leaving a net interest figure of £[✂] million. In paragraph 6.258 we noted that the return on capital for this period was approximately [✂] per cent.

6.264. In so far as the margin for asset finance ([✂] per cent) is concerned, it is worth mentioning that this is before taking account of business acquisition costs. These costs, such as payment of commissions to brokers, introducers etc, of [✂] per cent reduce the margin to approximately [✂] per cent.

6.265. In the year ended February 2001, asset finance had the highest net interest margin at [✂] per cent. Net interest margins for the other types of service were as follows: [✂] per cent for loans, [✂] per cent for deposits, [✂] per cent for current accounts with no overdrafts and [✂] per cent for overdrafts.

6.266. We asked BoS to provide us with an analysis of operating profits by type of service to SME customers. However, BoS told us that it was unable to do so, because it was not able to separate operating expenses and bad debt charges by type of service.

TABLE 6.70 **BoS: analysis of operating income by type of service to SMEs, year ended February 2001**

	£m	Balances and margins*
Loans		
Interest income		
Allocated cost of funds		
Net interest income		
Arrangement fees		
Other		
Net income†		
Average lending balance on balance sheet (£m)		
Annualized net interest (%)*		
Current accounts utilizing an overdraft facility		
Interest income		
Allocated cost of funds		
Net interest income		
Fees for lending		
Other		
Net income†		
Average overdraft balance on balance sheet (£m)		
Annualized net interest* (%)		
Other current accounts‡		
Benefit of funds from SMEs		
Interest paid		
Net interest income		
Service charge		
Net income§		
Average current account balance on balance sheet (£m)		
Annualized net interest* (%)		
Deposits		
Benefit of funds from SMEs	✂	
Interest paid		
Net interest income§		
Average deposit balance (£m)		
Annualized net interest* (%)		
Asset finance		
Interest income		
Allocated cost of funds		
Net interest income		
Fees		
Net income†		
Average current account balance on balance sheet (£m)		
Annualized net interest* (%)		
Other financing		
Interest income		
Allocated cost of funds		
Net interest income†		
Fees		
Net income		
Average current account balance on balance sheet (£m)		
Annualized net interest* (%)		
Other net income from		
Merchant acquiring		
Other		
Total net income from SMEs		

Source: BoS.

---

*Net interest as percentages of average balances. For the current accounts this is only an approximate measure as there will be interest from some accounts categorized as having utilized their overdraft facility that at some point in the year may have been in credit. Similarly other current accounts may have been in overdraft at some point over the year.

†Before deducting operating costs and bad debt charges, to derive the operating profit from this service to customers.

‡Includes current accounts without an overdraft facility and current accounts with an overdraft facility that has not been utilized. Of the current accounts without an overdraft facility, this classification will include those accounts that have an unauthorized overdraft. The related interest charged on these balances has also been accounted for under this classification.

§Before deducting operating costs, to derive the net operating profit from this service to customers.

6.267. Table 6.71 provides an analysis of operating cost for services to BoS 'Business Banking' customers for the year ended February 2001. BoS defined 'Business Banking' as customers with a turnover of up to £10 million. 'Business Banking' also includes all asset finance customers irrespective of customer size. BoS did not provide a breakdown of costs for the SME banking business as defined by us. Within direct costs, staff cost was the largest cost category at £[✀] million, or [✀] per cent of total costs. Indirect costs accounted for £[✀] million or [✀] per cent of total costs.

TABLE 6.71   **BoS: analysis of Business Banking operating costs, year ended 28 February 2000**

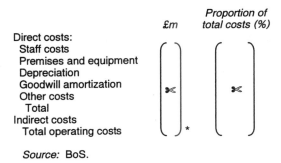

	£m	Proportion of total costs (%)
Direct costs:		
Staff costs		
Premises and equipment		
Depreciation		
Goodwill amortization	✀	✀
Other costs		
Total		
Indirect costs		
Total operating costs	*	

Source: BoS.

*The above costs have been derived from BoS's published results for Business Banking which include £[✀] million representing overseas activities. These costs do not form part of the operating costs in Table 6.66.

6.268. BoS told us that indirect cost allocation was, whenever possible, done on an 'actual' basis relating to appropriate measures such as activity volumes, number of staff or asset and liability volumes. Central overheads were allocated on a variety of bases. The methods were consistent with internal and historical methods and the allocation to the SME banking business was believed to be fair and reasonable but will continue to be refined.

6.269. BoS told us that, for the year ended February 2001, there were on average 4,100 people employed in Business Banking in the UK. All were involved in delivering banking services and related products such as Asset Finance (hire purchase, leasing, contract hire), and Cashflow Finance (factoring and invoice discounting). Approximately 500 staff involved in selling activities worked from home.

6.270. Table 6.72 shows an analysis of BoS's personnel serving SMEs in the year to February 2001, by function, in terms of FTE personnel.

TABLE 6.72 **BoS UK Group: summary of direct personnel serving SME customers as at 28 February 2001, analysed by function**

	Number of persons 100% serving SMEs
Analysis of direct personnel by function	
Selling and marketing	
Management	✀
Administration	
Other	
Total number of staff in SME banking business—UK	4,085*
Other staff not involved in SME banking business—UK	12,415
Total number of FTE staff (whole bank)—UK	16,500†

Source: BoS.

*Total annualized employment costs for UK SME banking business were £[✀] million, which equated to an average cost of £[✀] per employee.
†Total annualized employment costs for all activities were £491 million, which equated to an average cost of £29,757 per employee.

6.271. In February 2001 there were the equivalent of 4,085 personnel 100 per cent involved in the provision of services to UK SME customers. BoS could not provide details of the number of staff who had a partial involvement in the provision of services to SMEs. Overall, the annualized cost of personnel serving SME customers was £[✂] million at an average cost per FTE of £[✂] which compared with the whole bank's average cost of £26,757.

6.272. BoS told us that, for the six months to August 2000, advertising and marketing expenditure for the SME sector was less than [✂] per cent of total income for the sector.

Balance sheet items

6.273. Table 6.73 shows BoS's total average lending to SME customers as at February 2001. Total average lending to SME customers was £[✂] billion, which included loans at £[✂] billion, overdrafts at £[✂] billion, and asset finance at £[✂] billion. Deposits for the 12 months to February 2001 averaged £[✂] billion, while current accounts in credit were on average £[✂] billion in total.

TABLE 6.73 **BoS: loans to SME customers and other average balance sheet items, February 2001**

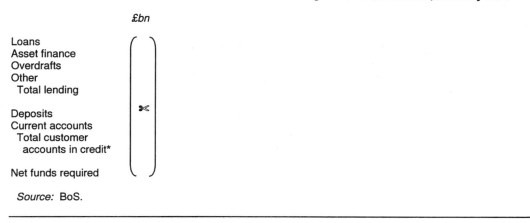

£bn

Loans
Asset finance
Overdrafts
Other
  Total lending

Deposits
Current accounts
  Total customer
    accounts in credit*

Net funds required

Source: BoS.

*Includes both deposit accounts, and current accounts in credit.

Capital expenditure and development costs

6.274. BoS told us that it was continuously updating its IT systems, telecommunications and properties to meet customer needs and to develop group business. Such expenditure was either capitalized and amortized, or written off to revenue, depending on its nature. On IT and telecommunications alone, its annual group budget was currently £[✂] million, of which over £[✂] million was for strategic projects.

6.275. [

Details omitted. See note on page iv.

]

Bad debts

6.276. We asked BoS to provide data on the level of bad debt charge and bad debt provision attributable to the SME sector over the past ten years. BoS told us that this data was only available at the UK group level and not at the SME segment level. Table 6.74 shows the level of bad debt provision and bad debt charge for services to SMEs in the years ended February 2000 and February 2001.

TABLE 6.74 BoS: summary of bad debt charges and year-end provision for services to SMEs, 2000 and 2001, based on BoS's definition of SMEs*

	February 2000	February 2001
Provision for bad debts (£m)		
Bad debt charge (£m)		
Lending balance (£bn)	✂	
Provisions as a percentage of lending (%)		
Bad debt charge as a percentage of lending (%)		

Source: BoS.

---

*BoS definition of SME excludes overseas activities and includes some corporate customers.

6.277. [

Details omitted. See note on page iv.

]

6.278. BoS said that it considered lending to SMEs as being more risky than lending to other business areas. It quoted a recent report from 'R3' (the Association of Business Recovery Professionals) which suggested that Scottish start-up businesses were more likely to fail than in England and indicated management and inadequate funding as two of the main reasons for failure. However, the job preservation rate in Scotland is 29 per cent against a national average of 19 per cent.

6.279. BoS noted that compared with larger businesses SMEs were more likely to be:

(a) weak on management;

(b) more reliant on external funding, ie little equity and a reluctance to dilute shares to bring some more in;

(c) more highly geared;

(d) limited in the security they could provide;

(e) short on accounting information; and

(f) possibly reliant on a small customer base making them more vulnerable from loss of key customers.

6.280. BoS noted that there was no evidence that in asset finance SMEs were more risky as this form of lending was based/secured upon the type of asset and its current or project value. Similarly its experience in factoring and invoice discounting did not suggest that SMEs were more risky, as the exposures were dependent upon the quality of the receivables secured to them. BoS noted that in this case the experience suggested that lending to SMEs could be less risky than lending to other business areas.

Future strategy in serving the SME banking business

6.281. With the recent business restructure, and the establishment of the Business Banking division (an amalgamation of both the banking services and the Asset Finance business), BoS told us that it was now gearing up its SME banking business in the UK. It was in the process of putting together teams that would service all the SME product ranges, rather than having a team for asset finance and a separate team for banking services. It was putting in place separate sales and marketing teams: one focused on gaining new customers, and another to look after relationship management with its existing customers. [*Details omitted. See note on page iv.*] BoS told us that it was putting together some fairly aggressive marketing campaigns in England. In particular, it would focus on its interest-bearing current accounts and would be offering the customer the choice of either dealing directly with a relationship manager at a business centre, or doing banking on a direct basis with a branch. Customers choosing to bank directly would have a slightly restricted service (but no bank charges), higher interest on deposits and more competitive interest rates on borrowings.

Ulster Bank

Overview of its business in serving SMEs

6.282. Chapter 5 deals in detail with Ulster Bank's position and activities generally. This section deals with its services to SMEs.

6.283. Ulster Bank told us that in Northern Ireland approximately 92 per cent of business customers had a turnover of less than £1.0 million, 7 per cent had a turnover between £1 million and £5 million and only 1 per cent had a turnover over £5 million. Therefore with very few exceptions all businesses within Northern Ireland fell within our definition of SME banking business.

6.284. Ulster Bank said that it did not manage its business in line with our definition of SME banking business. Instead SME customers were spread across several Ulster Bank business units: Retail, Business Banking, Cards, Lombard & Ulster Ltd (Ulster Bank's asset finance arm in Northern Ireland) and JCB Finance Ltd (Ulster Bank's asset finance arm in Great Britain). Ulster Bank used borrowing requirement as the primary indicator of the range and complexity of services which an SME customer was likely to require. It believed that the larger an SME became, the more likely it was to have a dedicated finance function, and to require specialist banking services, specifically:

(a) customers with a borrowing requirement of £1 million or more were serviced by the Business Banking unit; and

(b) customers borrowing up to £1 million were serviced by the Retail business unit.

6.285. Ulster Bank told us that its asset finance subsidiaries, Lombard & Ulster Ltd and JCB Finance Ltd, placed all non-personal finance almost exclusively into the SME sector. Its Cards business covered both issuance (personal and corporate) and merchant acquisition across the whole spectrum of SMEs in Northern Ireland.

Financial performance of the SME banking business

6.286. We asked Ulster Bank to provide us with profitability data on its SME banking business for the period between 1998 and 2000. It said that it did not manage its SME banking business as an identifiable unit, and that the SME banking business was spread across several business units. As a result, Ulster Bank gave us combined profitability data for the business units that provided services to SME customers in Northern Ireland. It defined these business units as 'in-scope' business units. However, as these business units also provided services to other, non-SME customers, this data needed adjustment before it could be used to draw conclusions on Ulster Bank's SME banking business. As the bank does not manage its SME banking business as a discrete unit, it does not make any income or cost allocations at the SME banking business level. We therefore had to make estimates that we considered appropriate of Ulster Bank's profitability from services to SMEs. SME loans and advances constituted [✂] per cent of its total lending to customers in 1998, [✂] per cent in 1999 and [✂] per cent in 2000. We therefore applied these proportions to the income and expense totals provided to us, using the loans balance as an indication of the size of the SME banking business. The results are analysed below.

6.287. Table 6.75 shows the estimated profitability of Ulster Bank's SME banking business from 1998 to 2000. Operating income was £[✂] million in 1998 and increased to £[✂] million in 2000, while operating expenses were £[✂] million in 1998 and increased to £[✂] million in 2000. The level of bad debt charge was around £[✂] million in each year. As a result, operating profit before tax was estimated at £[✂] million in 1998, £[✂] million in 1999 and £[✂] million in 2000. The cost:income ratio for 2000 was estimated at [✂] per cent.

TABLE 6.75 **Ulster Bank: estimated profit and loss account from SME banking business, 1998 to 2000**

£ million

	1998	1999	2000
Total operating income			
Operating expenses		*Figures omitted.*	
Operating profit before provisions		*See note*	
Bad debt charge		*on page iv.*	
Operating profit before tax*			

		per cent	
Performance indicators			
Cost:income ratio	(	✂	)

Source: CC based on information provided by Ulster Bank.

---

*As requested by us, these figures were calculated on the basis that all lending is financed from borrowing in wholesale markets. In fact, a proportion will be financed by the bank's equity, and it is therefore necessary to make an adjustment for this (see Table 6.76) before comparing returns on capital derived from these profit figures with the bank's cost of capital.

6.288. When our estimates were put to Ulster Bank, it commented that the estimates:

(a) ignored the expectation that income and cost structures would vary across the different businesses within the overall loan (and resource) portfolios;

(b) did not recognize the differential in costs of support for high-volume customers as opposed to low; and

(c) ignored the existence of central functions, such as risk, IT, finance and audit which incurred considerable time and expense supporting customer-facing businesses. It was inevitable that some businesses would benefit from this support more than others, for example agriculture, personal services including cards, and mortgages.

6.289. However, Ulster Bank did not provide us with any alternative estimates or adjustments to take account of its objections.

Attributable capital to support the SME banking business and potential returns

6.290. Table 6.76 considers Ulster Bank's profits from its SME banking business. In order to form a view on the significance of such profits we also consider the capital base of Ulster Bank. We look at this subject in greater detail in Chapter 7. In our discussion with Ulster Bank on determining the attributable capital to support its services to SMEs, we made a number of calculations for the years 1998 to 2000, based on our methodology as discussed in paragraphs 6.22 and 6.23.

6.291. Applying our methodology, we put to Ulster Bank our initial assessment that its attributable capital to support its SME banking business (based on an apportionment of its closing balance sheet capital) would be £[✲] million for 1998, £[✲] million for 1999 and £[✲] million for 2000.

6.292. In Table 6.75 we noted that Ulster Bank's estimated profits from SME banking business were based on it calculating net income from lending as if wholly financed from the wholesale markets at its internal transfer pricing rate. However, in identifying the rate of return to compare with the cost of capital, an adjustment must be made to reflect that a proportion of lending was funded from capital and not from the wholesale markets. This is necessary to avoid double counting, and for our purposes we considered that the appropriate adjustment is attributable capital times the average three-month LIBOR for each year. The rates used for each of the years 1998, 1999 and 2000 were 7.3 per cent, 5.45 per cent and 6.1 per cent respectively.

6.293. Ulster Bank said that when assessing its profitability from SME banking business, we should make an adjustment to take into account the amortization of its pension surplus, which had accumulated to over £70 million. These adjustments were £[✲] million for 1998, £[✲] million for 1999 and £[✲] million for 2000.

6.294. Table 6.76 incorporates these adjustments, together with the information shown in Table 6.75 on profitability, and shows estimates of returns (subject to adjustments discussed in Chapter 7). For 2000, which was a year with relatively low bad debt levels, Ulster Bank's pre-tax return on capital was [✲] per cent, based on closing capital. In Chapter 7 we consider Ulster Bank's appropriate cost of capital, and what adjustments we considered were necessary regarding these returns. In Chapter 2 we give our conclusions on this issue.

TABLE 6.76 **Ulster Bank: summary of estimated profits, capital and returns from services to SMEs, 1998 to 2000**

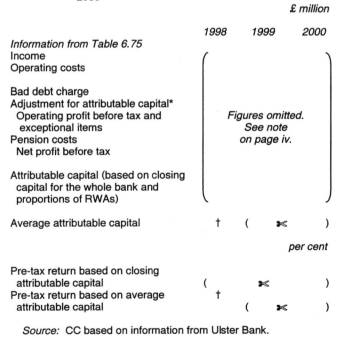

£ million

	1998	1999	2000
Information from Table 6.75			
Income			
Operating costs			
Bad debt charge			
Adjustment for attributable capital*			
Operating profit before tax and exceptional items		*Figures omitted. See note on page iv.*	
Pension costs			
Net profit before tax			
Attributable capital (based on closing capital for the whole bank and proportions of RWAs)			
Average attributable capital	†	(✲)	

per cent

	1998	1999	2000
Pre-tax return based on closing attributable capital		(✲)	
Pre-tax return based on average attributable capital	†	(✲)	

Source: CC based on information from Ulster Bank.

---

*At 7.3 per cent for 1998, 5.45 per cent for 1999 and 6.1 per cent for 2000 based on three-month LIBOR.
†Not available.

6.295. A further alternative method of calculating the capital attributable to the SME banking business would be to use an average capital figure, for example the average of the opening and closing capital base, rather than a return based on the closing figure. For 1999 we calculated that the effect on the pre-tax return would be an increase of one percentage point.

Further analysis of income and expenses

6.296. Ulster Bank told us that the three main sources of fee and commission revenues from SMEs were: money transmission services, lending-related services and card fees and commissions.

6.297. We asked Ulster Bank to provide a breakdown of net operating income from the SME banking business into net interest income and net fees and commission income by product type between 1998 and 2000. As previously advised to us, Ulster Bank does not manage its business in a manner which would enable them to provide this information for all of the years we requested it. Ulster Bank was able to provide this data only for 2000 and only according to its definition of 'in-scope' business units. Further, product type was limited to total lending including loans and overdrafts, and total deposits including current accounts and deposits.

6.298. Table 6.77 shows the income by type of banking service, for business units that provided services to SME customers, in 2000. Net interest income as a percentage of average loan balances in 2000 was [✂] per cent in 2000. Interest income as a percentage of average deposit balances was [✂] per cent.

TABLE 6.77 **Ulster Bank: income by type of banking service, from business units that provided services to SME customers in whole or in part during 2000**

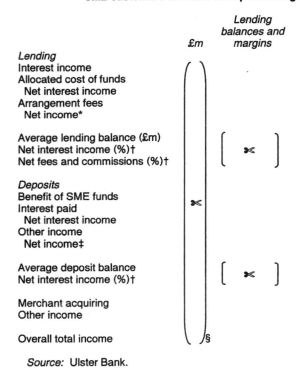

Source: Ulster Bank.

*Before deducting operational costs and bad debt charges, to derive the net operating profit from this service to customers.

†Net interest and net fees and commissions as percentages of average balances.

‡Before deducting operational costs, to derive the net operating profit from this service to customers.

§We estimated that [✂] per cent of total income for 2000 was from SME customers. This estimate is shown in Table 6.75.

6.299. Table 6.78 provides an analysis of operating costs for business units that provided services to SME customers. As with the income numbers in Table 6.77, the data includes costs of non-SME banking business as well. We have taken 66 per cent of these costs in 1999, and 69 per cent in 2000, as an estimate of costs attributable to SME customers in Table 6.78. Staff costs made up the largest cost categories for both years. However, Ulster Bank said that because it had no discrete unit that dealt exclusively with SMEs, it was unable to tell us how many FTE staff worked on providing services to SME customers. Consequently, Ulster Bank did not provide us with any estimates as to the amount of overhead cost that would be attributable to the SME banking business. It noted that all services provided to the SME banking business were also provided to larger corporate customers. Therefore the infrastructure in place supported all customers and it did not consider it meaningful or practical to estimate how much cost related solely to SME.

TABLE 6.78 **Ulster Bank: analysis of operating costs for business units that served SME customers, 1999 and 2000**

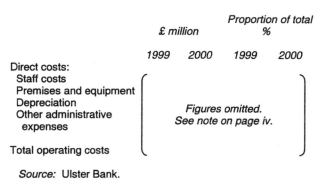

	£ million		Proportion of total %	
	1999	2000	1999	2000
Direct costs:				
Staff costs				
Premises and equipment				
Depreciation		*Figures omitted.*		
Other administrative expenses		*See note on page iv.*		
Total operating costs				

Source: Ulster Bank.

6.300. Ulster Bank told us that in 1999 it spent a total of £[✂] million on advertising, marketing and promotion in those business units that provide services to SMEs. Of this, it estimated that £[✂] was directly attributable to SMEs. It noted that over the last three years advertising of business services and products has been of a general nature to position its brand. There were no specific initiatives directly targeting start-ups or other banks' customers.

Balance sheet items

6.301. Table 6.79 shows Ulster Bank's total lending to SME customers between 1996 and 2000. Total lending to SME customers was £[✂] billion in 2000, while total customer accounts in credit was £[✂] billion.

TABLE 6.79 **Ulster Bank: SME balance sheet, 1996 to 1999**

£ million

	1996	1997	1998	1999	2000
Loans and advances to customers	(✂)		*Figures omitted.*		
Customer accounts	*		*See note*		
Funds required	*		*on page iv.*		

Source: Ulster Bank.

*Data not available.

Bad debts

6.302. Table 6.80 shows the specific provision movements for the SME banking business from 1996 to 2000, and the bad debt charges for business units that serviced SME customers. As the general bad debt provision is not allocated wholly or in part to the SME banking business, Ulster Bank said that it was not possible to state the total amounts of bad debt expenses relating solely to SMEs as the business

391

was not managed or accounted for in that way. That is, the general bad debt provision could not be allocated to the SME banking business. Bad debt charges for all business units that provided services to SME customers were [✂] per cent of total lending in 2000 and [✂] per cent of total income.

TABLE 6.80 **Ulster Bank: summary of specific bad debt provision for SME customers, and bad debt expense for business units which provided services to SME customers, 1996 to 2000**

	1996	1997	1998	1999	2000
Specific provision:*					
Balance at start of year	†	(✂)			
Charge against profits	(✂)				
Amount written off	†	†	*Figures omitted.*		
Recoveries	†	†	*See note*		
Balance at end of year	(✂)		*on page iv.*		
Total bad debt charge	†	(✂)			

			per cent		
Bad debt charge as a percentage of lending‡	†	*Figures omitted.*			
Bad debt charge as a percentage of income‡	†	*See note on page iv.*			

Source: Ulster Bank.

---

*Ulster Bank said that in providing this data, it had assumed that all non-personal bad debts arose among SMEs. Information was provided using Standard Industrial Classification Code data as the source.
†Not available.
‡As the bad debt charge provided was for all business units that provided services to SMEs (not just SME bad debts), the total lending and total income figures for these calculations are also those for the whole business units. Total income for all business units that provided services to SMEs in 2000 was £[✂] million, and total lending was £[✂].

6.303. In respect of the level of bad debts going forward, Ulster Bank said that Northern Ireland was heavily dependent on the overall performance of the UK economy, given its extensive trade with Great Britain and common fiscal policy. Ulster Bank believed, however, that the Northern Ireland economy was more exposed to the euro due to trade links with the Republic of Ireland. Public expenditure was also relatively much more important in Northern Ireland, and was continuing to rise at a faster pace than elsewhere in the UK. Combined with structural shifts in manufacturing from textiles into information, communications and technology, and retail, this had allowed the Northern Ireland economy to shed its traditional laggardly image. Unemployment had fallen to record lows, although it still remained above the UK average. Ulster Bank also told us that the current high exchange rate for sterling was posing problems for the agricultural sector which, although declining, was still relatively important. There was anecdotal evidence that the retail sector was suffering in border regions, as business from the Republic of Ireland had significantly contracted in real terms. Tourism, which was expected to do better from the peace process, had grown but was still a long way short of its potential.

6.304. Ulster Bank highlighted agriculture as the only sector that had caused concern over the last three years and which continued to do so. It told us that agriculture was generally cyclical, although never before had all parts of the sector been in such difficulty at the same time.

6.305. Ulster Bank's view was that most other industry sectors were performing well, particularly property and construction, although there was some concern that supply might outstrip demand, particularly for speculative office and apartment buildings. The local economy had also benefited from the very strong economic growth in the Republic of Ireland, and a significant element of the property development had been funded by Republic of Ireland investors.

6.306. Ulster Bank told us that there had been ongoing refinement of its risk management procedures but there had been no recent substantive changes, as the practices employed had proved to be robust. Going forward it was likely that it would adopt proven automated techniques to assist in the management of the lending portfolio, such as credit scoring and risk grading. Ulster Bank told us that it had not, in recent years, experienced bad debt levels comparable with those of financial institutions in

Great Britain. This, it believed, was primarily due to the fact that, while Northern Ireland had not benefited to the same extent as other parts of the UK from 'peaks' in the economic cycle, neither had it suffered the 'lows', reflecting, in part, the ongoing level of government expenditure in the province.

6.307. In commenting upon the riskiness of SME banking business, Ulster Bank repeated the views made by its parent bank, RBS, which are covered in earlier in this chapter.

Future strategy in serving the SME banking business

6.308. Ulster Bank told us that it had and would continue to invest in products, services and infrastructure to meet the needs of customers and to keep abreast of technological developments. In the three years from 1997, the bank had invested £1.5 million in the development and launch of an Internet banking service specifically aimed at personal and SME customers. To date, a telephone banking service had not been made available to SMEs because when the service was originally developed, Ulster Bank's research indicated that SMEs did not view telephone banking as a viable business service and would prefer an Internet or PC-based service. This decision might be revisited, as there were now indications that SMEs would use a telephone banking service. In addition to the above, Ulster Bank told us that it had spent a further £1.3 million on other e-banking initiatives, including the development of www.ulster bank.com and the provision of a BACS package specifically targeted at SME customers.

6.309. Ulster Bank told us that the group had recently announced a major restructure programme which it estimated would cost £87 million and was designed to develop and grow its operations across a range of businesses, and to streamline certain functional services. This programme would, among other things, impact on the SME sector and how it was serviced, although specific details were not available.

AIB, including First Trust and Allied Irish Bank (GB)

Overview of its business in serving SMEs

6.310. Chapter 5 dealt with AIB and the general activities of its divisions, First Trust and AIB (GB). First Trust provided services to SMEs in Northern Ireland, while AIB (GB) provided services on the British mainland. The following sections deal with their SME banking business.

First Trust

Financial performance of the SME banking business

6.311. We asked First Trust to provide us with profitability data on its services to SMEs for the period between 1997 and 1999. It told us that it recorded transactions and account balances on product reporting lines and did not record or analyse SMEs by turnover. Costs were not allocated to accounts of a particular turnover band or industry sector and it did not differentiate interest margins or fees charged between sectors or by customer account size. Further, because of its size, it had only minor costs that could be attributed to specific customer businesses. First Trust told us that it therefore could not complete the cost analysis, under the headings we requested, and it could only provide best estimates for certain other data.

6.312. Table 6.81 shows the profitability of First Trust's SME banking business for 1998 to 2000. Operating income for 1998 to 2000 was £[✂] million, £[✂] million and £[✂] million respectively, which resulted in operating profit before tax of £[✂] million in 1998, £[✂] million in 1999, and £[✂] million in 2000.

TABLE 6.81 **First Trust: profit and loss account from SME banking business, 1998 to 2000**

£ million

	1998	1999	2000
Net interest income			
Net fees and commissions			
Total operating income		*Figures omitted.*	
Operating expenses*		*See note*	
Operating profit before bad debts		*on page iv.*	
Bad debt charge			
Net profit before tax†			

per cent

Performance indicators			
Cost:income ratio	(	✂	)

Source: First Trust.

*Estimated by us based on cost:income ratio estimates provided by First Trust.

†As requested by us, these figures were calculated on the basis that all lending is financed from borrowing in whole-sale markets. In fact, a proportion will be financed by the bank's equity, and it is therefore necessary to make an adjustment for this (see Table 6.82) before comparing returns on capital derived from these profit figures with the bank's cost of capital.

6.313. First Trust told us that it considered the cost:income ratio for its services to SMEs, excluding cost of capital, as [✂] per cent in 1999. We used this estimate to calculate First Trust's SME banking business operating expenses for 1998, 1999 and 2000. First Trust also said that it planned cost:income targets at bank level only and had no specific cost:income target for a hypothetical SME banking business. We noted that this imputed cost:income ratio for services to SMEs was higher than that for the whole bank (discussed in Chapter 5), which was shown as [✂] per cent.

Attributable capital to support the SME banking business and potential returns

6.314. Table 6.82 shows the results for First Trust's profits from its services to SMEs. In order to form a view on the significance of such profits we also consider the AIB UK statutory entity's capital base. We look at this subject in greater detail in Chapter 7. In our discussion with First Trust on determining the attributable capital to support its services to SMEs, we made a number of calculations for the years 1998 to 2000, based on our methodology as discussed in paragraphs 6.22 and 6.23.

6.315. First Trust did not calculate a stand-alone capital adequacy ratio, but rather its RWAs were combined with those of AIB (GB) and reported as AIB Group (UK) plc.

6.316. Applying our methodology, we put to First Trust our initial assessment that its attributable capital to support its SME banking business (based on an apportionment of AIB UK's closing balance sheet capital) would be £[✂] million for 1998, £[✂] million for 1999 and £[✂] million in 2000.

6.317. In Table 6.81 we noted that First Trust's profits from SME banking business were based on it calculating net income from lending as if wholly financed from the wholesale markets at its internal transfer pricing rate. However, in identifying the rate of return to compare with the cost of capital, an adjustment must be made to reflect that a proportion of lending is funded from capital and not from the wholesale markets. This is necessary to avoid double counting, and for our purposes the appropriate adjustment is attributable capital times the average three-month LIBOR. The rates used for each of the years 1998, 1999 and 2000 were 7.3 per cent, 5.45 per cent and 6.1 per cent respectively.

6.318. Table 6.82 incorporates this adjustment, together with the information shown in Table 6.81 on profitability, and shows estimates of returns (subject to adjustments discussed in Chapter 7). For 1999, which was a year with relatively low bad debt levels, First Trust's pre-tax return on capital was [✂] per cent based on closing capital. In Chapter 7 we consider First Trust's appropriate cost of capital, and what adjustments are necessary regarding these returns. In Chapter 2 we give our conclusions on this issue.

TABLE 6.82 **First Trust: summary of profits, capital and returns from services to SMEs before any adjustments by the CC, 1998 to 2000**

£ million

	1998	1999	2000
Information from Table 6.81			
Income			
Operating costs			
Operating profit before bad debts			
Bad debt charge			
Adjustment for attributable capital*	*Figures omitted.*		
Net profit before tax and exceptional items	*See note on page iv.*		
Attributable capital (based on closing capital for AIB UK and proportions of RWAs)		†	
Average attributable capital	‡	(✂	)
Pre-tax return based on closing attributable capital	(	✂	)
Pre-tax return based on average attributable capital	‡	(✂	)

Source: CC based on information from First Trust.

---

*At 7.3 per cent for 1998, 5.45 per cent for 1999, and 6.10 per cent for 2000, based on three-month LIBOR.

†The attributable capital for 1999, which is shown as based on the closing capital level for First Trust, could alternatively be based on the average of the closing attributable capital figures for each year. For 1999, the resultant figure would therefore be £[✂] million, and the pre-tax return, based on this average attributable capital, would be [✂] per cent, ie an increase of [✂] percentage point.

‡Not available.

6.319. A further alternative method of calculating the capital attributable to the SME banking business would be to use an average capital figure, for example the average of the opening and closing capital base, rather than a return based on the closing figure. For 1999 we calculated that the effect on the pre-tax return would be an increase of one percentage point.

Further analysis of income and expenses

6.320. Table 6.83 provides an analysis of First Trust's operating income by type of banking service to SME customers for 1998 and 1999. The three main types of banking services from which First Trust earned income were loans (including overdrafts), deposits and current accounts with no overdraft facilities. In 1999 income from these services accounted for [✂] per cent of total income respectively.

TABLE 6.83 **First Trust: analysis of income by type of banking service to SME customers, 1998 and 1999**

	£ million		Income share %	
	1998	1999	1998	1999
Net income* from:				
Lending and overdrafts				
Current accounts (with no overdraft facilities)	*Figures omitted.*			
Deposits	*See note*			
Other†	*on page iv.*			
Total				

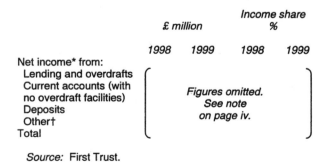

Source: First Trust.

---

*Includes net interest income and net fees and commissions. Operational costs and bad debt charges are then deducted from this income to derive net operating profit.

†Includes net non-interest-bearing balance sheet items, creditors and debtors.

6.321. Table 6.84 provides a further breakdown of net operating income from the SME banking business into net interest income and net fees and commission income for 1998 and 1999. The table shows actual income earned, as well as the notional cost of funds to finance the lending, and the benefit of funds deposited by SMEs.

6.322. The table also shows the net interest margin earned by First Trust from different types of banking relationships with the SMEs.

TABLE 6.84 **First Trust: analysis of operating income by type of service to SMEs, 1998 and 1999**

	£ million		Lending balances and margins	
	1998	1999	1998	1999
Loans and overdrafts				
Interest income				
Allocated cost of funds				
Net interest income				
Other income				
Net income*				
Average lending balance (£m)			[✂]	
Net interest (%)†				
Other current accounts				
Benefit of funds from SMEs				
Interest paid				
Net interest income				
Account management fees				
Money transmission services				
Net income‡				
Average current account credit balance (£m)			[✂]	
Net interest on credit balances (%)†				
Deposits		✂		
Benefit of funds from SMEs				
Interest paid				
Net interest income‡				
Average deposit balance (£m)			[✂]	
Net interest (%)†				
Other				
Interest income				
Benefit of funds from SMEs				
Allocated cost of funds				
Net interest income				
Account management fees				
Foreign exchange services				
Other fees and commissions				
Net income*				
Total income				

Source: First Trust.

*Before deducting operational costs and bad debt charges, to derive the net operating profit from this service to customers.
†Net interest as percentage of average balances.
‡Before deducting operational costs, to derive the net operating profit from this service to customers.

6.323. In 1999 First Trust earned income from providing the following types of services to SME customers:

(a) Loans: income earned was £[✂] million (of which £[✂] million was interest and £[✂] million was fees and commissions).

(b) Deposits: income earned was £[✂] million (all of which was the imputed net interest benefit of the customer deposits).

(c) Other current accounts (no overdraft facility or not utilizing a facility): net income earned was £[✕] million (of which £[✕] million was the net interest benefit of funds, £[✕] million was account management fees, and £[✕] million was money transmission charges).

6.324. In 1999 other current accounts had the highest net interest margin, at [✕] per cent. First Trust told us that the decline in margin was caused by the lower average base rate in 1999 at [✕] per cent as against [✕] per cent in 1998. Over the same period the margin on lending was [✕] per cent while the margin on deposits was [✕] per cent.

6.325. First Trust told us that interest income and interest payable represented the net amount above or below the transfer price paid or received by the customer. In the case of variable rate loans or instant access deposits, the transfer price used was the BoE base rate rather than LIBOR. In the case of fixed-rate lending or fixed-rate deposits the transfer price was the market fixed cost of funds for the period and amount in question. First Trust told us that the effect on income from using LIBOR rather than the above rates would be an additional cost of 0.07 per cent based on historical analysis. This would equate to approximately £0.5 million of additional funding costs.

6.326. First Trust told us that it was unable to provide cost data analysed by type of banking service to SMEs. With regard to total costs for services to SMEs, it told us that it did not differentiate between direct and indirect costs and that its main costs between 1997 and 1999 were staff ([✕] per cent), technology ([✕] per cent), marketing ([✕] per cent), accommodation ([✕] per cent) and depreciation ([✕] per cent).

6.327. We asked First Trust for details on the number of personnel who served the SME market in 1999. It said that selling to and servicing SME customers was predominantly the responsibility of the branch network. Their efforts were supported by a business banking team based at the bank's Head Office in Belfast. This central team was made up of senior lenders, accountants and trainee lenders. Their role was to advise branch managers and assist in the management of larger customer relationships. First Trust told us that in total it had 49 people involved in servicing the SME banking business full time, ie those in the central banking business unit, with an average cost per employee of £[✕]. First Trust was unable to provide details of the number of FTE employees who serviced the SME banking business within the branch network.

6.328. First Trust said that it did not incur material costs when targeting start-up or new customers. The average expenditure to the total SME banking business in 1997 to 1999 was £[✕] a year. A large percentage of this amount was for the provision of product and service literature.

Balance sheet items

6.329. Table 6.85 shows First Trust's total lending to SME customers for 1998 and 1999. Total lending in 1999 was £[✕] million, of which £[✕] million was loans and £[✕] million overdrafts. Total customer accounts in credit was £[✕] million for the same period. First Trust told us that its lending to the business sector had seen double-digit growth for a number of years.

TABLE 6.85 **First Trust: balance sheet items attributable to SME customers, 1998 and 1999**

£ million

	1998	1999
Loans		
Overdrafts		
Total lending		
Deposits	✕	
Current accounts		
Total for customer accounts in credit		
Funds required		

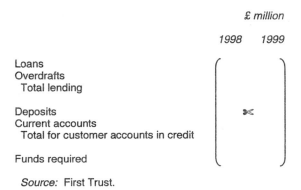

Source: First Trust.

Capital expenditure and development costs

6.330. First Trust pointed out the relatively small size of Northern Ireland with a population of 1.7 million. Although the bank had invested in both telephone and electronic banking services, the business market was of a size to caution against major investment. For example, it said that only [✂] customers had used its electronic banking package, which had been available for three years. Future investment would more likely be linked to the customization of its web-based products, developed for the parent company. It was not able to estimate costs associated with such customization at present.

Bad debts

6.331. We asked First Trust to provide data on the level of bad debt charge and bad debt provision attributable to servicing SMEs over the past ten years. First Trust told us that bad debt write-offs and provisions were monitored only for the total portfolio and not for individual sub-groupings, and therefore a time series of bad debt data for SME banking business customers was not available. First Trust estimated that bad debt charges for SME customers in 1998 were £[✂] million, and £[✂] million in 1999. This was around [✂] per cent of the total SME loan book.

6.332. First Trust told us that it sought to mitigate risk from SMEs through the quality of security, the use of the Small Firm Loan Guarantee Scheme and, in the case of foreign exchange exposure, through the provision of hedging instruments. It considered that the key factor in reducing risk exposure was a close and open relationship with the customer. The main factors currently influencing bad debt levels were industry forces, ie issues particular to certain sectors, the strength of sterling, the economic cycle, and local politics and its impact on the retail, leisure and tourism sectors.

6.333. First Trust said that, in general, agriculture had gone through a difficult period in recent years: however, historically it had never been able to acquire significant market share in this sector. Retailers in border areas and car dealers in general were also under considerable pressure owing to euro/sterling exchange rate movements.

6.334. There were also a number of issues which First Trust felt might particularly have impacted upon the Northern Ireland economy. These were:

(a) *Public expenditure.* Following the agreement of both the EC and UK Governments on funding levels to the Northern Ireland public sector, First Trust believed it was clear that the region would see increased capital expenditure on infrastructure projects over the next few years. In addition to the direct employment effect of these projects, they would provide opportunities and impetus to the local economy in the short/medium term.

(b) *Employment.* Northern Ireland was witnessing its highest levels of employment and the lowest levels of unemployment in decades. This increase in personal wealth was creating additional consumer demand in the local economy.

(c) *Retailing sector.* The sustained gap between the euro and sterling and the variance in duties and excise rates was causing difficulties across the retailing sector. These difficult trading conditions were not expected to improve in the medium term.

(d) *Political stability.* Inward investment, indigenous investment and tourism were directly linked to local political stability. First Trust's future bad debt charges were inextricably linked to the performance of the local economy, which was dependent to a significant degree upon the short-term political situation.

6.335. When asked to comment on the riskiness of SME banking business, First Trust stated that it did not view SME banking business as being more risky than normal banking activities. It noted that the Northern Ireland economy was essentially an SME market, and consequently the risk in lending to SMEs was essentially the same as providing business banking services generally for any bank. It believed that the risk of lending money to business customers was higher than lending to the personal customer market, mortgage lending, or providing any non-risk products such as savings, investments and insurance.

Future strategy in serving the SME banking business

6.336. First Trust told us that it had no specific investment plans in relation to its SME banking business. It invested in its network and products across the whole range of banking services and did not specifically segregate SME or other activities.

6.337. First Trust said that it was developing a system that would facilitate more detailed reporting and analysis of performance by customer. This was in the course of implementation and testing during 2001, and the first full financial year of using this system would be 2002.

AIB (GB)

Financial performance of the SME banking business

6.338. We asked AIB (GB) to provide us with profitability data on its services to SMEs for the period between 1997 and 1999. It told us that it did not have specific information on operating profitability of providing services to SME customers in comparison with other activities because costs were charged to the business as a whole, ie it did not allocate costs to customer accounts by turnover or to industry segments. It therefore provided us with 1999 data only, in so far as it was available. AIB (GB) excluded reference to clubs, charities and associations in the data provided to us as it considered that its involvement in these sub-sectors was immaterial.

6.339. Table 6.86 shows the profitability of AIB (GB)'s SME banking business for 1999. Operating income was £[✂] million, operating expenses were £[✂] million, and the bad debt charge was £[✂] million, which resulted in an operating profit before tax in 1999 of £[✂] million.

TABLE 6.86 **AIB (GB): profit and loss account from SME banking business, 1999**

	£m
Net interest income	
Net fees and commissions	
Total operating income	
Operating expenses*	✂
Operating profit before bad debts	
Bad debt charge	
Net profit before tax†	
	%
Performance indicators	
Cost:income ratio	(✂)

Source: AIB (GB).

*Estimated by us based on cost:income ratio estimates provided by AIB (GB).

†As requested by us, these figures were calculated on the basis that all lending is financed from borrowing in wholesale markets. In fact, a proportion will be financed by the bank's equity, and it is therefore necessary to make an adjustment for this (see Table 6.87) before comparing returns on capital derived from these profit figures with the bank's cost of capital.

6.340. AIB (GB) told us that it believed an appropriate cost:income ratio for services to SMEs was [✂] per cent. It based this assertion on its 1999 management accounts pertaining to the whole bank. This imputed cost:income ratio for services to SMEs was higher than that for the whole AIB (GB) business (discussed in Chapter 5), which was shown as [✂] per cent.

Attributable capital to support the SME banking business and potential returns

6.341. Table 6.87 shows the results for AIB (GB)'s profits from its services to SMEs. In order to form a view on the significance of such profits we also consider the AIB UK capital base. We look at this subject in greater detail in Chapter 7. In our discussion with AIB (GB) on determining the attributable capital to support its services to SMEs, we made a number of calculations for 1999 based on our methodology as discussed in paragraphs 6.22 and 6.23.

6.342. AIB (GB) did not calculate a stand-alone capital adequacy ratio, but rather its RWAs were combined with those of First Trust and reported as AIB Group (UK) plc.

6.343. Applying our methodology, we put to AIB (GB) our initial assessment that its attributable capital to support its SME banking business (based on an apportionment of its closing balance sheet capital for 1999) would be £[✂] million.

6.344. Table 6.86 shows that AIB (GB)'s profits from SME banking business were based on it calculating net income from lending as if wholly financed from the wholesale markets at its internal transfer pricing rate. However, in identifying the rate of return to compare with the cost of capital, an adjustment must be made to reflect that a proportion of lending was funded from capital and not from the wholesale markets. This is necessary to avoid double counting, and for our purposes the appropriate adjustment is attributable capital times the average three-month LIBOR for 1999 of 5.45 per cent.

6.345. Table 6.87 incorporates this adjustment, together with the information shown in Table 6.87 on profitability, and shows estimates of returns (subject to adjustments discussed in Chapter 7). For 1999, which was a year with relatively low bad debt levels, AIB (GB)'s pre-tax return on capital was [✂] per cent based on closing capital. In Chapter 7 we consider AIB (GB)'s appropriate cost of capital, and what adjustments are necessary regarding these returns. In Chapter 2 we give our conclusions on this issue.

TABLE 6.87 **AIB (GB): summary of profits, capital and returns from services to SMEs before any adjustments by the CC for 1999**

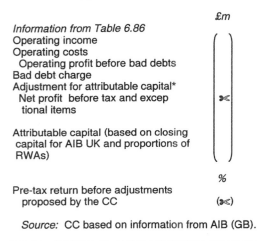

£m

Information from Table 6.86
Operating income
Operating costs
  Operating profit before bad debts
Bad debt charge
Adjustment for attributable capital*
  Net profit before tax and excep
  tional items   ✂

Attributable capital (based on closing
  capital for AIB UK and proportions of
  RWAs)

%

Pre-tax return before adjustments
  proposed by the CC   (✂)

Source: CC based on information from AIB (GB).

---

*At 5.45 per cent for 1999, based on three-month LIBOR.

6.346. A further alternative method of calculating the capital attributable to the SME banking business would be to use an average capital figure, for example the average of the opening and closing capital base, rather than a return based on the closing figure. However, this approach was not practicable for all banks, because data was not available. We note that AIB (GB) could not provide data for 1998 in order to calculate an average of opening and closing capital.

Further analysis of income and expenses

6.347. Table 6.88 provides an analysis of AIB (GB)'s operating income by type of banking service to SME customers for 1999 only. The three main types of banking services from which AIB earned income were loans, current accounts and deposits. Income from these services accounted for [✂
  ] per cent of total income respectively.

TABLE 6.88 **AIB (GB): analysis of income by type of banking service to SME customers, 1999**

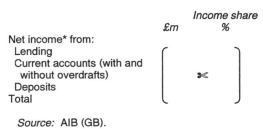

	£m	Income share %
Net income* from:		
Lending		
Current accounts (with and without overdrafts)		✄
Deposits		
Total		

Source: AIB (GB).

---

*Includes net interest income and net fees and commissions. Operational costs and bad debt charges are then deducted from this income to derive net operating profit.

6.348. Table 6.89 provides a further breakdown of AIB (GB)'s net operating income from the SME banking business into net interest income and net fees and commission income for 1999. The table shows actual income earned, as well as the notional cost of funds to finance the lending, and the benefit of funds deposited by SMEs. The table also shows the net interest margin earned from different types of banking relationships with the SMEs.

TABLE 6.89 **AIB (GB): analysis of operating income by type of service to SMEs, 1999**

	£m	Lending balances and margins
Loans		
Interest income		
Allocated cost of funds		
Net interest income		
Other income		
Net income*		
Average lending balance (£m)		
Net interest (%)†		
Current accounts with and without overdraft facilities		
Interest income		
Allocated cost of funds		
Benefit of funds from SMEs		
Interest paid		
Net interest income	✄	
Account management fees		
Money transmission services		
Foreign exchange commission		
Net income*		
Average current account debit balance (£m)		
Net interest on debit balances (%)†		
Average current account credit balance (£m)		
Net interest on credit balances (%)†		
Deposits		
Benefit of funds from SMEs		
Interest paid		
Net interest income‡		
Average deposit balance (£m)		
Net interest (%)†		

Source: AIB (GB).

---

*Before deducting operational costs and bad debt charges, to derive the net operating profit from this service to customers.
†Net interest as percentage of average balances.
‡Before deducting operational costs, to derive the net operating profit from this service to customers.

6.349. In 1999 current accounts with credit balances had the highest net interest margin, at [✄] per cent. Over the same period the margin on lending was [✄] per cent while the margin on overdrafts was [✄] per cent and the margin on deposits was [✄] per cent.

6.350. AIB (GB) told us that branch lending was funded at base rate, while commercial mortgages and some business loans were funded at the finance house rate. Funds lent to customers at a fixed rate were transfer-priced internally at LIBOR. Demand deposits and current account credit balances were transfer-priced at the BoE base rate, while term funds attracted LIMEAN pricing.

6.351. With relation to costs of the SME banking business, AIB (GB) told us that its main cost categories were standard items such as staff salaries, rents, rates and utilities.

Balance sheet items

6.352. Table 6.90 shows AIB (GB)'s total lending to SME customers for 1999. Total lending was £[✂], of which £[✂] was loans and the balance was overdrafts. Total customer accounts in credit was £[✂] million for the same period.

TABLE 6.90 **AIB (GB): balance sheet items attributable to SME customers, 1999**

£m

Loans	
Overdrafts	
Total lending	
	✂
Deposits	
Current accounts	
Total customer accounts in credit	
Funds required	

Source: AIB (GB).

Capital expenditure and development costs

6.353. [

Details omitted. See note on page iv.

]

Bad debts

6.354. We asked AIB (GB) to provide data on the level of bad debt charge and bad debt provision attributable to the SME sector over the past ten years. It told us that bad debt records for services to SMEs for the period 1989 to 1998 were not available. However, it was able to supply us with the following data for the whole AIB (GB) business.

6.355. Table 6.91 shows bad debt charges for the whole AIB (GB) business from 1994 to 1999. Since 1996 bad debt charges for the AIB (GB) business have decreased and in 1999 represented only [✂] per cent of the total loan book outstanding.

TABLE 6.91   **AIB (GB): bad debt analysis for whole AIB (GB) business, 1994 to 1999**

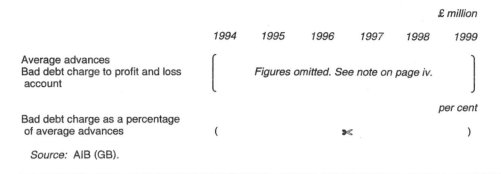

£ million

	1994	1995	1996	1997	1998	1999
Average advances						
Bad debt charge to profit and loss account			*Figures omitted. See note on page iv.*			
						per cent
Bad debt charge as a percentage of average advances	(		✂			)

Source: AIB (GB).

6.356.   Table 6.92 analyses SME bad debt provisions that AIB (GB) raised on a section of its lending book between 1989 and 1993. It noted that bad debt charges during the early 1990s were high and peaked at [✂] per cent of outstanding loan balances in 1992.

TABLE 6.92   **AIB (GB): bad debt analysis for SME banking business, 1989 to 1993**

£ million

	March 1989	March 1990	March 1991	March 1992	December 1992	December 1993
Advances						
Bad debt charge to profit and loss account			*Figures omitted. See note on page iv.*			
						per cent
Bad debt charge as a percentage of average advances	(		✂			)

Source: AIB (GB).

6.357.   AIB (GB) told us that its experience would indicate that the SME sector had been disproportionately influenced by adverse economic conditions, the interest rate environment and business confidence levels. SME banking businesses in AIB (GB)'s portfolio were typically engaged in activities relating to building and construction, and leisure and retail, which were particularly affected by cyclical movements. Other factors that played a part in business performance included financial expertise, quality of management and adequate capitalization. AIB (GB)'s experience suggested that SMEs often encountered difficulties in these areas. It considered that its bad debt levels during the early 1990s showed the effect of a poor economic climate, high interest rates and reduced business activity on its SME sector.

Future strategy in serving the SME banking business

6.358.   AIB (GB) told us that it was committed to growing its SME banking business over the coming years. It noted that, although there were very sizeable bad debt losses in the early 1990s, this had stemmed from a general problem with industry as a whole at the time. It believed that lessons had been learned and it would not turn away from supporting satisfactory businesses in the future.

6.359.   [

Details omitted. See note on page iv.

]

BoI

Overview of its business in serving SMEs

6.360. Chapter 5 deals with BoI's activities generally. This chapter deals with its services to SMEs. Although BoI operates in both Northern Ireland and Great Britain, this chapter focuses on BoI's Northern Ireland (BoI NI) operations.

6.361. BoI told us that it segmented its services to business customers, based on the size of debt facility required by them. The 'Corporate Banking' business unit was responsible for customers with a debt facility in excess of £1 million. Business centres managed relationships with customers that required debt facilities of between £25,000 and £1 million, while branches were responsible for relationships with customers that had a borrowing requirement of less than £25,000.

6.362. BoI stated that it offered a range of business services to SMEs, which it categorized into three groups: money transmission products, debt finance and deposit facilities. All SMEs had access to the complete range of products. BoI told us that since 1997 it had expanded its offering to include online banking for business customers, via Internet or direct dial facilities. This service allowed customers to view 'real time' information on all accounts held with BoI and to initiate BACS payments, foreign currency payments and same-day money transfers. BoI did not offer a telephone banking service to SMEs.

Financial performance of the SME banking business

6.363. We asked BoI to provide us with profitability data on its SME banking business for the period between 1998 and 2000. It provided us with data for the three years, split into three customer categories: business, retail and other. BoI told us that it had attempted to include all customers under our SME definition in the business category. However, in doing so, it had also included 10 to 12 customers that exceeded the £25 million threshold. Data on charities was excluded from BoI's SME customer data.

6.364. Table 6.93 shows the profitability of BoI NI's SME banking business between 1998 and 2000. Operating income for 1998, 1999 and 2000 was £[✂] million, £[✂] million and £[✂] million respectively, while operating expenses were between £[✂] million and £[✂] million over the period. The level of bad debt charge was up to £[✂] million a year. As a result, operating profit before tax was £[✂] million in 1998, £[✂] million in 1999 and £[✂] million in 2000.

TABLE 6.93 **BoI NI: profit and loss account from services to SMEs, 1998 to 2000**

£ million

	1998	1999	2000
Net interest income			
Net fees and commissions			
Total operating income	Figures omitted.		
Operating expenses	See note		
Operating profit before bad debts	on page iv.		
Bad debt charge			
Net profit before tax*			

Source: BoI.

---

*As requested by us, these figures were calculated on the basis that all lending is financed from borrowing in whole-sale markets. In fact, a proportion will be financed by the bank's equity, and it is therefore necessary to make an adjustment for this (see Table 6.95) before comparing returns on capital derived from these profit figures with the bank's cost of capital.

6.365. Table 6.94 further analyses the performance of BoI NI's SME banking business between 1998 and 2000, by showing all items as a percentage of operating income. Net interest income was constant at around [✂] per cent of total income for all three years. The cost:income ratio was [✂] per cent in 1998 and 1999, and fell to [✂] per cent in 2000. This fall was a result of operating income increasing more quickly than allocated costs. BoI noted that this was due to:

(a) an increase of [✂] per cent in income due to substantial increases in business volumes (advances increased by [✂] per cent and deposits increased by [✂] per cent) and increased fee income from lending, current account and foreign exchange services; and

(b) efficient cost management that contained cost increases to under [✂] per cent during the year.

TABLE 6.94 **Bol NI: operating profit and loss items as a percentage of operating income from SME banking business, 1998 to 2000**

per cent

	1998	1999	2000
Net interest income			
Net fees and commissions			
Total operating income		*Figures omitted.*	
Operating expenses		*See note*	
Operating profit before bad debts		*on page iv.*	
Bad debt charge			
Net profit before tax			

Source: Bol.

Attributable capital to support the SME banking business and potential returns

6.366. Tables 6.93 and 6.94 show the trend in Bol NI's profits from SME banking business. In order to form a view on the significance of such profits we also consider the capital base of Bol NI. We look at this subject in greater detail in Chapter 7. In our discussion with Bol on determining the attributable capital to support its services to SMEs, we made a number of calculations for the years 1998 to 2000 based on our methodology as discussed in paragraphs 6.22 and 6.23.

6.367. Bol NI operates as a branch of Bol, and not as a separate legal entity. As a result Bol NI was not required to submit a capital adequacy return to the FSA, but rather was included in an aggregate capital adequacy return for the Bol group which was submitted to the Central Bank of Ireland, the relevant regulator in the Republic of Ireland. Although Bol is subject to the capital adequacy regulations set by the Central Bank of Ireland, these regulations apply the same risk-weighting principles that are used by the FSA in the UK. In particular, these principles reflect credit risk, which (among others) was a key factor in the variability of banks' profitability over a long-term economic period, as shown by the variability of bad debt levels.

6.368. Applying our methodology, we put to Bol NI our initial assessment that its attributable capital to support its SME banking business (based on an apportionment of its closing balance sheet capital) would be £[✂] million for 1998, £[✂] million for 1999 and £[✂] million for 2000.

6.369. In Table 6.93 we noted that Bol NI's profits from SME banking business were based on it calculating net income from lending as if wholly financed from the wholesale markets at its internal transfer pricing rate. However, in identifying the rate of return to compare with the cost of capital, an adjustment must be made to reflect that a proportion of lending was funded from capital and not from the wholesale markets. This is necessary to avoid double counting, and for our purposes the appropriate adjustment is attributable capital times the average three-month LIBOR for each year.

6.370. Table 6.95 incorporates this adjustment, together with the information shown in Table 6.93 on profitability, and shows estimates of returns (subject to adjustments discussed in Chapter 7). For 1999, which was a year with relatively low bad debt levels, Bol NI's pre-tax return on capital was [✂] per cent, based on closing capital. In Chapter 7 we consider Bol NI's appropriate cost of capital, and what adjustments are necessary regarding these returns. In Chapter 2 we give our conclusions on this issue.

TABLE 6.95 BoI NI: summary of profits, capital and returns from services to SMEs, 1998 to 2000

£ million

Years ended 31 March

	1998	1999	2000
Information from Table 6.93			
Operating income			
Operating costs			
Operating profit before bad debts			
Bad debt charge			
Adjustment for attributable capital*			
Net profit before tax and exceptional items	Figures omitted. See note on page iv.		†
Attributable capital (based on closing capital for the whole bank and proportions of RWAs)			
Average attributable capital			

per cent

	1998	1999	2000
Pre-tax return based on closing attributable capital	✄		
Pre-tax return based on average attributable capital			

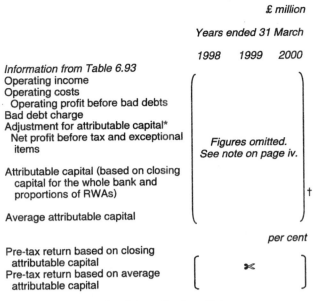

Source: CC based on information from BoI.

---

*At 7.3 per cent for year ended 31 March 1999 and 5.45 per cent for year ended 31 March 2000.

†The attributable capital for 2000, which is shown as based on the closing capital level for BoI, could alternatively be based on the average of the closing attributable capital figures for each year. For 2000, the resultant figure would therefore be £[✄] million, and the pre-tax return, based on this average attributable capital, would be [✄] per cent, ie an increase of [✄] percentage point.

6.371. A further alternative method of calculating the capital attributable to the SME banking business would be to use an average capital figure, for example the average of the opening and closing capital base, rather than a return based on the closing figure. For 1999 and 2000 we calculated that the effect on the pre-tax return would be an increase of three percentage points and one percentage point respectively.

Further analysis of income and expenses

6.372. Table 6.96 provides an analysis of operating income by type of banking service to SME customers between 1998 and 2000. In 2000, lending and current accounts contributed [✄] per cent of total income, deposits contributed [✄] per cent, asset finance [✄] per cent and other income [✄] per cent.

TABLE 6.96 BoI NI: analysis of income by type of banking service to SME customers, 1998 to 2000

Years ended 31 March

	£ million			Percentage of income		
	1998	1999	2000	1998	1999	2000
Lending						
Current accounts utilizing overdraft facility						
Other current accounts*			Figures omitted. See note on page iv.			
Deposits						
Asset finance						
Other income†						
Total income						

Source: BoI.

---

*Includes current accounts without an overdraft facility and current accounts with an overdraft facility that has not been utilized. Of the current accounts without an overdraft facility, this classification will include those accounts that have an unauthorized overdraft.

†Made up of income from foreign exchange services and personal IFA services. IFA services represent its Independent Financial Advisory business, providing investment services to personal customers.

6.373. We asked BoI to provide a further breakdown of net operating income from the SME banking business into net interest income and net fees and commission income between 1998 and 2000. BoI provided the following:

(a) With regard to loans, BoI estimated a net interest margin of [✂] per cent on balances for 1999. It did not provide a year-end balance nor a figure for net interest income for either of the years 1999 or 2000.

(b) Current accounts had a year-end balance in 1999 of £[✂] million and in 2000 this increased to £[✂] million. Net interest income earned during 1999 and 2000 on current accounts was £[✂] million and £[✂] million respectively, with a net interest margin of [✂] per cent and [✂] per cent.

(c) On overdrafts, BoI was unable to provide any information with regard to year-end balances, net interest earned or net interest margins. The CC made an estimate of net interest margin at [✂] per cent for 1999, which BoI did not object to or provide an alternative figure.

(d) Total deposits had a year-end value of £[✂] million in 1999. During the year the net interest income earned on these balances was £[✂] million with a net interest margin of [✂] per cent. In 2000 the year-end balance was £[✂] million, the net interest income earned was £[✂] million and the net interest margin was [✂] per cent.

6.374. Table 6.97 provides an analysis of operating costs for services to SME customers. BoI estimated that [✂] per cent of the branch network costs were attributable to business banking services, and therefore it allocated such costs to the SME banking business on this basis. Staff costs made up the largest cost categories for all years. BoI told us that the number of staff servicing the SME sector was 420 in 1998, 481 in 1999 and 392 in 2000. In 2000 allocated costs accounted for £[✂] million or [✂] per cent of total costs.

TABLE 6.97 **BoI NI: analysis of SME operating costs, 1998 to 2000**

	£ million			*Proportion of total costs %*		
	1998	*1999*	*2000*	*1998*	*1999*	*2000*
Direct costs						
Staff costs						
Premises and equipment						
Other costs						
Total						
Allocated costs			*Figures omitted. See note on page iv.*			
Staff costs						
Premises and equipment						
Other costs*						
Total						
Total operating costs						

Source: BoI.

*Other costs for 2000 include £[✂] million for the allocation of central Northern Ireland management overhead and £[✂] million of allocated central overhead from the Dublin Head Office. It should be noted that the Dublin Head Office allocation includes the operational costs of IT services (including mainframe bookkeeping and transaction processing) for Northern Ireland accounts. This equates to £[✂] million for 2000.

Balance sheet items

6.375. Table 6.98 shows BoI NI's total lending to SME customers between 1998 and 2000. [*Details omitted. See note on page iv.*]

TABLE 6.98   BoI NI: SME balance sheet, 1998 to 2000

£ million

As at 31 March

	1998	1999	2000
Loans and advances to customers			
Fixed assets (tangible and intangible)		✕	
Customer accounts			

Source: BoI.

Bad debts

6.376. We asked BoI NI to provide data on the level of bad debt charge and bad debt provision attributable to the SME sector over the past three years. Table 6.99 shows the level of SME bad debt charge for 1998 to 2000. Bad debt charges were [✕] per cent of total lending in 1998, fell to [✕] per cent in 1999 and then again increased to [✕] per cent of total lending in 2000. The 1999 published accounts included a write-back of around £[✕] million in relation to the downgrade of a single customer relationship included in the 1998 accounts. BoI NI told us that it believed a reasonable ongoing average level of annual bad debt provision to be [✕] per cent of the advances book.

TABLE 6.99   BoI NI: summary of bad debt charges for SME customers, 1998 to 2000

£ million

	1998	1999	2000
Bad debt expense	(	✕	)

per cent

	1998	1999	2000
Bad debt charge as a percentage of lending			
		✕	
Bad debt charge as a percentage of income			

Source: BoI.

Future strategy in serving the SME banking business

6.377. BoI NI told us that it did not set specific targets for gaining new customers. Instead financial targets were set which included increase in total business volumes (overdraft, loan, current account and deposit balances) from both existing and new clients. The bank also obtained ad hoc information from customers regarding their use of the bank's services and had employed regular 'customer satisfaction' surveys which tracked customer views on products, services and prices. BoI NI said that this information enabled it to understand better the views and needs of business customers and to tailor future products and services accordingly.

6.378. [

Details omitted. See note on page iv.

]

6.379. [

Details omitted. See note on page iv.

]

NAB

Overview of its business in serving SMEs

6.380. Chapter 5 deals in detail with NAB's general activities, and the sections below discuss its services to SME types of customers. As discussed in Chapter 5, NAB's operations in the UK are carried out by its three subsidiaries: Northern, Clydesdale and Yorkshire.

6.381. NAB described its role in the UK SME market as being a small and innovative player offering differentiated products and services through each of the above banks. In 2000 NAB formed the Global Specialist and Emerging Businesses division, to provide international banking services, leasing and asset finance, cards, payments and securities as well as investment, insurance and superannuation products.

Financial performance of the SME banking business

6.382. NAB provided separate profit and loss and balance sheet figures for services to SMEs in respect of its three subsidiary banks. However, it was only able to produce this SME information for the year ended 30 September 2000. The figures provided were for the Business and Financial Services (BFS) unit across the UK. While BFS does not fit precisely within our definition of SME banking business, it is a close match, but includes provision of services to some companies with turnover greater than £25 million (unless they were FTSE 350 companies), and excludes clubs and charities. NAB also told us that the figures provided for each of the three subsidiary banks exclude approximately 75 per cent of what it termed micro SME accounts for Yorkshire and Clydesdale, but included 100 per cent of micro SME accounts for Northern. Micro SME accounts were defined by NAB as accounts with a turnover of less that £100,000.

6.383. NAB acknowledged that there were various effects of these omissions of micro SME accounts on margin and cost figures for Clydesdale and Yorkshire. However, it said that they would not be considered significant for the purpose of the following analysis.

Allocation of profit and loss and balance sheet figures to Clydesdale, Northern and Yorkshire for 2000

6.384. NAB provided a breakdown of SME balances for each of the individual subsidiaries Clydesdale, Northern and Yorkshire for the profit and loss account and balance sheet, which are detailed below.

Clydesdale

Financial performance of the SME banking business

6.385. Table 6.100 shows the profit and loss summary for Clydesdale's services to BFS customers for 2000. Operating income was £[✕] million, while operating expenses were £[✕] million resulting in a cost:income ratio of [✕] per cent. Bad debt charges were £[✕] million. As a result, net profit before tax was £[✕] million.

TABLE 6.100 **Clydesdale: estimated profit and loss account from services to BFS customers, year ended 30 September 2000***

	£m	%
Net interest income		
Net fees and commissions		
Total operating income†		
Operating expenses	✄	
Operating profit before bad debts		
Bad debt charge		
Operating profit before tax		

Source: NAB.

*The BFS category does not perfectly match the CC's definition of SME banking business and includes some customers with turnover greater than £25 million.

†As requested by us, these figures were calculated on the basis that all lending is financed from borrowing in wholesale markets. In fact, a proportion will be financed by the bank's equity, and it is therefore necessary to make an adjustment for this (see Table 6.118) before comparing returns on capital derived from these profit figures with the bank's cost of capital.

6.386. Clydesdale's annual report stated that it had drawn significant competitive advantage from the sharing of centralized services with its sister banks in the UK and Ireland. Services such as human resources, finance, collections and a wide variety of back-office administrative tasks were managed globally but delivered locally, bringing significant economies of scale and scope to Clydesdale and its sister banks.

Further analysis of income and expenses

6.387. Table 6.101 analyses Clydesdale's operating income by type of banking service to BFS customers for 2000. Lending and current accounts was the largest source of operating income, and contributed [✄] per cent of operating income. In comparison, deposits contributed [✄] per cent of operating income.

TABLE 6.101 **Clydesdale: analysis of estimated income by type of banking service to BFS customers, 2000***

	£m	%
Net income† from:		
Lending and current accounts‡		
Deposits	✄	
Other		
Total		

Source: NAB.

*The BFS category does not perfectly match the CC's definition of SME banking business and includes some customers with turnover greater than £25 million.

†Includes net interest income and net fees and commissions. Operational costs and bad debt charges are then deducted from this income to derive net operating profit.

‡NAB was not able to provide information for lending and current accounts separately.

6.388. Table 6.102 provides a further breakdown of net operating income from services to BFS customers into net interest income and net fees and commission income for 2000. The table shows actual income earned, as well as the notional cost of funds to finance the lending, and the benefit of funds deposited by BFS customers.

410

TABLE 6.102 **Clydesdale: analysis of estimated operating income by type of service to BFS customers, 2000***

	£m	Margin and lending balances
Loans and current accounts		
Interest income†		
Cost of funds		
Net interest income		
Fees and commissions‡		
Net income		
Average balance		
Net interest—Loans and overdrafts (%)§		
Net interest—current accounts in credit (%)§		
Deposits		
Benefit of funds from customers		
Interest paid		
Net interest income		
Average deposit balance		
Net interest (%)§		
Other interest income		
Total net income		

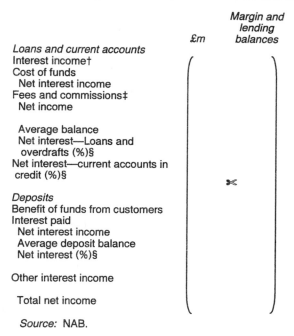

Source: NAB.

---

*The BFS category does not perfectly match the CC's definition of SME banking business and includes some customers with turnover greater than £25 million.
†NAB analysed the lending income at £[✄] million and the current account income at £[✄] million.
‡NAB analysed the lending income at £[✄] million and current account income at £[✄] million.
§Net interest as percentages of average balances.

6.389. NAB told us that the method used to calculate internal transfers of interest was to apply base rate as opposed to LIBOR. It did not consider that the application of base rate would cause a material impact on the figures.

6.390. Table 6.103 provides an analysis of operating cost for Clydesdale's services to BFS customers for 2000. Within direct costs, staff costs were the largest direct cost category at £[✄] million, or [✄] per cent of total costs. Indirect costs accounted for £[✄] million or [✄] per cent of total costs.

TABLE 6.103 **Clydesdale: analysis of estimated BFS operating costs, 2000***

	£m	Proportion of total %
Direct costs:		
Staff costs		
Other costs		
Total		
Allocated costs		
Total operating costs		

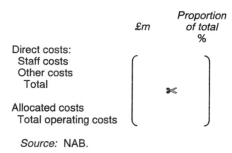

Source: NAB.

---

*The BFS category does not perfectly match the CC's definition of SME banking business and includes some customers with turnover greater than £25 million.

6.391. We estimated the total number of personnel for Clydesdale's SME banking business (based on the proportion of loans to customers) to be 529. NAB told us that the numbers included centrally-based staff such as senior management, marketing, finance and other support staff.

Balance sheet items

6.392. Table 6.104 shows Clydesdale's total lending to BFS customers for 2000 of some £[✄] billion.

TABLE 6.104 **Clydesdale: estimated balance sheet items attributable to BFS customers, 2000***

£m

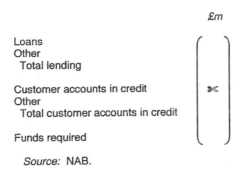

Loans
Other
  Total lending

Customer accounts in credit
Other
  Total customer accounts in credit

Funds required

Source: NAB.

*The BFS category does not perfectly match the CC's definition of SME banking business and includes some customers with turnover greater than £25 million.

Bad debts

6.393.   We asked Clydesdale to provide data on the level of bad debt charge and bad debt provision attributable to its SME customers for the last three years, but NAB was only able to provide information for 2000 in respect of its BFS customers. Table 6.105 shows the level of bad debt for 2000, at the BFS unit level. The level of bad debt charge as a proportion of lending was [✂] per cent, and [✂] per cent of income.

TABLE 6.105 **Clydesdale: summary of specific bad debt provision and charges for the BFS unit, 2000***

£m

General provision
Specific provision
  Bad debt provision   [✂]

Total bad debt charge

%

Bad debt charge as a
  percentage of lending
Bad debt charge as a   [✂]
  percentage of income

Source: NAB.

*The BFS category does not perfectly match the CC's definition of SME banking business and includes some customers with turnover greater than £25 million.

Future strategy in serving the SME market

6.394.   Clydesdale told us that the bank's primary strategy remained to provide its customers with an appropriate variety of channels through which they could access financial products and services which were tailored to their customers' needs. Clydesdale said that it would continue to capitalize on the existing strength of the Clydesdale brand and the growing value of its wider global resources in the NAB group.

6.395.   Clydesdale said that it had deliberately held back from the wider development of Internet banking services until it was fully satisfied that all security and resilience issues relating to the infrastructure have been addressed fully. Rather than attempt to gain advantage through being among the first to offer such services, Clydesdale chose to focus on selecting the best alliance partners with whom it could develop an Internet offering.

Northern

Financial performance of the SME banking business

6.396. Table 6.106 shows the profitability of Northern's services to SME customers for 2000. Operating income was £[✂] million, while operating expenses were £[✂] million resulting in a cost:income ratio of [✂] per cent. Bad debt charges were £[✂] million. As a result, net profit before tax was £[✂] million.

TABLE 6.106 **Northern: estimated profit and loss account from services to BFS customers, year ended 30 September 2000***

	£m	%
Net interest income		
Net fees and commissions		
Total operating income†		
Operating expenses	✂	
Operating profit before bad debts		
Bad debt charge		
Operating profit before tax		

Source: NAB.

*The BFS category does not perfectly match the CC's definition of SME banking business and includes some customers with turnover greater than £25 million.

†As requested by us, these figures were calculated on the basis that all lending is financed from borrowing in wholesale markets. In fact, a proportion will be financed by the bank's equity, and it is therefore necessary to make an adjustment for this (see Table 6.118) before comparing returns on capital derived from these profit figures with the bank's cost of capital.

Further analysis of income and expenses

6.397. Table 6.107 analyses Nothern's operating income by type of banking service to BFS customers for 2000 on the same basis as calculated for Clydesdale.

TABLE 6.107 **Northern: analysis of estimated income by type of banking service to BFS customers, 2000***

	£m	%
Net income† from:		
Lending and current accounts‡		
Deposits	✂	
Other		
Total		

Source: NAB.

*The BFS category does not perfectly match the CC's definition of SME banking business and includes some customers with turnover greater than £25 million.

†Includes net interest income and net fees and commissions. Operational costs and bad debt charges are then deducted from this income to derive net operating profit.

‡NAB was not able to provide information for lending and current accounts separately.

6.398. Table 6.108 provides a further breakdown of net operating income from services to BFS customers into net interest income and net fees and commission income for 2000. The table shows actual income earned, as well as the notional cost of funds to finance the lending, and the benefit of funds deposited by BFS customers.

TABLE 6.108 **Northern: analysis of estimated operating income by type of service to BFS customers, 2000***

	£m	Margin and lending balances
Loans and current accounts with and without overdrafts		
Interest income†		
Cost of funds		
Net interest income		
Fees and commissions‡		
Net income		
Average lending balance		
Net interest—Loans (%)§		
Net interest—overdrafts (%)§		
Net interest—current accounts in credit (%)§		
Deposits		
Benefit of funds from SMEs		
Interest paid		
Net interest income		
Average deposit balance		
Net interest (%)§		
Other interest income		
Total net income		

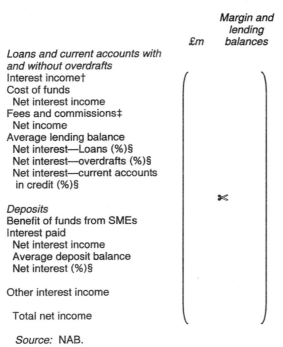

Source: NAB.

*The BFS category does not perfectly match the CC's definition of SME banking business and includes some customers with turnover greater than £25 million.
†NAB analysed the lending income at £[✂] million and the current account income at £[✂] million.
‡NAB analysed the lending income at £[✂] million and current account income at £[✂] million.
§Net interest and net fees and commissions as percentages of average balances.

6.399. Table 6.109 analyses operating costs for Northern's services to BFS customers on the same basis as for Clydesdale for 2000. Staff costs were £[✂] million, or [✂] per cent of total costs. Indirect costs were £[✂] million.

TABLE 6.109 **Northern: analysis of estimated BFS operating costs, 2000***

	£m	Proportion of total (%)
Direct costs:		
Staff costs		
Other costs		
Total		
Allocated costs		
Total operating costs		

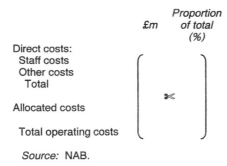

Source: NAB.

*The BFS category does not perfectly match the CC's definition of SME banking business and includes some customers with turnover greater than £25 million.

6.400. We estimated the total number of personnel for Northern's SME banking business (based on the proportion of loans to customers) to be around 210.

Balance sheet items

6.401. Table 6.110 shows Northern's total lending to BFS customers for 2000, at £[✂] billion compared with accounts in credit of £[✂].

414

TABLE 6.110 **Northern: estimated balance sheet items attributable to BFS customers, 2000***

£m

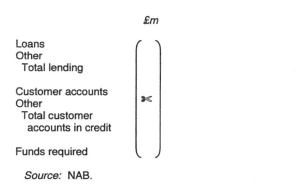

Loans	
Other	
Total lending	
Customer accounts	
Other	✂
Total customer	
accounts in credit	
Funds required	

Source: NAB.

*The BFS category does not perfectly match the CC's definition of SME banking business and includes some customers with turnover greater than £25 million.

Bad debts

6.402. Table 6.111 shows the level of bad debt charge for 2000, at the BFS unit level. The bad debt charge as a proportion of lending was [✂] per cent.

TABLE 6.111 **Northern: summary of specific bad debt provision and charges for the BFS unit, 2000***

£m

General provision	
Specific provision	
Bad debt provision	✂
Total bad debt charge	

%

Bad debt charge as a	
percentage of lending	
Bad debt charge as a	✂
percentage of income	

Source: NAB.

*The BFS category does not perfectly match the CC's definition of SME banking business and includes some customers with turnover greater than £25 million.

Future strategy in serving the SME market

6.403. Northern told us that as part of the NAB group's integration for growth strategy in Europe, BFS and Personal Financial Services of both Northern and National Irish Bank were merged into all Ireland teams. Northern claimed that this would result in more geographically focused units, attuned with and better able to service business and personal customers.

Yorkshire Bank

Financial performance of the SME banking business

6.404. Table 6.112 shows the profitability of Yorkshire's services to BFS customers for 2000. Operating income for 2000 was £[✂] million, while operating expenses were £[✂] million.

TABLE 6.112 **Yorkshire: profit and loss account from services to BFS activities, year ended 30 September 2000***

	£m	%
Net interest income		
Net fees and commissions		
Total operating income†		
Operating expenses	✂	
Operating profit before provisions		
Bad debt charge		
Operating profit before tax		

Source: NAB.

*The BFS category does not perfectly match the CC's definition of SME banking business and includes some customers with turnover greater than £25 million.

†As requested by us, these figures were calculated on the basis that all lending is financed from borrowing in wholesale markets. In fact, a proportion will be financed by the bank's equity, and it is therefore necessary to make an adjustment for this (see Table 6.118) before comparing returns on capital derived from these profit figures with the bank's cost of capital.

6.405. Yorkshire's annual report noted that it drew significant competitive advantage from the sharing of centralized services with its sister banks in the UK and Ireland. Services such as human resources, finance, collections and a wide variety of back-office administrative tasks are managed globally but delivered locally, bringing significant economies of scale and scope to Yorkshire and its sister banks.

Further analysis of income and expenses

6.406. Table 6.113 analyses operating income by type of banking service to BFS customers for 2000.

TABLE 6.113 **Yorkshire: analysis of income by type of banking service to BFS customers, 2000***

	£m	%
Net income† from:		
Lending and current accounts‡		
Deposits	✂	
Other		
Total		

Source: NAB.

*The BFS category does not perfectly match the CC's definition of SME banking business and includes some customers with turnover greater than £25 million.

†Includes net interest income and net fees and commissions. Operational costs and bad debt charges are then deducted from this income to derive net operating profit.

‡NAB was not able to provide information for lending and current accounts separately.

6.407. Table 6.114 provides a further breakdown of net operating income from services to SME customers into net interest income and net fees and commission income for 2000. The table shows actual income earned, as well as the notional cost of funds to finance the lending, and the benefit of funds deposited by SME customers.

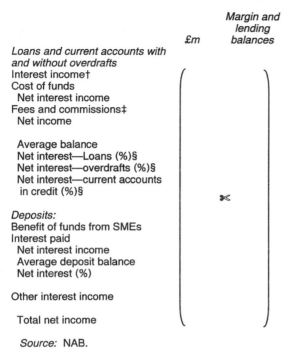

	£m	Margin and lending balances
Loans and current accounts with and without overdrafts		
Interest income†		
Cost of funds		
Net interest income		
Fees and commissions‡		
Net income		
Average balance		
Net interest—Loans (%)§		
Net interest—overdrafts (%)§		
Net interest—current accounts in credit (%)§		
Deposits:		
Benefit of funds from SMEs		
Interest paid		
Net interest income		
Average deposit balance		
Net interest (%)		
Other interest income		
Total net income		

Source: NAB.

*The BFS category does not perfectly match the CC's definition of SME banking business and includes some customers with turnover greater than £25 million.
†NAB analysed the lending income at £[✄] million and the current account income at £[✄] million.
‡NAB analysed the lending income at £[✄] million and current account income at £[✄] million.
§Net interest and net fees and commissions as percentages of average balances.

6.408. Table 6.115 analyses operating costs for Yorkshire's services to BFS customers for SME customers for 2000. Staff costs were estimated at £[✄] million. Indirect costs were estimated at £[✄] million.

TABLE 6.115 **Yorkshire: analysis of estimated SME operating costs, 2000***

	£m	Proportion of total %
Direct costs:		
Staff costs		
Other costs		
Total		
Allocated costs		
Total operating costs		

Source: NAB.

*The BFS category does not perfectly match the CC's definition of SME banking business and includes some customers with turnover greater than £25 million.

6.409. We estimated the total number of personnel for Yorkshire's SME banking business (based on the proportion of loans to customers) to be 450.

Balance sheet items

6.410. Table 6.116 shows Yorkshire's total lending to SME customers for 2000 of some £[✄] billion.

417

TABLE 6.116 Yorkshire: estimated balance sheet items attributable to BFS customers, 2000*

£m

Loans
Other
  Total lending

Customer accounts
Other
  Total customer accounts
  in credit

Funds required

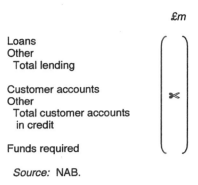

Source: NAB.

*The BFS category does not perfectly match the CC's definition of SME banking business and includes some customers with turnover greater than £25 million.

Bad debts

6.411. Table 6.117 shows the level of bad debt charge for 2000, at the BFS unit level. The level of bad debt charge as a proportion of lending was [✂] per cent, and as a proportion of income was [✂] per cent.

TABLE 6.117 Yorkshire: summary of specific bad debt provision and charges from services to BFS customers, 2000*

£m

General provision
Specific provision
  Bad debt provision

Total bad debt expense

%

Bad debt charge as a
  percentage of lending
Bad debt charge as a
  percentage of income

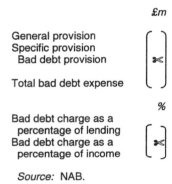

Source: NAB.

*The BFS category does not perfectly match the CC's definition of SME banking business and includes some customers with turnover greater than £25 million.

Future strategy in serving the SME market

6.412. Yorkshire's 2000 annual report noted that its primary strategy remained to provide its customers with an appropriate variety of channels through which they could access financial products and services which were tailored to its customers' needs. It said that it would continue to capitalize on the existing strength of the Yorkshire brand and the growing value of its wider global resources in the NAB group.

Attributable capital to support the SME banking business and potential returns for Clydesdale, Northern and Yorkshire

6.413. Tables 6.100, 6.106 and 6.112 considered each subsidiary's profits from its SME-type activities. In order to form a view on the significance of the profits we also consider each bank's capital base. We look at this subject in greater detail in Chapter 7. In our discussion with NAB on determining the attributable capital to support its services to SMEs, we made a number of calculations for 2000 based on our methodology as discussed in paragraphs 6.22 and 6.23.

6.414. Applying our methodology, we put to each subsidiary bank our initial assessment that its attributable capital to support its SME banking business (based on an apportionment of its closing balance sheet capital) would be: £[✂] million for Clydesdale; £[✂] million for Northern; and £[✂] million for Yorkshire.

6.415. In Tables 6.100, 6.106 and 6.112 we noted that NAB's estimated profits from SME-type activities were based on it calculating net income from lending as if wholly financed from the wholesale markets at its internal transfer pricing rate. However, in identifying the rate of return to compare with the cost of capital, an adjustment must be made to reflect that a proportion of lending was funded from capital and not from the wholesale markets. This is necessary to avoid double counting, and for our purposes we considered that the appropriate adjustment is attributable capital times the average three-month LIBOR for each year.

6.416. Table 6.118 incorporates this adjustment, together with the information shown in Tables 6.100, 6.106 and 6.112 on profitability and shows estimates of returns (subject to adjustments discussed in Chapter 7). For 2000 Clydesdale's pre-tax return on capital was [✂] per cent, Northern's pre-tax return on capital was [✂] per cent and Yorkshire's pre-tax return on capital was [✂] per cent. In Chapter 7 we consider each bank's appropriate cost of capital, and what adjustments are necessary regarding these returns. In Chapter 2 we give our conclusions on this issue.

TABLE 6.118 **NAB: summary of profits, capital and returns from services to BFS customers before any adjustments by the CC, 2000***

£ million

	Clydesdale	Northern	Yorkshire	Total
Information from Tables 6.100, 6.106 and 6.112				
Income				
Operating costs				
Operating profit before bad debts				
Bad debt charge				
Adjustment for attributable capital†		Figures omitted.		
Operating profit before tax and exceptional items		See note on page iv.		
Attributable capital (based on closing capital for the whole bank and proportions of RWAs)‡				

per cent

Pre-tax return before adjustments proposed by the CC	(	✂		)

Source: CC on information from NAB.

*The BFS category does not perfectly match the CC's definition of SME banking business and includes some customers with turnover greater than £25 million.
†At 6.1 per cent for 2000, based on yearly average for three-month LIBOR.

The Co-operative Bank

Overview of its business in serving SMEs

6.417. Chapter 5 deals in detail with the Co-operative Bank's position and activities generally. This chapter deals with its services to SMEs.

6.418. The Co-operative Bank told us that it was a small player in the provision of banking services to SMEs, and as such did not attempt to provide all SME services in-house. For example, cheque out-clearing and card services to retailers were performed by HSBC, RBS performed Scottish in-clearing, and its customers had access to post office counter services through Girobank. Of the services that it did provide in-house, the Co-operative Bank stated that they tended to be the activities that interacted directly with customers.

6.419. The Co-operative Bank handles most back-office and administrative functions for its SME customers through its call centre for business customers, which was opened in 1992. The exceptions to this are counter services and relationship management services, which operate from regionally-based corporate centres.

6.420. The Co-operative Bank launched its electronic banking service in 1993 and branded it 'Financial Director'. It was aimed initially at the large corporate treasurers. In 1995 it was upgraded, and a reduced functionality version was introduced for smaller businesses and branded 'Financial Director for Business'.

6.421. In 1996 the Co-operative Bank started Business Direct, a 24-hour telephone banking service, specifically designed for the bank's smaller commercial customers. The pricing proposition of this product was built especially to encourage use of the telephone banking service by offering reduced transaction prices. Since July 1999 a free Internet service has also been made available to Business Direct customers.

6.422. The Co-operative Bank told us that it segmented its Corporate and Commercial Banking customer base along the following lines:

(a) *Commercial:* includes distinct classes of business, of which the principal ones are local authority, clubs and charities.

(b) *Corporate:* businesses with account turnover greater than £500,000, credit balances greater than £250,000, or total lending greater than £50,000.

(c) *Other corporate and commercial:* businesses not falling into any of the above categories.

Financial performance of the SME banking business

6.423. We asked the Co-operative Bank to provide us with profitability data on its SME banking business for the period between 1997 and 2000. It was able to provide us with data for 1998 and 1999, but told us that income and balance sheet details at account level for 1997 did not exist.

6.424. The Co-operative Bank also said that the Corporate division had been analysed into UK clubs and charities, SMEs, customers with turnover greater than £25 million and 'other' corporate. The other corporate business included local authorities, leasing to third parties and other third party business. It also included income and bad debt costs relating to customers in its debt recovery section, as it was not possible to allocate these to businesses.

6.425. Table 6.119 shows the profitability of the Co-operative Bank's SME banking business for 1998 and 1999. Operating income for 1998 and 1999 was £[✂] million in both years, while operating expenses were £[✂] million in 1998, reducing to £[✂] million in 1999. The level of bad debt charge was constant at £[✂] million for both 1998 and 1999. As a result, operating profit before tax was £[✂] million in 1998 and £[✂] million in 1999.

TABLE 6.119 **The Co-operative Bank: profit and loss account from SME banking business, 1998 and 1999**

£ million

	1998	1999
Net interest income		
Net fees and commissions		
Total operating income		
Operating expenses	✂	
Operating profit before bad debts		
Bad debt charge		
Net profit before tax*		

Source: The Co-operative Bank.

*As requested by us, these figures were calculated on the basis that all lending is financed from borrowing in wholesale markets. In fact, a proportion will be financed by the bank's equity, and it is therefore necessary to make an adjustment for this (see Table 6.121) before comparing returns on capital derived from these profit figures with the bank's cost of capital.

6.426. Table 6.120 further analyses the overall performance of the Co-operative Bank's SME banking business for 1998 and 1999, by showing all items as a percentage of operating income.

TABLE 6.120 **The Co-operative Bank: operating profit and loss items as a percentage of operating income from SME banking business, 1998 and 1999**

per cent

	1998	1999
Net interest income		
Net fees and commissions		
Total operating income		
Operating expenses	✂	
Operating profit before bad debts		
Bad debt charge		
Net profit before tax*		

Source: The Co-operative Bank.

---

*As requested by us, these figures were calculated on the basis that all lending is financed from borrowing in wholesale markets. In fact, a proportion will be financed by the bank's equity, and it is therefore necessary to make an adjustment for this (see Table 6.121) before comparing returns on capital derived from these profit figures with the bank's cost of capital.

6.427. The Co-operative Bank noted that its activity-based management accounting systems provided financial analysis for the whole of the Corporate and Commercial banking activities, but did not separate the 'SME' sector as defined by us. As the vast majority of the bank's corporate customers were SMEs, the Co-operative Bank applied the same cost:income ratio to SMEs as to the rest of the corporate portfolio.

6.428. The SME activity's cost:income ratio was [✂] per cent in 1998, and fell to [✂] per cent in 1999. The Co-operative Bank told us that this fall was achieved from reorganizing central processing, improving the efficiency of its network and by the use of new technology. Economies were also achieved by outsourcing cash handling and cheque processing. The cost:income ratio for SMEs was slightly lower than that for the whole bank (discussed in Chapter 5), which was at 65 per cent.

Attributable capital to support the SME banking business and potential returns

6.429. Tables 6.119 and 6.120 show the results of the Co-operative Bank's profits from its SME banking business. In order to form a view on the significance of such profits we also consider the Co-operative Bank's capital base. We look at this subject in greater detail in Chapter 7. In our discussion with the Co-operative Bank on determining the attributable capital to support its services to SMEs, we made a number of calculations for the years 1998 and 1999 based on our methodology as discussed in paragraphs 6.22 and 6.23.

6.430. Applying our methodology, we put to the Co-operative Bank our initial assessment that its attributable capital to support its SME banking business (based on an apportionment of its closing balance sheet capital) would be £[✂] million for 1998 and £[✂] million for 1999.

6.431. Table 6.119 shows that the Co-operative Bank's profits from SME banking business were based on it calculating net income from lending as if wholly financed from the wholesale markets at its internal transfer pricing rate. However, in identifying the rate of return to compare with the cost of capital, an adjustment must be made to reflect that a proportion of lending was funded from capital and not from the wholesale markets. This is necessary to avoid double counting, and for our purposes the appropriate adjustment is attributable capital times the average three-month LIBOR. The rate used was 7.3 per cent for 1998 and 5.45 per cent in 1999.

6.432. Table 6.121 incorporates this adjustment, together with the information shown in Table 6.119 on profitability, and shows estimates of returns (subject to adjustments discussed in Chapter 7). For 1999, which was a year with relatively low bad debt levels, the Co-operative Bank's pre-tax return on capital was [✂] per cent, based on closing capital. In Chapter 7 we consider the Co-operative Bank's appropriate cost of capital, and what adjustments are necessary regarding these returns. In Chapter 2 we give our conclusions on this issue.

TABLE 6.121 **The Co-operative Bank: summary of profits, capital and returns from services to SMEs before any adjustments by the CC, 1998 and 1999**

	£ million	
	1998	1999
Information from Table 6.119		
Operating income		
Operating costs		
Operating profit before bad debts		
Bad debt charge	✂	
Adjustment for attributable capital*		
Net profit before tax and exceptional items		
Attributable capital (based on closing capital for the whole bank and proportions of RWAs)	(✂)	(✂)†
Average attributable capital	‡	(✂)
	per cent	
Pre-tax return based on closing attributable capital	✂	
Pre-tax return based on average attributable capital		

Source: CC based on information from the Co-operative Bank.

---

*At 7.3 per cent for 1998 and 5.45 per cent for 1999, based on three-month LIBOR.

†The attributable capital for 1999, which is shown as based on the closing capital level for the Co-operative Bank, could alternatively be based on the average of the closing attributable capital figures for each year. For 1999 the resultant figure would therefore be £[✂] million, and the pre-tax return, based on this average attributable capital, would be [✂] per cent, ie an increase of [✂] percentage points.

‡Not calculated.

6.433. A further alternative method of calculating the capital attributable to the SME banking business would be to use an average capital figure, for example the average of the opening and closing capital base, rather than a return based on the closing figure. For 1999 we calculated that the effect on the pre-tax return would be an increase of two percentage points. However, this approach was not practicable for all banks, because certain data was not available. The Co-operative Bank could not provide data for 1997.

Further analysis of income and expenses

6.434. Table 6.122 provides an analysis of operating income by type of banking service to SME customers for 1998 and 1999. The four main types of banking services from which the bank earned income were loans, current accounts utilizing an overdraft facility, deposits and other current accounts. Other current accounts was the largest source of operating income in both 1998 and 1999, and contributed [✂] per cent of operating income respectively. In comparison, loans contributed [✂] per cent of operating income, in 1998 and 1999 respectively, while deposits contributed [✂] per cent respectively. Current accounts utilizing an overdraft facility contributed [✂] per cent of operating income in both years.

TABLE 6.122 The Co-operative Bank: analysis of income by type of banking service to SME customers, 1998 and 1999

	£ million		Income share %	
	1998	1999	1998	1999
Net income* from:				
Lending				
Deposits				
Overdrafts utilizing an overdraft facility	*Figures omitted. See note on page iv.*			
Other current accounts				
UK clubs and charities				
Total				

Source: The Co-operative Bank.

---

*Includes net interest income and net fees and commissions. Operational costs and bad debt charges are then deducted from this income to derive net operating profit.

†Includes current accounts without an overdraft facility and current accounts with an overdraft facility that has not been utilized. Of the current accounts without an overdraft facility, this classification will include those accounts that have an unauthorized overdraft.

6.435. Table 6.123 provides a further breakdown of net operating income from the SME banking business into net interest income and net fees and commission income for 1998 and 1999. The table shows actual income earned, as well as the notional cost of funds to finance the lending, and the benefit of funds deposited by SMEs. Unlike some other banks, the Co-operative Bank pays interest on the majority of its current accounts, which significantly offsets the benefit of funds on these balances.

6.436. The table also shows the net interest margin, and net fees and commissions margin, earned by the bank from different types of banking relationships with the SMEs.

6.437. The Co-operative Bank told us that the method used to calculate internal transfers of interest was to apply the three-month LIBOR rate (7.25 per cent in 1998 and 5.36 per cent in 1999) to average daily balances. In fact, the bank funded and hedged interest-insensitive balances (current accounts) and fixed-rate lending with the appropriate medium-term instruments. Some lending was also 'match-funded', ie funded with liabilities that carry the same maturity and interest rate. The Co-operative Bank said that the effect of applying the short-term LIBOR rate as specified by the CC was to increase the Corporate division net interest by £5.6 million in 1999 and £3.3 million in 1998.

6.438. In 1999 the Co-operative Bank earned income from providing the following types of services to SME customers:

(a) Loans: income earned was £[✄] million (of which £[✄] million was interest and £[✄] million was lending commission).

(b) Deposits: income earned was £[✄] million (all of which was the imputed net interest benefit of the customer deposits).

(c) Current accounts with overdrafts: income earned was £[✄] million (of which £[✄] million was net interest income and £[✄] million was fees and commissions).

(d) Current accounts with no overdrafts: net income earned was £[✄] million (of which £[✄] million was the gross imputed interest benefit of the funds, £[✄] million was the interest paid to customers, and £[✄] million was fees, commissions and money transmission charges).

6.439. In 1999 current accounts with overdrafts had the highest net interest margin, at [✄] per cent for outstanding overdraft balances and [✄] per cent for credit balances held in a current account with an overdraft facility. In comparison, current accounts without an overdraft facility carried a net interest margin of [✄] per cent for credit balances and [✄] per cent for overdraft balances. This latter amount represents penalty interest rates for an unapproved overdraft. Other net interest margins were [✄] per cent for loans and [✄] per cent for deposits.

6.440. The Co-operative Bank told us that it derived more income from current accounts than any other SME service, because it included income from its highly successful Business Direct product, which was designed exclusively for customers who operated only in credit. Income from this product (both interest and non-interest) totalled £[✄] million in 1998 and £[✄] million in 1999.

TABLE 6.123   The Co-operative Bank: analysis of operating income by type of service to SMEs, 1998 and 1999

	£ million		Lending balances and margins	
	1998	1999	1998	1999

Loans
Interest income
Cost of funds to finance lending
  Net interest income
Other income
  Net income*
  Average lending balance (£m)
  Net interest (%)†

Current accounts with overdrafts
Interest income
Cost of funds to finance lending
Benefit of SME funds
Interest paid to customers
  Net interest income
Account management fees
Current account commission
Lending commission
  Net income*
  Average overdraft balance (£m)
  Net interest on debit balances (%)†
  Average credit balance (£m)
  Net interest on credit balances (%)†

Current accounts with no overdrafts
Interest income
Benefit of funds from SMEs
Interest payable to customers
Cost of funds
  Net interest income
Account management fees
Current account commission
Money transmission services
Corporate commission paid
  Net income‡
  Average debit balance (£m)
  Net interest on debit balances (%)†
  Average current account credit
balance (£m)
  Net interest on credit balances (%)†

Deposits
Benefit of funds from SMEs
Interest paid
  Net interest income‡
  Average deposit balance (£m)
  Net interest (%)†

UK clubs and charities
Interest income
Benefit of funds from SMEs
Interest payable to customers
Cost of funds
  Net interest income
Account management fees
Current account commission
Money transmission services
Lending commission
Corporate commission paid
  Net income*
  Total income
  Average debit balance (£m)
  Net interest on debit balances (%)†
  Average current account credit
balance (£m)
  Net interest on credit balances (%)†

*Figures omitted.
See note on page iv.*

Source: The Co-operative Bank.

---

*Before deducting operating costs and bad debt charges, to derive the net operating profit from this service to customers.
†Net interest and fees and commissions as percentages of average balances
‡Before deducting operational costs, to derive the net operating profit from this service to customers.

6.441. Table 6.124 provides a summary of the operating profits for the SME banking business by types of banking service for 1998 and 1999.

TABLE 6.124 **The Co-operative Bank: summary of operating profit by type of service to SMEs, 1998 and 1999**

| | £ million | | Proportion of total income (%) | |
	1998	1999	1998	1999
Lending				
Net income*				
Costs				
Bad debt charge				
Profit				
Deposits				
Net income*				
Costs				
Profit				
Overdrafts (authorized accounts)				
Net income*				
Costs				
Bad debt charge				
Profit				
Current accounts (no overdraft approved)				
Net income*				
Costs				
Profit				
Clubs and charities				
Income				
Costs				
Profit				
Total profit from SMEs				

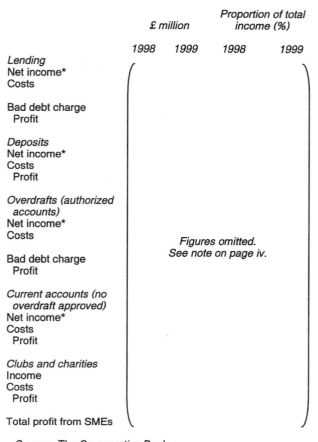

Figures omitted. See note on page iv.

Source: The Co-operative Bank.

*Net interest income plus fees and commissions.

6.442. Table 6.125 provides an analysis of operating costs for services to SME customers, which is subject to the allocation method noted above. Within direct costs, staff cost was the largest cost category in 1998 and 1999 at £[✂] million and £[✂] million respectively, or [✂] per cent of total costs. In 1999 indirect costs accounted for £[✂] million or [✂] per cent of total costs.

TABLE 6.125 **The Co-operative Bank: analysis of SME operating costs, 1998 and 1999**

| | £ million | | Proportion of total (%) | |
	1998	1999	1998	1999
Direct costs				
Staff costs				
Premises and equipment				
Other costs				
Total				
Allocated costs				
Staff costs				
Premises and equipment				
Other costs				
Total				
Total operating costs				

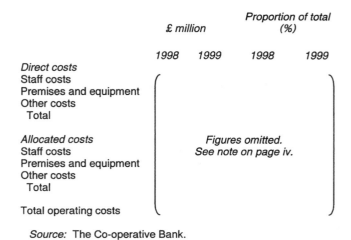

Figures omitted. See note on page iv.

Source: The Co-operative Bank.

6.443. We asked the Co-operative Bank for details on the number of personnel who serviced the SME sector in 1999. It told us that it was not possible to identify that element of head count dedicated to servicing SMEs, and that it felt unable to offer any 'qualified estimates' due to the inability to accurately apportion the costs of items such as:

(a) branch network cashiers servicing personal customers and SMEs;

(b) central support functions such as human resources and financial control; and

(c) third party supplier contracts such as cash processing arrangements with HSBC or clearing house arrangements with UPSL.

6.444. The Co-operative Bank said that during 1999 the total expenditure in respect of advertising and marketing for Corporate and Commercial Banking was £[✂] million, of which approximately [✂] per cent (or £[✂] million) related to SMEs. This represented an advertising expenditure to total income ratio of [✂] per cent for the SME banking business.

Balance sheet items

6.445. Table 6.126 shows the Co-operative Bank's total lending to SME customers for 1998 and 1999. Total lending to SME customers in 1999 was £[✂] million, of which £[✂] million was loans to customers. Total customer accounts in credit was £[✂] million for the same period.

TABLE 6.126 **The Co-operative Bank: balance sheet items attributable to SME customers, 1998 and 1999**

£ million

	1998	1999
Loans		
Overdrafts		
Loans and overdrafts to clubs and charities		
Total lending		
Deposits	✂	
Current accounts		
Deposits and current accounts from clubs and charities		
Total customer accounts in credit		
Funds available		

Source: The Co-operative Bank.

Capital expenditure and development costs

6.446. The Co-operative Bank told us that it was not possible to analyse development costs down to the SME sector. Its bank-wide development costs (ie marketing, consultancy and technology systems costs) for 1999 and 2000 amounted to approximately £[✂] million and £[✂] million respectively or [✂] per cent of its total income. Of this, approximately £[✂] million related to the corporate business in each year. The Co-operative Bank expected development costs for 2001 and 2002 to be broadly in line with 1999 and 2000.

Bad debts

6.447. We asked the Co-operative Bank to provide data on the level of bad debt charge and bad debt provision attributable to the SME sector over the past ten years. It told us that data on bad debt charges was available only at the total Corporate and Commercial Banking business unit level which included SMEs. It said that the total Corporate and Commercial Banking charge as a percentage of average balances reflected similar trends as the SME banking business.

6.448. Table 6.127 shows the level of bad debt charge for ten years to 1999, at the corporate business unit level. Bad debt charges were relatively high during the early 1990s, increasing to [✄] per cent of total lending in 1990. From 1996 to 1999 the bad debt charge has remained relatively constant at between [✄] per cent of total lending.

TABLE 6.127 **The Co-operative Bank: summary of bad debt charges compared with lending for the corporate business unit, 1989 to 1999**

£ million

	1989	1990	1991	1992	1993	1994	1995	1996	1997	1998	1999	Average 1989–93	Average 1994–99
Bad debt expense Average lending balance					*Figures omitted.* *See note on page iv.*								
Bad debt charge as a percentage of lending						✄							*per cent*

Source: The Co-operative Bank.

6.449. In terms of the future, the Co-operative Bank told us that at the end of 1999 it was calculating expected losses for Corporate and Commercial Banking bad debts at [✄] per cent. It further stated that it would anticipate the expected loss rate to be higher in the future as economic growth slows.

Future strategy in serving the SME banking business

6.450. The Co-operative Bank told us that during the next three years it would continue to benefit from cost efficiencies arising from internal developments and outsourcing arrangements while continuing to invest in customer services facilities, [*Details omitted. See note on page iv.*]. The cost:income ratio was expected to fall below [✄] per cent for the whole bank in 2003.

6.451. It told us that future investment plans relating to the SME sector were focused upon upgrading and improving systems to enable it to meet the anticipated needs of customers and to enhance services. [*Details omitted.* *See note on page iv.*] The cost of this project was estimated at approximately £[✄] million. It saw the investments as a measure to maintain a leading edge quality of service to existing customers.

6.452. The Co-operative Bank believed that the UK economy was generally stable and as a result was experiencing the lowest levels of corporate bad debt charge since the early 1990s. However, it said that growth was likely to slow within the next year and that a number of items were likely to have an impact on the cost base for SMEs including:

(a) upward pressure on inflation;

(b) unemployment falling rapidly and labour shortages in certain sectors leading to increased earnings;

(c) a weaker sterling, which would benefit exporters but place further pressure on inflation; and

(d) base interest rates might increase slightly to combat the inflationary pressures.

Alliance & Leicester/Girobank

Overview of its business in serving SMEs

6.453. Chapter 5 deals in detail with Alliance & Leicester's group position and activities generally. The section below deals with its services to SMEs and the financial performance of its SME banking business.

6.454. As noted in Chapter 5, Alliance & Leicester's SME banking business is conducted through its subsidiary Girobank. Until recently, Alliance & Leicester's services to SMEs were limited to the provision of deposit and current accounts without overdrafts, money transmission services and a limited amount of lending secured by property. In the latter part of 2000, Alliance & Leicester launched its Alliance Business Banking initiative, which primarily targets small businesses, ie up to £1 million turnover, and provides unsecured loans and overdraft facilities to sole traders, partnerships and limited companies up to a value of £25,000. Alliance & Leicester told us that larger facilities, for example secured lending up to £200,000, would be introduced shortly.

6.455. Alliance & Leicester told us that it currently provided services across the SME sector, but was developing a segment-specific approach to areas where it believed it could deliver additional benefits and added value, or where it could make contact with various industry segments via their trade associations or trade publications.

Financial performance of the SME segment

6.456. We asked Alliance & Leicester to provide us with profitability data on its SME banking business for the period between 1997 and 1999. It told us that it was able to provide us with data for 1998, 1999 and 2000.

6.457. Table 6.128 shows the profitability of Alliance & Leicester's SME banking business from 1998 to 2000. Operating income increased from £[✂] million in 1998 to £[✂] million in 2000, while operating expenses were £[✂] million in 1998, increasing to £[✂] million in 2000. As a result, operating profit before tax was £[✂] million in 1998 and £[✂] million in 2000.

TABLE 6.128 **Alliance & Leicester: profit and loss account from SME banking business, 1998 to 2000**

£ million

	1998	1999	2000
Net interest income			
Net fees and commissions			
Total operating income			
Operating expenses		*Figures omitted.*	
Operating profit before bad debts		*See note*	
Bad debt charge		*on page iv.*	
Net profit before tax			

Source: Alliance & Leicester.

6.458. Table 6.129 further analyses the overall performance of Alliance & Leicester's SME banking business from 1998 to 2000, by showing all items as a percentage of operating income. Net interest income was [✄] per cent of operating income in 1998 and [✄] per cent in 2000. Total non-interest income over the same periods was [✄] and [✄] per cent respectively.

TABLE 6.129 **Alliance & Leicester: operating profit and loss items as a percentage of operating income from SME banking business, 1998 to 2000**

per cent

	1998	1999	2000
Net interest income			
Net fees and commissions			
Total operating income			
Operating expenses	*Figures omitted. See note on page iv.*		
Operating profit before bad debts			
Bad debt charge			
Net profit before tax			

Source: Alliance & Leicester.

6.459. The SME activity's cost:income ratio was 83 per cent in 1998 and decreased to around 79 per cent in 2000. We noted that Alliance & Leicester allocated overhead costs so that the SME banking business's cost:income ratio equated with that of the whole Girobank business in each year.

6.460. [

Details omitted. See note on page iv.

]

Attributable capital to support the SME banking business and potential returns

6.461. Tables 6.128 and 6.129 show the trends in Alliance & Leicester's profits from its SME banking business, which as noted were generated by its Girobank operations. In order to form a view on the significance of such profits we also consider these profits in relation to Girobank's capital base. In our discussion with Alliance & Leicester on determining the attributable capital to support its services to SMEs we made a number of calculations for 1998 and 1999. Our methodology for allocating Girobank capital is briefly discussed below.

6.462. First, Girobank was required to maintain its own capital adequacy ratio. Therefore we considered that equity in relation to Girobank statutory entity should be used in our calculations rather than the equity for the entire Alliance & Leicester group.

6.463. Next, we noted that Girobank's SME banking business was distinct from other banks in that its lending portfolio was relatively insignificant. This indicated to us that allocation of Girobank equity to SME banking business activities by reference to SME-generated RWAs was inappropriate in this instance, because it was not a true reflection of the capital being used to support the SME banking business.

6.464. We therefore proposed two methods to Alliance & Leicester for allocating Girobank capital to its SME banking business activities which focused on the activity drivers behind the Girobank business, namely customer accounts in credit and money transmission services. Under method 1, which seemed to be the best proxy in the circumstances, we suggested allocation of capital in accordance with the proportion of customer accounts in credit. However, we recognized the importance of money transmission services revenue to Girobank and also looked at an alternative method of allocation, which allocated capital to areas of business according to turnover.

6.465. Applying the first allocation method, we calculated that the capital requirement of the SME banking business (based on an apportionment of its closing balance sheet capital) would be £[✂] million for 1998 and 1999 and £[✂] million for 2000. Using the second method for allocation, we calculated that the capital requirement of the SME banking business would be £[✂] million for 1998, £[✂] million for 1999 and £[✂] million for 2000. Table 6.130 incorporates both these initial estimates of attributable capital, together with the information shown in Table 6.128 on profitability and shows estimates of returns based on both capital allocation methodologies and subject to the adjustments discussed in Chapter 7. Because Girobank had minimal lending, an adjustment for the benefit of capital funding was not required. For 2000 Girobank's SME banking business's pre-tax return on capital was [✂] per cent under the first capital allocation method and [✂] per cent under the second.

6.466. Table 6.130 summarizes Alliance & Leicester's profits, attributable capital and returns from services to SMEs before any adjustments.

TABLE 6.130 **Alliance & Leicester: summary of profits, attributable capital and returns from services to SMEs before any adjustments by the CC, 1998 and 1999**

£ million

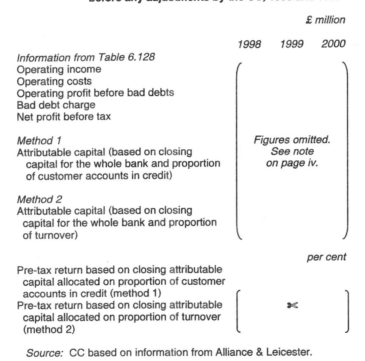

	1998	1999	2000
Information from Table 6.128			
Operating income			
Operating costs			
Operating profit before bad debts			
Bad debt charge			
Net profit before tax			
Method 1			
Attributable capital (based on closing capital for the whole bank and proportion of customer accounts in credit)	Figures omitted. See note on page iv.		
Method 2			
Attributable capital (based on closing capital for the whole bank and proportion of turnover)			

per cent

	1998	1999	2000
Pre-tax return based on closing attributable capital allocated on proportion of customer accounts in credit (method 1)		✂	
Pre-tax return based on closing attributable capital allocated on proportion of turnover (method 2)			

Source: CC based on information from Alliance & Leicester.

6.467. The differences in terms of rate of return between our two suggested methods of allocating capital were not significant, and we have used method 1 in our further analysis, which gives slightly lower returns.

6.468. A further alternative method of calculating the capital attributable to the SME banking business would be to use an average capital figure, for example the average of the opening and closing capital base, rather than a return based on the closing figure. For 1999 we calculated that the effect on the pre-tax return would be an increase of one percentage point.

Further analysis of income and expenses

6.469. Table 6.131 provides an analysis of operating income by type of banking service to SME customers from 1998 to 2000. As previously noted, prior to 2000 Alliance & Leicester provided only limited lending facilities to SMEs. Therefore Alliance & Leicester's income from SMEs up to 2000 was predominantly from deposits and current accounts with no overdraft facilities. Current accounts with no overdraft facilities was the largest source of operating income for all three years, and contributed approximately [✂] per cent of operating income in 1999 and 2000 respectively.

TABLE 6.131 **Alliance & Leicester: analysis of income by type of banking service to SME customers, 1998 to 2000**

	£ million			Income share (%)		
	1998	1999	2000	1998	1999	2000
Net income* from:						
Loans						
Current accounts utilizing an overdraft facility						
Other current accounts†		Figures omitted. See note on page iv.				
Deposits						
UK clubs and charities						
Other						
Total						

Source: Alliance & Leicester.

*Includes net interest income and net fees and commissions. Operational costs and bad debt charges are then deducted from this income to derive net operating profit.

†Includes current accounts without an overdraft facility and current accounts with an overdraft facility that has not been utilized. Of the current accounts without an overdraft facility, this classification will include those accounts that have an unauthorized overdraft.

6.470. Table 6.132 provides a further breakdown of net operating income from the SME banking business into net interest income and net fees and commission income from 1998 to 2000. The table shows actual income earned as well as the benefit of funds deposited by SMEs. Alliance & Leicester earned income from money in SME deposit and current accounts as well as from account management and money transmission fees. The table also shows the net interest margin on deposit accounts and current accounts earned by the bank. A large proportion of Alliance & Leicester's income, £[✂] million out of £[✂] million in 2000, arose from money transmission charges. A further £[✂] million arose from net interest income from current accounts in credit. Alliance & Leicester also derived considerable income ([✂] per cent of total income) from clubs and charities customers.

6.471. Alliance & Leicester told us that the method used to calculate internal transfers of interest was an internally agreed net treasury earnings rate of 6.2 per cent in 2000, 5.95 per cent in 1999 and 7.02 per cent in 1998. These figures were based on Girobank receiving one-month LIBID on deposits and paying one-month LIBOR on any borrowings. Alliance & Leicester confirmed that this transfer pricing rate was consistent across all the Girobank businesses. In 2000 current accounts without overdrafts had the highest net interest margin, at [✂] per cent. In comparison, deposits carried a net interest margin of [✂] per cent.

TABLE 6.132 **Alliance & Leicester: analysis of operating income by type of service to SMEs, 1998 to 2000**

	£ million			Lending balances and margins		
	1998	1999	2000	1998	1999	2000
Loans						
Interest received*	*					
Allocated cost of funds	*					
Net interest income	*	✂				
Fees and commissions	*					
Net income†	*					
Current accounts utilizing an overdraft facility						
Interest received	*	*				
Allocated cost of funds	*	*				
Net interest income	*	*	✂			
Fees and commissions	*	*				
Net income†	*	*				
Other current accounts‡						
Benefit of funds from SMEs						
Interest paid						
Net interest income						
Account management and other fees						
Money transmission services						
Net income§						
Average current account credit balance (£m)					✂	
Net interest on credit balances (%)¶						
Deposits						
Benefit of funds from SMEs						
Interest paid		Figures omitted.				
Net interest income§		See note				
Average deposit balance (£m)		on page iv.			✂	
Net interest (%)¶						
UK clubs and charities						
Benefit of funds from SMEs						
Interest paid						
Net interest income						
Account management fees						
Net income†						
Average current account credit balance (£m)					✂	
Net interest on credit balances (%)¶						
Other income						
Merchant services						
Overall total income						

Source: Alliance & Leicester.

---

*Not applicable as Alliance & Leicester did not provide SME services in these years.

†Before deducting operational costs and bad debt charges, to derive the net operating profit from this service to customers.

‡Includes current accounts without an overdraft facility and current accounts with an overdraft facility that has not been utilized. Of the current accounts without an overdraft facility, this classification will include those accounts that have an unauthorized overdraft.

§Before deducting operational costs, to derive the net operating profit from this service to customers.

¶Net interest and net fees and commissions as a percentage of average balance.

6.472. Table 6.133 provides a further analysis of fee income by type of SME customer from 1998 to 2000. Variable tariff clients with turnover between £1 million and £25 million represented the highest source of fee income in all years.

TABLE 6.133 **Alliance & Leicester: analysis of fee income by type of SME customer, 1998 to 2000**

£ million

	1998	1999	2000
Account management fees			
Fixed tariff			
Variable tariff:			
Less than £1m	*Figures omitted.*		
Between £1m and £25m	*See note*		
Merchant services	*on page iv.*		
Lending fees			
Other*			

Source: Alliance & Leicester.

*Includes bank and building society charges.

6.473. Alliance & Leicester told us that:

(a) Account management, fixed tariff and merchant services fees were taken directly from the profit and loss accounts and represented business obtained using the bank's published tariffs.

(b) Variable tariff fees represented business obtained by the sales force and the figures were based on analyses taken from the customer profitability system. Alliance & Leicester noted that, as this system provided an analysis only on a 12-month period, the 1998 figures were derived from the 1999 analysis, adjusted for account volumes and interest rates.

6.474. Table 6.134 provides an analysis of variable operating costs for services to SME customers. Recharges from Girobank incorporating post office and overhead costs were the largest category in 1998, 1999 and 2000 at £[✂] million, £[✂] million and £[✂] million respectively. As a percentage of operating costs these values equate to [✂] per cent respectively. Recharge income reflects costs within Girobank, which are recharged to the Personal Banking division. In the 1998 published accounts this was presented as income received, although in the 2000 published accounts the recharge has been netted off against costs.

TABLE 6.134 **Alliance & Leicester: analysis of SME operating costs, 1998 to 2000**

	£ million			Proportion of total costs %		
	1998	1999	2000	1998	1999	2000
Variable costs:						
Staff costs						
Premises and equipment						
Marketing						
Other variable costs	*Figures omitted. See note on page iv.*					
Third party processing costs						
Net recharges for post office costs and overheads*						
Total costs						

Source: Alliance & Leicester.

*Alliance & Leicester said that whenever a customer transacted over the post office counter, it incurred a charge.

6.475. We asked Alliance & Leicester for details on the number of personnel who serviced SME customers in 1999. It told us that there were several groups of people dedicated or identifiable with providing services to small businesses within the definition of SMEs including staff in account management in the Midland regional office, telebusiness staff in Bootle, and 'account-opening' staff in Bootle. In total, Alliance & Leicester estimated that there were 76 FTE staff (excluding Post Office staff) providing services to small businesses at a total employment cost of £[✂] million, or an average cost per employee of £[✂]. If the larger businesses within the definition of SMEs are included, the total employment cost figure rises to £[✂] million for 1999.

6.476. Alliance & Leicester advised us that the total advertising and marketing expenditure for Girobank alone, for 1999, was £[✄] million. Alliance & Leicester was unable to split this balance into that which related to SMEs and 'other'. It said that this expenditure was for the attraction of both existing customers and new customers. Historically the bank only targeted customers who already banked with competitor banks. New 'start-up' businesses could open an account, but there was no specific product proposition designed to attract these customers.

Balance sheet items

6.477. Table 6.135 shows Girobank's total deposits from SME customers and total lending to SME customers, for 1998 to 2000. Total customer accounts in credit increased [✄] per cent over the past three years, from £[✄] million in 1998 to £[✄] million in 2000. In contrast, the balance of overdrafts to SMEs has remained relatively small, with the overdrafts up to 2000 mostly secured against property. Alliance & Leicester confirmed that pending the Alliance Business Banking initiative, there was no explicit focus on small business lending within Girobank.

TABLE 6.135 **Alliance & Leicester: balance sheet items attributable to SME customers, 1998 to 2000**

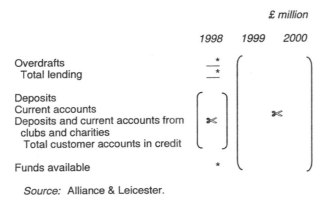

£ million

Source: Alliance & Leicester.

*Not available.

Capital expenditure and development costs

6.478. Alliance & Leicester told us that the capital forecast for Girobank for 2001 was £[✄] million and £[✄] million for 2002. There was no specific allocation to SME; however, Alliance & Leicester believed that it would only equate to a small proportion of systems/processes and be hard to differentiate.

Bad debts

6.479. We asked Alliance & Leicester to provide data on the level of bad debt charge and bad debt provision attributable to its services to SMEs over the past five years. It said that as Girobank did not historically provide any significant lending products to SMEs, the level of bad debts to this business was insignificant. Alliance & Leicester said that as the commercial lending emphasis has been on term lending with only very modest amounts of overdraft lending, any analysis based on provisions relating to overdrafts alone would not be meaningful.

6.480. Alliance & Leicester considered that SME lending activities were likely to carry potentially higher risks than corporate sector risk. It was, however, seeking to mitigate these risks, by implementing exacting approval criteria and robust scoring techniques. It would also use experienced and qualified underwriters with industry-wide knowledge, and sector risk management to avoid known problem areas.

Future strategy in serving the SME banking business

6.481. As noted previously, Alliance & Leicester through its Alliance Business Banking initiative began lending to small businesses in the latter part of 2000. It told us that it had instigated a careful

434

approach to developing its credit/finance offering in order to manage carefully the risks involved. An aggregate lending limit of £1 million had been reached at the end of February 2001 and it was envisaged that by the second quarter 2001 the product range would be expanded to include secured loans up to £200,000.

6.482. Alliance & Leicester told us that the lending business would primarily be conducted centrally, or by a team of relationship managers. Branches would only play a role in initial prospect customer interviews. It said that initially there would be a small team of five mobile relationship managers, and expansion would depend upon performance. It did not see a substantial role for the Post Office in developing the SME lending business.

6.483. [

Details omitted. See note on page iv.

]

6.484. [

Details omitted. See note on page iv.

]

Abbey National

Overview of its business in serving SMEs

6.485. As noted in Chapter 5, Abbey National said that it served business customers, although not exclusively, through a number of business units administered by its subsidiary First National Bank Plc. These businesses are: First National Vehicle Holdings, First National Invoice Finance, First National Commercial Banking, First National Asset Finance, First National Country Capital, Abbey National Business and Professional Banking and First National Business Equipment Leasing.

6.486. We asked Abbey National to provide us with profitability data for its SME banking business for the period between 1997 and 2000. It was unable to do so because there was no segmentation in its business customer data between SME and non-SME banking business. However, it provided a best endeavours estimate of the extent of SME banking business included in its total figures for 1999 only. This consisted of summary profit and loss data for the five main businesses concerned, with percentage estimates of the extent of SME banking business included in the total figures of each business, which we summarized to derive results for a hypothetical SME banking business.

6.487. Table 6.136 shows the estimated profitability of Abbey National's SME banking business for the year ended 31 December 1999. Operating income for the year was £[✕] million, while over the same period operating expenses were £[✕] million. The level of bad debt charge was £[✕] million. As a result, operating profit before tax was £[✕] million.

TABLE 6.136 **Abbey National: estimated profit and loss account from services to SMEs, 1999**

	£m	%
Net interest income		
Non-interest income		
Total operating income		
Operating expenses	✕	
Operating profit before bad debts		
Bad debt charge		
Net profit before tax*		

Source: Abbey National.

*As requested by us, these figures were calculated on the basis that all lending is financed from borrowing in whole-sale markets. In fact, a proportion will be financed by the bank's equity, and it is therefore necessary to make an adjustment for this (see Table 6.137) before comparing returns on capital derived from these profit figures with the bank's cost of capital.

435

6.488. Table 6.136 further analyses the overall performance of Abbey National's SME banking business for the year ended December 1999, by showing all items as a percentage of operating income. Net interest income was around [✂] per cent of operating income for the year.

6.489. The SME activity's cost:income ratio was [✂] per cent. This compared to a cost:income ratio for the consolidated bank of 43 per cent for the same year, noted in Chapter 5.

Attributable capital to support the SME banking business and potential returns

6.490. Table 6.136 sets out the estimated profits of Abbey National's SME banking business for 1999. In order to form a view on the significance of such profits, we need to consider its capital base. We look at this subject in greater detail in Chapter 7. In our discussion with Abbey on determining the attributable capital to support its services to SMEs, we made a number of calculations for 1999 based on our methodology as discussed in paragraphs 6.22 and 6.23.

6.491. Applying our methodology, we calculated that the capital requirement of the SME banking business (based on an apportionment of its closing balance sheet capital) would be £[✂] million for 1999.

6.492. Table 6.136 shows that Abbey National's profits from SME banking business were based on it calculating net income from lending as if wholly financed from the wholesale markets at its internal transfer pricing rate. However, in identifying the rate of return to compare with the cost of capital, an adjustment must be made to reflect that a proportion of lending was funded from capital and not from the wholesale markets. This is necessary to avoid double counting, and for our purposes the appropriate adjustment is attributable capital times the average three-month LIBOR for 1999 of 5.45 per cent.

6.493. Table 6.137 incorporates this adjustment, together with the information shown in Table 6.136 on profitability, and shows estimates of returns (subject to adjustments discussed in Chapter 7). For 1999, which was a year with relatively low bad debt levels, Abbey National's pre-tax return on capital was [✂] per cent, based on closing capital. In Chapter 7 we consider Abbey National's appropriate cost of capital, and what adjustments are necessary regarding these returns. In Chapter 2 we give our conclusions on this issue.

TABLE 6.137 **Abbey National: summary of profits, capital and returns for services to SMEs before any adjustments by the CC, 1999**

	£m
Operating income	⎧
Operating costs	⎪
Operating profit before bad debts	⎪
Bad debt charge	⎪
Adjustment for attributable capital†	✂
Net profit before tax	⎪
	⎪
Allocated capital (based on closing capital for the whole bank and proportions of RWAs)	⎩
	%
Pre-tax return based on closing allocated capital	(✂)

Source: CC based on information from Abbey National.

---

*The attributable capital for 1999, which is shown as based on the closing capital level for Abbey National, could alternatively be based on the average of the closing attributable capital figures for each year.
†At 5.45 per cent for 1999, based on three-month LIBOR.

6.494. A further alternative method of calculating the capital attributable to the SME banking business would be to use an average capital figure, for example the average of the opening and closing capital base, rather than a return based on the closing figure. However, this approach was not practicable for Abbey National, because relevant data was not available.

Further analysis of income and expenses

6.495. We asked Abbey National for a detailed breakdown of income earned by its SME banking business according to product type, being loans, asset finance, overdrafts, deposits and current accounts. Information on profitability and performance measurement in these areas was also requested. It was unable to do so, however, because there was no segmentation in its data between SME and non-SME banking business.

6.496. Consequently we have not been able to carry out detailed analyses on the components of income and expense or profit for the SME portion of Abbey National's business.

6.497. It told us that advertising and marketing expenditure for the SME banking business was not separately identifiable and that such costs were set by business units based on various factors such as new business volume target, profitability and growth and market conditions. Further it told us that no indirect central costs were allocated to the SME banking business as, given the small proportion of business which is currently SME related, it is deemed not material. In addition, there was no specific unit, or allocation of staff, which targeted the SME banking business.

Balance sheet items

6.498. We asked Abbey National for detailed balance sheet information for the SME banking business. Table 6.138 shows the estimated assets and liabilities for 1999 for SME banking business based on a summary of balance sheet items for the five business units concerned with servicing business customers, including SMEs.

6.499. The liabilities figure represents deposits taken by Business and Professional Banking. Abbey National also showed these amounts as assets because the funds are on-lent to Abbey National Treasury Services. Part of the interest receivable represents the interest earned on these on-lent deposits which is at a rate of LIBOR plus [✂] basis points, consistent with the rate paid by the business for funds borrowed from the treasury business. No attempt has been made to replicate the commercial cost of funds to stand-alone businesses. Using a true arm's length price could be expected to increase the net cost of funds of the business, in this case Business and Professional Banking.

TABLE 6.138 **Abbey National: balance sheet items for the SME banking business, 1999**

	£m
SME assets	
SME liabilities	✂
Funds available	

Source: CC based on information from Abbey National.

Capital expenditure and developmental costs

6.500. With regard to capital expenditure, for example IT systems, telecommunications and properties to meet customer needs, these were all budgeted as costs for the Abbey National group and not allocated to the separate businesses. Only direct costs of running each business are allocated to the individual businesses.

6.501. Abbey National told us that its budgeted capital expenditure over the next three years for the group's Business Finance division was expected to be £[✂] billion, which includes the use of capital for lending. The budget for new investment, for product development and related capital infrastructure was £[✂] million and the area that this would be concentrated towards was [✂]. No analysis of this expenditure was provided by Abbey National.

Bad debts

6.502. Abbey National was unable to provide information on its long-term bad debt history from servicing SMEs, but its involvement to date has been recent and on a relatively small scale compared with its total activities. It did not provide authorized overdrafts to business customers (although board approval for a programme for overdrafts was subsequently granted in March 2001) and the total of commercial mortgages did not exceed £[✂] million.

6.503. Abbey National told us that historically SME lending has been riskier than lending to larger companies—riskiness being measured by the ratio of bad debts to lending assets.

Future strategy in serving the SME banking business

6.504. As the Abbey National group does not identify SMEs as a separate category of customer, it did not have projections relating to reference activities. In Business and Professional Banking, the group hopes to grow its share of business bank accounts from 1 to 5 per cent over the next five years.

6.505. [

Details omitted. See note on page iv.

]

7 Comparison of banks' returns from services to SMEs with their cost of capital

Contents

Introduction

7.1. Chapter 5 summarized the financial results for the clearing banks that supply services to SMEs in the UK, and looked at all their main activities, of which services to SMEs were a part. Chapter 6 presented results for these banks from services to SMEs in England and Wales (mainly Barclays, Lloyds TSB, NatWest and HSBC), in Scotland (mainly RBS, BoS and Clydesdale), and in Northern Ireland (mainly Northern, Ulster Bank, First Trust and BoI). Other banks that serve SMEs on a regional basis were also discussed.

7.2. The purpose of this chapter is to provide the information and analysis that we use in Chapter 2 for the purpose of determining whether the banks concerned are making returns more than that necessary to finance their services to SMEs. We identify:

(a) the capital at the whole-bank level, and the proportion allocated to the SME banking business, together with a number of possible adjustments thereto;

(b) the returns achieved from the supply of banking services to SMEs using results for the three years to 2000, together with a number of possible adjustments thereto; and

(c) the cost of capital for the respective banks.

We deal first with the six largest clearing groups and, later in the chapter, with the smaller banks.[1]

7.3. Finally we set out our methodology for determining the returns which it is appropriate to compare with the banks' respective cost of capital. In doing so we set out the initial figures that we sent to the banks on an illustrative basis in order to seek their views and then set out various arguments that the banks put to us, some of which are noted in greater detail in the views chapters. In Chapter 2, we set out our views on the appropriateness of the adjustments proposed by the banks to our suggested methodology, and our assessment of whether the banks have made returns at a level higher than necessary to finance their services to SMEs. Some of the banks disagreed with the methodology or considered that it was not practicable to measure with any degree of precision whether profits were being made in excess of cost of capital. Many banks emphasized that they did not operate services to SMEs on a stand-alone basis, and therefore there was a significant degree of judgement in arriving at profits from their respective services to SMEs, or the capital attributable to such activities. Some banks also queried whether it was possible to compare their performance in the reference activity with other banks. As appropriate, we refer to the banks' comments on particular points of our methodology in this chapter.

Capital—whole-bank issues for the largest six UK banking groups

7.4. We first identify the capital base for the banks at the whole-bank level to serve as a basis for attributing capital to the SME banking business. However, some items attributable to the whole bank's capital base have no connection with SME activities, and therefore such items will have a zero allocation to the SME banking business.

7.5. We noted in Chapter 5 that banks generally (including those providing services to SMEs) are highly geared with only a small proportion of shareholders' capital compared with total assets. Moreover, most of their balance sheets consist of financial assets and liabilities with differing lengths of time to maturity or settlement. The banks also pool deposits from customers for use in a range of activities, including lending and investment. The banks also have considerable central costs that support a number of income-generating activities, which some said resulted in economies of scope that would not have arisen if the various activities had been undertaken by separate independent businesses. Chapter 5 also showed that the banks have an overall capital base (shareholders' funds) that is retained in the business to support all their respective activities, and which must meet FSA capital adequacy requirements.

7.6. Finally, we noted that over the 1990s, some banks providing services to SMEs bought back their shares from the market because they considered they had capital above their requirements at the time, for example:

---

[1] We use the terms 'smaller' and 'larger' banks in this chapter by reference to their presence in the SME market in the UK, rather than to their absolute size.

(a) Barclays spent £2.3 billion in the five-year period to 1999 in repurchasing shares, which left it with shareholders' funds of around £9 billion at the end of the 1999 financial year (see Table 5.9); and

(b) NatWest spent £1.4 billion over the same period that left it with shareholders' funds of some £9 billion at the end of the 1999 financial year (see Table 5.55).

Barclays said that the consequence of its active share buy-back programme was that the bank did not believe that it currently had capital above its requirements.

7.7. Capital for our purpose means equity capital (shareholders' funds) as reported in the published financial statements, and where appropriate, this included preference capital.[1] As a separate matter, we have computed capital so as to exclude intangible assets, including, for example, goodwill capitalized on acquisitions. This accords with the FSA's definition of Tier 1 capital for regulatory purposes. However, the banks suggested that a number of adjustments to this measure of equity capital were necessary as follows:

(a) Goodwill on acquisitions[2] should be recognized as an asset and added to shareholders' funds: prior to 1998 two different treatments were allowed in annual financial statements for the acquisition of goodwill: one method allowed companies to write off goodwill on acquisitions to reserves, while method two allowed such goodwill to be capitalized as an asset in the balance sheet and amortized over a period of years. For accounting periods ending on or after 23 December 1998, companies have been required by UK GAAP to capitalize goodwill on acquisitions, subject to (i) impairment tests, and (ii) amortization where indicated by the nature of the assets.[3] We noted that prior to 1998, some of the largest banks made significant acquisitions, and the goodwill was written off to reserves. Barclays said that the CC should standardize its treatment of goodwill. For the purposes of our initial discussions with the banks, we deducted goodwill capitalized on acquisitions from shareholders' equity. This was because the goodwill could have represented the present value of excess profits to be earned in the future. Barclays considered that an attempt should be made to say how much of the goodwill arose from this factor, but made no proposal on the matter. RBSG on this point added that even if there was a possible risk that some goodwill might reflect excess profits from SME activities, goodwill should not be entirely excluded. In some cases goodwill arose from the acquisition of businesses that were not connected with the supply of reference services. We also noted that for the FSA's regulatory purposes goodwill acquired is disregarded when determining capital to comply with the capital adequacy targets.[4]

---

[1]We noted for 1999 that BoS and NatWest had preference shares in issue. Lloyds TSB and Barclays had no preference shares in issue. HSBC had some 70 million non-cumulative preference shares of US$0.01 each in issue, which was a small proportion of its total issued share capital. RBS had preference shares amounting to £1,350 million (£1 million nominal and £1,349 million of related share premium) in issue in 1999, but with the acquisition of NatWest in 2000 it issued further preference shares. Barclays noted that it had a small amount of preference capital issued by its main subsidiary (Barclays Bank PLC) but as we used the relevant capital figure from its consolidated accounts that incorporated this item, no further action was required.

[2]Transactions that meet the merger accounting rules under FRS 6 give rise to no goodwill.

[3]Paragraph 15 of FRS 10 says: 'Where goodwill and intangible assets are regarded as having limited useful economic lives, they should be amortised on a systematic basis over those years.' Paragraph 17 says: 'Where goodwill and intangible assets are regarded as having indefinite useful economic lives, they should not be amortised but should be subject to periodic impairment tests.' Paragraph 19 says: 'There is a rebuttable presumption that the useful economic lives of purchased goodwill and intangible assets are limited to periods of 20 years or less. This presumption may be rebutted and a useful economic life regarded as a longer period or indefinite only if (a) the durability of the acquired business or intangible asset can be demonstrated and justifies estimating the useful economic life to exceed 20 years; and (b) the goodwill or intangible asset is capable of continued measurement (so that annual impairment reviews will be feasible).' Paragraph 33 says: 'The useful economic lives of goodwill and intangible assets should be reviewed at the end of each reporting period and revised if necessary. If a useful economic life is revised, the carrying value of the goodwill or intangible asset at the date of revision should be amortised over the revised remaining useful economic life. If the effect of the revision is to increase the useful economic life to more than 20 years from the date of acquisition, the additional requirements of the FRS that apply to the goodwill and intangible assets that are amortised over periods more than 20 years or are not amortised become applicable.' Paragraph 37 says: 'Goodwill and intangible assets that are amortised over a period exceeding 20 years from the date of acquisition, or are not amortised, should be reviewed for impairment at the end of each reporting period.'

[4]Lloyds TSB suggested that the FSA's practice of disregarding goodwill was irrelevant to our purposes. It said that the FSA's objective was to look for a measure of capital which was apt to ensure that the bank could, if necessary, realize assets to repay depositors. Goodwill was disregarded because it was illiquid/unrealizable in the context of a bank's failure. Barclays expressed similar views. HSBC said that goodwill was disregarded for FSA purposes because it was recognized that such an asset was not available to support any losses of investors. But it added that goodwill was included in the calculation of capital invested in a business because the goodwill represented paid-for investments, on which it was appropriate to earn a return.

442

(b) Accrued dividends should be added to the capital base. This was because, although shown as a liability in the accounts, they should not be treated as a real liability at the year end as they still required both board and shareholder approval before becoming a liability. By the time the dividend would be paid in the next year, further profits, approximately equal to the dividends accrued, would be expected to have been earned.[1]

(c) Pension surpluses should form part of shareholders' equity: one bank, with a large pension surplus, was not making pension contributions, and was in fact recording the benefit each year as it recognized the effect of the surplus. It therefore suggested that instead of disregarding such a credit to income in assessing its performance, we should impute an amount of capital equivalent to the surplus from which this credit was derived. The bank included this adjustment to capital as if it were an asset on the balance sheet based on the actuarial value of the surplus. As an alternative, another bank suggested that for those banks which were not making pension payments we should impute a pension charge to the profit and loss account of the SME banking business, as if there were no pension fund surplus, and not therefore adjust the capital base.

(d) Intangibles, such as the cost or economic value of training, acquired expertise, customer databases, brands, reputation etc, should be included in the asset base.

(e) Properties should be revalued to replacement cost, in so far as not already so valued in the financial statements.

(f) Provisions made in prior years against emerging market debts, now assessed not to be necessary, should be treated as released although such release was not reflected in the bank's accounts.

(g) Various provisions, made in the ordinary course of business and accepted as necessary, including bad debt provisions, should be added back to equity capital, because investment analysts made such adjustments in considering the value of companies. However, the bank that proposed this later withdrew the suggestion.

7.8. In the paragraphs below, we discuss the adjustments proposed by the six largest clearing groups to their equity capital. We also noted that returns preferably should be based on the average of opening and closing equity capital, rather than on the closing figure, unless there was no great difference between these two figures. Some banks moreover suggested that monthly figures should be averaged over a year for greater accuracy.

Barclays

7.9. Table 7.1 shows the shareholders' funds for Barclays in respect of the financial periods ended in the years 1998 to 2000 with various adjustments. We proposed the removal of capitalized goodwill to derive a baseline capital figure. We also show additional adjustments either as proposed by Barclays or suggested by other banks, such as an add-back for accrued dividends, and inclusion of a value for intangibles. As explained in paragraph 7.3, our conclusions on each of these possible adjustments to the baseline capital are contained in Chapter 2.

---

[1]HSBC commented that the view that dividends should not be treated as a real liability was contentious. It said that although not constituting a liability under FRS 12, provision was made for dividends in accounts, and they should therefore be treated as a liability.

TABLE 7.1 **Barclays: adjustments to shareholders' funds, 1998 to 2000**

£ billion

	1998	1999	2000
Shareholders' funds as per statutory accounts	8.2	8.8	14.8
Removal of capitalized goodwill*	−0.2	−0.2	−4.3
Baseline capital	8.0	8.6	10.5
Adjustments proposed by Barclays:			
Accrued dividends	(✄)		(✄)
Value of intangibles†	‡		‡
Property revaluation	‡	✄ §	‡
Pension fund surplus	‡		‡
Revised figure for capital	†		†

Source: CC based on information from Barclays.

---

*This removes the capitalized goodwill shown on Barclays' balance sheet.

†To be determined, based on comments in paragraphs below. Barclays suggested that the SME portion would be £[✄] billion for 1999.

‡Not provided, but see paragraphs below.

§Barclays suggested that the SME portion would be £[✄] million for 1999.

7.10. Barclays said that intangible assets had a considerable value, and that we should recognize the value of brand image, systems, training and expertise, which were not at present included in arriving at shareholders' equity. It acknowledged the difficulties of estimating the value of intangible assets owned by the banks, and said that we should instead compare banks' profitability with that of other organizations, particularly those that had considerable intangible assets. Initially, it did not propose a value for the intangible adjustment since it did not believe there was an accurate methodology for reflecting the value of intangible assets and would introduce too many areas into our analysis. It suggested that, if we compared its average return for its SME banking business over 11 years with those of various business indices, such as the FTSE 100 or a selection of UK companies with strong brands (which included Boots, British Telecom, Cadbury Schweppes, Marks & Spencer, Sainsbury, Tesco and Vodafone), we would find that its return was below that of these companies. Although Barclays continues to hold this view, at a later stage it provided a figure of between £[✄] billion and £[✄] billion for the intangible assets of its SME banking business, based on the estimates of a third party. Barclays suggested that, in the absence of comparisons with other companies, the CC should include this figure as an appropriate valuation for its intangible assets arising from services to SMEs. However, it added that in July 1999, an external party attributed a brand value of £[✄] billion to the Barclays Group. Barclays believed it was possible to allocate this sum in a number of ways to the SME banking business, for example by reference to capital allocated to different businesses, or according to revenue, based on the assumption that the value derives from the willingness of customers to use the bank.

7.11. It also indicated that the value of its pension fund surplus should be added to capital, if the notional cost of the pension was not included as a cost for determining its profits from services to SMEs.

7.12. Barclays argued that costs could be incurred for a future benefit although being treated as revenue. However, it did not identify such costs or seek to quantify them because it did not believe this was the right approach to valuing intangibles. Barclays said that brands were or could be valued other than by reference to the value of the company, and accordingly that brands theoretically had an includable value. Barclays stated that the practical difficulties were such as to make it difficult for brand values to be included as assets for the purpose of the CC, and suggested instead that profitability should be assessed by comparison with appropriate other companies.

Lloyds TSB

7.13. Table 7.2 shows the shareholders' funds for Lloyds TSB in 1998 to 2000 with various adjustments. We proposed the removal of capitalized goodwill to derive a baseline capital figure. We also show additional adjustments either as proposed by Lloyds TSB or suggested by other banks, such as an add-back for accrued dividends, pension surplus, and other items. As explained in paragraph 7.3, our conclusions on each of these possible adjustments to the baseline capital is contained in Chapter 2.

TABLE 7.2 **Lloyds TSB: adjustments to shareholders' funds, 1998 to 2000**

£ billion

	1998	1999	2000
Shareholders' funds as per statutory accounts*	7.5	8.7	10.3
Removal of capitalized goodwill†	−0.2	−0.2	−2.6
Baseline capital	7.3	8.5	7.7

Adjustments proposed by the banks:
 Accrued dividends
 Property revaluations
 Emerging market debt surplus after tax
 Reinstatement of capitalized goodwill
  as removed above
 Goodwill on acquisitions arising from:
  TSB merger
  Lloyds Abbey Life acquisition
  Cheltenham & Gloucester acquisition
 Other acquisitions

Capitalized pension value arising from
 surplus

Revised figure for capital proposed by
Lloyds TSB

*Figures omitted.
See note
on page iv.*

Source: CC based on information from Lloyds TSB.

*Lloyds TSB told us near the end of the inquiry that the figures for the years 1998 to 2000 should be amended to £[✂] billion, £[✂] billion and £[✂] billion respectively because of recent restatements in its accounts. We did not amend our figures for baseline capital because the impact of this change on the amounts allocated to the SME banking business would have been minor.

†This removes the capitalized goodwill shown on Lloyds TSB's balance sheet.

7.14. Lloyds TSB noted two accounting policy changes for our consideration. The first, which was implemented in the 30 June 2000 interim accounts to accord with FRS 15, was to restate fixed assets to historical cost. This resulted in the carrying value of tangible fixed assets at 1 January 1999 being reduced by £112 million. The second, which was implemented in the 30 June 2001 accounts, was to change the accounting policy for debt securities issued by countries experiencing payment difficulties not collateralized by US Treasury Securities. This resulted in the carrying value of bonds being increased by £731 million and reserves, net of deferred tax, being increased by £286 million (as at 30 June 2001).

7.15. Lloyds TSB proposed the following adjustments to increase shareholders' funds to what it considered was a more appropriate level:

(a) Replacement cost adjustments. Lloyds TSB said that the book value of shareholders' funds for all years should be increased by £[✂] because the replacement cost of its property exceeded the book value, and was therefore a more accurate representation of its economic value.

(b) Regarding the emerging market debt adjustment, it said that the securities were held under its current accounting policy at an amount based on market value at the date of the original exchange, as adjusted for the amortization of the discount on acquisition. The adjustment of some £[✂] was to increase this amount to current market value.

(c) Goodwill adjustments. Lloyds TSB said that the book value of shareholders' equity in 1999 should be increased by £[✂] billion for goodwill on acquisitions/mergers that were not capitalized in its accounts, for example relating to the merger in 1995 with TSB. It calculated this adjustment as £[✂] billion for the TSB merger, £[✂] billion for the Abbey Life acquisition, £[✂] billion for the Cheltenham & Gloucester acquisition, and £ [✂] billion for other acquisitions. However, we noted that only the TSB merger had any aspect that included services to SMEs and therefore this was the only item where, if added to the whole bank's capital base, an allocation to the SME banking business might be appropriate. Lloyds said that in arguing that goodwill arising on certain acquisitions should be brought into account in the capital employed for the group, it was not seeking to argue that the whole or any part of those amounts related to the SME banking business: it said the purpose was to demonstrate that, in its view, Lloyds TSB

as a whole had not earned excessive returns on capital. Lloyds TSB suggested that its adjustments would bring the accounting into line with the current standard on goodwill.

(d) *An adjustment for the bank's pension surplus of £[✂] in 1999.* Lloyds TSB said that the pension surplus credit recorded in the profit and loss account was attributable to prudent funding policies and investment performance in earlier years, and was not attributable to current trading. Whilst a pension surplus credit is recorded in the profit and loss account of the Group, the actuarial surplus which gave rise to the profit and loss account entry is not recorded as part of the accounting capital base. A mismatch would therefore exist if unadjusted accounting returns were to be calculated as a proportion of such an unadjusted accounting base. To reflect this, Lloyds TSB proposed including the actuarial surplus as part of the capital base, at £[✂] in 1999. Alternatively if capital were not adjusted, it would be necessary to adjust the profit and loss account to disregard the pension surplus credit when considering returns as a proportion of capital. In addition, for comparability purposes between banks, a figure should be imputed for the forgone pension charge, which it estimated as £[✂] million for 1999 relating to the segment providing services to SMEs, as we noted in Chapter 6. Lloyds TSB said it would be incorrect to consider that if the bank had made smaller funding contributions in the past so that there was not a current surplus, past accounting profits would have been greater because the accounting profits were based on actuarial costs rather than cash contributions. Lloyds TSB suggested that its adjustment would bring the accounting into line with the current standard on pensions, and it expected to implement the standard in the near future. [

Details omitted. See note on page iv.

] It emphasized that no one could accurately ascertain for how long a pension surplus could arise because this would depend on equity market movements.

(e) *A proposed dividend adjustment.* Lloyds TSB said that equity should be increased by £[✂] for 1998, to remove the accrued final dividend of £[✂] from liabilities, and add it to shareholders' funds. It said that this was not a genuine liability at the year end as it would not have received both board and shareholder approval before the year-end date, although UK company law requires it to be treated as such in the statutory financial statements. It would become a true liability in the following year, being funded from the profits of that year. Lloyds TSB said that its proposed adjustment would bring the accounting into line with International Accounting Standards and US GAAP.

7.16. Lloyds TSB said that the baseline capital figure was not appropriate for use as a base to determine disaggregated capital of the SME banking business. It added that the baseline capital figure, which increased from £7.3 billion in 1998, to £8.5 billion in 1999, and then fell back in 2000 to £7.7 billion (or £8.0 billion upon restatement of Lloyds TSB's financial statements) also had a high degree of fluctuativity, which could produce amounts allocated to the SME banking business that also exhibited that fluctuativity. Lloyds TSB considered that such results would be inaccurate. It said that the reduction in the 2000 figure was after accounting for the Scottish Widows acquisition, where considerable goodwill arose from the purchase consideration exceeding the value of tangible assets acquired. Its preferred approach is discussed in paragraph 7.66ff.

7.17. Given the poor performance of TSB in making profits from the commercial banking market, as discussed in paragraph 5.137, we asked Lloyds TSB to explain why any goodwill imputed to the merger with TSB should be added to the capital needed to support its SME banking business's activities, or be considered when calculating returns on capital for the SME activities. Lloyds TSB said that the poor performance of TSB in the commercial banking market was irrelevant to the SME market as the primary customer base of the TSB Commercial Banking business was corporates which did not meet the CC's definition of an SME. In addition, Lloyds TSB said, when the goodwill on acquisition of TSB was considered, it appeared that some was attributable to SME activities. In particular Lloyds Bank plc had acquired the UDT asset finance business as part of the combination with TSB, and UDT was a successful business that justified goodwill being attributed to its activities. Moreover, the combination of Lloyds and TSB businesses created the opportunity to generate synergy savings, and part of the goodwill represented the capitalized value of the expected synergy savings. Because those synergy savings arose in upstream business units which provided services to the SME units (IT, branch network, central transmission services, etc), some part of the synergy savings should be allocated to the SME banking business.

7.18. Lloyds TSB added that it was also willing to pay a premium over the book value of TSB's assets to reflect the value of TSB's existing intangible assets. Lloyds TSB said that in the four years after the merger, it reduced total operating costs by £400 million a year. It therefore considered that much of the goodwill attributable to the merger represented the capitalized value of achieving future operating cost efficiencies. It suggested that in a competitive market, a firm which makes a risky capital investment in the hope of securing a competitive advantage (for example, reducing operating costs as a result of the acquisition) would expect to earn a return on this investment, ie to continue to charge prices that produced a return on this expenditure until competitors' costs fell to levels where they were able to catch up with efficiencies achieved by the firm concerned. When we asked Lloyds TSB to estimate how much of the £1.5 billion noted above for TSB goodwill should be included in the SME capital base, it did not consider it practicable to do so.

7.19. Lloyds TSB commented on the possible future benefit of revenue costs, and accepted the definition of intangible assets in International Accounting Standard 38.[1] Lloyds TSB said that what was often called goodwill might sometimes reflect more definable elements, although in other instances it might not, and urged us to consider individual acquisition transactions by the banks concerned that had given rise to the goodwill. Lloyds TSB accepted that, if individual elements giving rise to a brand value were included (for example, training costs of a superior workforce), the brand itself should be excluded so as to avoid double counting.

NatWest, RBS and RBSG

7.20. Table 7.3 shows shareholders' funds for NatWest in 1998 and 1999, and for RBS from 1998 to 2000, with various adjustments. We proposed the removal of capitalized goodwill to derive a baseline capital figure. We also show additional adjustments proposed by RBSG or suggested by other banks. As explained in paragraph 7.3, our conclusions on each of these possible adjustments to the baseline capital are contained in Chapter 2. RBS acquired NatWest in March 2000 and shareholders' equity for RBS in 2000 of £23.7 billion is for the enlarged group (including NatWest).

7.21. At the whole-bank level, RBSG said in its early submissions that the best estimate of its capital base was replacement cost (shareholders' funds plus intangibles) and that this was best approximated by the Group's market capitalization. Rather than taking shareholders' funds and making upward adjustments for the intangibles, RBSG favoured the use of market values directly, which it believed took account of all the relevant factors of the SME banking business, including the value of intangible assets not shown on the balance sheet. RBSG believed it was possible, using the proxy of market value, to estimate the capital base associated with certain parts of the Group that were separately identifiable and could be compared with other similar quoted companies. If there was a concern that the use of market values could give rise to circularity in that such values might reflect excess profits, it suggested that the CC could use an iterative approach. In the case of the SME banking business, RBSG accepted that this approach was not possible because the SME banking business was an integrated part of three divisions: Retail Banking, CBFM and Manufacturing; and also because of the lack of a separately quoted bank concentrating exclusively on SMEs.

7.22. RBSG referred to an academic paper (reproduced in Appendix 13.1—see also paragraph 13.129) which suggested that the use of accounting-based returns on shareholders' funds (or even returns based on 150 per cent of shareholders' funds) when used in conjunction with the economic measure of cost of equity would be tantamount to a predisposition that a substantial proportion of its profits were 'excess', which it did not accept. RBSG believed that shareholders' funds excluding intangibles, as reported in NatWest's balance sheet of £9.4 billion at the end of 1999, understated its capital base, as shareholders' funds did not take into account the following items:

(a) adjustment to allow for the impact of inflation;

---

[1] Paragraph 7 defines an intangible asset as 'an identifiable non-monetary asset without physical substance held for use in the production or supply of goods and services, for rental to others, or for administrative purposes'. An asset is further defined as a resource *(a)* controlled by an enterprise as a result of a past events; and *(b)* from which future economic benefits are expected to flow to the enterprise. Paragraph 19 says that and intangible asset should be recognized if, and only if, *(a)* it is probable that the future economic benefits that are attributable to the asset will flow to the enterprise; and *(b)* the cost of the asset can be measured reliably. An intangible asset should be measured at cost.

TABLE 7.3 RBSG: adjustments to shareholders' funds, 1998 to 2000

£ billion

	NatWest 1998	NatWest 1999	RBS 1998	RBS 1999	RBSG 2000*
Shareholders' funds as per statutory accounts†	8.6	9.4	3.0	4.3	23.7
Removal of capitalized goodwill‡	−0.6	−0.5	0.0	0.0	−12.1
Baseline capital	8.0	8.9	3.0	4.3	11.6
Adjustments proposed by the bank for value of intangibles:§					
Employee base					*
Capitalized software					*
Brands					*
Products					*
Reputation					*
Licences/infrastructure					*
Capitalized pension value arising from surplus	Figures omitted. See note on page iv.		Figures omitted. See note on page iv.		*
Value of intangibles					(✄)
Revised figure for capital proposed by NatWest/RBS before addition of a value for the customer base					(✄)
Value of customer base for the SME business§					¶

Source: NatWest, RBS, RBSG.

---

*These are the consolidated RBSG figures as shown in the published RBSG annual report as at 31 December 2000.
†NatWest figure includes some £480 million preference shares for both 1998 and 1999, which were part of its Tier 1 capital base. In 1998 and 1999, RBS had preference shares of £1 million in issue, which were part of its Tier 1 capital base. For 2000, RBSG issued further preference shares at a premium.
‡This removes the capitalized goodwill shown on the balance sheets.
§RBSG provided a figure for its estimate of value of the customer base only for the SME banking business, rather than for the whole bank.
¶Not provided.

(b) internally generated goodwill;

(c) goodwill purchased in the past but written off; and

(d) other intangibles such as brands and intellectual property.

7.23. RBSG said that if the items above were incorporated in the balance sheet for most UK banks and reflected in shareholders' funds, the value of the capital would be increased by a factor of up to 3 and correspond with market value. On a conservative basis, to take account of the above factors, it considered that RBSG's capital should be around twice shareholders' funds assuming that its shareholders' funds included capitalized goodwill from the acquisition of NatWest. This capital could then be allocated to the constituent businesses, including the SME banking business, by reference to RWAs using Basle 1 or Basle 2 principles. As discussed further below, RBSG near the end of the inquiry expressed a preference for the use of Basle 2 principles.

7.24. RBSG initially said that if book value was be used as an alternative to use of market values in deriving whole-bank capital, then shareholders' funds for 1999 should be increased by the following three adjustments:

(a) The value of the employee base: it initially estimated this by reference to the cost to recruit and train employees at between £[✄] billion and £[✄] billion for the whole bank for 1999. Later RBSG submitted calculations for employee acquisition costs totalling £[✄] billion for NatWest and RBS combined ([✄] per cent of equity).

(b) The costs to acquire the customer base: it initially estimated this between £[✄] billion and £[✄] billion for NatWest as a whole, and between £[✄] million and £[✄] million for NatWest's

SME segment, as shown in Table 7.4. The costs included advertising and promotion costs, cost of staff associated in setting up new accounts, performing credit checks, etc. It later supplied us with point estimates for the SME segment of the Group (ie NatWest, RBS and Ulster Bank), along with some analysis into cost components for RBSG, as shown in Table 7.5, totalling £[✂] million.

(c) The replacement cost of technology assets not included in the accounts: it initially estimated this between £[✂] and £[✂] billion for the whole bank. At a later stage of the inquiry, RBSG confirmed this range and also gave a point estimate of £[✂] million. By way of substantiation of this amount, a second report by consultants for RBSG stated that, inter alia, NatWest's spend on software development activities was £[✂] million in 1999 which was seen as necessary to maintain the value of this intangible asset, and which RBSG capitalized under US GAAP.

RBSG told us that it believed the intangible assets in each of (a), (b) and (c) would in effect have indefinite lives because they did not need any amortization, and on a replacement basis these assets do not depreciate. In a steady state, it considered, for example, that 'depreciation' (marked by loss of customers) would be made good by investments to acquire new customers, leaving a like-for-like customer base with the same value.

TABLE 7.4 **RBSG: initial submission of NatWest's SME customer acquisition costs, 1999***

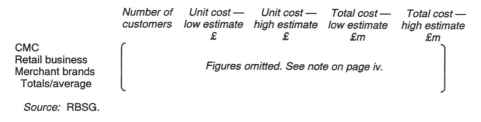

	Number of customers	Unit cost — low estimate £	Unit cost — high estimate £	Total cost — low estimate £m	Total cost — high estimate £m
CMC					
Retail business					
Merchant brands		Figures omitted. See note on page iv.			
Totals/average					

Source: RBSG.

*Sent to the CC in April 2001.

TABLE 7.5 **RBSG: second submission of RBSG's SME customer acquisition costs, 1999***

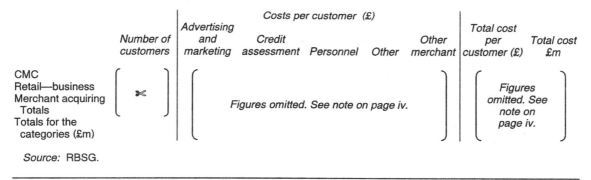

	Number of customers	Advertising and marketing	Credit assessment	Personnel	Other	Other merchant	Total cost per customer (£)	Total cost £m
		Costs per customer (£)						
CMC								
Retail—business	✂						Figures omitted. See note on page iv.	
Merchant acquiring		Figures omitted. See note on page iv.						
Totals								
Totals for the categories (£m)								

Source: RBSG.

*Includes estimates for NatWest, RBS and Ulster Bank. Sent to the CC in July 2001.

7.25. At a later stage, in addition to the three categories noted in paragraph 7.24, RBSG also suggested that the value of capitalized pension surpluses should be included in the calculation of equity and similarly added to the shareholders' funds at the whole-bank level. This adjustment totalled £1,410 million in 1999.

7.26. In relation to the estimated employee acquisition costs provided by RBSG it was noted that some of the component costs included within the 1999 total figure were:

(a) £[✂] million for maternity leave and career breaks;

(b) £[✂] million for the acquisition of temporary staff;

(c) an uplift of [✂] per cent to reflect a disproportionate number of staff members in 1999 compared with other years;

449

(d) costs that appear to be in the nature of on-the-job training and supervision;

(e) costs for additional time required by staff—both supervisors and colleagues—consequent upon the arrival of new employees; and

(f) relocation costs for staff who earn less than £15,000 a year.

7.27. RBSG engaged consultants to help them quantify the values to enable it to provide estimates for the above adjustments. In attempting to make the estimates of replacement cost, the consultants' report noted that RBSG's management information systems were not configured to provide readily available information for this purpose. This was because the SME banking business as defined was run as an integrated part of three separate divisions, and so the consultants employed the following steps:

(a) They defined the costs and activities for staff, customers and the IT systems for which a replacement cost was needed.

(b) They held meetings to enable the bank's divisional management to use the definitions to produce consistent replacement cost estimates. The bank staff suggested a range of estimates, referred to as high and low.

(c) Then they collated the estimates and checked that they were reasonable by comparing the results between divisions with overlapping product mixes, for example the mainland bank and Ulster Bank.

7.28. The method employed was described by the consultants in their final report as a piecemeal approach which entailed assessing the piecemeal costs associated with recruiting the bank's staff, gaining the customer base and purchasing and developing the bank's IT systems. It was viewed as the more conservative approach and was believed to reflect more closely the way in which these intangible assets were developed over time. The alternative approach was to assess the start-up costs of building the bank from scratch which would involve paying a premium to recruit staff and to gain market share. It was acknowledged that a complete replacement of all these intangibles, or replacement to the scale of the bank, would not be necessary for a competitor bank to conduct business in the SME market segment. RBSG stated that its higher costs reflected its full-service, national offer for all types of business customers. We questioned RBSG on its methodology and the following points emerged:

— RBSG included credit-scoring costs, which the customers had already paid for, in the cost of the assets on which it proposed that we should allow a return. It said it believed it to be appropriate to consider all expenditures, whether apparently reimbursed by customers or not, as costs incurred in the acquisition of those customers. Similarly, any income, even if charged on the basis of reimbursement of costs, should be regarded as income, not as a reduction in the acquisition cost.

— RBSG first suggested that its intangible assets should be valued on a 'new for old' basis, rather than on the basis of depreciated replacement costs. In terms of technology assets, it suggested that replacement costs were going down so that 'new' is less than old. It added that the amount of money that its shareholders had invested and the assets that were being used at the end of 1999 were higher than the replacement cost because advances in technology were bringing costs down—in other words RBS put forward the proposition that its shareholders should not only earn a return on the new replacement value, but should be entitled to a return on what they actually paid at an earlier date, and that that was an even higher figure because in relation to technology the new value was falling. It later clarified that these valuations were based on the costs of recreating the then current state of operational capacity of RBSG, ie they were on a like-for-like basis, not new for old.

— RBSG produced information on, for example, customer acquisition costs for NatWest (that included SMEs and other categories) of some £[✂] million for 1999, but later it provided a point estimate of £[✂] million for the SME banking business of NatWest. RBS and Ulster Bank were estimated to have a customer base valued at £[✂] million and £[✂] million respectively for the SME banking business in 1999.

450

— RBSG estimated staff acquisition costs as an intangible asset. These costs were not directly determined from individual cost components—rather RBSG assessed average cost percentages and multiplied the result by numbers of people in salary bands. This produced results that it acknowledged could be higher than benchmarks derived from studies carried out by the Chartered Institute of Personnel. In particular, NatWest's staff recruitment costs (expressed as a high and a low figure) were [✂] per cent and [✂] per cent respectively of salary for all grades of staff, of all types, in all divisions. RBSG, however, considered that the surveys it had used to prepare its figures should be helpful in supporting its position.

7.29. In addition to the adjustments to shareholders' funds noted in paragraph 7.24, RBSG suggested that allowance should be made to whole-bank equity for the following intangible assets shown in Table 7.6. For example, a basis of calculation was provided for computing the replacement valuation of NatWest's brand in a letter to RBSG from M&C Saatchi, [

Details omitted. See note on page iv.

].

TABLE 7.6 **RBSG: assessment of additional whole-bank intangible assets to be included in the determination of equity, 1999**

£ million

	NatWest	RBS	Ulster Bank	Total RBSG
Brand				
Reputation				
Licence	*Figures omitted. See*			
Product	*note on page iv.*			
Infrastructure				
Total				

Source: RBSG.

7.30. Table 7.7 summarizes the effect on equity for the SME banking business of RBSG as a result of the inclusion of the above adjustments by RBSG.

TABLE 7.7 **RBSG: effect on SME equity of adjustments to include intangibles and capitalized pension surpluses, 1999**

£ million

	NatWest	RBS	Ulster Bank	Total
Customer base				
Replacement costs*	*Figures omitted. See*			
Pension fund surplus	*note on page iv.*			
Total				

Source: RBSG.

*Includes replacement costs for employee base, brands, licences, reputation, products, IT software and infrastructure.

7.31. RBSG suggested a third possible approach, which values capital as if it were calculated based on regulatory capital requirements of a stand-alone business whose services were exclusive to SMEs. RBSG told us that in this situation, the level of capital required to support a business would be based upon the underlying risk of loss to that business, and that the regulatory requirements to hold capital, when assessed by the FSA, would be significantly higher than any value calculated as a pro rata of its group capital. Based on recommendations by external consultants, RBSG said it considered that the smaller end of the SME market was up to twice as risky as normal activities for which risk capital target figures were set by the FSA. Therefore capital of twice the value of regulatory capital should be held for this segment. Based on estimates provided by RBSG, this would equate to between £[✂] and £[✂] billion for NatWest for the year ended 1999. This estimate, however, was not based on a model or methodology and assumed that the SME banking business would be a stand-alone business, and a new entrant, on which the FSA would impose a higher target capital ratio than the Basle 1 minimum. RBS/NatWest noted that it was impossible to be precise about what level of regulatory capital should be assigned to a portfolio of SME loans. However, it believed the SME banking business should require double the amount of capital that would arise from normal risk-asset regulations for the whole bank. It later added that the Basle 2 proposals supported its view that lending to SMEs needed more capital, although the delay in the implementation of the proposals demonstrated that precise quantification was difficult.

7.32. In response to our suggestions on the approach to value capital, RBSG sought to refer us to US authorities, primarily the debate in the USA about the use of 'fair value', as a basis for asset valuation. Fair value is defined by the US Financial Accounting Steering Board (FASB) in terms of the amount at which an asset can be bought in current transactions between willing parties. RBSG said that measuring an asset at fair value would not normally involve the recognition of all the future gains that a reporting entity would expect to generate by using the asset. Only those gains that a hypothetical business purchasing the asset in the market would be able to generate would be reflected in its fair value. As a result any special gains that the reporting entity could generate from the asset (for instance, by the use of its peculiar expertise or reputation that a third party purchasing the asset could not achieve) would be included in future earnings statements. By contrast, if assets were measured at their 'value in use', such gains would be recognized immediately. This was an argument for the use of fair value that had been put forward by the FASB on a number of occasions. RBSG said that while the use of fair value might be considered less objectionable than value in use, it was inconsistent with the deprival value model, which normally required assets to be measured at replacement cost, ie as an entry cost. It would therefore be appropriate to view fair value as such an entry cost if the asset involved could be replaced at that amount. However, for the type of intangible asset being considered (which it viewed as being irreplaceable) fair value could only be an exit price for the reporting entity (ie net realizable value).

7.33. RBS also suggested that investment analysts made adjustments to equity as contained in company accounts, inter alia by adding back provisions made in the ordinary course of business (such as bad debt provision), and that such adjustments would add [✂] per cent to NatWest's whole-bank equity capital. It added that this adjustment should reflect all the reserves that might have been created on the balance sheet through time, and reserves against any anticipated expenses that are common and usual for the business to grow with the business activities. It believed that these reserves/provisions should be considered part of the equity base and that this was accepted financial analysis. In the case of NatWest for 1999, the provision against loans and advances was around £[✂] billion. It later withdrew this suggestion.

HSBC

7.34. Table 7.8 shows the shareholders' funds for HSBC in 1998 to 2000 with various proposed adjustments. We proposed the removal of capitalized goodwill to derive a baseline capital figure. We also show additional adjustments either as proposed by HSBC or suggested by other banks, such as an add-back for accrued dividends, and inclusion of a value for intangibles, each of which we discuss in the following paragraphs. As explained in paragraph 7.3, our conclusions on each of these possible adjustments to the baseline capital are contained in Chapter 2.

7.35. HSBC said that shareholders' funds were understated and should be adjusted to include goodwill written off, and unrecorded intangible investments. It noted that unrecorded intangible investments arose because investments in internal growth, relating to marketing and other customer acquisition costs, cost of free banking, training, brand, reputation, and product/system developments had been expensed rather than capitalized. It said that in its view, equity markets attributed a value to intangible investments, and that this explained a significant part of the difference between the market value and the book value of shareholders' equity. It said that the average market to book equity ratios for UK banks was 301 per cent between 1995 and 1999, which compared to 341 per cent for the FTSE 100 Index. HSBC also said that this compared with 223 per cent and 222 per cent for the ten largest US and Continental European banks respectively.

TABLE 7.8 **HSBC: adjustments to shareholders' funds, 1998 to 2000**

£ billion

	1998	1999	2000	2000 restated*
Shareholders' funds as per statutory accounts†	4.8	4.9	15.4	
Removal of capitalized goodwill‡	0.0	−0.1	−8.2	✄
Baseline capital	4.8	4.8	7.2	
Adjustments proposed by the banks:				
Value of intangibles§	*Figures omitted.*			
Revised figure for capital	*See note on page iv.*			

Source: HSBC.

---

*HSBC restated its 2000 figures to exclude the effect of principal overseas acquisitions. It considered that its own calculations were more appropriate and should be used by the CC. The calculations show average shareholders' funds for the year, excluding the effect of foreign acquisitions. It noted that the alternative figures would affect the risk-weighted proportion of assets which we discuss later in this chapter in deriving a capital figure attributable to the SME banking business—see also Tables 7.12 and 7.13.

†2000 reflects the increase in average shareholders' funds attributable to new share capital subscribed in respect of subsidiary acquisitions during the year amounting to £9.0 billion.

‡This removes the capitalized goodwill shown on the balance sheets.

§Discussed in the following paragraphs. This is essentially estimated development expenditure, multiplied by [✄] years (assuming this is the average useful life), times one-half to arrive at a depreciated replacement cost. HSBC said that its estimate of development costs/intangibles represented approximately [✄] per cent of total operating costs. HSBC assumed that its intangibles in 2000 were at the same level as in 1999.

7.36. We put a number of arguments to HSBC regarding intangibles and their relevance to assessing returns, which we cover in the following paragraphs. It emphasized that development costs that it had treated as operating expenses should be recognized as assets from an economic/commercial standpoint, and therefore included in capital. It added that its investment in training, marketing, brand, reputation, free banking, products and systems were assets attributable to shareholders. It did not believe that the omission of such assets from its accounts undermined the need to make an adjustment to add a value for intangibles to shareholders' funds for the purposes of assessing returns. It said that in order to show a true and fair view, financial accounts were prepared in accordance with UK GAAP, which precluded the recognition of such amounts if, for example, the related benefits were not reasonably certain. It believed this presentation would not always be consistent with financial accounts prepared from a commercial/economic viewpoint, which it considered would give rise to the recognition of such assets. HSBC believed that, after such adjustments had been made to equity, it would be seen as having made no excess profits, and if there was a gap between its adjusted returns on this basis and its cost of capital, this could be explained by its competitive advantage relative to the UK bank sector, and the timing of the economic cycle. It considered that other industry sectors had returns on equity above the cost of equity, which it said could most obviously be explained by the existence of intangibles.

7.37. HSBC illustrated its argument by using information from 1999. It said that its overall bank operating income was £4.5 billion, operating expenses were £2.5 billion (including depreciation of £316 million), pre-tax profits were £1.72 billion and average shareholders' funds were £5.0 billion. On this basis, it calculated its return on equity at around 35 per cent. It then suggested, for example, that capitalizing [✄] per cent of the current operating expenses, assuming an average economic life of [✄] years, would reduce pre-tax return on equity from 35 per cent to around [✄] per cent.[1] Table 7.9 shows the results of HSBC's calculations of the effect on returns on equity for a number of alternative scenarios where a proportion of operating costs are capitalized and amortized over a number of years.

---

[1]Based on 1999 data, HSBC explained this calculation for year [✄] (assuming that [✄] per cent of operating costs at £[✄] million a year are capitalized and amortized over [✄] years) as follows:
— Operating income remains unchanged at £4.5 billion.
— Operating expenses fall from £[✄] billion to £[✄] billion, being the [✄] per cent capitalized costs.
— Depreciation increases from £[✄] million to £[✄] million, being the effect of amortizing seven years' capitalized costs under this new methodology, ie capitalized operating costs at £[✄] million a year, for [✄] years, divided by [✄].
— The effect on reported operating profits is unchanged at £[✄] billion, ie the depreciation increase offsets the operating costs reduction.
HSBC then said that the effect on shareholders' funds at £[✄] billion would be an increase of £[✄] billion (being the cumulative effect of capitalized costs after amortization) to £[✄] billion. Hence the original return of around [✄] per cent ([✄]) would fall to around [✄] per cent ([✄]).

TABLE 7.9 **HSBC: illustrations of various scenarios showing the percentage point change in returns on equity from the following scenarios**

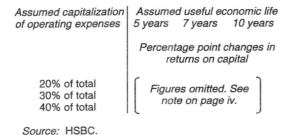

Assumed capitalization of operating expenses	Assumed useful economic life 5 years 7 years 10 years
	Percentage point changes in returns on capital
20% of total 30% of total 40% of total	*Figures omitted. See note on page iv.*

Source: HSBC.

7.38. HSBC believed that the value of intangible assets for economic purposes (ie to include in its capital base even though not shown as an asset in the financial statements prepared under UK GAAP,[1] because these items are expensed rather than capitalized) could be derived from a review of its expenditure levels for training, marketing, sales development and cost of 'free' business banking, customer acquisition costs, special offers, and product and system developments. It told us that such expenditure for the whole UK bank was between £[✂] million and £[✂] million a year in the three years to 1999, as summarized in Table 7.10. It compared these totals with the average annual operating costs of £2.3 billion over this period. It therefore suggested that its development costs were some [✂] per cent of its total operating costs in recent years. It believed that a large part of the development costs gave rise to internally generated intangible assets and goodwill, in particular in its brand value and reputation, which ought to be viewed as having a long life. On this basis, HSBC therefore believed that it was acceptable to assume a life of [✂] years for its expenditure on development costs, which it believed would reduce its observed returns if such costs were capitalized and amortized, and produced the results noted in paragraph 7.37. Notwithstanding this approach, it still attributed useful lives to each type of expenditure.

TABLE 7.10 **HSBC: summary of HSBC's estimates for whole-bank development expenditure between 1997 and 1999, and the estimate expenditure for 1999 relating to the SME banking business**

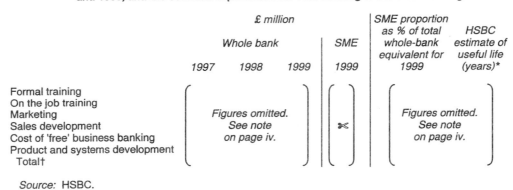

	£ million Whole bank 1997 1998 1999	SME 1999	SME proportion as % of total whole-bank equivalent for 1999	HSBC estimate of useful life (years)*
Formal training On the job training Marketing Sales development Cost of 'free' business banking Product and systems development Total†	*Figures omitted. See note on page iv.*	[✂]	*Figures omitted. See note on page iv.*	

Source: HSBC.

*See paragraph 7.39 for HSBC's explanation regarding these lives.
†HSBC said that this represented approximately [✂] per cent of its total UK operating expenditure in each year.

7.39. HSBC explained its estimates of useful lives as follows:

(a) *Training:* The average remaining service life of individuals in the bank's defined benefit scheme was over [✂] years and therefore HSBC assumed that the training took place on average halfway through this period.

(b) *Marketing:* HSBC said that its advertising to SMEs was an important part of its overall strategy to establish the HSBC brand. It felt the useful life of the expenditure was [✂] years, and needed to be replenished/stimulated on a regular basis to continually raise and improve awareness.

---

[1]HSBC said that the conditions to be met before an asset could be recognized for accounting purposes were more onerous than would be required in a commercial/economic context, and this was particularly significant in relation to quantifying the benefits associated with such expenditure, which in reality meant that it might not be possible for it to demonstrate with reasonable certainty the benefits that could arise. Hence the expenditure could not be capitalized under UK GAAP.

HSBC considered that its estimate was consistent with the average duration of a current account of [✂] years. It also said that its products/services delivered to the SME market tended to have enduring features and it therefore anticipated that a minimum [✂] years' product life cycle was sustainable. It also considered that its marketing spend to the personal sector had benefits in the SME market by attracting new customers. HSBC said, however, that it could not quantify with sufficient certainty the extent of related benefits and therefore such expenditures could not be capitalized under UK GAAP.

(c) *Sales development and free banking:* Based on the average length of current account relationships of [✂] years.

(d) *Systems development:* HSBC said that its experience of asset useful life was [✂] years. It gave examples of its online risk management system introduced in 1992 and still in use; the system administering branch cheque returns introduced in 1994 and still in use; and its mainframe computer system introduced in the early 1970s and only replaced in the last two years.

7.40. HSBC believed that it incurred a significant investment in staff training which in its view had benefits to the bank as follows:

(a) a significant proportion of HSBC's training created non-transferable skills which would be of little value in outside employment;

(b) there was a strong mutual commitment between the bank investing in training staff to have transferable skills and them being loyal and productive; and

(c) training increased the productivity of employees without significant loss of staff or higher staff costs.

7.41. HSBC contended that, although its investment in personnel training was not a permanent benefit because staff could leave of their own volition, employee goodwill in practice was a reality in terms of the value of worker expertise and loyalty. The cost of this to the bank was stated by HSBC to be [✂] per cent of operating costs, directed at informal on-the-job training. HSBC also said that the corollary that training was not an asset was that HSBC would not have an incentive to invest in training if training did not create future economic benefits. It added that there was also literature on management, economics, and accounting, to suggest that staff training could represent an asset for a business. It said that the UK Government's 2000 Pre-Budget Report proposals on tax relief for companies investing in, or acquiring, intangible assets was recognition that employee goodwill was an intangible asset. HSBC, however, said that recognizing the amounts as assets under UK GAAP was difficult.

7.42. In response to our questions regarding its brand and reputation, HSBC considered that this had significant value, because the service proposition could not be readily observed at the point of sale of banking services. Customers placed a value on the service proposition. In this context, brand and reputation was a signal of service proposition and represented the value of HSBC's customer base to the bank. It did not, however, consider that this brand and reputation issue was a barrier to entry as other entities could enter the market with this feature—ie brand and reputation could be easily transferred from other businesses. Its view was that there were many other businesses (banking and non-banking) with an appropriate brand and reputation to enable them to enter the banking services market. It added that its brand and reputation differentiated it from competitors, provided competitive advantage and required continuous investment to prevent loss of market share. HSBC emphasized that it had fought long and hard to win its reputation and establish its brand, which involved significant ongoing investment in product, marketing, promotion and customer relationships.

7.43. HSBC did not see it as relevant that intangible assets were not included for the purpose of computing regulatory capital. It considered that the purpose of regulatory capital was to provide security for depositors and other creditors against bad debts and other losses incurred by the bank. Accordingly the bank must hold an appropriate level of readily realizable assets. Intangible assets did not fulfil this role, as their value could not be realized without disposing of the business. HSBC therefore considered that regulatory treatment of intangible assets was irrelevant to the calculation of economic profits and returns.

7.44. HSBC also regarded it as irrelevant that intangibles were not treated as meaningful security when lending decisions were made. It stated that staff training and other intangible assets typically did not represent lending security, as the value could not be readily realized without disposing of the business. There were exceptions: lending with a floating charge, which represented security over both recognized and unrecognized assets of the business; lending conditional on key man insurance, which represented security over elements of the human capital of the business; and unsecured lending, which also represented lending against the intangible assets of a business. However, HSBC did not consider that this issue was relevant to the determination of HSBC's intangible assets.

7.45. It added that although typically intangible assets were not used as security for lending, teams of skilled staff might be recognizable as an asset because of the expectation of future economic returns from their efforts. However, in the absence of a legal right to retain the staff, an employer would have insufficient control over the expected future benefits to justify recognizing such costs as assets in financial statements.[1] HSBC recognized that financial reports prepared under UK GAAP are intended to show a true and fair view, but this basis of presentation might not always produce financial reports that presented transactions in a way consistent with the commercial/economic view of transactions.

7.46. HSBC said that from a commercial/economic standpoint, it viewed its development of software as an intangible asset. It said that its policy was to capitalize purchased software where it considered such to be of a capital nature, on a basis consistent with that of related hardware, but in the case of software developed in-house by its IT personnel the cost was expensed as it was incurred. We asked HSBC whether it would capitalize internal development costs in accordance with provisions in FRS 10 which say: 'software development costs that are directly attributable to bringing a computer system or other computer operated machinery into working condition for its intended use within the business are treated as part of the cost of the related hardware rather than as a separate intangible asset'. HSBC responded that where it could be demonstrated that the conditions for capitalization were met under FRS 10 (goodwill and intangible assets), or FRS 15 (tangible fixed assets), software could be capitalized and amortized over its useful life.

7.47. HSBC said that in relation to systems development described in paragraph 7.39(c), the costs had been expensed to the profit and loss account as incurred. It also said that such treatment did not mean that it considered that the IT expense was not of a capital nature from a commercial/economic standpoint. We also asked that if HSBC considered that such IT expenses had a capital nature to them, how was it able to assess that they were not abortive expenditure that did not produce an asset. HSBC responded that such a consideration was irrelevant as the expenditure was incurred with a view to achieving commercial/economic benefits (otherwise the spend would not be incurred in the first place), even if such benefits could not be anticipated and quantified with sufficient certainty to justify capitalizing such costs for accounting purposes. It said that its projects were based on anticipation of future benefits. HSBC's 2000 financial statements referred to differences between UK and US GAAP and noted that its accounts under US GAAP capitalized £54 million of 'costs of software developed for internal use' which it wrote off under UK GAAP, which compared with the UK profit after tax and minority interests of £1.35 billion. For 1999, the equivalent figure was £50 million, and nil for 1998. It noted that US GAAP restricts software spend to be capitalized; for example, related administration and overhead costs are excluded, as are any preliminary costs. Hence the costs capitalized under US GAAP are lower than the costs set out in Table 7.9 which includes all costs relevant to software development.

7.48. We also asked HSBC why, when considering its capital base, any allowance should be made for goodwill on the acquisition of Midland, given that Midland had incurred losses and was in a near breakeven position at the time when HSBC made the acquisition (see paragraph 5.151 and Table 5.37). HSBC said that goodwill of £1.9 billion arose on the acquisition of Midland by HSBC. The goodwill represented the difference between the price paid for the business and the aggregate of the fair values of separable net assets. Hence goodwill would have related to unrecognized assets.

---

[1]HSBC further acknowledged UK financial reporting standards (SSAP 13) which require that development expenditure should be written off in the year of expenditure except in the following circumstances when it might be deferred to future periods: (a) there is a clearly defined project; (b) the related expenditure is separately identifiable; (c) the related outcome can be assessed with reasonable certainty; and (d) costs deferred are reasonably expected to be exceeded by related future benefits.

BoS

7.49. BoS did not have any comments on adjusting its equity base for special factors. However, it noted that its equity consisted of both ordinary shares and preference shares, and it was paying a fixed dividend on preference shares at a rate of around 13.4 per cent gross, which was close to its cost of capital. It stated that for internal purposes only, BoS allocated capital to divisions based upon the RWAs within these divisions. It said that if ordinary shares were used as its equity base, a deduction from profits should be made for the dividend on preference shares. An alternative would be to include the preference shares with the equity and make an allowance for cost of equity in assessing returns, which would produce a similar result. Its equity comprising ordinary and preference share capital and reserves totalled £3.43 billion at February 2000, and £4.86 billion in February 2001, which represented an increase of some 42 per cent. Table 7.11 shows the shareholders' funds for BoS with various adjustments at the whole-bank level. The revised figure at February 2001 was also some 24 per cent higher than the level at February 2000.

TABLE 7.11 **BoS: adjustments to shareholders' funds, February 2000 and 2001**

£ billion

	February 2000	February 2001
Share capital and reserves	3.43	4.86*
Removal of capitalized goodwill†	−.08	−.10
Removal of securities—Feb 2001	-	−.52
Revised figure for capital	3.35	4.24

Source: BoS.

---

*Capital issues in March 2000 and February 2001 amounted to approximately £0.9 billion. Excluding these items growth in the bank's share capital and reserves was approximately 15 per cent.
†This removes the capitalized goodwill shown on the balance sheets.

Basis for allocating capital to the SME banking business

7.50. Whatever figure emerges as the capital base of the bank for all its activities, a further step is required to attribute capital to support the SME banking business, in order to determine returns. In the following paragraphs we discuss our methodology, starting from the figures described above as baseline capital (bank's capital after deducting any capitalized goodwill). Earlier in this chapter we discussed a number of possible adjustments to this baseline capital and in Chapter 2 we show our conclusions on each adjustment and our assessment of each bank's SME capital.

7.51. Table 7.12 shows total on-balance-sheet assets, RWAs, and proportion of SME RWAs to whole-bank equivalent for 1998 to 2000 for the largest six banking groups. By RWAs we mean assets as given the risk weightings imposed by the current regulatory regime in computing minimum capital requirements. Later in the chapter, we show similar information for the smaller banks—see paragraph 7.248. In order to allocate baseline capital to the SME banking business, we calculated the RWAs for the SME banking business as a proportion of the total RWAs, and applied this proportion to the baseline capital figure for each bank. We asked the banks to provide us with data for the RWAs of their SME banking businesses. Loans to SME customers are the main identifiable asset in the banks' SME balance sheets; we assumed that such loans to SME customers had 100 per cent risk weightings, and some banks did not dispute this; Barclays, as an example, preferred its own approach to determining capital, as discussed in paragraph 7.55. For our purposes, Barclays said that the RWAs of the SME banking business in 1999 were £[✂] billion. For some of the other banks we had to estimate the RWAs for their SME banking businesses. NatWest said that total loans to SME customers were £[✂] billion and hence we assumed for our purposes that total SME RWAs were also £[✂] billion. Excluding BoS, the banks had a proportion of SME to whole-bank RWAs in the range 13 to 18 per cent for 1998 and in the range 11 to 18 per cent for 1999. In 2000 Barclays had a proportion of [✂] per cent, Lloyds TSB's proportion was [✂] per cent, that for NatWest was [✂] per cent, HSBC was [✂] per cent, BoS was [✂] per cent (of its UK group's RWAs), and RBS had the lowest proportion at [✂] per cent. Barclays argued that this was an inappropriate basis for allocating capital to SME banking, and considered that its approach gave a better indication of capital. Barclays also suggested that the risk-weighted proportion should also take account of the interbank lending of a surplus of deposit balances in excess of lending because a stand-alone SME bank would have to use such funds.

TABLE 7.12 **Summary of assets, RWAs and proportion of SME RWAs to whole-bank equivalent, 1998 to 2000**

	Barclays	Lloyds TSB	NatWest	HSBC	Largest four banks	BoS*	RBS
1998							
Total on-balance-sheet assets (£bn)	219	168	186	105	678	60	80
RWAs for whole bank (£bn)†	110	83	96	71	360	47	49
RWAs for SME banking business (£bn)†					58.1	‡	
Proportion of SME RWAs to whole-bank equivalent (%)	[Figures omitted. See note on page iv.]				16	‡	[✂]
1999							
Total on-balance-sheet assets (£bn)	255	176	186	106	723	72	89
RWAs for whole bank (£bn)†	116	84	97	72	369	51	57
RWAs for SME banking business (£bn)†					60.4		
Proportion of SME RWAs to whole-bank equivalent (%)	[Figures omitted. See note on page iv.]				16	[✂]§	[✂]
2000							
Total on-balance-sheet assets (£bn)	316	218	186	185¶	905	86	134
RWAs for whole bank (£bn)†	147	94	98	107¤	446	62	77
RWAs for SME banking business (£bn)†					68		
Proportion of SME RWAs to whole-bank equivalent (%)	[Figures omitted. See note on page iv.]				15	[✂]§	[✂]

Source: CC based on information from the banks.

---

*BoS data in 1999 and 2000 is for the year ended February 2000 and 2001 respectively. BoS provided information to exclude the RWAs of foreign subsidiaries, ie for the UK group.

†This is for on- and off-balance-sheet assets. For Lloyds TSB as an example in 1998, the off-balance-sheet figure was around [✂] per cent of the total RWAs.

‡Not available.

§SME RWAs represented [✂] per cent of UK group and [✂] per cent of total group RWAs.

¶Information from published accounts of HSBC and includes foreign subsidiaries.

¤The £107 billion shown is the RWAs for the bank including foreign subsidiaries. We used this figure to derive the SME proportion shown in the table of [✂] per cent. However, HSBC suggested that we could use an RWA figure of £[✂] million excluding the foreign subsidiaries (acquired in 2000) to derive an alternative proportion of [✂] per cent, rather than the [✂] per cent disclosed above. Depending upon the proportion used, it would be applied to baseline capital (including or excluding foreign subsidiaries) to derive a figure for SME capital for 2000, as shown in Table 7.13.

7.52. Table 7.13 shows the methodology we used to allocate baseline shareholders' equity at the whole-bank level to the SME banking business, and which we put to the banks for their comments. The baseline equity was defined as shareholders' funds excluding capitalized goodwill and intangibles. We, however, informed the banks that in presenting our conclusions in Chapter 2, we would replace the baseline equity figure with what we determine for each bank as the appropriate whole-bank capital base, based on our assessment of the adjustments needed. We applied the SME proportion of RWAs to the baseline equity to determine the capital to be allocated to the SME banking business in the figures which we sent to the banks. For example, in 2000 for Barclays we applied [✂] per cent to its baseline equity of £[✂] billion and as a result estimated the capital attributable to the SME banking business to be £[✂] billion, but Barclays insisted that its own estimate of £[✂] billion by its own methods (discussed separately in paragraph 7.55 etc) was more correct. We used RWAs under the Basle 1 accord as an appropriate basis for allocating baseline equity to the SME banking business.

7.53. Because NatWest had merged with RBS in 2000 it could not provide a baseline capital figure for 2000 that was consistent with that for earlier years. RBSG provided a 2000 capital figure for NatWest of £7.1 billion and, using a proportion of [✂] per cent based on RWAs, this would give an SME baseline capital figure of £[✂] billion. However, this would be some [✂] per cent lower than the 1999 baseline capital figure of £[✂] billion and would be a much-reduced base on which to calculate returns for the purpose of determining potential profits in excess of the cost of capital. RBSG said that the inconsistency was as a result of RBSG taking significant dividends from NatWest upon the acquisition of NatWest by RBSG. Accordingly we substituted a figure of £[✂] billion being the 1999 baseline capital figure uplifted by [✂] per cent to reflect the increase in NatWest's 2000 SME income.

458

	Barclays	Lloyds TSB	NatWest	HSBC	BoS*	RBS
1998						
Proportion of SME RWAs to whole-bank equivalent (%)	[*Figures omitted. See note on page iv.*]				§	[✂]
Baseline capital for the whole bank (£bn)	8.0	7.3	8.0	4.8	3.1	3.0
Allocated capital for SME banking business (£bn)	*Figures omitted. See note on page iv.*				§	[✂]
1999						
Proportion of SME RWAs to whole-bank equivalent (%)					[✂]	[✂]
Baseline capital for the whole bank (£bn)	8.7	8.5	8.9	4.8	3.4	4.3
Allocated capital for SME banking business (£bn)	*Figures omitted. See note on page iv.*				[✂]	[✂]
2000						
Proportion of SME RWAs to whole-bank equivalent (%)			†	‡	[✂]	[✂]
Baseline capital for the whole bank (£bn)	10.5	7.7	7.0†	7.2‡	4.2	4.3
Allocated capital for SME banking business (£bn)	[	✂	]†	[✂]‡	[✂	]
Summary of SME RWAs as a proportion of the whole-bank equivalent:						*per cent*
1998	*Figures omitted. See note on page iv.*				§	[✂]
1999					[✂]*	[✂]
2000				‡	[✂]*	

Source: CC based on information from the groups.

---

*BoS data in 1999 and 2000 is respectively for the year ended February 2000 and 2001. For 2000, BoS's whole-bank baseline capital increased by some 27 per cent to £4.2 billion, but there was no equivalent change in SME income. It stated that SME RWAs increased by [✂] per cent during the year, which necessitated a higher capital allocation to support the business. The BoS proportions of RWAs at [✂] per cent were significantly greater than for comparable banks. BoS stated that this reflected the different customer mix (including asset and motor finance) prevalent within BoS. It also stated that business banking accounted for some [✂] per cent of combined UK group lending.

†A directly comparable baseline capital figure for NatWest in 2000 was not available. RBSG noted that reductions in baseline capital were as a result of RBSG taking significant dividends from NatWest upon its acquisition. Accordingly, we estimated an attributable capital figure of £[✂] billion for 2000, based on the allocated capital figure for 1999 of £[✂] billion, uplifted by [✂] per cent to reflect the increase in NatWest's 2000 SME income.

‡As noted in Table 7.12, HSBC provided a figure of £[✂] billion as RWAs of foreign subsidiaries acquired in the year which resulted in an SME proportion of [✂] per cent for 2000. Applying this to baseline capital as shown in Table 7.8 (excluding foreign subsidiaries) of £[✂] billion produced a figure of £[✂] million as capital for the SME banking business. However, as shown above, our methodology uses [✂] per cent based on the SME proportion of RWAs (inclusive of foreign subsidiaries), which we applied to baseline capital shown in Table 7.8 of £7.2 billion (also inclusive of foreign subsidiaries) to produce a figure of £[✂] million as capital for the SME banking business, which was almost equal to that derived by HSBC's approach.

§Not provided.

Note: Figures rounded.

7.54. The following section discusses the banks' comments on our methodology for allocating adjusted shareholders' equity at the whole-bank level to the SME banking business.

Barclays

7.55. Barclays said that the allocation of shareholders' equity pro rata to RWAs was inappropriate for the following reasons:

(a) The measure only took into account credit risk on the lending book, and failed to take into account business, operational and market risk, and operating capital.

(b) The measure did not allocate capital to deposit or money transmission activities.

(c) The measure did not take into account the variation in risk of different classes of lendings, and treated loans to large corporations on the same basis as loans to SME customers.

(d) The measure did not have a matching numerator and denominator, as it included capital for lending activities but included the return for the entire SME banking business. Taken to the extreme, the approach would show an infinite return on equity for an SME bank that took deposits and provided money transmission services but had no lending. The approach would also overestimate returns from services to SMEs in boom years when customers borrowed less and deposited more and would show lower returns in other periods.

7.56. Barclays concluded that the correct approach to allocating shareholders' equity to its SME banking business was to use its economic capital allocation model, which it believed was the best measure of the relative riskiness of different parts of the Barclays group. Using this approach, Barclays told us that the equity capital base of its SME banking business in 2000 was £[✄], which we noted was higher than our estimates discussed in this chapter.

7.57. Table 7.14 shows Barclays' estimate of capital in the SME banking business, based on its economic capital model, from 1989 to 2000. For 1999, [✄] per cent of the total economic capital represented credit risk, [✄] per cent represented operational and business risk, and [✄] per cent represented property and equipment risk.

TABLE 7.14 **Barclays: summary of equity allocation to SME banking business by risk type, 1989 to 2000**

£ million

Risk type	1989	1990	1991	1992	1993	1994	1995	1996	1997	1998	1999	2000
Credit risk Business and operational risk Property and equipment risk Market risk Total					*Figures omitted. See note on page iv.*							

Source: Barclays.

7.58. Barclays said that its calculation of economic capital was based on a bottom-up measure of risk in the SME banking business. Its view was that the various business units of a bank contributed different levels of risk to the group, and were a result of a mixture of lending balances, risk profile of borrowers, net income, cost structure, investment assets, market value at risk, insurance balances, etc.

7.59. The Barclays approach identified four main types of risk inherent in each business and calculated economic capital on the basis of each risk as follows:

(a) Credit risk: Credit risk arose from the volatility of loans to third parties. The measure of credit risk was based on the bank's 'exposure in event of default',[1] 'the expected default frequency'[2] and the 'severity of any possible losses'[3] after security had been taken into account. The economic capital required was calculated on a loan by loan basis.

(b) Business and operational risks: Business risk arose from the volatility of earnings as a result of changes in volumes and margins generated by the general economy. Operational risk was the volatility of earning arising from events in the operations of the business, such as system failure or fraud.

---

[1]This represents the credit exposure (the amount of an advance) outstanding when a default occurs. It is usually based on the anticipated utilization of lending agreed facilities at the point of default.

[2]This is the statistical probability of a customer defaulting within a 12-month period. This is expressed as a percentage (ie the number of defaults per hundred customers of a similar type).

[3]This is the expected percentage of credit exposure which will be lost in the event of default. This takes account of the value of any security, the time value of money pending realization of any security and the costs of recovery.

(c) *Property and equipment risk:* Property risk was the fluctuation in returns as a result of holding a fixed asset portfolio. The risk was measured by taking the book value of property and equipment, multiplying by the asset beta of property and equipment, and dividing by the equity 'beta' used in Barclays' cost of equity calculation.

(d) *Market risk:* Market risk arose from the volatility that the business unit was exposed to because of changes in market prices. It was calculated on the basis of the actual daily value at risk to which Barclays was exposed in the wholesale markets.

7.60. As economic capital was calculated from the bottom up, Barclays noted that total economic capital, as summed across all business units, would not necessarily be equal to total shareholders' funds as shown in the statutory financial statements, although this was its intention when the first estimates were made and remains its intention for the future. However, since 1996, this total was less than equity in the financial statements. For the assessment of returns, Barclays stated that the actual equity capital should be used as the appropriate benchmark, but allocated on the basis of risk as measured by its economic capital methodology. Accordingly, to achieve this result it scaled up the credit risk and business and operational risk components of economic capital, until the sum of economic capital for all risks across all business units equated to actual capital. The scaling factor applied to credit risk and business and operational risk for the SME banking business in 1999 was around [✂] per cent; this is included in Table 7.15.

7.61. In light of the complexity of the above model and the recognition that other banks may use a different economic capital basis, Barclays suggested to us that an alternative method for allocating capital to the SME banking business could be developed, which could be applied consistently to all banks. This method was based on the draft Basle 2 capital adequacy framework as interpreted by Barclays; and Barclays told us that it produced an SME capital figure from individual components of £[✂] in 2000. This, it noted, was similar to that of its own internal economic capital allocation figure of £[✂], as scaled up to actual equity.

7.62. Table 7.15 shows the proposal capital allocation calculation performed by Barclays.

7.63. The steps by which Barclays attained these figures are set out below:

(a) *Step 1:* Barclays calculated, under the proposed Basle 2 capital adequacy approach for credit risk, an RWA balance of £[✂], that would arise from the SME lending book as at 30 December 2000.

(b) *Step 2:* Where Barclays SME deposits exceeded loans, it applied a 20 per cent risk weighting to surplus deposits as if they were lent on the interbank market, as prescribed by Basle 2. RWAs attributable to the excess deposits were £[✂].

(c) *Step 3:* Barclays converted the above RWA figures to a capital requirement of £[✂], by applying an internal capital ratio.

(d) *Step 4:* Barclays added to this number an operational risk capital requirement of £[✂] million, equal to [✂] per cent of gross income for the SME banking business, as prescribed by Basle 2.

(e) *Step 5:* Barclays performed the same calculations for all its other business units and summed the results to obtain total group regulatory capital of £[✂], and then calculated the SME portion as a percentage of the total as around [✂] per cent.

(f) *Step 6:* Barclays applied this percentage to the group equity of £[✂] billion to determine the equity to be allocated to SME banking of £[✂].

TABLE 7.15 **Barclays: proposed capital allocation calculation, 2000**

£ million

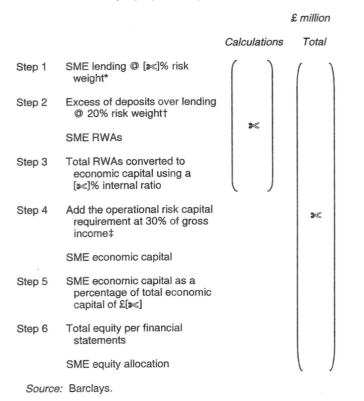

		Calculations	Total
Step 1	SME lending @ [✂]% risk weight*		
Step 2	Excess of deposits over lending @ 20% risk weight†		
	SME RWAs		
Step 3	Total RWAs converted to economic capital using a [✂]% internal ratio		
Step 4	Add the operational risk capital requirement at 30% of gross income‡		
	SME economic capital		
Step 5	SME economic capital as a percentage of total economic capital of £[✂]		
Step 6	Total equity per financial statements		
	SME equity allocation		

Source: Barclays.

---

*The [✂] per cent arises from Barclays' calculations using the Basle 2 rules. It applied its internal risk-based ratings to particular classes of lending, and overall these calculations resulted in an RWA figure that was [✂] per cent higher than the book value of the loans.
†Barclays said that the 20 per cent risk weighting to interbank lending assets was a Basle 2 requirement.
‡This is [✂] per cent of [✂] overall SME economic capital, or [✂] per cent of [✂] subtotal.

7.64. Barclays suggested that it would be possible to simplify the model further, if the information was not available on the same basis from all the banks, by making the following amendments:

(a) In step 1, the banks should apply a generic [✂] per cent risk weighting to all SME lending, which it believed was a reasonable estimate, based on its own calculations using the draft Basle 2 rules.

(b) In step 5, the banks should calculate the total of SME RWAs as a percentage of Basle 1 group regulatory assets. This was based on the proposition in Basle 2 that overall regulatory capital in the industry should not change significantly.

7.65. Barclays told us that although this method was not perfect it believed that it was more appropriate than under the current regime of using Basle 1 risk asset proportions. Barclays summarized its position on the issue of capital and returns from services to SMEs as follows:

(a) It believed that equity capital (ie shareholders' funds plus minority interests) is the right capital base on which to assess profitability and returns to shareholders.

(b) Equity capital should be allocated to business units according to risk, which was the most important determinant of the level of capital required.

(c) It believed that the most accurate assessment of risk capital requirements was economic capital, and that equity capital should therefore be allocated to business units on the basis of economic capital. Because the total equity capital of the group was larger than Barclays' assessment of its total economic capital, the allocation of equity capital in proportion to relative economic capital weightings would be greater than the economic capital for that unit. Barclays did not consider that this result was a scaling up of economic capital but rather an allocation of equity capital and was acceptable because, in its view, not all the actual capital was captured in the risk evaluation exercise; for example: (i) because group capital was held for other purposes; (ii) because there were imperfections in existing risk assessment methodologies and the potential to discover new risks; (iii) because there was need to consider future growth of the bank and other strategic options; and (iv) so that there was a buffer above regulatory levels so that its degree of freedom would not be constrained and it could raise funds at an optimal price, and to maintain a high credit rating of AA/AA+.

(d) As an alternative to the economic allocation approach, it suggested that equity could be allocated in accordance with Basle 2 estimates of capital requirements. It offered this idea not in preference to economic capital, but so that we could apply a consistent methodology to all banks. It acknowledged that Basle 2 was not finalized and was subject to consultation and change, but thought that use of Basle 2 would not give a result very different from its allocation approach using economic capital because they both used similar assessment information as to the riskiness of SME banking relative to other activities of Barclays.

(e) Barclays considered that it was not overcapitalized, and its ratio of equity capital to RWAs was slightly below the level it sought to maintain. Barclays added that it had actively managed its capital base over the past few years by share buy-backs and dividend policies, but the Woolwich acquisition had temporarily left it with capital at a slightly lower level than would normally apply.

Lloyds TSB

7.66. Lloyds TSB said that there were a number of possible methodologies that could be followed to derive an assessment of capital to support its SME activities. It said that the most robust approach to calculating the assets employed by its management units serving the SME banking business would be to use a 'bottom-up' methodology. One approach would be to take the book/accounting value of fixed assets (premises, plant, etc), and add an amount in respect of intangible assets and the loan book. However, one of the problems with this approach was that equity requirements could not be directly linked to specific balance sheet categories or balance sheet size—two businesses with identical balance sheets could have significantly different equity requirements.

7.67. To address this issue in relation to measuring the minimum capital required by each of its business streams, Lloyds TSB had developed an 'equity attribution' model to derive equity required by a business as a function of the various risks attaching to its products and customer relationships. A more risky business would attract a higher equity requirement. As an illustration, Lloyds TSB presented the model's results for its Business Banking unit (which provided services to business customers with turnover less than £2 million). This indicated a minimum equity requirement in 2000 of £[✂] million (compared with a much lower figure of £[✂] million based on a simple 'top-down' allocation of total Group minimum regulatory capital in line with RWAs). For Commercial Banking, Lloyds TSB estimated an equity attribution figure in the region of £[✂] million for services to SMEs, and around £[✂] million for its Asset Finance services to SMEs.

7.68. Lloyds TSB introduced its equity attribution model in 2001, and suggested that the CC could use its results to determine equity for the SME banking business. Lloyds TSB worked backwards from 2001 to estimate a minimum equity figure for the SME banking business in 1999 of £[✂] billion.

7.69. If this approach were to be applied to the SME banking business, the resulting equity figure would reflect all the equity required for the SME banking business, including any equity required to achieve any business growth envisaged in relevant business plans, and to undertake planned capital investments. However, Lloyds TSB told us that this estimated equity ought to be increased, so as to allow for a 'cushion' to ensure that the bank was sufficiently capitalized to take advantage of opportunities for acquisitions or other strategic developments, as they presented themselves. Lloyds TSB suggested that such a 'cushion' could fall within a range of between 10 and 50 per cent of attributed equity.

7.70. Lloyds TSB's equity attribution model was broadly as follows:

(a) It identified five risk types: credit, market,[1] insurance, business[2] and operational.

(b) It estimated the equity required to support each of the business units (that included services to SMEs), having regard to the above risks. It did this by multiplying a risk driver (percentage of risk exposure) by a risk indicator (for example, the level of lending balances, level of operating expenses, level of income) for each business unit of the bank. Therefore in the case of credit risk as an example for 2001, it estimated the risk factor as [✂] per cent of exposure (ie lending) for SME customers, compared with [✂] per cent of exposure for personal business, and [✂] per cent for large corporates. These factors resulted in credit risk equity values of £[✂] for the business units serving the SME sector, £[✂] million for the personal banking sector, and £[✂] million for large corporate relationship banking. Accordingly, for its business units serving the SME sector in 2001, Lloyds TSB calculated the budgeted equity required to cover all risks to be £[✂], which was the sum of £[✂] for credit risk, plus £[✂] million for business risks, plus £[✂] million for operating risk, and £[✂] million for market risk. Lloyds TSB then worked backwards to estimate a total figure specifically for the SME banking business within the business units of £[✂] billion in 1999 subject to upward adjustment because:

— the estimate represented only the minimum capital required to cover the risks implicit in the business but, in a competitive market, a bank would need to invest additional capital to compete effectively; and

— its estimate made no allowance for the holding of a 'cushion' of additional equity to provide resources to take advantage of strategic opportunities (for example, acquisitions, and other means of business development).

7.71. We noted, however, that Lloyds TSB's guide to the equity attribution method suggested that the results from the basic approach already took account of dividends, investments and business growth plans, and therefore there might not be any need for an uplift.

7.72. Lloyds TSB also provided other measures of capital employed in its SME banking business, drawn up on a variety of different bases, to illustrate the wide range of figures which could be used:

(a) regulatory capital—this was £[✂] million in 1999 and £[✂] million in 2000 and was derived by applying the equity component of the bank's internal capital ratio, times a factor of [✂] under present rules, to the RWAs of the SME banking business (the [✂] being the proportion of total regulatory capital represented by equity capital);

(b) economic capital of around £[✂] in 1999 and £[✂] in 2000, derived by applying a Basle 2 type method of allocation to a whole-bank equity figure; and

(c) economic capital of around £[✂] in 1999 and £[✂] in 2000, based on Basle 1 principles, scaled up to its estimate of a whole-bank equity figure. This means it includes the added components of equity suggested by Lloyds TSB in Table 7.2.

Lloyds TSB said that the figures were illustrative and no further elaboration was required.

RBSG

7.73. Following on from RBSG's view on how its capital at whole-bank level should be assessed (see paragraph 7.20), it suggested, in relation to the allocation to the SME banking business, that RBSG (excluding NatWest) should have an imputed capital value in 1999 of between £[✂] million and £[✂] million.

7.74. In relation to NatWest, it suggested that the SME banking business should have an imputed capital base in 1999 as follows:

---

[1]Such as adverse price changes in financial instruments, including interest rates, exchange rates, equities, options and commodities.
[2]Such as macroeconomic influences, competitor actions and market events.

(a) using market value—between £[✂] billion to £[✂] billion;

(b) using replacement costs—between £[✂] billion and £[✂] billion;

(c) using regulatory capital—between £[✂] billion and £[✂] billion; this was based on RBSG's view that a free-standing SME bank, if such existed, could be required to have a regulatory Tier 1/Tier 2 capital level of between [✂] per cent of lending, compared with a level of around 8 per cent under current Basle 1 rules. It added that a level higher than [✂] per cent would not be surprising.

In summary, it therefore suggested that we should use a range of from £[✂] billion to £[✂] billion for the capital value of its SME banking business.

7.75. Following our invitation for RBSG to make further comments on the derivation of its capital base, it made a subsequent submission at a late stage in the inquiry, which suggested that the appropriate capital base could also be determined using Basle 2 principles, as opposed to current regulatory principles. Under Basle 2, the group capital requirement would be calculated based on consideration of all risk exposures, including operational and market risks. RBSG's proposals involved the following steps:

(a) It estimated SME RWAs using a Basle 2 approach of some £[✂] billion for 2000, compared with £[✂] billion for the whole group. It thereby suggested that the SME proportion of RWAs should be [✂] per cent, which compared with its estimate under a Basle 1 approach of [✂] per cent. RBSG accordingly inferred that attributable capital determined under the Basle 1 approach should be uplifted by some [✂] per cent.

(b) For 1999, using an estimated figure of £[✂][1] as the attributable capital for the SME banking business of NatWest using Basle 1 RWAs, it suggested that the revised estimate using Basle 2 principles should be increased by [✂] per cent to £[✂].

(c) It then added estimated values for the cost of intangibles supporting the SME banking business of £[✂] as follows:

— Customer base—£[✂] million;

— Staff training costs—£[✂] million;

— IT costs—£[✂] million;

— Brands—£[✂] million;

— Products—£[✂] million;

— Reputation—£[✂] million; and

— Licences—£[✂] million.

(d) The resulting total was £[✂] to which it added an estimate for the value of a pension surplus of £[✂] million to give a final estimate of attributable capital for the SME banking business of £[✂].

HSBC

7.76. HSBC first said that shares of RWAs were the best proxy for disaggregating the capital base, but it later noted that they were not an unreasonable proxy for this purpose. It believed, however, that there were some imperfections with use of RWAs, such as:

---

[1]Table 7.21 shows this figure, which was noted in Chapter 6 as an original estimate.

(a) RWAs did not result in an allocation of capital to non-asset activities (for example, deposit-taking and money transmission).

(b) RWAs did not result in an allocation of capital to assets with zero risk weights, although they recognized that this was not a relevant consideration for services to SMEs where 100 per cent risk weightings applied.

(c) RWAs did not take into account the incidence of non-credit risks (for example, operational risk) for different businesses.

(d) RWAs depended on the allocation of fixed assets to different activities.

(e) RWAs did not take into account the shares of intangible assets relevant to different activities.

7.77. HSBC did not propose any particular methodology for determining capital to support services to SMEs, but suggested that the figure should take account of intangible assets, which we have discussed in paragraphs 7.36 to 7.47. HSBC also stated that the RWAs attributable to the SME banking business could increase significantly as a result of the introduction of the 2001 Basle 2 draft capital accord. Hence, capital attributable to the SME banking business would increase.

7.78. Regarding capital that should be attributed to the SME banking business, it compared its whole-bank Tier 1 ratio in 1999 of 6.8 per cent with other banks, such as Barclays (7.5 per cent), BoS (6.8 per cent) and RBS (8.1 per cent). It therefore suggested that because it was a subsidiary of a larger international group, it did not need to hold as much Tier 1 capital as other banks, and we should therefore make an uplift of its capital attributable to SME activities for this factor.

BoS

7.79. BoS did not indicate an alternative to the RWA methodology. It agreed that Tier 1 capital broadly equated to the group capital and reserves and was therefore an appropriate basis against which to assess performance. It also agreed with the principle of allocating equity by reference to RWAs among the business segments. However, it stated that the capital of its overseas subsidiaries should be excluded. Accordingly, BoS provided full UK group data on which to base SME allocations of capital. BoS said that SME RWAs represented [✂] per cent of the UK group equivalent, and [✂] per cent of total group equivalent.

Other banks

7.80. On issues of capital, the other banks did not make any proposals additional to those discussed above for the six largest clearing groups, except for the Co-operative Bank, First Trust and NAB.

The Co-operative Bank

7.81. The Co-operative Bank told us that it did not calculate economic capital, and instead used regulatory capital to allocate capital among its business segments. This was done using the bank's internal standard of 11 per cent of RWAs. Regulatory capital was calculated as:

Total shareholders' funds

Plus: General provisions
        Subordinated liabilities

Less: Regulatory amortization of subordinated liabilities.

7.82. The Co-operative Bank noted that a better method of allocating economic capital to segments would be to use a robust risk-based approach that correctly determined the true amount of capital required given the level of risk undertaken by the bank. This would be better than allocating capital on a simple regulatory basis where the risk reward balance may not be aligned. However, it noted that this would require sophisticated models and large volumes of data, particularly over an economic cycle.

7.83. In addition, the Co-operative Bank said that it felt the CC's calculation of RWAs did not recognize that the Co-operative Bank in general, and the SME banking business in particular, had an excess of deposit funds over assets. It said that the CC had appeared to take consideration of retail lending only in the composition of RWAs that appeared to ignore the requirement to provide an adequate return on surplus deposits. The Co-operative Bank said that its approach was to allocate a 25 per cent risk weighting to excess deposits on the basis that the surplus had to be lent on the market. It said that a 25 per cent risk weighting reflected the risk weighting of Treasury assets. The effect of adopting this approach would be to increase the RWA figure used to allocate capital to the SME banking business.

First Trust

7.84. First Trust told us that it did not calculate, make reference to, or benchmark itself against any form of economic capital in determining pricing to SMEs or any part of its business. First Trust used a post-tax cost of capital of [✀] per cent or a pre-tax rate of around [✀] per cent, which had been determined by the parent company to ensure that the various banks within the Group evaluated business decisions in a consistent manner. It used cost of capital estimates only for investment decisions, property development, technology investment and acquisitions.

7.85. First Trust told us that it was part of AIB and as such did not have a separate measurable capital base to support its business activities. It said that capital should be allocated to the different business units in direct proportion to the underlying risk/lending within those business units. It said that AIB was currently in the process of developing models to allocate capital to business units, for example First Trust, and subsequently to individual sectors and loan products. The capital that would be required to support any individual business unit would vary from that required for regulatory purposes, due to the risk profile of the unit's portfolio. First Trust was unable to estimate what these balances would be, but said that in the future this shareholder value-based management approach would be used to assess capital efficiency and risk-adjusted profitability.

National Australia Bank

7.86. NAB told us that for management purposes it allocated capital using a five-step allocation methodology, not according to regulatory requirements or Basle 1 principles.

7.87. First, it determined the overall required capital level (the target level of capital) for allocation to global divisions within the group. The target level of capital was assessed annually taking into account its credit rating, analysts' views, regulatory requirements etc. Currently it was set as a figure equivalent to a core Tier 1 ratio of [✀] per cent.

7.88. The target level of capital was then allocated to businesses according to their relative historical earnings volatility, which NAB described as a top-down approach. Earnings are defined as revenues less bad debt provisions, because these are the most volatile components. The bank used statistical simulation to measure earnings volatility.

7.89. It then calculated the actual risk capital required for each division using a bottom-up approach, which was the sum of its assessments for market risk capital, credit risk capital and operational risk capital for the bank.

7.90. In order to address any differences between the total target capital, which had been allocated according to earnings volatility, and the total amount of capital required under a bottom-up approach, a residual risk value was calculated. This residual risk value was a scaling factor and was calculated by dividing the top-down risk capital for a business unit by the unit's bottom-up risk capital. If the top-down process resulted in £1,400 and the bottom-up figure was £1,000, a scaling factor of 1.4 would be applied. The target capital applied to a business unit using the top-down approach would be multiplied by a factor of 1.4 to arrive at the final allocated capital amount. NAB applied a maximum scaling factor of 2 and a minimum of 1.1.

7.91. It then analysed the scaling factors in each division, and if any was outside the permitted range of 1.1 to 2.0, capital would then be further reallocated.

7.92. In relation to calculating capital attributable to the SME banking business, NAB felt that the most appropriate whole-bank capital base to start from was Tier 1 plus Tier 2 capital including the full value of subordinated debt. This was preferred to the allocation by the CC of baseline capital being shareholders' equity reduced by any capitalized goodwill. The inclusion of the subordinated debt balance had the effect of increasing the whole-bank capital base for Yorkshire, Northern and Clydesdale to £[✄] million, £[✄] million and £[✄] million respectively for 2000. This compared to £[✄] million, £[✄] million and £[✄] million as calculated by the CC.

Cost of capital

7.93. In this section we describe our approach to the cost of capital and provide details of our estimates of it for the banks for the years 1998 to 2000. Some banks provided their own estimates and these are also given. Later we compare the estimates of the cost of capital with the banks' return on adjusted equity from their SME banking business.

7.94. The cost of capital needs to reflect the returns that investors require, in order to be compensated for investing their money in the bank's shares and bearing the associated non-diversifiable risks. Generally, the cost of capital is calculated as a weighted average of a company's cost of equity and its cost of debt (including subordinated debt), and hence is referred to as the weighted average cost of capital. For non-financial firms the weighted average cost of capital relates to the cost of total capital (equity and debt) employed to support net operating assets. In the case of banks, the customers' deposits and other customer accounts have a dual nature, being both a liability (or means of financing lending activities) and a retail product in their own right, ie forming part of working capital. Accordingly the concept of weighting the cost of capital is not relevant for banks and we decided that the appropriate cost of capital was the cost of equity. Barclays, however, said that banks could be considered like other businesses to have 'net assets' which were the assets net of the liabilities used as part of the ongoing operations of the business. For banks, this number would include customer deposits in the same way that other businesses have current liabilities. Like other businesses, banks financed their net assets from two main sources: equity and debt capital. In a bank, however, it said that the debt capital must be subordinated to the interests of depositors. Barclays therefore suggested that we could examine profitability of banks in two ways: by examining the return to equity holders (after the cost of subordinated debt), or by examining the return on total capital, which would include subordinated debt. It added that these two approaches should not produce fundamentally different results, if used correctly.

Cost of equity

7.95. The method we have used to estimate the bank's cost of equity is the capital asset pricing model (CAPM), which states that a company's post-tax cost of equity is equal to the risk-free rate of return, plus the equity risk premium (ERP), multiplied by the company's beta. Beta measures the riskiness of a company's shares in relation to that of the markets. For example, the beta of all shares quoted on the Stock Exchange is 1. A higher beta, say 1.4, suggests that the share has 40 per cent more non-diversifiable risk than the Stock Exchange as a whole. If the Stock Exchange index increased or decreased by 10 per cent, one would expect the share with a beta of 1.4 to increase or decrease by 14 per cent.

The risk-free rate

7.96. The current real risk-free rate represents that amount of the return that would be earned, or the minimum cost of capital, if there were no risk associated with a given investment. The redemption yields on UK government-issued index-linked gilts provide a direct estimate of the real risk-free rate over different maturities. It is the one component of the CAPM model that is readily observable from trading in liquid markets because the future cash flows of such stocks can be mapped with certainty. Recent reports by the CC have taken account of these factors, and have discussed them in some depth. We saw no reason not to use the real risk-free rate of 3.0 per cent plus 2.5 per cent to take account of inflation that we used in recent reports for the purpose of our inquiry. This rate compares with a range of 4 to 6 per cent used by the six largest clearing groups. HSBC said that the risk-free rate in 1999 was at a historical low for the period 1988 to 1999, having fallen from a maximum for the period of 11.7 per cent. HSBC suggested that the rate of 5.5 per cent was not sustainable in the medium term.

Equity risk premium

7.97. The ERP represents the additional return that investors require to compensate for the additional risk associated with investing in equities rather than risk-free securities. It is not directly measurable from market data because the future payout from equities (unlike gilts) is uncertain. In determining the value of the ERP, the objective is to estimate the investor's expectations of the return over the life of the investment. In prior CC inquiries the ERP has largely been determined based on an historical average of the difference between past equity returns and risk-free rates.

7.98. For the purpose of this inquiry we reconsidered the issues involved in determining the appropriate ERP and decided to use a figure of 4 per cent. This is consistent with the rate used in recent CC reports and it was felt that the rationale that led to the calculation of this figure had not significantly changed. The rate of 4 per cent compares with the six largest clearing groups' range for the year ended 31 December 1999, which was 3 to 6 per cent (see Table 7.17).

Equity betas and illustrative cost of equity figures for the banks

7.99. As with the ERP, beta is not measurable directly from market data. However, statistical estimates of beta are made by regression analysis (total returns from holding a particular share or portfolio of shares are regressed against total returns from the market portfolio).

7.100. Table 7.16 shows the components of the CAPM model for the six largest clearing groups, as estimated by us. We have applied equity betas to each of the banks using rates supplied by the London Business School, with some modification in the case of HSBC.[1] As discussed above, the post-tax nominal risk-free rate applied for all banks was 5.5 per cent, and the post-tax equity risk premium was 4 per cent. The estimates of beta differed among the banks. To arrive at the pre-tax cost of equity, we grossed up the post-tax cost by applying a tax rate of 30 per cent.[2] For 1999, the pre-tax cost of equity was accordingly in the range of 14 to 16 per cent.

7.101. HSBC's figure as calculated by the London Business School was 1.79. It represented the beta for the holding company, and therefore included HSBC's global activities. We thought it was not appropriate to use this figure, as it was so different from the betas of the other large banks. As a proxy, we calculated a beta for HSBC based on the average of the other five largest banks for each year.

---

[1]Source: London Business School Risk Measurement Service, July–September 2000, page 50.
[2]HSBC said that this rate should be 31 per cent for 1998.

TABLE 7.16 **Illustrations of nominal cost of equity for the six largest clearing groups serving SMEs in the UK, 1998 to 2000**

	Barclays	Lloyds TSB	NatWest	HSBC	BoS	RBS
1998						
Risk-free rate (%)	5.5	5.5	5.5	5.5	5.5	5.5
Beta	1.38	1.32	1.20	1.28*	1.25	1.27
ERP (%)	4	4	4	4	4	4
Post-tax cost of equity (%)	11	11	10	11	11	11
Pre-tax cost of equity (%)	16	15	15	15	15	15
1999						
Risk-free rate (%)	5.5	5.5	5.5	5.5	5.5	5.5
Beta	1.49	1.50	1.13	1.35*	1.40	1.21
ERP (%)	4	4	4	4	4	4
Post-tax cost of equity (%)	11	12	10	11	11	10
Pre-tax cost of equity (%)	16	16	14	16	16	15
2000						
Risk-free rate (%)	5.5	5.5	5.5	5.5	5.5	5.5
Beta	1.30	1.39	1.14	1.25*	1.25	1.14
ERP (%)	4	4	4	4	4	4
Post-tax cost of equity (%)	11	11	10	10	11	10
Pre-tax cost of equity (%)	15	16	14	15	15	14

Source: CC.

*The beta as calculated by the London Business School in 1999 was 1.79 for the holding company, and therefore included its global activities. Consequently, we calculated an estimate based on the average of the betas for the five other larger banks.

7.102. Table 7.17 shows the CAPM components and resulting cost of capital calculation for each of the six largest clearing groups, based on their own assessments for their whole business. The banks' estimates were not greatly out of line with our calculation, and the simple average across the six banks was virtually identical. There were, however, some differences in the values ascribed to some components of the CAPM calculation. The banks generally considered that the SME banking business, if considered on its own, was more risky than the business of the whole bank, and therefore the cost of equity should be higher for the SME banking business than that for the whole bank. We noted first that should the SME beta be different from that of the whole bank, we could not observe it; and second, it was not by any means certain that returns to the SME banking business would vary more than overall returns in the market. Third, in the event that SME banking business was more risky, this increased risk would more than likely be attributed to increased default risk which would be reflected in the allocation of capital, rather than necessarily being the determinant of a higher cost of equity.[1] Moreover, the banks did not themselves normally calculate a separate cost of capital on a business segment basis. For example, RBSG said that it applied a group hurdle rate, which was [✂] than its computed cost of capital, in order to cover any risks associated with individual parts of the business. The risk on such business parts was not quantified and their approach is judgemental in relation to the allocation of a group hurdle rate. However, RBSG suggested that the appropriate cost of capital for any one year was the cost of capital that applied at the beginning of the year when price decisions could be assumed to be made.

7.103. For the smaller banks, we were not able to determine reliable beta factors that could be applicable for their SME activities. However, we would not expect their cost of equity figure to diverge greatly from the average for larger banks in 1999 of around 15 per cent pre-tax.

[1]HSBC did not agree with the comment, given its view that the capital allocated reflected the proportion of SME RWAs to total bank RWAs. The capital allocation therefore reflected the risk weightings attaching to SME exposures, ie 100 per cent. HSBC said that this could be the same weighting attaching to non-SME exposures. It could therefore be seen that the approach used to calculate SME capital would not necessarily reflect the increased volatility.

TABLE 7.17 **Comparison of cost of capital calculations for the six largest clearing groups, as calculated by the banks for 1999, compared with the CC's illustrative figures**

	Barclays	Lloyds TSB	NatWest	HSBC	BoS	RBS
Estimates by banks						
Risk-free rate (%)						
Beta						
ERP (%)		*Figures omitted.*				
Post-tax cost of equity (%)		*See note on page iv.*				
Pre-tax cost of equity (assuming tax of 30%)						
Comparison to						
Pre-tax cost of equity as calculated by CC	<u>16</u>	<u>16</u>	<u>14</u>	<u>16</u>	<u>16</u>	<u>15</u>
Difference (+ if bank estimate is greater than CC figure)	(✂)*		(✂)†	(✂)‡	(✂)	

Source: CC based on information provided by the banks.

---

*Lloyds TSB used an ERP of [✂] per cent, compared with our assessment of 4 per cent.

†NatWest had a risk-free rate of [✂] per cent compared with our assessment of 5.5 per cent, but its ERP at [✂] per cent was higher than our estimate of 4 per cent.

‡HSBC used an ERP of [✂] per cent compared with 4 per cent used by us.

Income and profit allocated to the SME banking business for the six largest clearing groups

7.104. Barclays, Lloyds TSB and HSBC provided us with more than two years' profitability data on their SME banking business, and Barclays' profitability information was the most comprehensive covering 12 years. BoS provided profitability data for the two years ended 28 February 2000 and 2001. NatWest provided only 1999 income data for its SME banking business, from which we estimated its profitability. RBS provided only 1998 and 1999 income data for business customers with turnover less than £10 million, from which we estimated profitability for the SME banking business. For 2000, RBSG combined the RBS and NatWest businesses except for income figures which it provided for each of the two banks, from which we had to make our own estimates of profitability, as we discussed in Chapter 6. Generally the six largest clearing groups predicted improving profitability and no serious economic downturn over the next three years from their services to SMEs, although some (for example, Barclays) mentioned scenarios that were less optimistic. HSBC said that circumstances could change rapidly. In addition, as this inquiry progressed, the banks said that the recent foot-and-mouth epidemic in the UK might have a potentially serious negative effect on their lending portfolio, and asserted that this crisis demonstrated the sectoral risks that banks faced. [

Details omitted. See note on page iv.

]

7.105. HSBC noted that there had been numerous surveys and reports published in recent months showing increases in SME liquidations and bankruptcies, and falls in business confidence. To give some examples, on 2 July 2001, it said, Dun & Bradstreet published research which found that the number of UK businesses being liquidated or going bankrupt reached 10,804 between April and June 2001, an increase of 15 per cent on the previous quarter. The rise was said to be in part due to the drop in tourism and other adverse factors caused by the foot-and-mouth epidemic, but also revealed a continuing high number of manufacturing failures. Quarterly figures on company profitability published by Experian in mid-July showed that for the economy as a whole, the average return on capital fell over the final quarter of 2000, signalling the longest period of falling profitability since the recession of the early 1990s.

7.106. Barclays, Lloyds TSB and RBSG proposed some specific adjustments to SME profitability, which we discuss in the following sections. These adjustments were:

(a) a deduction for pension costs, where the pension scheme was in credit;

(b) removal of profits from structural hedges;

(c) allowing deductions for restructuring costs; and

(d) disregarding the recoveries from earlier bad debt charges, when considering profits over a short period of a few years. However, over a longer period, covering an economic cycle, recoveries should be included in assessing profitability.

Tables 7.18 and 7.19 quantify these adjustments for Barclays and Lloyds respectively and illustrate the potential effect they would have on operating profit. Paragraph 7.114 discusses adjustments proposed by RBSG. HSBC and BoS did not propose any additional adjustments to the profit and loss figures they initially provided and their figures are summarized, together with those of Barclays, Lloyds TSB and RBSG, in Table 7.20.

Adjustments for attributable capital

7.107. As discussed in Chapter 6, the banks provided figures for profit derived from lending, calculated on the basis that the cost of lending was financed from borrowing in wholesale markets. In fact, a proportion was financed by the bank's shareholders' funds, as was noted by, for example, Lloyds TSB and Barclays. We (and some banks) therefore noted that an adjustment to profits would be necessary to reflect the capital attributable to this lending. Without this adjustment, the attributable interest cost set against interest income received would have been overstated and this would have resulted in double counting when we came to allow a return on the attributed capital. The following subparagraphs summarize the banks' position on this issue:

(a) Barclays accepted that there was need for this adjustment, based on the level of capital attributed to the SME banking business.

(b) Lloyds TSB accepted that there was need for this adjustment, based on the level of capital attributed to the SME banking business. It suggested, however, that a three-year rolling average swap rate should be used rather than three-month LIBOR that we proposed.

(c) HSBC accepted that there was need for this adjustment, based on the level of capital attributed to the SME banking business, but suggested that three-month LIMEAN ought to be used.

(d) RBSG commented on this adjustment for NatWest, RBS and Ulster Bank. First, it suggested that not all the attributable equity capital would be available to fund business lending. It said that at 31 December 2000, RBSG's fixed assets were £6.1 billion, compared with shareholders' funds of some £11 billion, ie a proportion of around 55 per cent. It therefore considered that this proportion of shareholders' funds was not available to support lending and therefore should be disregarded for the purpose of an attributable capital adjustment. It also added that any intangible assets created and capitalized in the balance sheet would need to be funded by equity. We noted, however, that some £2.7 billion of the £6.1 billion fixed assets represented operating leases and therefore were already 'income earning'. Of the remaining fixed assets, RBSG stated that they were in the form of premises and computer hardware, some of which, it said, should be apportioned to the SME banking business. RBSG said that an adjustment should be made to reflect this issue. Second, RBSG said that NatWest was in a net placement position, ie its accounts in credit from SMEs exceeded the lending, and if the SME banking business was a separate stand-alone business with this balance sheet mix, it would not be able to achieve the interbank offer rate, but surplus funds could be invested at around one-eighth of a percentage point below the offer rate. Third, it suggested that subordinated debt should also be considered in arriving at the adjustment for attributable capital on equity. It believed that the ratio of subordinated debt to equity should be 40:60, and as a highly-rated bank its subordinated debt had a margin cost of around 0.8 per cent. For a stand-alone SME bank, this could rise to 1.1 per cent. Fourth, it suggested that the value of the attributable capital should be based on LIBID, which, it said, for 1999 was 5.33 per cent. It summarized these points for NatWest using an example of equity of £[✂] for the SME banking business. It said that 45 per cent of the equity totalled £[✂] million, which at a LIBID cost of 5.33 per cent had a value of £[✂] million. It then took

472

account of a margin on subordinated debt of 1.1 per cent at a value of £[✂] million, to result in a net adjustment of £[✂] million.[1]

(e) BoS accepted that there was need for this adjustment, based on the level of capital attributed to the SME banking business.

7.108. Having noted the banks' comments on the need for an attributable capital adjustment, we now consider the profit and loss adjustments suggested by the banks, in particular Barclays, Lloyds TSB and RBSG, in the paragraphs below.

Barclays—suggested adjustments to profits

7.109. Barclays said that the calculation of SME profits should take account of:

(a) Pension cost. Barclays said that its pension scheme was in surplus and hence its pension cost was below the normal rate. In its view we should allow a deduction of £[✂] million in 1998 and £[✂] million in 1999 for notional pension contributions in arriving at SME profits. It said that its own calculations of SME profits took account of this cost.

(b) Special profits from structural hedges. Barclays said that SME operating income had been artificially inflated by structural hedges. It said that we should reduce operating income by £[✂] million in 1998 and £[✂] million in 1999.

(c) Restructuring costs. Barclays said that it incurred restructuring costs of £[✂] million in 1998 and £[✂] million in 1999, and we should accept the inclusion of these costs in arriving at the profits it reported to us.

(d) Recoveries of earlier bad debt charges. Barclays said that recoveries had significantly distorted the profit profiles of the SME banking business, in particular from 1994 to 1999. It proposed that we remove recoveries of £[✂] million in 1998 and £[✂] million in 1999 from our analysis, which would decrease operating profits if periods of less than the whole economic cycle were analysed.

7.110. Table 7.18 shows the adjustments to profitability proposed by Barclays for 1998 to 2000. In Chapter 2 we give our conclusions on its profits from services to SMEs for the purpose of determining its returns.

TABLE 7.18 **Calculation of SME operating profit, based on adjustments proposed by Barclays, 1998 to 2000**

£ million

	1998	1999	2000
SME operating income:			
As submitted			
Adjustment for attributable capital*			
Revised income			
Operating expenses	*Figures omitted.*		
Bad debt charge	*See note on*		
Revised operating profit	*page iv.*		
Adjustments proposed by the bank to the			
CC's revised figure for operating profits:			
Pension costs			
Structural hedges			
Restructuring			
Recoveries of earlier bad debt charges			
Operating profit after adjustments			
Attributable baseline capital for the SME			
banking business from Table 7.13			

Source: CC based on information provided by Barclays.

*At 7.3 per cent for 1998, 5.45 per cent for 1999, and 6.10 per cent for 2000, based on yearly average of three-month LIBOR.

[1]The £[✂] million was calculated by applying a funding ratio of 40 parts subordinated debt to 60 parts equity. The calculation becomes equity times the funding ratio, multiplied by the margin on subordinated debt, £[✂]*(40/60)*1.1% = £[✂] million.

Lloyds TSB—suggested adjustments to profits

7.111. Lloyds TSB proposed an adjustment to SME profits for the overfunded pension scheme as discussed in paragraph 7.15(d). The long-term pension cost adjustment was the charge that would have arisen if its current pension scheme were not in surplus. It said that in 1999 the notional adjustment for pension costs for the SME banking business was £[✂] million (which represented [✂] per cent of the staff costs attributable to the businesses serving SMEs).

7.112. Table 7.19 shows the adjustments to profitability proposed by Lloyds TSB for 1998 to 2000. In Chapter 2 we give our conclusions on these adjustments for the purpose of determining its returns. Lloyds TSB also emphasized that allowance was required for effects of profit cyclicality, adjustment for attributable capital, and bad debts over an economic cycle (which we consider separately in this chapter and in Chapter 2).

TABLE 7.19 **Calculation of SME operating profit, based on adjustments proposed by Lloyds TSB, 1998 to 2000**

£ million

	1998	1999	2000
SME operating income:			
As submitted			
Adjustment for attributable capital*			
Revised income			
Operating expenses			
Bad debt charge	Figures omitted.		
Revised operating profit	See note on		
	page iv.		
Adjustment proposed by the bank to the			
CC's revised figure for operating profits:			
Pension costs†			
Operating profit after adjustments			
Attributable baseline capital for the SME			
banking business from Table 7.13			

Source: CC based on information provided by Lloyds TSB.

*At 7.3 per cent for 1998, 5.45 per cent for 1999, and 6.10 per cent for 2000, based on yearly average of three-month LIBOR. Lloyds TSB, however, considered that the rate should be based on the three-year rolling swap rate.
†We have assumed similar figures in 1998 and 2000 for pension costs, based on information supplied by Lloyds TSB for 1999.

7.113. Lloyds TSB suggested that the CC should look at profits earned in recent years (it suggested the period from 1996 to date), on the basis that the profits earned in the recent past might be expected to provide the best guide to the present state of competition and the likely future state of competition. It added that the banking industry was cyclical: firms competed with each other over the long term, and could expect profits to fluctuate over the economic cycle, according to the prevailing economic climate. In particular, during times of economic recession, banks could expect to incur higher levels of bad debt and higher operating costs in managing problematic loans, and to sell lower volumes of other products (for example, insurance and savings products) as SME demand for such products fell. Hence, at the least it would be necessary to look at profits over a longer period, covering at least one economic cycle, or to adjust profits for the most recent period to take account of cyclical downturns. Nonetheless, Lloyds TSB said that even if one adjusted profits for the most recent period to take account of cyclical downturns, it considered that the resulting figures were likely to offer little insight into the state of competition in the market. Lloyds TSB did not consider that profits in excess of cost of capital were indicative of market power. It suggested that in competitive markets, one or more firms might, for short periods, earn profits that deviated significantly from the cost of capital.

7.114. RBSG said that a deduction for pension costs of some £[✂] million a year should be made to take account of its estimated pension surplus from the SME banking business for NatWest and RBS. In addition, an adjustment to income was required to reflect that amount of interest on equity already accounted for in the profit results of NatWest. The effect of this adjustment was to reduce income by £[✂] million in each of the years 1998 to 2000. Other main banks did not note any special adjustments to their reported income and expenses as shown in Chapter 6. Table 7.20 shows SME income, cost and profitability figures for the six largest clearing groups before inclusion of any of the proposed adjustments described above (except, for reasons of comparability, the pension cost adjustment for banks where this applied). These adjustments are evaluated in Chapter 2. The table therefore includes income as stated, adjusted only for attributable capital (see paragraph 7.107); costs as stated excluding extraordinary items; and bad debt charges to the profit and loss account.

TABLE 7.20 **The six largest clearing groups: summary of SME operating profit based on discussions with the banks (including the attributable capital adjustment made by the CC), 1998 to 2000**

£ million

	Barclays	Lloyds TSB	NatWest	HSBC	BoS*	RBS
1998						
Operating income					†	
Operating expenses					‡	
Unadjusted operating profit before provisions‡					†	
Adjustment for attributable capital§					†	
Pension cost adjustment		¶			(✂)	
Operating profit before provisions					†	
Bad debt charge					‡	
Revised operating profit					‡	
1999						
Operating income					¤	
Operating expenses						
Unadjusted operating profit before provisions‡						
Adjustment for attributable capital§		Figures omitted. See note on page iv.				
Pension cost adjustment		¶				
Operating profit before provisions						
Bad debt charge						
Revised operating profit						
2000						
Operating income					¤	#
Operating expenses						
Unadjusted operating profit before provisions						
Adjustment for attributable capital§						
Pension cost adjustment		¶				
Operating profit before provisions						
Bad debt charge						
Revised operating profit			#			

Source: CC based on information from the banks.

*BoS data in 1999 and 2000 is for the years ended February 2000 and 2001 respectively. BoS's returns were lower than for comparable banks. Chapter 6 describes its services to SMEs in greater detail and notes, for example, that it was paying significant interest on current accounts in credit.

†Not provided.

‡Barclays, Lloyds TSB and BoS accounted for operating leases until 1999 in a different manner from that adopted in 2000, but the operating profit for all the years was not affected. In Table 7.24 we adjust income and operating costs for this factor to achieve comparability with 2000 information.

§At 7.3 per cent for 1998, 5.45 per cent for 1999, and 6.10 per cent for 2000, based on yearly average for three-month LIBOR.

¶We have assumed similar figures in 1998 and 2000 for pension costs, based on information supplied by Lloyds TSB for 1999.

¤1999 and 2000 figures include £[✂] million and £[✂] million share of net income from investments in associates.

#RBS provided the figure £[✂] million as income from customers with turnover of £10 million for the 15 months to 31 December 2000, which equated to £[✂] million income on a 12-month pro-rata basis. In addition, it noted £[✂] million income from mid corporate business customers for the 15 months, of which we assumed that 25 per cent related to customers with turnover from £10 million to £25 million. This income on a 12-month pro-rata basis equated to £[✂] million, and resulted in our estimate of total income of £[✂] million.

Note: N/A = Not applicable.

Return on capital for the six largest UK banks, before any further adjustments by the CC

7.115. Table 7.21 shows the SME capital and revised operating profit (discussed above) for the six largest UK clearing banks from 1998 to 2000 before any adjustments (that we discuss later in the chapter). The table also shows the initial estimates of differences between pre-tax returns and cost of capital that we discussed with the banks during the course of the inquiry as a basis for considering whether excess returns were being made from services to SMEs.

TABLE 7.21 **The six largest clearing groups: comparison of pre-tax returns with the cost of equity capital for their SME activities, 1998 to 2000 (as put to the banks before any further adjustments by the CC)**

	Barclays	Lloyds TSB	NatWest	HSBC	BoS*	RBS	Total
1998							
Attributable capital derived from baseline capital as per Table 7.13† (£m)	1,219	1,115	1,389	802	‡	372	‡
Revised operating profit as per Table 7.20 (£m)	[	Figures omitted.		]	‡	[✂]	‡
Pre-tax return on capital (%)§		See note on page iv.			‡		‡
Cost of equity as per Table 7.16 (%)§	16	15	15	15	15	15	15¶
Difference between pre-tax return and the cost of capital (%)§	[	Figures omitted.		]	‡	[✂]	‡
Value of the difference between pre-tax return and the cost of capital (£m)		See note on page iv.			‡		‡
1999							
Initial capital figure that we reported to the banks for illustrative purposes (£m)	1,362	1,358	1,628	866	901	477	6,592
Attributable capital derived from baseline capital as per Table 7.13† (£m)	1,334	1,322	1,535	857	881	476	6,405
Revised operating profit as per Table 7.20 (£m)	[	Figures omitted.				]	2,295
Pre-tax return on capital (%)§		See note on page iv.					35¶
Cost of equity as per Table 7.16 (%)§	16	16	14	16	16	15	16¶
Difference between pre-tax return and the cost of capital (%)§	[	Figures omitted.				]	19¶
Value of the difference between pre-tax return and the cost of capital (£m)		See note on page iv.					1,295
2000							
Attributable capital derived from baseline capital as per Table 7.13 (£m)†	1,454	1,194	1,643	958¤	1,098	403	6,750
Revised operating profit as per Table 7.20 (£m)	[	Figures omitted.				]	2,662
Pre-tax return on capital (%)§		See note on page iv.					40¶
Cost of equity as per Table 7.16 (%)§	15	16	14	15	15	14	15¶
Difference between pre-tax return and the cost of capital (%)§	[	Figures omitted.				]	25¶
Value of the difference between pre-tax return and the cost of capital (£m)		See note on page iv.					1,648

Source: CC based on information from the banks.

*BoS data in 1999 and 2000 was for the years ended February 2000 and 2001 respectively.
†This capital figure may differ from that shown in Chapter 6 because of changes in basis for calculations as the inquiry progressed. For 2000, HSBC provided an alternative figure of £[✂] million based on average capital and excluded acquisitions of foreign subsidiaries.
‡Not available.
§Figures rounded.
¶This is a simple average.
¤HSBC calculated this on its alternative approach discussed in footnote ‡ to Table 7.13 as £[✂] million.

7.116. We considered certain additional adjustments to SME profitability. The adjustments were:

(a) an additional allowance for bad debts;

(b) an efficiency adjustment; and

(c) further cyclicality adjustments, which considered profit effects arising from changes in GDP and the scope for the banks to increase income in times of downturn in economic activity.

Lloyds TSB, however, suggested that banks experienced increased costs, lower business volumes and lower profits in times of economic downturn.

Additional allowance for bad debts

7.117. In the relevant sections of Chapters 5 and 6, we have summarized the bad debt record for each bank as a whole and in relation to their services to SMEs, to the extent that data was available.

7.118. Table 7.22 summarizes the six largest clearing groups' bad debt charges as a percentage of lending to SMEs over the 12 years to 2000. Only Barclays was able to give us a full series of data, but the other banks made estimates for us on a best endeavours basis. In the case of Lloyds TSB, the information for SME banking services was available only from 1995, as is shown in the table. However, for illustrative purposes to show the long-term trend, it provided a series for the majority of its SME activities over the period, which it said was indicative of the SME results. Similarly, for HSBC the information up to 1994 that it was able to present was not considered comparable for direct inclusion in this table, but is shown in footnote §, as well as Chapter 6. HSBC explained that the early 1990s results reflected not only the economic downturn at the time, but also Midland's adoption of an inappropriate strategy in terms of the way it serviced its SME customers. NatWest carried out a special exercise to provide 'high' and 'low' estimates as shown in the table, but its low estimate was not very different from the figures noted in Chapter 6. RBS was able to provide information only from 1992. BoS had information only for the years ended February 2000 and 2001. The table also shows the averages for the five years to 1995, the five years to 2000, and the 12 years to 2000. We also show in the case of Barclays and HSBC figures for their respective bad debt charges (before recoveries) as a percentage of lending, to show the extent to which recoveries impacted on the ratio. [*Details omitted See note on page iv.*]

7.119. Regarding the future, the banks suggested during 2000 that they expected the immediate future to continue to be benign and this was reflected in their economic forecasts to around 2002/03. In 2001 the banks indicated that the foot-and-mouth problem and threats of an economic downturn had changed their views. However, RBSG noted that if there was going to be a recession (and it thought there was certainly going to be a downturn in economic activity), it would not be as bad as was experienced in the early 1990s. The banks also generally accepted that their credit assessment and debt control systems had improved compared with the position in the early 1990s, but Barclays added that such would have little bearing on its future bad debt rates, relative to its forecasts. HSBC also suggested that the likely effect of a recession would nevertheless be a decline in profitability and that the financial consequences of the early 1990s could occur again. The following summarizes the position of the six largest clearing groups over the next three years (based on their forecasts and estimates, where available):

(a) Barclays had a central plan forecast that included an economic slowdown. Its forecast from April 2000 showed that the bad debts to lending ratio would rise to [✁] per cent in a non-recession scenario, and [✁] per cent in a recession scenario.

(b) Lloyds TSB noted that no 2000–2002 business plan for the SME banking business was separately prepared, and a single expected ratio was therefore difficult to derive with accuracy. It added that Business Banking (which accounted for 56 per cent of average lending to SMEs) had a plan, which showed a ratio of [✁] per cent for this period, [

Details omitted. See note on page iv.

]. It said that this stretching target applied to both SME and non-SME activities, and might be exceeded in worsening economic conditions.

(c) RBSG said that it was not sensible to guess the future when assessing a norm for bad debt to lending ratios, and rather its historical figures should be used for this purpose. In any event, for the combined Group of NatWest, RBS and Ulster Bank, it said that SMEs were not a recognized business segment within RBSG and accordingly it did not have bad debt to lending ratio predictions relating thereto. Moreover, the data it used to provide historical figures was not available on a projected basis.

TABLE 7.22 **The six largest clearing groups: comparison of bad debt charges as a percentage of loans from services to SMEs, 1989 to 2000**

per cent

	1989	1990	1991	1992	1993	1994	1995	1996	1997	1998	1999	2000
*Based on information in Chapter 6**												
Barclays	(			✂			)					)
Lloyds TSB—SME	†	†	†	†	†	†	†					
Lloyds TSB‡—estimate	(			✂			)		*Figures omitted.*			
HSBC	§	§	§	§	§	§	(✂)		*See note on page iv.*			
NatWest (high estimate)	[			*Figures omitted.*								
NatWest (low estimate)				*See note on page iv.*			]					
RBS	†	†	†	(		✂	)					)
BoS¶	†	†	†	†	†	†	†	†	†	†	(✂	)
Bad debt charge (before recoveries) as a percentage of lending												
Barclays	(			*Figures omitted. See note on page iv.*								)
HSBC	†	†	†	†	†	†	(		✂			)

Summary	5-year average 1991–95	5-year average 1996–2000	12-year average 1989–2000
*Bad debt charge as percentage of lending**			
Barclays	(✂)	0.2	1.5
Lloyds TSB	†	0.8	†
Lloyds TSB‡—estimate	(✂)	0.9	2.0
HSBC	§	0.4	§
NatWest (high estimate)	(✂)	0.6	1.6
NatWest (low estimate)	(✂)	0.5	1.4
RBS	†	0.5	†
BoS	¶	¶	¶

Source: CC based on information from the banks.

---

*After recoveries.

†Reliable data was not available.

‡These figures relate to the Business Banking and Commercial Banking units, and exclude asset finance and AMC activities. Lloyds TSB provided this information to show a long-term trend in this ratio, as it was not able to provide SME figures for 1995 and earlier years. Lloyds TSB said that it was unable to determine any ratio for asset finance activities, because to do so required detailed customer analysis as high level apportionment was not an appropriate approach to determine a figure for the SME proportion because the asset finance business was not homogenous.

§In the case of HSBC, it considered that we should note ratios of [✂] per cent for 1990, [✂] per cent for 1991, [✂] per cent for 1992, [✂] per cent for 1993, and [✂] per cent for 1994. These figures were very different to the results from other banks, and the five-year average from 1991 to 1995 would be [✂] per cent.

¶BoS was not able to provide its SME bad debt to lending ratios, but suggested that we should use its whole-bank figures as an indicator of the significance of its bad debt history. Chapter 5 records this information, which showed ratios as follows: 1.2 per cent for 1991, 1.4 per cent for 1992, 1.8 per cent for 1993, 1.4 per cent for 1994, 0.9 per cent for 1995, and 0.5 to 0.6 per cent in later years.

(d) In September 2000, HSBC predicted improving profitability and no serious economic downturn over the next three years from its services to SMEs, but noted that circumstances could change rapidly. It said that halfway through 2001, the threat of economic recession was now real and could seriously impact on the business in terms of bad debt and income reduction arising from a lower level of customer activity. Hence it considered that its improving profitability scenario was now, with hindsight, optimistic. HSBC was not able to say how high the bad debt ratio might reach going forward to 2002/03, but it considered that a figure significantly in excess of 0.7 per cent ought to be a norm going forward to take account of adverse events that might arise, as well as the bad debt charges over the last ten years. We suggested to HSBC that its indications of bad debt ratios were orders of magnitude greater than comparator banks and could not be factored into sustainable long-term figures, for example when margins are compared with such suggestions of potential lending losses. HSBC acknowledged this area as being one involving a judgement for the CC to make. In summary, HSBC noted that its plan prepared in the light of economic conditions at that time assumed that the UK would continue to benefit from a benign economic environment.

(e) BoS had plans prepared at January 2001 for the businesses serving SMEs which indicated that the bad debt to lending ratio would be no higher than [✂] per cent going forward to 2002/03.

7.120. In Chapter 2 we show how we used this information to determine our estimate of an appropriate figure to include in our calculation of whether and, if so, to what extent profits in excess of cost of capital have been earned.

Comparisons of SME banking business cost:income ratios of the six largest clearing groups, including issues of business mix, and efficiency

7.121. We discussed with the largest UK banks our use of cost:income ratios as a basis for identifying relative efficiency, and we note their main comments below. In the respective sections of Chapters 5 and 6 we showed the trends in cost:income ratios for the largest banks, and the data included in costs and income for recent years. Table 7.23 summarizes such cost:income ratios for the major banks' services to SMEs, where information was available, in order to illustrate the trends, but some banks pointed out that not all years were presented on a consistent accounting basis. HSBC, for example, said that there were no accounting standards governing the calculation of cost:income ratios; therefore there was scope for banks to place their own interpretation on the content and treatment of the constituent elements of the calculations.

TABLE 7.23 **The six largest clearing groups: comparison of cost:income ratio trends for services to SMEs, 1996 to 2000, before adjustments**

per cent

	1996	1997	1998	1999	2000	Prediction 2002/03
Barclays	61	59	61	56	53	⎫ *
Lloyds TSB	57	57	59	49	52	⎬ ✂ †
HSBC	69	63	62	63	61	⎪
NatWest	‡	‡	68	68	64	§
RBS	‡	‡	62	58	56	§
BoS¶	‡	‡	‡	(✂)	¤

Source: CC based on information from the banks as shown in Chapter 6.

---

*From baseline plan. This falls to [✂] per cent by 2004. Barclays said that this was not wholly comparable with the earlier years' figures because it related to Business Banking and not SME banking.

†Table 6.34 shows a cost:income ratio of [✂] per cent for business banking, and [✂] per cent for commercial banking, equating to [✂] per cent for the two units by 2002.

‡Not available.

§[

Details omitted. See note on page iv.

]

¶The year end is to February.

¤See paragraph 7.123.

7.122. The banks predicted reductions in future cost:income ratios. RBSG noted potential annual cost savings of some £[✂] billion by 2003 arising from the integration with NatWest. If the SME banking business only accounted for up to [✂] per cent of total activities, some £[✂] million of savings could be attributable to services to SMEs for RBS and NatWest combined, but RBSG did not consider that a pro-rata approach could give any indication of efficiency savings, or savings from elimination of de-duplication costs. RBSG said that only a small proportion of the cost savings would be for the Corporate Banking unit (which serves large SMEs), and cost savings from Retail and Manufacturing divisions would be spread over services to both personal and corporate customers. It added that in order to implement the savings, it would also have to incur integration costs of at least £[✂] billion between 2000 and 2003, as well as capital expenditure of around £[✂] billion. It told us that the savings from integration were expected to arise primarily in support areas but there were no plans to reduce the variable costs attributable to SME services because all branches were to remain open and no headcount was envisaged in customer-facing activities.

7.123. HSBC objected to the CC's use of cost:income ratios, as we discuss below, but it predicted that its ratio of 61 per cent in 2000 would fall to [✂] per cent by 2003. Barclays suggested a cost:income ratio of [✂] per cent for its Business Banking unit by 2003 (which included services to SMEs), but indicated that it did not use such a measure for its business purposes. Lloyds TSB suggested a ratio of around [✂] per cent by 2002, based on its business plans for Commercial and Business Banking (but emphasized that these two business units alone did not account for the whole of the businesses serving the SME sector, as the Asset Finance and AMC activities were excluded from this ratio). BoS was not able to suggest a future cost:income ratio for its SME banking business but, regarding its overall business, it noted that at August 2000 the group cost:income ratio was [✕] per cent [*Details omitted. See note on page iv.*].

7.124. Lloyds TSB described the cost:income ratio in its published financial statements as its efficiency ratio. In 2001 Lloyds TSB announced that it no longer considered it appropriate to target a specific cost:income ratio. However, Lloyds TSB's medium-term incentive plan for executive directors in 2000[1] referred to efficiency ratios as targets, and said: 'The two minimum performance targets are a reduction in the group's efficiency ratio to 37 per cent by the end of 2002 and a return on equity of 28 per cent by the end of 2002. No payment will be made under the plan unless both these minimum targets are met.' Lloyds TSB said that the medium-term incentive plan was now superseded and was therefore irrelevant because the new share option plan for 2001 did not include any cost:income targets as a basis for incentivizing staff performance. It said that cost:income ratios were only one useful measure of efficiency for the purpose of business performance, when set at an appropriate level for a specific bank based on its particular circumstances, and when coupled with other performance targets (such as achieving particular investment outputs, or volumes). Without the additional measures, it felt there was no way of knowing whether a particular cost:income ratio had been achieved by simply cutting back on investment expenditure or underperforming against volume targets.

7.125. Lloyds TSB also considered that it was incorrect to compare cost:income ratios between banks, and they would be of limited value for our purposes. It considered that in addition to the level of efficiency, differences between banks' cost:income ratios could be due to other factors, such as:

(a) failure to undertake investment in new business products;

(b) lower than projected growth in existing business lines;

(c) difference in business mix; and

(d) difference in service quality.

It therefore suggested that banks operating with different business strategies/plans, and at different stages of implementation of their plans, were not comparable in terms of cost:income ratios.

7.126. As a guide to recent trends in costs, we looked at the banks' results in the three years to 2000. Table 7.24 shows a summary of income, costs and cost:income ratios for the services to SMEs of the six largest UK banks between 1998 and 2000, with revisions for adjustments discussed in Chapter 6, and restatement of income and costs for net income from operating leases. In 1999, after the adjustments, NatWest had the highest ratio at 69 per cent, followed by BoS with [✕] per cent, HSBC at 63 per cent, Barclays at 60 per cent, RBS at 59 per cent and Lloyds TSB at 52 per cent.

7.127. Initially we suggested to the banks that profits should be adjusted to take account of a notional cost:income ratio of 50 per cent based on performance of the most efficient banks providing services to SMEs, and a downward trajectory in costs. The banks objected and claimed that several factors might account for variances between their own performance and a norm of 50 per cent. Barclays said that if a downward trajectory of costs was considered, a downward trajectory in prices also required consideration. Several banks said that cost:income ratios at the whole-bank level were not comparable, as each bank had a different mix of activities. At the SME level, the banks said that different mixes of income-earning activities would affect cost:income ratios, as well as some accounting presentation differences. Other factors which could have an influence were price levels (because they affected income levels) and quality of service (because this would have an impact on costs), which have been addressed in Chapter 4. In any event, the banks all considered themselves to be efficient with those exhibiting higher cost:income ratios attributing this to one or more of the factors noted above. In addition to any effect of inefficiency, we noted that differences might also arise from different cost allocations or income mix, and we now consider these two factors in turn.

---

[1]This was approved by shareholders in April 2000, as reported on page 40 of its report and accounts.

TABLE 7.24 **The six largest clearing groups: comparison of performance and relative cost:income ratios from services to SMEs, 1998 to 2000**

£ million

	Barclays	Lloyds TSB	NatWest	HSBC	BoS*	RBS†
1998						
Operating income	(	‡	(	§	¶	(
Operating expenses		‡			¶	
Operating profit before provisions and adjustments					¶	
Adjustments				✂		
Pension costs					(✂)	
Bad debt charge					¶	
Operating profit before adjustment for attributable capital				)	¶	
1999						
Operating income		‡		§	¤	
Operating expenses		‡			¤	
Operating profit before provisions and adjustments						#
Adjustments	✂		✂			✂
Pension costs						
Bad debt charge						
Operating profit before adjustment for attributable capital				✂		
2000						
Operating income				§	¤	
Operating expenses					¤	
Operating profit before provisions and adjustments						
Adjustments						
Pension costs						
Bad debt charge						
Operating profit before adjustment for attributable capital	\		)	)	)	)

Performance indicators						per cent
Cost:income ratios before above adjustments:						
1998	61	60‡	68	62	¶	62
1999	56	50‡	68	63	[✂]¤	58
2000	53	52	64	61	[ ]¤	56
Cost:income ratios after above adjustments:						
1998	65~	61‡	69#	62	¶	62#
1999	60~	52‡	69#	63	[✂]¤	59#
2000	58~	53	65#	61	[ ]¤	57#

Source: CC based on information from the banks.

---

*BoS has an accounting period ending 28 February. The figures for the 1999 and 2000 calendar years are those of BoS for the years ended February 2000 and 2001 respectively, and exclude £[✂] million and £[✂] million share of net income from investments in associates.

†RBS provided us with estimates of its operating costs, which included specific and memorandum recharges.

‡These figures have been adjusted to make Lloyds TSB's treatment of operating leases accord with that of other banks. For 1999 and earlier years it treated depreciation as a deduction from income, rather than as a cost. For 1998 and 1999 it said that this adjustment was £[✂] million and £[✂] million respectively on a 'best estimate' basis. Accordingly, we increased the income and operating cost figures reported by Lloyds TSB by £[✂] million and £[✂] million respectively which increased its cost:income ratio by almost one percentage point for both years. From 2000 Lloyds TSB has treated depreciation in the same manner as other banks and no adjustment is needed.

§In calculating cost:income ratios for NatWest, we used income figures as originally submitted. Later in the inquiry these figures were revised downwards by £[✂] million for each of the years 1998, 1999 and 2000 to reflect income on equity earned and accounted for in its profit figures. The reduction was necessary to ensure that the attributable capital adjustments made by the CC did not overstate the benefit of equity. The adjusted income figures became £[✂] in 1998; £[✂] in 1999; and £[✂] in 2000. This change did not significantly distort the following analysis and so the income figures used were the unadjusted ones.

¶Not provided.

¤These figures have been adjusted to make BoS's treatment of operating leases accord with that of other banks. It treated depreciation as a deduction from income, rather than as a cost. For 2000, it said that this adjustment was £[✂] million on a 'best estimate' basis. Accordingly, we increased the income (£[✂] million) and operating cost (£[✂] million) figures reported by BoS by £[✂] million which increased its cost:income ratio by [✂] percentage points to [✂] per cent. For the 1999 year, the adjustment was £[✂] million to increase income of £[✂] million to £[✂] million, and to increase costs from £[✂] million to £[✂] million. The effect of the lease adjustment has been to increase cost:income ratios to [✂] per cent compared with [✂] per cent.

#NatWest said that its leasing activities were not included in the above figures, but were in the business results of Lombard, which are separately noted in Chapter 5. NatWest confirmed that the SME proportion of its leasing activities were small, as covered in paragraph 5.196. RBS told us that its leasing activities to SMEs were small.

~Barclays said that its operating lease activities were not material from a group point of view. Accordingly, it accounted for them as finance leases. It added that the depreciation charge from operating leases is deducted from net interest income rather than being treated as an operating cost.

Note: N/A = not applicable.

Cost allocations

7.128. We asked the banks to provide us with cost breakdowns for activities in a consistent manner for 1999, based on a pro-forma template. The banks provided us with data but it was not comparable among banks on a line-by-line basis. For example, each bank had a different way of treating direct and indirect costs, and the proportions varied widely between banks. Moreover, for some banks, costs were allocated directly to the sub-unit as incurred, and central costs were not allocated. This made detailed comparisons between the banks on a line-by-line basis impracticable. We therefore made our comparisons at the total cost:income ratio level.

7.129. To explore the costs of the largest banks, we looked at a breakdown of Barclays, HSBC and Lloyds TSB's SME costs for 1999. NatWest, RBS and BoS said that they were not able to provide such information and, for example, BoS explained that this was because it did not allocate costs to a product level.

7.130. Table 7.25 shows the income and costs as allocated by Barclays between product categories for 1999. Barclays indicated that its current accounts with authorized overdraft facilities had a cost:income ratio of [✄] per cent, but this fell to [✄] per cent for current accounts with no overdraft facilities. For loans the cost:income ratio was [✄] per cent, but for deposit accounts was only [✄] per cent. Total costs were shown as £[✄] million, of which direct costs were £[✄] million ([✄] per cent) and allocated and other costs were £[✄] million.

TABLE 7.25 **Barclays: summary of costs and income mix from services to SMEs, 1999***

£ million

	Current account—authorized overdraft facility	Current account—no overdraft facility	Deposit account	Loans	Merchant acquiring	Other	Total
Direct costs							
Staff costs							
Premises and equipment							
Depreciation							
Legal and professional							
Travel and entertaining							
Stationery, postage and phones							
Advertising and marketing							
Other							
Total direct							
Allocated and other costs							
Staff costs							
Premises and equipment							
Depreciation		Figures omitted.					✄
Allocated—customer services		See note on page iv.					
Allocated group costs							
Share option costs							
Other							
Total allocated							
Total costs							
Net interest income							
Fees and commissions, etc							
Total income (excl clubs, etc)							
Cost:income ratios (%)							55†
Average cost:income ratio (%)							

Source: Barclays.

---

*Figures exclude clubs and charities. Such income was £[✄] million and costs were £[✄] million.
†The overall cost:income ratio shown of 55 per cent increases to [✄] per cent if clubs and charities are included.
Note: Items without figures mean not applicable.

7.131. Table 7.26 shows the income and costs as allocated by Lloyds TSB between product categories for 1999. Lloyds TSB indicated that its current accounts in credit had a cost:income ratio of [✄] per cent, which was close to the [✄] per cent for loans and current accounts with overdrafts. For deposit accounts, the cost:income ratio was [✂] per cent. Total costs were shown as £[✂] million, of which direct costs were £[✂] million and allocated costs were £[✂] million.

TABLE 7.26 **Lloyds TSB: summary of costs and income mix from services to SMEs, 1999***

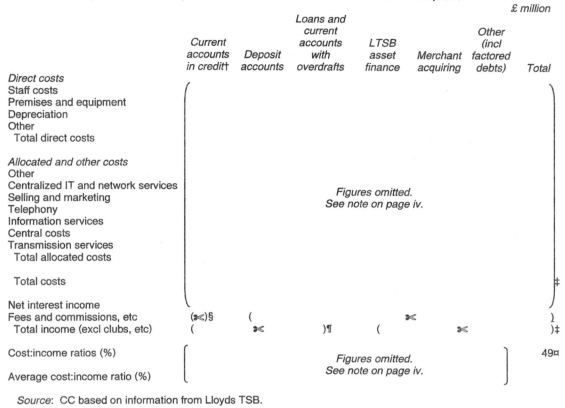

£ million

	Current accounts in credit†	Deposit accounts	Loans and current accounts with overdrafts	LTSB asset finance	Merchant acquiring	Other (incl factored debts)	Total
Direct costs							
Staff costs							
Premises and equipment							
Depreciation							
Other							
Total direct costs							
Allocated and other costs							
Other							
Centralized IT and network services			*Figures omitted.*				
Selling and marketing			*See note on page iv.*				
Telephony							
Information services							
Central costs							
Transmission services							
Total allocated costs							
Total costs							‡
Net interest income							
Fees and commissions, etc	(✂)§	(			✂		)
Total income (excl clubs, etc)	(	✂	)¶	(		✂	)‡
Cost:income ratios (%)			*Figures omitted.*				49¤
Average cost:income ratio (%)			*See note on page iv.*				

Source: CC based on information from Lloyds TSB.

*Figures exclude clubs and charities. Such income was £[✂] million and costs were £[✂] million. Lloyds TSB indicated that it could only split net interest income between current accounts with overdrafts and current accounts in credit.
†Including those with unauthorized overdrafts.
‡Per Table 7.24, income of £[✂] is equal to £[✂] shown above, plus £[✂] million from clubs and charities, plus £[✂] million from adjusting for operating leases. The costs figure in Table 7.24 of £[✂] million is equal to £[✂] million shown above, plus £[✂] million from clubs and charities, plus £[✂] million from adjusting for operating leases.
§This includes income from current accounts with overdrafts, as Lloyds TSB was not able to separate from current accounts in credit.
¶Analysed as income from loans at £[✂] million, and £[✂] million from current accounts utilizing overdraft facilities.
¤The overall cost:income ratio shown of 49 per cent increases to [✂] per cent if clubs and charities are included.
Note: Items without figures mean not applicable.

7.132. Table 7.27 shows the income and costs as allocated by HSBC between product categories for 1999. It indicated that its current accounts (with and without overdrafts) had a cost:income ratio of [✂] per cent, but for loans and asset finance the combined ratio was [✂] per cent. For deposit accounts the cost:income ratio was [✂] per cent. Total costs were shown as £[✂] million (excluding costs of clubs, charities and associations), of which direct costs (related to loans only) were £[✂] million ([✂] per cent) and allocated costs were £[✂] million. Costs for other services were allocated on the basis of the cost of the activity associated with those services. HSBC said that all bank costs were fully absorbed into product costs. It said that its approach might not be the same as for other banks that, for example, might not allocate central costs. Regarding the very high cost:income ratio for current accounts, we suggested that this may reflect an overallocation but HSBC emphasized that its cost allocations were appropriate, and explained its belief in this cost:income ratio as is covered in paragraphs 7.161 to 7.164.

7.133. Next, we summarized the cost:income ratios by type of product, based on information from the banks, as shown in Table 7.28. From this, we estimated a lending ratio of 55 per cent, 66 per cent for current accounts with overdrafts, 49 per cent for current accounts without overdrafts, and 25 per cent for deposit accounts. We disregarded the cost:income ratios from other activities. Information on cost:income ratios at the overall SME level for NatWest, RBS and BoS are shown in Chapter 6 and reproduced in the table, but they were not able to provide cost:income ratios by type of service.

TABLE 7.27 HSBC: summary of costs and income mix from services to SMEs, 1999*

£ million

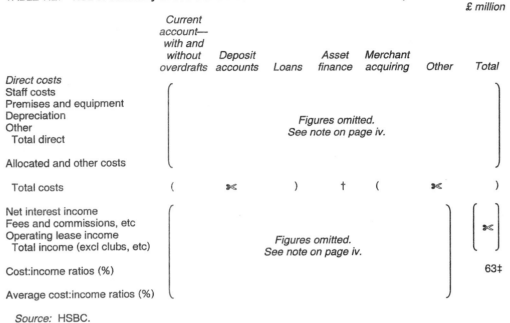

	Current account— with and without overdrafts	Deposit accounts	Loans	Asset finance	Merchant acquiring	Other	Total
Direct costs							
Staff costs							
Premises and equipment							
Depreciation			*Figures omitted. See note on page iv.*				
Other							
Total direct							
Allocated and other costs							
Total costs	(	✂	)	†	(	✂	)
Net interest income							
Fees and commissions, etc							✂
Operating lease income			*Figures omitted. See note on page iv.*				
Total income (excl clubs, etc)							
Cost:income ratios (%)							63‡
Average cost:income ratios (%)							

Source: HSBC.

*Figures exclude clubs and charities. Such income was £[✂] million and costs were £[✂] million.
†Not provided.
‡The overall cost:income ratio shown of around 63 per cent remains unchanged if clubs and charities are included.
Note: Items without figures mean not applicable.

TABLE 7.28 The six largest clearing groups: estimation of imputed cost:income ratios for particular bank services to SME customers in 1999

per cent

	Barclays	Lloyds	HSBC	NatWest	RBS*	BoS†	Imputed CIR	Based on:
Lending	‡					55		2 bank average
Asset finance	‡					N/A		
Current accounts with overdrafts						66		3 bank average
Current accounts in credit	✂	✂				49		2 bank average
Deposits						25		3 bank average
Other, including merchant acquiring etc¶						70		3 bank average
Overall cost:income ratio	56	50	63	68	58	(✂)		

Source: CC based on information from the banks.

[✂] could only provide a combined figure for lending and current accounts with overdrafts.
*RBS was able to provide data only for SME customers with turnover less than £10 million.
†Based on year to February 2001, which was the only year for which BoS was able to provide disaggregated income. The figure for the year ended February 2000 was [✂] per cent.
‡Information provided by Barclays. The combined cost:income ratio is [✂] per cent.
¶Excludes clubs and charities.

7.134. We then sought to adjust for the fact that different banks have different ratios of lending (loans and current accounts with overdrafts) to deposits (current accounts in credit and deposit accounts). As the deposit-taking[1] activity has a lower cost:income ratio than lending,[2] a shortfall of deposit-taking

---

[1]We mean by this term both the activity of operating deposit accounts and running current accounts in credit, rather than a pure deposit account service.
[2]We mean by this term both the activity of lending and running current accounts with overdrafts, rather than a pure lending service.

484

income will, all other things be equal, raise a bank's cost:income ratio. Lloyds TSB said, however, that the shortfall would need to be more in deposit account income, rather than from current accounts in credit, as its data suggested that the cost:income ratio from current accounts were broadly similar, whether the accounts were in credit or overdrawn.

7.135. To allow for different ratios of loans to deposits, we calculated the average value of this ratio across the banks and then calculated the cost:income figures that would occur if a bank had exhibited this average ratio of loans to deposits. This allowed us to identify the impact of different mixes of SME banking activities. Specifically (as shown in Tables 7.30 to 7.35):

(a) we included income from lending in 1999 as reported by the banks; but

(b) we used a figure of 127 per cent for the ratio of income from deposits to income from lending (as discussed in the following paragraph), this being the average ratio for the five largest banks, and we adjusted income from deposits accordingly. The difference between a bank's actual income from 'deposits' and its 'normalized' value, calculated this way, is identified as a 'balance of deposit income' item;

(c) we calculated costs on the same basis—ie using actual costs of lending but with costs of 'deposits' adjusted to reflect a level of 'deposit' income equal to 127 per cent of income from lending. Hence again, the difference between the actual and adjusted (or normalized) value is shown as a balancing item; and

(d) we derived adjusted cost:income ratios from the above. This gives the cost:income ratios that would have been observed if all the banks had had the same ratio of loan income to 'deposit' income.

7.136. Table 7.29 shows the analysis of income[1] information for the six largest clearing groups in 1999. Overall the final column of the table shows the totals for Barclays, Lloyds TSB, HSBC, NatWest and RBS, and shows that 56 per cent of income was from current accounts in credit and deposit accounts, compared with 44 per cent from lending and overdrafts, ie income from deposits was 127 per cent of income from lending. We used this ratio as a benchmark to take account of differences in mixes between banks, as we discuss in later paragraphs. However, the summary at the bottom of the table shows that for Lloyds TSB and NatWest, around [✂] per cent of their total income from lending and deposit services had come from the benefit of current accounts in credit and deposits; compared with [✂] per cent which came from lending and overdrafts. In contrast, Barclays and HSBC show total income from current accounts in credit and deposit accounts that are below the benchmark of 56 per cent. BoS was excluded from the average because its ratio was dramatically different from the other banks and might be seen as distorting the norm. We noted that some banks claimed there might have been some distortion of fee income allocated to current accounts in credit, compared with current accounts with overdrafts, in cases where an account had changed its status over the year. However, we used the overall ratios derived as a basis to consider all the banks on a similar basis in terms of income mix, so any distortion effect is unlikely to be significant in the context of this analysis.

---

[1]Net interest income plus fees and commissions.

TABLE 7.29 **The six largest clearing groups: comparison of income contribution mixes from services to SMEs, 1999**

£ million

	Barclays	Lloyds TSB	HSBC	NatWest	RBS*	BoS†	Total (excluding BoS)
Income from							
Lending	‡						1,087
Current accounts with overdrafts			§				783
							1,870
Current accounts in credit		¶	§				1,639
Deposits							718
							2,357
Total income from lending and deposits							4,227¤
Other income							
Asset finance contribution	‡						264
Merchant acquiring							273
Foreign exchange services							87
Factored debt	✂	✂	✂	✂		✂	44
Cards							36
Other							200
Trade commissions							19
Contribution							923
Total income from SMEs							5,150¤
Income from clubs, etc							139
Overall total income					*		5,289
Summary of proportions							
Lending and overdrafts (%)	‡						44
Current accounts in credit and deposit accounts (%)	‡						56
							100

Source: CC based on information from the banks.

---

*RBS was able to provide data only for SME customers with turnover less than £10 million. The £[✂] million total represents income from customers with turnover up to £10 million. In addition we estimated some £[✂] million income from customers with turnover from £10 million to £25 million, which is excluded from this analysis, resulting in a revised income figure of £[✂] million.

†Based on year to February 2001, which was the only year for which BoS was able to provide disaggregated income. The equivalent figure for the year to February 2000 was £[✂] million.

‡£[✂] million includes income of £[✂] million from asset finance lending, resulting in a revised figure of £[✂] million for general lending. The ratio of [✂] shown for lending:deposits reflects this reallocation.

§This was estimated information provided by HSBC.

¶Includes £[✂] million fees and other income, some of which Lloyds TSB said was from current accounts with overdrafts, but it was not able to separate from current accounts in credit.

¤Income from lending and deposits for the largest five banks was 82 per cent of total income of £5,150 million.

Comparison of cost:income ratios between the six largest clearing groups when allowance is made for differences in income mix from services to SMEs in 1999

7.137. In the following paragraphs to 7.178 discussing comparisons of cost:income ratios between the banks shown, the term 'five largest banks' means Barclays, Lloyds TSB, HSBC, NatWest and RBS. Table 7.30 summarizes our calculations for 1999 in respect of Lloyds TSB to show that the actual cost:income ratio of 44 per cent from the four income activities was not affected by restating it to a norm for the five largest banks (see column 1), which remained at 44 per cent (see column 2). For control purposes, we also reconciled the total income from the four categories of activity, to the overall total income reported by Lloyds TSB from services to SMEs.

£ million

Based on five largest banks' benchmark

	Lending and deposits Actual*	Adjusted income	Balance of deposit income
Income from			
Lending			
Current accounts with overdrafts			
Current accounts in credit			
Deposits income		†	
Combined income	✂	✂	✂
Total costs		‡	§
Profit before provisions			
Percentage lending (%)			
Percentage accounts in credit (%)			
Cost:income ratio (%)	44	¶	

	Income	Costs	Operating profit before bad debts £m	Cost: income ratio %
Summary reconciliation				
Lending and deposits (as above)				44
Asset finance	Figures omitted.			[✂]
Merchant acquiring, others, CACs	See note on page iv.			
Total for SME activities				50

Source: CC based on information from the banks.

---

*Excludes the capital charges adjustments and pension costs adjustments noted separately in Chapters 5 and 6.

†The total is 127 per cent of lending income. This income is then allocated between current accounts in credit, and deposit accounts in the same ratio as for the equivalent actual income in column 1. See also paragraph 7.148, which discusses an alternative calculation for the apportionment of this income.

‡Actual total costs minus costs of balancing deposits.

§Calculated as £[✂] million times [✂] per cent for current accounts, and £[✂] million times [✂] per cent for deposit accounts (see Table 7.28).

¶Figure rounded as impact of change is less than 1 per cent.

7.138. Table 7.31 summarizes these calculations regarding Barclays' activities to SMEs for 1999. It shows that the actual cost:income ratio of 53 per cent from the four income activities was revised to [✂] per cent when adjusted to a norm for the five largest banks.

7.139. Table 7.32 summarizes the calculations regarding HSBC's services to SMEs for 1999. It shows that the actual cost:income ratio of 62 per cent from the four income activities was revised to [✂] per cent when corrected to a norm for the five largest banks. These results were on the assumption that the cost:income ratio of asset finance activities was [✂] per cent, based on information from HSBC, and our estimate for the cost of the 'deposit' income shown in column 3 of [✂] per cent, based on information from other banks.

487

TABLE 7.31 **Barclays: application of assumptions to arrive at a cost:income ratio for comparison with other large banks providing services to SMEs, 1999**

£ million

Based on five largest banks' benchmark

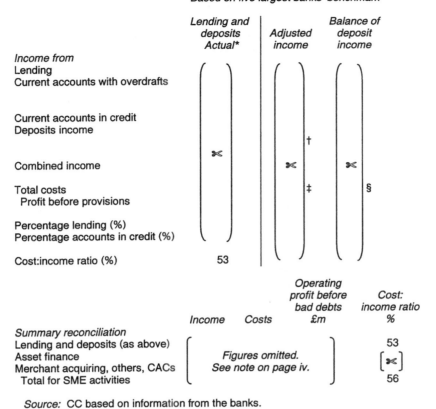

	Lending and deposits Actual*	Adjusted income	Balance of deposit income
Income from			
Lending			
Current accounts with overdrafts			
Current accounts in credit			
Deposits income		†	
Combined income	✂	✂	✂
Total costs		‡	§
Profit before provisions			
Percentage lending (%)			
Percentage accounts in credit (%)			
Cost:income ratio (%)	53		

	Income	Costs	Operating profit before bad debts £m	Cost: income ratio %
Summary reconciliation				
Lending and deposits (as above)				53
Asset finance	Figures omitted.			[✂]
Merchant acquiring, others, CACs	See note on page iv.			
Total for SME activities				56

Source: CC based on information from the banks.

---

*Excludes adjustments noted separately in Chapters 5 and 6.

†The total is 127 per cent of lending income. This income is then allocated between current accounts in credit, and deposit accounts in the same ratio as for the equivalent actual income in column 1. See also paragraph 7.148, which discusses an alternative calculation for the apportionment of this income.

‡Actual total costs plus costs of balancing deposits.

§Calculated as £[✂] million times [✂] per cent for current accounts, and £[✂] million times [✂] per cent for deposit accounts, being percentages derived from Barclays' submission (see Table 7.28).

TABLE 7.32 **HSBC: application of assumptions to arrive at a cost:income ratio for comparison with other larg banks providing services to SMEs, 1999**

£ million

Based on five largest banks' benchmark

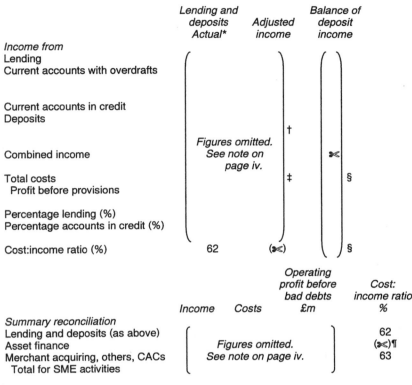

	Lending and deposits Actual*	Adjusted income	Balance of deposit income
Income from			
Lending			
Current accounts with overdrafts			
Current accounts in credit			
Deposits		†	
	Figures omitted. See note on page iv.		✂
Combined income			
Total costs		‡	§
Profit before provisions			
Percentage lending (%)			
Percentage accounts in credit (%)			
Cost:income ratio (%)	62	(✂)	§

	Income	Costs	Operating profit before bad debts £m	Cost: income ratio %
Summary reconciliation				
Lending and deposits (as above)				62
Asset finance	*Figures omitted.*			(✂)¶
Merchant acquiring, others, CACs	*See note on page iv.*			63
Total for SME activities				

Source: CC based on information from the banks.

---

*Excludes adjustments noted separately in Chapters 5 and 6.

†The total is 127 per cent of lending income. This income is then allocated between current accounts in credit, and deposit accounts in the same ratio as for the equivalent actual income in column 1. See also paragraph 7.148, which discusses an alternative calculation for the apportionment of this income.

‡Actual total costs plus costs of balancing deposits.

§Calculated as £[✂] million income from current accounts at [✂] per cent cost:income ratio, and £[✂] million income from deposit accounts at a cost:income ratio of [✂] per cent, which gave an average ratio of [✂] per cent (see Table 7.28). These cost:income figures were taken from results for other banks, despite HSBC's suggestion that we should use its own overall estimate of [✂] per cent.

¶Estimated by the CC as HSBC did not provide this information. If the ratio is lower, the cost:income ratio for the other activities will increase.

7.140. Table 7.33 summarizes the calculations regarding NatWest's activities to SMEs for 1999. It shows that the actual cost:income ratio of 68 per cent from the four income activities was revised to [✂] per cent when corrected to a norm for the five largest banks.

TABLE 7.33 **NatWest: application of assumptions to arrive at a cost:income ratio for comparison with other large banks providing services to SMEs, 1999**

£ million

Based on five largest banks' benchmark

	Lending and deposits Actual*	Adjusted income	Balance of deposit income
Income from			
Lending			
Current accounts with overdrafts			
Current accounts in credit			
Deposits		†	
Combined income	*Figures omitted. See note on page iv.*		
Total costs		‡	✂ §
Profit before provisions			
Percentage lending (%)			
Percentage accounts in credit (%)			
Cost:income ratio (%)	68	(✂)	

	Income	Costs	Operating profit before bad debts £m	Cost: income ratio %
Summary reconciliation				
Lending and deposits (as above)		*Figures omitted.*		68¶
Merchant acquiring, others, CACs		*See note on page iv.*		(✂)¶
Total for SME activities		¤		68

Source: CC based on information from the banks.

---

*Excludes adjustments noted separately in Chapters 5 and 6.

†The total is 127 per cent of lending income. This income is then allocated between current accounts in credit, and deposit accounts in the same ratio as for the equivalent actual income in column 1. See also paragraph 7.148, which discusses an alternative calculation for the apportionment of this income.

‡Actual total costs minus costs of balancing deposits.

§Calculated as £[✂] million times notional cost:income ratio of [✂] per cent, plus £[✂] million times notional cost:income ratio of [✂] per cent. NatWest did not provide any analysis of costs for these activities, and these cost:income figures were taken from results for other banks (see Table 7.28).

¶NatWest told us that we should use the overall cost:income ratio for this calculation, and therefore attribute a similar ratio to its lending and deposit activities.

¤This figure was the original total provided by NatWest, but late in the inquiry it was revised to £[✂]. We have not revised these workings for the change.

7.141. Table 7.34 summarizes the calculations regarding RBS's activities to SMEs for 1999. It shows that the estimated cost:income ratio of 58 per cent from the four income activities remained at [✂] per cent when corrected to a norm for the five largest banks.

TABLE 7.34 RBS: application of assumptions to arrive at a cost:income ratio for comparison with other large banks providing services to SMEs, 1999

£ million

Based on five largest banks' benchmark

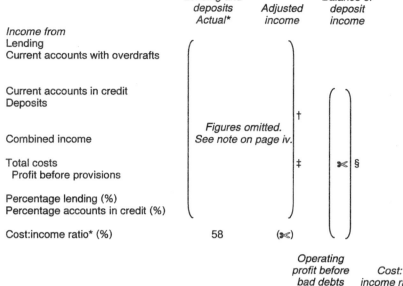

	Lending and deposits Actual*	Adjusted income	Balance of deposit income
Income from			
Lending			
Current accounts with overdrafts			
Current accounts in credit			
Deposits			
Combined income	Figures omitted.	†	
Total costs	See note on page iv.	‡	✂ §
Profit before provisions			
Percentage lending (%)			
Percentage accounts in credit (%)			
Cost:income ratio* (%)	58	(✂)	

Summary reconciliation	Income	Costs	Operating profit before bad debts £m	Cost: income ratio %¶
Lending and deposits (as above)				58
Merchant acquiring, others, CACs				
For customers with turnover to £10m	Figures omitted.			✂
For customers with turnover from £10m to £25m	See note on page iv.			
Total for SME activities				58

Source: CC based on information from the banks.

---

*Excludes adjustments noted separately in Chapters 5 and 6.

†The total is 127 per cent of lending income. This income is then allocated between current accounts in credit, and deposit accounts in the same ratio as for the equivalent actual income in column 1. See also paragraph 7.148, which discusses an alternative calculation for the apportionment of this income.

‡Actual total costs plus costs of balancing deposits.

§Calculated as £[✂] million times notional cost:income ratio of [✂] per cent for current accounts, and £[✂] million times [✂] per cent for deposit accounts. RBS did not provide any analysis of costs for these activities, and these cost:income figures were taken from results for other banks (see Table 7.28).

¶RBS told us that we should use the overall cost:income ratio for the individual calculations by product category, and therefore attribute a ratio of 58 per cent to its lending and deposit activities.

7.142. Table 7.35 summarizes the calculations regarding BoS's activities to SMEs for the year to February 2001. It shows that the estimated cost:income ratio of [✂] per cent from the four income activities changed to [✂] per cent when corrected to a norm for the five largest banks. These results were on the assumption that the cost:income ratio of asset finance activities was [✂] per cent as calculated by BoS.

TABLE 7.35 BoS: application of assumptions to arrive at a cost:income ratio for comparison with other large banks providing services to SMEs, based on the year to February 2001

£ million

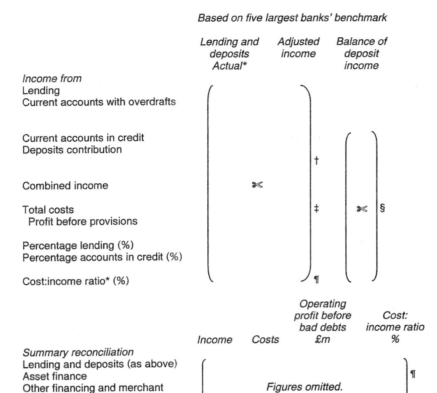

Based on five largest banks' benchmark

	Lending and deposits Actual*	Adjusted income	Balance of deposit income
Income from			
Lending			
Current accounts with overdrafts			
Current accounts in credit			
Deposits contribution			
Combined income			
Total costs			
Profit before provisions			
Percentage lending (%)			
Percentage accounts in credit (%)			
Cost:income ratio* (%)			

	Income	Costs	Operating profit before bad debts £m	Cost: income ratio %
Summary reconciliation				
Lending and deposits (as above)				
Asset finance				
Other financing and merchant acquiring		Figures omitted. See note on page iv.		
Investment profits				
Total for SME activities				

Source: CC based on information from the banks.

*Excludes adjustments noted separately in Chapter 6.

†The total is 127 per cent of lending income. This income is then allocated between current accounts in credit, and deposit accounts in the same ratio as for the equivalent actual income in column 1. See also paragraph 7.148, which discusses an alternative calculation for the apportionment of this income.

‡Actual total costs plus costs of balancing deposits.

§Calculated as £[✂] million times notional cost:income ratio of [✂] per cent for current accounts, and £[✂] million times [✂] per cent for deposit accounts. BoS did not provide any analysis of costs and these cost:income figures were taken from results for other banks (see Table 7.28).

¶Calculated by BoS.

7.143. Table 7.36 summarizes the results from the methodology, as discussed above. The table shows the total income from all services to SMEs for the largest banks (line A). It then shows the income from the four services discussed, and the respective cost:income ratios (line B). The table then notes each bank's lending:deposits ratio and compares this with the benchmark ratio of 44:56 (deposits set at 127 per cent of lending). The table then shows the adjusted income from the four services on the revised basis and the revised cost:income ratio for this theoretical income (line C). Finally the table compares the revised cost:income ratios with the two lowest-cost main banks.

TABLE 7.36 **The six largest clearing groups: summary of cost:income comparisons, using data mainly from 1999***

Label		Barclays	Lloyds	HSBC	NatWest†	RBS‡	BoS§
A	Total income from services to SMEs (£m)	(		✂		)	
	Original cost:income ratio (%)	56	50	63	68	58	
	Of which actual income from lending/deposits totalled	(		✂		)	
	And resulted in: cost:income ratios (%) (see tables						
B	above)	53	44	62	68	58	¶
	and lending:deposit income ratios of (see tables above)						
	Does the bank have more income from deposits than the 44:56 norm?						
	Adjusted lending income plus income from deposits assuming a similar mix of income from lending/accounts in credit (see tables above)		*Figures omitted. See note on page iv.*				✂
C	Adjusted cost income ratio on similar mix of income from lending/accounts in credit (%) (see tables above)	51	44	60	73	58	
	Impact of adjustment, ie C minus B	−2	0	−2	+5	0	
D	Difference from lowest-cost main bank, ie Lloyds TSB—see line C	+7	0	+16	+29	+14	
E	Difference from alternative low cost main bank, ie Barclays—see line C	0	−7	+9	+22	+7	

Source: CC based on information from the banks.

*Using 1999 data the largest five banks (excluding BoS); the lending to accounts in credit ratio is 44:56.

†Figures estimated by the CC from management accounts of NatWest.

‡Figures estimated by the CC from management accounts of RBS. The £[✂] million represents income from customers with turnover up to £10 million. In addition we estimated some £[✂] million income from customers with turnover from £10 million to £25 million, which is excluded from this analysis.

§BoS information is for year ended February 2001, which was the only year for which it had disaggregated income information.

¶Estimate based on information from BoS.

7.144. As a check on our calculations, we calculated the average value across the banks of the cost:income ratio for each of the four main activities (where information was available as shown in Table 7.28)—namely for overdrafts, loans, current accounts in credit and deposit accounts—and applied these imputed cost:income ratios to the actual income figures for each bank.

7.145. Table 7.29 shows the basic data from which the income figures were extracted; and Table 7.37 shows the income data used, together with the imputed cost:income ratios. The variation in the overall imputed cost:income ratios identified in line F (for the four main activities) cannot be due to differences in cost:income ratios between banks because the same ratios have been used in the calculation for all of them. The variations observed therefore reflect the difference in business mix as between the banks. The difference between the imputed figures in line F and the actual ratios, reproduced in line B, therefore reflect differences in cost:income ratios, having allowed for business mix. These differences are shown in line G and these figures can then be expressed in relation to the lowest cost ratio observed as shown in line H. For comparison, line D shows the equivalent figures calculated in Table 7.35. Alternatively the figures in Table 7.36 can be expressed in relation to the second lowest cost: income ratio observed, as shown in line J and compared with the equivalent figures from Table 7.36, ie line E.

TABLE 7.37 **The six largest clearing groups: summary of method applying an imputed cost:income ratio to the actual income from lending and customer accounts in credit for 1999***

Label		Barclays	Lloyds TSB	HSBC	NatWest	RBS†	BoS‡	£ million | Imputed cost:income ratio§ %
	Income from							
	Lending							55
	Current accounts with overdrafts							66
	Current accounts in credit							49
	Deposits							25
K	Total income from lending and deposits							
				Figures omitted. See note on page iv.				
	Calculations of costs based on imputed cost:income ratios as above							
	Lending							
	Current accounts with overdrafts							
	Current accounts in credit							
	Deposits							
L	Total imputed costs for lending and deposits							
							per cent	
F	Imputed CIRs based on company mix (ie L divided by K)	51	50	52	48	49		
B	Original cost:income ratio for lending/ deposit activities	53	44	62	68	58		
G	Difference between lines B and F	+3	–6	+10	+20	+9		
H	Difference from lowest-cost main bank (Lloyds TSB) using standard cost:income ratios on actual income from services—see line G	+9	0	+16	+26	+15		
D	Difference from lowest-cost main bank (Lloyds TSB) using standard mix of income from lending and accounts in credit—see Table 7.36	+7	0	+16	+29	+14	✂	
J	Difference from alternative low-cost main bank (Barclays) using standard cost:income ratios on actual income from services—see line G	0	–9	+7	+17	+6		
E	Difference from alternative low-cost main bank (Barclays) using standard mix of income from lending and accounts in credit—see Table 7.36	0	–7	+9	+22	+7		

Source: CC based on information from the banks.

*Using 1999 data the largest five banks (excluding BoS).

†Figures estimated by the CC from management accounts of RBS, based on services to customers with turnover to £10 million. The total income from such customers was £[✂] million, and in addition we estimated some £[✂] million income from customers with turnover from £10 million to £25 million, which is excluded from this analysis.

‡BoS information is for the year to February 2001, which was the only year for which it could produce disaggregated income information.

§Based on information in Table 7.28.

Note: Some figures rounded.

7.146. Table 7.38 summarizes the overall results of adjusting for business mix. Line A shows the original cost:income ratio for each bank's total services to SMEs as a whole, and line B for the four main activities of overdraft, loans, current accounts in credit, and deposit accounts. Line M shows an illustrative adjustment suggested by the last four lines of Table 7.37 to reflect the differential cost:income ratios from having allowed for the impact of business mix, and for the moment, presuming that no other adjustments are appropriate (for example, for price or quality characteristics). It is roughly a mid-point between the comparative results using the lowest- and next-lowest cost banks. Line N shows the resulting adjusted ratios for the four main activities. Line K reproduces the actual income from those four activities, and line Q the difference between actual costs and the costs that would have arisen in generating the income shown if the banks had all exhibited the lowest cost:income ratios, having allowed for the differences in business mix. Line R shows the cost:income ratio for all services to SMEs (as reflected in line A) if the banks' cost:income results reflected the line M adjustment, ie having allowed for the differences in business mix as between the main four activities which accounted for 82 per cent of all SME income for the largest five banks as shown in Table 7.29.

TABLE 7.38 **The six largest clearing groups: summary of methods to calculate the potential cost:income ratio adjustment for each bank to achieve parity with lowest-cost bank***

Label		Barclays	Lloyds TSB	HSBC	NatWest	RBS†	BoS‡
A	Original cost:income ratio for all SME activities (%)	56	50	63	68	58	(✂)
B	Cost:income ratio on the four main banking activities for lending and deposits (%)§						
M	Suggested cost:income adjustment based on lines D, E, H and J from Table 7.37 (%)						
N	Revised cost:income ratio for lending/accounts in credit only (%)		*Figures omitted.*				✂
K	Actual income from lending and accounts in credit (£m)		*See note on page iv.*				
Q	Evaluation of cost:income ratio variance (£m) (line K times M)					¶	
R	Equivalent for all services to SMEs (%) (line A – M)						

Source: CC based on information from the banks.

---

*Using 1999 data the largest five banks (excluding BoS where figures were used for the year to February 2001).
†RBS provided us with estimates of its operating costs, which included specific and memorandum recharges.
‡BoS information is based on the year to February 2001.
§Based on information in Table 7.36.
¶Figures estimated by the CC from management accounts of RBS, based on services to customers with turnover to £10 million. The total income from such customers was £[✂] million, and in addition we estimated some £[✂] million income from customers with turnover from £10 million to £25 million, which is excluded from this analysis.
Note: Some figures rounded.

7.147. As a further check on the above results, we applied a similar approach, but this time increasing the costs to take account of accounting differences such as additional pension costs for Barclays, Lloyds TSB, NatWest and RBS; and to correct for the treatment of operating leases in 1999 as shown in Table 7.24. The results from this exercise were not dissimilar to those shown above.

7.148. Footnote † to Tables 7.30 to 7.35 also showed that the analysis of adjusted income in column 2 into current accounts in credit, and deposits, was in the same proportion as the total income equivalents shown in column 1. On this basis, the balance of 'deposit' income in column 3 was calculated, and costs relating to this income were estimated. We noted, however, that Table 7.29 showed that the total income from the five largest banks from current accounts in credit was some 88 per cent of lending income (ie £1,639 million divided by £1,870 million); and for deposit income the ratio was 38 per cent (£718 million divided by £1,870 million), and that the relative weights of such income between banks was not the same. As an alternative approach, we therefore did workings for each bank that apportioned 'deposit' income in column 2 (assuming a similar overall income mix of 44:56 from lending:deposits) between current accounts in credit and deposit income, using the 88 per cent of lending ratio, and the 38 per cent ratios respectively. Accordingly, we were able to calculate a new balance of 'deposit' income in column 3, from which costs relating to such income were estimated. When we summarized the results, we found again that they were not dissimilar to those shown in the above tables.

7.149. The above analysis excluded from income the attributable capital adjustment, as discussed in Chapter 6, in arriving at cost:income ratios for comparison between the banks. The attributable capital adjustment takes account of the cost of capital used to support lending and, if this was included in the cost:income ratios, then, to the extent that this made any difference to the comparison of these ratios across the banks (reflecting different capital structures), it would have created a distortion that was not relevant to the analysis between the banks.

7.150. In the following paragraphs we summarize the main additional responses on cost:income ratios for HSBC, Barclays and RBSG; and their views on perceived cost differences between banks. HSBC indicated various matters that it considered should be taken into account regarding its circumstances, when considering its relative efficiency with other banks, as described in paragraph 7.151ff. BoS did not provide any special comments on cost:income ratios from services to SMEs.

HSBC's views on cost:income ratios

7.151. HSBC stated that it disagreed strongly with the CC's approach in this area, and that cost:income ratios were generally imperfect measures of comparative efficiency. It said that cost:income ratios could only be regarded as meaningful measures for like-for-like businesses where cost and income were reported on a like-for-like basis, and businesses had the same capital structure. Furthermore all the businesses must be 'price takers' or there must be no significant differentiation in prices because otherwise there would be non-efficient parameters being reflected in income. HSBC also requested that, if the cost:income ratio was a good measure of operating efficiency, the CC should use return on equity as a measure of operating and capital efficiency. Return on equity would reflect both effects and would seem a logical extension of the CC's approach. This would lead to businesses with high returns on equity being regarded as efficient. HSBC then suggested that this would create the result that the businesses earning in excess of the cost of capital would be the same as those considered to be earning 'excess profit'. HSBC added that a low cost:income ratio did not necessarily imply low costs and therefore efficiency, but only that costs were a low proportion of income, and that feature could be income as well as cost related.

7.152. HSBC said that there were other measures available to the CC which, in its view, would have been more relevant to measuring efficiency, such as cost per unit of output (for example, cost per customer, or cost per branch); the number of customers served; the number of cheques cleared; and the number of accounts managed. As a minimum, other comparators should have been used. HSBC said that in recent water merger cases, at least five comparators had been used. Moreover, the concept of economic efficiency, as used by economic regulators, related to the relationship between inputs and outputs. However, outputs and, wherever possible, inputs were not measured in financial but in physical terms—this was because any financial measure of inputs and outputs included both price and quantity effects and could not therefore isolate efficiency from other factors.

7.153. HSBC then said that there was extensive literature relating to measuring efficiency in the banking markets—it suggested that there were studies that did not use cost:income ratios as an efficiency measure. HSBC also considered that UK banks had the lowest cost:income ratios in Europe.

7.154. HSBC agreed that differences in cost:income ratios between banks could be explained by differences in business mix, cost allocation, financial reporting, and efficiency, in principle. However, HSBC contended that there was insufficient information to estimate all such differences. It did not believe that differences in SME banking business mix could be easily isolated or that adjustments could be immediately made for differences in relation to:

(a) Product mix.

(b) Customer mix (in terms of size, risk profile and industry sector)—it said that a bank that serviced smaller customers would incur more cost for the same level of income than a bank that serviced larger customers. HSBC added that its customers were towards the smaller end of the turnover range, reflecting the bank's free banking offers and Community Banking strategy.

(c) Service proposition mix, particularly on the balance between price and cost, but also on issues such as customer responsiveness, attention to individual customer requirements, customer satisfaction, and complaints procedures. HSBC added that it was differentiated from its competitors by its Community Banking, which involves higher costs due to the presence of a high number of senior staff in branches.

(d) Distribution channel mix, for example by remote delivery, business/service centre, or branch delivery. For example, a bank that offers customers a choice of delivery channels will have higher costs than a bank that offers services only over the Internet.

496

(e) Operations/processing mix—a bank with very centralized processing would have a different cost structure to one that had more branch-based processes. Furthermore, a bank that outsourced processes could have a lower cost:income ratio than a bank that kept those processes in-house to the extent that the cost of outsourcing was presented as fees and deducted in arriving at income rather than inclusion in costs.

7.155. HSBC strongly objected to any view that it was not efficient or that its costs should be compared with a benchmark based on another bank's activities. When we discussed the gap between HSBC's overall cost:income ratio and those of other banks, HSBC did not accept, for example, that its costs could be as much as [✂] percentage points higher than other banks. It added that it could not reconcile some statistics put forward by the CC to the published financial statements of competitor banks. It suggested that [✂] percentage points of any difference—if the CC believed there to be such a difference, which it refuted—was due to its Community Banking strategy, [✂] percentage points were due to accounting differences between banks, such as the treatment of operating leases, and [✂] percentage points were due to other reasons. We discuss these possible causes in the following paragraphs. HSBC also provided workings comparing itself, for example, with Lloyds TSB (as a bank that was acknowledged as having placed emphasis on cost controls), using data from the latter's published financial statements, but said that it was unable to reconcile any estimate of Lloyds TSB's cost:income ratio from SME activities with its own.

7.156. Dealing first with HSBC's Community Banking point, it said that the key to its success in serving customers was its locally-focused service delivery by means of branches at which local managers were given considerable autonomy in how they ran their operations to achieve high customer satisfaction levels and to win new business. It said that this strategy originated from 1992/93 when HSBC's market share had dipped from 14 to 12 per cent, compared with its current estimate of 16 per cent. It emphasized that it had not reduced its branch structure compared with its four largest competitors. Table 7.39 summarizes changes in branch numbers between 1992 and 1999. HSBC said that its strategy had not been to compromise the level of service by reducing its branch network. HSBC considered that the closure of branches and restructuring of many bank services (for example, by moving functions to central or regional offices) by its principal competitors might have led to loss of confidence in the quality of advice they could offer to their small business customers, and to a reduction in service levels, and might have been a possible reason for the lower satisfaction levels of their customers.

TABLE 7.39 **The largest five banks: summary of branch changes (based on information in Chapter 3)**

	Branches in 1992	Branches in 1999	Change 1992 to 1999	Percentage change
Barclays	2,274	1,895	−379	−17
NatWest	2,541	1,712	−829	−33
RBS	786	648	−138	−18
Lloyds TSB	3,253	2,309	−944	−29
	8,854	6,564	−2,290	−26
HSBC*	1,734	1,676	−58	−3
Total	10,588	8,240	−2,348	−22

Source: CC based on information from the BBA and HSBC.

---

*HSBC subsequently made small changes to this table. For example, it changed 1,734 to 1,716 as branches in 1992; and 1,676 in 1999 to 1,662 in 1999, being a revised reduction of 54 branches, compared with 58 as noted above.

7.157. HSBC therefore said that its commitment to Community Banking came at a cost which it estimated at [✂] percentage points in terms of cost:income ratio. It based this calculation on the assumption that:

(a) the impact on the cost:income ratio could be estimated by calculating the cost of keeping open branches that otherwise would have been closed if it had not adopted the Community Banking strategy; and

(b) its personnel costs per outlet were at a similar level to those of competitor banks.

7.158. In order to assess the impact of its Community Banking approach on its cost:income ratio, HSBC said that had it closed around 26 per cent of its branches, this would have resulted in a reduction in its network of a further 392 outlets, leaving it with around 1,270 branches. It estimated the average cost per branch as £[✂]¹ and that SMEs accounted for [✂] per cent of branch costs. It therefore estimated the total costs of such branches at £[✂] million, which, compared with income of £[✂] million for 1999, would amount to around [✂] percentage points in terms of cost:income ratio. Table 7.40 shows the number of SME customers and accounts per branch for the largest banks, based on statistics in Chapter 3. HSBC had 263 SME customers per branch compared with 248 for Lloyds TSB, and 326 SME accounts per branch compared with 289 for Lloyds TSB. The changes from 1992 to 1999 could have reflected:

(a) that Barclays and NatWest were overbranched; and

(b) Lloyds TSB's rationalization following its merger with TSB in 1995.

We asked HSBC whether it would have been able to operate with only 65 per cent of the average number of the three main competitor banks' branch networks (around 1,300 branches), without a fall in income. It said that closure of a significant number of branches would not only be a reversal of current HSBC strategy, but would inevitably have a detrimental impact upon its service proposition, given that HSBC considered that it currently had a number of branches which was appropriate to its proposition. Income could clearly be affected as would the ability of the bank to deliver 'Community Banking' and to provide a good value-for-money service for customers.

TABLE 7.40 **Summary of SME accounts and customers per branch in 1999 for the largest four clearing groups**

	Number of current accounts '000	Number of SME customers* '000	Number of branches	Accounts per branch	Customers per branch
Barclays	729	521	1,895	385	274
NatWest	725	653	1,712	423	381
RBS	233	182	648	360	281
HSBC	542	437	1,662	326	263
Lloyds TSB	667	572	2,309	289	248

Source: CC based on information from the BBA and the banks.

*Excluding clubs and charities. The NatWest and RBS numbers are for customers with turnover to £100 million, but this additional group is small.

7.159. HSBC also indicated that the difference between its and Lloyds TSB's respective approach to operating leases was also a cause of distortions in the comparison of cost:income ratio. It noted that it (HSBC) showed depreciation on operating leases as an expense in accordance with its accounting policies. It suggested, however, that Lloyds TSB as a comparator bank had offset depreciation on operating leases against the relevant income, rather than showing it as an expense in 1999 and in earlier years. Accordingly it said that to compare itself with Lloyds TSB, it should offset depreciation of £[✂] million against income of £[✂] million (including income from clubs, charities and associations), and make an offsetting adjustment to reduce costs from £[✂] million to £[✂] million. Accordingly, it calculated that the change could result in a reduction in its perceived cost:income ratio of [✂] per cent.

7.160. As explained in footnote ‡ to Table 7.24, prior to 2000 Lloyds TSB's policy was to deduct operating lease depreciation in arriving at its income, whereas the other banks treated this depreciation as a cost. When we discussed the treatment of operating leases as a factor in explaining the gap between Lloyds TSB and other banks, Lloyds TSB quantified the difference as being less than one percentage point on its whole bank and SME cost:income ratio, and said that the scale of the Lloyds TSB operating lease business was deemed immaterial. It added that Lloyds TSB had changed the accounting treatment in 2000 following the publication of the Statement of Recommended Practice on leasing, which established the GAAP in respect of the treatment of operating leases in the books of the lessor. Prior to 2000, there had been no such published guidance.

7.161. HSBC emphasized that it believed business mix also caused major differences in perceived cost:income ratios between banks. We have discussed the impact of business mix on cost:income ratios earlier in this chapter. We noted, however, that HSBC reported a relatively high cost:income ratio from

¹Calculated as the total costs of the branch network in 1999 (£[✂] million) divided by the number of branches in 1999 of 1,662.

current account services of [✂] per cent. It said that the ratio appeared high because it allocated the cost of money transmission to costs for current accounts. Table 7.41 shows the summarized results that HSBC provided to show the cost and income on its most commonly used accounts, and its money transmission services. It allocated costs of [✂] per cent of 'income' on its money transmission services. It hypothesized that its competitor banks might not have allocated 100 per cent of their money transmission costs to their current accounts, and might have allocated their costs in a different way.

7.162. HSBC said that in addition to the differences between banks in the underlying basis of preparation (described in more detail in Chapter 6), differences in cost:income ratios between banks could also be explained by accounting differences, as calculation of the ratio was not prescribed by accounting standards. The policies and methods for calculating income and costs could be different between banks, and although, for example, HSBC fully absorbed all its costs (including central overheads) in arriving at the profitability of its products, other competitor banks might not do the same. HSBC also said that while not affecting SME activities, the presentation of insurance income and costs illustrated well the flexibility in accounting presentation—while not applicable to HSBC, it was the general practice for related income to be included as income in the cost:income ratio, but for related costs to be ignored. The alternative treatment was to include both related income and related costs in the cost:income ratio. HSBC also said that the treatment of pension costs or surpluses would also affect the cost:income ratio. It noted that some banks had pension credits at a whole-bank level (for example, Lloyds TSB), while HSBC had a pension charge increasing its costs. HSBC considered that removing its pension charge from its UK banking operations (which includes services to SMEs) would reduce its cost:income ratio by two percentage points.

TABLE 7.41 **HSBC: analysis of costs and income from its current account services to SMEs (including some large corporates with turnover greater than £25 million served by its branch network) for 1999***

£ million

	Negotiated tariff	Money transmission	Small business	Total*
Income				
Cost	✂	†	✂	
Operating profit/loss				
Cost:income ratio (%)				

Source: HSBC.

*HSBC said that the information was derived from its management information system. However, it said that the figures shown in this table were not directly reconcilable to the overall income and costs from services to SMEs as shown in Chapter 6 and in this chapter because this analysis includes:
— income and costs of these services provided to SMEs and large corporates dealt with by the branch network, but will not reflect all income and costs of such services to large corporates; and
— income and costs of fewer services than are included in the comparable SME information.
†HSBC said that the information was derived from its management information system, with the costs being determined on a fully absorbed level.

7.163. HSBC said that it could not reduce its cost:income ratio by increasing its income from taking on more deposits which carried a lower cost:income ratio ([✂] per cent compared with [✂] per cent), because it did not manage its business in this way. HSBC said that it could not just focus on raising funds. It said that deposit-taking formed part of the whole banking service offering and that it was up to the SME customer to choose the extent to which they held surplus cash with the bank. HSBC added that any further deposits would need to be reinvested in new loans to customers, which depended on customers' appetite for new credit.

7.164. HSBC also said that it considered its prices were below most of its competitor banks, and hence its income would be lower than its competitors for a given volume of products, which could result in an increase of up to [✂] percentage points in cost:income ratio. Chapter 4 covers prices and our analysis of relative pricing between the main banks. HSBC also added that its free-banking proposition to customers with turnover less than £1 million could result in forgone income of up to £[✂] million a year and this too could result in its cost:income ratio being [✂] percentage point higher than those of its competitors.

7.165. We noted that HSBC rebranded its UK branch network from 'Midland Bank' to HSBC in 1999. It told us that most of such costs were met by its holding company bank, but total costs for 1999 from this process totalled approximately £[✂] million.

Barclays' views on cost:income ratios

7.166. Barclays indicated various adjustments to its costs, which we cover separately in paragraph 7.109. It said that the cost:income ratio was a measure of return as it was logically equal to one minus the operating profit margin, and not of efficiency. As a result, a higher ratio could equally be the result of lower prices or of higher costs. It emphasized its view that cost:income ratios were not an appropriate measure of cost inefficiency. Barclays also added that any adjustments for business mix, as covered by the workings in Tables 7.28 to 7.38, were flawed and it gave us some calculations using what it described as extreme examples to illustrate its view that reliance should not be placed on the results of the analysis.

7.167. Barclays said that it was essential to allow for differences in relative prices if cost:income ratios were to be used as a measure of relative cost efficiency. Income was the product of output multiplied by prices, whereas efficiency is measured by cost divided by output. Barclays' cost:income ratio could be higher than others because its prices were lower. Its view was that the CC's research in Chapter 4 showed that its prices were lower. Barclays argued that evidence showed it was price competitive rather than cost inefficient. It noted that its product mix could also be a source of differences between banks, as well as factors such as the degree of investment in the future development of the business, participation in money transmission systems, treatment of restructuring provisions, and the extent of its branch network. In assessing the overall adequacy of its cost:income ratio, it pointed out its quality in relationship management and its quality in customer service. It added that it did not primarily use cost:income ratios as a tool for assessing performance of its activities.

7.168. In addition to price differences as a source of cost:income variances, Barclays summarized the following factors as sources of differences in cost:income ratios between banks' services to SMEs:

(a) there could be differences in costs and income allocations between product groups within an SME banking business;

(b) full service banks could have a higher cost structure than those offering more limited services;

(c) investment expenditure that was not capitalized but treated as revenue costs could distort relative ratios;

(d) the treatment of intangibles could distort ratios;

(e) survivor bias could explain differences in ratios;

(f) ratios were sensitive to the period over which profits were assessed, in particular to take account of changes in GDP across the cycle—it said that using the years 1998 to 2000 as a key measurement period was not appropriate as these were benign years in the economic cycle; and

(g) an attributable capital adjustment should be made before calculating relative cost:income ratios.

7.169. Barclays also referred to a need to compare rates of return with those of other leading companies, when assessing the significance of cost:income ratios.

7.170. Barclays stated that it could not accept any view that another bank could demonstrate substantially superior levels of service in a like-for-like comparison with itself. It considered that it had high levels of customer satisfaction on a number of factors, and paragraphs 4.254 to 4.256 summarize results from a market research survey of perceptions on customer satisfaction, and value for money.

RBS's and NatWest's views on cost:income ratios

7.171. RBSG believed that using the most efficient costs would be wrong in principle and would lead to serious practical problems. It considered that cost:income ratios were only appropriate in principle if new competitors could build up market share very rapidly, based solely on price, as was the case in some industries, whereas in banking even strong competitors such as RBS had taken some time to build up their market shares.

7.172. RBSG said that cost:income ratios were not appropriate if low-cost firms' offerings differed in quality from those of other providers (a frequent result of cost-cutting innovations in banking such as branch closures) or where the impact of cost cutting on profits emerged only slowly (as was often the case for management innovations).

7.173. On a practical basis, RBSG said that cost:income ratios, as absolute comparators, were not appropriate indicators of efficiency in banking, because they were strongly affected by the different mixes of different banks. Banks that had focused on cutting their cost:income ratio had tended to cease to carry on low-margin but profitable businesses that banks with a contribution-based business model had persisted with. It added that there was still a debate as to whether the differences in banks' cost:income ratios that had emerged over the last five years would be sustained. It suggested that the apparent efficiency of cost-cutting banks such as Lloyds TSB might not produce superior long-term performance, as the financial markets seemed to be realizing. It concluded that entrants would therefore look to the profitability of the least—not the most—efficient firm as the benchmark.

7.174. In response to the initial suggestion of an achievable cost:income ratio of 50 per cent from services to SMEs, RBSG provided its own estimate. While it suggested that it had no established methodology for estimating the cost:income ratio of its services to SMEs as defined by the CC, it arrived at a range between 55 and 75 per cent. This was based on the ratio for NatWest Retail in 1999 which was 75 per cent, and RBSG stated that it had no reason to suppose that the cost:income ratio for services to SMEs would be lower than for personal banking or corporate banking. Subsequently, as discussed in Chapter 6, we were able to derive a cost:income ratio for NatWest's and RBS's SME banking businesses. RBSG added that:

(a) NatWest's cost:income ratio reflected its view that it suffered from low income rather than high costs.

(b) Its academic adviser suggested that adjustment to a bank's cost:income ratio on the basis of its presumed inefficiency on costs was circular.

(c) Allocation of shared costs was an arbitrary process, and RBSG did not do this in practice. It therefore suggested ranges, which by discussion with the CC became specific estimates, as noted in Chapter 6.

(d) RBSG did not believe that a 50 per cent cost:income ratio was achievable by NatWest for 1998 or 1999. RBSG also believed that shareholders, not customers, suffered as a result of NatWest's poor performance. Regarding the future, and RBSG's commitment at a group level to reduce the cost:income ratio below 50 per cent, this did not apply to the SME banking business, and its shareholders would have to support the management's efforts and investment decisions to achieve this objective. It believed the CC should allow, for example, the integration costs, in an assessment of cost:income ratios. RBSG said that it was transforming NatWest following its acquisition, and therefore suggested that detailed analysis of NatWest's historic cost:income ratios was irrelevant. It said that the takeover of NatWest was partly in response to the advantage gained by Lloyds TSB from its merger with TSB, and showed that the market for banking services was efficient and effective, although the transition period during which banks' cost:income ratios had fallen (including NatWest's) had lasted several years.

(e) RBSG did not believe it was appropriate to assess one variable (cost:income ratios) on a forward-looking basis, in relation to historic measures of other variables.

(f) RBSG regarded only Barclays as being comparable to NatWest. RBS also rejected any approach that sought to compare its performance with other banks, or applied a standardized income mix ratio of, for example, 127 per cent for 'deposits' to lending, as discussed in paragraph 7.136, or that any conclusions from the exercise of comparisons could be made. RBSG said that in practice, banking costs were a mixture of fixed and variable costs, and of shared and direct costs, and the mix comparative analysis discussed above did not reflect such realities.

Paragraph 13.224ff summarizes further its views on cost:income ratios.

Profit cyclicality

7.175. In order to consider whether banks' income and profits before bad debts were influenced by the economic cycle, we asked the largest banks to provide us with whole-bank and SME data to compare with changes in UK GDP for the period from 1989 to 2000. Barclays and HSBC provided us with such data. As neither bank had made any material acquisitions in the period, and as both had had significant shares of the UK SME market over the period, we considered that such data could help us to form a view on the extent to which income and profitability varied with changes in GDP.

7.176. HSBC provided data from 1989 for the whole bank and from 1990 for the SME segment (regarding the former Midland). We were told by HSBC that the data had been provided on a 'best endeavours' basis and that information from 1990 to 1994 was not strictly comparable with information for later years. This was due to the change in business structure that occurred in 1995, and the limited ability of information systems prior to 1995 to reproduce the information that we requested. As a result, the data points plotted for the periods prior to 1995 are included for indicative purposes only and are illustrated with a broken line. Data points for the years 1995 to 1999 are illustrated with a continuous line in the charts.

7.177. Lloyds TSB said that its inability to provide information relating to an economic cycle was due to difficulties associated with a reconciliation of information prior to its merger with TSB. Lloyds TSB added that any exercise to consider the effect of income and profitability with changes in GDP should be carried out with caution. It considered that a simple regression analysis of these variables with GDP over time was unlikely to present a fully representative picture of the bank's exposure to revenue and profit falls if growth in GDP were to slow or to decline. It suggested that further work was needed such as changes in SME customers' buying patterns, changes in the mix in banks' revenues, changes in the banks' lending policies (such as the extent to which different sectors have been targeted), and changes in the propensity of customers to buy products from their main supplier of banking services.

7.178. Lloyds TSB added that economic downturns differed in their length and severity, which meant it could not be assumed that the experience of the last recession would be repeated should GDP decline. Similarly the nature of economic downturns could vary. For example, it said that the recession of the late 1980s and early 1990s was in part a consequence of an unsustainable expansion of credit which had a disproportionate impact on the housing, property and construction sectors, whereas the previous recession in the early 1980s was a consequence of high interest rates which had a disproportionate effect on the manufacturing sector.

Barclays: comparison of performance to GDP

7.179. First, we looked at Barclays' whole-bank results. Table 7.42 shows whole-bank income data for Barclays from 1989 to 2000, which we illustrate in Figure 7.1 by plotting the changes (at constant 1995 prices) against GDP changes also at constant prices. The table shows how we converted Barclays' nominal results to constant prices.

TABLE 7.42 **Barclays: comparison of whole-bank income from 1989 to 2000 with changes in GDP at constant 1995 prices**

	1989	1990	1991	1992	1993	1994	1995	1996	1997	1998	1999	2000
Nominal GDP (£'000 bn)	513.3	556.2	584.5	608.2	639.4	677.6	713.9	756.1	805.4	851.7	891.1	934.9
Nominal whole-bank total income (£m)	5,639	5,754	6,366	6,776	7,416	6,990	7,251	7,566	7,589	7,382	8,361	9,596
Adjustment factor to constant 1995 prices	1.28	1.19	1.11	1.07	1.04	1.03	1.00	0.97	0.94	0.91	0.89	0.88
GDP at constant 1995 prices (£'000 bn)	655.2	659.5	649.8	650.3	665.4	694.6	713.9	732.2	757.9	777.9	794.4	820.2 ⎤
Annual change (%)	2.1	0.7	−1.5	0.1	2.3	4.4	2.8	2.6	3.5	2.6	2.1	3.3 ⎦
Whole-bank total income at constant 1995 prices (£m)	7,198	6,822	7,077	7,245	7,718	7,166	7,251	7,327	7,142	6,743	7,453	8,418 ⎤
Whole-bank annual change in constant income (%)	*	−5	4	2	7	−7	1	1	−3	−6	11	13 ⎦

Source: CC based on information from Barclays.

---

*Not available.

FIGURE 7.1

Barclays' comparison of the whole-bank changes in income, compared with changes in GDP in constant 1995 price

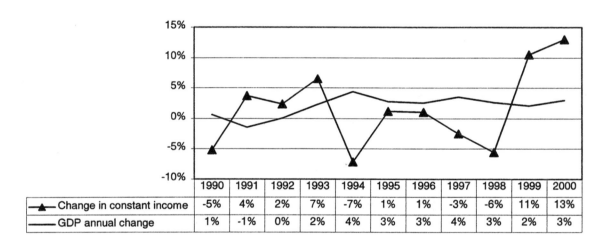

	1990	1991	1992	1993	1994	1995	1996	1997	1998	1999	2000
—▲— Change in constant income	-5%	4%	2%	7%	-7%	1%	1%	-3%	-6%	11%	13%
—— GDP annual change	1%	-1%	0%	2%	4%	3%	3%	4%	3%	2%	3%

Source: CC based on information from Barclays.

7.180. Table 7.43 shows profit before bad debt charges data for Barclays from 1989 to 2000, which we illustrate in Figure 7.2 by plotting the changes (at constant 1995 prices) to GDP changes also at constant prices. The table shows how we converted Barclays' nominal results to constant prices.

503

TABLE 7.43 **Barclays: comparison of whole-bank profit before bad debt charges from 1989 to 2000 with changes in GDP at constant 1995 prices**

	1989	1990	1991	1992	1993	1994	1995	1996	1997	1998	1999	2000
Annual change in GDP in constant 1995 prices as shown in Table 7.42 (%)	2.1	0.7	−1.5	0.1	2.3	4.4	2.8	2.6	3.5	2.6	2.1	3.3
Nominal whole-bank profit before bad debt charges (£m)	2,089	1,993	2,080	2,434	2,590	2,418	2,247	2,478	2,389	2,486	3,217	4,104
Adjustment factor to constant 1995 prices	1.28	1.19	1.11	1.07	1.04	1.03	1.00	0.97	0.94	0.91	0.89	0.88
Whole-bank profit before bad debt charges at constant 1995 prices (£m)	2,667	2,363	2,312	2,603	2,696	2,479	2,247	2,400	2,248	2,271	2,868	3,600
Whole-bank change in constant profit before bad debt charges (%)	*	−11	−2	13	4	−8	−9	7	−6	1	26	26

Source: CC based on information from Barclays.

*Not available.

FIGURE 7.2

Barclays' comparison of whole-bank changes in profit before provisions, compared with changes in GDP in constant 1995 prices

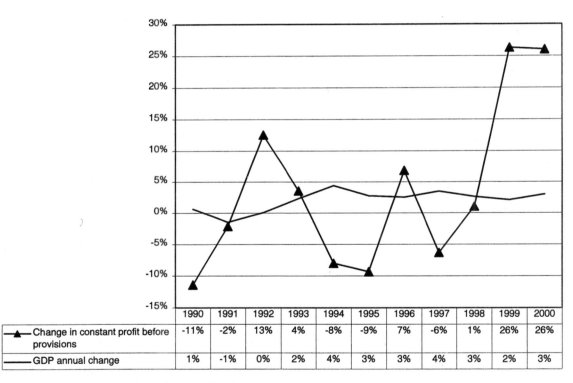

	1990	1991	1992	1993	1994	1995	1996	1997	1998	1999	2000
—▲—Change in constant profit before provisions	-11%	-2%	13%	4%	-8%	-9%	7%	-6%	1%	26%	26%
——GDP annual change	1%	-1%	0%	2%	4%	3%	3%	4%	3%	2%	3%

Source: CC based on information from Barclays.

7.181. Figure 7.2 shows the percentage change in Barclays' whole-bank operating profit before bad debt charges against the percentage change in GDP in constant 1995 prices. The changes in economic activity are the same as those in Figure 7.1. Changes in the whole bank's pre-bad-debt income display a similar pattern to changes in income over the early 1990s, and from 1996 to 1999. But there is a more prolonged period of decline over 1994 to 1995 with a return to positive growth not occurring until 1996. In addition, the recovery to positive growth, after a fall in real terms in 1997, had occurred by 1998 rather than by 1999 as was the case with income.

7.182. Next we compared levels of economic activity as measured by GDP (in constant 1995 prices) with:

— Barclays' income from services to SMEs (in constant 1995 prices); and

— Barclays' operating profit from services to SMEs (also in constant 1995 prices.

7.183. Table 7.44 shows the data used for this exercise from 1989 to 2000, and the results are shown in Figure 7.3. The data showed no obvious relationship between real levels of SME income with levels of GDP, or between SME profits before bad debts and levels of GDP.[1]

TABLE 7.44　**Barclays: comparison of levels of SME bank income, and operating profits before bad debt charges with GDP levels, 1989 to 2000**

	1989	1990	1991	1992	1993	1994	1995	1996	1997	1998	1999	2000
Nominal GDP (£'000 bn)	513.3	556.2	584.5	608.2	639.4	677.6	713.9	756.1	805.4	851.7	891.1	934.9
Nominal SME total income (£m)												
Nominal SME operating profits before bad debt charges					Figures omitted. See note on page iv.							
Adjustment factor to constant 1995 prices	1.28	1.19	1.11	1.07	1.04	1.03	1.00	0.97	0.94	0.91	0.89	0.88
GDP at constant 1995 prices (£'000 bn)	655	659	650	650	665	695	714	732	758	778	794	820
SME total income at constant 1995 prices (£m)												
SME operating profits before bad debt charges at constant 1995 prices (£m)					Figures omitted. See note on page iv.							
Indexed GDP at constant 1995 prices (1989=100)	100	101	99	99	102	106	109	112	116	119	121	125
Indexed SME total income at constant 1995 prices												
Indexed SME operating profits before bad debt charges at constant 1995 prices					Figures omitted. See note on page iv.							

Source: CC based on information from Barclays.

7.184. We then considered whether there was any relationship between the changes in SME income and changes in GDP, and the same for profits before bad debts and changes in GDP. Table 7.45 shows the change in Barclays' income from services to SMEs from 1989 to 2000 converted to constant 1995 prices. Figure 7.4 illustrates in chart form the changes in SME income (at constant prices), with GDP changes also at constant prices for this period.

[1]Regressing real levels of SME income against real levels of GDP produced a negative GDP coefficient ([✂]) that was statistically significant. The same regression for real levels of SME profits before bad debts and real levels of GDP also produced a negative GDP coefficient ([✂]) but it was statistically insignificant.

FIGURE 7.3

Barclays: comparison of indexed (constant 1995 prices) SME income, profits before bad debt charges, and GDP changes (based on base year 1989 = 100)

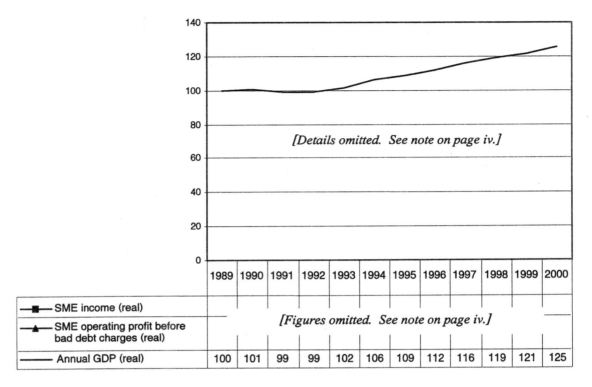

	1989	1990	1991	1992	1993	1994	1995	1996	1997	1998	1999	2000
■ SME income (real)												
▲ SME operating profit before bad debt charges (real)												
—— Annual GDP (real)	100	101	99	99	102	106	109	112	116	119	121	125

[Figures omitted. See note on page iv.]

Source: CC based on information from Barclays.

TABLE 7.45 **Barclays: comparison of changes in SME income from 1989 to 2000 with changes in GDP at constant 1995 prices**

	1989	1990	1991	1992	1993	1994	1995	1996	1997	1998	1999	2000
Annual change in GDP in constant 1995 prices as shown in Table 7.42 (%)	2.1	0.7	−1.5	0.1	2.3	4.4	2.8	2.6	3.5	2.6	2.1	3.3
Nominal SME income (£m)	(					*Figures omitted. See note on page iv.*						)
Adjustment factor to constant 1995 prices	1.28	1.19	1.11	1.07	1.04	1.03	1.00	0.97	0.94	0.91	0.89	0.88
SME income at constant 1995 prices (£m)	(					*Figures omitted. See note on page iv.*						)
SME change in constant income (%)	*	(				*Figures omitted. See note on page iv.*						)

Source: CC based on information from Barclays.

*Not available.

7.185. Figure 7.4 shows the percentage change in Barclays' SME income against the percentage change in GDP in constant 1995 prices. The economic activity line is the same as that in Figures 7.1 and 7.2. The data does not suggest any particular relationship between SME income and GDP in recent years.[1]

7.186. Table 7.46 shows the changes in Barclays' profit before bad debt charges from services to SMEs from 1989 to 2000 converted to constant 1995 prices. Figure 7.5 shows in chart form the changes (at constant prices) in SME profit before bad debts, with GDP changes also at constant prices.

---

[1]Regressing real changes of SME income against real changes of GDP produced a positive GDP coefficient, that was not statistically different from zero.

FIGURE 7.4

Barclays' SME changes in SME income at constant 1995 prices, compared with changes in GDP at constant 1995 prices

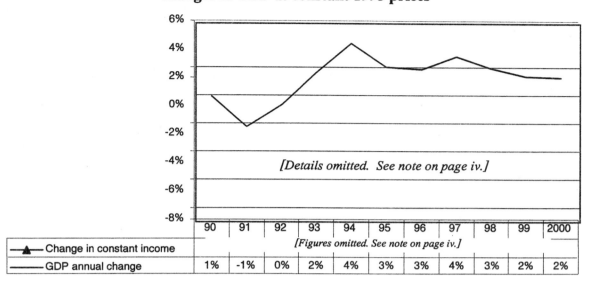

	90	91	92	93	94	95	96	97	98	99	2000
▲ Change in constant income	*[Figures omitted. See note on page iv.]*										
GDP annual change	1%	-1%	0%	2%	4%	3%	3%	4%	3%	2%	2%

Source: CC based on information from Barclays.

TABLE 7.46 **Barclays: changes in SME profit before bad debt charges at constant 1995 prices compared with changes in GDP at constant 1995 prices, for 1989 to 2000**

	1989	1990	1991	1992	1993	1994	1995	1996	1997	1998	1999	2000
Annual change in GDP in constant 1995 prices as shown in Table 7.42 (%)	2.1	0.7	–1.5	0.1	2.3	4.4	2.8	2.6	3.5	2.6	2.1	3.3
Nominal SME profit before bad debt charge (£m)	(				*Figures omitted. See note on page iv.*							)
Adjustment factor to constant 1995 prices	1.28	1.19	1.11	1.07	1.04	1.03	1.00	0.97	0.94	0.91	0.89	0.88
SME constant profit before bad debt charge (£m)	(				*Figures omitted. See note on page iv.*							)
SME change in constant profit before bad debt charge (%)	*	(				*Figures omitted. See note on page iv.*						)

Source: CC based on information from Barclays.

---

*Not available.

7.187. Figure 7.5 shows the comparison between changes in Barclays' SME profit before bad debt charge at constant 1995 prices to changes in GDP at constant 1995 prices. The data on the change in GDP at constant prices and the change in SME profit before bad debt charges at constant prices again do not suggest any particular relationship between the two data series.[1]

7.188. In summary, we found no particular relationship between changes in SME income and changes in GDP, and between changes in profits before bad debt charges and changes in GDP. We also examined whether there was a relationship between the deviation of SME income from its trend and the deviation of GDP from its trend, and the same for profits before bad debts and GDP. Again, we found no particular relationship.[2]

---

[1]Regressing real changes of SME profit before bad debts against real changes of GDP produced a positive GDP coefficient that was not statistically different from zero.
[2]Regressing the deviation of SME income from its trend against the deviation of GDP from its trend produced a positive GDP coefficient that was not statistically different from zero. The same regression for the deviation of SME profits before bad debt from its trend and the deviation of GDP from its trend produced a positive GDP coefficient was also not statistically different from zero.

FIGURE 7.5

Barclays: change in SME profit before bad debt charge at constant 1995 prices compared with changes in GDP at constant 1995 prices

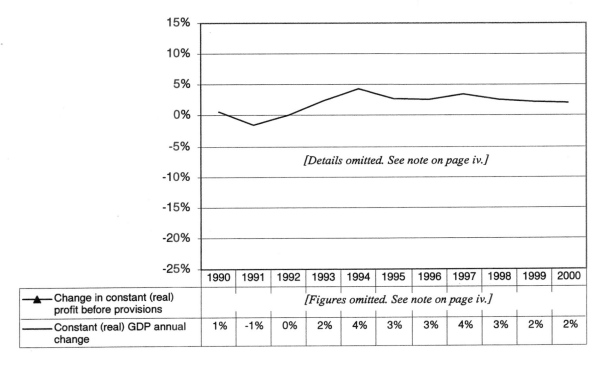

	1990	1991	1992	1993	1994	1995	1996	1997	1998	1999	2000
—▲—Change in constant (real) profit before provisions				*[Figures omitted. See note on page iv.]*							
——Constant (real) GDP annual change	1%	-1%	0%	2%	4%	3%	3%	4%	3%	2%	2%

Source: CC based on information from Barclays.

7.189. Barclays suggested that the operating return[1] for its SME banking business had a trend and moved with the growth in GDP and that the growth in GDP lagged by one year. As we explain next, these movements would lead to relatively small changes in operating profits when compared with long-term behaviour.

7.190. We examined a regression analysis produced by Barclays where the annual change in operating return was modelled by a time trend, and by the annual change in GDP, and the change in GDP lagged by one year (both at constant 1995 prices). The analysis suggested that a 1 per cent decline in GDP would produce a [✂] per cent decline in pre-bad debt profitability in that year: but that there would also be a delayed effect that would largely reverse the change in the following year. In other words, the coefficients of the GDP effect were statistically significant but their sum was not statistically different from zero. Barclays suggested this GDP effect might be the result of feedback in the market. According to the model, operating return declined by [✂] per cent each year, after GDP effects were excluded. Barclays believed this was statistical evidence of long-run pressure on the profitability of SME banking arising from competition in the market.

7.191. Consequently, we looked for predicted effects that would be substantial in the long run. The model predicted operating returns of [✂] per cent for the years 1998, 1999 and 2000 respectively. We compared these predictions, which were based upon actual GDP growth, with its predictions when GDP growth was set to a long-term average rate. We used two long-term growth scenarios.

7.192. First, we assumed that the UK's long-term average annual growth of GDP was 2.25 per cent. The model predicted that, were GDP to have grown at this long-term rate, Barclays' operating returns would have been [✂] per cent for the years 1989, 1999 and 2000 respectively. Based on Barclays' equity capital for these years, the model implied that the short-term deviations from the long-term average growth of GDP might have led to an annual average increase in its operating profits of £[✂] million over the three years 1998, 1999 and 2000. This is a net increase in profits of [✂] per cent

---

[1]Operating return = (Operating profits + Capital profits) / (Equity Capital).

over the three years, which is negligible compared with the standard error of prediction of [✂] per cent. The corresponding figures for the years 1989 to 2000 were an annual average decrease of £[✂] million and a net decrease of [✂] per cent.

7.193. Second, we assumed that the UK's long-term average annual growth of GDP is 2.5 per cent. Under this scenario, the model implied that the short-term deviations from long-term average growth of GDP may have led to an annual average decrease in operating profits of £[✂] million over the three-year period 1998, 1999 and 2000. The corresponding figure for the years 1989 to 2000 was an annual average decrease of £[✂] million. These are relatively small changes when compared with the levels of Barclays' operating profits.

HSBC: comparison of performance with changes in GDP

7.194. Table 7.47 shows whole-bank income data for HSBC from 1992 to 2000, which we illustrate in Figure 7.6 by plotting the changes (at constant 1995 prices) against GDP changes also at constant prices. The table shows how we converted HSBC's nominal results to the constant prices.

TABLE 7.47 **HSBC: comparison of whole-bank income from 1989 to 1999 with changes in GDP at constant 1995 prices**

	1989	*1990*	*1991*	*1992*	*1993*	*1994*	*1995*	*1996*	*1997*	*1998*	*1999*	*2000*
Nominal GDP (£'000 bn)	513.3	556.2	584.5	608.2	639.4	677.6	713.9	756.1	805.4	851.7	891.1	934.9
Nominal whole-bank total income (£m)	†	†	2,698	2,767	3,556	3,091	3,428	3,638	4,042	4,042	4,537	5,421
Adjustment factor to constant 1995 prices*	1.28	1.19	1.11	1.07	1.04	1.03	1.00	0.97	0.94	0.91	0.89	0.88
GDP at constant 1995 prices (£'000 bn)	655	659	649	650	665	694	713	732	757	777	794	820
Annual change (%)	2.1	0.7	−1.5	0.1	2.3	4.4	2.8	2.6	3.5	2.6	2.1	3.3
Whole-bank total income at constant 1995 prices (£m)	†	†	2,999	2,959	3,701	3,169	3,428	3,523	3,804	3,692	4,044	4,756
Whole-bank annual change in constant income (%)	†	†	†	−1	25	−14	8	3	8	−3	10	18

Source: CC based on information from HSBC.

*Adjustment factor to convert current (nominal) to constant (real) 1995 prices.
†Not available.

7.195. Figure 7.6 shows a recession in the economic cycle at the beginning of the 1990s, positive growth from 1992 and further improvement in economic activity by 1994. There was a small slackening in the rate of growth between 1994 and 1997 when growth increased, and then another slowing in the rate of growth. Looking at HSBC's whole-bank income, there was slightly negative growth in 1992 (the earliest date being 1991); a highly significant rate of growth in 1993 (explained as being due to significant dealing income) which reversed to a highly negative rate of growth in 1994 (explained as being due to a decline in dealing income), when the economy was displaying signs of increased positive growth. There was another large recovery to positive growth in 1995 followed by a fall in growth in real terms in 1996 after which time growth continued until 1997, but turned negative again in 1998, and since turned positive.

7.196. Table 7.48 shows profit before bad debt charges for HSBC from 1992 to 2000, which we illustrate in Figure 7.7 by plotting the changes (at constant 1995 prices) to GDP changes also at constant prices. The table shows how we converted HSBC's nominal results to constant prices.

FIGURE 7.6

HSBC: comparison of the whole-bank changes in income, compared with changes in GDP in constant 1995 prices

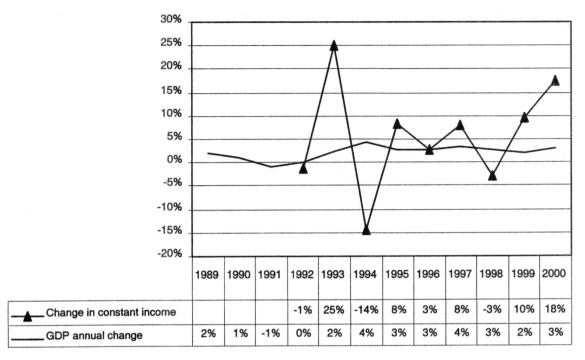

	1989	1990	1991	1992	1993	1994	1995	1996	1997	1998	1999	2000
▲ Change in constant income				-1%	25%	-14%	8%	3%	8%	-3%	10%	18%
GDP annual change	2%	1%	-1%	0%	2%	4%	3%	3%	4%	3%	2%	3%

Source: CC based on information from HSBC.

TABLE 7.48 **HSBC: comparison of whole-bank profit before bad debt charges from 1989 to 1999 with changes in GDP at constant 1995 prices**

	1989	1990	1991	1992	1993	1994	1995	1996	1997	1998	1999	2000
Annual change in GDP in constant 1995 prices as shown in Table 7.47 (%)	2.1	0.7	−1.5	0.1	2.3	4.4	2.8	2.6	3.5	2.6	2.1	3.3
Nominal whole-bank profit before bad debt charges (£m)	†	†	682	795	1,419	925	1,121	1,374	1,719	1,745	2,070	2,282
Adjustment factor to constant 1995 prices*	1.28	1.19	1.11	1.07	1.04	1.03	1.00	0.97	0.94	0.91	0.89	0.88
Whole-bank profit before bad debt charges at constant 1995 prices (£m)	†	†	758	850	1,477	948	1,121	1,331	1,618	1,594	1,845	2,002
Whole-bank change in constant profit before provisions (%)	†	†	†	12	74	−36	18	19	22	−1	16	8

Source: CC based on information from HSBC.

*Adjustment factor to convert current (nominal) to constant (real) 1995 prices.
†Not provided.

7.197. Figure 7.7 shows the percentage change in HSBC's whole-bank operating profit before bad debt charges against the percentage change in GDP in constant 1995 prices. The changes in economic activity are similar to those shown in Figure 7.6 for the bank's income. The whole-bank profit before bad debt provisions line displays a similar pattern from 1992 to 1995. However, there is a continuation of positive growth from 1995 to 1997, where there is a decrease in the rate of growth for whole-bank income in 1996. HSBC noted that consistent with whole-bank changes in income, there was negative growth in profits before bad debt charges in 1998 followed by a significant recovery to positive growth in 1999. In 2000 there was a reduction in the rate of growth from 1999 but it was still positive.

FIGURE 7.7

HSBC: comparison of whole-bank changes in profit before bad debt charges, compared with changes in GDP in constant 1995 prices

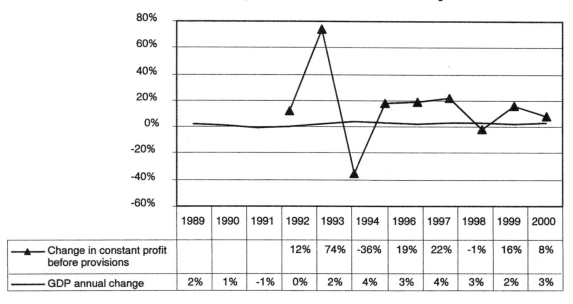

	1989	1990	1991	1992	1993	1994	1996	1997	1998	1999	2000
—▲— Change in constant profit before provisions				12%	74%	-36%	19%	22%	-1%	16%	8%
—— GDP annual change	2%	1%	-1%	0%	2%	4%	3%	4%	3%	2%	3%

Source: CC based on information from HSBC.

7.198. Table 7.49 shows HSBC's income from services to SMEs from 1990 to 2000 converted to constant 1995 prices. We illustrate the trend in this income in Figure 7.8 by plotting the changes (at constant prices) to GDP changes also at constant prices.

TABLE 7.49 **HSBC: comparison of changes in SME income from 1990 to 1999 with changes in GDP at constant 1995 prices**

	1989	1990	1991	1992	1993	1994	1995	1996	1997	1998	1999	2000
Annual change in GDP in constant 1995 prices as shown in Table 7.47 (%)	2.1	0.7	−1.5	0.1	2.3	4.4	2.8	2.6	3.5	2.6	2.1	3.3
Nominal SME income (£m)	†	(			*Figures omitted. See note on page iv.*							)
Adjustment factor to constant 1995 prices*	1.28	1.19	1.11	1.07	1.04	1.03	1.00	0.97	0.94	0.91	0.89	0.88
SME income at constant 1995 prices (£m)	†	(			*Figures omitted. See note on page iv.*							)
SME change in constant profit before provisions (%)	†	†	(			*Figures omitted. See note on page iv.*						)

Source: CC based on information from HSBC.

---

*Adjustment factor to convert current (nominal) to constant (real) 1995 prices.
†Not available.

7.199. Figure 7.8 shows the percentage change in HSBC's SME income against the percentage change in GDP in constant 1995 prices. The changes in economic activity are the same as that in Figure 7.6. The SME income line displays consistent positive growth in SME income from 1991 to 1993, and a sharp increase in income in 1994. HSBC said that the reasons for this sharp increase in income included the increase in business generated from the restructuring that occurred when Midland and HSBC merged. There was also a reallocation of income (which had previously been classified as corporate) to the SME banking business. In addition, HSBC suggested that less reliance should be placed on information provided for years prior to 1995. The systems in existence up to 1995 were not able to accurately break down information into the SME banking business and information provided for this period was on a best endeavours basis. After 1995, income grew but at a decreasing rate, remaining positive to the end of the period in 1999, although in 1998 and 1999 the rate of growth approached [✂]. In 2000 the rate of positive growth had increased to [✂] per cent.

FIGURE 7.8

HSBC: changes in SME income at constant 1995 prices compared with changes in GDP at constant 1995 prices

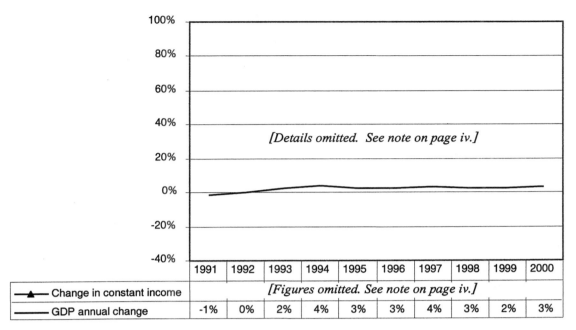

	1991	1992	1993	1994	1995	1996	1997	1998	1999	2000
——▲—— Change in constant income	*[Figures omitted. See note on page iv.]*									
—— GDP annual change	-1%	0%	2%	4%	3%	3%	4%	3%	2%	3%

Source: CC based on information from HSBC.

7.200. Table 7.50 shows HSBC's operating profit before bad debt charges from services to SMEs from 1990 to 2000 converted to constant 1995 prices. We illustrate the trend in this profit before bad debt charges in Figure 7.9 by plotting the changes (at constant prices) against GDP changes also at constant prices.

TABLE 7.50 **HSBC: comparison of SME profit before bad debt charges at constant 1995 prices compared with changes in GDP at constant 1995 prices**

	1989	1990	1991	1992	1993	1994	1995	1996	1997	1998	1999	2000
Annual change in GDP in constant 1995 prices as shown in Table 7.47 (%)	2.1	0.7	−1.5	0.1	2.3	4.4	2.8	2.6	3.5	2.6	2.1	3.3
Nominal SME profit before bad debt charges (£m)	*	(			*Figures omitted. See note on page iv.*							)
Adjustment factor to constant 1995 prices	1.28	1.19	1.11	1.07	1.04	1.03	1.00	0.97	0.94	0.91	0.89	0.88
SME constant profit before bad debt charge (£m)	*	(			*Figures omitted. See note on page iv.*							)
SME change in constant profit before bad debt charge (%)	*	*	(		*Figures omitted. See note on page iv.*							)

Source: CC based on information from HSBC.

*Not available.

7.201. Figure 7.9 shows the comparison between changes in HSBC's SME profit before bad debt charge at constant 1995 prices to changes in GDP at constant 1995 prices. It shows a recession in the economic cycle at the beginning of the 1990s, positive growth from 1992 and further improvement in economic activity by 1994. There was a small slackening in the rate of growth in 1995 and 1996. However, growth increased in 1997 after which there was another dip in the rate of growth. Comparing this with HSBC's SME profit before bad debt charges, the data points for the two series do not suggest any discernible relationship. HSBC provided data prior to 1995 on a best estimates basis which did not appear to be reliable for further interpretation, and the post-1995 data series was too short for a reliable trend line to be derived to take account of the 1990s recession.

FIGURE 7.9

HSBC: changes in SME profit before bad debt charges compared with changes in GDP at constant 1995 prices

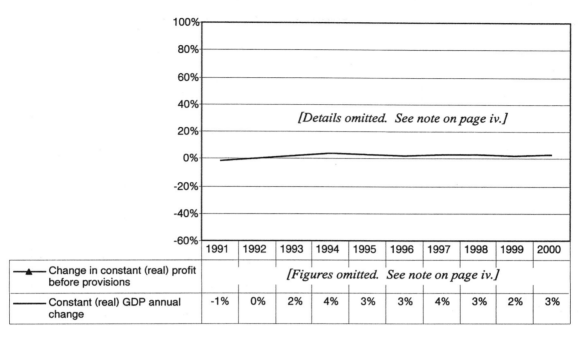

	1991	1992	1993	1994	1995	1996	1997	1998	1999	2000
▲ Change in constant (real) profit before provisions				*[Figures omitted. See note on page iv.]*						
Constant (real) GDP annual change	-1%	0%	2%	4%	3%	3%	4%	3%	2%	3%

Source: CC based on information from HSBC.

7.202. HSBC also provided a chart of returns on equity before and after bad debt provisions for the period 1989 to 1999 as evidence of a relationship between its SME banking business and the economic cycle. Its claim implied that that part of the variation in before-bad-debt returns on equity for its SME banking business could be explained by GDP. As we have noted, some of its data was affected, inter alia, by structural and financial reporting changes. Despite this, we sought to identify the magnitude of any GDP effect.

7.203. Both HSBC's returns on equity and GDP exhibited an increasing secular trend over the period 1989 to 1999. Thus, to identify any effect due to GDP that was distinct from this trend, we fitted a model that allowed returns on equity to be explained by a steady trend and by the changes in GDP. Diagnostic leverage statistics from this analysis showed that HSBC's before-bad-debt return on equity in 1989, which was unusual, disproportionately affected the results. When this datum was discounted the model ceased significantly to explain the variance in before-bad-debt returns on equity. However, setting aside considerations of statistical significance, the magnitude of the effect of changes in GDP on returns on equity was typically less than the prediction errors of the model, with or without the datum for 1989. This may reflect the weakness of the link between profits and changes in GDP and the uncertain nature of the data prior to 1995.

Summary of potential returns in excess of the cost of capital for the six largest clearing groups serving SME customers in the UK

7.204. As a basis for investigating whether, and if so to what extent, returns on equity were in excess of the cost of equity capital, we put to the banks illustrative calculations based on baseline capital allocated to the SME banking business (see Table 7.13), and income adjusted for attributable capital (see Table 7.20). We also made two further adjustments.

7.205. The first was to recognize that current bad debt:lending ratios were likely to be below the figures sustainable over forthcoming years, because of the likelihood that the economic environment was currently more benign than could be expected over the whole economic cycle. HSBC, for example, said that the situation could change rapidly, and in its view the threat of economic recession was now real. In the light of the figures in Table 7.21 we included an adjustment to give the profitability that would have occurred if the bad debt ratio had been 0.7 per cent rather than the actual value in each of the years 1998 to 2000. This raised the values on average across the five largest banks, and across all three years by 55 per cent (from 0.45 to 0.7 per cent). The banks' responses to this are summarized below, but in essence all the large banks objected to the ratio of 0.7 per cent. Our conclusion on this issue is given in Chapter 2.

7.206. The second further adjustment was to eliminate costs in excess of a 50 per cent cost:income benchmark (see Table 7.51 and paragraphs 7.120 to 7.173) as being costs which might reflect inefficiency. The amount of costs we deducted is shown in Table 7.51 for 1998 to 2000 for illustrative purposes. Table 7.52 then incorporates these two adjustments into the comparison of returns with the cost of equity for 1998, 1999 and 2000. The 50 per cent illustrative benchmark was originally derived for 1999. The banks did not feel a 50 per cent cost:income ratio benchmark was appropriate and was not indicative of a measure of efficiency. A 1999 benchmark may constitute too low a figure for 1998, but by the same token may constitute too high a figure for 2000. Our overall conclusion on this issue is also given in Chapter 2.

TABLE 7.51 **The largest six UK banks: potential adjustments to profits for 1998 to 2000 to take account of differences in cost:income ratios**

£ million

	Barclays	Lloyds TSB	NatWest	HSBC	BoS*	RBS	Total/ average
1998 cost:income adjustment							
Operating income (excluding attributable capital adjustment)†					‡		4,995
Operating expenses (including pension adjustment for Barclays, Lloyds TSB and RBS/NatWest)§		Figures omitted. See note on page iv.			‡	✂	−3,216
SME cost:income ratio (%)	65	61	69	62	‡	62	64
CC estimated cost:income ratio of SMEs (%)¶	50	50	50	50	(✂)	50	50
Difference (%)	15	11	19	12	‡	12	14
Further cost:income adjustment	[Figures omited. See note on page iv.]				‡	(✂)	720
1999 cost:income adjustment							
Operating income (excluding attributable capital adjustment)†							5,998
Operating expenses (including pension adjustment for Barclays and Lloyds TSB)§		Figures omitted. See note on page iv.					−3,676
SME cost:income ratio (%)	60	52§	69	63	✂	59	62
CC estimated cost:income ratio of SMEs (%)¶	50	50	50	50		50	50
Difference (%)	10	2	19	13		9	11
Further cost:income adjustment	(Figures omitted. See note on page iv.					)	677
2000 cost:income adjustment							
Operating income (excluding attributable capital adjustment)†							6,383
Operating expenses (including pension adjustment for Barclays and Lloyds TSB)§		Figures omitted. See note on page iv.					−3,818
SME cost:income ratio (%)	58	53	65	61	✂	57	56
CC estimated cost:income ratio of SMEs (%)¶	50	50	50	50		50	50
Difference (%)	8	3	15	11		7	10
Further cost:income adjustment	(Figures omitted. See note on page iv.					)	627

Source: CC based on information from the banks.

*This is for years to February 2000 and 2001.

†The attributable capital adjustment is excluded for the purpose of this calculation.

‡Not available.

§The pension adjustment is included for comparability purposes as Barclays and Lloyds TSB had pension holidays, compared with the other banks. For 1999, the Barclays total is costs of £[✂] million plus a pension charge of £[✂] million. The Lloyds TSB figure is costs of £[✂] million plus a pension charge of £[✂] million. For NatWest the total cost is £[✂] million plus a pension charge of £[✂] million and RBS had total costs of £[✂] million plus a pension charge of £[✂] million.

¶For illustrative purposes. Chapter 2 deals further with this subject.

TABLE 7.52 The largest six UK banks: summary of illustrative returns in excess of the cost of capital from their services to SMEs after further CC adjustments, 1998 to 2000

£ million

	Barclays	Lloyds TSB	NatWest	HSBC	BoS*	RBS	Total
1998							
Value of the difference between return on capital and the cost of capital per Table 7.21					†		†
Adjustments proposed by CC							
Further bad debt adjustment					†		†
Cost:income adjustment		Figures omitted. See note on page iv.			‡	✂	‡
Value of the difference between return on capital and the cost of capital after adjustments					†		†
Return on capital (before adjustments)* (%)					†		†
Return on capital (after above adjustments)‡ (%)					†		†
1999							
Value of the difference between return on capital and the cost of capital per Table 7.21							1,295
Adjustments proposed by CC							
Further bad debt adjustment							−152
Cost:income adjustment							677
Value of the difference between return on capital and the cost of capital after adjustments							1,820
Return on capital (before adjustments)* (%)							35§
Return on capital (after above adjustments)‡ (%)							43§
2000		Figures omitted. See note on page iv.					
Value of the difference between return on capital and the cost of capital per Table 7.21							1,648
Adjustments proposed by CC							
Further bad debt adjustment							−283
Cost:income adjustment							627
Value of the difference between return on capital and the cost of capital after adjustments							2,991
Return on capital (before adjustments)* (%)							40§
Return on capital (after above adjustments)‡ (%)							44§

Source: CC based on information from the banks.

---

*As per Table 7.21, computed as revised operating profit divided by attributable capital based on baseline capital. This is after the CC's initial adjustments for capital, income and expenses. Some banks commented that the returns should be calculated using a capital figure that included an allowance for intangibles, and therefore the returns shown were overstated. We address the subject of intangibles in Chapter 2.

†Not available.

‡Computed as revised operating profit per Table 7.20, plus adjustments above, divided by attributable capital based on baseline capital.

§Simple average for six banks.

Further comments by the banks on the methodology for considering returns in excess of cost of capital

7.207. In this section we note the main comments from the largest banks on our methodology, as discussed above.

Barclays

7.208. Barclays referred to the unadjusted numbers that it provided to the CC. In its view these showed that the average return on capital for the SME banking business over the economic cycle was within [✂] per cent of its cost of capital. Barclays said that it was clear from this data that it had not made profits from SME banking significantly in excess of its cost of capital over the cycle. It stated that the CC's assertion that it had made returns in excess of the cost of capital was only the result of what it claimed were arbitrary adjustments to its figures, which it suggested were unjustified. Chapter 10 gives a more detailed statement of its views on these matters, but the following briefly summarizes its position on these calculations, and the main elements of our methodology. It said that its average post-tax return on capital over the 12 years from 1989 to 2000 was [✂] per cent, as shown in Table 7.53. It suggested that this result was within [✂] per cent of its cost of equity over the same period. Barclays said that in this calculation, it used the equity capital base derived from the internal economic capital model that it used to manage its business. Barclays considered that this was the most accurate assessment of the capital requirements of SME banking. These requirements were considerably higher than the estimates that we put to Barclays during the inquiry. It said that in 2000, its post-tax return based on its own assessment of capital was [✂] per cent, which it did not consider was excessive at this point in the economic cycle.

TABLE 7.53 **Barclays' estimate of its return for services to SMEs, 1989 to 1999**

£ million

	1989	1990	1991	1992	1993	1994	1995	1996	1997	1998	1999	Average %
Operating profit/loss as per Table 6.1*												
Adjustment for attributable capital†												
Profit/loss after capital adjustment												
Barclays' internal estimate of capital						*Figures omitted.*						
Rate used by Barclays for the attributable capital adjustment (%)†						*See note on page iv.*						
Pre-tax return on capital (%)												
Post-tax return on capital (%)												

Source: Barclays.

---

*These figures were calculated on the basis that all lending was financed from borrowing in wholesale markets. In fact, a proportion was financed by the bank's equity, and Barclays therefore made an adjustment for this before comparing returns on capital derived from these profit figures with the bank's cost of capital.

†Barclays' estimate of the adjustment using the rates shown. In the early 1990s the value of this adjustment was much higher than in later years because of high interest base rates at the time. However, during these years, the cost of capital would also have been higher than in the late 1990s when bank base rates were at low levels.

7.209. Barclays told us that it did not believe the adjustment for attributable capital could be related to lending activities alone. It stated that capital profits did not relate only to lending activities but to all products provided by Barclays' SME banking business, ie current accounts, deposit accounts and other products as well as loans and overdrafts.

7.210. Barclays consistently objected to the use of RWAs as a basis for allocating capital, which it regarded as understating the capital needed for the SME banking business. It urged us to use its own methodology to assess its capital base, or a methodology based on Basle 2 proposals. It argued that the CC should not use RWAs, which it considered were widely believed to be flawed for the purpose of assessing business unit profitability.

7.211. Regarding bad debts, it insisted that the figure that we had suggested during the inquiry, of 0.7 per cent of lending as the annual bad debt charge to reflect the long-term norm, was incorrect and too low for its SME banking business. It consistently argued that the CC should use its long-term historical average bad debt rate of 1.5 per cent. It did not believe that the recession years (1990 to 1994) should be discounted, when compared with the improved bad debt rates in the next seven years to 2000, as it said the CC had no objective basis for doing so. It also considered that the improved bad debt rates in the late 1990s reflected the benefit of recoveries from earlier provisions. It suggested that that the CC's estimate of 0.7 per cent might have been based on an expectation that there would not be a recession in the foreseeable future. It said that the business cycle was not dead, and suggested that there was a high probability of a recession of some magnitude at some point over the next ten years. Barclays also added its expectation of an economic slowdown in the near term. In addition, it believed the foot-and-mouth disease problem in the UK in the first half of 2000 was an example of the unexpected risks that it faced, as well as the recent terrorist events in New York.

7.212. Barclays added that much of the risk inherent in SME banking pertained to the exposure of SME banking to the macroeconomic cycle as a whole. It therefore believed that in a recession, a large proportion of SME loans would default at the same time. This factor made SME banking more risky than personal banking or corporate banking. It said that there was no reason to believe that the future would be less risky than the past. [*Details omitted. See note on page iv.*] Barclays added that a recent BoE report outlined a new model of corporate insolvencies which suggested that, using the bank's own central economic forecast, the insolvency rate could rise by between [✄] and [✄] per cent by the end of 2001. It suggested that DTI statistics indicated that long-term corporate insolvency rates were increasing, compared with earlier decades. Barclays therefore concluded that there were good reasons to believe that the future might be more risky than the past. It further added that technological change across industry as a whole increased its lending risks to SMEs, and made the economy much more volatile than in the past. However, we noted from another bank that the historical corporate failure rate in England and Wales in the recession of the early 1990s was 2.6 per cent in 1992, compared with a current rate in 1999/2000 of around 1.2 per cent. Barclays, however, considered that this was an inappropriate comparison as default rates in a recession were not comparable with those occurring after a long period of growth.

7.213. Barclays believed that its econometric models of bad debt charges were a good basis for considering the future. It was using this model in the bank in the management of its lending activities. It was statistically robust and had been quality assured by external academic economists. The model suggested that bad debt charges could rise to about [✄] per cent in a coming recession, compared with about [✄] per cent in the 1990s recession.

7.214. Finally on bad debts, it added that the provisions were a function of a bank's appetite for risk and therefore the assumption that there should be a uniform optimum ratio for all banks was inappropriate. As noted in paragraph 7.211, Barclays' bad debts:loans ratio for the 12 years to 2000 was 1.5 per cent. Barclays provided forecast data that provided an estimate of this ratio peaking at some [✄] per cent around 2003, assuming a period of recession.

7.215. Barclays also added that it did not accept any view that it was possible for banks to increase prices in times of economic recession, to offset the damaging effect of increased bad debts. Barclays said that if it put its lending rates up in a manner substantially out of line with the market, this would be a powerful signal that it was pricing itself out of the SME banking market as a whole, and it would expect to see new business volumes deteriorate substantially. Barclays also believed that such a policy could also lead to a problem of 'adverse selection', ie attracting a preponderance of the riskier lending propositions. Barclays also said that regarding its existing lending book, there was nothing it could do to renegotiate any lending margins agreed under established contracts, unless the customers breached the terms of agreement. Very often, its experience was that customers only breached their terms when it was too late to do anything about the riskiness of the advance, ie the customers were already experiencing financial difficulties.

7.216. Barclays emphasized that its aim was to support customers so long as they had viable long-run financial prospects, and that simply stopping lending, or pricing itself out of the market in expectation of increases in bad debt rates, was not consistent with its brand promise. It said that the expected present value of customer relationships might be positive over the lifetime of that relationship, even if the profit was negative in some years. Barclays said that it could tighten its lending rate to new customers marginally, but it could not move far from the terms prevailing in the market, or to a position that was radically different from the prevailing view of competitors regarding future bad debts. Barclays also said that banks might be expected to put up lending rates if they all expected a recession at the same time, but its evidence provided to the CC of the recession in the early 1990s did not suggest that this had occurred, ie it did not increase its margins.

7.217. Barclays also commented on 'risk pricing' (ie prices and margins and their relationship to risk), and its linkage to capital requirements. Barclays said that the average expected default rates were priced into lending margins, but unexpected losses from default were not. Unexpected losses around the expected average (ie the volatility) gives rise to risk and capital requirements. It stated that loan prices take account of average expected losses and the cost of capital required to support unexpected losses. Unexpected losses were taken into account by capital requirements driven by risk, such as its economic capital or Basle 2 capital (but not RWAs). Barclays noted that equity investors typically would make a trade-off between risk and reward in investment decisions, and risk was usually the volatility of earnings compared with 'reward' being the expected average level of earnings. For higher-risk investments, investors required higher expected average earnings, and for any given volatility of earnings, investors preferred higher average earnings. Barclays considered that the same logic applied to lending portfolios, in that for a given level of bad debt volatility, higher margins made the loans more attractive as an investment opportunity, but did not change the capital requirement to take account of unexpected bad debts, ie margins from lending were an irrelevant consideration for determining capital requirements. The higher average earnings would, however, increase the rate of return on the capital.

7.218. We now summarize Barclays' views on the use of cost:income ratios. It believed that a 50 per cent ratio as a norm was not correct. It said that efficiency measures were concerned with the level of inputs, or the level of costs required to supply a given level of output. It did not believe that income was a valid output measure, unless businesses had similar product mixes, strategies and prices. It gave some examples to illustrate its views.

7.219. Barclays emphasized that it was an efficient bank which, by considerable management effort, had reduced its operating cost base in SME banking by [✀] per cent in real terms over the 11 years from 1989 to 1999. This was despite the fact that about [✀] per cent of its operating cost base consisted of staff costs that had risen in real terms, year on year. This reduction in its cost base had not reduced its cost:income ratio substantially because the benefit of cost reductions was passed on to customers in lower prices. Barclays said that prices in all product areas had fallen over the last six years in real terms (1994 to 1999), which was why its profit margins had hardly moved.

7.220. Barclays believed that to conclude that a bank was inefficient, the CC must conduct empirical analysis of the unit costs of standard processes within each bank. This would allow comparison of costs to specific units of output, and then further comparison with difference in mix, strategy and investment.

7.221. When considering differences between banks on cost:income ratios, Barclays listed a number of variables that it considered could explain differences, such as:

(a) relative prices of SME banking products and services;

(b) business mix across product categories (ie current accounts, deposit accounts, loans and over-drafts); or product mix within product categories (for example, asset financing compared with loans and overdrafts, or agriculture versus retail lending); or size of customers; or percentage of lending that was secured;

(c) quality of service issues, extent of branch network, geographical concentrations, and business risk profiles;

(d) IT developments, product developments, customer channel developments, advertising and marketing expenditure, and degree of restructuring activity;

(e) strategic choices affecting a bank's cost base, for example use of direct banking, telephone banking, and Internet banking; or acquisitions compared with organic growth; or the impact of scale on costs;

(f) differences in cost allocation policies between banks, and whether the costs were fully allocated to the correct business segment;

(g) differences in accounting treatment, for example structural hedges income, operating leasing income, pension holidays, restructuring costs, investment expenditure (whether capitalized or treated as an expense when incurred); and

(h) changes in year-to-year cost:income ratios for particular banks.

7.222. Finally it suggested that the use of a cost:income ratio was circular. It said that by imposing a ratio, this in turn imposed a profit margin that was then deemed to be excessive. It felt this was a flawed and unreasonable process.

Lloyds TSB

7.223. Table 7.54 shows some calculations of estimated returns in excess of the cost of capital for 1999, produced by Lloyds TSB to illustrate results from different assumptions from those made by the CC. It stressed that by doing so, it was not endorsing the approach that we adopted. Lloyds TSB indicated a variety of alternative methods to calculate capital for the purposes of determining the value, if any, of returns in excess of the cost of capital from services to SMEs, using 1999 as a benchmark year. The table shows different calculations of returns that Lloyds TSB presented, some of which had negligible returns in excess of the cost of capital. Lloyds TSB said that the purpose of the calculations was to show that on what it considered were reasonable assumptions, it could demonstrate that the bank did not make supernormal profits at all from services to SMEs.

7.224. Scenario A shows a calculation of excess profits using our assumptions, but with a three-year rolling average swap rate of 7.1 per cent for the attributable capital adjustment, as recommended by Lloyds TSB. This compared with the CC's assumption for the attributable capital adjustment, to use a three-month LIBOR rate of 5.45 per cent. This would have revised the attributable capital adjustment to £[✂] million, compared with our estimate of £[✂] million.

7.225. Scenario B used the results of Lloyds TSB's equity attribution methodology for determining its capital base, which it expected to be compatible with, but not dependent upon, adoption of Basle 2 principles. This calculation took a base equity figure of £[✂], being the minimum capital allocation required to address the various risks of the bank: credit risk; market risk; business risk; operational risk; and insurance risk. It then applied a series of 'uplift' percentages to provide examples of potential levels of equity required to reflect the fact that the equity attribution model does not make allowance for the 'cushion' of equity needed to allow for the SME banking business units to invest in the additional assets which it needed to compete effectively, and to take advantage of new business opportunities as they presented themselves. In effect, it is an additional amount of equity required to effectively run the business and to take account of unexpected risks attaching to its products and customer relationships. The figures shown in Table 7.54 took the equity attribution figure originally calculated of £[✂], and uplifted it to [✂] per cent. [*Details omitted. See note on page iv.*   ]

7.226. The third calculation of returns in excess of the cost of capital (Scenario C) performed by Lloyds TSB showed the result of using capital derived from making adjustments to the group's accounting capital as indicated in Table 7.2 (totalling some £[✂] billion) and apportioning the result to the SME banking business under the principles of Basle 1 (ie using RWAs).

7.227. In both scenarios B and C, Lloyds TSB adopted a pre-tax cost of equity of [✂] per cent. Lloyds TSB adopted a higher cost of equity to reflect the belief that, in the absence of a stand-alone listed SME bank carrying on an SME banking business, it must be recognized that the CC's estimate could be no more than a rough estimate of such a business. It said that according to a joint survey, carried out by external consultants, the true cost of equity of SME banking business could well exceed the level assumed by the CC. In order to show the effect of assuming a higher cost of equity, Lloyds TSB adjusted the CC's calculation on the basis of an assumed cost of equity of [✂] per cent.

7.228. Scenarios B and C also include an adjustment of £[✂] million (effectively an increase in operating costs) to reflect the fact that, in 1999, the SME banking business enjoyed the benefit of a contributions holiday in respect of Lloyds TSB pension schemes, a situation which is independent of the trading performance of the business. This is in effect a cost which would have been incurred had the pension schemes not been in surplus.

7.229. Lloyds TSB did not propose any adjustment in respect of cost:income ratio, as it did not consider it appropriate to measure different banks' relative efficiency by reference to their respective cost:income ratios.

7.230. The bad debt adjustment made by Lloyds TSB in scenarios B and C takes the actual bad debt charge:loans ratio of [✂] per cent in 1999, and increases it to [✂] per cent. This has the effect of a

£[✂] million adjustment on a loans balance of £[✂] in 1999. This results in the replacement of the unrepresentatively low bad debt charge in 1999 (reflecting the benign phase of the economic cycle) with an average related to the whole economic cycle.

TABLE 7.54 Lloyds TSB: range of estimated excess profits from services to SMEs, to compare hypothetical estimates prepared by the CC with alternative assumptions proposed by Lloyds TSB, 1999

£ million

Assumptions by Lloyds TSB and the CC	A Based on CC's assumptions, but using Lloyds TSB's attributable capital adjustment	B Equity attribution [✂]% of the base calculation	C Economic capital —adjusted shareholders' funds 'top-down' Basle 1 allocation	Based on CC's assumptions, and the CC's attributable capital adjustment
Cost:income ratio (%)	50.0	50.0	52.5*	50.0
Income				
Operating costs				
Bad debt charge				
Bad debt adjustment†				
Cyclicality adjustment‡				
Adjustment for attributable capital (see below)				
Adjustment for normal pensions				
Pre-tax normalized profit				
Cost of capital (see below)				
Excess profit (pre-tax)				
Adjustment for attributable capital				
Imputed capital		Figures omitted.		
Earnings on equity rate (%)		See note on page iv.		
Adjustment for attributable capital				
Imputed capital				
Imputed pre-tax cost of capital (%)§				
Imputed pre-tax profit based on imputed cost of capital, and capital level¶				

Source: Lloyds TSB and CC.

*Lloyds TSB showed costs of £[✂] million under scenario C, compared with costs of £[✂] million under scenario B, the difference of £[✂] million being a year's amortization of goodwill to maintain symmetry with its approach to calculate capital, which included goodwill.

†Lloyds TSB in scenarios B and C used a bad debt to loan ratio of [✂] per cent, compared with our estimate of 0.7 per cent, representing the average ratio expected over the next economic cycle.

‡Lloyds TSB made this adjustment based on its view of the effects of an economic downturn, which could result in SMEs holding smaller levels of accounts in credit, the SME banking business selling fewer insurance and pension products, and the SME banking business incurring additional costs in managing the debt portfolio. Lloyds TSB said that it lacked reliable data from the last economic cycle to support its assessment of such costs.

§The CC's figure was based on the CAPM methodology for the whole group. The Lloyds TSB figure of [✂] per cent was its assessment of a figure appropriate to a freestanding SME banking business.

¶Lloyds TSB said that in a competitive market some firms would earn more than the cost of capital.

7.231. Lloyds TSB also responded to our comment that it was not appropriate to view costs for the SME banking business as though it were a stand-alone bank. It indicated that when assessing the cost of capital of the SME segment, there might be some areas within a bank that had a lower cost of capital, such as a domestic mortgage business. It said that the impact this had in the whole bank's cost of capital needed to be considered in arriving at a suitable cost of capital figure for the SME segment.

7.232. Lloyds TSB prepared a range of estimates for equity for 2000 using the same basis of calculations as shown in Table 7.51. Equity calculated under scenario A gave a figure of £[✂] (increase of 18 per cent from £[✂] in 1999), scenario B gave a figure of £[✂] in 2000 which was the same as for 1999, and scenario C gave a figure of £[✂] (increase of 10 per cent from £[✂] in 1999).

HSBC

7.233. HSBC said that it did not consider it was making excess profits. It believed that the baseline capital figure as calculated by the CC was too low and failed to address the adequate inclusion of intangible assets. Product and systems development, training, free banking, marketing, brand recognition, sales and development expenditure, and the value of its customer base should all have an attributed value that was recognized in its capital base to determine the existence of any excess profit. Furthermore, it was HSBC's view that it was wrong to assume that any profit over and above the perceived cost of equity should be regarded as excessive. Competitive markets required profits as a signal of success, and the competitive advantage of individual businesses could result in returns exceeding the cost of capital.

7.234. In addition, HSBC stated that it was concerned that the CC was considering profits only for 1998 to 2000. The CC's analysis considered the years when the economic environment was more benign and not representative of the full economic cycle and therefore it was important to consider results over the full cycle. HSBC stated that, in its view, its annual post-tax return on equity over the period 1989 to 1999 was close to its cost of capital. It suggested that this compared favourably with the CC's cost of equity set out in Table 7.20 in respect of 1998 to 2000, which might have been higher in earlier years. It claimed that on this basis, HSBC was not making excess profits over the full economic cycle. HSBC's view was that this cycle should cover at least ten years, and include at least one recession. It added that the three-year period 1998 to 2000 was too short, and even five years was not sufficient. It believed strongly therefore that it was inappropriate for the CC to use 1998 to 2000 information as the only years on which to make its assessment of whether HSBC was making excessive profits.

7.235. Further, HSBC, in relation to the potential adjustment for bad debt charges, expressed the view that a high bad debt to loans ratio was necessary to take account of the economic cycle. It did not produce an alternative figure to the 0.7 per cent of loans as an acceptable benchmark ratio, but emphasized that it had suffered very large bad debt charges in the previous recession, and therefore, on that basis, the bad debt ratio should be substantially higher. HSBC considered that one of the main reasons for the 0.7 bad debt ratio adjustment being too low was that this figure failed to consider the economic cycle as a whole. It calculated that over the period 1990 to 2000, its average annual bad debt charge as a percentage of total loans and total income was 5.3 per cent and 34.3 per cent respectively (see Table 6.47). HSBC stated that it was inappropriate to calculate an average bad debt ratio based on an assessment of bad debt charges over merely the past couple of years, and a prediction of macroeconomic conditions in the future which might turn out to be incorrect. Notwithstanding improvements in HSBC's credit risk assessment techniques in recent years, the financial consequences of the early 1990s could recur, particularly now that an economic recession was a real possibility.

7.236. HSBC also noted recent developments in the area of bank security, which it considered should be included in the CC's assessment of bad debt risk. It noted a recent White Paper, 'Insolvency—A Second Chance', which proposed that floating charge-holders would lose the ability to appoint administrative receivers. A modification/streamlining of the existing administration procedures for holders of floating charges was instead proposed. In addition, HSBC pointed out a recent Privy Council decision on the New Zealand case, known as Brumark, which resulted in some doubts of the validity under English law of lenders' fixed charge on book debts. HSBC considered that both developments had created some uncertainty that might potentially lead to a detrimental effect on the availability of credit and the risk of higher bad debt charges through the inability to crystallize appropriate security.

7.237. With regard to an efficiency or cost:income ratio adjustment suggested by the CC, HSBC felt that this was wholly inappropriate. It believed its actual costs should be taken as an acceptable reflection of efficiency in line with the way in which HSBC conducted its business. In addition, HSBC did not believe that differences in efficiency between banks were relevant for determining excess profits. It felt that the cost:income ratio was really only useful for comparing the same business over time and, at best, it suggested that cost:income ratio comparisons were a snapshot at one point in time of the relationship between cost and income. Its more detailed views on its cost:income ratio in 1999 are covered in paragraph 7.151, and Chapter 11 shows its more general views.

RBSG

7.238. Table 7.55 shows illustrations of deficits between returns on capital and cost of capital that RBSG said were applicable to NatWest in 1999 under the various assumptions shown for services to

521

SMEs. It provided a range of estimates, low and high for each element involved in the calculation of excess profit that we identified for this inquiry. It adopted this approach because RBSG had not been able accurately to identify costs, which were critical in determining profits from services to SMEs. It stressed that because a substantial proportion of banking costs were shared, any allocation was arbitrary, and it did not make such allocations for its own purposes. It had, however, assisted the CC to derive a result on a 'best estimates' basis as discussed in Chapter 6 for RBS and NatWest in 1999. In addition, RBSG said that it was more meaningful to provide a range of estimates as it did not believe there was a definitive answer to the profitability of SME banking business because of the different possible methods of calculating the variables involved in calculating profitability. It therefore felt that a range of figures for the key inputs as shown in the table would prove useful in arriving at a result to compare with the one that we had suggested to the bank. As a result, NatWest suggested that, far from making profits of £[✂] million in excess of the cost of capital as calculated in the figures we had sent, NatWest's results fell short of the cost of capital by between £[✂] million and £[✂] million.

TABLE 7.55 **RBSG: estimated excess/deficit of profits from services to SMEs that NatWest could have earned for 1999, based on assumptions, compared with the hypothetical example prepared by the CC**

Assumptions	NatWest low range	NatWest high range	CC's hypothetical example
Cost:income ratio (%)	65	70	50
Bad debt to loans ratio (%)		Figures omitted.	
Imputed capital (£bn)		See note on page iv.	

£ million

Resulting in:		
Income*		
Costs		
	Figures omitted.	
Bad debt charge†	See note on page iv.	
Interest on equity		
Normalized pre-tax profit		
Cost of capital‡		
Excess/deficit of profit		

Source: RBSG and CC.

*Subsequently revised to £[✂], as shown in Table 7.20.
†Equal to [✂] and [✂] per cent for the low and high estimate respectively.
‡RBSG used a pre-tax rate of [✂] per cent on the imputed capital under the low basis, and [✂] per cent under the high estimate based on the CAPM methodology, which compared with the CC's estimate of [✂] per cent.

7.239. RBSG said that the 1999 profits of NatWest already included the £[✂] million representing interest on equity and said that the income used by the CC would need to be reduced by this amount when calculating returns on equity to avoid overstating income when making its adjustment for attributable capital.

7.240. Later in the inquiry and at the request of the CC, RBSG provided point estimates of excess profits/deficit of profits that NatWest could have earned for 1999, based on its own assumptions, compared with the estimate calculated by the CC. Table 7.56 shows these estimates. While the estimated interest on equity figure increased from £[✂] million to £[✂] million, it said that the amount already included in the 1999 profit figures remained at £[✂] million.

7.241. RBSG's views on its cost:income ratio, based on information for 1999, are covered in paragraph 7.171ff, and Chapter 13 shows its more general views. It did a further calculation on the same basis as shown in Table 7.57 using information for 1999 in respect of its combined banks (NatWest, RBS and Ulster Bank). RBSG suggested that, under its assumptions, the three banks together were not covering their cost of capital. At best, it noted that RBSG showed a deficit of £[✂] million when its returns, revised to take account of long-term bad debt rates and its assessment of capital, were compared with an appropriate cost of capital. It added, however, that the deficits also reflected NatWest's poor performance and that it was taking steps to restore NatWest's profitability to a more acceptable level.

TABLE 7.56 RBSG: revised estimated excess/deficit of profits from services to SMEs that NatWest could have earned for 1999, based on assumptions, compared with the hypothetical example prepared by the CC

Assumptions	NatWest	CC's hypothetical example
Cost:income ratio (%)	68	50
Bad debt to loans ratio (%)	[✂	]
Imputed capital (£bn)		

	£ million
Resulting in:	
Income	( )
Costs	
Bad debt charge*	✂
Interest on equity	
Normalized pre-tax profit	
Cost of capital†	
Excess/deficit of profit	( )

Source: RBSG and CC.

---

*Equal to [✂] per cent for NatWest and 0.7 per cent for the CC.
†RBSG used a pre-tax rate of [✂] per cent on the imputed capital based on the CAPM methodology, which compared with the CC's estimate of [✂] per cent.

7.242. In addition, RBSG objected to deriving a measure of excess profit by comparing the returns achieved on the book value of shareholders' funds with the cost of capital. RBSG argued that this was an inconsistent approach as the cost of equity was derived directly from market value and shareholders' funds is at book value. For the cost of capital to be used in an appropriate manner, RBSG believed the value of shareholders' funds needed to be adjusted, as mentioned previously, to reflect the market value or full replacement cost of its assets (see paragraph 7.20ff).

TABLE 7.57 RBSG: estimated excess/deficit of profits from services to SMEs that NatWest, RBS and Ulster Bank could have earned for 1999, based on assumptions, compared with the hypothetical example prepared by the CC

£ million

Assumptions*	RBSG low estimates	RBSG high estimates	CC's hypothetical example
Normalized pre-tax profit			†
Cost of capital‡	Figures omitted. See note on page iv.		
Excess/deficit of profit			§

Source: RBSG.

---

*RBSG's assumptions are the same as shown in Table 7.55. Capital reflects that estimated for all three banks.
†Table 7.20 shows adjusted operating profits of £[✂] million for NatWest, and £[✂] million for RBS. Table 7.66 shows £[✂] million operating profit for Ulster Bank. These results total £[✂] million based on actual costs.
‡RBSG used a pre-tax rate of [✂] per cent on the imputed capital under the low basis, and [✂] per cent under the high estimate, based on the CAPM methodology, which compared with the CC's estimate of [✂] per cent.
§Table 7.52 shows the results of the CC's illustrative examples on returns in excess of cost of capital that were discussed with RBSG during the inquiry. It shows that assuming a cost:income ratio of 50 per cent as a benchmark for making a cost adjustment in 1999, the excess return for NatWest would have been £[✂] million, and that for RBS would have been £[✂] million. Table 7.74 shows the equivalent information for Ulster Bank as £[✂] million. These results total £[✂] million, and the CC's conclusions on returns for the banks are given in Chapter 2.

7.243. As with the other aspects of profitability, RBSG provided point estimates for the estimated excess profits that NatWest, RBS and Ulster Bank could have earned for 1999 at our request at a later stage in the inquiry. These are shown in Table 7.58.

RBSG: revised estimated excess/deficit of profits from services to SMEs that NatWest, RBS and Ulster Bank could have earned for 1999, based on assumptions, compared with the hypothetical example prepared by the CC

£ million

Assumptions	RBSG	CC's hypothetical example
Normalized pre-tax profit		*
Cost of capital†	✂	
Excess/deficit of profit		‡

Source: RBSG.

---

*Table 7.20 shows adjusted operating profits of £[✂] million for NatWest, and £[✂] million for RBS. Table 7.66 shows £[✂] million operating profit for Ulster Bank. These results total £[✂] million based on actual costs.

†RBSG used a pre-tax rate of [✂] per cent on the imputed capital based on the CAPM methodology, which compared with the CC's estimate of [✂] per cent.

‡Table 7.52 shows the results of the CC's illustrative examples on returns in excess of cost of capital that were discussed with RBSG during the inquiry. It shows that, assuming a cost:income ratio of 50 per cent as a benchmark for making a cost adjustment in 1999, the excess return for NatWest would have been £[✂] million, and that for RBS would have been £[✂] million. Table 7.74 shows the equivalent information for Ulster Bank as £[✂] million. These results total £[✂] million, and the CC's conclusions on returns for the banks are given in Chapter 2.

BoS

7.244. BoS did not make any special comments on the methodology to calculate returns in excess of the cost of capital, although it suggested that its profits were not excessive, and pointed out that it was paying interest on its current accounts. On valuation of capital, it said that it would support the principle of depreciated replacement cost of assets as a basis for valuation, and noted that its intangible assets were insignificant. It agreed that stock market values were not appropriate for valuing capital. It added that Basle 2 proposals were likely to result in higher capital allocation requirements for the SME segment. BoS said that it was currently unable to quantify the effect of Basle 2 on its portfolio, but considered that the risk weights under the standardized and IRB foundation approaches (see paragraphs 5.490 and 5.491) were penal compared with current practice. It said that there was a link between the issues surrounding capital allocation where capital was expected to cover both expected and unexpected loss and to allow for the stresses of a serious recession.

7.245. BoS accepted that cost:income ratios could be affected by more than efficiency factors, but that this ratio was a reasonable performance measure. On bad debts to lending ratios, it said that it was correct to note that assessment models had improved, but it considered that property risks were still present as value comparisons to earnings multiples were currently running at close to their peak. BoS considered that it would be imprudent to ignore events such as the early 1990s recession. BoS added that its last three years' performance to February 2001 was under benign economic conditions.

7.246. It stated that profits needed to exceed the cost of capital to enable:

(a) reinvestment in the business (for example, IT expenditure to deliver efficiencies for the benefit of customers);

(b) growth of the lending book; and

(c) maintenance of regulatory conditions.

7.247. BoS concluded that if its internally generated profits were restricted, this would most likely constrain its ability to support ongoing business growth and could limit competition. It emphasized that, unlike competitor banks, it had not returned capital to shareholders, and in the last year it had issued preferred capital, and managed its balance sheet by securitizing mortgages and loans.

Considerations of profits in excess of the cost of capital for the smaller banks serving SMEs in the UK

7.248. Chapter 6 showed the results of smaller banks' services to SMEs in the UK, as well as calculations of returns based on their results in 1998 and 1999 and in some cases 2000. Earlier in this chapter we dealt with the assessment of capital for the larger banks, and their profits for the purposes of calculating potential profit in excess of the cost of capital. The tables below summarize the equivalent information for the smaller banks serving SMEs in the UK. In Chapter 2 we show how we used this information to determine our estimate of an appropriate figure to include in our calculation of whether and, if so, to what extent profits in excess of cost of capital have been earned.

7.249. First, we address the allocation of capital to support the smaller banks' services to SMEs, and distinguish those serving England and Wales (which will include some Scottish activities for some banks) from banks in Northern Ireland and those in Scotland.

Capital allocated to support the smaller UK banks' services to SMEs

7.250. We applied the same methodology to allocate capital to the SME banking business as we used for the larger banks. The main basis of allocation was the proportion of RWAs held by the SME banking business compared with the whole bank. This proportion was then applied to the baseline capital figure for the whole bank to allocate a portion to the SME banking business. As covered in paragraph 7.7, we defined baseline capital as shareholders' funds excluding capitalized goodwill and intangibles.

7.251. An exception to this methodology was Alliance & Leicester. As noted in Chapter 5, Alliance & Leicester's services to SMEs are conducted through its subsidiary Girobank. As discussed in Chapter 6, Girobank's SME banking business was distinct from those of other banks in that its lending portfolio was relatively insignificant and it operated through a post office counter network. This indicated to us that allocation of Girobank equity to an SME banking business by reference to SME-generated RWAs was inappropriate in the case of Girobank, and could not give a true reflection of the capital used to support its SME banking business. Therefore, as covered in Chapter 6, capital was allocated to a hypothetical SME banking business in proportion to turnover. In addition, we noted that because Girobank had minimal lending, an adjustment for attributable capital was not required.

7.252. We asked the banks to provide us with data for the RWAs for their SME banking business. For the smaller banks serving SMEs mainly in England and Wales, Table 7.59 shows total on-balance-sheet assets, RWAs, and proportion of SME RWAs to whole-bank equivalent for 1998 and 1999.

7.253. NAB was able to produce information only for the year ended 30 September 2000 for each of its three subsidiaries servicing SMEs in the UK: Yorkshire, Northern and Clydesdale. In the case of Yorkshire, the information for 2000 has been included alongside the information for 1999 for the other smaller banks serving SMEs mainly in England and Wales. We did not require the other banks from this region to provide 2000 figures because of their small size in the overall market for services provided to SMEs and because of the small proportion of the banks' business as a whole that was represented by services to SMEs.

7.254. Table 7.60 shows total on-balance-sheet assets, RWAs and proportion of SME RWAs to whole-bank equivalent for 1998 and 1999 for the four smaller banks serving SMEs mainly in Northern Ireland. As noted above, NAB was able to provide information only for 2000 for its subsidiaries serving SMEs in the UK. With regard to the smaller banks in Northern Ireland serving SMEs, each of them provided relevant information for 2000 and so we were able to provide a complete comparative analysis for that year.

7.255. Table 7.61 shows total on-balance-sheet assets, RWAs and proportion of SME RWAs to whole-bank equivalent for 2000 only for the banks servicing SMEs mainly in Scotland. NAB was able to provide information only for the year ended 30 September 2000, as noted previously. The analysis of BoS and RBS is discussed earlier in this chapter as part of the assessment of the six largest clearing groups servicing SME customers in the UK. These two banks have a large amount of business in England and so are not separated on a regional basis in the earlier part of Chapter 7. In particular, RBS told us that approximately 42 per cent of its income from Retail, Cards and Corporate originates from Scotland. These two banks have been included for the purpose of this section to provide comparability with Clydesdale as the other bank servicing SME customers in Scotland.

TABLE 7.59 **Smaller banks servicing SMEs mainly in England and Wales: summary of assets, RWAs and proportion of SME RWAs to whole-bank equivalent, 1998 and 1999**

£ billion

England and Wales*

	Co-operative Bank	Alliance & Leicester	Abbey National	AIB (GB)	Yorkshire	Total
1998						
Total on-balance-sheet assets			(✂)	(✂)	†	‡
RWAs for whole bank§	Figures omitted.		¶	(✂)	†	‡
RWAs for SME banking business§	See note on		¶	¤	†	‡
Proportion of SME RWAs to whole-bank equivalent (%)	page iv.		¶	¤	†	‡
1999						
Total on-balance-sheet assets						‡
RWAs for whole bank§			Figures omitted.			‡
RWAs for SME banking business§			See note on page iv.			‡
Proportion of SME RWAs to whole-bank equivalent (%)						‡

Source: CC based on information from the banks.

*May include Scotland activities for some banks.

†NAB was not able to provide information for 1998 or 1999 but did provide figures for 2000. The 2000 figures have been shown as 1999 to provide additional comparability between the smaller banks serving SMEs mainly in England and Wales.

‡Not able to be calculated.

§Includes on- and off-balance-sheet assets.

¶Abbey National was not able to provide information for 1998 because there was no segmentation in its data between SME and non-SME banking business. However, it provided a best endeavours estimate of the extent of SME banking business included in its total figures for 1999.

¤Not provided.

Note: N/A = not applicable for Alliance & Leicester as it refers to Girobank, which is discussed in paragraph 7.251.

TABLE 7.60 **Smaller banks serving SMEs mainly in Northern Ireland: summary of assets, RWAs and proportion of SME RWAs to whole-bank equivalent, 1998 to 2000**

£ billion

Northern Ireland

	Ulster Bank	First Trust	BoI	Northern	Total
1998					
Total on-balance-sheet assets	10.0	✂	32.1	*	†
RWAs for whole bank‡	6.4		17.8	*	†
RWAs for SME banking business‡	Figures omitted.			*	†
Proportion of SME RWAs to whole-bank equivalent (%)	See note on page iv.			*	†
1999					
Total on-balance-sheet assets	9.3	✂	36.2	*	†
RWAs for whole bank‡	6.8		20.7	*	†
RWAs for SME banking business‡	Figures omitted.			*	†
Proportion of SME RWAs to whole-bank equivalent (%)	See note on page iv.			*	†
2000					
Total on-balance-sheet assets	11.2	§	40.7	✂	†
RWAs for whole bank‡	7.9	§	23.9		†
RWAs for SME banking business‡	✂	§	✂		†
Proportion of SME RWAs to whole-bank equivalent (%)		§			†

Source: CC based on information from the banks.

*NAB was not able to provide information for 1998 or 1999 but did provide figures for 2000.

†Could not be calculated due to lack of data.

‡Includes on- and off-balance-sheet assets.

§Not provided for 2000.

TABLE 7.61   **Banks servicing SMEs mainly in Scotland: summary of assets, RWAs and proportion of SME RWAs to whole-bank equivalent, 2000**

£ billion

	Scotland			
	Clydesdale*	BoS†	RBS†	Total
Total on-balance-sheet assets	8	86	134	228
RWAs for whole bank‡	7	62	77	146
RWAs for SME banking business‡		✂		26
Proportion of SME RWAs to whole-bank equivalent (%)				29§

Source: CC based on information from the banks.

*NAB was not able to provide information for 1998 or 1999 but did provide figures for 2000.
†May include some England and Wales activities.
‡Includes on- and off-balance-sheet assets.
§Simple average.

7.256. We now summarize the capital attributable to the SME banking businesses for the smaller banks in the following three tables, first by reference to England and Wales, next for Northern Ireland, and then for Scotland. We informed the banks that, in presenting our conclusion in Chapter 2, we would substitute the baseline capital figure with what we determine for each bank as the appropriate whole-bank capital base.

7.257. For the smaller banks operating mainly in England and Wales, Table 7.62 shows the figures we used to allocate baseline capital at the whole-bank level to their respective SME banking businesses, and which we put to the banks for their comments. For 1999 the Co-operative Bank had capital attributed to the SME banking business of £[✂] million; Alliance & Leicester had capital of £[✂] million; Abbey National had capital of £[✂] million; AIB (GB) had capital of £[✂] million; and Yorkshire had capital of £[✂] million.

TABLE 7.62   **Smaller banks operating mainly in England and Wales: application of RWAs to baseline capital to determine capital for the respective bank's services to SMEs, 1998 and 1999**

	England and Wales*					
	Co-operative Bank	Alliance & Leicester	Abbey National	AIB (GB)	Yorkshire	Total
1998						
Proportion of SME RWAs to whole-bank equivalent (%)	(✂)	N/A	†	†	‡	§
Baseline capital for the whole bank (£m)	280	1,853	†	†	‡	§
Allocated capital for SME banking business (£m)	(✂)§		†	†	‡	§
1999						
Proportion of SME RWAs to whole-bank equivalent (%)	(✂)	N/A	(	✂	)	21¶
Baseline capital for the whole bank (£m)	341	1,752	6,078	(✂)	459	9,105
Allocated capital for SME banking business (£m)	(✂)¤		(	✂	)	447

Source: CC based on information from the groups.

*May include Scotland activities for some banks.
†Not provided.
‡NAB was not able to provide information for 1998 or 1999 but did provide figures for 2000. The 2000 figures have been shown as 1999 to provide additional comparability between the smaller banks serving SMEs mainly in England and Wales.
§Not able to be calculated.
¶Simple average.
¤Allocated in proportion to turnover of the SME banking business—see paragraph 7.251.
Note: N/A = not applicable for Alliance & Leicester as it refers to Girobank, which is discussed in paragraph 7.251.

527

7.258. Table 7.63 shows similar information for the smaller banks operating in Northern Ireland. For 1999 and 2000 respectively, Ulster Bank had capital allocated to the SME banking business of £[✂] million and £[✂] million, First Trust £[✂] million and £[✂] million, BoI £[✂] million and £[✂] million, and Northern in 2000 had £[✂] million.

TABLE 7.63 **The smaller banks operating mainly in Northern Ireland: application of RWAs to baseline capital to determine capital for the respective bank's services to SMEs, 1998 to 2000**

	Northern Ireland				
	Ulster Bank	First Trust	BoI	Northern	Total
1998					
Proportion of SME RWAs to whole-bank equivalent (%)	(	✂	)	*	†
Baseline capital for the whole bank (£m)	619	(✂)	1,333	*	†
Allocated capital for SME banking business (£m)	(	✂	)	*	†
1999					
Proportion of SME RWAs to whole-bank equivalent (%)	(	✂	)	*	†
Baseline capital for the whole bank (£m)	675	(✂)	1,956	*	†
Allocated capital for SME banking business (£m)	(	✂	)	*	†
2000					
Proportion of SME RWAs to whole-bank equivalent (%)	(✂)	‡	(	✂	)	25§
Baseline capital for the whole bank (£m)	799	‡	2,012	(✂)	3,075
Allocated capital for SME banking business (£m)	(	✂		)	550

Source: CC based on information from the groups.

*Not provided.
†Not able to be calculated.
‡Not provided for 2000.
§Simple average.

7.259. Table 7.64 shows the similar information for the banks operating in Scotland. For 2000, BoS had capital allocated to SME banking business of £[✂], RBS £[✂] million and Clydesdale had £[✂] million.

TABLE 7.64 **Banks operating mainly in Scotland: application of RWAs to baseline capital to determine capital for the respective bank's services to SMEs, 2000**

	Scotland			
	Clydesdale*	BoS†	RBS†	Total
Proportion of SME RWAs to whole-bank equivalent (%)	(	✂	)	29‡
Baseline capital for the whole bank (£m)	550	4,239	4,259	9,048
Allocated capital for SME banking business (£m)	(	✂	)	1,776

Source: CC based on information from the banks.

*NAB was not able to provide information for 1998 or 1999 but did provide figures for 2000.
†May include some England and Wales activities.
‡Simple average.

Adjustments for attributable capital

7.260. As discussed in paragraph 7.54, and in Chapter 6, the banks provided figures for lending, calculated on the basis that all lending was financed from borrowing in wholesale markets. In fact, a proportion was financed by the bank's equity. We therefore noted that an adjustment to profits would be necessary for the capital attributable to this lending. Without this adjustment the attributable interest cost set against interest income received would have been overstated and this would have resulted in double counting when we came to allow a return on the attributed capital. We noted that a proportion of the banks' lending was financed by equity and not wholly from the wholesale markets. We suggested that the adjustment should be based on attributable capital times the average three-month LIBOR for the year, which was 7.3 per cent for 1998, 5.45 per cent for 1999 and 6.1 per cent for 2000. The following subparagraphs summarize the smaller banks' position on this issue:

(a) The Co-operative Bank suggested that the attributable capital adjustment to profit as suggested by us could be overstated because the value of the benefit at LIBOR did not take account of the additional cost of funding by way of subordinated debt which would be [✂] per cent. For 1998 and 1999 it calculated the attributable capital adjustment as £[✂] for both years, compared with the figure of £[✂] million which we suggested for both years.

(b) As discussed in paragraph 7.251, we did not consider that an attributable capital adjustment was required for Alliance & Leicester, and it did not comment on this issue.

(c) Abbey National did not comment on either the methodology or the value we assigned to the attributable capital adjustment for 1999, which we estimated at £[✂] million.

(d) AIB (GB) did not comment on either the methodology or the value assigned to the attributable capital adjustment 1999, which we estimated at £[✂] million.

(e) NAB commented that it believed the attributable capital adjustment as calculated by the CC required three amendments:

— It should be reduced to reflect the increased cost of using subordinated debt as a source of funding the SME banking business. It told us that subordinated debt is provided by National Australia Bank Ltd at a cost of three-month LIBOR plus [✂] per cent. The impact of the cost of subordinated debt on each of the three NAB banks (Yorkshire, Northern and Clydesdale) for 2000 is a reduction in the attributable capital adjustment of £[✂] million, £[✂] million and £[✂] million respectively.

— NAB applied a rate of 6.163 per cent for 2000 instead of our 6.10 per cent when calculating the attributable capital adjustment as a percentage of baseline equity. The difference was due to NAB having a 30 September year end rather than a 31 December year end.

— NAB also suggested that the attributable capital adjustment needed to be further reduced by the amount which represented the use of equity to fund the purchase of non-income-generating assets, ie fixed assets. NAB said that the value of the reduction required should be calculated by the proportion of total fixed assets to shareholders' funds.

The overall impact of these changes would be to make an attributable capital adjustment as calculated by NAB for each of Yorkshire, Northern and Clydesdale of £[✂] million, £[✂] million and £[✂] million respectively.

(f) RBSG's response, as discussed in paragraph 7.107(d), included its views for Ulster Bank. We calculated this adjustment as £[✂] million in 1998 and £[✂] million in 1999.

(g) First Trust commented that it had included the income benefit earned on capital in the total income figure it provided to us. It estimated this amount to be £[✂] million for the year ended 31 December 2000. This compared to the £[✂] million calculated by us for 2000. Comparable figures for 1998 and 1999 could not be provided by First Trust.

(h) BoI commented that it had already included an adjustment for the attributable capital figure in its profit and loss figures within the other interest income line. This line included notional income on capital, calculated using the formula (capital × average swap rate). The notional income BoI calculated for 1998 and 1999 was £[✂] million and £[✂] million respectively, compared with the £[✂] million and £[✂] million calculated by us. For 2000, the notional income BoI calculated was £[✂] million compared with the £[✂] million calculated by us.

7.261. In the following tables we summarize the results of the smaller banks' services to SMEs by regions: England and Wales, Northern Ireland and Scotland. For the five smaller banks serving SMEs mainly in England and Wales, Table 7.65 shows the SME profitability figures. Only NAB suggested an adjustment to the calculation of the capital base to be allocated to the SME banking business. This was the addition of the value of staff training costs. However, NAB was not able to provide a figure for this adjustment in the absence of an appropriate measurement technique. The only other adjustment therefore made to either profit or capital adjustment was the attributable capital adjustment. The five banks in 1999 showed operating profits between £[✂] million and £[✂] million. For 2000, as noted above, we requested information only from Yorkshire and this is included with the 1999 results for the other banks.

TABLE 7.65 **Smaller banks serving SMEs mainly in England and Wales: summary of operating profit, taking account of an attributable capital adjustment, but before any adjustments made by the CC, 1998 and 1999**

England and Wales*

£ million

	Co-operative Bank	Alliance & Leicester	Abbey National	AIB (GB)	Yorkshire	Total
1998						
Operating income			†	†	‡	§
Adjustment for attributable capital			†	†	‡	§
Operating expenses			‡	‡	‡	§
Operating profit before provisions			†	†	‡	§
Bad debt charge			‡	‡	‡	§
Revised operating profit	*Figures omitted. See note on page iv.*		‡	‡	‡	§
1999						
Operating income						324
Adjustment for attributable capital						23
Operating expenses			*Figures omitted.*			−188
Operating profit before provisions			*See note on page iv.*			159
Bad debt charge						−23
Revised operating profit						136

Source: CC based on information from the banks.

*May include Scotland activities for some banks.
†Not provided.
‡NAB was not able to provide information for 1998 or 1999 but did provide figures for 2000. The 2000 figures have shown as 1999 to provide additional comparability between the smaller banks serving SMEs mainly in England and Wales.
§Not calculated due to lack of data.

7.262. Table 7.66 shows SME profitability data for 1998 to 2000 for the four smaller banks serving SMEs mainly in Northern Ireland, with the only adjustment being the attributable capital adjustment. The banks in 1999 and 2000 showed operating profits between £[✂] million and £[✂] million, and £[✂]million and £[✂] million respectively.

£ million

	Ulster Bank	First Trust	BoI	Northern Ireland Northern	Total
1998					
Operating income	(	✄	)*	(✄)†	‡	§
Adjustment for attributable capital§	(	✄	)*	(✄)†	‡	§
Operating expenses					±	§
Operating profit before provisions		*Figures omitted. See note on page iv.*			‡	§
Bad debt charge					±	§
Revised operating profit					±	§
1999					
Operating income	(	✄	)*	(✄)†	‡	§
Adjustment for attributable capital¶	(	✄	)*	(✄)†	‡	§
Operating expenses					±	§
Operating profit before provisions		*Figures omitted. See note on page iv.*			‡	§
Bad debt charge					±	§
Revised operating profit					‡	§
2000					
Operating income	(	✄	)*	(✄)†	(✄)	283
Adjustment for attributable capital¶	(	✄	)*	(✄)†	(✄)	34
Operating expenses						−182
Operating profit before provisions		*Figures omitted. See note on page iv.*				135
Bad debt charge						−16
Revised operating profit						119

Source: CC based on information from the banks.

*As discussed in paragraph 7.60, First Trust suggested that its operating income already reflected this adjustment and therefore there was an element of double counting income if the adjustment was shown without reducing the operating income figure. The income figure provided by First Trust was £[✄] million, £[✄] million and £[✄] million for 1998, 1999 and 2000 respectively. These figures have been reduced by the attributable capital figure as calculated by the CC.

†As discussed in paragraph 7.60, BoI suggested that its operating income already reflected this adjustment and therefore there was an element of double counting income if the adjustment was shown without reducing the operating income figure. The income figure provided by BoI was £[✄] million, £[✄] million and £[✄] million for 1998, 1999 and 2000 respectively. These figures have been reduced by the attributable capital figure as calculated by the CC.

‡NAB was not able to provide information for 1998 or 1999 but did provide figures for 2000.

§Not calculated due to lack of data.

¶At 7.3 per cent for 1998 and 5.45 per cent for 1999 based on yearly average of three-month LIBOR.

7.263. Table 7.67 shows revised SME profitability data for 2000 for the three banks serving SMEs mainly in Scotland, adjusted in the same manner as discussed above. The three banks in 2000 had operating profits between £[✄] million and £[✄] million.

£ million

| | Scotland | | | |
	Clydesdale*	BoS†	RBS†	Total
Operating income	(	✂	)‡	(✂)	1,228
Adjustment for attributable capital§				109
Operating expenses		Figures omitted.		−739
Operating profit before provisions		See note on page iv.		592
Bad debt charge				122
Revised operating profit				476

Source: CC based on information from the banks.

---

*NAB was not able to provide information for 1998 or 1999 but did provide figures for 2000.
†Includes England and Wales activities.
‡Includes £[✂] million other income which is from investments in associates and is net of expenses.
§At 7.3 per cent for 1998 and 5.45 per cent for 1999 based on yearly average of three-month LIBOR.

Return on capital for the smaller banks serving SMEs in the UK, before any adjustments by the CC

7.264. We now summarize returns for the smaller banks by region in the following three tables. For the smaller banks serving SME customers mainly in England and Wales, Table 7.68 shows the SME capital and profit for 1998 and 1999, before any adjustments for bad debt charges or cost:income ratio adjustments. Our conclusions on these are presented in Chapter 2. The table also shows the initial estimates of differences between actual pre-tax returns and the cost of capital that we sent to the banks during the course of the inquiry for them to comment on. For the smaller banks, we were not able to determine reliable beta factors that could be applied to their SME banking business. However, we would not expect their cost of equity to diverge greatly from the average for larger banks in 1999 of around 15 per cent pre-tax.

7.265. NAB, however, commented that it felt its cost of capital should reflect that of its parent company which is based in Australia. The reason for this was that the three NAB subsidiaries in the UK had no direct access to the UK capital markets over the period under review and the capital was provided by the parent company. NAB told us that it believed the relevant cost of capital was that which applied to the location where funds were raised rather than the location where the funds were utilized. The cost of capital proposed by NAB should have been [✂] per cent for the year ended 30 September 2000.

TABLE 7.68 **Smaller banks serving SMEs mainly in England and Wales: comparison of returns with the cost of equity capital for their SME banking business before any bad debt or cost:income adjustments by the CC, 1998 to 1999***

£ million

England and Wales

	Co-operative Bank	Alliance & Leicester	Abbey National	AIB (GB)	Yorkshire†	Total/ average
1998						
Initial capital figure that we reported to the banks for illustrative purposes shown in Chapter 6			‡	‡	‡	§
Attributable capital derived from baseline capital as per Table 7.62¶			‡	‡	‡	§
Revised operating profit as per Table 7.65			‡	‡	‡	§
Pre-tax return on capital (%)			‡	‡	‡	§
Cost of equity (%)			‡	‡	‡	§
Difference between pre-tax return and the cost of capital (%)			‡	‡	‡	§
Value of the difference between return on capital and the cost of capital			‡	‡	‡	§
1999						
Initial capital figure that we reported to the banks for illustrative purposes shown in Chapter 6						450
Attributable capital derived from baseline capital as per Table 7.62¶						447
Revised operating profit as per Table 7.65						136
Pre-tax return on capital (%)						31
Cost of equity (%)						15
Difference between pre-tax return and the cost of capital (%)						16
Value of the difference between return on capital and the cost of capital						69

Source: CC based on information from the banks.

---

*May include Scotland activities for some banks.

†NAB was not able to provide information for 1998 or 1999 but did provide figures for 2000. The 2000 figures have been shown as 1999 to provide additional comparability between the smaller banks serving SMEs mainly in England and Wales.

‡Data not provided.

§Not calculated due to lack of data.

¶This capital figure may differ from that shown in Chapter 6 because of changes in basis for calculations as the inquiry progressed.

7.266. Table 7.69 shows the SME capital and profit for the smaller banks serving SME customers mainly in Northern Ireland for 1998 to 2000, before any adjustments for bad debt charges or cost:income ratio adjustments. Chapter 2 gives our conclusions on these adjustments. The table also shows initial estimates of differences between actual pre-tax returns and cost of capital that we sent to the banks during the course of the inquiry for them to consider.

£ million

	Ulster Bank	Northern Ireland First Trust	BoI	Northern*	Total/ average
1998					
Initial capital figure that we reported to the banks for illustrative purposes				†	‡
Attributable capital derived from baseline capital as per Table 7.63§				†	‡
Revised operating profit as per Table 7.66				†	‡
Pre-tax return on capital (%)				†	‡
Cost of equity (%)				†	‡
Difference between pre-tax return and the cost of capital (%)				†	‡
Value of the difference between the return on capital and the cost of capital				†	‡
1999					
Initial capital figure that we reported to the banks for illustrative purposes				†	‡
Attributable capital derived from baseline capital as per Table 7.63§				†	‡
Revised operating profit as per Table 7.66		✄		†	‡
Pre-tax return on capital (%)				†	‡
Cost of equity (%)				†	‡
Difference between pre-tax return and the cost of capital (%)				†	‡
Value of the difference between the return on capital and the cost of capital				†	‡
2000					
Attributable capital derived from baseline capital as per Table 7.63§					550
Revised operating profit as per Table 7.66					119
Pre-tax return on capital (%)					22¶
Cost of equity (%)				✄	15¶
Difference between pre-tax return and the cost of capital (%)					6¶
Value of the difference between the return on capital and the cost of capital					35

Source: CC based on information from the banks.

*Northern is a subsidiary of NAB. NAB was not able to provide information for 1998 or 1999.
†Not provided.
‡Not calculated due to lack of data.
§This capital figure may differ from that shown in Chapter 6 because of changes in basis for calculations as the inquiry progressed.
¶Simple average.

7.267. Table 7.70 shows the SME capital and profit for the banks serving SME customers mainly in Scotland for 2000, before any adjustments for bad debt charges or cost:income ratio adjustments which are the subject of our conclusions in Chapter 2. The table also shows initial estimates of differences between actual pre-tax returns and cost of capital that we sent to the banks during the course of the inquiry for them to consider. The table repeats information shown for BoS and RBS in earlier tables because of their significant share in Scotland of services to SMEs.

£ million

| | Scotland | | | |
	Clydesdale*	BoS†	RBS†	Total/ average
Attributable capital derived from baseline capital as per Table 7.64‡				1,776
Revised operating profit as per Table 7.67				476
Pre-tax return on capital (%)				29§
Cost of equity (%)				15§
Difference between pre-tax return and the cost of capital (%)				15§
Value of the difference between the return on capital and the cost of capital				212

Source: CC based on information from the banks.

*NAB was not able to provide information for 1998 or 1999 but did provide figures for 2000.
†Includes England and Wales activities.
‡This capital figure may differ from that shown in Chapter 6 because of changes in basis for calculations as the inquiry progressed.
§Simple average.

7.268. We considered certain additional adjustments to SME profitability as discussed for the larger banks. The adjustments were:

(a) a further bad debt adjustment; and

(b) a cost:income ratio adjustment.

Further bad debt adjustment

7.269. None of the smaller banks serving SME customers in the UK were able to provide data for bad debt charges over a 10- to 12-year period. At best, some banks were able to provide data for 1998 to 2000 which were likely to be benign years in the economic cycle. We noted from the data provided, however, that the ratio of bad debt charges to loans and advances for most of the smaller banks was quite low, with the highest being 0.5 per cent and the average being around 0.2 per cent for these recent years.

7.270. Given the lack of data available to conduct an assessment of bad debt charges over a longer period for these smaller banks, we put to them an initial benchmark of the bad debt charges to loan ratio of 0.7 per cent as was suggested to the larger banks. Chapter 2 gives our conclusions on this issue.

Comparisons of cost:income ratios between the smaller banks serving SMEs in the UK

7.271. Some of the smaller banks were able to provide information to calculate the cost:income ratios of the SME banking business only for 1999. For the smaller banks serving SMEs mainly in England and Wales, Table 7.71 summarizes their respective cost:income ratios, based on information provided to us. The range was between 48 and 77 per cent, though some of these banks lacked scale, compared with the six largest clearing groups, in providing services to SMEs.

TABLE 7.71 **Smaller banks serving SMEs mainly in England and Wales: cost:income ratios for the SME banking business, 1998 and 1999**

per cent

	1998	1999
Co-operative Bank		
Alliance & Leicester		
Abbey National	✂	✂
AIB (GB)	*	
Yorkshire	†	

Source: CC based on information from the banks.

---

*Not provided.

†NAB was not able to provide information for 1989 and 1999 but provided figures for 2000 which have been included for comparative purposes.

7.272. For Scotland, the main banks serving this market are RBS, BoS and Clydesdale. RBS and BoS have been discussed in our analysis for the large six banks above, and Clydesdale had a cost:income ratio of [✂] per cent for 2000.

7.273. Table 7.72 shows the cost:income ratios for the smaller banks serving SMEs mainly in Northern Ireland, based on information provided to us. The range was between 65 and 76 per cent (excluding Northern), though all these banks lacked scale, compared with the six largest clearing groups in providing services to SMEs.

TABLE 7.72 **Smaller banks serving SMEs mainly in Northern Ireland: cost:income ratios for the SME banking business, 1998 to 2000**

per cent

	1998	1999	2000
Ulster Bank	(	✂	)
First Trust	(✂)*	(✂)*	(✂)*
BoI	(✂)†	(✂)†	(✂)
Northern	‡	‡	(✂)

Source: CC based on information from the banks.

---

*The ratio shown should be based on income excluding the attributable capital adjustment, ie on the basis that all lending was financed from money markets. The figure shown for 2000 is based on costs of £[✂] million and expenses of £[✂] million. 1999 is based on costs of £[✂] million and income of £[✂] million as shown in Table 7.66. The figure shown for 1998 is based on costs of £[✂] million and income of £[✂] million as shown in Table 7.66. These ratios have been calculated on the adjusted income figure, reduced for the amount that represents an attributable capital adjustment.

†The ratio shown should be based on income excluding the attributable capital adjustment, ie on the basis that all lending was financed from money markets. The figure shown for 1999 is based on costs of £[✂] million and income of £[✂] million as shown in Table 7.66. The figure shown for 1998 is based on costs of £[✂] million and income of £[✂] million as shown in Table 7.66. These ratios have been calculated on adjusted income figure, reduced for the amount that represents an attributable capital adjustment.

‡NAB was not able to provide information for 1989 and 1999.

7.274. For the purpose of discussions with the smaller banks, we applied a similar approach to determining a cost:income ratio adjustment, as was considered for the six largest clearing groups, as discussed above, ie a 50 per cent benchmark. Chapter 2 gives our conclusions on this issue.

7.275. The following three tables summarize the results for the smaller banks in England and Wales, Northern Ireland and Scotland. For the smaller banks serving SMEs mainly in England and Wales, Table 7.73 shows illustrative calculations of profitability for 1998 and 1999 incorporating the further adjustments for bad debts and efficiency. Chapter 2 gives our conclusions on this.

TABLE 7.73 **Smaller banks serving SMEs mainly in England and Wales: summary of illustrative returns in excess of the cost of capital after further adjustments, 1998 and 1999***

£ million

England and Wales

	Co-operative Bank	Alliance & Leicester	Abbey National	AIB (GB)	Yorkshire†	Total/ average
1998						
Value of difference between pre-tax return and the cost of capital as shown in Table 7.68			‡	‡	‡	§
Adjustments proposed by CC						
Further bad debt adjustment			‡	‡	‡	§
Cost:income adjustment			‡	‡	‡	§
Difference after adjustments			‡	‡	‡	§
Return on capital (before adjustments) (%)			‡	‡	‡	§
Return on capital (after above adjustments) (%)			‡	‡	‡	§
1999						
Value of difference between pre-tax return and the cost of capital as shown in Table 7.68						69
Adjustments proposed by CC						
Further bad debt adjustment						−9
Cost:income adjustment						29
Difference after adjustments						87
Return on capital (before adjustments) (%)						31¶
Return on capital (after above adjustments) (%)						40¶

Source: CC based on information from the banks.

---

*May include Scotland activities for some banks.

†NAB was not able to provide information for 1998 or 1999. The 2000 figures have been presented in the 1999 column to provide some comparability between the other banks.

‡Not available.

§Not calculated due to lack of data.

¶Simple average.

Note: Figures rounded and therefore may not add to the totals shown.

7.276. For the smaller banks serving SMEs mainly in Northern Ireland, Table 7.74 shows calculations of profitability for 1998 to 2000 incorporating the further adjustments for bad debts and efficiency. Chapter 2 gives our conclusions on this.

	Ulster Bank	Northern Ireland First Trust	BoI	Northern*	£ million Total/ average
1998					
Value of difference between pre-tax return and the cost of capital per Table 7.69				†	‡
Adjustments proposed by CC					
Further bad debt adjustment				†	‡
Cost:income adjustment				±	±
Difference after adjustments				†	‡
Return on capital (before adjustments) (%)				†	‡
Return on capital (after above adjustments) (%)				†	‡
1999	*Figures omitted. See note on page iv.*				
Value of difference between pre-tax return and the cost of capital per Table 7.69				†	‡
Adjustments proposed by CC					
Further bad debt adjustment				†	‡
Cost:income adjustment				±	±
Difference after adjustments				†	‡
Return on capital (before adjustments) (%)				†	‡
Return on capital (after above adjustments) (%)				†	‡
2000					
Value of difference between pre-tax return and the cost of capital per Table 7.69					35
Adjustments proposed by CC					
Further bad debt adjustment		*Figures omitted.*			−18
Cost:income adjustment		*See note on page iv.*			43
Difference after adjustments					60
Return on capital (before adjustments) (%)					22§
Return on capital (after above adjustments) (%)					25§

Source: CC based on information from the banks.

*NAB was not able to provide information for 1998 or 1999 but did provide figures for 2000.
†Not available.
‡Not calculated due to lack of data.
§Simple average.
Note: Figures rounded and therefore may not add to the totals shown.

7.277. For the banks serving SMEs mainly in Scotland, Table 7.75 shows calculations of profitability for 2000 incorporating the further adjustments for bad debts and cost:income ratios. Chapter 2 gives our conclusions on this.

TABLE 7.75 **Banks serving SMEs mainly in Scotland: summary of illustrative returns in excess of the cost of capital after further adjustments, 2000**

£ million

	Clydesdale*	BoS†	RBS†	Total/ average
		Scotland		
Value of difference between pre-tax return and the cost of capital per Table 7.70				212
Adjustments proposed by CC				
Further bad debt adjustment				−56
Cost:income adjustment	*Figures omitted.*			133
Difference after adjustments	*See note on page iv.*			189
Return on capital (before adjustments) (%)				29‡
Return on capital (after above adjustments) (%)				31‡

Source: CC based on information from the banks.

*NAB was not able to provide information for 1998 or 1999 but did provide figures for 2000.
†May include England and Wales activities.
‡Simple average.
Note: Figures rounded and therefore may not add to the total shown.

Printed in the UK for The Stationery Office Limited
On behalf of the Controller of Her Majesty's Stationery Office
ID86747   3/2002   709679   19585

Published by The Stationery Office Limited
and available from:

The Stationery Office
(Mail, telephone and fax orders only)
PO Box 29, Norwich NR3 1GN
General enquiries 0870 600 5522
Order through the Parliamentary Hotline *Lo-call* 0845 7 023474
Fax orders 0870 600 5533
Email book.orders@theso.co.uk
Internet http://www.clicktso.com

The Stationery Office Bookshops
123 Kingsway, London WC2B 6PQ
020 7242 6393 Fax 020 7242 6394
68–69 Bull Street, Birmingham B4 6AD
0121 236 9696 Fax 0121 236 9699
33 Wine Street, Bristol BS1 2BQ
0117 9264306 Fax 0117 9294515
9–21 Princess Street, Manchester M60 8AS
0161 834 7201 Fax 0161 833 0634
16 Arthur Street, Belfast BT1 4GD
028 9023 8451 Fax 028 9023 5401
The Stationery Office Oriel Bookshop
18–19 High Street, Cardiff CF1 2BZ
029 2039 5548 Fax 029 2038 4347
71 Lothian Road, Edinburgh EH3 9AZ
0870 606 5566 Fax 0870 606 5588

Accredited Agents
(See Yellow Pages)

and through good booksellers

ISBN 0-10-153192-

9 780101 531924